BY THE SAME AUTHOR

Invitation to the Dance:
A Guide to Anthony Powell's Dance to
the Music of Time
(1977)

IVY

IVY

THE LIFE OF I. COMPTON-BURNETT

HILARY SPURLING

Columbia University Press
New York
1986

Columbia University Press Morningside Edition   1986
Columbia University Press
New York

Library of Congress Cataloging-in-Publication Data

Spurling, Hilary.
Ivy, the life of I. Compton-Burnett.

First published in Great Britain as two works with
titles: Ivy when young and Secrets of a woman's heart.
Bibliography: p.
Includes index.
1. Compton-Burnett, I. (Ivy), 1884–1969—Biography.
2. Novelists, English—20th century—Biography.
I. Spurling, Hilary. Secrets of a woman's heart. 1985.
II. Title.
PR6005.03895Z93   1985   823'.912 [B]   85-22372
ISBN 0-231-08383-1 (pbk.)

Manufactured in the United States of America

This edition published by arrangement with Alfred A. Knopf, Inc.

For Maureen

CONTENTS

Illustrations follow pages 174 and 430.

PREFACE

READERS on both sides of the Atlantic first discovering Ivy Compton-Burnett at the end of the 1920s were in no doubt that she represented the last word in modernity. She was favourably compared with the young Hemingway and Faulkner when *Brothers and Sisters* came out in the U.S. in 1929; nearly twenty years later *Bullivant and the Lambs* more than held its own with reviewers against stiff competition from Norman Mailer, who made his debut in the summer of 1948 with *The Naked and the Dead;* while in the sixties she was roped in as, on the one hand, a direct forerunner of the *nouveau roman* in France and, on the other, a potentially disruptive force in the general questioning of socio-politico-cum-moral conventions that preoccupied that effervescent decade. 'In her own eccentric way, Compton-Burnett is a radical thinker, one of the few modern heretics,' wrote Mary McCarthy (who said that Ivy, lunching at the Ritz in her long black skirts, velvet hairband and buckled shoes, resembled nothing so much as her redoubtable Catholic Grandmother McCarthy). 'It is the eccentricity that has diverted attention from the fact that these small uniform volumes are subversive packets.'[1]

This is the central puzzle of Ivy Compton-Burnett's life and work. She dressed and behaved all her life like a Victorian maiden lady, and she thought in ways so unconventional that even now in 1984—the centenary of her birth—the full implications of her writing have scarcely yet sunk in. For half a century and more, readers enchanted by the subversive content of her books, baffled by their author's old-world air, have speculated furiously as to what lay behind the gap. But this was only the first of many lesser mysteries surrounding Ivy, who became towards the end of her life something of a literary legend, austere, aloof and so inscrutable that nobody dared press her on points she did not care to discuss.

I never met her, but her public image was so intimidating that, when I started talking to her friends a year or so after her death, I found it hard at first to credit the gentle, considerate, affectionate and amusing private person many of them described. More disconcerting still was their blankness about her origins and early life. Conflict, crime and violent upheaval among the families in her books had naturally roused intense curiosity about her own home life. But the many, mostly sensational rumours which were all I had to go on at the start of this biography turned out to be as misleading as Ivy's own characteristically dismissive claim: 'I have had such an uneventful life that there is little to say.'[2]

Certainly Ivy herself seldom if ever broke her rule of silence about the tragic family history that lay on the far side of the First World War. By the early 1920s, when she started writing her extraordinary novels, she had already drawn a line beneath the past: from now on she saw almost nobody connected with it, never revisited its sites and steadfastly resisted questioning about it. The split was so drastic that, biographically speaking, the only answer seemed to be to write her life, as she had lived it, in two separate, more or less self-contained halves divided by the first war, which is why the first section of this book, *Ivy When Young,* was finished (and originally published in England) in 1974, ten years before its sequel, *Secrets of a Woman's Heart.*

Ivy When Young is the story of the passionate, sensitive, vulnerable girl whose life was darkened by a series of disasters—sudden death, grief, tyranny, isolation and near-madness—and eventually destroyed by the public and private catastrophes of 1914–18. By the end of the war, Ivy had lost her home, her occupation, everyone she had ever loved or needed and, with them, all but the faintest inkling of her will to live. Long afterwards she said or implied to several people that her life was over—she told Rosamond Lehmann that it had gone under-ground[3]—after 1914; and, ten years ago when I wrote *Ivy When Young,* it seemed to me that she was right.

But it was of course preposterous to suppose her life was over in any but the most superficial sense. *Secrets of a Woman's Heart* is the story of the writer who learnt, over forty years or more, to draw on her own past for books based firmly in the present: Ivy's view of the pre-1914 world in which nearly all her books are set was never literal, still less nostalgic, nor did it impose any kind of constraint. On the contrary, it freed her to write about what seemed then and still seem some of the most threatening issues of the time. Almost from the start Ivy used the domestic novel, distanced by her ostensibly Victorian style and setting, to explore atrocity, violence, the corruption of language and the totalitarian abuse of power. She was not interested in conventional politics, and she had no patience with radical or any other sort of chic. She visited none of the world's trouble spots, indeed she travelled at all only under protest. What interested her was people (apart from writing—and a celebrated weakness for expensive chocolates, soft fruit and garden flowers—she had almost no other interests). Above all she was concerned with the lengths to which the strong are prepared to go to exploit and crush the weak. No enormity was hidden from her, which perhaps explains why her popularity increased dramatically in England in the Second World War when uncertainty and fear played so large a part in everyday reality. Nervous readers, before and since, have echoed the protesters in her books:

'Oh, must we be quite so honest with ourselves, my dear?'
'We do not know how to avoid it,' said Terence. 'That is why there is horror in every heart, and a resolve never to be honest with anyone else.'[4]

It is Ivy's honesty that makes her at once so exhilarating, consoling and disturbing. She set exacting standards for a biographer, and what little she herself said on the subject—'biography has to be looking back, or it may have to be keeping back, anyhow an autobiography'[5]—confirmed that the only hope of solving the many puzzles she set in fact and fiction lay in some attempt to see what Ivy saw in her own heart. The first part of this biography is an excursion into the Victorian and Edwardian past that subsequently supplied so much of the background to her books. Life for the Compton-Burnetts at home was perhaps no fuller of struggle and tension than for many comparable large Victorian families ruled by an all-powerful parent: Samuel Butler's notorious father and Elizabeth Barrett Browning's—or for that matter several aspects of Virginia Woolf's—approximate more closely than Ivy's own what we now think of as the Compton-Burnett model. It was a pattern of cant, repression and double think that commonly filled her contemporaries with gloom, and a fierce determination to escape. Liberation is a constant theme in Ivy's early writing and, when I wrote *Ivy When Young,* I was unequivocally on the side of the younger generation in her books: victims cowed and persecuted by authoritarian elders, their courage and humour heightened by their helplessness in what was, as Ivy said,[6] essentially a world of power politics.

But Ivy also said that it would never do to underestimate her tyrants, and she remonstrated gently with people siding too indignantly against the powermongers. It was a point of view I came only slowly to understand in the ten years that separated the two parts of this book (perhaps because they were the years in which I had children, and so found myself willy-nilly changing sides in the domestic power struggle); and it brought me as close as I shall ever come to a solution to my puzzle. Ivy found her tyrants in herself, but she also found their victims, together with the observers who stand, appalled and impotent, on the edges of the action in her books. In the first half of her life she was cruelly oppressed, before becoming briefly the oppressor herself; in the second half she came to comprehend both roles with extraordinary tolerance, wisdom and generosity. The Victorian disguise she eventually adopted in both fact and fiction was not so much a retreat from modern life as a distancing device: a way of contemplating objectively, if not with equanimity, horrors which she saw, whether in herself or in the world at large, too clearly for comfort.

Ivy left no explanations, no journal and comparatively few letters: even to her dearest friends she was generally terse, rarely intimate and always punctiliously obedient to her generation's rule against gossiping by post. Gossip—'simple candid probing of our friends' business'[7]—was her delight, but she understood inquisitiveness too well—'Our curiosity is neither morbid nor ordinary. It is the kind known as devouring'[8]—not to take precautions. When she died her private papers amounted to little more than a shoebox half full of engagement diaries, and a small, apparently random selection of fanmail. By far the greater part of my information reached me therefore by word of mouth, and here I owe more than I can say to Ivy's sisters, Vera and the late Juliet Compton-Burnett, for their unfailing kindness, patience and perseverance in reconstructing for me things that happened in the Compton-Burnett household before 1915. I could not have written this book without them, nor without constant encouragement, advice and insight from Ivy's many friends, among whom I should particularly like to thank Madge Garland, Robert Liddell, the late Herman Schrijver and Sonia Orwell.

My other great debt is to Anthony Compton-Burnett for permission to quote from Ivy's published and unpublished works, and to the late Hester Marsden-Smedley for her unpublished memoir, her practical help and the long loan of both Ivy's papers and those of her companion, Margaret Jourdain (chief among these were the minute diaries in which both intermittently recorded visits and visitors, parties given and attended, professional contacts, trips and holidays; Ivy's press cuttings, practically complete from 1925 to Margaret's death in 1951, after which the collection lapsed; Margaret's Account Book, 1902–24, address books and a few odd scraps of correspondence).

Next to these I owe most to the novelist Elizabeth Taylor, who gave me permission before she died to quote from the remarkable letters she wrote to Robert Liddell about Ivy, and to all the others who took notes at the time, in particular Barbara and the late Walter Robinson, Rosamond Lehmann, Lady Anne Hill and James Lees-Milne, whose published diaries and private conversation have been invaluable. Among Ivy's other friends who spared neither time nor trouble to help me I am especially grateful to members of the Beresford, Kidd and Felkin families—the late Mrs J. B. Beresford and Mrs Alan Kidd, Rosemary Beresford, Mr and Mrs Benedict Beresford, Mr and Mrs Roger Kidd, Joyce Felkin and Penelope Douglas; also to Sybille Bedford, James Brandreth, Rex Britcher, Professor Charles Burkhart (whose pioneering books remain indispensable to anyone interested in Ivy), Lettice Cooper, Kay Dick, Marjorie and the late Ralph Edwards, Kathleen Farrell, Dr George Furlong, Livia Gollancz, the late Cicely Greig, Heywood Hill, the late Soame Jenyns, Francis King, the late Viva King, the late Olivia Manning, Julian Mitchell, Elka Schrijver, the late Elizabeth Sprigge and Vere Watson-Gandy.

Among people who helped me with *Ivy When Young,* I should like to thank Professor S. T. Bindoff for access to Charles Webster's papers, for a survey of activities among historians at King's College, Cambridge, before the First World War and for reading and assessing Noel Compton-Burnett's thesis for me; the late Dr Frank Bodman for much information about homoeopathic history in general and Dr James Compton Burnett's career in particular; L. R. Conisbee for investigating Ivy's schooldays in Bedford; Hilda Stowell for combing Hampshire records in pursuit of Richard Burnett and his son Charles Compton; and the Clacton historian, Kenneth Walker, for countless details about Ivy's maternal relations in northeast Essex, for examining the topographical references in *Dolores* and for a guided tour of the sites which provided the setting for that novel. I am also very grateful to Ivy's contemporaries at school and college: Marjorie E. T. Andrewes, Isabel M. Bremner, Mabel Eastaugh, Mrs J. A. Elliott, Grace J. Fothergill, Lady MacAlister and Mrs A. E. Rampal; and, among her brother's friends at King's, to Leigh Farnell, W. H. Haslam, Raisley Moorsom and the late Philip Noel-Baker.

For help with *Secrets of a Woman's Heart* my best thanks go to Margaret Hawkins, Gertrude McCracken, K. E. Currey and the other inhabitants, past and present, of Sutton Veney who told me about the Noyes sisters—Liza Banks, Joan McWilliam, Anne Northcroft and Caroline Walker; to Peter Thornton and his staff at the Furniture and Woodwork Department of the Victoria and Albert Museum for information, advice and access to Margaret Jourdain's furniture notes (specially interesting to me because they were jotted down on the backs of discarded letters, receipts, income tax returns, royalty statements, etc., including odd pages of typescript from Ivy's novels and even her torn-up contracts with Heinemann); and to Dr John Rollett, the connoisseur and collector of Jourdainiana, but for whom much in Margaret's early life might have remained a blank.

I am also grateful to the following for help, information and permission to reproduce or quote from material in their possession: Jennifer Adamson; Margaret Aldridge; C. G. Allen of the London School of Economics; Messrs Edward Arnold, T. A. Baker of the Clacton branch of Essex County Library; the Rev A.J.W. Barker, Vicar of Dent; Patricia Bell, Bedfordshire County Archivist; Margaret Birch; the late Katherine Blackie; Simon Blow; Violet Bower; Professor Ian A. Boyd; Livia Breglia; Gerald Brenan; Anna Browne; Dr Peter Burnett; Richard Burton of Royal Holloway College; John and Sheila Bush; Christopher Carter ('Touchstone' of the *Bedfordshire Times*); Glen Cavaliero; Sir Michael Clapham; Sara Coffin; Mr and Mrs Percy Compton-Burnett; Raymond A. Cook; Professor Christopher Cornford; John Cornforth; Arthur Crook; Anne Doe; Jack Dove, Librarian of Hove Central Library; Messrs Duckworth; Mrs T. S. Eliot; Elizabeth Ellem of King's College Library; Dr Ulick R. Evans; Renée Fedden; Yvonne ffrench; David Fletcher of William Blackwood and Sons; Professor John Fletcher; Eva Fox; Roy Fuller; P. N. Furbank; the late David Garnett; Victoria Glendinning; Cecil Gould; I. W. Green; Lionel Hale, General Secretary of the British Homoeopathic Association; John B. Hall of Dover Harbour Board; Dr M. A. Halls, Modern Archivist, King's College, Cambridge; Rupert Hart-Davis; Norah Harvey-Lloyd; Gwenda Haynes-Thomas; the Rev Edward Hayward; Violet Henriques; Iseult Hickie of Kensington Central Library; Kathy Huff (for an unpublished bibliography); Mrs Leonard

Humphreys; J. L. Hurn, Registrar of Royal Holloway College; Lucille Iremonger; Colonel Johnson; Enid Johnson; M. Jolliffe, Librarian of Royal Holloway College; Arthur J. Jourdain; Joy Jourdain; Richard Kennedy; Dorothy Kerr; A.J.B. Kiddell of Sotheby's; Edith Lamont; Moll Lampard; J. A. Laurence; Mary Maguire; Lady Mander; Douglas Matthews and the staff of the London Library; Mary McCarthy; the late Robin McDouall; Lady Medawar; Peter Mellors; Esther Millar; the late Raymond Mortimer; W. R. Mowll; Hugh Noyes; L. D. O'Nions, Librarian of Hastings Public Library; Dr Stephen Pasmore; Derryan Paul, Archivist of Royal Holloway College; Eric J. B. Pearson; Dulcie Pendred; Michael Pinney; Sir John Pope-Hennessy; Anthony Powell; Margaret Powell; the late Mario Praz; the Rev. J. Pringle, Vicar of Owlesbury; Sir Dennis Proctor; Maurice G. Rathbone, Wiltshire County Archivist; Marion Rawson; Graham Reynolds; Professor O. L. Richmond; A. J. Ricketts, Dover Borough Librarian; Lucy Robertson of Edinburgh University Library; Neil Robertson of Glasgow University; Joanna Routledge; Carol Rygate; Seeley M. Sherbrooke; Constance Babington Smith; L. I. Smith; Natasha Sokolov; Humphrey and Sir Stephen Spender; Dame Freya Stark; Jane Stockwood; Mrs Stoll of the Faculty Library, Royal London Homoeopathic Hospital; Mr Storey of the Historical Manuscripts Commission; Jenny Stratoford; Dorothy Stroud; Christopher Sykes; Michael Tayler; Mr and Mrs Richard Thesiger; R. J. Thomas of Messrs Mowll and Mowll; Mrs Geoffrey Toulmin; Stephen Toulmin; Clissold Tuely; Dame Janet Vaughan; Alison Waley; the Rev. Canon C. Wells, Rural Dean of Winchester; N. C. Wilde of Bedford Central Library; Henrietta Williamson; Sir Angus Wilson; Sir Peter Wilson; Norman Wright; and Francis Wyndham.

HILARY SPURLING
London, 1984

ONE

IVY WHEN YOUNG

1884–1919

It is better to be drunk with loss and
to beat the ground, than to let the
deeper things gradually escape.

Ivy to Francis King,
22 June 1969.

PARENTS AND GRANDPARENTS

'Fools, imbeciles, idiots and donkeys'

I

THE BURNETTS OF HAMPSHIRE lived, at the turn of the eighteenth century, in a place called Gavelacre on the banks of the River Test, some eleven miles from Winchester along the old Roman road to the east of Salisbury plain. There are records of fishing and farming Burnetts in the county for hundreds of years before that, many of them as humble and no doubt as difficult to trace as the Gavelacre Burnetts who seem to have lived in the parish at least since 1737, and who remained there until well into the nineteenth century as labourers or small tenant farmers. Gavelacre Farm was not large enough to support more than one tenant so that younger sons like Richard and William Burnett, born in 1779 and 1790, had to seek their fortunes elsewhere. Both described themselves as yeomen, though neither was strictly entitled to the claim, since their family owned no land. Judging by gaps in the registers at their own and the half-dozen neighbouring parishes, these Burnetts were probably nonconformist; but all that can be said with certainty is that both left home in their early twenties, and both married sisters called Compton.

The Comptons of Winchester were well-to-do tradesmen: John Compton (who was born in 1749) was a blacksmith, his only son was a watchmaker and, by way of a dowry for his two daughters, he lent each of his sons-in-law £300. Richard Burnett married Catherine Maria Compton at St Maurice's, Winchester, on 29 October 1803. Eight years later his younger brother William married her sister Anne. The younger couple had six children, the elder seven who were nearly all baptized in their mother's name of Compton, so that in the early years of the nineteenth century there were two young families of Compton Burnetts growing up on small, rented farms close to Winchester. By the middle of the century several of the more ambitious sons of the first marriage had moved to the large coastal towns, Southampton or Portsmouth, where they became shopkeepers, coal merchants, corn dealers, while the abler of their sons in turn entered the professions. Within three generations at least one branch of the family had abandoned farming, left Hampshire and severed all connection with trade. Richard Burnett's grandson James was an eminently successful doctor, with a large London practice and a country villa at Pinner, by the time that the seventh of his thirteen children, Ivy Compton-Burnett, was born on 5 June 1884.

How much Ivy knew of this family history is doubtful. Intermarriage between pairs of brothers and sisters, a recurrent theme in her books, was a common enough pattern among cousins and uncles and aunts on both sides of the family in her own and her parents' generations, producing sometimes rather more complex relationships than the fairly straightforward union of the Compton sisters with the Burnett brothers some eighty years before she was born. Family tradition seems to have been vague on the matter, asserting only that the Burnetts descended originally from the seventeenth-century historian Bishop Burnet; this belief is repeated in a biography of Ivy's father by his friend Dr Clarke,* who probably had it at first hand from Dr or Mrs Compton Burnett. Dr Clarke's description of more immediate ancestors is short but suggestive: 'The name Compton was taken about the year 1770, on the marriage of James' grandfather with a Miss Compton of Hampshire, a lady of large fortune, at whose desire the addition was made.' The summary is accurate (except for the date), and interesting because it seems likely that none of her great-grandchildren knew that this Miss Compton was a blacksmith's daughter, and her fortune a loan of £300. Ivy herself, when asked where her family came from, gave much the same account as her father's biographer: 'James Compton Burnett descended from an old Scotch family, the younger branch of which

---

* *Life and Work of James Compton Burnett, M.D.*, by J. H. Clarke. This is a strictly professional life (the few facts in Dr Clarke's brief biographical section evidently reached him on hearsay and are often misleading), written shortly after Dr Burnett's death and intended as at once a valediction and a vindication of the homoeopathic faction to which both Clarke and Burnett belonged. Though somewhat sketchy at times, for reasons of professional discretion (see chapter six), it provides a sympathetic portrait by a close friend and colleague.

came south. A notable member of this branch was Gilbert Burnet, Bishop of Salisbury . . . who flourished from 1643 to 1715. From him James Compton directly descended.'[1]

Gilbert Burnet (the younger son of an Aberdeen advocate, and nephew to the ancient Scottish family of baronets called Burnet or Burnett whose line still continues) left Scotland round about 1675 for London where, being a Whig of stern moral principles and fond of speaking his mind on both counts, he pursued a fairly tricky course at court. He reformed the Earl of Rochester in a spectacular deathbed conversion, but failed signally to do the same for Charles II. Withdrawing to The Hague he was outlawed under James for high treason, and returned at the abdication in high favour with William and Mary. He had three wives, three sons and two daughters (one of whom was mother to the poet Gray's friend Richard West, who died young, believing that his mother had murdered his father); his fame rests chiefly on his skill as a brilliantly racy though by no means impartial historian of his own times. Dr Clarke detected in this ancestry 'the source whence Dr Burnett's mental vigour was derived' and, even allowing for a gap of two centuries, the resemblance between the two men is sufficiently striking. The Bishop's robust prose style is informed by vast knowledge and an equally prodigious memory; his nature was fiery and furiously inquisitive; his contemporaries were divided between those who marvelled at his extraordinary personal magnetism and those who, like Swift, smarted under his reforming zeal, his vituperative pamphlets and 'a boisterous vehement manner of expressing himself'[2] peculiarly exasperating to his enemies. On all these counts, and perhaps especially the last, one might well argue a close affinity between Bishop Burnet and his supposed descendant, James Compton Burnett; and one might even extend the likeness to some of the formidable fathers depicted in James' daughter's books.

But, appropriate though the Bishop may seem as an ancestor for I. Compton-Burnett, he must unfortunately be discarded for at least two reasons. In the first place, there were Burnetts living in the Test valley near Winchester long before the Bishop left Scotland; and even supposing that one of his sons or grandsons had happened to settle in Hampshire, among a whole tribe of completely unconnected English Burnetts, it is barely conceivable that the descendants of so prominent a statesman, diplomat and churchman should have sunk, in so short a time, to become obscure nonconformist tenant farmers, marrying the daughters of a Winchester tradesman and showing no sign whatever of patronage from anyone more important than their local squire.* In the second place, the Bishop's male line ended with a single great-grandson, born in 1740, who was a surgeon at Chigwell in Essex and died there, leaving one unmarried daughter.[3]

It is not hard to see how the claim to the Bishop arose in a family as energetically determined to rise in the world as the Compton Burnetts seem to have been. Little is known of Ivy's great-grandfather, the Richard Burnett of Gavelacre who had left home to be married in 1803, save that he obtained enough money from his father-in-law to take a tenancy from the lord of the manor of Wherwell (the next hamlet, a mile or so downstream from Gavelacre Farm) where he impressed the vicar sufficiently to become in the next ten years his church warden and parish overseer. Charles Compton Burnett, Ivy's grandfather and the youngest of Richard's four sons, was born at Wherwell in 1811. He was married on 5 June 1834 to Sarah Wilson, the daughter of a small farmer some thirty miles south at Alverstoke. His sister, Martha Compton Burnett, had married Sarah's brother Jesse one month before. Two years later Charles' eldest brother, Richard, married Agnes Wilson and, when Martha died in her twenties, Jesse Wilson took as his second wife Ann Compton Burnett, youngest sister to Charles and Richard and Martha (an illegal match, since it was not until 1907 that a man was permitted by act of parliament to marry his deceased wife's sister). Ivy's ancestors might well have agreed with the girl who said in one of her books: 'I think we are overdoing this intermarrying.'†

Ivy's father, James, the youngest child of the second of these four marriages, was born on 21 July 1840, 'at Redlynch near Salisbury, his father being', according to Dr Clarke, 'a considerable landowner in the neighbourhood'.[4] But Charles Compton Burnett had moved just over

---

*See Appendix One for a fuller account of Ivy's ancestry. Anthony Powell, in a letter to the author, confirms that the extraordinary number of mariners, seafaring characters and husbandmen named Burnett recorded in the Winchester and Southampton areas before and during the eighteenth century 'clearly indicates that the Hampshire Burnetts were modestly placed over a long period. . . . If one accepts this, the conclusion is that there was *not enough time* for the Bishop's family to have emigrated to Hampshire and gone down hill on quite such a steep and numerous scale. . . .'

† *Elders and Betters*, p.227. The *Cambridge Review* for 29 October 1907 reported a telling speech by Ivy's brother Noel in his first debate at the Union against the motion, 'That this House regrets the Deceased Wife's Sister's Act'; but there is no means of knowing whether Noel's support of the new bill had anything to do with the marriages of his great aunts, Martha and Ann Compton Burnett.

the Wiltshire border to Redlynch less than a year before James was born. He described himself (like his father before him, and with no better claim) as a yeoman but, since he does not appear on the local Tithe Apportionment or on the electoral register, he can hardly have owned any land in the district. He moved about and switched jobs all his life, and he seems to have been a farm labourer in the early part of James' boyhood. James himself acquired in these years an abiding love of the country which he later shared with his daughter Ivy. His own recollections of birds nesting and fishing, of collecting tips from wood-men on the cure of snake-bite or how to charm warts, are invariably happy (save that once, 'with the help of a village apothecary and half-a-hogshead of mixture', he had nearly died of pleurisy). Otherwise he was a dreamy child, tall and sturdy, dark-eyed, dark-haired and clear-skinned, fond of exploring the woods alone and 'always thoughtful beyond his years'. He had a brother Charles, who was five years his senior, and sisters Sarah and Mary, but he seems to have been closest to his brother John who was one year older; and he was especially devoted to his mother, often recalling her later to his own children, and writing always with the utmost respect and enthusiasm of mothers in general.

When James was ten or eleven his father moved to Southampton and set up shop at 74 French Street, in what was then one of the poorer parts of the city. James' uncle, Richard Compton Burnett, had been living for some time in West Street where he worked as a labourer and his wife, Agnes, as a dress- and straw-bonnet-maker. Another uncle, William, was a general dealer in Gosport. Charles himself a few years later started a small coal-and-corn-dealing business which (with help from his brother Richard) he ran for the next ten years from the same address. Southampton possessed already several families of rather more prosperous Burnetts, among them an accountant named John James Burnett who, though evidently unrelated to the Compton Burnetts, is interesting because of his ancestry. John James claimed descent from the naval physician-general Sir William Burnett, a surgeon in Nelson's fleet who was decorated as a young man at Trafalgar and knighted a quarter of a century later for medical reforms in the navy. What is interesting is that John James' ancestor was a Scotsman who came south to make his career in England like the seventeenth-century Bishop Burnet; and perhaps it was this which suggested a similarly illustrious pedigree to John James' neighbour, the coal dealer, Charles Compton Burnett. The claim was unquestioningly accepted by Charles' descendants, and the whole affair passed so rapidly into family legend that by the time Ivy grew up her father even had an engraving of Sir William Burnett hanging on his walls for good measure.*

Times must often have been hard for James and his brothers in the days when their father was attempting to establish a footing for himself in Southampton. All hands were needed in the family business and, though the three boys were no doubt already destined by their parents for the professional classes, they may well have been required to help alongside their uncle and various cousins in the shop, or with the numerous sidelines started by their father in the 1850s. Charles and John both eventually became Congregationalist ministers, harking back perhaps to the original Gavelacre Burnetts who had probably attended the Congregationalist chapel at Andover. James himself had always wanted to be a doctor. He afterwards held strong views on a sound education, and proved a liberal parent in this respect to his daughter Ivy; but, though he seems to have attended the village school as a small boy at Redlynch, there are no records of James or his brothers at King Edward's grammar school in Southampton. His biographer is vague at this point, saying only that he left school at sixteen, finished his education in France and 'travelled for several years, principally on the continent' before he arrived round about 1865 at the medical school in Vienna. Tuition at Vienna was free, a subject on which James later felt keenly: 'It is right to explain that this has been a common thing in German universities from time immemorial, and it is not there thought by any means an undignified thing to receive gratuitous instruction, as it is the *right* of poor students, especially such as matriculate with honour. . . .'† James' father can have been in no position to support him at this time for, though he seems to have flourished in the 'fifties and early 'sixties as a dealer and carrier of corn and coal (operating at one point, jointly with his brother Richard, from three different

* Listed in the estate agent's brochure when the contents of Dr Burnett's house were sold in 1915.

Sir William (1779–1861) came from much the same part of Scotland as Bishop Burnet's family, but there seems to have been no more connection between the Stuart bishop and the Victorian surgeon than between the two Southampton families named Burnett who severally laid claim to these ancestors. A fanciful turn of mind in the Compton Burnetts is borne out by a later and even wilder claim, on the part of Ivy's cousins, to be related to the romantic authoress Frances Hodgson Burnett (*née* Hodgson in 1849 at Manchester, emigrated as a child to America where she married and later divorced a citizen of Knoxville, Tennessee, named Swan Moses Burnett).

† *Ecce Medicus*, p.17. According to Kay Dick (*Ivy and Stevie*, p.27), Ivy said that her father had studied under Freud in Vienna, but Freud was nine years old at the time.

addresses), he had abandoned the business by 1865, becoming instead a dairyman at Millbrook, two miles outside Southampton. Four years later, just before his son left Vienna to take an M.B. at Glasgow, Charles had moved again to Pinks Farm at Dibden, where he leased three fields (one arable, two pasture, just enough to keep a horse) and remained for the next decade. One may perhaps detect fellow feeling in Dr Compton Burnett's word, delivered years later, on another brilliant medical student: 'he knew but too well the pinch of poverty and the weirdness of want'.[5]

Ivy never knew her paternal grandfather, who died the year before she was born. Her father, who was fond of recalling in middle age the woods and fields of his boyhood, seldom spoke of his early struggles or indeed of anything that had happened in the fifteen years between his leaving Redlynch and reaching Vienna. Ivy's own friends in later life generally assumed that she came, as the families do in her books, of a long line of country squires settled for hundreds of years in the same place.* In fact she had moved with her family four times before she was fourteen, living on housing estates or in brand new suburban developments and hearing practically nothing about her Compton Burnett relations. The setting she later chose for her novels was the traditional one, hallowed by literary precedent, providing ample scope and a stable background for the tyrannical passions which chiefly absorbed her attention. She herself had always known comfort and material security in a provincial society where class distinctions seemed paramount and immutable; the family history remained in her childhood largely unknown save for what might be built on a few Wilson teaspoons, the engraving of Sir William Burnett and a photograph of Compton village church in Wiltshire which hung in one of the bedrooms. In so far as she cared about her ancestors at all, Ivy accepted the story that her great-grandfather had married a Miss Compton who brought him a fortune. This fortune was said to have been recklessly squandered by her great-uncles, 'all of whom died on the hunting field save one, and he was kicked to death by his horse in the stable'.[6] But the second part

* 'Originally, she [Ivy] told me, her family came from Wiltshire, the village of Compton; she was a descendant of a Bishop Burnett [sic] who married a Miss Compton. The family, to use her word, was "raised" on an estate, and one appreciated the truth of this in her fiction.' (Ivy and Stevie, p.27.) Miss Dick's account may conveniently serve to typify the muddled impression Ivy contrived to leave on her friends; whether or not she actively put it about that she was raised on an estate, the assumption was certainly one she did nothing to contradict.

of this story had mellowed with time as much as the first since, of Ivy's three Compton Burnett great-uncles, one was in middle age a labourer whose wife sold straw bonnets in Southampton; and another was a grocer who died at seventy-six of bronchitis, leaving £46 14s. 2d, when Ivy was one year old.

Her father by this time had long since lost sight of his Hampshire connections. But the break with his family was probably not as decisive, and certainly not as dramatic, as the break he had also made at the very start of his career with the medical profession. As a young man in the medical school at Vienna James Compton Burnett seems to have been in his element, charmed by his studies, by the place itself and by the German language. For the rest of his life his conversation and writings were peppered with anecdotes of his student days on the continent, with Viennese proverbs, quotations from Schiller and practical cures picked up on his travels. He is said to have spent an extra two years studying anatomy for pleasure at Vienna—'my own dear old alma mater', as he afterwards called it—and acquitted himself so well that, when he finally returned to enrol at the Glasgow medical school, he was permitted to take his M.B. in one year instead of the usual three or four. But, on graduating in 1872 amid the congratulations of his professors, he took a post at the Barnhill Parochial Hospital and Asylum in Glasgow where he was promptly converted to homoeopathy, a step which in those days meant professional death.

Dr Burnett had left university with strictly orthodox medical views, 'having been taught by good men and true that Homoeopathy was therapeutic Nihilism'.[7] This was the current view at the time, often expressed with a great deal more virulence. Homoeopathy in Britain was confined to a more or less persecuted sect, actively ridiculed in the universities and widely despised outside them. Its followers were looked upon as quacks or cranks, its practice had narrowly escaped being declared illegal in the 1850s and the British Medical Association prohibited homoeopaths from joining its ranks. The professor of anatomy at Glasgow in 1873 had begged his most promising pupil not to throw his life away, for it was true that, as Dr Burnett himself afterwards bitterly put it, 'the social value of [surgery] is—a baronetcy. The social value of [homoeopathic remedies] is—slander and contempt.'* When

* *Tumours of the Breast*, p.15. One cannot help suspecting that the source of this particular outburst was Sir James Paget (George Eliot's physician and serjeant-surgeon to Queen Victoria, created a baronet in 1871) whose consulting rooms were across the road from Burnett's, and who regularly figures in the doctor's writings as a notorious enemy.

urged not to abandon orthodox medicine, Dr Burnett had declared that 'he could not buy worldly honours at the cost of his conscience',[8] but one may readily detect behind his conscientious objection an equally keen resentment of received authority. Perhaps because of his early hardships, there was something about social ostracism which suited him. The aggressive and dictatorial impulses which play such a large part in the novels of I. Compton-Burnett were by no means unknown to her father. He remained all his life uncompromisingly independent and furiously scornful of nervous hesitation or compromise in other people. His immediate reaction, on resolving to try a first experiment in homoeopathy, suggests already the belligerent streak in his character which was later to be fully developed: 'I would try the thing at the bedside, prove it to be a lying sham, and expose it to an admiring profession'.

He was thirty-two years old. He had reached without help against substantial odds a point at which a brilliant career was confidently predicted ahead of him. But he had been increasingly discouraged for some time and, considering the wretched conditions under which poor medical students and inexperienced young doctors then worked in the ill-ventilated, overcrowded, smallpox- and cholera-ridden tenements of Glasgow, it is scarcely surprising that Dr Burnett, in his first post at Barnhill, had half determined to throw up medicine altogether and emigrate as a farmer to America. His own account of what happened next admirably conveys both the extreme vehemence of his nature, whether in passive despair or energetic reaction, and the tender, even shrinking sensibility which is evident in all his clinical writings and which—together with his passionate regard for truth and his considerable gifts as a storyteller—he later passed on to his daughter Ivy:

A number of years ago, on a dull dreary afternoon, which I had partly occupied at B— Hospital with writing death certificates, I suddenly rose and felt something come over me, for the fiftieth time at that period. I hardly knew what, but it grew essentially out of my unsatisfactory clinical results. I had been an enthusiastic student of medicine originally, but an arrantly sceptic professor quite knocked the bottom out of all my faith in physic, and overmuch hospital work and responsibilities, grave beyond my age and experience, had squeezed a good deal of the enthusiasm out of me. After pacing up and down the surgery, I threw myself back into my chair and dreamily thought myself back to the green fields and the early bird's-nesting and fishing days of my childhood. Just then a corpse was carried by the surgery window, and I turned to the old dispenser, and enquired in a petulant tone, 'Tim, who's that dead now?' 'Little Georgie, sir.'

Now little Georgie was a waif who belonged to nobody, and we had liked him and had kept him about in odd beds, as one might keep a pet animal. Everybody liked little Georgie; the most hardened old pauper would do him a good turn, and no one was ever more truly regretted than he.

It all came about in this way: One day I wanted a bed for an acute case, and I ordered little Georgie out of his bed in a warm, snug corner, to another that was in front of a cold window; he went to it, caught cold, had pleurisy, and Tim's reply gives the result.

Said I to myself: If I could only have stopped the initial fever that followed the chill by the window, Georgie had probably lived. But three medical men besides myself had treated Georgie—all in unison —and all hospital men; still pleurisy followed the febricula, dropsy followed the pleurisy, and poor little Georgie died. Old Tim was a hardened man, and I never saw him shew any feeling or sentiment of any kind, or regret at anybody's death, but I verily believe he was very near dropping just one wee tear over Georgie's memory, for I noticed that his attention was needlessly and unwontedly fixed on the surface of the bottles he was washing. Be that as it may, Georgie was no more, and I FELT SURE HE NEED NOT HAVE DIED, and this consciousness nearly pressed me down into the earth.[9]

Confiding his despondency that night to his friend Alfred Hawkes at the Royal Infirmary, who recommended homoeopathy, Dr Burnett furtively purchased—'very much as if I were contemplating a crime'— Richard Hughes' two manuals, on pharmacodynamics and therapeutics, which at that time provided the standard introduction in English to this dangerous ground:

I mastered their main points in a week or two, and came from a consideration of these to the conclusion either that Homoeopathy was a very grand thing indeed, or this Dr Hughes must be a very big ——. No, the word is unparliamentary. You don't like the word ——? Well, I do, it expresses my meaning to a T; on such an important subject there is for me no middle way, it must be either good clear God's truth, or black lying.

One hundred years later, the sequel is still remembered with awe in homoeopathic circles. Hughes had suggested aconite as a remedy for simple fever and Dr Burnett determined to test the advice on his children's fever ward, dosing all the patients down one side with Fleming's Tincture of Aconite and treating the others as usual. Within twenty-four hours all the aconite children were cured (save one who had measles) and smartly discharged, while the rest still languished in hospital. The experiment was repeated with the same startling results until a truculent nurse, impatient of the doctor's hard heart, dosed all the patients indiscriminately from 'Dr Burnett's Fever Bottle' and emptied the ward.

The doctor was 'simply dumbfounded', spent his nights reading homoeopathic literature and, having suffered a conversion which he afterwards compared to St Paul's on the road to Damascus, instantly resolved 'to fight the good fight of homoeopathy with all the power I possess: were I to do less I should be afraid to die'.[10] His M.D. thesis, submitted when his year's term at Barnhill elapsed, was rejected for heretical, homoeopathic tendencies (a second thesis was accepted in 1876). But early in 1874 Dr Burnett had found an opening in Chester, attracted no doubt by its nearness to Liverpool which rivalled London as a centre of homoeopathic activity. Liverpool was the seat of Dr John Drysdale, founding editor of the *British Journal of Homoeopathy*, who very soon became 'Burnett's chief hero among his contemporaries'. Drysdale was then in his late fifties, had qualified at Edinburgh and spent several years in the great continental medical schools before settling in Liverpool, where his successes in the cholera epidemic of 1849 had so 'roused the envy of his allopathic colleagues' that he was forthwith 'expelled from the Liverpool Medical Institute'. Eight years later the Liverpool Homoeopathic Society was founded, and it was largely because of Drysdale's perseverance that there grew up around him a group of ambitious young homoeopaths (including Burnett's future biographer, John Clarke, and his Glasgow friend Alfred Hawkes), among whom Dr Burnett evidently found himself in congenial company.

He does not seem to have had consulting rooms of his own in Chester, though he afterwards described treating patients at the Chester dispensary which operated from Pepper Street in rooms given free by a homoeopathic chemist named Edward Thomas.[11] Edward Thomas' son John later became a homoeopathic physician, and so did his brother Henry who lived in Whitefriars where Dr Burnett also had lodgings.

Homoeopaths in those days had no choice but to hang together in cliques which perhaps explains why, almost as soon as he arrived in Chester, Dr Burnett began paying court to Edward Thomas' daughter Agnes. She was twenty-one when she met him, presumably through her father or uncle, and they were married shortly afterwards on 6 July 1874. It was a bold move for a newly qualified young doctor without means of his own, especially since Agnes (who was the eldest of ten) cannot have brought him much of a dowry. Her father had inherited a printing business (later producing, among other homoeopathic works, several of his son-in-law's books) in Bridge Street Row next door to his chemist's shop (which stocked 'Homoeopathic Cocoa, Tooth Powder, Pomade etc. etc.' as well as homoeopathic medicines and literature); he was also a practising homoeopathic vet, much in demand among local farmers to look over their diseased pigs, cattle and horses. Within a few months of his marriage Dr Burnett had moved to Liverpool, setting up his plate in what were probably rented premises at 51 Hamilton Square, Birkenhead, where his first child, Olive, was born in 1875. He had a son, James, two years later and another daughter, Margaret (called Daisy), in 1878, by which time he could afford to move his family and consulting rooms a few doors down the square to a house of his own at number seventeen.[12]

He had prospered from the start in Liverpool where he was house surgeon at the homoeopathic dispensary in Hardman Street, pursued a stiff programme of scientific research, read papers to the Homoeopathic Society, became a voluminous contributor to medical journals and built up for himself a practice so thriving that, years later, devoted patients still travelled down from the north to consult him in London. He seems to have drawn this practice chiefly from the local gentry, regularly visiting the country seats of neighbouring squires (where he noted that the horses sent to fetch him in a trap from the station were impressively faster and smarter, in cases of grave illness, than the ambling grass-fed ponies considered quite adequate for routine calls) and growing exceedingly familiar with what he called 'your thoroughly gouty individual' (for whom, in spite of his local reputation as a fierce teetotaller, Dr Burnett prescribed Scotch whisky as often as not). His fame spread fast. Dr Clarke, who was himself no mean physician, considered Dr Burnett 'one of the most remarkable Healers of modern times';[13] and certainly the doctor's own clinical records contain several instances of what must have seemed to his patients little short of miraculous cures.

As 'a struggling young doctor'[14] he had against all expectation speedily cured one important lady in the north of hepatalgia, earning both her gratitude and a notable access of patients. He rescued two maniacal ladies—one of them so violent that it took three or four people to fetch her away in a reinforced carriage—in the nick of time from imprisonment in lunatic asylums for life, being stoutly resisted in both cases by sceptical friends and relations. He was called in May 1875 to examine a case of acute ophthalmia which, being 'specially anxious to make a hit', he cured right away to his patient's amazement; whereupon he treated her cataract so dramatically that, hearing a commotion in his hall one day, he found his door burst open as she stormed his consulting room crying aloud that she had recovered her sight. The case 'made a considerable stir', all the more so because the lady had been distinctly ashamed (as his patients commonly were) of having any truck with a homoeopath in the first place: one testy squire, suffering horribly from eczema, made the dire mistake of consulting in 1874 an eminent skin specialist who 'used such language about me professionally that my patient would not allow my name to be mentioned in his house for nearly three years'. Repenting too late, the luckless old gentleman returned to Dr Burnett only to die of an ossified heart brought on by the ministrations of the malevolent skin doctor.

This cautionary tale, narrated with marked relish, is typical of Dr Burnett's many subsequent encounters with orthodox practitioners—'our friends, the enemy' as he habitually called them—in a lifelong campaign which reached major proportions when, in August 1879, he was appointed editor of the *Homoeopathic World*. This mild and comparatively obscure monthly paper became an offensive weapon in the hands of its new editor, who devoted his very first leader that September to rallying the homoeopathic troops behind him against the medical establishment: 'We are free men, and we refuse to allow our rights to free thought and free action to be trampled under foot by any earthly powers whatsoever. It is useless to prate about peace, there is no peace but the peace of the manacled and the fettered.'

For the next five years Dr Burnett breathed flame, waging a regular feud with the *Lancet* ('The Egyptians worshipped their leeks and onions, in fact grew their gods in their own gardens, and British surgeons worship their *Lancet*, and of course are bound by their religious vows. . . .')[15] which that paper returned with interest. It was common practice in his day for both doctors and eminent patients to disclaim publicly any connection with homoeopathy. Professional medical bodies forbade their members to consult with, or even to meet, their homoeopathic colleagues: 'We shall not condescend to treat such vulgar trade-unionists and ratteners other than with contempt,' wrote Dr Burnett when the Royal College of Surgeons of Ireland passed a resolution to this effect. 'They must feel their position insecure, and so it is, or they would not so far forget themselves. THEY MERELY WANT THE MONOPOLY, and no means seems too bad to get it.' Orthodox chemists refused to stock, and orthodox medical journals to advertise, homoeopathic medicines or literature. The medical journals would not willingly print contributions which so much as mentioned the name of homoeopathy or its founder: 'Now we will not only not omit them, but WE WILL have them WRIT LARGE,' wrote Dr Burnett excitedly in his own journal.

As a freedom fighter, a furious polemicist, an outstanding diagnostician and a scientific researcher whose name had penetrated even orthodox medical circles, he rapidly became one of the acknowledged leaders of homoeopathy. He had left Liverpool for London a few months before he took over the *Homoeopathic World*, moving his family to Lewisham, where his son James died of concussion in May 1879,[16] and where his second son, Richard, was born the following October. Iris was born at 4 Harley Place sixteen months later, by which time Dr Burnett must already have been looking for a larger place with a garden in the more salubrious air outside London. By 1881 he had reached a position sufficiently solid to do so. He had published the first six of his twenty-six medical books, had a seat on the medical committee of the London Homoeopathic Hospital and two years later a lectureship at the hospital's medical school. He had begun treating patients at the homoeopathic headquarters in Finsbury Circus but very soon moved to a better address near Harley Street, retaining both practices to the end of his life. He started at much the same time to invest in speculative property development and, in September 1881, acquired a house deep in the country—No. 2 Onslow Villas, Woodridings, Pinner—in which to install his wife and children while he himself travelled daily to London.

Agnes presumably welcomed this arrangement. Relations between Dr Burnett and the Thomases seem to have been cordial, judging at any rate by the fact that Agnes' father began contributing veterinary notes to the *Homoeopathic World* soon after his son-in-law became editor, starting with a case of Red Mange in a dog named Percy in January 1882. Shortly afterwards Agnes' uncle was writing on gallstones from Llandudno (where he had opened a hydro); and one may perhaps deduce from an energetic defence by the editor of homoeopathic chemists in general ('A special training is absolutely needful, and also capacity, and above all *conscientiousness. . . .*'),[17] printed immediately below Edward Thomas' first article, that Dr Burnett thoroughly approved of his father-in-law. Agnes had spent all her life in the north, surrounded by a large and affectionate family from whom she had scarcely been parted for, even when she moved to a home of her own, it was still no great distance to her father's house in Pepper Street, Chester. She was greatly attached to her nine younger brothers and sisters who, according to one of her nieces, were all 'deeply fond of her' in return. In Birkenhead she had lived above the consulting rooms but, considering the vast amount of work her husband accomplished in their first seven years of marriage, she can never have been used to spending much time in his company. She bore him six children and died, survived by the last, in childbirth at Pinner on 8 September 1882. Twelve months and three days later Dr Burnett was married again to Katharine Rees, the beautiful daughter of Alderman Rowland Rees, J.P., civil engineer, architect and prospective Mayor of Dover.

2

KATHARINE REES WAS twenty-seven when she married and had long been accustomed to admiration. Her father, the Alderman, was a prominent citizen of Dover, a prime mover in local controversy and a pillar of the Methodist chapel. She herself had 'the high, arched nose and high, arched brow, the full blue eye and short but finished build'[18] which, nearly half a century later, her daughter Ivy passed on to Sophia Stace in *Brothers and Sisters*. Her long golden hair was famous in her family and so was the story that, when Queen Victoria came to Dover, Katie joined the procession and rode round the town with her sister Lizzie acknowledging applause and bowing to the populace from an open carriage. Years later she liked to tell over to her daughters the long list of suitors rejected in her youth, among them a future judge whom she had seriously considered but turned down for his pompous address; whereupon her stepmother said, 'My dear, be careful. You may do this once too often.'

She fell ill not long afterwards and is said to have been convalescing with her married sister Lizzie when she met her husband by chance in the winter of 1882. The Reeses were already homoeopathic enthusiasts and they had relations in Liverpool named Thomas who, whether or not they belonged to the same family as Dr Burnett's first wife, were probably the indirect means of introducing him to his second.[19] Whatever the connection, rumours from Liverpool had so impressed Katharine's brother-in-law that he took her up to town to consult Dr Burnett, who instantly fell in love with her. Five years after their marriage her husband gave, as the twenty-sixth of his *Fifty Reasons for Being a Homoeopath*, his own account of this meeting:

It may be half a dozen years ago that an unusually beautiful, sweet girl, a good way in her twenties, residing in an important provincial town, was noticed to fade and get weak, with peculiar ill-defined throat symptoms, weakness in her back, rectal and uterine irritation, weakness and emaciation. People could not think what had come over her. She is one of those human high-breds who will not cave in, but, if duty calls, will go on till they drop: till then, existing on their 'go' rather than on their physique.

In life they are commonly misunderstood, and because they can put on a spurt or clear a very high-fenced difficulty *au besoin*, the un-knowing and non-observant think they are really strong, but are lazy or sham.

'Oh! she nursed her nieces for weeks and never had her clothes off, but did not seem to mind it a bit, and now she would have you believe she is so delicate; she shams, it's all put on.' But it is not put on at all; if you will examine their heads you will find the animal sphere almost entirely absent. . . .

The lady in question has the most exquisitely intellectual development, a wonderful arch of cerebrum, but no occipital power worth while.

Well, the patient in question had been through a domestic trial and had *bent*; some thought she had *broken*.[20]

Dr Burnett's attitude to his wife's nervous temperament is revealing in the light of what happened later, and so is his report of uncharitable comments passed by her friends and relations in whom family pride, family possessiveness and the family temper were all apt to run high. The passage goes on to describe how the local physician diagnosed Bright's Disease, recommended that the patient wear flannel all over and predicted that, though she might last for some time with care, she could never get well: 'Much family council was held together, and the outlook being dark and hopeless, the young lady was brought to me.' Dr Burnett cured her in eight months with *Mercurius vivus*,* whereupon she got married, had 'several bouncing children' and afterwards remained in excellent health. Mrs Compton Burnett was naturally charmed with this public tribute to her beauty and goodness and, since her conduct as mother and stepmother exposed her to criticism and 'misunderstanding' after her marriage quite as much as before, her husband's enthusiastic defence of her character must have been a particular satisfaction. The date puts their first meeting not later than January 1883. They were married on 11 September by Katharine's elder brother, the Rev. Allen Rees, at the Wesleyan Centenary Chapel in Dover, spent their honeymoon in Paris and returned in October to Pinner where, nine months later, Ivy was born.

Dr Burnett ever after maintained that his second wife was 'the love of his life'. But she was also gay, imperious, exacting, fond of town life and 'not at all maternal' when she married a widower fifteen years older than herself, becoming stepmother to his five small children, and went to live in the country. By 1883, her five brothers and three elder sisters had nearly all long since left home. Elizabeth, who was two years older and remained all their lives Katie's closest sister, had been married at twenty-two in 1875. Their mother died in 1877, whereupon Katie kept house for her father until in his sixties he suddenly married again. Her stepmother was not unkind but, as the only unmarried daughter at home, Katie must have been glad four years later of the chance to become mistress of her own establishment. She seems to have taken much the same view as the second Mrs Hutton (who is similarly placed in Ivy's first novel): 'The father, whose home she ordered, had himself taken a second wife; and though her late esteem of stepmothers had not been flattering to the class, she found that their sway appeared less repellant regarded as wielded than obeyed.'[21]

Dealings between a stepmother and her stepchildren are scrutinized with minute, even reckless, attention in the works of I. Compton-Burnett. 'A family is itself. And of course there are things hidden in it. They could hardly be exposed,' says Hugo Middleton in *The Mighty*

---

* 'In Bright's disease a past grandmaster in therapeutics has all his work cut out, and he will need all his knowledge, however great, of climate, diet, raiment and therapeutics,' wrote Dr Burnett seven years later (*Gout and Its Cure*, p.155) when he found tincture of cloves a great help, though *Mercurius* remained his chief standby.

and Their Fall, while watching the first meeting between a second wife and an eldest daughter supplanted, as Dr Compton Burnett's eldest daughter had been, by her father's new marriage. The second Mrs Middleton had hoped for a life without constraint or concealment, and had been by no means prepared by her future husband for the shock of meeting his family:

'He simply said he was a widower with a mother and five children.'
'Simply!' said Hugo. 'And you thought you could live a life that was what it seemed!'[22]

Ivy's mother never cared greatly for small children, her own or anyone else's. When she married Dr Burnett she took on his first wife's two sons and three daughters—all under eight years old, and the eldest at least fiercely hostile towards their new mother—and had seven more of her own. She disliked living in the country, and her new home was not even in Pinner itself but a few miles outside on a recently built housing estate reached by a muddy lane from the village. She was passionately devoted to her husband, as he was to her, but for most of their married life Dr Burnett lived at an hotel in London, joining his family at weekends, seldom taking more than five days' holiday together, and only towards the end of his life allowing himself one day at home in the middle of the week, which he allotted to writing. Katharine possessed in abundance the magnetism that goes with decided views and a forceful personality. But she had also intense nervous energy for which she can have found little outlet, living in isolation with the children's nurse, increasing numbers of nursery maids, governesses and household servants, moving in the next fourteen years to a series of steadily larger houses, making few friends and no intimate companions outside her own family, always without her husband, and surrounded always by more and more children.

Dr Burnett's eldest daughter, Olive, had her eighth birthday in October 1883, when her father brought home a new wife almost the same age as her own mother had been when she died. In the interval before his second marriage Olive had come to think of herself as her father's especial companion, allowed downstairs after her brothers and sisters were in bed to dine with him alone on the nights when he came back from London. What must have been particularly bewildering for a small child—and made her dismissal even harder to bear, when she was abruptly banished to the nursery again—was the fact that her father was so evidently in love with the newcomer. Courtship and marriage had occupied rather less than a year in an affair which, as both parties later declared, had begun with love at first sight; and by all accounts Ivy's mother took few pains to conceal the feelings that had lain behind her precipitate romance, and afterwards came to dominate her life. Olive, who remembered her own mother clearly, never forgave this usurpation and always bitterly resented her stepmother's presence. Her sister Daisy, who was five, may also have remembered their mother but the others were probably too young: Richard had been three, Iris eighteen months and Charlie a few days old at her death. They never spoke of her afterwards, or not at any rate in front of their half-brothers and -sisters. They called their father's second wife Mother, except for Olive who spoke of her always as 'Mrs Burnett'; her own children called her Mummy or Mum. In a few years Olive was old enough to be sent away to boarding school (which was not then usually considered, as it was to be later, the proper place for young girls from respectable families) where Daisy and Iris soon followed her. Ivy and her four younger sisters were educated at home.

There seems to have been a break with the Thomas family much as there was with Dr Burnett's own Hampshire relations round about the time of his second marriage. His father, Charles Compton Burnett, had died on 21 August 1883, three weeks before the wedding. His father-in-law, Edward Thomas, who had been a regular contributor to the *Homoeopathic World* in Agnes Burnett's lifetime, sent in his last paper in October 1883, the month in which the editor returned from his second honeymoon. After that contributions from Edward and Henry Thomas abruptly ceased, and the Thomases never came south to visit Agnes' children, though Olive and Daisy were several times sent on their own to stay with their grandparents and their four maiden aunts in Chester. They had five Thomas uncles only one of whom had children, all born long after the little Compton Burnetts, who apparently said nothing on their visits to the north about their own difficulties at home.[23] This loss of contact must have contributed to the stepchildren's loneliness in a home where their background counted for nothing, their father was seldom available and their own concerns were increasingly overshadowed by the arrival of Ivy and, after her, of six more half-brothers and -sisters.

It is perhaps small wonder that earlier ties should have receded in Dr Burnett's household before the claims of his second wife's numerous

Rees connections. Katharine Compton Burnett took no small pride in her own side of the family. 'We are descended from Ap Rees ap Rees ap Madoc' was one of her favourite sayings, and her children often teased her about this vague but princely ancient Welshman thought to to have bequeathed royal blood to later, more humdrum nineteenth-century Reeses. Katharine's father, from whom she had inherited a strong partiality for her own relations as well as much else in her character, became Mayor of Dover less than two months after her marriage. James Compton Burnett inscribed his next book, published just before Ivy was born, 'To that Eminent Christian Citizen and Ardent Champion of Liberty Rowland Rees J.P. Mayor of Dover the following pages are admiringly dedicated by their author'.[24] The admiration was mutual, for after his retirement, the Mayor moved to be near his son-in-law's family and spent the next eleven years a few streets away from the house where Ivy grew up. She was eighteen when he died, and must have heard a great deal in her childhood about his exploits in public and private life. His first wife, Ivy's grandmother, was christened Sophia Sabine; his second wife's surname was Stace; all three names were borrowed by his granddaughter when she came to choose names for her fearsome domestic tyrants and, in so far as one can trace any of her material back to a single source, her grandfather himself may be said to live on in the novels of I. Compton-Burnett.

Rowland Rees was the 'peremptory man'[25] whom, towards the end of her life, Ivy described to Julian Mitchell. He himself boasted that the notorious temper, for which he was famed and feared in Dover, had descended to him from another 'ardent champion of liberty', Ap Rice ap Howell ap Rowland ap Rees. But all that is known for sure is that Rowland's father was a John Rees from Wales who arrived, probably round about 1808, at Great Clacton in Essex where he built the eleven Martello towers on the east coast, put up to withstand Napoleon after the French invasion scare at the start of the century. Seven of John Rees' towers still stand,[26] though they proved useless after the peace of 1815 and were never even garrisoned. Rowland, who was the second of John's eight children, was born and baptized in 1816 at Great Clacton, and grew up in a house within the curtilege of one of the towers on a desolate site (now Butlins' holiday camp) overlooking the North Sea at Clacton Wash.

Ivy and her Rees cousins later maintained that both Rowland and his father had been army officers but, since neither appears on the army lists, family memories on the Rees side seem to have been no more dependable than they were on the Burnetts'. John Rees had come to Clacton as Clerk of Works to the Royal Engineers; he was remembered long afterwards by an ancient inhabitant who said that old Mr Rees carried on a business as coal merchant at the Wash (which was then a popular landing place for smugglers, as well as for legitimate cargoes) when the Napoleonic wars were over; what is certain is that, some time after 1825 when his eighth child was baptized at Great Clacton, John Rees moved with his family to Dover where enormous defensive works were under construction on the Western Heights. He had married in 1813 Nancy Sadler, one of the sixteen children of George Sadler of 'Three Chimneys' who belonged to solid, East Anglian farming stock. Ivy said that her great-grandmother 'had the misfortune to stand too close to a cannon one day when it went off and deafened her'. This was why, when Nancy Rees later lived as a widow with her son Rowland, his children were all obliged to learn sign language, being forbidden to speak in her presence: 'Ivy's mother and her brothers and sisters could all talk on their hands'.[27]

Rowland had followed his father at nineteen as a clerk to the Royal Engineers, and had married at twenty-one Sophia Sabine Broad,[28] daughter of Charles Broad, a carver and gilder of Bench Street. The Broads had attended St Mary's, Dover, for generations but Rowland, who was posted as a young married man to Gibraltar and there converted by the local Methodist missionary, brought up his children as staunch Wesleyans. Piety combined with a marked inclination to power made him at various times circuit steward, class leader, six times lay representative at Methodist conferences and a celebrated local preacher. He was active in the cause of total abstinence, a leading member of the Dover Temperance Reformers and a fervent supporter in the 'seventies and 'eighties of the Social Purity Movement, resembling in this as in much else the elder Andrew Stace in *Brothers and Sisters*: 'One of the religious movements had swept him away in his youth; and a stern and simple Protestantism had mingled with his pride of race, had leavened his mind and his outlook, had given him a passionate zest for purity of life, and an eager satisfaction in the acknowledged rectitude of his own.'[29]

The force which had swept Rowland Rees away in his youth was embodied in William Rule, the formidable Methodist minister who had chosen Catholic Gibraltar of all places to become the chief Wesleyan missionary outpost in the British army. Dr Rule, whose ambition was no less than the wholesale conversion of Spain, had been persecuted on, and twice expelled from, the mainland. His activities in Gibraltar itself had meanwhile so exasperated the commander of the British garrison that soldiers were permitted to attend the Wesleyan chapel only after direct intervention from Whitehall; and he had simultaneously caused such perturbation among the Roman Catholic clergy that Pope Gregory VI was moved to issue a specific warning against him. Matters came to a head in 1839, the year of Wesley's centenary and also of Rowland Rees' conversion, when a new Bishop and Vicar Apostolic—'once an Inquisitor in Seville, in the last days of the Horrible Tribunal'[30]—was dispatched to the Rock expressly to crush Dr Rule. The intrepid missionary merely redoubled his efforts to enlighten the priest-ridden papists, ably assisted in his six mission schools as in his more daring evangelical exploits by Rowland Rees, who delighted long afterwards to relate to his grandchildren how he had smuggled satchels full of Bibles over the border to Spain* (a feat which would have gladdened the heart of the lay preacher in Ivy's first novel who, though he shuddered perfunctorily at agnosticism and atheism, thought Roman Catholicism far more pernicious than either). After two years at Gibraltar and a brief spell at Portsmouth, Rowland Rees was posted next to Hong Kong where he won fame as the first man to organize Methodist class meetings in China; and, before he left, had extracted recognition of the Lord's Day observance from the government of 'that densely populated and thoroughly idolatrous empire'.

After ten years or so in the ordnance civil service, he retired in the mid-1840s to Dover where he set up in private practice as an architect and surveyor, embarking simultaneously on a strenuous career of public appointments. Many of the best houses built in the town between 1850 and 1860 were his, and so was the National Provincial Bank. As Surveyor to the Paving Commissioners, he had charge from 1849 of lighting, maintaining, draining and paving the streets of Dover. As Engineer and Surveyor to the corporation (when the Paving Board

---

* Dr Rule (who had personally visited the spot where the last Spanish Quaker was hanged by the Inquisition in 1821) describes how, round about 1839, he ventured over the border again 'with a young man then acting as assistant missionary' in a 'carriage well packed with New Testaments', distributed them free to a grateful crowd, narrowly outwitted the constable sent to arrest him, whipped up his horse, galloped back to Gibraltar and 'did not slacken speed till we were beyond the possibility of being overtaken'. (*Recollections*, p.160.) Contemporary accounts of Rowland Rees' career in the Methodist press confirm his prowess as a Bible smuggler, so I see no reason why this young assistant should not have been Ivy's grandfather.

was dismantled in 1850), he reformed the town's sewage, initiating a vast new arterial system of drainage and water supply which cost £70,000 and took thirty years to pay off (the citizens of Dover groaning the while under an unprecedented rate of three shillings in the pound). Resigning this post not without acrimony in 1861, he became Engineer, Architect and Receiver of Rents to the Harbour Board and stayed there for practically a quarter of a century; his plan for extending Dover harbour was turned down in 1882 (as were all the other plans submitted at that time). He had been elected town councillor in 1862, an alderman three years later, and remained Alderman Rees with barely a gap until on 9 November 1883—at an election so tense that the police were flung aside and the great burnished bar of the Council Chamber torn down 'by the rush of the outside burgesses to be present'[31]—he became Mayor by the chairman's single casting vote.

The following Sunday the Mayor, 'being a Wesleyan and a much stauncher political nonconformist than Wesleyans usually are', broke the established mayoral custom of attending church in state: a shrewd conclusion to a singularly intransigent career devoted, on at least two major and innumerable minor occasions in the past thirty-four years, to vigorous agitation for local reform. Wesleyan Methodism remained for most of the nineteenth century a stoutly conservative body, Tory by inclination though officially non-political, and distinctly timid, when not positively repressive, in its attitude to the comparatively few but conspicuous radical agitators whom the movement was nonetheless bound to produce: laymen trained to manipulate the democratic processes of church government, accustomed to public speaking and anxious to command a wider audience than their own humble chapel-going congregations. Rowland Rees was 'in his element', as a contemporary account nicely said, 'in putting his shoulder to the wheel, helping to get the car of public business out of the ancient ruts'. Inefficiency annoyed him; but, though his principles were libertarian, his temperament was autocratic, obstinate, overbearing, quick to take umbrage and mortally offensive when crossed.

Throughout his career the Dover papers regularly record Rowland Rees taking part amid 'uproar' in the exchange of 'smart blows', reporting the first and one of the fiercest of these turbulent scenes barely six months after his début, on 14 June 1849, as a newly appointed young officer to the Paving Board. Complaints were constantly laid that summer against the lamentable ineptitude, parsimony and pro-crastination of the Paving Commissioners who, in spite of rising cholera and the repeated remonstrances of their Surveyor, could by no means be brought to approve the newfangled notion of paving and sewaging the town. They were moreover implacably, and not unnaturally, opposed to the Public Health Act of 1848 (a measure in their own words 'fraught with mischief, pregnant with litigation, tyrannical in its machinery and tending most materially to interfere with constitutional rights, and to the subversion of the liberty of the subject'),[32] one of the great reforming bills of the nineteenth century whereby the Board itself would inevitably be abolished. Accusations of lying, forgery, fraud and threats of libel were freely bandied at the Board's meetings between the conservative majority and the Surveyor's small radical faction. In Christmas week 1849, the Commissioners flatly rejected the Act's adoption; four days later, at a specially convened and 'densely crowded Common Hall', Rowland Rees' counter motion was carried by two to one over the heads of his employers, who were shortly afterwards obliged to assist at their own dissolution.

At its first meeting on 3 August 1850, the corporation unanimously invited Mr Rees to continue in his old post under the newly constituted Board of Health. But the Surveyor's path ran no more smoothly than before and, by October, he had already detected 'dishonourable and unprincipled' plotting against him, protesting that he 'would rather resign his office and go out of every public thing'[33] than tolerate interference from his new employers. In the next ten years he was frequently accused of petty offences (charging too much in fees, appropriating too many perquisites and percentages, neglecting public for private business) and angrily retaliated, expostulating against the 'malignity' of his enemies, observing that 'those who had attacked him had mistaken their man', denouncing their complaints as 'calumnious', 'incapable of proof', 'abusive, low and contemptible'. In November 1858, the Board of Health proposed to reduce his salary, a resolution instantly repudiated by the Surveyor who declined thereafter to draw so much as a penny; matters were still unresolved two years later, when he submitted simultaneous plans for a new reservoir and for doubling his pay. His supporters declared him 'the worst paid man in town'. His opponents argued that, since the Surveyor had 'frequently insulted the Board', 'had never performed his duties to their satisfaction, and had invariably set them completely at defiance', he was entitled neither to his salary nor to his post as their officer.

In May 1861, at a sensational meeting which several times threatened to turn into a riot to the vast amusement of a packed public gallery, the Surveyor was finally dismissed by a manœuvre which one of his only three supporters pronounced 'unmanly, un-English and un-paralleled in the history of public bodies'.[34] Freely distributing threats, abuse, charges of conspiracy and promises to sue on all hands, the victim himself declared that 'of all the scandalous doings that had come to his knowledge this was the most cowardly, the most unjust attack that had ever been made upon him in his lifetime'. But Mr Rees had put in much time that summer campaigning against the commissioners of Dover harbour—'dragging those gentlemen through their own harbour mud' as a friend loyally said—till in June they resigned in a body. Whereupon, the ancient authority being declared obsolete under the 1861 Harbour Act, the first move of the new Harbour Board which replaced it was to employ Rowland Rees at twice his old salary.

What had maddened his previous employers was the suspicion that the Surveyor was 'too strong for them, too long-headed and would over-ride them, as many believed he had over-ridden them for a long time'. Precisely the same suspicion maddened his colleagues on the town council for the next twenty years and more: 'If Rees had been "at it", men read the papers to see what Rees had been "at".'[35] More often than not his agitations promoted the noblest causes—liberty of the citizen, religious tolerance, freedom of speech—privileges he seldom cared to extend to any persuasion except his own. Views with which he disagreed were dismissed as moonshine or claptrap, aldermen stout enough to oppose him were grievously badgered and bullied although, as one of them plaintively said, 'the Council was not composed wholly of fools, imbeciles, idiots and donkeys, as he had heard Alderman Rees call the members'.[36]

If Ivy's grandfather was as gruff with his family as he was with his colleagues in public, he could also on occasion be excellent company. A pleasant account of evenings at the Reeses' is given by the Rev. Hugh Price Hughes, another belligerent Welshman who had begun his career in 1869 as a Methodist minister in Dover and afterwards gratefully remembered his welcome by the Alderman's family. Old Mrs Rees, for whose sake the Alderman had forbidden his children to speak save in sign language, died at the age of eighty-one in 1868. Nine years later his wife died, 'respected and beloved by all who knew her' according to the *Methodist Recorder*, on 6 July 1877, when she was sixty-three. In the eighteen months before he re-married, his household was run by his daughters Katie and Lucy (who had been widowed young, and returned to her parents' house with slender means and two small children). According to a family tradition which Ivy later put to memorable use in *A House and Its Head* and *The Mighty and Their Fall*, her grandfather had spoken no word of his intentions until shortly before the wedding when, summoning his family about him, he formally announced that he meant to marry again, had made due provision for Lucy and desired his children to meet his betrothed.

Teresa Miriam Stace was then in her mid-fifties, the daughter of a surgeon in Southampton who had recently died, leaving her with a house of her own and a comfortable income to run it.[37] She was married by licence on 21 January 1879, at a Presbyterian church in Southampton; how or when she had first met her husband his family never discovered. She was handsome, intelligent, humorous, and seems to have got on well with her stepchildren though there are indications that she could not wholly approve Katharine's behaviour when she in turn acquired stepchildren. Katharine herself liked and perhaps admired her stepmother for, however irascible Rowland Rees may have been, his second wife had a will as strong. Nearly ninety years later, Ivy told Julian Mitchell that her grandfather 'disapproved very strongly indeed of the Married Women's Property Act. He spent all his first wife's money—"not unvirtuously, but on setting up sons in foolish businesses and so on". When she died, "he lamented her", then married again. But he was quite unable to get control, as he wished, of his second wife's fortune, and when she died, she left it back to her own family "as she had every right to do". He was furious, being a tyrannical as well as a peremptory man.'[38] Rowland Rees' first wife had not been a rich woman but he certainly disinherited three of his sons because, as he said in his will, they had 'already had more than their share of my property'; and it was true that, when his second wife died without children of her own many years later, she left what remained of her marriage portion—£6,726—back to her Stace nephews and nieces.

Her husband's employees at the Harbour Board had been so moved by the marriage that they drew up a congratulatory address to their chief 'when he took upon himself sweet bondage for the second time'.[39] He was elected Mayor four years later; and his term of office was marked not so much by any outstanding civic achievement as by the tremendous scenes regularly enacted within the mayor's parlour, scenes so disreputable and sometimes so hilarious that the local reporters took to recording them under the headline BAITING THE MAYOR. Minor points of procedure ostensibly prompted these brisk bouts of name-calling but what was at issue was clearly the Mayor's own domineering personality. A skilled heckler himself, he now found his victims uniting against him, the timid egging on the brave to open revolt, so that the Mayor—protesting that his mutinous council had perpetrated 'the greatest breach of order that has ever been offered to any Mayor in England'—came on at least one occasion perilously close to deposition. It is a situation by no means uncommon, in a domestic setting, in the novels of I. Compton-Burnett; and readers accustomed to the sophistries of arbitrary parents and grandparents in her fiction may well find something oddly familiar in, for instance, the accents of mingled grief, rage and mortification with which, having signally failed to impose his will on a recalcitrant watch committee, her grandfather in fact promptly proclaimed himself the injured party:

> Public objects, public duty and public convenience alone influenced me. . . . To suggest that I am setting up my will in opposition to that of the Committee is perfectly absurd. I hate assumptions of personal power. There is no man in Dover who is more opposed to the assumption of personal power than I am, particularly in corporation affairs, therefore the idea that I should set up my arbitrary power in opposition to the wish of the Committee is perfectly absurd. I never assumed anything of the kind. That resolution was passed, I said: 'Pass your resolution, it will be inconvenient for me, and I shall not be able to attend, but pray do not consider me in the matter.' . . . I am the Mayor and you having chosen to elect me to that office, although I attach very little importance to these attacks personally, I do not wish indignity to be done to the office of Mayor by an insult offered to me. . . . Pass your resolution by all means, but for the reasons I have given I could not attend those meetings, and I am sure my fellow townsmen would not ask me to allow myself to be shut up in a private room to be insulted and called all sorts of names, behind the back of the public.[40]

But, if Alderman Rees was widely detested in Dover, he was also greatly esteemed. He had been 'loved and reverenced'[41] by Hugh Price Hughes, who never forgot the debt incurred as a young man in his first ministry at Dover. Hughes later became (after Wesley himself and the conservative Jabez Bunting who dominated the movement in the first half of the nineteenth century) the third major influence on Wesleyan Methodism. A tireless enemy to social and moral corruption in the 'eighties and 'nineties, founding editor of the *Methodist Times*, keeper of the nonconformist conscience (a cliché he had himself coined) and pioneer of the Forward Movement in Methodism, he was also largely responsible for rallying the nonconformist vote behind Gladstone. By his savage denunciations at the height of the Parnell scandal, Hughes precipitated Gladstone's ultimatum and subsequent disaster for the Liberal Government, a feat for which we may thank Ivy's grandfather. It was Alderman Rees who, as a 'red-hot Radical', had first turned the young Hughes into a Liberal, introduced him to Josephine Butler (promoter of Social Purity and an early exponent of women's liberation), encouraged him to take up his lifelong crusade as a public saviour and generally pointed him in the direction of what, some thirty years later, the *Spectator* called 'his noble advocacy of social righteousness'.

On a humbler level the men of the Harbour Board seem to have been especially fond of their chief. They had waited on him in a body at the time of his second marriage; they waited again when his daughter Katharine left home, and on his election as Mayor two months later; and some thirty or forty of them crowded into the dining room of his house on the Esplanade to console and salute him, and to give him a barometer when, in February 1885, he retired after 'a difference of opinion at the Harbour Board'.[42] This one arose, as differences commonly did throughout his career, from a dispute over money; and it is perhaps not altogether surprising to find that, on leaving the post he had held for twenty-four turbulent years, Alderman Rees also left Dover for good three months later. 'In bidding goodbye to the Alderman, with whom we have often differed but oftener agreed,' wrote the *Dover Express* in guarded farewell, 'we cannot help feeling that taking him for all in all, we ne'er may see his like again.'

The Alderman moved with his wife to Great Clacton, where he built himself a capacious, pink-and-white house in the decorative seaside style of the period, and moved again seven years later to a house in Hove round the corner from his son-in-law, James Compton Burnett. These two, who had presumbly met for the first time in 1883, had each instantly recognized in the other a kindred spirit. What seems to have drawn them together was their common support for the campaign against compulsory vaccination which was at its height in the year of their meeting. 'Every right-minded man knows that compulsory vaccination is a criminal act against the sacredness of the person and an infamous outrage on human nature. . . . For the love of God and man, for love of home and country, the people should resist this horribly wicked law,' wrote the Mayor of Dover in a letter dated December 1883, which was widely publicized in the press, cruelly derided in the *Lancet*, and which went on to demand 'the infliction of condign punishment on the wretch who should dare to perpetrate such an act as compulsory vaccination'.[43] In his book *Vaccinosis* (dedicated to the wrathful Mayor) Dr Burnett had argued much the same case, in terms no less heated, on medical grounds. Both were men of far-sighted, radical views which both were apt to forget in the delight of confounding their enemies. 'They have their just reward—the spittle of contempt,' wrote James Compton Burnett in one of the many fighting editorials whose language equals, and often surpasses, the vigour of his father-in-law's political invective.

Dr Burnett had abandoned allopathy because he was convinced that the future of scientific medicine lay with the homoeopaths; but his propagation of this new creed was undertaken more often than not for the sheer pleasure of war, as he himself was well aware—'I do it just to ... slap the jeering ignorance of orthodoxy in the face.' This was all his life a favourite pastime of Alderman Rees, and indeed the atmosphere of schoolboy ragging and baiting which pervaded the mayor's parlour at Dover in 1884 is not a thousand miles away from the piratical exuberance with which the Editor of the *Homoeopathic World* hands out the Black Spot to orthodox medicine: 'We wish to say that we mean *war*, and not peace; we know allopathy, root and branch, and we condemn it as *bad*, altogether *bad*, and pernicious. We will have nothing but war to the bitter end with allopathy *because it is bad, false in principle and pernicious in practice*, and we know whereof we write. We ask nothing better from the allopaths than *war*, and the fiercest fighting till they or we kiss the dust.'[44]

This intransigent, ambitious, independent, progressive and radical background is not perhaps what might have been expected for I. Compton-Burnett. One might legitimately have supposed her the daughter of an impoverished country squire, living in a house inhabited by generations of her forbears on a dwindling income from its ancestral lands, such as provides the setting for practically all her twenty novels. But nonconformity—whether medical, political or religious—was the characteristic expression of iron wills on both sides of her family. Her Burnett ancestors, who had almost certainly been nonconformist as far back as the eighteenth century, had risen in three generations from farm labourers to the prosperous middle classes; the same stubborn energy is evident throughout her maternal grandfather's career; both Burnetts and Reeses might have taken as their guiding rule the rousing words with which her father concluded his New Year editorial for 1881: 'Let our motto be—Forward! We have dangled our legs on the banks of the river of expectancy long enough.'

1884–1896

'I was a child of passion'

I

ON 13 JUNE 1885, eight days after Ivy's first birthday, her brother Guy was born. The two were inseparable as small children, 'like twins' as she said long afterwards;[1] their next brother, Noel, who was three and a half years younger than Ivy, tagged on after his elders or, as they all three passed into the schoolroom, sometimes repaired to the nursery to play with the four younger sisters who arrived at intervals over the next decade. Already Ivy's family background has become recognizably the world of her novels (which practically all take place in the 1890s, or the early years of the next century, roughly the period between her tenth and twentieth birthdays): a large and sequestered Victorian household permitting small contact with people outside it, staffed by domestics who all slept under its roof, and running to a rigid timetable which sharply divided parents and children, masters and servants, nursery, schoolroom and drawing room parties.

Except perhaps for the unusually large number of strong wills shut up together inside it, the Compton Burnetts' seems to have been a perfectly conventional establishment. It followed what must then have been a commonplace pattern whereby those families who had only comparatively lately, and at the expense of considerable effort, attained middle class status were also those who had most to lose by any relaxation of the social code, and therefore those who most stringently enforced and perpetuated the crushing load of respectability which bore down on so many Victorian childhoods. Ivy herself said that the society which allowed later generations to live and mix more freely produced people less dangerous but duller:

Isolation and leisure put nothing into people. But they give what is there, full play. They allow it to grow according to itself, and this may be strongly in certain directions.

I am sure that the people who were middle-aged and elderly when I was young, were more individualized than are now my own contemporaries. The effect of wider intercourse and self-adaptation seems to go below the surface, and the result is that the essence of people is controlled and modified. . . .

Imagine a Winston Churchill, untaught and untrained and unadapted in the sense we mean, and then immured in an isolated life in a narrow community, and think what might have happened to his power, what would have happened to it.[2]

Already one may begin to suspect how deeply she drew later on things she had seen as a child. Her grandfather's unrestrained appetite for power; her mother's similarly imperious temperament aggravated by 'isolation and leisure', and the effect of so much pent-up, frustrated energy on her own children as much as on her stepchildren; the strain under which the first family grew up; Ivy's absorption from infancy in the lives of her two brothers, both of whom died young: all these provided dimly outlines which were to take shape in the novels of I. Compton-Burnett, and so did her father's partial withdrawal from family life. Arthur Waley, who was one of the very few visitors admitted to stay with the Compton Burnetts before the first war, maintained that the doctors in her books—for the most part gentle and perceptive, but invariably peripheral characters—were taken from Ivy's father. She lived at home according to an outward routine which scarcely changed, though it grew harsher towards the end under the shadow of sudden death and perpetual mourning, until the household dissolved in 1915. This dissolution, the deaths of her father and mother and her two brothers, together with the war itself, broke for ever the world in which she had lived for thirty-one years and on which her mature imagination drew for the rest of her life.

'I was a child of passion,' said Ivy looking back, and described how when Guy was given a ball while she was presented with a useful pinafore, she was so maddened by the injustice that she stamped and roared 'till my family feared for my life'.[3] One might have expected a passionate nature from the violent undercurrents as much as from the fearful explosions in her books but, outside the immediate circle bounded by her nurse and her brothers, Ivy seems to have been a

resolutely reticent small girl, learning early that principle of concealment which was afterwards invariably central to her theory of
survival:

'Our true selves should not be anything to be ashamed of,' said
Faith.
'I don't think it would be nice not to be ashamed of them,' said
Hope. 'I am ashamed and terrified of mine, and even more of other
people's.'[4]

Ivy's sisters Vera and Juliet, who were six and eight years younger,
could barely remember even once seeing her lose her temper, though
their nurse often said she had been a difficult baby, much given to
tantrums. This was 'before she had learnt to hide herself', and both
agreed that the hiding began very soon. Throughout the time when
they lived together at home, including a period when Ivy taught them
herself in the schoolroom, they had never known her break those habits
of reserve and watchfulness—'eyes that roved and suddenly withdrew
as if their owner were informed'[5]—well known to her friends in later
life. Probably she had herself and her family under close observation
by the time she was three years old, the age at which Freud held that
the essential foundations of character have already been laid down. It is
also the age of the youngest (and some of the most idiosyncratic as well
as the most enchanting) characters in her books who—since Ivy shared
her mother's lack of maternal feeling and, once she had left the nursery
herself, never again voluntarily had anything to do with small children
—must have been drawn from her own recollections of desire and gratification and the struggle for power at that age. Few other novelists
have caught so sharply the desperate emotions of very small children,
or noted how quickly they acquire worldly wisdom—something sadly
familiar to Nevill Sullivan, in *Parents and Children*, who at three years
old is sufficiently shrewd to have grave misgivings when his mother
promises him a present for tomorrow:

'No, today,' said Nevill, with rising feeling. 'Today.'
'Tomorrow will soon be here,' said Luce.
'It won't,' said Nevill, in a tone of experience.[6]

Nevill, who was the first of her three-year-olds, veers as rapidly
between resignation and rage as the last, Henry Egerton in *A God and*

His Gifts, whose days are darkened by the prodigious virtues of a small relation named Maud (' "Come and let us tell you about Maud," said Merton. "Very good girl. Not at all spoilt. Not stamp and cry," said Henry, openly forestalling information.').The clash of wills may be less ruinous in infancy but it is no less bitter than in middle or old age, and not to be soothed by a chorus of interfering adults when Maud's arrival interrupts Henry, who is making a drawing:

> [Maud] entered, glanced at Henry and stood in silence. Henry returned the glance and looked away.
> 'Say good-morning to Great-Grandma,' said Merton.
> Maud remained silent.
> 'Come, surely you can say a word.'
> 'Pencil,' said Maud, looking at Henry's occupation.
> The latter did not raise his eyes, and Maud's also maintained their direction.
> 'Let her have the pencil, Henry,' said Ada. 'She is younger than you, and she is your guest.'
> Henry put it smoothly behind his back.
> 'Come, the house must be full of pencils,' said Hereward, glancing at his son.
> Maud looked round for signs of this, and seeing none, made an advance on the pencil and acquired it.
> Her host broke down.
> 'Come, what a way to behave!' said Ada.
> 'Paper,' said Maud.[7]

But it was not until she was nearly sixty that small children began to play any great part in the novels of I. Compton-Burnett. Her first eight books dealt almost entirely with relations inside much older families, and one may perhaps gauge how hard this particular knot had been to untie by the fact that, for ten years after her own family broke up, she wrote nothing at all though the bulk of her material had lain ready to hand, almost from birth, in the years before she left home. Samuel Butler, whose *Note-Books* came as a crucial formative influence at the start of her career as a novelist, describes what must have been a familiar precaution of Ivy's in his note, 'On Wild Animals and one's Relations': 'If one would watch them and know what they are driving at, one must keep perfectly still.'[8]

. . .

Not that her early childhood was by any means unhappy. Ivy's mother, always inclined to prefer her sons, was nonetheless fond of this eldest child who had inherited her own colouring—dark blue eyes and golden hair—combined with her husband's sturdy build, his clear complexion, broad brow and the curious set of his eyes, what Ivy called 'the cut of the face'.[9] She was a delicate baby and remained to the end of her life peculiarly prone to colds on the chest. All her brothers and sisters, except Noel, 'were more or less puny at birth', and all but Noel 'were oiled daily during the first year of their lives' with excellent results, on their father's instructions. For all his pugnacity in public, Dr Burnett at home was a tender and thoughtful parent, recommending that cod liver oil be discarded in favour of salad oil 'which is much less nasty', and leaving a charming description of his scheme for the Compton Burnett nursery:

> The mother, or nurse, in charge of the child to have a large pinafore of flannel. . . . She is to be seated in front of a good fire, an ample screen at her back to keep off the draughts. A large soup-plate full of fine salad oil to be slightly warmed and standing near at hand. The babe to be held naked in the lap and the whole of the oil very gently and very slowly and *playfully* rubbed into its entire body, excepting its face and hands, and then the babe to be dressed for the night.[10]

By far the most important person in the children's lives was their nurse, Ellen Smith—Ivy's beloved Minnie—who had come at the age of twenty-three to keep house for their father and take charge of the nursery when his first wife Agnes died, and who remained with the family for the rest of her life, bringing up all twelve children in turn. For most of their lives she was the only mother the stepchildren had known, and they loved her as dearly as the second family did. '"You love Mummy and you love Daddy," said Mrs Compton Burnett, to which Ivy replied: "But I love Minnie best."'[11] Ivy's sisters remembered Minnie as imperturbable and selflessly kind: she had 'very large eyes—very dark, almost green, a wonderful colour—a long nose, soft hair, large capable hands. Nothing put her out of her stride, she could put up with anything—and she had a lot to put up with, too.' She gave up her own independent existence without regret or the least trace of sanctimoniousness because 'it was her pleasure to do so', and she became, as successive catastrophes darkened their childhood, 'prop and mainstay' to the whole household. Much the same might be said of Miss Patmore who was nurse to Sophia Stace's unfortunate children in *Brothers and Sisters* and who bears, in character as much as in looks, an unmistakable likeness to Minnie: 'Miss Patmore was a spare young woman of Sophia's age with a thin, sallow face, a narrow, long nose, and large, kind eyes. Her chief qualities, almost her only ones, for she was built on simple lines, were a great faithfulness, a great kindness and a great curiosity.'[12]

Miss Smith, like Miss Patmore, was a haberdasher's daughter, a fact which set her well above most nurses since it meant that she had a home of her own and was not obliged to earn a living. Her father, Joseph Smith, kept a large and prosperous draper's shop in St Matthews Street, Ipswich, had sent his daughter to boarding school, and subsequently left her a competence in his will.[13] Minnie might have lived at home if she chose but she disliked her stepmother and returned only on occasional visits, causing consternation in the Compton Burnett nursery. 'Well, if this goes on I shall go for a holiday,' she would say when the children became obstreperous, a threat which they parried with the constant refrain: '*Promise* you won't go away for a holiday this year'. Guy had named her on one of these visits to her sisters in Ipswich when, as a baby of two, he had cried himself sick till consoled with her dressing gown which he made into a doll and called 'Minnie', so that the name was waiting for her when she got back.

Minnie's disposition may have been exceptionally sweet, but selflessness was the price then automatically exacted from nannies in return for their charges' devotion. Nineteenth-century autobiographies commonly describe children who lived in terror of their nurses' departure, who would have thought it gravely improper to be bathed or dressed or even to have had their hair brushed by their mothers and indeed, except when sent for downstairs or on formal rounds of the nursery and schoolroom, seldom encountered their mothers at all. ' "She loved us but she didn't like us very much," Ivy said. . . . "Well, she showed great interest when we were ill and so on, you know. We knew she cared. But we really loved Minnie." '[14] It was Minnie who took Ivy for the first time to the seaside to visit her grandfather at Clacton and said, when Ivy asked uneasily if the water would come any nearer, 'Not if you're a good girl, Miss Ivy';* and it was Minnie who first introduced her to 'Puss in Boots and Jack the Giant Killer

---

* Or was this perhaps the 'under-nurse', who made Ivy feel guilty and 'always said, when it thundered, "That is God, angry with you," because she, Ivy, had hit one of her brothers or stolen a chocolate'? (*Ivy and Stevie* by Kay Dick, p.29; Ivy's first sight of the sea is described by Julian Mitchell in the *New Statesman*, 5 September 1969.)

at an age when it is right that giants should be killed, and even bearable that Red Riding Hood should be eaten by the wolf in the bed'[15] (though Minnie had a milder version in which the heroine escaped). It is evidently Minnie who stands behind a long line of capable, inquisitive, absolutely dependable nurses who provide a secure retreat in the disasters of infancy—the death of a hen or a surfeit of Ring-a-ring-o'-roses—as from the treacherous, veiled brutalities of the adult world: a line which begins with Miss Patmore in *Brothers and Sisters* and runs through Hatton in *Parents and Children*, Fanshawe in *Darkness and Day*, Bennet in *The Present and the Past*:

> Bennet was a small, spare woman of forty-five, with a thin, sallow face marked by simple lines of benevolence, long, narrow features and large, full eyes of the colour that is called grey because it is no other. She took little interest in herself, and so much in other people that it tended to absorb her being. When the children recalled her to their world, she would return as if from another. They loved her not as themselves, but as the person who served their love of themselves, and greater love has no child than this.[16]

Minnie took great pleasure in the country round Pinner and often talked afterwards of its woods and paddocks and orchards, and the beautiful garden at No. 2 Onslow Villas. Ivy had inherited from her father an abiding love of 'the real country, where I can pick primroses', but her mother still hankered after town life so, early in 1887, the family moved nearer London to a house called Chesilbank at Twickenham where Noel and Vera were born. Ivy remembered, from well before her third birthday, a miniature dustpan and brush with which she used to sweep the step of the house at Pinner; and she told Julian Mitchell a story about herself and Guy at Chesilbank which illustrates the inadvertent harshness of advanced Victorian parents who, like Dr Burnett, did not believe in coddling children: 'One day . . . she and her brother were out in the garden. It was so cold that they cried to be let in. Their mother appeared at a window and promised them each a penny booklet with a bright cover if they would stay outside for another half hour. Cold was thought good for children.'[17]

So was simple living and plain food. The children's rooms had bare cork linoleum fitted throughout; convention decreed a 'miserable fire' in the nursery and no fires at all in the bedrooms ('if you saw the girl coming in with the kindling, you knew you were ill and the doctor was coming'). The bedsteads were iron, the basket chairs decrepit and the nursery table top had a ledge underneath on which the children were accustomed to deposit layers of unwanted food. Thrift collaborated with accepted medical opinion on nursery diets: meat was considered too rich, sugar unwholesome, jam morally unwise and sponge cakes were only for visitors, which perhaps explains why, when Ivy later did her own housekeeping, she paid particular attention to copious helpings of roast meat, boiled hams, substantial puddings and sumptuous teas with three courses, hot, savoury and sweet. Dr Burnett, progressive in this as in much else, believed that fruit and vegetables led to longevity and brought up his children as vegetarians for the sake of their health (though meat and drink were allowed downstairs which suggests that he had somewhat relaxed his earlier teetotalism). His attitude to infant malpractices like masturbation or bed-wetting—generally held to be vicious, and often punished with astonishing violence—was invariably liberal, and so were his views on dress at a time when girls were regularly put into stays at thirteen, and when respectable children wore for playing, even in the height of summer, thick, black, woollen stockings, laced boots and high-necked, long-sleeved overalls. 'If Daddy had had his will,' said Mrs Compton Burnett, 'you'd all have gone barefoot.'

Sea air was a tonic of which he approved, and probably the reason why, at the beginning of December 1891, he moved his wife and nine children—three of whom at least were already delicate and dangerously susceptible to the pneumonia which in the end killed Guy and nearly killed Ivy—to Hove, then just beginning to become a fashionable adjunct to Brighton. 'From August to the end of December the climate of Brighton is probably the best in England, but the spring is boisterous, windy and often very cold,' advised the *Homoeopathic Directory* and Dr Burnett had devised his own mysterious system for rating in order of precedence the coastal resorts which he prescribed for ailing small children: 'a few years' residence at the seaside, preferably the first year or so at Worthing, the second at Brighton, and then a year or two at Eastbourne or Folkestone'.[18]

It is a curious thing that, whereas the people in her books live mostly on their family estates in manor houses built by their ancestors, Ivy herself had known only brand-new houses of the kind put up in suburban developments all over the Home Counties in the late nineteenth century to cope with the demands of the rising business and professional classes. It is doubtful whether, before she was thirty, she has so much as visited what is generally meant by an English country house. The nearest approach to a 'place' in her family was probably the original home of her great-grandfather Burnett at Gavelacre (a pleasant compact farmhouse which still stands), but Ivy can scarcely have known of its existence. Otherwise there was Valley Farm, a farmhouse not much bigger than a fair-sized cottage with a pretty, pillared porch at Great Clacton, which several times changed hands among her mother's relations and which she remembered from her first visit to the seaside before she was six. Her grandfather's new house, Hillside in Burr's Road, could be seen at Clacton until quite recently; and one of her uncles built himself in 1886 a solid, roomy, red-brick residence, called Soetrana or Clay Hall, which may still be seen nearby. From the time of his second marriage, her father had begun to invest systematically in speculative property development, buying land and putting up houses on the Woodridings Estate at Pinner; at Great Clacton, on the Greens round about where his wife's relations owned property, and at Clacton-on-Sea (then a seaside settlement barely ten years old and developing swiftly on rather humbler lines than the middle-class suburbs of Brighton); and on the outer fringes of Hove.

The houses he built were nearly all small shops or semi-detached cottages, two rooms up and two down, designed for the working classes. The houses he lived in were considerably grander, and grew more so as his family increased: No. 2 Onslow Villas was one of a pair (Dr Burnett soon bought the other half) of handsome, plain but substantial, red-brick, three-storied dwellings which stood in their own grounds at Woodridings. The estate itself, the very first in a district since smothered by housing estates, had been built for wealthy London commuters (Mrs Beeton had lived at Woodridings, and so had Nelson's daughter by Lady Hamilton) after the railway reached Pinner in 1844. It was three minutes' walk from Hatch End railway station, and a mile or so across fields from Pinner itself along a footpath 'impassable for mud for five months out of twelve'.[19] Chesilbank at Twickenham stood in Cambridge Park on the banks of the Thames, a suburb much like Woodridings and built for much the same purpose. When Ivy was seven and a half, and the family moved to Hove, they lived at 30 First Avenue which, as its name implies, was one of the original avenues running down to the sea when the town was laid out in the 'sixties and 'seventies.

Hove at the beginning of the last century had been a decayed fishing village with barely a hundred inhabitants. The coming of the railway and the westward expansion of Brighton meant that, by the time the

Compton Burnetts arrived, it was a wilderness of raw red brick with a population of 26,097 which has continued to grow ever since. In 1891 there were five churches, all newly built or still under construction in styles running from Early Decorated to Romanesque and Italian Gothic. Waterhouse's town hall was finished in 1882, and the public library in 1891; the school to which Ivy was sent at fourteen was new, as was her brothers' prep school and Brighton College itself which they later attended. The family moved for the last time, in 1897, a few streets westward to The Drive 'in the midst of fashionable Hove', a spot where, as a contemporary directory proudly records, the stranger 'cannot help being struck with the air of wealth and refinement'[20] and where the Compton Burnetts settled at number twenty: a thirteen-bedroomed slab in red brick with white facings known ever after among Dr Burnett's children as 'that hideous house'.

Carriages, waiting while their owners paid calls, filled the road outside the new house two or three deep every afternoon (though the first motor car had already caused a commotion in The Drive two years before the Compton Burnetts arrived). Opposite lived a General Basden who, taking umbrage as most people did at having a homoeopath for a neighbour, refused to permit his wife to call which was a great grief to Mrs Compton Burnett. 'He was a thorn in my mother's flesh for many a long year,' said her daughter Vera. Margaret Powell gives a startling account of libertinism, alcoholism, even outright violence practised behind closed doors by the master or mistress in two highly respectable establishments on The Drive when her mother (who was four years older than Ivy) worked there in the 1890s, first as a fourteen-year-old kitchen maid to a family named Benson and later to another family as a plain cook. The Bensons had 'kept a satisfactory staff as mum puts it. A butler, footman, housemaid and under-housemaid, a lady's-maid and a valet, a gardener, a coachman and a stable-boy.'* The Compton Burnetts had roughly the same number of servants, except

---

* *My Mother and I* by Margaret Powell, p.40. This book gives a fascinating account of life both above and below stairs in fashionable Hove when Ivy was young (for the occasion on which the Bensons' servants were roused one night by their mistress's curses as she attempted to split her husband's bedroom door with an axe, see p.43; for further lecherous exploits among the Compton Burnetts' neighbours, see p.68); and I am grateful to Mrs Powell for asking her mother if she had any recollection of Dr Burnett: 'although she vaguely remembers the name I'm afraid that she cannot recall any incidents of that period. As Mother explained, she was always in the kitchen, these being basements naturally the view was somewhat restricted.'

that they kept no carriage, their footman was replaced by a boy and their butlers doubled as valets (one made a habit of filching the fees from Dr Burnett's coat pockets and later absconded with the family silver).

Under-servants, known in the family as 'squalors', had no claim in those days to names or clothes of their own: the page's suit was handed down whatever the shape or size of each new boy and a nursemaid called Leeney passed on her name to two more, the three being distinguished for their mistress's convenience as Fat, Thin and Dignified Leeney. But the cook, a Plymouth Brother with a repertoire of Temperance hymns, held her own even with Mrs Compton Burnett who loved cooking though she entered the kitchen at some risk to herself: 'My mother was a woman who feared neither God nor man, but she did fear that cook,' said Ivy.[21] Next in order of consequence was the manservant Ager, an imposing person, 'fond of long, important words' and so lordly that the whole family trembled when Ager was asked to help the nursemaid lift the perambulator up the front steps. Ager had succeeded George Harvey, whom Mrs Compton Burnett had once been obliged to reprove for drowning the cook's voice when she sang. Vera Compton-Burnett has a curious memory of Harvey performing before her one day when she was a baby and he found her alone in her high chair at First Avenue: 'I can see him now, making faces and dancing in front of me'. None of the children was allowed in the kitchen and, according to her sisters, Ivy even as a small girl had scarcely set foot below stairs. But it must have been from things seen and heard in these years that she drew the sad procession of page boys hopelessly aspiring to higher things in her books, the sardonic and self-assured cooks, the butlers whose vocabulary is so much more ambitious than their masters' and the manservants who pull furtive faces or mimic their betters behind their backs to an audience of conspiratorial children.

Ivy detested Hove to the end of her life and steadfastly refused to visit friends who lived in Brighton. 'It's a horrid, horrid place,' she said with unaccustomed venom to one[22] who had happened to mention it shortly before she died. Throughout the twenty-four years that the family lived there, Hove was rapidly rising and sprawling around them, 'showing an activity on the part of the speculative builder almost more remarkable than one could have believed', as the *Hove Gazette* noted when the census figures were published for 1901. But much of the land later sold for building was still wild fields and there were open downs at the back of the town. The Drive was a piecemeal extension of Grand Avenue, a grandiose thoroughfare running from Church Street to the sea front and bordered by what was then a rough meadow full of buttercups and daisies, wild rose and apple trees. The little Compton Burnetts on their walks picked clover and sea pinks and took sugar to feed the donkey who lived in a field beside the town hall. Thrift grew on the marshes westward towards Portslade (where Dr Burnett later bought building plots to erect small villas in rows), and Ivy told Sonia Orwell long afterwards that her pleasantest memory was of great swathes of wild flowers growing between the downs and the sea.

She had small, delicate hands and always loved small things—single flowers better than double ones, wild flowers better than either and harebells best of all. Long after she had left off playing dolls' houses, she kept a collection of minute dolls in an old dress box and, when she was sixteen or so, she would make dolls for her sisters out of petals and twigs, fastened with thorns and exquisitely dressed. Some sixty years years later, Elizabeth Taylor lunched with her just before Christmas: ' "My mother", Ivy said, "told me that, when I was a child, she spent all the year looking out for small things to put in my stocking. I remember those more than all the dolls I had—especially a little box of glass beads." '[23] Once she was taken by Minnie to stand against the railings and watch the Prince of Wales drive by. On a visit to London designed as a treat, she had been thoroughly bored by the Tower; what she liked best was to be put in a cab with Guy by their father, and driven about the streets.

Dr Burnett, having settled his family at Hove, had taken to staying in London at the Holborn Viaduct Hotel, returning twice a week to spend Wednesdays and weekends at home. He arrived by cab from the station late at night and would visit the children at breakfast next morning to make sure they had swallowed their compulsory porridge —'It's no good having a big brain box if you don't put anything in it' was a regular saying of his—before taking the five eldest, from Ivy down to Juliet (called Judy), along the street to a fruit shop where each might choose whatever he or she pleased. The party then proceeded a few minutes' walk to the sea where he would throw down his small change and, in the early morning before anyone much was about, the children would scramble for pennies on the front (the money was not to spend but to fill money boxes). On Sunday evenings there were sweets and games when their father played bear, crouching under the furniture and growling 'Hinaus' and 'Herein'; the smallest children would dip in his pockets for coins, or he would tell stories from the fire. This was after family prayers with a procession of manservants and maids, hymns and readings from the Family Bible. On ordinary nights one may suppose that Ivy and Guy economized with something more like the prayer— 'May I be forgiven and saved'[24]—invented by Rose Lovat, aged ten, for her younger sister Viola in *Darkness and Day*: a formula which, as Rose explains, avoids time and effort being wasted on 'a long prayer and a hymn', while neatly covering all the salient points.

2

ROSE AND VIOLA share a world of their own, secure from the disturbing vagaries of grown-ups and sheltered even from their nurse's intrusion, a withdrawal common enough in the novels of I. Compton-Burnett though the relationship is generally between an elder or dominant girl and a boy, a year or so apart in age. The theme of brother and sister runs through every single one of her books, from the six- to thirteen-year-olds—Honor and Gavin Sullivan in *Parents and Children*, Julius and Dora Calderon in *Elders and Betters*, Clemence and Sefton Shelley in *Two Worlds and their Ways*, Henry and Megan Clare in *The Present and the Past*, Claud and Emma Challoner in *A Heritage and its History*, Leah and Hengist Middleton in *The Mighty and their Fall*—to Emily and Nicholas Herrick (who is seventy) in *Pastors and Masters*. It is first elaborated in *Brothers and Sisters* where—apart from the central incestuous pair—there are no less than five sets of brother and sister, all living in the same village, all in their middle or late twenties, all contemplating, and several of them actually attempting without success, intermarriage with one another. The relationship itself, beginning for mutual comfort and protection in the nursery, strengthening on contact with harsh or intemperate adults into a deeper protective bond, ripening often in middle age when fear no longer obtains, provides an intimacy more satisfactory and closer—or at any rate examined in greater depth—than even the happiest marriages in her books. Honor Sullivan, aged ten, expounds the practical aspects to her younger brothers:

'Why can't brothers and sisters marry?' said Gavin.
'Because they have to start a family,' said his sister. 'If they married people in the same one, there would never be any new ones. But they can live together.'

'Do they have any children then?'

'I don't think they do so often. But they can adopt some.'

'He will be your little boy,' promised Nevill in full comprehension.[25]

The relationship between Honor and Gavin Sullivan was the one which Ivy's sisters thought came closest to Ivy's with Guy. Gavin is his mother's favourite, a slow, shy child, the younger by 'a year all but two days' and dependent on Honor for leadership whether in tormenting the governess, misleading their mother or simply in construing the mysterious undercurrents of adult conversation which Honor can follow and he can't. Guy Compton-Burnett was also his mother's favourite. Ivy had been 'quicker than Guy as a little girl' but, as he grew older, 'even Ivy looked up to Guy' who developed into a brilliant as well as an uncommonly sweet-tempered boy with a strength of character which, in times of crisis, was recognized by the whole family. He had dark curly hair, grey eyes and 'a steadfast face'.* Minnie loved him especially, his younger sisters adored him and there can be small doubt that, as Honor loved Gavin, so Ivy loved Guy more than anyone else in the world.

Noel, who shared the schoolroom with Ivy and Guy, was a backward child, often left out by his elders and obliged to fall back on his sister Vera who was three years younger. He seems to have been one of those solitary children isolated in a large family between older and younger pairs, like the twelve-year-old James Sullivan in *Parents and Children*:

The two sisters lived for each other, as did Honor and Gavin; and James lived to himself like Nevill, but with less support, so that his life had a certain pathos. He would remedy matters by repairing to the nursery, where Hatton's welcome and Honor's inclination to a senior brought Nevill to open, and Gavin to secret despair. The suffering of his brothers was pleasant to James, not because he was malicious or hostile, but because the evidence of sadness in other lives

---

* Guy and Noel Compton-Burnett are described in the persons of Fabian and Guy Clare on p.12 of *The Present and the Past*: 'Fabian at thirteen had a broad face and brow, broad, clear features and pure grey eyes that recalled his sister's. Guy was two years younger and unlike him, with a childish, pretty face, dark eyes that might have recalled [his baby brother's], but for their lack of independence and purpose, and a habit of looking at his brother in trust and emulation.' (Ivy's sisters confirm that this is an exact likeness of their own brothers.)

made him feel a being less apart. He showed no aptitude for books, and this in his sex was condemned; and he carried a sense of guilt which it did not occur to him was unmerited. It was a time when endeavour in children was rated below success, an error which in later years has hardly yet been corrected, so that childhood was a more accurate foretaste of life than it is now.[26]

Often, in the novels, the gap between an elder pair and a tiresome younger brother narrows with time so that—as happened with Ivy and Guy and Noel when they reached their teens—the pair becomes a trio. But as a small boy Noel, who was handsome and dreamy like his father in childhood, had been young for his age and 'imaginative but not clever'; his sisters remembered him still at nine or ten years old galloping up and down the street alone, pretending to be a horse with invisible reins at the corners of his mouth. He was a secret poet, like James Sullivan ('James could not refer to . . . the poems which to himself were proof of [his cleverness], as he had revealed them to no one, and was postponing publication until his maturity')[27] and several of the other lonely children in his sister's books ('"People can't be very open about poems," said Guy, with a flush. "Anyone who is a poet knows that."'). All the Compton Burnett children were dab hands at composing limericks and verses in competition to see who was fastest; and they all wrote poems, encouraged by their father who would reward them with pennies—'so much for a poem, so much less for a hymn, because hymns were easier'. But only Noel retained his childhood facility as a grown-up ambition to the point at which, in 1914 just after he had been elected a Fellow at Cambridge, he proposed abandoning scholarship and turning poet instead.

None of his early verses survive, but there is a fragment written by Ivy (with Guy's help) about their governess, a Miss Mills commonly known as 'Miss Smills' to her pupils:

> There once was a lady, Miss Mills was her name,
> She wrote a bad novel and thought to get fame.
> But when she found no one would publish her book
> To gambling she very wickedly took.
> And worse than all her troubles yet
> She very soon got into debt. . . .

This was only the beginning of a long and fearsome saga, remorselessly chanted aloud in the Compton Burnett household, which followed the

lady as she took to stealing to pay off her gambling debts, was imprisoned for theft and sank steadily through a great many stanzas to
touch the bottom of crime and ignominy. There was not a word of
truth in it: if Miss Mills had written a novel, it was unknown to her
pupils whose gloomy notion of a literary career was prompted as much
by their own literary ambitions as by their naturally dim view of
authority.

Ivy and Guy were ringleaders in the nursery, experts at dressing up
and make-believe, pressing the others into service as pall bearers or
corpses when they staged a funeral, as the Clare children and the
Middletons do in her books. They invented an octopus, which lived
behind a grating in the garden and terrorized their brothers and sisters,
and when Ivy was ten or eleven they organized a Royal Academy to
which all the children contributed paintings. A few years later the two
boys would come up to the nursery to amuse the younger ones on
Sunday mornings ('All the heathen practices we had were on a Sunday
morning,' because there were lessons the rest of the week) with 'horrific
games which terrified us out of our lives'. The most impressive of these
took place behind locked doors with the blinds drawn when Guy,
wearing a mask with lighted candles at the eye holes, became an idol
known as 'The Holy Beckle'. The Beckle would issue pronouncements
as to what had to be done (generally the decapitation of one of the
dolls) whereupon their mother, hearing agitated screams from above,
would call from downstairs: 'Which one of you's hurt?'

Ivy by this time was too old to take part any longer in idolatrous
rites. But as small children she and Guy had their own gods, named
Polio and Elephantas, enshrined on two little ornamental stucco pillars
in the back garden. All the children were obliged to kneel and pray to
these gods, and to make sacrifices ordained by Ivy and Guy as high
priests: 'The gardener was furious when Polio ordained that all young
leaves be picked as a sacrifice,' said Juliet Compton-Burnett. Similar
offerings ('Flowers and grasses and acorns and things') are made by
Dora and Julius Calderon, aged ten and eleven in *Elders and Betters*, in
the hope of propitiating their god and averting disasters which loom
when a family of unknown relations settle in the neighbourhood:

'O great and good and powerful god, Chung,' said Theodora
Calderon, on her knees before a rock in the garden, 'protect us, we
beseech thee, in the new life that is upon us. For strangers threaten
our peace, and the hordes of the alien draw nigh. Keep us in thy

sight, and save us from the dangers that beset our path. For Sung Li's sake, amen.'

'For Sung Li's sake, amen,' said her brother.

'Guard us from the boldness of their eyes and the lewdness of their tongues,' went on Theodora. 'For their strength is great, and the barbarian heart is within them. Their eyes may be cold on the young, and harsh words may issue from their lips. Therefore have us in thy keeping. For Sung Li's sake, amen.'

'Sung Li is a good name,' said Julius as they rose from their knees. 'Enough like Son and yet not too much like it. It would not do to have them the same.'

'Blasphemy is no help in establishing a deity,' said his sister, in a tone of supporting him. 'And the power of Chung is real, though it is only used for those who believe in him. And he would always help people's unbelief.'[28]

'I do not claim that the children in my books, any more than their elders, resemble the actual creatures of real life,'[29] said Miss Compton-Burnett just after *Elders and Betters* was published. What is extraordinary about these particular children is not so much their habit of serving strange gods, nor the liturgical language reserved for this purpose, but rather their power of articulating the miseries generally endured by actual children with a dumb sense of injustice and falsehood. Dora and Julius are past masters at dissimulation: 'It was held that their amusement was their own affair, and confidence on the point was not misplaced, as their pastimes included not only pleasure, but religion, literature and crime. They wrote moral poems that deeply moved them, pilfered coins for the purchase of forbidden goods, and prayed in good faith to the accepted god and their own, perhaps with a feeling that a double share of absolution would not come amiss.'[30] They keep a strict confessional account of daily transgressions like fibbing and fighting ('"O great and good and powerful god, Chung," prayed Dora, "forgive us, we beseech thee, the lie that has passed our lips. For we have uttered to thy handmaid, our governess, the thing that is false, yea and even to our mother...."') but they also intercede to be rid of the subtler duplicities commonly visited on children by even the most well-meaning adults.

Worst of these is the obligation, imposed involuntarily to their mutual embarrassment, to simulate the frank, winning ways considered by their parents proper to childhood: shifty, shame-faced caperings

performed with a wholly fraudulent artlessness which makes them considerably more wretched than the comparatively straightforward
predicaments evaded by the lie direct. Other novelists have written
without sentimentality about children but few have portrayed them on
such absolutely equal terms as beings no less intelligent than grown-ups
but powerless and hopelessly vulnerable, dwarfed in an alien world
whose customs they must obey without understanding. Conversely,
the grown-ups in this book are reflected from below as fickle, careless,
remote and incalculable giants whose casual actions rebound ominously
on the children, whose motives can only be dimly grasped and pieced
together with difficulty, whose slipperiness has to be met as best one
may with nervous prevarication. These things make for a life of constraint and oppression, further shadowed by the children's guilt at their
own double dealing. Small wonder that Dora prays to the god for a
ripe old age: 'For it would not be worth while to suffer the trials of
childhood, if they were not to lead to fullness of days'.

The trials of childhood naturally foster, at first by instinct, later from
hard experience, the growth of reticence and caution. Absolute loyalty
requires that the children present a united front to their father when he
comes to enquire into a fight which—though it leaves Julius bitten and
scratched, Dora with hair torn out and her ribbon undone—both
stoutly and promptly deny ('"You did not hit your sister, did you, my
boy?" said Thomas, struck by something battered in his daughter's
aspect, but assuming that his son would not transgress a certain limit.').
Ivy's sisters remembered her being driven, on at least one occasion, to
retaliate with tooth and nail on Guy. But such matters, like religion and
poetry, were covered by the code of concealment and mutual support
between brother and sister which (in youth and middle age as much as
in childhood) is violated only by hypocrites or fools in her books.

There were, in any case, other distractions in the Compton Burnett
schoolroom. Miss Mills, who was homely and kind but not what her
pupils called clever, was fair game to Ivy and Guy who 'played her up a
good deal'. She had come to take over the education of the elder trio
from Minnie when Ivy was six or seven years old, and she remained
until superseded by the daily tutor who taught them Latin and Greek.
She was reluctant to leave and tried unsuccessfully, many years later, to
persuade Mrs Compton Burnett to take her back for the two youngest
of Ivy's four sisters. But her position, like that of so many dependents in
Victorian households, cannot have been easy. She lived with the family,
took meals in the schoolroom where her word was supposedly law, and

remained in her free time awkwardly placed between the servants' hall and the downstairs drawing room, neither welcomed in nor officially excluded from either. A governess's lot was seldom happy, as one of them points out in *Daughters and Sons* to a visitor who had tried to defend it:

> 'What is a little impatience, hastiness—tyranny if it must be said, compared with a real isolation and loneliness?'
> 'I am afraid it must be said, and they are a great deal worse.'[31]

Ivy, who early acquired a reputation for wit and had never been backward at passing remarks, often 'got the better of Miss Mills'. One may suppose that, like Honor in *Parents and Children* (who had already had two governesses when she grimly prepared to do battle with a third), she knew 'the tricks of the trade' and 'the nature of the beasts'. Probably no one now will ever know what passed between Ivy and Guy and Miss Mills in the schoolroom but it is perhaps not entirely unfair to detect some faint reflection of past personal triumphs in the fiendish ingenuity with which Honor Sullivan and Rose Lovat, each ably abetted by her younger brother or sister, persecute their respective governesses. Governesses in the novels fall roughly into two categories: on the one hand those who, possessing like Miss Lacy in *Elders and Betters* an understanding of children not often shared by their parents, are involuntarily respected and occasionally feared by both parents and pupils; and on the other those who, like the Sullivans' Miss Pilbeam or the Lovats' Miss Hallam, have neither the learning nor the moral ascendancy required to keep order. Greed in a governess is always a prime cause for mirth in her pupils, and so are dowdy or insecure clothes—hats which come off in a wind, skirts which unravel at the back or get torn in scuffles with a schoolroom chair. The Compton Burnetts' Miss Mills belonged more or less to the second division, a class well represented by Mildred Hallam in *Darkness and Day* whose first lesson ends in outright defeat by her pupils, and whose second lesson drives her almost to tears:

> 'You think you are patient,' said Viola, wiping her brush. 'But I can tell from your voice that you are not.'
> 'Well, people's patience does not last for ever. It is as well to learn that.'
> 'Yours did not last even for half-an-hour,' said Rose, looking at the clock. 'We have never had anyone with so little.'

'I have any amount if there is a reasonable demand on it.'

'Well, then you would not want it.'

'And you have less even than you pretend to have,' said Viola.

'And so I suppose you expect me to lose it?'

'Well, we were waiting for that,' said Viola, in an almost engaging tone.

'And then what is to happen?' said Mildred.

'You will say you can't teach us, and stop coming, and we shall go back to learning with Fanshawe. But I daresay you will have your pay for the month. The last governess did.'[32]

But, however poorly the Compton Burnetts may have thought of their governess, she had given them at least one cause for gratitude. It seems to have been Miss Mills who first set Ivy on the track of losing her religion, something she had always mistrusted, gradually ceased to credit and finally discarded as easily as she had earlier relinquished Polio and Elephantas. As a small child she had accepted without question what her elders taught her: 'But I never liked the religion. I never liked it,' she said in a tape-recorded conversation with Kay Dick in 1963. 'I didn't like all the atonement and all that, you know. I didn't like it at all. I thought it was a disagreeable and humiliating religion . . . I questioned it because, of course, science came into the air, you see, and Darwin came, and I remember when I was very tiny, about seven, the governess told us that men—I suppose she was modern—descended from monkeys. I remember telling my nurse that she said that, and she said it was very wicked to say that men were not created by the Almighty.'[33] Ten years before this conversation with Miss Dick took place, Ivy had put the identical scene into *The Present and the Past*, where the nursemaid Eliza takes much the same dubious view as Minnie had done when Megan and Henry Clare, aged seven and eight, are launched on modern thought by their governess:

'Are animals of the same nature as we are?' said Henry. 'Monkeys look as if they were.'

'Yes, that is the line of the truth. A scientist called Darwin has told us about it. Of course we have developed much further.'

'Then weren't we made all at once as we are?' said Megan. 'Eliza says that would mean the Bible was not true.'

'It has its essential truth, and that is what matters.'

'I suppose any untrue thing might have that. I daresay a good many

have. So there is no such thing as truth. It is different in different minds.'
'Why, you will be a philosopher one day, Megan.'[34]

Mr Salt, the tutor who taught Ivy and her brothers, inspired confidence, unlike Miss Mills, and found unusual aptitude in at least his
two elder pupils. All three of them liked him and, long after the boys
had been dispatched on various, more or less disastrous forays to prep
and public schools, Ivy continued to take Latin and Greek lessons alone
with Mr Salt, who prepared her for the entrance examination when she
finally left home to read classics at college. Such a thing, for a nicely
brought-up girl who had no need to earn her living, was almost
unheard of: history and literature, a little French, music lessons and
sums were as much as was generally considered advisable, or even
decent. Clever daughters of liberal parents might be permitted to share
lessons with their brothers at first but to insist on continuing was worse
than eccentric, and almost bound to end in tears—as it did in Charlotte
M. Yonge's *The Daisy Chain* when, for the sake of 'all the little common
lady-like things' prized by her dear mamma, Ethel May was reluctantly
forced at fifteen to give up learning Latin and Greek with her brother.
   The Daisy Chain was a book much beloved by the younger Compton
Burnetts, partly no doubt because its account of nursery and schoolroom life in a doctor's household so closely resembled their own. The
eleven May children divide up by age and sex as the Compton Burnetts
did, the boys preparing for Oxford, the church or the navy, the girls in
fee to dull and crotchety governesses. Worst of Ethel's troubles is her
beloved brother's heartless condescension, when she confides the cause
of her misery to him: 'I assure you, Ethel, it is really time for you to
stop, or you would get into a regular learned lady, and be good for
nothing'.[35] What had been accepted as a matter of course in the 1850s,
when *The Daisy Chain* was published, had become an issue hotly
debated by the time Ivy reached the schoolroom. Alarming examples
of the New Woman—'Not bold or bad she had yet lost that ineffable
something which gives womanhood its essential charm, endows it with
its special power, and throws over it, as it were, a veil of mystic beauty'
—are depicted in Mrs Lynn Linton's *The One Too Many* (1894), a novel
devoted to exposing in dreadful detail the dire effect on a Girton girl of
'that boasted Higher Education which had ruined her nervous system,
prematurely initiated her into the darker secrets of life, and by these two
things destroyed the very well-springs of her health and happiness'.
That Dr Burnett agreed with the general opinion is evident from a

passage in his *Delicate, Backward, Puny and Stunted Children* (published when Ivy was eleven years old, and presumably nearing the stage at which Guy would begin to outstrip her) on the relative powers of boys and girls:

> . . . most of what is commonly said on this point is nothing but weak twaddle. Only the Almighty can make a New Woman. Put broadly, up to the age of puberty, the girl, all other things being equal, beats the boy; with puberty the damsel throws away every month a vast amount of fluid power in the order of Nature. Let us call this *pelvic power*. Assuming the girl to be the superior of the boy up to the pelvic power stage,—which, indeed, anyone can observe for himself, in his own sphere,—but once arrived at the stage of pelvic power, and the girl is left behind in her lessons by her brother in the natural order of things, or else the girl's brain saps the pelvis of its power, when she will also lose in the race with the boy, because he will be physically well, while she, with disordered pelvic life, must necessarily be in ill-health, more or less. The whole thing is a question of energy. . . .
>
> The New Woman is only possible in a novel, not in nature . . . I have very many times watched the career of exceedingly studious girls who spent the greater mass of their power in mental work, and in every case the pelvic powers decreased in even pace with the expenditure of mental power. Not one exception to this have I ever seen . . . I have sat at the feet of Nature a good many years, and I give it as my opinion that to be a mother in its best sense is the biggest thing on earth, and comes nearer the Creator's work than anything else under heaven; to be a learned girl or woman graduate is a very good and respectable thing enough, and twelve of them make a dozen.
>
> At the same time, genius has no gender; it can be in a female or in a male, as the case may be.[36]

Dr Burnett can have had small grounds at this stage for detecting genius under his roof, but he was by no means an autocrat, or not at least in his family circle; and his wife, who had herself acquired the usual accomplishments including embroidery and the singing of drawing-room ballads at a Miss Hadden's academy in Dover, shared his respect for intelligence and a sound education. 'We came of a booky family,' said Ivy[37] and, however heartily her father may have deplored the New Woman, there seems to have been no question but that his daughter should learn Latin and Greek like her brothers.

But it was only the middle three who were booky. The four youngest daughters were musical, an interest which absorbed them almost from the nursery onwards; and the five stepchildren, having no pretentions to learning, were separately educated. Although the youngest, Charlie, was only eighteen months older than Ivy and considerably closer to her than Noel in age, it was apparently never contemplated that he or any of the others should share a governess, let alone a tutor, with his half-brothers and -sister. Relations between the two families were on the whole cool. Olive, Daisy and Iris had been sent as soon as they were old enough to a boarding school kept by their aunt, Mrs John Compton Burnett, in Bedford, and so were out of the house for most of Ivy's time in the schoolroom. Dick and Charlie attended a day school in Hove and when they left, at the age of fifteen or so, were both articled to solicitors in London. This suited Dick, who was stolid and competent, but not Charlie who was always a daredevil, never cared for the law and had been the kind of boy who could take to the sea and swim without being taught, or jump on a bicycle for the first time at seven years old and ride it away. Of Dr Burnett's four sons, he was the wildest and by far the best-looking, with classical features and blazing blue eyes. The neighbours would send over in a high wind, when Charlie was little, to ask did his mother know there was a small boy flying a kite on the roof?

Charlie can have had little in common with the three immediately below him, who were none of them fond of outdoor pursuits. Olive and Dick were too old to impinge much on the schoolroom party and Iris, being practical and good with her hands, interested them as little as Charlie. Daisy, however, liked children: she was pious, domesticated, 'a home bird', and when she left school would preside over nursery meals at one end of the table with Minnie at the other and the little ones, from Ivy down to the baby in its high chair, ranged in between. Only Daisy got on with their stepmother, and only Olive bore her an open grudge. The others kept whatever they felt to themselves, and none of them was on particularly easy or intimate terms with the rest of the family. Their father being mostly away, their stepmother resenting his absence and never in any case markedly well-disposed towards her stepchildren, their lives had always been hard: Olive and the two boys took the earliest possible chance to leave home, an escape which cost Olive at least a prolonged and desperate struggle.

Ivy and her brothers must have seen enough as small children to grasp the causes of unhappiness and tension, and they saw a great deal more later. But the three lived to themselves, constrained in the company of grown-ups, wholly at ease only with each other and Minnie, impervious to their elder brothers and sisters, ignoring the younger ones and scarcely meeting the outside world except for occasional cousins. It was a conventionally sheltered upbringing, and Ivy took from it things of which she can have been barely aware at the time—except in so far as she was an attentive and thoughtful child, like Fabian Clare in *The Present and the Past*, who at thirteen years old is rebuked by his governess for saying that a good many people can't think:

'And you are one of the fortunate ones who can?' said Miss Ridley, using a dry tone.

'I am one of the unfortunate ones who do. That is how I should put it.'[38]

1897–1901

'No good can come of it'

I

THE COMPTON BURNETTS had a family pew at St John's Church, Hove, a few minutes' walk from First Avenue and not much further on foot or by carriage from The Drive. In so far as one may judge from his habit of unselfconsciously proclaiming God's truth, calling down God's blessing and committing himself to God's will in his books, Dr Burnett seems to have held the accepted beliefs of his day without qualms, and perhaps without attaching any special importance to them. Religion, or the lack of it, plays no great part in his daughter's books except as a convenient indication of social and intellectual standing. An active faith is generally a sign of mental or moral obtuseness, a passive faith the outcome of a civilized tolerance towards the ways of the world; and since (after the first one) the novels deal exclusively with the educated classes and more particularly with the landed gentry, religion as a matter of course means allegiance to the established church. Vicars (apart from the excellent Rev. Oscar Jekyll in *A House and Its Head* whose Christmas sermon 'was to earn a parishioner's comment, that faith as deep as his would hardly appear on the surface. In fact, his concern with his faith was limited to this level, as it was years since it had existed on any other. . . . He hoped his duties would be less well done by a stupider man, as a believer would probably be; and his views, though of some inconvenience to himself, were of none to his congregation, as they were beyond the range of its suspicions')[1] are usually odious, fools and toadies or worse. Dissent is relegated more or less to the servants' hall, or to occasional minor characters like the schoolmaster Mr Bigwell in *Two Worlds and Their Ways*—an early, high Victorian example of a type which in both life and literature was becoming increasingly familiar and fashionable by 1949, when the novel was published—who came of a working-class, chapel-going family in the north and lost no opportunity of proclaiming in public that he was not ashamed of the fact.

Dr Burnett's first wife's family, the Thomases, had been church people and her children, unlike their half-brothers and -sisters, maintained a strong religious bias. Daisy, who in her twenties twice underwent nervous breakdowns which took the form of a mild religious mania, eventually 'gave herself to Jesus' and set out, to Ivy's amusement, as a missionary for Northern Nigeria; Iris, who became a nurse before the first war at the Temperance Hospital in London, remained like her elder sister an ardent and active churchwoman to the end of her life. Katharine Compton Burnett's position was more equivocal. There was still in the late nineteenth century a gulf fixed between church and chapel whose adherents, ranking low in the social hierarchy, kept themselves to themselves, confined their evangelical attentions as a rule to the labouring classes and had indeed only reluctantly and after long altercation been admitted to such elementary privileges as attendance at the older universities or entry to the learned professions. Methodists in particular traditionally looked with suspicion on any but the most limited education, and mistrusted all reading matter (John Wesley's own annotated Shakespeare had been burnt shortly after his death by a zealous disciple, on the ground that it was 'useless lumber') save the Bible and the Methodist Hymn Book, supplemented on occasion by tracts and sermons. Rowland Rees himself had been converted during a campaign directed almost entirely at the lowest ranks of the army; and the social limitations involved in his choice of religion afterwards inevitably proved a sore point with later generations of Reeses.

It cannot have been pleasant for anyone as sensitive as Ivy's mother to find herself exposed, when she left home, to the kind of slights for which nothing in her background could have prepared her. Family pride was her delight, as it had been her father's, and perhaps also a consolation, even a form of self-defence, in the peculiarly difficult and lonely position imposed by her marriage. Certainly she always considered that, in the choice of his first wife, her husband had married beneath him and, though she took her place at his side without question in public, in private she deplored the unorthodoxy which blocked his professional career. James Compton Burnett would do anything to please her short of changing his medical faith: she had to be content with extolling his achievements, despising a profession which ostracized him, and inserting a hyphen into his name to make it look better. But it must have been a further blow to discover that her father's prominence in Wesleyan circles, which had been a source of rejoicing at Dover, was likely to prove a grave disadvantage in fashionable Hove; and, having suffered much from the handicap of being a homoeopath's wife, she saw no reason why she should suffer for being a Methodist's daughter as well.

But her transfer of allegiance was made discreetly, and never wholly completed. Rowland Rees was not a man easily flouted, though what later became a widespread retreat from chapel to church among his descendants had already begun in his lifetime when his youngest son George became an Anglican priest ('a spanking parson' was Ivy's phrase for her Uncle George, who had impressed her as a child by consuming a whole haddock for breakfast besides quantities of bacon and eggs). It was Rowland Rees' elder son Allen, however, who regularly officiated at the marriages of his brothers and sisters. One of Ivy's cousins was a Methodist missionary in China while her mother's favourite sister, Elizabeth, and Elizabeth's husband, Robert Blackie, continued the family tradition as strong chapel people. Of all their relations the Compton Burnetts saw most of their Aunt Lizzie, Uncle Robert and the ten Blackie cousins who overlapped them in age downwards from Olive to the four youngest daughters. The two families exchanged visits, spent holidays together and, in Ivy's early childhood, several times foregathered at Clacton where her grandfather had settled in 1885 and the Blackies a few years before. Nearly eighty years after that summer at Clacton when she first saw the sea, Ivy 'remembered driving in the governess cart, pulled by a donkey, with her brother, the governess and the nurse. "They are all gone now," she said, "the village has gone, the donkey has gone, the governess cart has gone, and certainly the governess and the nurse have gone."'[2]

Robert Blackie, who looked forward to a substantial inheritance from his father's engineering business in Liverpool, had moved to Essex round about 1880, established his family at Valley Farm a mile or so over fields to the sands of Clacton-on-Sea, promptly built himself a handsome and much larger mansion on the site of what had once been a thatched cottage called Clay Hall, and generally set up in some style as a gentleman farmer.* He was elected Sea Defence Commissioner

* Robert Blackie and his father, who had come south to marry one of Rowland Rees' Pudney cousins at Clacton, between them bought up all the small properties (Valley Farm, the Pudneys' Coppins Hall and Coppins Wick, the Sadlers' Clay Hall) associ-

shortly after he arrived, besides sitting on the Board of Guardians and the parochial committee for Clacton-on-Sea. As a keen local preacher, an impassioned teetotaller and steward of the Clacton Methodist circuit from 1882 to 1887, he took no small pleasure in supervising local religious affairs. He was known as 'the Squire' to his Compton Burnett nephews and nieces on account of his lavish notions of the state due to a gentleman, resembling at any rate in this respect Sir Godfrey Haslam in *Men and Wives* who also came of dissenting stock, had inherited an industrial fortune from his 'dear old parents', purchased a country house in which to install his family and his newly acquired family portraits, and lived comfortably thereafter on an income which, though a source of considerable discomfort to his butler Buttermere, caused none to himself. ('Nothing to be ashamed of in my heritage, Buttermere, in a useful little fortune and title earned by providing people with things they need, by putting at their hand what sufficed unto them. I should blush for myself if I blushed for it.')[3] Like Sir Godfrey, Robert Blackie was fond of delivering long extempore prayers to his family in private.

Together with his father-in-law, Rowland Rees (many of whose strong views he shared), Mr Blackie was frequently at the centre of local controversy in what proved a comparatively short but stormy career at Clacton. Always an enthusiastic speaker on behalf of the Liberal party, he was convicted in 1885 of assault at a Clacton election meeting; he was brought before the magistrates again in 1886 for failing to pay sea defence and general rates, and yet again the same year for refusing to vaccinate his children (whereupon, with support from Rowland Rees, he organized an anti-vaccination meeting as part of a campaign which culminated in the local doctor's resigning his seat on the Sanitary Committee, of which Robert Blackie was then chairman); and he was so vehemently in favour of signing the pledge that, in 1888, he notified the local press that he 'desired henceforward to work his farm on total abstinence principles'.[4]

For the past few years he had managed the farm at Coppins Hall for his two maiden aunts, Miss Eliza and Miss Mary Grace Pudney, the

---

ated with their wives' families; several of these (Coppins Wick, parts of Valley Farm and Clay Hall Farm, sites at Magdalen Green) later passed to their still more prosperous relation, James Compton Burnett, who also acquired the Clacton Mansion House, Foots Farm at Little Clacton and High Birch Farm at St Osyth. Terrace houses put up on these building plots would have been the nearest thing to an ancestral estate in the Compton Burnett family.

last of a line which had owned Coppins Hall Farm for nearly two hundred years. The Misses Pudney were renowned in their lifetimes, and remembered locally for another quarter of a century, as outstanding—whether for piety, good works or missionary zeal—among the 'elect ladies' of Clacton. They organized charity bazaars in the 'eighties, held weekly prayer meetings in their farm kitchen and drove out on Sundays in an old-fashioned carriage to Trinity Methodist Church at Great Clacton. They also dominated the Trinity Ladies' Sewing Meeting, an 'ever-green and ever-fruitful organization' which was perhaps the precursor of Lady Haslam's ineffable working parties in *Men and Wives*, where the sterner business of scandal, gossip and long-standing feuds leaves the ladies scant time for the manufacture of flannel petticoats for orphans:

> 'Really this is not fit for the poor. I don't see how any unfortunate person could wear it, not anyone already unfortunate.'
> 'It is plain and strong,' said Mellicent.
> 'I hardly liked to put it into words, but it is, isn't it?'[5]

Missionary work among the neighbouring hamlets was vigorously prosecuted by local evangelists 'eager for more conquests in Christ', and nowhere more so than at Coppins Hall where the labouring population was 'greatly blessed' and 'soundly converted' at first in open air services, later in a barn owned by the Misses Pudney, and finally in a brand-new chapel built on land given 'in answer to prayer'[6] by Dr Compton Burnett. Since the doctor all his life could refuse his wife nothing, the prayers were presumably hers for Mrs Compton Burnett, though she had preferred church to chapel for herself and her children, seems always to have retained some misgivings about the exchange.

Ivy had probably been taken as a small child to visit, and would certainly have heard stories about, the Misses Pudney and their widowed sister Georgiana Blackie (mother to her Uncle Robert), who all three lived to a great age, Miss Eliza dying in 1892 at eighty years old, Mrs Blackie at eighty-four in 1901, and Miss Mary Grace at ninety-one on 29 January 1911, a month before I. Compton-Burnett's first novel was published. They were first cousins to her grandfather Rowland Rees (his mother and theirs had been sisters, Nancy and Lucy Sadler) as well as connections twice over by the simultaneous marriages in 1875 of their nephew and niece, Robert and Esther Blackie, to Mrs Compton Burnett's sister and brother, Elizabeth and Charles Rees. Ivy's uncle and grandfather had both left Clacton by the time she was eight years old (Robert Blackie moving to Norfolk, Rowland Rees to a house in St John's Road, Hove) but when she began work in her early twenties on a novel startlingly different in both kind and quality from any of her later work, she drew copiously on material supplied by her Methodist connections. The complicated family tree linking Pudneys, Reeses, Blackies and Burnetts is reproduced almost branch for branch in *Dolores*, and the atmosphere of pious ferment at Clacton in the 'eighties and 'nineties is as faithfully drawn in the Wesleyan background to that novel. The Coppins Hall barn, the public conversions, the local preachers patronizing a chapel congregation composed of small shop-keepers and cottagers all reappear in *Dolores*, and so does the evangelical fervour prevalent for at least two generations on the Rees side of the family: "'No, I don't agree with you there, Mrs Cassell,'' said Mr Blackwood loudly; "I don't agree with you. I remain a staunch up-holder of *Temperance* myself. We Wesleyans don't shrink from showing our colours for a cause we honestly have at heart; and I shall never shrink from showing mine for Temperance. Ah, yes; there are Wes-leyans in every part of the world, showing their colours for what they believe in their hearts to be right." '7

On Ivy's father's side of the family colours were less strident, and not so insistently shown. Generations of Burnetts seem to have switched back and forth as a regular thing between nonconformity and the established church, but the Congregational movement belonged to an older, staider and rather more cultivated tradition of dissent than John Wesley's society. James Compton Burnett's brother John, when Ivy first knew him, was a Congregational minister without a congregation of his own, occupied in preaching and teaching at Bedford. He had begun his career with churches at Burnham in Essex and Saxmundham in Suffolk but, being obliged by poor health to retire from the ministry in his late thirties, had moved to Bedford in 1877 where he joined first Howard Congregational Church (named for the philanthropist and prison reformer John Howard, who was a founder member in 1772) and later Bunyan Meeting (named for John Bunyan who became its minister shortly after the meeting began in 1650). Both these churches organized classes, lectures, Sunday schools and a well-established net-work of lesser churches, for Bedford had been since Cromwell's time a centre of religious independence. Bunyan Meeting especially—which had connections with Whitbreads, Wilberforces, Kingsleys and is several times depicted in the novels of Mark Rutherford, whose father was superintendent of Sunday schools in the 'forties—flourished in the second half of the nineteenth century under the Rev. John Brown, a man of considerable energy, charm and resource, ecclesiastical historian, author of the standard life of John Bunyan, and grandfather to Maynard and Geoffrey Keynes. The Rev. John Compton Burnett was a friend of Dr Brown, and his active supporter at Bunyan Meeting. Ivy's uncle took services, gave lectures, preached in its five village churches and was for ten years an able and unusually popular secretary of the Bedford Union of Christians.[8] His wife's school for girls, Howard College (where Ivy herself was sent for a couple of terms at the age of seventeen), had a reputation for 'careful Christian training, high class teaching, physical training'[9] and was one of the more select establishments in a town noted for its private schools.

Ivy's Uncle Jack and Aunt Sarah (their four children were older even than Dr Burnett's first family) paid fairly frequent visits to Hove. Sarah Compton Burnett was an imposing figure, stout and stately, dressed generally in black, with a black satin reticule and a manner calculated to inspire awe rather than affection in her nephews and nieces, as in her pupils. Her husband was more approachable; he took Scripture lessons at Howard College where the girls both liked and looked up to him. The two brothers seem to have shared much the same disposition. Both were by inclination gentle and genial and, both having married formidable wives, they remained so fond of one another that, whether fairly or not, one cannot help recalling the two mild and amiable middle-aged brothers, Edgar and Dudley Gaveston in *A Family and a Fortune*, whose devotion was grounded in a 'friendship which dated from their infancy'.[10] Dr. Burnett was a huge man, tall and so broad that the desk in his library at The Drive had had to be specially built for him; his brother was as tall but slighter, less robust, with a stoop imposed by a delicate constitution; and it is at least possible that the characteristic image of the Gavestons—'two tall figures', the one bending towards the other, strolling arm in arm on the terrace and watched from the windows by Edgar's children—may have been suggested by a memory of Jack and Jim Compton Burnett walking and talking together at Hove.

Other members of the family were less in evidence, Dr Burnett's eldest brother and sister (another Aunt Sarah) being both for similar reasons disgraced. Ivy's Uncle Charles, who was a Congregational minister at Sheerness and Newmarket in the 'sixties, had emigrated in 1873 to America and shortly afterwards died there; he was said to have married his cook, a scandal mentioned only with bated breath in the Compton Burnett household. His sister had married a policeman in

Bournemouth and, for all the good it did her in the family, 'might as well have married a convict and gone to Botany Bay'. Both were effectively erased from the family annals, along with the fact that their father had been a shopkeeper, coal merchant and dairyman. It is difficult to overestimate the importance of such social considerations in middle-class, high Victorian England: one of the things which had disgusted Ivy, and presumably shaped her attitude to the church, was her memory of 'our parson in Hove telling my mother he wanted a curate to call on the trades people'.[11] This parson was occasionally invited to dine but the Compton Burnetts were not over strict about church attendance: they went sometimes to St John's, sometimes to the parish church of All Saints which was nearer The Drive, and only on special occasions (when the girls had new frocks) to church parade on the front which was then the high spot of the week for fashionable Hove. Mrs Compton Burnett liked driving out with Ivy or another of her daughters to hear the Rev. A. D. Spong (namesake of the unspeakable Dominic Spong in *Men and Wives*) of Cliftonville Congregational Church, whose sermons were much admired and regularly reported in the local press; but though she publicly attended the Anglican service with her family in the morning, she would often slip out privately at night with her stepdaughter Daisy for evening worship at the Methodist chapel.

Ivy was duly baptized, confirmed and sent at fourteen to a High Church school. She herself on different occasions and to different people later set the date of her own disillusionment at various ages, ranging from ten to seventeen: 'I was brought up perfectly ordinarily in the Church of England but when I was sixteen or seventeen my reason naturally rejected such nonsense. No good can come of it. Its foundations are laid in fostering guilt in people—well, that obviously makes it easier for our Pastors and Masters when we are young,' she told Elizabeth Taylor in 1957. In the same decade she told Barbara and Walter Robinson that 'My brother gave up believing in God at the same time as Father Christmas, he realized they couldn't both be true. And it was a terrible shock.' The brother in question was almost certainly the ten-year-old Guy at Christmas 1895, when Ivy was eleven years old. Probably their scepticism grew gradually, encouraged by a series of shocks like this one (or Miss Mills' revelation when Ivy was seven) and sharpened in reaction to the kind of treatment meted out by his grandmother to Hengist Middleton, who with his sister had played a shabby trick on their governess: '"Hengist, you thought we did not

know. But there was Someone Who knew. Can you tell me Who saw
what you did, and saw into your hearts as you did it?" Selina had no
religion herself, but feared to let her grandchildren do without it.'[12]

It is not now easy to gauge the misery and resentment inflicted on
small children taught to believe literally in hell fire or (as Ivy remembered being told by the under-nurse) that thunder was a sign of God's
anger, in retaliation for some nursery crime, and would shortly be followed by His punishment. Ivy and her brothers seem to have reached
their position of humorous incredulity easily and early, without assistance and apparently without any of the torments suffered by an older
generation of conscientious Victorians who, like Henry Sidgwick in
fact and Robert Elsmere in fiction, lost their faith as adults and whose
lives were blighted, even broken, by agonizing problems of conscience.
But appearances may be deceptive. Religious guilt was a part of that
oppressive burden cast off with such an immense sense of relief at the
turn of the century by Ivy's generation, and from which she herself had
not escaped entirely unscathed. Dolores' prolonged career of self-
sacrifice, in I. Compton-Burnett's first novel, recalls in its frantic, unrelieved gloom the conflicts commonly endured by Victorian heroes
and heroines in the throes of religious doubt, a struggle at its most
tortuous in Edmund Gosse's *Father and Son*, at its most hectic in Mrs
Humphry Ward (whose heroine's doctrine of self-sacrifice, in *Robert
Elsmere*, repays comparison with Dolores'), and which casts a shadow
even over the cheerful domesticity of Charlotte M. Yonge (when
Norman May's faith is sorely tried in *The Daisy Chain*). Religious
pressure varied from the simpler nursery forms of emotional blackmail
to the curdled cruelty systematically practised by the Rev. Theodore
Pontifex on his son in Samuel Butler's *The Way of All Flesh*. In her late
thirties, Ivy still felt strongly enough on the subject to mark with a
pencil line this passage in her copy of Butler's *Note-Books*:

Religion.
Is there any religion whose followers can be pointed to as distinctly
more amiable and trustworthy than those of any other? If so, this
should be enough. I find the nicest and best people generally profess
no religion at all, but are ready to like the best men of all religions.[13]

Butler's view coincides exactly with what later became Ivy's own
characteristic position, given sombre expression by France Ponsonby
discussing her Aunt Hetta in *Daughters and Sons*:

'She goes to church,' said Muriel. 'And she does not have to go, does she?'

'If she were religious, she would not go,' said France. 'She would have thought about her religion and lost it.'[14]

We know something of what this relaxed and rational attitude had cost Samuel Butler, from his letters and his father's and from his own scarifying account of an upbringing which left him in some ways at least emotionally crippled for the rest of his life. Ivy's childhood, at any rate on this count, bears no comparison with Butler's; but long after-wards she would sometimes speak with a vehemence that suggests an abiding grudge against religion, all trace of which is expunged from her books where the customary attitude among the astute, young or old, is the kind of amused scepticism she had once shared with her brother. Her bitterness in later life may be seen perhaps as a measure of her pain at their loss, strengthened possibly by the fact that Guy and Noel—who both naturally possessed, in their sister's phase, 'a religious temper and no beliefs'[15]—had each severally turned at the end to the Bible for consolation in face of death.

However that may be, religious difficulties apparently caused no particular friction in the Compton Burnett household. It was accepted as a matter of course that Ivy and Guy and Noel (known as Jim to his family and friends because he disliked his baptismal name, or Noll to his younger sisters) should attend church 'under duress at times', and it later became a question as to which one should accompany their mother if she were going. 'My mother, I think, rather lost her beliefs because we did, or sort of half lost them,' Ivy said to Kay Dick. By this time Dr Burnett had died, and his wife seems to have made no bones about her children's rationalism—tolerating it perhaps as a sign of intelligence, and so a source for pride, as she had earlier tolerated Ivy's learning Greek with her brothers.

2

THE CONCEIT OF parts, which Boswell discerned and Dr Johnson approved in Mrs Thrale, was rife in the Compton Burnett schoolroom as it will be among clever and competitive children brought up, as these were, to furnish their brain boxes with nourishing porridge in a family whose other members were duller, and despised on that account. Ivy had inherited from her father his studious temperament and respect for learning, from her mother that 'exquisitely intellectual development' which had inspired such detached, professional pleasure in Dr Burnett when they first met. Her children's intelligence was a keen satisfaction to Mrs Compton Burnett, as it is to other strongminded mothers in her daughter's books. Anxiety on this score comes naturally to Eleanor Sullivan who, in spite of evidence daily supplied to the contrary by her son James, still cannot entertain 'the possibility of an absolutely ordinary child'; or to Sophia Stace whose habit of comparing her own children favourably with their humbler cousins, the Batemans, sustains her rare moods of complacency: 'My family could hardly escape intelligence, with their parents what they are.'[16] Ivy's achievements and Guy's were a congenial topic whenever the Blackies came to stay at Hove, and a cause of some asperity between the two sisters: 'Well, my dear, your children may have all the brains,' said Aunt Lizzie, 'but mine have the looks.'

Intelligence was evidently a weapon in Ivy's childhood, as it is in her books. It is also the moral principle which underlies all her work, the source of perception (without which there can be no self-knowledge) and so of all generosity. Conversely, ignorance is the pretext which enables the insensitive safely and with a good conscience to practise all forms of meanness:

'I can do no more for you, Mortimer. The truth is the kindest thing.'
'Is that so? I wonder what would be the unkindest.'[17]

The same code is advanced in book after book, by shrewd and experienced adults like Mortimer Lamb in *Manservant and Maidservant* or Rachel Hardistie in *Men and Wives* ('Being cruel to be kind is such dreadful cruelty. Being cruel to be cruel is better'), as by inexperienced and unhappy children like Clemence Shelley in *Two Worlds and Their Ways*. It is curious to note the clumsiness with which Clemence (whose schoolmistresses, having convicted her of cheating at school, casually smash her security at home by sending a full account to her mother) painfully works out for herself the doctrine unobtrusively practised, and so much more gracefully expressed, by sophisticates like Rachel or Mortimer: 'I don't think they were kind. No kind person would have told about it. They knew what that meant, or knew part of it. I could see they did. They were too stupid to know all of it, but stupidity is not kindness. I don't think a really kind person would ever be stupid.'[18]

Clemence Shelley at thirteen bears much the same relation to Ivy herself in childhood as the ten-year-old Honor Sullivan in *Parents and Children*. Both Clemence and Honor are bright little girls, both inclined to disparage their governesses, both naturally adopting an attitude at once encouraging and protective towards a timid younger brother who is his mother's favourite. Both excel at arithmetic, Honor ostentatiously outstripping her maladroit governess at sums, Clemence doing hers so much faster than the rest of the form that she has to be checked by her maths mistress: 'Clemence has done it in her head! So I will ask her not to answer the next one. We must all be given a chance, and mere quickness is not everything.' In 1965, Elizabeth Taylor encountered much the same situation when, on being asked if she could do a tricky income tax calculation in her head, Ivy replied: 'I have done so. I am very good at arithmetic. When I was at school, I was so good that I wasn't allowed to answer the questions, but had to give the other girls a chance'.

Like Ivy, Clemence (who had already begun Latin and Greek at home with her brother's tutor) has specially arranged private Greek lessons at school, proudly refuting 'the theory that classical and mathematical ability do not meet'. Clemence has her fourteenth birthday in her first term at school, Ivy was just turned fourteen when she was sent in the autumn of 1898 to Addiscombe College for the Daughters of Gentlemen in Hove. The two establishments have so much in common that it is unreasonable not to suspect some admixture of personal experience underlying Clemence's dreadful first day at school, and her first encounter with that surreptitious, sly brutality cultivated with such expertise by hardened schoolgirls—a brutality barely concealed when, having subjected the newcomer to a ruthless interrogation on her cleverness, age, future prospects, her parents, home and family circumstances, the other girls crowd into the dormitory while matron unpacks to inspect Clemence's clothes, and pass biting remarks on her lack of a party frock:

'What are those things?' said Esther, indicating some linen in Miss Tuke's hands. 'Underclothes?'

'Now what do you think they would be?' said Miss Tuke, shaking them out.

'I don't know,' said Verity, in a low tone, as though good manners deterred her from going further.[19]

Clemence's hair is another incentive to wit among her companions who tirelessly draw each other's, the matron's and their form mistress's attention to what strikes them as an odd and conspicuous hair style. Ivy had been proud of her long curly hair which she wore loose, tied back with a ribbon when she was fifteen or so, till she had it put up in a roll at the back of her head. Both her clothes and her hair had given rise to comment when, at eighteen, she went away to college: 'No one could deny her brains and probably her coaches had a better opinion of her than we did, but she did not really fit into ordinary academic life,' wrote a contemporary who wishes to remain anonymous. 'My chief recollection of her is as a rather badly dressed—but most of us were—girl with an incredible head of peroxide golden hair dressed in defiance of any fashion in a top-knot.'

Five different schools are examined in the novels of I. Compton-Burnett, but the only other small girl at school is Amy Grimstone in *The Last and the First* (the novel on which Dame Ivy was still at work when she died, published posthumously in 1971). Amy suffers under all the same heads as Clemence: painfully shy and self-conscious, agonized at school functions, going in mortal shame of her shabby clothes, her embarrassing relations and of not having a new dress for the school play. When her school is threatened with extinction, Amy is philosophical:

> 'How will you feel if the school is given up, and you have to go to another?'
> 'I am not sure, Grannie,' said Amy, seeing no prospect of real change unless all schools met this fate.[20]

That the system is unfair, inevitable and 'part of a great wrong' is also the view of Oliver Shelley, Clemence's older stepbrother in *Two Worlds and Their Ways*, who retains a vivid memory of his own school: 'It taught me to trust no one and to expect nothing. . . . To keep everything from everyone, especially from my nearest friends. That familiarity breeds contempt, and ought to breed it. It is through familiarity that we get to know each other.' The same point is put later in the same book from the opposite side, in a discussion between the matron and the headmaster's wife on the cruelty of older boys:

> 'The new boys do not meet that here.'
> 'Might they not be asked the number of their sisters and their fathers'

Christian names? The rumours cannot be quite without foundation.'
'That would not hurt them.'
'I never know why it hurts them so much. But it seems to be recognized.'[21]

Clemence and her younger brother Sefton are rightly apprehensive when the time comes for them to move on from governess and tutor. Ivy and her brothers had also made scenes when all three were dispatched simultaneously to school, Ivy to Addiscombe College, the boys to a prep school in Cromwell Road near The Drive kept by a Mr Charles Holland. Noel, who at eleven years old was already an accomplished mimic, privately regaled his sisters with imitations of Mr Holland extolling the merits of his 'little fellows' to their parents: 'But when the little fellows were in class, it was quite another story,' said Noel darkly. He and Guy later became weekly boarders, coming home on Friday evenings after school tea. When they were asked by their headmaster what was the first thing they did on reaching home, both replied with one voice: 'Have tea'. But neither was the kind of small boy likely to cause a moment's uneasiness to nervous adults like Terence Calderon, who has doubts of his cousin Reuben in *Elders and Betters*: 'I hope he is not a great hearty creature. If he is, I have been misled. I know he is thirteen, and that is a suffering age.'[22]

The Compton-Burnetts were not hearty creatures. Guy's chest had always been weak, and his health so frail that, when he was sent on to Tonbridge at fourteen, he was brought home desperately ill after two terms and nearly died of pneumonia. Noel who, according to his father, had been 'so strong and robust at birth that it was thought needless to bother' about oiling him, had fallen back by the time he was eight years old to become 'by far the least fine and strong'[23] of them all. At thirteen or fourteen he strained his back while running downhill with Vera and Judy, was laid up for weeks and could never again play strenuous games. Guy was similarly forbidden on account of his chest. Addiscombe College had its own sports ground on The Drive where in the afternoons there were games of hockey in winter, tennis and cricket in summer, in which neither Ivy nor her sisters took part.

Vera had been sent to school in 1899, in hopes of avoiding a fresh outbreak of the fuss and tears which had afflicted her elders the year before. Judy joined her in 1901 and so did their next sister, Katharine (called Topsy), a particularly bright and self-possessed child of five. Topsy was once caught and reproved by the headmistress, Miss

Cadwallader, for laughing at another small girl in the kindergarten: 'But, Topsy, you don't know everything yourself, do you?' 'No,' replied Topsy firmly. 'And neither do you, Miss Cadwallader, do you?' The Compton Burnett girls were remembered by their contemporaries at school as shy, hesitant, withdrawn and shabbily dressed. They took no extras save elocution, attended no dances, plays or painting exhibitions, didn't mix, made few friends and never asked anyone home to play—'When school was over they packed their satchels and spoke to no one, they came straight down, took their hats from their pegs and went home to work.' But they were undeniably clever. Vera, coming downstairs one day as Miss Cadwallader was interviewing the anxious parent of a prospective pupil in the hall below, overheard her say with emphasis: 'There goes one (we have them all) of a very gifted family.'

There were three Misses Cadwallader: the two eldest—Miss Catherine who was the nominal headmistress, taught poetry and scripture, took prayers and received the parents, and Miss Laura who took the top classes and was widely feared by her duller pupils—ran the school in partnership with Miss Katherine Marsland, a mathematician from Newnham. The youngest sister, Miss Frances (known as 'Fussy Frances' to her charges), did the housekeeping together with the Matron, Miss Lane, who looked after the boarders' clothes. Addiscombe College occupied two adjoining houses, numbers 39 and 41 Tisbury Road (which runs directly behind The Drive), and prided itself on its excellent tone, drawing its pupils mainly from the professional classes, among them a good many doctors' daughters, holding cricket matches in the summer with Roedean, and boasting a dancing mistress who had once taught the Prince of Wales and his brother. It was also devoutly High Church—'rather too high for comfort', as one of its pupils recalled. Ivy herself remembered with distaste interminable lessons on 'history of the prayer book, history of Collects and all kinds of such things'. The Misses Cadwallader wore black in Lent ('And I can remember Miss Laura coming into prayers on Ash Wednesday with the most dismal countenance you can imagine'),[24] celebrated Ascension Day with a school picnic on the downs and on Sundays conducted a crocodile of the twenty-five boarders, dressed in the school uniform of green skirts, white blouses and white hats with a Welsh dragon badge (the Cadwalladers, like the Reeses, claimed descent from a royal Welsh line), to St Barnabas church.

But their views on education for girls were considered distinctly advanced. They were unusually particular about their staff and its qualifications, retaining a resident mademoiselle (though the standard of compulsory French speaking remained fairly elementary: '*Donnez-moi un bun*'), a visiting German Fräulein, and visiting masters for music, elocution and riding. Miss Laura and Miss Marsland had read English and mathematics at London and Cambridge respectively, a great thing in those days as Ivy confirmed in *The Present and the Past* ('Miss Ridley had obtained a degree, a step whose mystic significance for a woman was accepted at that date even by those who had taken it').[25] Their pupils learnt Latin but no Greek, overstepping even in this the bounds of Mrs Lynn Linton's ideal (a maiden 'not attuned to aught but the tender things of everyday life—innocent, unsuspicious, affectionate— just the good, dear girl of a quiet English home'), but conforming to the conditions exacted from poor Ethel May in *The Daisy Chain*, who had been induced to give up her dearest wish on the grounds that she could not both learn Greek and remain 'a useful, steady daughter and sister at home . . . The sort of woman that dear mamma wished to make you, and a comfort to papa.'[26] Ivy, however, remained adamant, neither innocent nor unsuspicious, unattuned to the tender, everyday things ('Which finger do I put the thimble on?' she asked once to tease in a needlework class), and content to study Greek alone in private coaching sessions at school with Mr Salt. Any girl not positively incapable at Addiscombe College was expected to sit the Cambridge Local Board examinations, but Ivy was again unique in proposing to go on to university.

Vera Compton-Burnett remembered Miss Laura Cadwallader as 'rather the New Woman, very shirty' (that is, she wore a shirt and tie and was 'as like a man as it is possible to be, without actually being one'). She was grave, stern, highly esteemed for her awesome B.A., and took small part in the everyday affairs of the school. One may suspect that, of all the mistresses, Miss Laura was the one most likely to appeal to Ivy who recounted with the respect of one wit for another her remark, on handing back the form's work, to one Florence who was not much of a hand at writing essays: 'Mean little handwriting, Florrie, and mean little ideas.' Miss Laura's particular friend was Miss Marsland (the two had been colleagues at Portsmouth High School before taking over Addiscombe College in 1896), who had 'a high, shiny forehead, long hair oiled and coiled like a great Chelsea bun', and whose geometry lessons are still remembered with pleasure by several of her pupils: 'Miss Marsland was *quite different* from the Cadwalladers. She was gentle and kind and, if you were naughty, she dissolved into tears.'[27] By all accounts the pair closely resembled two of the three partners at Clemence's school in *Two Worlds and Their Ways*:

Miss Marathon's upright figure, pronounced nose and prominent, expressionless eyes gave her a somewhat forbidding aspect, that was hardly borne out by her pupils' demeanour towards her. She sat among them and supervised their needs in a manner at once precise and kindly, critical and tolerant. Miss Laurence was recognized as too intellectual for tangible affairs, and remained aloof and did nothing, thereby both creating and fulfilling a part. Her pupils regarded her with affection and fear, or merely with the latter. Miss Marathon they regarded with neither, and with no other particular feeling.[28]

Miss Catherine Cadwallader, who cultivated a winning manner and a penchant for pastel shades, pale fawn, grey lace, floating draperies, was 'the opposite of her sister', though equally formidable in a different way. An associate of Cheltenham Ladies' College, her function was to cajole, reassure and entertain the parents—a part she played as expertly as Amy Grimstone's headmistress or Mr Merry in *Pastors and Masters*, both insinuating, equivocal, even sinister creatures, both strangely relaxed among the various forms of uneasiness which inevitably exist in a school, both adept at making capital out of a natural vagueness as to the identity and achievements of any particular pupil:

'Well, Mr Merry,' said a father, 'so you haven't put my boy among the prize-winners? Of course, I don't mean that. But he doesn't go in for taking prizes, does he?'

'Ah, your boy,' said Mr Merry, who knew the ill policy of honesty with parents; 'and a nice boy too! No, he doesn't go in for taking prizes. No, not yet. But I tell you what.' Mr Merry's voice became intimate. 'If I had a boy, I should like him to be your boy. I will tell you that.'[29]

Like Mr Merry, Miss Cadwallader was in her element at the school prize-giving for which Hove Town Hall was taken every year, and for which the staff and parents (Dr Burnett only after stiff protest) wore evening dress, the children their party frocks.

Ivy took her matriculation when she had just passed her seventeenth birthday in the summer of 1901, and was then sent for a couple of terms to Howard College at Bedford so that she might grow accustomed to life away from home. Bedford in those days was in its late Victorian heyday, a centre for private boarding schools and a favourite retreat of the army and navy (a local directory for 1902 lists among the town's residents a retired vice-admiral, a paymaster-in-chief, a deputy inspector-general R.N., two naval captains, a commander and two lieutenants, four generals, one lieutenant-general, two major-generals, thirty-five colonels, sixteen majors and twenty-two captains). The countryside came right up to the rim of the town, nightjars sang in the outskirts and the corncrake could still be heard within half a mile of Howard College at 77 Bromham Road; 'old gentlemen on tricycles, riding three abreast, in authoritative measured tones would discuss their afternoon's golf or the iniquities of the latest budget, as they returned home along Bromham Road'; the town's peace was broken only by 'furiously driving butcher boys' or, on market days, by sheep which 'ran down any available turning and through garden gates left open (those of Howard College among others)'.[30] The school itself was another enlightened establishment, run on much the same lines as Addiscombe College and pluming itself, according to the Rev. John Compton Burnett, on moral guidance, physical training and mental work in that order.* It took some thirty or forty boarders, half a dozen day girls, and drew special attention in advertisements and prospectus to its site on gravel soil, its lighting, ventilation, sanitary arrangements and the exertions of its drill sergeant.

Ivy's Aunt Sarah ran it, though she did no teaching herself, ruling her staff, her pupils and her husband—who was 'a little retiring as he was very much dominated by his wife'[31]—with a despot's authority. Ivy's uncle had in fact died a few months before she reached Howard College but, so far as the school was concerned, his departure meant only that

---

* Ivy's uncle died before he knew that she would amply fulfil a prophecy he had made in an address to the school in 1899: 'He found it difficult to give any adequate report of the real work they were doing. Theirs was largely a sowing of seed which would produce its harvest in the characters and lives of their pupils in after years. . . . They aimed first of all at the true physical training of their pupils. They were careful not only about diet and light, about ventilation and drill. They went further; they were specially considerate of means for the expansion of the chest, which was not only of such prime importance in the child's development, but enriched the blood and told powerfully on the whole physical life. In their mental work they tried really to educate, to guide and strengthen the mind for gaining and assimilating knowledge in the future of the pupil's life. The higher moral results they valued most of all. They remembered that true refinement is of the heart—"Tis only noble to be good".' (Report in the local press, supplied by the Bedfordshire County Archivist.)

his widow became its nominal as well as its actual head. A contemporary of Ivy well remembered saying to another girl, 'Oh, we are making a row,' and being overheard, called back and curtly rebuked by Mrs Compton Burnett: 'Never say "row", say "hubbub".' Ivy herself long afterwards described her cousin Maude, who helped in the school and was then nearly thirty, being treated before company as tersely as if she were still in the nursery: 'Maude, leave the room'. The family lived in the school buildings (which had been specially built in 1878, now converted into flats), and left a vivid memory with Ivy's contemporary: 'I enjoyed the Rev. Compton Burnett's scripture lessons immensely, he was a very good teacher . . . Maude Compton Burnett was just like her mother. I was afraid of her. Not a bit like her father.'

It is difficult to avoid the conclusion that memories of both Howard College and the day school at Hove contributed later to the school in *Two Worlds and Their Ways* whose headmistress is also a connection by marriage and Clemence's courtesy aunt, the redoubtable Lesbia Firebrace. 'This place is a nest of professional eavesdroppers,' complains one of her discomfited pupils, unwisely goaded by Miss Firebrace's habit of being neither seen nor heard:

'It is true that I have a profession, Esther, but it is not that of eavesdropper. I have a right to walk where I will in my own house, and I shall continue to use it. And it is a pity you so often say things that you do not wish to be heard, that is, that you are a little ashamed of. If you broke yourself of the habit, you would not need to be concerned about what you choose to call eavesdropping.'

There was a silence over this choice of Esther's, and Lesbia continued in an even, distinct tone.

'I do not take a harsh or narrow view of the intercourse amongst you. No, I do not, Esther. You are allowed more latitude than is often the case. You would not meet it everywhere. I know that young people must talk, and that it is idle to look for much weight or worth in what they say—or to listen for it, if you will.' Miss Marathon just raised her eyes at this open appraisement. 'But things must be kept within certain bounds, and within those bounds they will be kept. Do you understand me, Esther?'[32]

Miss Firebrace is one of those demanding, implacable, by no means unintelligent but disingenuous women, common enough in the novels of I. Compton-Burnett, devoured by an urge to power whose full implications are hidden even from herself. It was the force of her will, dreaded as much by Clemence's parents as by the school's staff and pupils, which brought her niece to the school in the first place. It seems at least possible that Ivy, too, had been sent like her stepsisters to boarding school at her aunt's insistence, and certainly the reasons for which she was sent were much the same as those Lesbia exploits for bullying Clemence's parents. One cannot build much on a novel written nearly fifty years later, and which has its own independent existence; but it is perhaps worth noting that when the other girls—driven to retaliate by dominating someone even younger and weaker than themselves— close in on Clemence, one of their favourite needling points is her relation to the headmistress. It is a subject expressly forbidden by Miss Firebrace, and one to which Clemence's tormentors are irresistibly drawn:

> 'Is it anything to be ashamed of?' said Gwendolen, again. 'I don't see so much disgrace in keeping a school. Perhaps there isn't any.'
>
> 'I should say there is no occupation that carries less disgrace, Gwendolen. Miss Firebrace merely meant that no difference was to be made.'
>
> 'Does it make any other difference to come to a school kept by a relation, by a connection?' said Esther, in a tone at once blunt and innocent.
>
> 'I suppose not, if it is to be forgotten,' said Clemence.
>
> 'I meant any difference of any kind.'
>
> 'Does Miss Firebrace do you charity, or do you do her charity?' said Gwendolen, laughing at her own openness.
>
> 'Oh, I expect we do her charity,' said Clemence, finding the situation taken in hand by something outside herself, and surprised at her ease in it. 'That is how it would be.'[33]

This is the beginning of a career of inexperienced lies and evasions which lead inevitably to humiliating public exposure. The cause of Clemence's final undoing is her mother's ambition: Maria Shelley, being like Sophia Stace and Eleanor Sullivan inordinately proud of her children's intelligence and anxious for them to excel, conveys her anxiety to her daughter who, coming head of her class effortlessly at first, later with increasing difficulty, desperate to win and maintain her mother's approval, embarks on a course of systematic cheating which is detected as easily as her earlier, wretchedly inept attempts at duplicity had been, and punished the more cruelly in proportion as the mistresses' power exceeds the girls'. Whether or not Ivy herself had come similarly to grief is immaterial. What matters is that it is at school that Clemence first learns by necessity ('. . . necessity is the mother of invention. The hard mother of a sad and sorry thing') the harsh lessons formulated again and again in the novels of I. Compton-Burnett.

Ivy at school had been aloof and self-contained, discouraging intimacy with the other girls—'she had her tongue in her cheek with most of them'—and no doubt as vulnerable as other intelligent, sensitive children dispatched alone from the seclusion of family life to an alien world mined with traps for the unwary. Precisely this experience is described in the autobiography of Charles Darwin's granddaughter, Gwen Raverat, who was a year younger than Ivy and who, after a happy Cambridge childhood spent at home with her family, her nurse and her brother's tutor, was sent at sixteen to a boarding school where, 'with all the bewildered avidity of an anthropologist trying to understand the minds of the natives', she attempted to fathom unintelligible and hitherto unknown schoolgirl customs like games and gossip and hat-pin-knobbing: '. . . the chief thing I learnt at school was how to tell lies. Or rather, how to try to tell them; for, of course, I did it very badly. Still, I did my best to pretend that I liked what I didn't and that I didn't like what I did. But it was no good; they knew perfectly well that there was something wrong about me, so that I always felt inferior and out of it, just as I did at a party. . . .'[34] Five years before Gwen Raverat's autobiography was published in 1952, I. Compton-Burnett, looking back over the same distance of half a century, had given the same dispassionate insight to her fourteen-year-old heroine in a scene where Clemence sums up for her younger brother her own experience at school: '. . . there is not much that I don't know now. I know such a lot of unexpected things. Things that are said and not thought, and things that are thought and not said. And there are so many of both. I should never have known, if I had stayed at home, or never have known that I knew. That is another thing you learn, to know what you know.'[35]

We know that school had come as a severe emotional shock to Ivy, a shock doubly painful because it meant that she was for the first time detached from her brothers and from the mutual security, protection and imaginative sympathy that had enclosed her from infancy—something which consoles even the solitary Amy Grimstone, questioned by her elder brother and sister after a school concert has taxed her powers of endurance beyond breaking point:

'It is nothing,' said Amy . . . 'Or nothing you would understand.'

'Was it everything?' said Erica, in a tone that denoted understanding.

'Yes it was,' said Amy, in one that accepted it.[36]

We may perhaps suspect that Ivy had suffered at public functions, as
Amy and Clemence do in her books, from the strain of mediating
between the two incompatible worlds of home and school. We know
that her classical learning set her apart from the other girls; that she
never willingly took part in games, clubs, debates or organized social
activity of any kind at school or college; that she made no particular
friends at her first school, and only one at her second—a certain Daisy
Harvey, also a boarder at Howard College, who went on with Ivy to
Royal Holloway College and remained there her only close companion.
We know that, at two at least of these establishments, she was considered odd and unapproachable by girls who inclined more readily to
the atmosphere of boisterous juvenile domesticity combined with
moral earnestness which obtained at all three. And we know that round
about the time when she went to school—the age at which her younger
sisters first clearly remember her—she was already beginning to assume
at will a mask impenetrable outside the family circle, and penetrated
within it only by her two brothers.

What is curious about *Two Worlds and Their Ways* is that its author
here examines the process whereby Clemence acquires a similar mask;
and what is perhaps even more curious is to compare Clemence at
fourteen with a long line of older heroines in whom one may divine
the same vulnerability, though age and experience conceal it rather
more successfully than Clemence's miserably frail defences. It is
precisely this mask of frivolous indifference, assumed with such gaiety
and grace in face of catastrophe, which has caused so much difficulty to
readers who find in I. Compton-Burnett a disconcerting heartlessness.
The misunderstanding is natural enough, since it means that the delicate
veneer of wit maintained by her characters has concealed, as its ingenious inventors mean it to do, the turbulent emotions beneath. But it is
nonetheless interesting to find that in *Two Worlds and Their Ways*—
published in 1949, mid-way through her career as a novelist—I.
Compton-Burnett explicitly acknowledges the underlying perturbation and fear so often elaborately disguised elsewhere in her books. The
source of courage is made transparently clear when Clemence, exposed
as a cheat before a tribunal of schoolmistresses who remain unmoved by

her painful, blurted explanations as by her agonizingly controlled pleas for mercy, is saved from abject collapse (though not from despair) by the cold eye of Miss Firebrace: 'what Clemence saw as relentless and shallow penetration, struck her pride and gave her a calm front'. Clemence dreads above all that her parents should learn of her downfall, the school report threatening destruction of her world at home as well as at school. She moves with a sense of unreality through the end-of-term party, her first indication that outsiders may remain perfectly unruffled even by another's unendurable distress—'The lack of imagination staggered her and wrought in her a lasting change'—and through the farewells when school breaks up next morning: 'She followed her companions to the cab and the train with no sign of her inner tumult.'[37]

'A calm front', 'inner tumult', and a staggering lack of imagination on the part of those who accept the one without discerning the other beneath it, are constant themes throughout the work of I. Compton-Burnett. It is pride which gives Clemence courage, pride which sustains her and lends her a sense of superiority, even in her utmost unhappiness, towards those blind or indifferent to the suffering they cause. Greater sufferings than Clemence's are endured by older heroines with incomparably greater sang-froid; but it is not perhaps too much to suggest that Clemence's very rawness and immaturity may shed some light on how and why Ivy herself acquired in childhood the beginnings of that stoical composure which enabled her afterwards to endure pain and loss with a calm front.

IV

JAMES COMPTON BURNETT

'It darkened the day'

I

JAMES COMPTON BURNETT died suddenly of heart failure at his hotel in London during the night of Monday, 1 April 1901, two months before Ivy's seventeenth birthday. He had travelled up to town as usual that morning and spent the day visiting patients. Almost the only warning noticed by his family beforehand had been that, while taking his customary walk on Sunday, he turned back half way because of a pain at the chest which he attributed to indigestion, '"though", he added in a casual way, half speaking to himself, "it's rather like angina pectoris"'.[1] Ivy had never seen a great deal of her father. In what little time he spent at home she had been one among twelve although, as the eldest child of his beloved second wife, she had no doubt a special claim on his affections. 'In human life we have our favourites; we have them in our families,'[2] he said and, in a family with one parent as openly partial as the second Mrs Compton Burnett, it must have been hard to avoid attempts to redress the balance. But the self-contained trio in the schoolroom can have had no more than their fair share of his attention when so much of it was devoted to amusing the younger ones and, with the older ones, to easing the tensions which tended to spring up around his wife. His death marked the end of what had hitherto been, at any rate for the second family, a secure and cheerful childhood. 'It had been so joyous till then,' said Vera Compton-Burnett. 'The sun suddenly went out.'

Their father's death brings a similar eclipse on the Stace children in *Brothers and Sisters* which, of all the novels of I. Compton-Burnett (except for the early *Dolores*, an indiscretion in several senses and so immature that it can scarcely be seen as belonging to the main body of her work), is the one most intimately connected with her own life. *Brothers and Sisters*—published in 1929, when Ivy was in her mid-forties—was her third book and the only one in which she directly retraces the period between the last year of her father's life and her mother's death ten years later. Other books may contain characters and incidents drawn, more or less distinctly, at greater or less distance, from memories of her childhood and adolescence; but *Brothers and Sisters* contains recognizable portraits of Ivy and her brothers, her parents, her grandfather Rowland Rees and her nurse Minnie. They are of course well disguised: transposed to an ancestral manor house in the country, stripped of extraneous trappings, accompanied by a charming attendant cast of wholly imaginary characters and subjected to an eventful plot involving family skeletons, missing documents, long-lost parents and a steady flow of marriage proposals. But the central situation—the death of Christian Stace, his wife's tyrannical grief and his children's subsequent suffering—reflects all the more soberly for its extravagantly fictional setting events in the Compton Burnett household.

Christian Stace is the first of Ivy's doctors (again, apart from Dr Cassell in *Dolores* who was taken from quite another model), and the one who most closely resembles her father: 'He had a slow, strong brain and a personality felt as a support, a religious temper and no beliefs, a gentle opinion of others and a high one of himself. As a physician and a man, he was becoming much beloved, a fact that called for no surprise, and from him had none.'[3] Dr Stace, like Dr Burnett, travels up to town to attend to a large London practice which keeps him away from home by day and consequently aloof from family affairs; he, too, diagnoses in himself the signs of impending heart failure which shortly afterwards kills him; and his conversation (as, for instance, when his wife asks if there is any chance of a cure: '"All the chances," said Christian . . . "I am as busy as can be with my precious self. So are one or two others of the trade. We all think I shan't be got out of the way so easily."') reproduces both the tone and the turns of phrase characteristic of Ivy's father. 'Simple goodness' is the phrase most readily applied by his family and friends to Christian, as it commonly was to Dr Burnett: 'He was a remarkably strong character of a rugged, massive type, straightforward and direct to a degree,' wrote the *Monthly Homoeopathic Review* when he died. 'He was simply a grand man, a lover of his kind, a faithful physician, the impersonation of kindness and sweetness . . .' wrote Dr Frank Kraft in the *American Homoeopathist*. His bio-

grapher and friends abound in tributes to the 'merry twinkle in his
eye', his 'uncommonly potent personality', 'that magnetism, that
witchery, that individuality which held his auditor from the first
moment'; and indeed one may still sense from his books, nearly a
hundred years after they were written, something of the forcefulness
and charm of a bonhomous nature revealed with perfect unselfcon-
sciousness for, unlike Sir Roderick Shelley in *Two Worlds and Their
Ways*, Dr Burnett was accustomed to 'write the word he spoke'.
Reading him is much like being subjected to his bluff handshake which
'left a feeling of heartiness and good will'.[4]

Simplicity, heartiness and good will are generally ominous signs in
his daughter's books, indicating an alarming lack of self-knowledge
which allows the ostensibly simple and hearty to vent their underlying
ill will unmolested and with undiminished, often greatly enhanced,
self-esteem. But Dr Burnett's straightforwardness was genuine, the
outcome of that furious appetite for work typical of so many professional men in the second half of the nineteenth century, which left
neither time nor taste for introspection. His practice was vast—'one of
the largest consulting practices in London' according to his obituary in
the *Westminster Gazette*—and, judging by the patients singled out in his
case histories, select: 'a lady of rank', 'a gentleman of position and
means', 'an author of eminence', 'the little son of a distinguished clergyman' are typical of a clientèle drawn occasionally from the nobility and
soundly based on the country squires who journeyed to consult him
from Cheshire and from the Home Counties, on London merchants,
professional men, staff officers and their dependents. In all his voluminous writings, I find reference among his patients to one seaman in
Liverpool, one Kentish servant and one charwoman with a bad heart
whom he cured free of charge on her mistress's recommendation, and
who thereafter became a legend to his children:

> . . . I saw no more of her for some time until one day she was ushered
> into my consulting room. She came up to where I was sitting, told
> me she was perfectly well, could do any work with ease, and—then
> occurred one of the sweetest incidents of my professional life—the
> old lady (and *what a lady*!) put a tiny packet on my desk, tried to say
> something, burst into tears and rushed out!
>
> I never saw her again, and have often since wished I had kept that
> particular sovereign and had it set in diamonds.[5]

But there was another side to his character not seen by his family and friends, the bellicose and litigious side uninhibitedly expressed throughout his career at the expense of 'our friends, the enemy', his orthodox professional colleagues. Religious imagery was frequently necessary to convey the fury of his feelings on this point: having compared his own conversion to St Paul's, he liked later to see himself as marshalling the forces of homoeopathy 'in the obscurity of schism' against the medical establishment, the soi-disant 'true *Ecclesia medica catholica*'. 'Though one rose from the dead they would not believe' was a favourite slogan in his battle against a profession which he habitually characterized as dishonest, dense-minded, insolent, imbecilic and afflicted by 'the traditional dementia of all who are doomed to extinction'.[6] The *Homoeopathic World* under his editorship became a convenient campaign ground for goading his enemies, confounding their politics, frustrating their knavish tricks and rallying support in turn for the gallant fighting homoeopaths of Norwich, Halifax (the editor's jubilation in December 1880 at the downfall of 'the dapper allopaths of Halifax' is pleasant to see), Bath and Liverpool. His *Fifty Reasons for Being a Homoeopath* was provoked in 1888 by a young doctor who called him a braggart and a quack and who was in return chastised by Dr Burnett as a liar for whose ignorance 'I have the most absolutely unspeakable contempt'. Quackery was a sore point with homoeopaths, being a charge constantly laid against them and one which Dr Burnett returned with energy, calling down vengeance in his pages on all quacks, gulls (among them Sir William Jenner who regularly earned his displeasure as President of the Royal College of Physicians) and 'eye-carpenters' (or ophthalmic surgeons), on 'Mrs Dr Grundy' and all those led astray by 'the apron-strings of Mrs Lancet', and, with especial venom, on all pseudo- and crypto-homoeopaths ('the mean men that have crawled into professional chairs with the aid of purloined portions of the homoeopathic *Materia Medica* and simultaneous abjurations thereof. These creeping things inspire disgust').[7]

His wrath scarcely abated when in April 1885 he resigned his editorship because of pressure of work. He was still liable to harry those of his patients rash enough to object to the time he took to effect a cure (long, slow healing was a crucial point in his treatment) or, blackest of crimes, to suggest recourse to another branch of the profession. His satirical outbursts on these occasions recall the tirades of his daughter's domestic tyrants who, like Dr Burnett, are apt to complain of people 'banding together and baiting me as if I were just a person to be put right about everything!'[8] Something very like their characteristically self-righteous assumption of divine right is evident in, for instance, his aggrieved account of a country clergyman's wife with a tumour at the breast whose husband, after two years' apparently ineffectual treatment, requested a second opinion from the distinguished surgeon, Sir James Paget (whose consulting rooms were opposite Burnett's, and a perpetual mortification to him):

> To this I declined to assent. . . . Truth to tell, I am sick and weary of the lying statements that the knife is even any, and least of all the only cure for tumours. . . .
>
> But to return to my patient and her choleric husband, I absolutely declined any second opinion.
>
> Why?
>
> Simply because a very considerable number of people with tumours literally die of doctors' opinions, and then what is the use or value of the opinion of never so eminent a pathologist on a therapeutic point? Just none.
>
> Of course, I know it is said to be very unprofessional to decline an eminent colleague's opinion in a given case. But I did it for my patient's good, *not* for my own; and, moreover, they do the same to me when people want my opinion.[9]

One may readily detect in this and similar passages a resemblance to the many intemperate fathers who, like Ninian Middleton in *The Mighty and Their Fall*, are commonly compared to God ('There are the anger, jealousy, vaingloriousness, vengefulness, love, compassion, infinite power. The matter is in no doubt')[10] in the novels of I. Compton-Burnett. But what drives Ninian and his like to excess is their lack of occupation, the fatal sense of mighty powers unfulfilled in a life with no outlet beyond the immediate domestic circle. Dr Burnett was fully occupied by a professional round which afforded more than sufficient outlet for his considerable energies; and we have his younger daughters' evidence that his character at home revealed nothing more intimidating than the soothing mildness of Christian Stace. The most one can say is that, like his fourth daughter, Dr Burnett well understood the urge to intolerance and tyranny and that—also like her, though for wholly different ends—he exploited to the full its dramatic possibilities. He clearly derived the greatest enjoyment from hurling his thunder-bolts like Jove; from the biblical precedent which he selected for the crypto-homoeopaths who betrayed his creed ('Well, they serve a purpose. So did Judas'); and from the god-like vantage point whence he contentedly surveyed the trail of humiliation and havoc left in his wake: 'The frankness and honesty of one's allopathic colleagues are wonderful articles. However, they have, as usual, had to munch the leek.'[11]

Many of his harshest judgements come from *Tumours of the Breast*, a peculiarly fiery work published in 1888 and full of that long rankling bitterness which invariably consumed Dr Burnett when he contemplated the ravages inflicted by contemporary surgery. But it should be remembered that, if homoeopathy in the 'eighties and 'nineties was under constant fire from without, it was torn simultaneously by civil war within. Dr Burnett had to contend not simply with crypto-homoeopaths like Joseph Kidd, who had attended Disraeli in his last illness, publicly renounced his homoeopathic allegiance and became the object of a blistering, often libellous onslaught in the *Homoeopathic World* for eight months thereafter; or allopaths like Robert Koch who, as the first to isolate the drug tuberculin which ultimately eradicated consumption, won a renown in the early 'nineties which Burnett (who claimed to have pioneered the same methods five years before Koch) held to be rightfully his. Homoeopathy itself was meanwhile split into two warring factions, the one led by Burnett and a group of his friends (among them his future biographer, John Clarke), the other by the immensely influential Richard Hughes. It was Hughes' *Manual of Pharmacodynamics*, the first authoritative homoeopathic textbook published in English, which had recruited Burnett himself and practically the whole of Burnett's generation of rising young homoeopaths in Britain. But Hughes was severely puritanical by temperament, a fundamentalist and a purist, resenting on the one hand all attempts to tamper with his own interpretations of what he regarded as revealed truth laid down by the movement's founder, Samuel Hahnemann, and detesting, on the other, an *ad hoc*, empirical or individual approach to clinical symptoms. Both views are vigorously repudiated in Burnett's opening manifesto in the *Homoeopathic World* for September 1879. Hughes' ambition was to convert the allopathic world by presenting scientific evidence so codified and purged of extraneous detail as to be irrefutable on any objective reading, a dream which Burnett denounced as timid, conventional and dangerously restrictive.

The battle was at its fiercest in the last fifteen years or so of Burnett's life. Hughes, who was considerably older, finally achieved supreme authority in the homoeopathic world and managed thereafter to block

all roads to power as long as he lived. In 1883 he had selected John
Clarke, one of his own most promising medical students, as his assistant
editor on the *British Journal of Homoeopathy*; the appointment lasted two
years before Hughes realized his mistake, and it was the first and last
office Clarke ever held. In 1890 Clarke 'let his hair down and bared his
teeth'[12] in a paper, 'The Two Paths in Homoeopathy', intended as an
outright challenge to Hughes. Burnett meanwhile had been obliged,
whether by overwork or by hostile pressure from above, to resign his
own official appointments and to concentrate, as Clarke was forced to
do for the rest of his life, on private practice. The two combined with
Robert Cooper, another outstanding practitioner and Burnett's closest
friend, and Thomas Skinner (a celebrated renegade, once notorious as a
'persecuting allopath' in Liverpool, who had recanted dramatically in
the early 'seventies and became a leading homoeopathic authority on
the use of drugs at high potency) in a dining club, later known
as the Cooper Club, which met regularly on weekday evenings in
London to discuss problems of therapeutics and, no doubt, of medical
politics.

Clarke later described the other leading members of the Cooper Club
as 'the three most potent influences on the evolution of British Homoeopathy today',[13] and wrote in 1901: 'It is not too much to say that during
the last twenty years Burnett has been the most powerful, the most
fruitful, the most original force in homoeopathy'. Clarke was himself a
physician to be reckoned with, and in time the author of a medical
encyclopaedia which rivalled Hughes'. But it is possible that partisan
feeling affected his judgement of his contemporaries and that he was a
trifle hampered, in his enthusiastic life of his friend, by the professional
discretion which forbade any but the vaguest reference to Hughes or to
what he called 'the littlenesses and paltry jealousies that not infrequently
arise'. Many of Burnett's works (including the *Cure of Consumption*
which, according to Clarke, 'establishes beyond question his claim to
immortality and the eternal homage of his kind')* have inevitably been

---

* Burnett's book was published in November 1890 (shortly after Koch's discovery of
tuberculin) with a preface furiously denouncing the persecution of homoeopaths by
'the very men who now lie prone at Dr Koch's feet in abject adoration. . . . True, we
work in the obscurity of schism, but we work nevertheless; and although to him all
the honour, and to us ridicule, misrepresentation and hateful slander, still we pray we
may never be weary in well-doing.' I am grateful to Dr Frank Bodman for the information that Burnett's 'bacillinum' (which was considered superior to Koch's rival
preparation by its inventor) was in fact 'a much cruder agent prepared from tuber-
culous sputum and probably contaminated with secondary germs'.

superseded by twentieth-century developments. Recent opinion would argue that his single most important contribution to medical history was his first book, *Natrum Muriaticum* (1878), which demonstrated Hahnemann's cardinal theory of drug dynamization at a time when the point was hotly disputed by allopaths, and which was noticed with respect—a rare accolade for a homoeopath—even in the strictly orthodox *British Medical Journal*.

But, apart from this one closely reasoned argument, Burnett's twenty-six books and pamphlets consist for the most part of strings of case histories, jotted down 'in odd scraps of time, sometimes in carriages or at railway stations, and not infrequently when tired',[14] and interspersed with more or less random reflections, proverbs, rhyming jingles, quotations from Schiller and Goethe, snatches of conversation and anecdote, anything which happened to take his fancy as he wrote. He undeniably used medicines to cure cataracts and tumours, both then commonly subject to the surgeon's knife; and his caution on the use of the drug tuberculin, or on the dire effects of vaccination, was salutary in an age when dangerously, even murderously large doses were regularly prescribed by orthodox practitioners. But his brilliance lay not so much in his books—which are in any case so unspecific as to be virtually useless from the point of view of passing on scientific information—as in the originality of his individual diagnoses. He was an intuitive and deductive practitioner. His essential requirements were time, patience and 'the ladder of remedies', a series of different medicines prescribed at different potencies and subtly adjusted to the needs of a particular case. The trickiest problems pleased him most, and the quirkier the solution the better it suited him ('Now the homoeopathic treatment of the shingles after-pains is one of the prettiest bits of therapeutic sharp-shooting imaginable . . .'). Many of his remedies were known, as he frequently noted with engaging complacency, only to himself; and his pride was not easily mollified when patients made what he called 'tedious recoveries', thereby cheating him of a radical cure.

He was, as a great many early homoeopaths had to be, largely self-educated: an omnivorous reader not only of his contemporaries in German, French and English but of their predecessors who, long before Hahnemann first formulated the homoeopathic law of similars,* had

* The British Homoeopathic Association's official *Guide to Homoeopathy* defines this law as follows: 'Homoeopathy is a branch of medicine based on the principle that "like cures like", namely that a substance which, in certain forms and doses, causes disease symptoms may also be used to cure illnesses showing similar symptoms. The

speculated on the subject in the sixteenth and seventeenth centuries. His library at Hove contained volumes on mediaeval alchemy, obscure medical treatises in Latin and copies of Hahnemann's seminal translation of William Cullen's *Materia Medica*, 'two ragged old books'[15] published at Leipzig in 1790. In his own books, he is as likely to quote with approval from the sixteenth-century Johannes Fernelius or the seventeenth-century Robert Fludd, from Rademacher or Paracelsus (whom he especially revered as Hahnemann's immediate forerunner), as from the nineteenth-century experiments of Pasteur or Koch. He was, moreover, 'an intrepid prover', testing his prescriptions first on himself according to Hahnemann's teaching (often with disconcerting or disagreeably painful results), and boasting that anyone who lived in the country would find a pharmacopoeia sufficient to supply the needs of a lifetime in the plants growing within half a mile of his door.

He several times compares the practice of homoeopathy to gardening or chess, both favourite pastimes of his, both calculated to appeal to a temperament which derived particular satisfaction from protracted, crafty and crabwise manœuvres. Traces of his own country background are evident throughout his writings—in the truculent independence of mind which led him, on the one hand, to denounce received authority and, on the other, to startle conventional opinion with therapeutic tips collected from the most abstruse and arcane learned authorities; in his vigorous, unsystematic reading habits and in his simultaneous insistence on practical experiment. Something very like the countryman's contempt for book-learning emerges when, in the introduction to his *Fifty Reasons*, he loses his temper at dinner over the nuts and wine:

> My dear fellow, your mind is as full of scholastic conceit as an egg is full of meat, and you are therefore a doomed man so far as scientific medicine is concerned . . . your knowledge is like those Neapolitan walnuts there, which have been dried in a kiln, and thereby rendered sterile; plant them, and they will not germinate, and it is just thus with your scholastic learnings. . . . You have no living faith in living physic—so far as the really direct healing of the sick is concerned all your medicine is *dead*, as dead as a door-nail.[16]

---

homoeopathic physician seeks to correct the disorder which causes the symptoms. This requires a study of the individuality of every patient. The remedy, which is specially prepared, is usually given in very small doses, and acts by stimulating the natural defences and recuperative powers of the body.'

The ten-year-old schoolboy who had wandered alone in the woods round Redlynch, learning from woodmen how to charm warts or cure snakebite with snake venom, has much in common with the erudite doctor who, in late middle age, still took a mischievous pleasure in scandalizing his staider professional colleagues by recommending nettle-tea or a poultice of ivy leaves. All his life Dr Burnett delighted to experiment with esoteric, then almost unknown drugs and at the same time to prescribe the homeliest remedies drawn from the unlikeliest sources: essence of walnuts or acorns for a pain in the spleen (from a German carpenter who advised cracked acorns in brandy), tincture of nettles for ague (from a charwoman who cured one of his patients quicker than he could), greater celandine for jaundice, bruisewort for swellings, couch grass for the bowel and the common daisy for dermatitis.[17]

Burnett's shock tactics, his chatty tone and resolutely empirical attitude to clinical symptoms were anathema to Richard Hughes, who regularly gave him curt, dismissive reviews and a distinctly ungenerous obituary in the *Journal* when he died.[18] Worse even than Burnett's lack of scientific method was his defiantly popularizing approach, which Hughes regarded as little less than sabotage of his own more discreet efforts to further their common cause. Neither, as it turned out, proved in the long run especially successful. Burnett's reputation lived on, if at all, in the writings of a lone disciple, Dr Margaret Tylor; and his name in the Compton Burnett Chair of Homoeopathy, founded through the efforts of John Clarke who had hoped that his friend might hold it in his lifetime—a scheme effectively scotched by Hughes, so that the chair (which has since been held by some of the most distinguished names in homoeopathy) was established only after both Hughes and Burnett were dead. Hughes himself had been 'virtually forgotten' by the 1930s, his books unread and his battles unsung even in homoeopathic circles.

But, however dim the mark left on posterity, reverberations of turmoil and skirmish can hardly have escaped Dr Burnett's family in his lifetime. Hughes was something of an academic snob, though his qualifications (an Edinburgh L.R.C.P. and three honorary M.D.s from American colleges whose degrees were not recognized in England) were markedly inferior to Burnett's—a fact which, one may suspect, gave considerable satisfaction in the Compton Burnett household. It is perhaps worth noting that, in Ivy's first novel, one of Dr Cassell's many disadvantages is that 'his degrees were American'; and that Dolores' father 'had once, in talking with his wife, gone so far as to observe that

Cassell was an illiterate, canting fool'.[19] We have Dr Burnett's own word that his career was followed at home with keen attention, 'my wife urging me to publish my experience with Bacillinum two or three years before Koch's cure was heard of, but I hesitated, because I felt the world was not ripe for it, and a man with a very large family has no right to court ruin—so I held back'. The book's eventual publication was not well received and: 'when I showed the review to my wife, she exclaimed, "What a cruel shame!"'.[20]

It was not only Mrs Compton Burnett who took to heart her husband's setbacks and triumphs. His children were familiar from their earliest years with his characteristically independent and individualistic outlook, as with the country maxims which reinforced his demands for practical action: 'If you want roasted pigeon for dinner you must procure the pigeon and roast it; it will not fall ready roasted into your mouth.'[21] Ivy herself at the very end of her life still used in conversation or correspondence expressions she had heard from her father sixty or seventy years before; and, like her brothers and sisters, she must have imbibed in childhood something of his scorn for received opinion, his reliance on first-hand observation and analysis, his absolute regard for truth. Above all she must have noted the passion—nonetheless genuine for being expressed with such sonorous, rhetorical enjoyment—with which he held his libertarian principles:

> We are not believers in authority. . . . We shall try to keep constantly before us that theories and hypotheses are the curse of our art, and the bonds and fetters that make free minds slaves. . . . Prejudice, ignorance, authority, *a priori* tall talk, we will leave as fit food for the perennial babes of the *Lancet, et hoc genus omne.* . . .
>
> We were born free, we will live free, we will die free, and freedom shall be our children's heritage. To those who would forge fetters that they may lead us into bondage we declare war to the bitter end.[22]

2

IVY HAD INHERITED her father's looks (the 'wide face' and 'deep-set eyes' shared also by Christian Stace and his daughter Dinah), his love of gardening and of the open country, and traces at least of his robust disposition. A photograph taken when she was just turned eighteen shows a plump, smiling schoolgirl with an open expression and wavy hair. Arthur Waley, who met her for the first time some six or seven years after Dr Burnett's death, remembered Ivy in her early twenties as 'a vigorous, healthy, country-bred girl, big and bouncing'.[23]

Subsequent events, and the development of her own nature, worked a change which makes his description difficult to reconcile with the shy, inconspicuous, tart-spoken woman described by her friends in the 1920s and 30s, or the formidable Miss Compton-Burnett with delicate, austere features and a delicate, austere wit who became something of a legend to literary London after the second war. But Ivy had learnt from earliest childhood to treat people with a reserve and suspicion wholly foreign to her jovial, ebullient father who remained all his life forthright to the point of naïveté in his fervent reactions to other people and their machinations. For Dr Burnett there was 'no middle way, it must be either good clear God's truth or black lying'. One can't help feeling that he would have shown small patience with the subtle reservations familiar, in his daughter's books, to circumspect characters like Mortimer Lamb or Dudley Gaveston—though he would surely have warmed to Dudley's bluff, impetuous niece, Justine, who has no hesitation in making pronouncements as emphatic as Dr Burnett's own:

'Truth is truth and a lie is a lie', . . . [said Justine] . . . 'We ought not to mind a searchlight being turned on our inner selves, if we are honest about them.'

'That is our reason,' said Mark. ' "Know thyself" is a most superfluous direction. We can't avoid it.'

'We can only hope that no one else knows,' said Dudley.[24]

But, even in her later, mature self, it is not hard to detect traits which —however modified and adapted—Ivy shared with her father. The work of both shows the same driving energy, the same urge to diagnose any given situation to its furthest limits. 'We want to know the whole thing,' says a character in *Daughters and Sons*. 'Our curiosity is neither morbid nor ordinary. It is the kind known as devouring.'[25] Ivy and her father might have said the same. Both were intensely inquisitive about human nature whose moral workings, in the novels of I. Compton-Burnett, are subjected to a scrutiny as rigorous and uncompromising as the doctor's relentless concentration on its physical symptoms. A curious incident in his *Diseases of the Spleen* well illustrates both the indifference to material surroundings so marked in his daughter, and that severely professional eye for essentials which Ivy's friends found on occasion so disconcerting:

> Some time since I was casually sitting in a pretty garden with a gentleman. . . . And then in a twinkling he exclaimed—'Oh, what lovely tints, just look at the shade of the plum-tree across the path, and that green, I mean there just by the nut-tree.' Need I say he is an artist?
> I had not noticed any of the pretty things to which he called my attention, but I *had* seen a small issue—a tiny aperture in his skin covering his larynx.[26]

Both Ivy and her father often drew startling conclusions from direct, practical observation, both being perfectly indifferent to the dictates of convention or fashion: it was precisely its unconventional flexibility which, according to Dr Burnett, constituted the strength of the homoeopathic system, 'rendering, however, its practice disgustingly difficult'.[27] Certainly the doctor's intuitive approach to medicine—'I let my imagination play about a case' was one of his characteristic sayings— closely resembles what little Ivy vouchsafed to her friends about her own working methods. Dr Burnett, whose constant boast was that 'Homoeopathy wins by being in harmony with the spirit of the advanced men of the times', had preached revolutionary doctrines in medicine; his daughter, though she made no overt reference to the matter, actually achieved revolution in her own sphere, drawing the novel away from the overblown naturalistic school still lingering on from the nineteenth century towards a style which more nearly approaches the concise formality of the other major arts in the twentieth century.

It is, however, hard to imagine a technique more unlike Dr Burnett's diffuse, conversational essays, dashed down in cabs or at railway stations, than his daughter's compact prose, exquisitely balanced and refined by a process which involved several drafts. One might perhaps argue a similarity between the doctor's trained habit of precision when describing his patients—'Young Lord X . . . was pale, spare, neck long and thin, and in the neck his glands visible from their very considerable enlargement and induration, and his temper most miserable'; 'they [consumptives] are mum, taciturn, sulky, snappish, fretty, irritable, morose, depressed and melancholic, even to insanity'[28]—and I. Compton-

Burnett's descriptions of her own characters in terms so laconic that, at first reading, one is liable to underestimate the amount of information conveyed in the fewest possible words. But otherwise the two will bear no comparison. Dr Burnett had had in his youth a feeling for language so great that he had hesitated on the point of devoting his career to philology, 'but neither words nor the study of words could long suffice to absorb the energies of the young Burnett, and he finally decided to make medicine his profession'.[29] There remains in his books evidence of that spontaneous storyteller's gift which makes his case histories as absorbing to the layman, and often as entertaining, as Sherlock Holmes': a cab draws up at the door, from it descends a nervous clergyman, a veiled lady or an Indian army officer in distress who, on being ushered into the doctor's consulting rooms, pours out a tale of woe to which the doctor listens attentively, rapidly sifting out clues and proceeding via investigation and treatment to a more or less unexpected, almost invariably successful solution to what had hitherto frequently been, in the hands of less expert practitioners, an insoluble mystery. Conan Doyle (who wrote his first Sherlock Holmes story in April 1891, while waiting in vain for patients to arrive at his brand-new consulting rooms in Devonshire Place, just round the corner from Dr Burnett's establishment at 86 Wimpole Street) is said to have modelled Holmes' detective methods on the diagnostic system practised by Dr Joseph Bell of the Edinburgh Infirmary, so it is not perhaps surprising that Dr Burnett should have hit on the same excellent receipt for popular success.

One of the charges regularly laid against Dr Burnett by Richard Hughes was that he wrote 'ad populum'. The same is true, in *Daughters and Sons* (1937) and *A God and His Gifts* (1963), of the two successful authors, John Ponsonby and Hereward Egerton, each of whom has a child also determined to write. John Ponsonby's daughter, France, and Hereward Egerton's son, Merton, both mean to write books which, unlike their fathers', shall not pander to popular taste, an ambition which not unnaturally causes hard feeling between parent and child. The two fathers produce quantities of what seems to be fairly run-of-the-mill Victorian popular fiction, bringing tears to their readers' eyes, a mixture of pride, social embarrassment and gratitude ('of course people do earn by it, even more than by serious books they say. . . . And we welcome the help with expenses')[30] to their families, and making their children wince at their sentimental excesses. Both write to 'serve many thousands of people', both are household words (as the name Compton Burnett had been throughout Ivy's first twenty years in homoeopathic circles), and both are uneasily aware that their reputations are unlikely to outlast their own lifetimes. It is this dark suspicion which adds jealousy to the already awkward situation brought about by their children's loftier views: 'I would rather write nothing than write as he does', says Merton Egerton, to which his shrewd brother replies: 'Well, that should offer no problem'. France Ponsonby is more tender towards her father: 'He would have written better, if he had written for fewer and earned less. And it is for us that he earns; he does not spend on himself. It is all subtle and sad, and he is very pathetic.' Apart from his pathos, all we know of John Ponsonby's career is that he began to write early, driven to eke out a precarious income for the sake of his growing family (' "He could not hold his public without his popular touch", said Victor. "And we should be badly off, if he did not hold it. . . ." '); that his books, like Dr Burnett's, have prefaces in which he proposes to thank his friends for insights received; and that he has immortalized in his books, as Dr Burnett had done in his, the disingenuous saying that 'a woman's work is the highest in the world'.[31]

All of which is by no means to suggest that John Ponsonby resembles James Compton Burnett, only that Ivy made use in both novels of knowledge derived from her father's success as a popular writer. She herself had written, or at any rate disclosed, nothing in his lifetime though both she and her brothers were already determined to write,* and equally determined no doubt to avoid their father's artless and emotional 'popular touch'. The elaborate figures of speech in which Dr Burnett habitually indulged—'Homoeopathy is the winning horse at the Medical Derby of the world, and will presently be hurried past the winning post by Orthodoxy itself as her rider'[32]—are suspect more often than not in the novels of I. Compton-Burnett, where an injudicious use of words tends to reflect on the speaker's part a similar coarseness of moral fibre. But there can be small doubt, from the way she talked of him afterwards, that Ivy had loved her father dearly. His death was 'a deep sorrow' to her, the first of many in the next fifteen years which she bore with the same outward composure. If there are glimpses of Dr Burnett at all in his daughter's books, it is in the tenuous but wholly amiable character of Christian Stace; or perhaps in the type most fully developed in Justine Gaveston who, like Dr Burnett, is

* 'I think I always felt I should, and I think my brothers did too . . . I think we always assumed we should write, and talked as if we should. Our parents were interested in writing, and we grew up with the feeling.' (Ivy Compton-Burnett in *Review of Eng. Lit.*, October 1962.)

garrulous, demonstrative, overbearing and interfering, uninhibited in manner and self-congratulatory in tone: 'I sound my bracing note and snap my fingers at the consequences'. No type is further removed from the subtle, wary, introspective characters on whom the principle of virtue generally depends in the novels of I. Compton-Burnett. But, if Justine is without the restraints imposed by self-consciousness, she is also completely unselfish, and proves in the end the one dependable source of support in an unstable household. Her stepmother's comment on Justine might serve as an epitaph on Dr Burnett: '"I like good people," said Maria, with the simplicity which in her had its own quality, something which might have been humour if she could have been suspected of it. "I never think people realize how well they compare with the others."'³³

Dr Burnett's death came at a time when his family could ill afford to be without his support. His wife, who had never been strong, possessed none of the placidity which might have fitted her better to contend with the fatigue of constant child-bearing, a miscarriage and the strain of his absence in London. Her father had lived for the past ten years in St John's Road near The Drive but, though she saw them often, neither he nor her stepmother was particularly interested in domestic concerns, and neither can have provided much of a substitute for the intimate companionship she craved as an outlet for a possessive and passionate nature. The 'unusually beautiful, sweet girl' with whom Dr Burnett had fallen in love eighteen years before had become a demanding, imperious woman, still beautiful but increasingly dissatisfied with the monotony of life at Hove cooped up with Minnie and growing numbers of children in 'that hideous house'. Ivy, whom she loved as her first child, and the two sons she adored, had exhausted her admittedly small stock of maternal feeling. The four youngest daughters (Stephanie Primrose, called Baby, was born at The Drive on 19 April 1899) were apparently regarded almost from birth as a burden rather than a pleasure. Her five stepchildren meanwhile had reached the stage at which they contemplated escape or at least, since escape for the three girls could not easily be reconciled with propriety, some respite from the frustrations all five had endured since infancy. Mrs Compton Burnett seems to have reacted to what must at times have been a wretched situation with uncertain temper and occasionally spectacular displays of nervous irritation; Ivy described years later how, driving out one day in a carriage, her mother lost patience with her lap-dog and flung it suddenly straight through the open window.³⁴

How far Dr Burnett was aware of the underlying frictions in his household is impossible to say. We know that he had urged his wife to avoid working herself into a fury, and that long afterwards she would dispassionately repeat his warning that her fits of rage might lead to cancer (cancer of the breast, diagnosed nine years after his death, eventually killed her). He was constantly at hand 'to comfort her and smooth her path', to shield her as much as her children from the consequences of her own outbursts. But we know, too, that he took an optimistic view of her temperament: 'She is one of those human high-breds who will not cave in, but, if duty calls, will go on till they drop'. Having noted when they first met that 'in life' such high-breds 'are commonly misunderstood', he continued to the end of his life to take her part with unwavering loyalty. He himself, however, was often lonely, if one may judge by his descriptions of evenings spent dining with patients in London, with his colleagues in the Cooper Club or working alone at his hotel, and by the way in which every spare scrap of time was parcelled out between his books and his practice. His presence had always been a restraining influence, but much of what went on at home in his absence presumably escaped him. He seems to have been, like Christian Stace, 'happy that his wife should be the ruling spirit of his home. He knew her little and she knew him well, the relation between herself and her father, that seemed to her natural.'

If Christian unmistakably resembles James Compton Burnett, then Sophia Stace with her 'nerve storms' and her 'habitual fits of crying', her absorbing love of her husband and the jealous irritation she vents on her children, is in both looks and character the nearest Dame Ivy ever came to a direct portrait of her mother: '. . . Sophia made life easy only for her husband. Sophia was a woman to whom one man was her life. For her children her love demanded more than it gave.'[35] The secluded lives of the three Stace children—the intimacy between Dinah and Andrew, the comparative immaturity of their younger brother Robin, the 'literary gifts' of the elder pair accepted by the family as a natural outcome of 'the Stace fluency in words', and nurtured in long hours spent alone together in the schoolroom made over into a study—correspond to the Compton Burnetts' daily routine; and the parallel was in any case confirmed by Noel's friends, Arthur Waley and Elliott Felkin, who recognized in Sophia Stace their own memories of Katharine Compton Burnett.[36] The Stace children discuss their mother in private with a freedom which matches their restraint in her presence, and one can't help suspecting that their verdict is in some sense a version of the kind of conversation which took place in the Compton Burnett schoolroom between Ivy and her two brothers:

'What passes me is, how Father has never got to know Sophia,' said Robin. 'Day after day, year after year it goes on under his eyes, and he never sees it.'

'Not under his eyes, just away from them,' said Dinah. 'Don't you see how Sophia is on her guard?'

'Yes. Her cunning is on the scale of the rest of her,' said Andrew.

'I always have doubts about Sophia's scale,' said Robin. 'I think she is rather a small, weak person in many ways. It is known that I am a little like her. Now Father is on a more considerable scale, though I often think his simplicity is the most appreciable thing about him.'[37]

The few months before Dr Burnett's death had not been particularly easy ones. His first family were by now nearly all grown up. His eldest son Richard had qualified by November 1900 as a solicitor but the 'wild dog' Charlie, also articled in his teens and living in digs with his brother in London, showed signs of turning out less satisfactorily, and was perhaps already flirting with the kind of trouble ('spending what he shouldn't have') which overtook him after his father's death. Olive, who was twenty-five and 'very much the New Woman', had also left home that autumn. Of all the stepchildren Olive had always been the one who most stubbornly refused to acknowledge their stepmother's authority and, at a time when young ladies were expected to remain under their fathers' roofs till marriage or death removed them, she had paid dearly for her freedom. The ugly scenes between a stepmother and an eldest stepdaughter determined to leave home in Ivy's first and last books—separated by a gap of almost sixty years—suggest perhaps how deep an impression this upheaval made on the family. Olive, having gone to London to learn shorthand and typing, was 'regarded as somebody on the wrong path altogether'. Iris, who remained at home for another five years, was no happier than her eldest sister. Only Daisy at twenty-two seemed outwardly content with her lot, supervising the nursery, paying calls with her stepmother and cheerfully performing the domestic duties which Ivy detested. Guy, meanwhile, who had been sent alone to Tonbridge in the summer of 1900, fell ill with pneumonia at the end of the autumn term and was fetched home by his father in an ambulance. His condition had been critical, and he was still convalescent when Olive shocked her family again by coming down from London with her hair cropped short: 'I remember it was just before Christmas,' said Vera Compton-Burnett. 'It darkened the day.'

This was the last Christmas of their father's life, with all twelve children assembled at Hove from Olive to the baby who was twenty months old. Dr Burnett's last book was published that spring, and he continued to work as furiously as ever though several of his sayings, reported later, suggest that he was not unaware of approaching death. 'You can't work an old horse too long, but it will fall,' he said to a friend three or four weeks before he died and, to another, 'My only hope is that I may die in harness.' Some twenty years later Ivy marked with a pencil in her copy of Butler's *Note-Books* a passage on physical excellence as a criterion of morality, which runs in part: 'In the case of those who are not forced to over-work themselves—and there are many who work themselves to death from mere inability to restrain the passion for work, which masters them as the craving for drink masters a drunkard—over-work in these cases is as immoral as over-eating or drinking.'[38]

Dr Burnett's beloved brother Jack visited Hove for the last time in February or March and died, after a lingering illness, at Bedford on 21 March 1901; Charles Compton Burnett represented his father at the funeral, together with a wreath inscribed 'In loving memory from Jim'. On 23 March Dr Burnett made a new will and ten days later he was dead, an instance perhaps of his own theory set down twelve years before on the causes of Angina Pectoris: 'Fag is a potent factor in angina; and so is wounded pride and nerve shock. Not infrequently fag and shock combine to produce it.'[39]

He was sixty. Twelve of his thirteen children survived him. The eldest was twenty-five, the youngest not quite two when he died but, though both his wives had belonged to large families and though he himself came of a prolific and fertile line, Dr Burnett had no further descendants. Of his twelve children, one died young of pneumonia; another was killed in the first war; three committed suicide. Two of his four sons made brief, childless marriages, his eight daughters remained unmarried so that, though he himself had ardently believed that 'the true source of national greatness is large families of healthy children',[40] his only legacy to posterity lies in the novels of his fourth daughter: an astonishing and sometimes fearful monument to family life.

KATHARINE COMPTON BURNETT

'A figure in tragedy'

I

FROM THE DAY of Dr Burnett's death his children found their own world overthrown. 'It changed totally,' said Vera Compton-Burnett. 'And that was why Ivy lived so much in retrospect.' Accounts of what followed in the next weeks and months at Hove suggest much the same atmosphere as Ivy herself later described in the Stace household: 'Sophia's grief hung like a pall on the house, crushing its inmates with a load as if of guilt, that their sorrow was less great than hers.'[1] The news reached Hove on Tuesday, 2 April; Dr Burnett was thought to have died as he prepared for bed the night before and had been found that morning by the hotel staff when his breakfast remained untouched and his cab drawn up at the door. His wife started out at once alone for London, leaving the children at home in Minnie's charge with the blinds down. The funeral took place a week later at St Leonard's church, Aldrington, set back from the sea a mile or so from The Drive on the western outskirts of Hove. St Leonard's had been a favourite goal for the doctor's Sunday strolls, when the family would walk across fields by the sea to inspect his property at Aldrington where he had always said he would like to be buried. In the next ten years Marjorie Andrewes, who was in the same form as Vera at school and who lived with her parents on the road to St Leonard's, would regularly see Mrs Compton Burnett pacing slowly past their house with one or more of her daughters, all dressed in black, speaking to no one and carrying flowers to lay on his tomb—a plain cross in polished pink marble inscribed at the top *Semper Fidelis*, and at the foot: 'In tender loving memory of my dear husband James Compton Burnett M.D.

Who passed away 2nd April, 1901, aged 60. "In secure and certain hope."' More than seventy years later, Dr Burnett's cross, which now bears inscriptions for his wife and four of her children, is still noticeably taller, shinier and more imposing than any other monument in the graveyard.

'Ivy lived rather under the shadow of death,' said her sister, 'and death in those days had its trappings. Coal black from head to foot, and my mother in deepest widow's weeds.' Mrs Compton Burnett never again went out of mourning, indeed her behaviour recalls Josephine Napier's dramatic reaction to her own widowhood in *More Women Than Men* ('"Simply the deepest mourning that is made for a widow," said Josephine, in an almost light tone. "That is all I have to say."')[2] She wore streamers and crape to the knee for two years and, though she may then have made some concessions in dress, she wore full mourning again two years later when Guy died. She had put the whole family into black, down to the baby in her pram who could not remember her father and who had a dark grey pelisse tied over her bonnet with black ribbons. Topsy, at five years old, wore unrelieved black like her six elder sisters for at least a year ('I should think it was more than a year, because the things wouldn't have worn out'). When the Queen died, seven weeks before Dr Burnett, promenaders on the Hove sea front had all worn black for the next four Sundays but, even in those days, Mrs Compton Burnett's notions of mourning were considered extravagant, at any rate for small children: one of the things about the Compton Burnett girls which had most impressed their contemporaries at school was that 'they all always wore black—and perhaps that depressed them'. Ivy was still in mourning for her father when she went up to Royal Holloway College in the autumn of 1902, and she wore black again for Guy throughout her last year at college.

The three little girls—Vera was ten and Judy seven years old—were encouraged by their mother to make doleful tableaux in the graveyard, weaving daisy chains to hang on their father's tomb. Minnie taught Topsy to kiss her father's photograph ('Daddy's picture') so that she should never forget him. All three seem to have performed these sentimental observances with the same sense of dismay and obscure distaste as Julius and Dora Calderon, who are similarly obliged in *Elders and Betters* to serve as an outlet for adult emotions which they can neither understand nor appease. One may perhaps date from this time Ivy's acute sensitivity to the bewilderment of desolate small children placed as her own sisters had been, either forgotten altogether in a house overtaken by mourning, or as arbitrarily remembered and harshly rebuked for violating the solemnity due to bereavement; one thinks of Dora's 'peaked and staring face' on the day of her mother's death, or the Humes' nervous laughter in *Mother and Son* ('"Are we supposed to be joking?" said Adrian. "No, we are supposed to be sorrowing. We are joking."').[3] But the heaviest burden of their mother's grief fell on the older children. Mrs Compton Burnett was inconsolable and her despair took the form of open lamentation. 'My mother not being able to take the loss in an heroic way—and I'm afraid she wasn't,' she gave way to terrifying storms of crying which lasted sometimes all night and, though the younger ones would lie awake in bed and hear her, the older ones lived in her presence under what became an almost intolerable strain. 'She did grieve sincerely for her husband. But she expressed her grief vocally, and that was very hard on her children. On Guy and Ivy especially.'

Vera Compton-Burnett's description of her mother will be already familiar to readers of *Brothers and Sisters*. Sophia's self-dramatization as she sinks distraught to the ground or 'sends her cries through the house', her screams, 'her slow, solemn voice', her unsatisfactory last moments alone with her husband's body—'Sophia's lifelong exercise of her own will had led her almost to expect response from the dead'—together with the obligation to provide a less inadequate response as she kneels weeping beside his empty chair drive her two eldest children to the limits of their strength: 'Andrew and Dinah stood by, stunned and helpless. Sophia was just enough conscious of their presence to know that her laments were heard.'[4] The book was written long after both Ivy's brothers and her mother were dead, and it is no doubt fruitless to speculate as to how far the burden on Andrew and Dinah— 'Come with me, my dears. We three will go away and be together. . . . We will go apart, and try to meet together our great, great sorrow. Great for you all, but infinitely greater for me. You will have to remember that, in all your future dealings with me'—corresponds to the demands made, more than twenty years before, on Guy and Ivy at Hove; or what bitter memory may have underlain the moment when Sophia calls for Robin who, 'white and trembling' on the day of his father's death, lacks the courage to face his mother in her extremity: 'She went to the door and called, more clearly, as no answer came, unconscious that she sent a shiver through her son and daughter, that was to return to them all their lives.'

Noel Compton Burnett was thirteen when his father died, and young for his age. Robin Stace is twenty-two but, like Noel, he retains a childishness which at once protects him from his mother's deepest feeling and leaves him more pitilessly exposed in moments of crisis than his elder brother and sister. One of several traits which the two have in common is dependence on their former nurse, for the Staces' Patty ('Miss Patmore had been their nurse and nearly their mother in childhood, and they had for her much of the feeling that might have been Sophia's'), like the Compton Burnetts' Minnie, is the sole buttress between themselves and their mother's ruthless exploitation of her position:

'Well, I have said goodbye to him,' said Sophia. 'I have said my farewell that is to last my life, my life that will never be a life to me again. Your dear father! My husband!'

She stooped her face, contorted again with weeping, over her teacup, and Robin's face showed a spasm of stricken nerves. . . .

'He must go to bed early,' said Sophia to Patty. 'He had better go directly after this. Andrew and Dinah can sit up for a little while with me.'

'Oh, I think they all ought to go to bed,' said Patty, her tone bringing a change to Sophia's face. 'Dinah looks dreadfully shaken, and Andrew is very tired. And you ought to go to bed early too. You know you ought. You will be worn out.'

'Well, I will go to bed or I will sit up,' said Sophia in an aloof monotone. 'Nothing that I do will make any difference to me now. Nothing will ever help me again. But I will go to bed, so that other people may go. So that they will not feel that they have to wait up with me, to watch with me one hour.'

A sound as of hysteria came from Robin.

'Are you laughing, my son?' said Sophia, in a simply incredulous voice.

Ivy's two younger sisters maintain emphatically that her books contain no hint of a portrait of Guy: 'The quality was the same, but never the character.' Nonetheless, if one sets their account of their father's death beside the sixth chapter of *Brothers and Sisters*, one has the curious impression of seeing the same event reflected in two different mirrors. It was Guy who, like Andrew Stace, stood next to his father in his mother's affections, and Guy who 'bore the brunt with my mother. It took too much toll.' Both sisters repeated this phrase, 'too much'. Andrew, spent and desperate in the early days of Sophia's widowhood, becomes as Guy had done chief source of support to the household, attending on his mother and protecting his sister who meets Sophia's eyes, and Sophia's exaltation of her own loss as a means of detracting from other people's, in silence. When Dinah remains at home on the day of the funeral: 'The brothers knew which was the heavier part; and Dinah, white-faced in the black that was rather too plainly poorer than her mother's, was sadder to them than Sophia.' Guy would sit alone with his mother when no one else could do it. Noel was too young, Ivy too withdrawn and Minnie (whose growing importance in the household had made for an uneasy relationship with its mistress) preoccupied with the younger children. Daughters had in any case never been much consolation to Mrs Compton Burnett: 'She gave her maternal love to Guy, but she took far more than she gave.'

Both Ivy's sisters conjure up a horrifying image of grief, settling like a black cloud on the house, blotting out the happiness of their own childhood, disfiguring their mother, draining Guy's strength which was called on and unreservedly given to sustain the whole family. A light had gone out with their father's death and never returned. Their mother remained self-absorbed, sunk in immoderate mourning, increasingly forgetful of her younger children who turned instead to their brother. For the next four years Guy, not quite sixteen when his father died, took on responsibility not only for his mother's exorbitant emotional needs but also for the comfort and security of his small sisters. 'He was so *very* kind—kindness is the wrong word. He was our ideal,' said Vera Compton-Burnett. 'Guy was a saint,' said her sister, 'I can't remember a single thing he ever said or did to hurt anyone. He brought happiness to a household that lacked it totally. *How* he tried to take the place—to fill the hollow left by my father's death—for the young children.'

One may suspect something, if not of Guy's character, at least of his quality in Terence Calderon who, in a distracted and grief-stricken household in *Elders and Betters*, is the only person prepared to give time and attention to his little brother and sister after their mother has died. Dora and Julius are wholly at ease with Terence who takes them for granted, and whose humorous, matter-of-fact gravity comes as an inexpressible relief when, after the miseries and fears and nervous exhaustion of an impossible day, they come in from the garden to find him seated with his book in the firelight at the schoolroom table. Their father's unexpected severity, alternating with an even more disconcerting, exaggeratedly sentimental view of the dead, especially disturbs them:

'He would hardly be in form at the moment,' said Terence.

This allusion to the circumstances struck Dora as so boldly humorous, that she fell almost into hysterics.

'Take care. Shrieks of mirth are not the sounds expected at this juncture,' said Terence, forgetting how easily they occurred at such a point.

His sister's sense of the ludicrous received a further spur.

'I hope we shall be able to maintain the required deportment,' said Terence. 'I cannot say I detect any signs of promise.'

Dora shook in silent helplessness.[5]

Outbursts of nervous laughter, sharply checked in the presence of adults and exploding in hysterical reaction behind their backs, come again and again in I. Compton-Burnett's accounts of children subjected to emotional pressure beyond their bearing. It was a form of release familiar enough in her own family in the years after her father's death: the boys would come up on Sunday mornings to play boisterous games with their small sisters in the nursery but otherwise there were few outlets, let alone opportunities for pleasure or amusement, in the grim atmosphere imposed by their mother's grief. 'It was an incredibly clouded household—incredibly overshadowed,' said Juliet Compton-Burnett. 'You ask about the days—they were *completely uneventful*. Nothing happened. Outwardly the same thing happened every day.' Inwardly there was intense mental activity. For most of the week Guy, Ivy and Noel, attending to their literary gifts in the study, had little to do with the younger ones, engrossed in elaborate games of make-believe behind closed doors ('It was very private') in the nursery. School barely touched this inner world, and secrecy was essential when so many people lived in close physical proximity, pursuing imaginary lives of utmost vividness side by side under the same roof. 'We had few toys and not many books,' said Vera Compton-Burnett. 'I remember often hearing the word retrenchment as a small girl.'

Retrenchment is a subject with which, as with the cold, draughts and generally arrant inconvenience of country houses, Ivy was intimately acquainted and in which she took a particular pleasure. The Calderons, inventing their own gods, their own penal code and their own board games from a makeshift assortment of cast-off pieces, are by no means the only children in her books left to amuse themselves from their own resources. Writing is one of very few activities which, though it has other drawbacks, escapes criticism at least on the score of expense:

'Less ambitious things need training,' said Sabine. 'We will leave her her own occupation, as it costs us nothing.'

'It does not save us anything either. But I am glad she has some occupation, and is not too sunk in black sulks to mention it. We will leave her to waste her time in her own way.'[6]

But children are as well aware as their elders that their entertainment ranks low on the list of problems they pose. The Lambs and Ponsonbys are publicly mortified by outgrown, outmoded or handed-down clothes; the Shelleys, Lovats, Grimstones, Challoners and Staces by the meagre appointments of their nurseries, generously renamed schoolroom and study as a means of acknowledging their advancing years at no extra cost; and nearly all are accustomed, like the Humes and the Middletons, to forestall the accusations of reckless expenditure constantly cast up against them by making their own shrewd calculations as to the price of food, clothes and lessons ('"The girls do not cost us much," said Sabine. "It would not be right that they should, but it is a fact that they don't."').[7] The university education required by boys is an especially sore point—'Grinning and chattering like apes and costing like dukes!' as Sir Jesse Sullivan says bitterly of his two grandsons in their last year at Cambridge:

'And where will they spend the next ones? Behind bars, I should think. I hope that will be less expensive.' . . .

'If we are fed by the public through a grating,' said Daniel, 'it will take our keep off Grandpa.'

'We should still carry our debt to the grave,' said his brother. 'Or to Grandpa's grave we should.'[8]

Dr Burnett had left the bulk of his considerable estate—£67,166— to his wife, in trust for her children after her death, on terms pretty well identical with the terms of Christian Stace's will: 'It was clear that Sophia would hold not only her former place, but her own and her husband's. Her children were little affected by the knowledge. They would hardly have been surprised if the whole had been their mother's. They knew how well their father knew, and did not know, Sophia; how equal and unequal Sophia was to her life.'[9] The joint income, from Dr Burnett's trust estate and from Mrs Burnett's own marriage portion, must have amounted to several thousand pounds a year but frugal practices unknown in their father's lifetime became a recognized feature of the children's lives in the next ten years. The family no longer kept manservants, and the four maids eventually dwindled to two under Minnie with a boy to clean the steps (though Mrs Compton Burnett permitted a telephone and a refrigerator, she set little store by newfangled gadgets and the idea of importing a vacuum cleaner filled her with such dismay—'taking all the goodness out of the carpet! She wouldn't have such a thing in the house'—that the matter was dropped). A great deal was done for show, as it was in so many respectable Edwardian households: 'My mother very rarely gave dinner parties, but when she did they were grand and formal with countless courses'. The children would watch over the bannisters as the guests went in and would be called down afterwards to entertain them, but these cere-monial occasions were in sharp contrast to everyday thrift. Normally their mother ate high tea with the family in the early evening, main-taining at the same time a strict pretence of dining nightly since owning up to high tea would have been unthinkable in fashionable Hove.

The result of this and similar economies, as of their mother's growing melancholia, was to drive the family in on itself. Mrs Compton Burnett returned formal calls but otherwise visitors were not encouraged, and the children had none of their own. 'We could never ask our school friends to the house—*I wouldn't have*—it was so strange and so peculiar. It took away the desire to mix with other people,' said Vera Compton-Burnett. Later, the four youngest girls began to attend children's parties at Christmas ('Going down to supper with little boys in Etons who would fetch you ice cream.' There were cards for partners, each with a little pink pencil, and a huge tea followed by conjurors or dancing before supper) and even gave their own in return, occasions as often as not of memorable embarrassment. The party rage had gripped Hove after Ivy left school, though one of her cousins remembered a party given by their step-grandmother for 'Ivy and Jimmy and Guy', and she had presumably noted in her sisters, if not from her own sad experience, something of Amy Grimstone's agonizing shame at the prospect of inviting schoolfriends to tea, or the marked lack of enthu-siasm shown by the Lovats when asked what they know of other children:

> 'Well, we have been out to tea twice.'
> 'Both times I cried,' said Viola.
> 'Cried?' said Selina. 'Where they not kind to you?'

'Grown-up people have to be in a way. The children said we were different from them.'[12]

Much the same impression of strangeness and isolation was received by contemporaries of the younger Compton-Burnett girls at school. Their parties were considered 'very, very exclusive', and their mother uncomfortably strict. 'She never recognized you in the street or anything, and if they were with *her*, they'd hardly look at you,' said Marjorie Andrewes. 'I used to see the four little girls often, out walking with their nurse,' said Mrs Elliot who had been in the same form as Judy at school, and who remembered Minnie as 'a drab little figure—but I think they turned to her for everything.' One girl, who had gone to The Drive with a message, never forgot being shown into a room disused and covered with dustsheets, and being told to wait without moving or touching anything. Another, not even admitted to the hall, was kept waiting by the maid on the doorstep. At school the girls were reticent and given to stammering, with 'a terrible stutter' when called on to read or recite and a habit of giggling in class which their contemporaries attributed to nervousness. 'They were a funny family,' said Mrs Elliot. 'There was a sort of barrier up around them, you could feel it. They kept you off.'

It might be a description of the many families in the novels of I. Compton-Burnett who, like the Ponsonbys in *Daughters and Sons*, give rise to ceaseless speculation in their wondering visitors and a rather more sober reaction in the more experienced:

'Miss Hallam is seeing us as we are,' said Clare. 'Do families often stand revealed as soon as this?'

'Yes, fairly often,' said Edith. 'You would hardly believe about families. Or many people would not.'

'We have to belong to a family to believe it,' said France. 'But everybody does belong to one. It seems so odd, when you think of what is involved.'[11]

Muriel Ponsonby, a shy, plain eleven-year-old afflicted by dumbness which alternates with exasperating fits of the giggles ("'It is a nervous habit which we must hope she will leave behind." "It is hard to see how we can leave behind nervous habits," said Clare. "Probably most of our habits are of that nature"'), is the first of many whose inarticulate sufferings in childhood are as excruciating as anything endured by their elders. There can be small doubt that Oliver Shelley's attitude to

children in *Two Worlds and Their Ways*—'They are always pitiful'—
was Ivy's own, though this was far from the impression left on her
sisters. 'She had an incredible reserve,' said Vera Compton-Burnett.
'As a young girl she was never one with the family.' 'She put herself
into the books, and she was a secret otherwise—known only to herself,'
said her sister Juliet. Both remember Ivy in the years after their father's
death as someone who took no part in their lives and who, as they grew
older and were no longer confined to the nursery, became increasingly
a repressive influence. The Compton-Burnetts learnt early, as members
of large Victorian families had to do, to 'be alone in a room with other
people' but Ivy, who had thankfully abandoned piano lessons herself,
suffered much from the sound of her sisters' incessant practising and, as
soon as she was in a position to do so, categorically forbade it. For years
before that she would sit in the evenings between two candles at the
schoolroom table, intent on her book, while one or other of her sisters
'thundered away at the piano'. Throughout their own wretched
childhood, when the boys 'took great trouble to make us happy in what
was not a very happy home', the younger girls had scant sympathy
from Ivy. 'I can see her now standing at the window, twisting the blind
cord and swinging it round—while we rampaged round the schoolroom,' said Juliet Compton-Burnett. It was a trick her sister later
handed on to Isabel Sullivan in *Parents and Children*, another aloof
adolescent absorbed by her own unhappiness in the midst of a family
scene: 'Isabel went to a window and stood, throwing the blind cord
over her finger, taking no notice when the tassel struck the pane.'[12]

Isabel, like other sensitive older children in the novels of I. Compton-
Burnett, is by inclination a passive spectator, intervening only occasionally to protect her small brothers and sisters from their mother's
depredations, accepting (as her elders cannot) the folly of interfering in
and the impossibility of entering the children's world. Families in the
books divide as the Compton-Burnetts did into groups sealed off from
one another by age and occupation, and by 'that intense family shyness'
which makes it so hard for Terence Calderon to establish relations with
the schoolroom party ('"We have no idea what impression this tragedy
is making on them," said Terence. "We must wait for the time when
they write their lives."').[13] If Ivy, unlike Guy, had no feeling to spare
for her sisters, one cannot help suspecting that she watched them
intently, storing things which she could not express, perhaps scarcely
understood at the time. Beneath what seemed to them an impenetrable,
sometimes positively hostile indifference lay an incomparably delicate

understanding of the preoccupations and tensions of childhood. But it was something that remained dormant long after she had begun to explore other aspects of life before the first war. Children make only the most perfunctory appearances in her first six books and it was not until 1937, with Muriel Ponsonby in *Daughters and Sons*, that she turned her attention to the world of nursery and schoolroom: a world which to the end of her career as a novelist continued to cast strange shadows on the adults in the drawing-rooms below, and which must have been drawn in part from memories of her own early childhood, in part from what she had seen much later in these years of oppression at Hove.

2

'I THINK THAT actual life supplies a writer with characters much less than is thought,' said Miss Compton-Burnett in 1944. 'Of course there must be a beginning to every conception, but so much change seems to take place in it at once, that almost anything comes to serve the purpose —a face of a stranger, a face in a portrait, almost a face in the fire. And people in life hardly seem to be definite enough to appear in print. They are not good or bad enough, or clever or stupid enough, or comic or pitiful enough.'[14] Children gave satisfaction no more than their elders: 'When I meet them, they are open to the same objection, and fail to afford me assistance.'

By this time she had published ten of her twenty novels, and had long since set a sufficient distance between herself and the household at Hove which broke up in 1915 to look back on it with equanimity. All her books are sown with retrospective allusions, but only the first three show a demonstrably closer connection with her early life. Traits belonging to several characters in *Dolores* (written in her mid-twenties and published in 1911) were borrowed, on Ivy's own admission, from various close relations, their setting from her family's Wesleyan background, and the novel's almost unbroken gloom evidently to some extent reflects her own when she wrote it. *Pastors and Masters*, published after a gap of fourteen years, belongs as much for its irresistible, ebullient gaiety, as for its urbane account of love and intrigue among dons in a university town strongly reminiscent of pre-first war Cambridge, to the world opened up by her brother at King's College in the first decade of the century. In 1929, with *Brothers and Sisters*, she turned back again to the family setting which afterwards remained the delight of her life, as it was of Jane Austen's. Children, dependants and servants, brothers and sisters in infancy, youth, middle and old age, power, love, death and the step-relationship provided abundant material. But the theme which, being the most violently dramatic, has most attracted attention is that of domestic tyranny; and—bearing Ivy's repeated disclaimers in mind, and though one must also sharply distinguish between the mature novelist who drew on the experience of her early years and the shy, secretive, immature girl who lived through them without apparent rebellion against the tenets of her class and age—it is interesting to see how far Ivy's mother may be said to stand behind the long line of her domestic tyrants; and what other models (supplemented later no doubt, since Ivy in her forties and fifties built up a small but choice collection of domineering, elderly women among her circle of friends) may have lain to hand in her childhood and adolescence.

Mrs Compton Burnett, who married late having been the youngest and one of the handsomest daughters of an uncommonly forceful father, seems to have possessed the kind of wayward, wilful, magnetic attraction, together with the emotional obduracy, often found in an only child. Her feelings, channelled exclusively towards her own family, were both demanding and fiercely possessive. She had once found Vera seated on her husband's knee and turned the child smartly off it saying, 'half in jest but half not' and with sufficient intention to wound, 'That's my place'. Her devotion to her husband in his lifetime was exceeded only by her cult of his memory afterwards. Her pride in her children was boundless, especially at the expense of their half-brothers and -sisters or their 'rather more average' cousins; but it was a pride easily mortified, and often turned to exasperation ('Don't peer!' was her constant refrain to a short-sighted daughter, a phrase which Ivy also found useful as a critical elder sister). She had inherited from her father not only his excellent conceit of himself but also his histrionic gifts which, since they had no opportunity for public display, were freely developed in private. Her temper, never a strong point, grew reckless after her husband's death when 'she had nothing to hold her in': more than sixty years after her own death, her rages are still mentioned in awe-stricken undertones by the few outside her own immediate circle who witnessed them. 'She did get into terrible paddies,' said her daughter Vera. 'She made scenes over nothing at all, we never knew when she would have it. It was a pathological state.' The nervous uncertainty visited on her children grew steadily worse, exacerbated by Guy's sudden death, by their mother's increasing deafness, rheumatism and, in the final year of her life, by her painful last illness and a primitive and even more painful form of radium treatment.

All these quirks of a refractory personality devolved in turn on Sophia Stace: 'I sometimes find myself marvelling at the gulf between the average person and myself,'[15] says Sophia with the candour which is one of her more disarming traits. Another is the triumphant contrariness with which, having driven her children to their study, she interrupts them twice in a morning on grounds (that they are not working or, alternatively, moping over their work—work in any case so frivolous compared with her own that it barely merits the term) calculated to amount to a grievance of one sort or another. Attacks of the fidgets, common enough among Victorian ladies with no occupation beyond giving orders to a highly organized household, were a familiar complaint with Mrs Compton Burnett: 'She had *nothing* to do,' said her daughter Juliet. 'She had nothing to do with us—*she* bore no responsibility; if we were ill, *she* didn't do anything about it. She would look into the nursery or schoolroom in a kindly mood, or sometimes in the other. . . .' The daily routine was fixed, with times laid down for working, walking and meals. Permission was neither sought nor given to alter it, and it grew if anything stricter after their father's death. The three eldest children had possessed bicycles since Ivy was thirteen or so, a privilege later withdrawn by their mother: 'We weren't allowed bicycles in case we were run over, we weren't allowed to swim in case we were drowned, we weren't allowed to ride in case we had a fall.' Sophia, too, has vivid premonitions of death or disaster when her children leave the house, and vents this and other displeasures at the appalling meals which take place both before and after her widowhood:

> 'I don't think you all ought to sit, dreary and monosyllabic, and make no effort at intercourse, just because your mother is in great sadness and loneliness of heart, and never spare her an encouraging word. When my life is broken, I don't want less from people who are supposed to love me. I need more.'
>
> 'You exact too much from people in that position,' said Andrew. 'You have gone too far.'[16]

A similar constraint descended on the Compton Burnett household when, after Guy's death, Noel in his vacations from Cambridge was (like Robin Stace) often 'the only person at ease': 'At family meals

Noel would talk to my mother about politics—I don't think anyone
else ever said anything. I don't think any of the rest of the family
would have spoken to my mother in a spontaneous manner, not Ivy
even.'

Sophia is the first and closest but far from the only descendant of
Mrs Compton Burnett in her daughter's books. To the very end of
her career Ivy generously distributed among her characters touches
taken from her mother—her anxiety over her illness to the two masterful invalids, Matilda Seaton and Sukey Donne; her dangerous possessiveness to Josephine Napier; her ambitions for her children to Harriet
Haslam, Eleanor Sullivan and Maria Shelley; her critical asperity to
Sabine Ponsonby and others too many to mention. But the two who
most nearly resemble the original pattern come quite close together
near the end of their creator's life, Eliza Mowbray in *A Father and His
Fate* (1957) and Eliza Heriot in *The Last and the First* (1971)—both
described in almost the same terms as Sophia, whose looks had been
borrowed in the first place from Mrs Compton Burnett. Eliza Mowbray
'cared little for looks in men . . . but demanded them in women and
made much of her own. She was a short, fair, young-looking woman
of fifty, with an almost beautiful, aquiline face, clear, grey, deep-set
eyes, and lips and brows that were responsive to her emotions.' Eliza
Heriot 'was a fair, almost handsome woman of fifty-five, with solid
aquiline features and a short, upright frame, and active hands that
seemed their natural complement. . . . Autocratic by nature, she had
become impossibly so, and had come to find criticism a duty, and
even an outlet for energy that had no other.'[17]

The two Elizas' likeness in character is as marked as in looks. Both
are jealous, competitive women, both dramatically inclined ('"Mater
sees and hears herself," said Hermia. "That ends my pity for her and
transfers it to Father. He sees and hears her too'"),* both apt to congratulate themselves on the problem posed by an 'awkard temperament'
('"Oh, it is the highest type, you know," said Eliza. "But it is not so
easy for the person who has it"').† Each wields absolute power in her
family and each shares a humorous appreciation of the fact with her
children who, slaves to their mother as the Staces had been to Sophia,

---

* *The Last and the First*, p.16; compare *Brothers and Sisters*: 'Sophia in her extreme
moments, when she suffered more than most, never ceased to listen to herself.' (p.106.)
† *A Father and His Fate*, p.45; compare *Brothers and Sisters*: '"Oh, no one knows what
people go through, when they have such a temperament as I have," said Sophia . . .'
(p.161).

find themselves almost daily constrained to admire their ruler's wanton, foolhardy, sometimes positively diabolical but always masterly sense of foul play. By no means can either be said to be a portrait of Mrs Compton Burnett, except in so far as each embodies an aspect—Eliza Mowbray is an inconsolable widow, Eliza Heriot a resentful stepmother—in which Ivy's mother had once appeared. What seems to have happened is that Ivy used her early experience as other writers have used a body of myth, selecting from it images and archetypes which to the end of her life possessed her imagination and which, though they may retain certain essential and recognizable features, bear in the end no more resemblance to their starting point than to a face in the fire.

Vestiges of the original conception retained by Eliza Mowbray are easily identified. A widow with three sons, her considerable energies are equally divided between the past great romance of her marriage and the present great dudgeon aroused by her eldest son's desire for independence. Her brother-in-law, not a man easily daunted, is frankly frightened of Eliza, and says as much to her son:

'There is no one on this earth, whom I would not rather set myself against than your mother. I wondered how your father could undertake her. I put it in plain words. "My dear brother," I said, "you are a braver man than I am." But he heard no reason. And the marriage was a success. Believe it or not, it was.'

'I believe it,' said Malcolm. 'I was a witness of it. It lives in my memory. It casts its shadow over us. It was so great a success that nothing else can be so. No one can love her enough, admire her enough, give her enough. She can never be satisfied. And my brothers give a good deal.'[18]

The same dissatisfaction is evident in relations between Mrs Mowbray and her companion Miss Manders, known as Mandy, who serves at once as refuge and confidante to the young Mowbrays. Mandy has the 'long, thin face and large kind eyes'[19] bequeathed to Miss Patmore and others by the Compton Burnetts' Minnie, as well as the insatiable curiosity associated with this type (Miss Jennet, or Jenney, in Elders and Betters, Miss Griffon in A Family and a Fortune are obvious examples, besides a whole retinue of children's nurses); and her intimacy with the children provokes in Eliza a tirade of outraged betrayal preposterous in any but a person born, as one of her sons remarks, to be a figure in tragedy: 'I am a figure in tragedy, my dear. I was not born to be one. I was born for happiness and love and life. And they have been torn from me. You would think that people would extend to me a helping hand. But I am to have nothing; no kindness, no loyalty, no help in my hard place. I am a figure of tragedy indeed.'

Eliza Heriot, also a figure in tragedy and accustomed to trade on the fact, is interesting here chiefly in her capacity as disgruntled second wife. Her husband leaves the running of his home 'wholly in her hands', and has moreover bequeathed his property to her over the heads of his children in a will identical with Christian Stace's, or for that matter with Dr Burnett's. What is perhaps more curious is that in Ivy's last book (on which she worked intermittently for five or six years before her death) she returned to a situation which had loomed large in her first: Eliza Heriot's authority, in *The Last and the First*, is grimly challenged and ultimately routed by her eldest stepdaughter Hermia who leaves home just as, in *Dolores*, the eponymous heroine had done to escape the dominion of a coldly hostile stepmother. There is small point in setting the juvenile clumsiness of *Dolores* beside the breath-taking clarity and concision with which similarly gruelling battles are presented, at incomparably greater emotional pressure, in a book written almost sixty years later. But one may note in passing that the second Mrs Hutton in *Dolores* was in part at least a rough and superficial sketch of Mrs Compton Burnett ('let it not be thought that his wife was a virago or a termagant . . . Mrs Hutton was merely an irritable, jealous, sensitive woman'),[20] that her path is 'continually dogged by my stepchildren', and that she resents her husband's first marriage so acutely that he learns from 'dread of domestic friction' to suppress all trace of fondness for his eldest daughter. Hermia Heriot's father does the same; and both stepdaughters suffer not only from a loveless upbringing but also from the fact that any mention of their early childhood—Hermia was ten, Dolores nine years old when her own mother died—is forbidden on pain of their stepmothers' extreme displeasure.

Olive Compton-Burnett had been eight years old when her father brought home a second wife, and the first marriage was not thereafter a subject encouraged for conversation in her stepmother's household. Olive, like Hermia and Dolores, had once been especially dear to her father, and preserved the memory long after her privileged position had been undermined. But the gap in age and circumstances effectively prevented any great contact with the second family. She had been dispatched to boarding school when Ivy was two years old, returning for six or seven unhappy years before she left again for good ('A daughter leaving the family home to seek employment! It is not a thing she would be proud of,' says Eliza's son, discussing his mother in *The Last and the First* with a detachment matched in Hermia's sombre reply: 'There is no cause for pride. It has never been a home to me')[21] when Ivy was sixteen. Olive seems to have been the one who most actively smarted under the sense of inferiority fostered in all five step-children by their uncertain status at home, their separate education, their dullness when set beside the achievements of their half-brothers and -sisters, their own mother's comparatively humble origins as the daughter of a provincial chemist, and the more or less complete break with her family. Always 'a difficult person', forceful and clever but not intellectual, Olive had never slackened the feud with her stepmother and 'vented it all round'. Inevitably one thinks of the submerged cruelties ('"Of course stepmothers are cruel," said Hope, "but then so are stepchildren, though they don't have any of the discredit"')[22] inherent in this situation in the novels of I. Compton-Burnett. But one should remember that the two despotic second wives, Mrs Hutton and Lady Heriot, are easily outnumbered in the novels by stepmothers on excellent terms with their stepchildren—and that the kind of atmosphere which prevailed in the Compton Burnett household must have been widespread at a time when people had no alternative but to endure for years at close quarters what was perhaps no less a volume of suffering than the miseries of divorce, separation and broken homes which have since largely replaced it.

It was presumably a relief to both parties when Olive, after her father's death, severed close connections with her stepmother's family (though she retained to the end of her life a measure of financial dependence on her half-sisters). She earned a precarious living by journalism, mostly in London, always in straitened circumstances, and towards the end of the first war set up house with a friend called Emily Pope who remained her companion until she died at the age of eighty-seven in 1963. There are differing views of this ménage in which Olive, hardened no doubt by her early experience (to which she never afterwards referred), was the dominant partner, seeming something of a bully to outside observers who had small doubt that—at any rate when Olive was old and hearty, Miss Pope older and delicate—'there was tyranny there'.[23]

Iris and Daisy had spent more time at home though Iris, who helped with the housekeeping and maintained a mutual coldness with her stepmother, left home like her eldest sister at twenty-five to train at the Temperance Hospital in Hampstead (which she chose in preference to the Homoeopathic Hospital on the ground that she would not there be known as her celebrated father's daughter), where she eventually became a sister and remained—a faithful and respected nurse, a pillar of St Barnabas' Guild, the Bible Reading Fellowship and St John's Church, Ladbroke Grove—till shortly before her death in 1944. It is hardly surprising that Ivy had no special liking for any of her half-sisters. 'Though they lived cheek by jowl, and though there was certainly no enmity, I don't think there was any affinity,' said Vera Compton-Burnett. Ivy had cared perhaps least of all for Daisy, who was 'my mother's right hand. Daisy called her mother, which the others didn't, and I think she really felt herself to be her daughter. She was the daughter at home.' It was Daisy who paid calls with Mrs Compton Burnett, replaced on occasion unwillingly by Ivy who 'loathed calling. She didn't do it with a very good grace, and she hadn't a gift for it.' It was also Daisy who helped teach the small children, partly from inclination and partly because time spent in the nursery meant that so much less time need be spent in the company of Ivy and her brothers: 'She got out of the difficulty of relations with the older ones by being with the younger ones'. The chief difficulty seems to have been that Daisy, 'being so religious and Ivy so irreligious', provided an admirably accommodating butt for her younger sister's sharp tongue: while the pious and gentle Daisy sat staring dreamily into space 'Ivy would make remarks,' and turn poor Daisy's clumsy answers upside down. Part at least of Daisy's trouble was that she had too little to do. She would, according to her younger sisters, have made an excellent vicar's wife and, if one thinks of Ivy's attitude towards this calling as represented by the vicar's wife in *Men and Wives*—'I have had my fill of funerals, and mothers' meetings and parishioners' teas. The funerals are the best; they do get rid of somebody'[24]—one can very well see why the two had never got on. Guy sometimes held the peace between them ('And I should think he had his work cut out,' said Juliet Compton-Burnett), but 'Daisy was a target rather'.

Daisy's religious fervour first rose to a mania in the dark days after their father's death when Vera and Judy, coming home from school on weekday afternoons, would be captured and made to sing hymns at the piano by a sister who 'looked strange'. She was promptly sent away to visit her Thomas aunts in Cheshire, and came home restored again; but, round about her thirtieth birthday, after years of depression and strain brought on by the grinding monotony of life at Hove, her strangeness returned in a form which amounted to a serious breakdown. 'One Sunday afternoon, it was just after tea—we were so embarrassed we didn't ever speak about it—Daisy stopped at the door and said, "There is something I wish you all to know. I have given myself to Jesus." We nearly fainted, I remember the awful tension,' said Vera Compton-Burnett. 'My mother said something like, "Well, I'm sure it's very nice that Daisy has done this." The rest of us were dumb with horror.'

Shortly afterwards Daisy departed of her own accord for a missionary training school, leaving a note explaining what she had done and saying goodbye to no one. She never returned to Hove and, having regained her health, volunteered in 1913 for service under the Church Missionary Society at Panyam in Northern Nigeria where she was held in considerable esteem, established a homoeopathic dispensary for the tribespeople, and was known as Mat-yen (woman of medicine). On her retirement some years later she became head of the school to which she had originally fled, the Carfax Missionary Home (later a refuge for retired missionaries) in Bristol. Here she was remembered in the 'thirties by her doctor[25] as a tall, imposing, self-possessed lady dressed in grey with an Edwardian coiffure: 'A *very* dignified lady, very austere, who had high standards of behaviour for herself and for everybody else. She could be very critical if you didn't live up to her standards.' She bore no resemblance to her father in looks, and in character she had become by then 'too controlled'. A clerical friend from Panyam, who had travelled out on the same boat in 1913 to Africa, recalled that 'she seldom spoke of any relative. We knew however that the members of her own family had little sympathy with her Christian principles and outlook.'[26] Her family for their part had not unnaturally lost touch with Daisy. Ivy herself in later life was frequently humorous at the expense of her missionary sister, though one may perhaps detect a hint of sympathy in her account of Rosamund Burtenshaw, the senior member of a trio of zealous and meddlesome spinsters distributing tracts in *A House and Its Head*: 'Miss Burtenshaw had retired from missionary work owing to the discomfort of the life, a reason which she did not disclose, though it was more than adequate; and was accustomed to say she found plenty of furrows to plough in the home field. . . .'[27]

Daisy's two brothers in their early twenties had made an equally dramatic break with the family. Both had already left Hove in their father's lifetime and neither seems to have made any great impression on their half-brothers and -sisters before that. Charlie had had his first birthday ten days before his father remarried in 1883, Richard his fourth one month later; and Richard at any rate might have agreed with Fabian Clare in *The Present and the Past*, another melancholy small boy whose childhood had been overshadowed by his father's second marriage: 'My life was over when I was four. I wonder how many people can say that.'[28] Richard, who had come into a small income from property left him under his father's will, appears from the Law Lists to have practised as a solicitor in London between 1901 and 1903. Charlie never apparently qualified. He had been led astray by 'a set with money' and several times got into trouble, being finally discovered one night by the Salvation Army penniless on London Bridge with nowhere to go. Mrs Compton Burnett, who was promptly sent for from Hove, did her duty without hesitation on this occasion: 'My mother paid his debts and got him straight, and then he went abroad.' The rents from his share of his father's property—£28 10s. per quarter—had been paid to his stepmother until his twenty-first birthday, when he signed a formal discharge on 10 September 1903. Family legend later took a dim view of the doctor's two eldest sons: 'They were rotters and they ran through their money,' said a distant relative who remembered being taken up to London as a small child in the 'nineties to consult Dr Burnett for a sore throat.

Whatever the reason, the two brothers left the country some time in 1904, emigrating to America as their father in his youth had once half determined to do. Charlie, always a first-rate horseman, was last heard of by his half-sisters training cavalry in Canada during the first world war; he settled afterwards at Pasadena in California, was said to have become a fruit farmer, corresponded regularly with Olive, lived to a ripe old age and made a late marriage to 'an old friend' long after there was any prospect of children. Richard, who had set up as an attorney in Pasadena, was less fortunate: 'The financial slump in America in '29 ruined him and affected his health,' wrote Olive in 1949, 'and my brother Charles looked after him in his remaining years.'* He killed himself by jumping off a bridge in Los Angeles on 11 December 1935.

* Richard's death certificate says that he had been in the U.S. since 1900, Olive's letter (to her solicitor) that he emigrated 'just prior to 1905'. He died unmarried, childless and intestate, his sole possession consisting of a thirty-fifth share under the intestacy of his uncle, Alfred Henry Thomas, who had predeceased him in 1935; Richard's share, eventually made over by his brother Charles to Olive, came to £70.

3

WHATEVER MAY HAVE happened after Dr Burnett's death, there is no reason to suppose that his two eldest sons had not got on well with their father in his lifetime, though one may perhaps detect a certain mistrust in his having in one sense passed over them both in his will. Dr Burnett left small parcels of property (mostly working men's cottages, together with two or three small farms, at Great Clacton and Walton-on-Naze) to his first five children, who would each have received an annual income from tenants of round about £150, and sometimes considerably less. Ivy and her two brothers had also come into similar but smaller bequests. The rest (apart from a conditional legacy of £200 to Minnie) was left in trust to his wife, to be divided after her death between her own children. The disparity between provisions for his first and second families in what was evidently a scrupulously fair will probably reflects the fact that his first wife had brought him little or nothing (as a 'struggling young doctor' in 1874, he himself had presumably only his prospects to live on),* and his second wife a fairly substantial dowry. But Katharine Compton Burnett became trustee and sole guardian of his infant children (who included Iris and Charlie at the time of his death), to be succeeded, if she should die, by Guy when he reached the age of twenty-one. Guy was also to assist his mother as joint trustee although Richard, who was entrusted with no responsibility, had been already twenty-one when the will was made, and even Charlie was three years older than Guy. Apparently the doctor, who had held strong, indeed reverent views on the supremacy of duty, trusted his wife to be fair to her stepchildren (and, when she was not, her daughters contributed annually after her death to the comparatively meagre portions of their three half-sisters).

It is perhaps small wonder that Mrs Compton Burnett, left with nine children under twenty-one on her hands as well as two older, unmarried stepdaughters, should have been in the last years of her life so earnestly bent on retrenchment. She had moreover the additional

---

* No great capital outlay was required to set up in the late nineteenth century as a G.P.: Arthur Conan Doyle put up his plate at Southsea in 1882, in a villa rented at £40 p.a. and furnished for £3, having purchased '£12 worth of tinctures, infusions, pills, powders, ointments and bottles at a wholesale house', and prided himself on living expenses of sixpence a day. (*Conan Doyle* by Hesketh Pearson, Methuen, 1943, p.66.)

strain of contributing to the expenses of her father's household. Rowland Rees died at Hove, sixteen months after his son-in-law, at the age of eighty-six on 22 July 1902, leaving a will which, though it makes ominous mention of his sons' debts, also includes elaborate directions for the getting in of all moneys and properties in a trust fund to provide for his wife, various grandchildren and all but three of his seven surviving children (excluding his eldest son Rowland, something of a black sheep in the family, as well as Allen and Charles who had all three received and squandered their inheritance). But the estate, when got in, amounted to £1,850 13s. 2d., barely sufficient to cover his few preliminary bequests—a discrepancy which, taken with the earlier move from his large house at Clacton to a small terrace villa in Hove, the fact that James Compton Burnett had for some years supported him, and that Katharine continued after his death to make an allowance to her stepmother, points to some kind of financial catastrophe.

Dr Burnett and his father-in-law had been fond of one another, and often played chess in the evenings. Katharine in later years would frequently take 'an evening prowl' to call on her stepmother ('I think I'll just go and see Mater tonight') and the second Mrs Rees returned her affection, though not without reservations ('She disapproved of Katie, you know, she thought the first family should've been treated better,' said one of Rowland Rees' granddaughters). Ivy's sisters had had little to do with the Reeses who did not care for small children, and who 'played no part in our lives at all'; but Ivy, eighteen when her grandfather died, had been old enough to take note of his character as of his dealings with a family which over three generations acknowledged him as its head. Records of his tempestuous career in Dover suggest a striking affinity with the many stiff-necked, contumacious fathers and grandfathers ruling their households by terror, and by an unshakeable conviction of their own divine right, in the novels of I. Compton-Burnett; and accounts of his years in retirement confirm that his temper had by no means worn thin in old age. 'A very peppery, aristocratic sort of a man, of an irritable disposition,' said his granddaughter Vera; 'I should think his wife and family ran at his behest.' Vera never forgot her stepgrandmother, who was regularly snubbed at home, explaining that some indisposition was nothing worse than a cold, whereupon her grandfather growled: 'What would you have, woman—a plague?'

Rowland Rees shared with Sophia's father, the elder Andrew Stace in *Brothers and Sisters*, not only his early religious conversion and subsequent zeal but also his attitude to himself ('When he spoke of his Maker, he spoke simply of the being who had made him—and perhaps been pleased in this case to execute one of his outstanding pieces of work').[29] Indeed, when one considers Andrew Stace in his eighties— his gruff, disobliging manner with women, his likeness in temperament to his daughter and his preference for her husband's company, his habitual pose of self-pity, his genuine self-congratulation and his terrific fondness for self-dramatization—it is difficult to avoid the conclusion that the character must have been fairly closely modelled on Ivy's grandfather. Traces of his influence constantly recur in the novels, perhaps most forcibly in Miles Mowbray who (in *A Father and His Fate*) behaves abominably to his family and, when eventually thwarted, impudently turns his own public exposure into a scene of public self-applause: 'Everyone else has been able to be generous and heroic. And I have been ridiculous and pitiful and a sort of spectacle and butt. And doing more all the time than anyone else, and facing more into the bargain! Indeed no one else doing or facing anything! It has been a test on a large scale.'[30]

Alderman Rees had also frequently been, in the 'seventies and 'eighties, 'a sort of spectacle and butt' in Dover Town Hall, as in the local and national press. He had possessed, moreover, an ample share of that indomitable ebullience which enables Miles Mowbray, in common with many of Ivy's tyrants, not only to override other people with brutal indifference but, when his victims protest, to abuse them roundly for harbouring grudges. The Editor of the *Dover Chronicle*, writing evidently from personal experience, had hotly defended Councillor Rees in 1862 against this very charge: 'Mr Rees is the man to blurt out the fiery indignation of his Welsh ancestor, Ap Rice Ap Howell Ap Rowland Ap Rees; but when once the Welsh blood has effervesced in a genuine "tiff", he is the best-natured of good fellows.'[31] The celebrated vigour and obstinacy of the Mayor of Dover, his grief when his town clerk sought to 'insult and aggravate' him, his piteous remonstrances against 'dogmatic, impudent persons' who persistently gave him the lie, his blistering, virulent, but somehow absurdly fetching public tantrums, remind one again and again of Miles Mowbray whose particular talent lay, as Alderman Rees' had done, in carrying off impossible situations:

'I would rather be what I am, a weak, erring man, weaker than a woman I daresay, than a hard, hardly-judging person, who speaks with a second purpose all the time, and a malicious one at that. I bear no one ill-will, though something has been exposed, that I meant to be hidden, that had better have been hidden, as so many things in our lives had better be. Oh, I have not so much fault to find with myself.'

'But we hardly expected so much praise,' said Rudolf.[32]

A colleague and contemporary of Rowland Rees had been the chairman of the Gas Company, one W. R. Mowll, J.P., who, in company with the future Mayor, is several times reported in the local press as active in furthering the interests of the Young Men's Christian Association or relieving the poor in time of hard frost. William Rutley Mowll had several sons who entered the church or the law, and we have it on the authority of Arthur Waley (who presumably had it directly from Ivy herself)[33] that the figure whose shadow had lain over her childhood and who continued long afterwards to stand behind her tyrants was one of these sons—also in his day a prominent citizen of Dover, an evangelical churchman, staunch Tory, Town Councillor, East Kent's Receiver in Bankruptcy, Register of Dover Harbour and the Compton Burnetts' trusty family solicitor, Worsfold Mowll. Messrs. Mowll and Mowll of Dover had drawn up James Compton Burnett's marriage settlement in September 1883, and thereafter conducted his business transactions (including drawing up his will and his father-in-law's) to the end of his life. Worsfold Mowll had been named joint trustee with Mrs Compton Burnett during Guy's minority and much later, when Guy and Noel and Worsfold Mowll were all dead, his brother Martyn became joint guardian with Ivy to her four younger sisters. As a child, Ivy must often have seen Worsfold Mowll, who came with a clerk twice yearly to review the doctor's accounts and afterwards maintained the custom of lunching with his widow at Hove—solemn occasions which Ivy attended (and perhaps recalled, in a scene from *Men and Wives*, when another lawyer comes to condole with his client and review her finances: 'Dominic entered the house with a hushed tread, holding his bag as a secular object brought on a sacred occasion. He remained leaning over Harriet's hand in silence').[34] Worsfold Mowll, vastly tall, grave and portentous, ponderous in manner and person, made a memorable impression of omnipotence and omniscience on the small children who, though not present at lunch, would be dressed up and brought down for his inspection in the course of the afternoon. Vera Compton-Burnett, once reproved by her mother for stooping, remembered Mr

Mowll launching at once into the cautionary tale of Little Johnny Head-in-Air: what infuriated the child was the injustice of being squashed simultaneously for looking down one moment and looking up the next. Later, she retaliated by putting a bulb under the plate of his brother Martyn—'rather less Worsfold than Worsfold'—and squeezing it so subtly that he could never be certain whether it jumped or not. But Worsfold himself had been more intimidating, a fearsome disciplinarian and not to be trifled with. 'He *was* a person . . .' said Vera Compton-Burnett; 'only second to God, I would think,' said her sister.

The Mowlls had long been a leading family in Dover. Worsfold, born in 1850, had founded the family firm in 1881 in partnership with his brother. His son Rutley (also in turn Ivy's solicitor) later won brief and no doubt disagreeable fame when, as Coroner for East Kent, he gave evidence at the Old Bailey on the inquest of Bessie Munday, one of Joseph Smith's Brides in the Bath murdered at Herne Bay in July 1912. Some forty years earlier, Worsfold's father had won an equally brief and perhaps even more disagreeable notoriety when, as President of the local Y.M.C.A., he had on moral and religious grounds successfully banned Shakespeare from the library and *Punch* from the reading room. The ensuing commotion afforded considerable amusement to the national and even international press from *Le Figaro* to the *Daily Telegraph*, and *Punch* printed a derisive riposte under the heading, DOLTS OF DOVER: 'Oh Mowll, Mowll. We cannot be serious with *you*. . . . But what of Dover? What of its Young Christians? What of people who can choose such rulers and submit to them? Well . . . we apprise Dover that its unhappy dulness shall be respected and tenderly cared for. Our pictures shall henceforth be explained (in foot-note or otherwise) for the instruction of Dover, and as the Essex Calf has been improved into average sense, Punch hopes that years of cultivation may elevate the Dover Dolt.'[35]

W. R. Mowll's two sons seem to have held the same stern belief in their own righteousness as their father who, undaunted by strenuous local opposition, had determined in 1871 to persevere in 'the cause of religion and morality, despite the ungodly press of England'. 'I have always gone on in the *old* groove,' was a saying of Martyn Mowll's when, as guardian to the motherless Compton-Burnett girls until they were twenty-four, he had earnestly attempted to curb their desire for independence. Ivy's sisters proposed to lead a musical life, chaperoned by Minnie and sharing a house with Myra Hess, a scheme which dismayed the heart of their guardian who envisaged prospects too frightful to contemplate if they were permitted any truck with however respected and respectable a pianist: 'Miss Vera, these *artist people* are very charming—very charming, Miss Vera—but unreliable. This friendship of yours may end in the law courts.'

Worsfold Mowll was also as godly, inflexible and assiduous as his father had been before him in prosecuting good works for local orphans, athletes and police constables who were regaled at an annual cricket match with the villagers and his family (he had eleven children as well as numerous nieces and nephews, one of them later at King's College with Noel Compton-Burnett) in the grounds of his house outside Dover. 'The police force will lose a friend,' wrote the *Dover Telegraph* when he died on 26 January 1906, lamented by the whole town with flags at half mast and the bells of St Mary's tolling on the day of his death, muffled peals at St James' and funeral sermons preached in almost every church the following Sunday. The Mayor and corporation followed him to his grave, together with over a thousand mourners and six carriages loaded with two hundred wreaths (among them one 'In loving memory' from Mrs Compton Burnett), in a funeral procession half a mile long. He is commemorated by a memorial window in Dover Town Hall and the *Dover Telegraph*, mourning his loss, suggests perhaps some of the reasons why he should also long afterwards have been commemorated in the novels of I. Compton-Burnett:

> He was unlike other men. Worsfold Mowll was Worsfold Mowll. Without being pedantic, aesthetic or affected, he had a distinct individuality. . . . There was something great about Worsfold Mowll—one cannot bring oneself to prefix him with the ordinary Mr . . . a big man, truly, in every sense of the word—in stature, in the largeness of his heart, in his generosity and geniality. He had an overwhelming effect upon you—not the overbearing pettiness of the martinet, but a mannerism that enveloped you and drew you within its grasp with peculiar fascination. . . .[36]

Whatever the aspect uppermost in the minds of his townsmen in their hour of bereavement, there were undeniably traces of the pettiness of the martinet in Mr Mowll's relations with the Compton Burnetts. After their father's death, he had become their mother's chief guide and councillor and, though Mrs Compton Burnett may have found him congenial company, he seems to have appeared repressive and dictatorial to her children at a time when the three eldest were already beginning to assert their independence. One cannot help suspecting his influence on Dominic Spong, the Haslams' solicitor in *Men and Wives*, who exasperates the family by his interference in money matters ('"Oh, Spong is an old skinflint," said Godfrey rather uneasily. "... I don't know what we are coming to, if lawyers are to be father and mother and legal adviser all in one"'),[37] his laboured witticisms, his embarrassing habit of currying favour with their mother and his ill-concealed disapproval of the children's artistic and literary ambitions ('Dominic rose and took his leave, an extra heaviness in his breathing betraying his present unavoidable attitude to the house'). Both Arthur Waley and Jack Beresford, friends of Noel Compton-Burnett at King's, were familiar with Noel's imitations of Mr Mowll in a high, starched collar issuing oracular pronouncements from a great height, and both had the impression that he ruled the Compton-Burnett finances, as well as offering opinions on the children's education and upbringing, with an authority seldom gainsaid.[38] Ivy, too, made caustic comments on Mr Mowll; and it is perhaps worth noting that crushed and apprehensive children in the novels of I. Compton-Burnett often retaliate by aping the people who frighten them—Lesbia Firebrace, Duncan Edgeworth, Sabine Ponsonby and Jocasta Grimstone, four egregious tyrants, are all mimicked by their victims behind their backs.

Shapes and patterns which later sharply emerged in the novels must have surrounded Ivy in these years. Her mother, her grandfather and Worsfold Mowll all provided examples of the kind of moral turpitude which she afterwards accepted without rancour or indignation, and analysed with disturbing precision: '... I think that life makes great demand on people's characters, and gives them, and especially used to give them, great opportunity to serve their own ends by the sacrifice of other people. Such ill-doing may meet with little retribution, may indeed be hardly recognized, and I cannot feel so surprised if people yield to it.'[39] But Ivy at seventeen was in no position to formulate her later philosophy, though she may well have lived according to its law of stoical acceptance. What little indication survives—descriptions of her attitude at college, letters and verses written in her early twenties, the vicious doctrine of self-sacrifice embedded in her first novel—suggests that she hardly recognized, any more than her mother, the pattern underlying their mutual unhappiness.

Mrs Compton Burnett in the early part of her widowhood can have had little enough to deter her from temperamental excesses, with

Olive and Charlie both treading roads to ruin in London, Daisy sunk in religious melancholia at home, Ivy away at college, the four little girls turning wholly to Minnie for affection and supervision. Guy and Noel had been sent as day boys to Brighton College in the summer term of 1901, and both left again (whether on grounds of retrenchment, or because they had as much difficulty as their sisters in adjusting to a school where 'the day-boys were still pretty good mud, and the idea of a Day-boy House still a little strange,'⁴⁰ or because the school itself was at that time held in low repute and had even been up for sale the year before) the following Easter. For a year they were taught by their tutor at home until Guy, at nineteen, went up to King's to read classics in 1904. No records remain of his two terms at Cambridge, though his younger sisters were both convinced that 'he would have been quite remarkable. Guy could have put the other two in his pocket.' Dr Burnett had wanted Guy to take up medicine and they thought that, if their father had lived, Guy would probably have acquiesced: when pressed on the subject, he would reply that he meant to be a doctor of divinity and headmaster of a school. But the plan to be a clergyman, like Noel's to be a soldier, was no more than a childish ambition, and both Ivy and her sisters maintained that Guy would have been a writer. One should not perhaps attach much importance to a set of verses composed on his father's death in April 1901, which, though they show a certain 'fluency in words', reveal otherwise nothing beyond the average capacities of a fifteen-year-old boy writing in the conventional idiom of his period:

> There is a veiling curtain drawn before
> The eyes of men, concealing from their sight
> The hidden mysteries of the further shore,
> Till they were taught to bear the fuller light. . . .
>
> The curtain will be lifted, when 'tis time,
> The weary road will draw unto an end;
> They are the means to make the soul sublime
> To pass away, and meet each long-lost friend.

Noel, too, is said to have written a patriotic poem commemorating the deaths of his father and Queen Victoria, 'and God certainly came into it', so perhaps the earlier break with religion had not been as complete as it seemed to Ivy in retrospect. Her two younger sisters both agreed that (at any rate in the sense defined by France Ponsonby in *Daughters and Sons*) Guy had been truly religious. 'I think it was in a way his religious nature which supported us all,' said Juliet Compton-Burnett; and accounts of his forbearance towards their mother, his generosity to his sisters, suggest that he had reached in the last years of his life an extraordinary emotional maturity.

But the strain, coming so soon after his own dangerous illness on one whose health had always been delicate, must have taxed his strength beyond bearing. When the whole family caught influenza in the Easter holidays Guy, who had seemed to be getting well, suffered a sudden relapse and died within a few days of his apparent recovery on 29 May 1905. 'My mother put everything into Guy,' and she had received more in return up to the last few days of his illness when he would beg Minnie to prevent her coming into the sick-room: 'He hadn't the strength any more to stand it.' She never recovered from the two deaths. For months afterwards she would go for walks with Vera, urging her to talk about him, to dredge up memories of anything Guy had ever done or said, much as Sophia Stace in the early days of her widowhood 'begged with untiring eagerness for assurances of her virtues as a wife, that were given at first willingly, but by degrees with the last weariness'.[41] It was Noel, still young for his age at seventeen, who grew up to take the place of his father and Guy—'After Guy died, Noll changed almost overnight'—and Noel who became his mother's 'darling boy', though he could not respond to her as heroically as Guy had done: 'Noel had a lighter temperament than Guy, he didn't live in his nature so much.' Noel from this time became Ivy's inseparable companion. Both bore their own grief with resolute courage in silence; and both must have suffered from their mother's emotional collapse as the Stace children had done from 'the stress and pity of Sophia'.

But Ivy by this time was in her third year at Royal Holloway College and, having once escaped the confines of life at Hove, she never again submitted to complete subjugation. Guy's loss remained a source of almost unfaceable pain to the end of her life; and she was not able, as he had been, to offer their mother either consolation or intimacy. In later years the two would walk down to the sea together in the evenings, but it is unlikely that their conversation ever strayed beyond the bounds of Ivy's habitual reticence. 'Ivy very rarely put into words what was her real being,' said her sister; and Mrs Compton Burnett, though she was afterwards justly proud of her eldest daughter, was also, with reason, 'always a little bit in awe of Ivy'.

1902–1911

'Always secret and very dark'

I

ROYAL HOLLOWAY COLLEGE, when Ivy arrived there chaperoned by Minnie on 2 October 1902, was a small, isolated and inward-looking community regarded with some suspicion by the outside world. It stood alone on the borders of Berkshire and Surrey, twenty miles from London, forty miles from Oxford, just outside the tiny country town of Egham, on a hillside overlooking Virginia Water and Windsor Great Park. Strange rumours about the doings of its staff and students circulated in the established universities, and stranger still among the wider public who considered education for women an unhealthy, even sinister attempt to undermine the nation's fabric. The college had been founded sixteen years before by the philanthropist Thomas Holloway, a baker's son who had built his vast fortune on a patent pill advertised in his lifetime as a cure for 'inflammations, abscesses and ulcerations . . . indigestion, biliousness, sick headache, nervousness, sleeplessness, loss of appetite' as well as 'skin diseases of the most revolting character'; but which proved, when analysed by the British Medical Association after his death, to contain aloes, powdered ginger and soap. The pill remained long afterwards a source of embarrassment and vexation to the grateful recipients of Mr Holloway's bounty. Queen Victoria had opened the college in 1886, and the following year twenty-eight students arrived to occupy an enormous French château, newly-built of local red brick and covering, according to a boastful prospectus, 'more ground than any other college in the world'. The Dean of Windsor, watching this strange, scarlet edifice rising in the neighbouring fields, had said: 'It is intended for the higher education of women;

but the question I am asking is whether any women with facilities open to them at both Oxford and Cambridge are ever likely to go to Egham to be educated?'[1]

But education at Egham had several advantages over education elsewhere. Holloway College, for one thing, had an endowment of nearly a quarter of a million pounds which made it conspicuously richer than the foundations for women at Oxford and Cambridge. For another, its Founder's views had been in advance of his time and decidedly liberal: all students were to read for degrees (which was by no means the case for girls at the older universities), and their choice of subject was to be broader than the traditional curriculum based on Latin, Greek and mathematics—though these were still, in Ivy's day at Holloway, 'spoken of as genuine Schools and the others as soft options'.[2] Three years before she came up, the college, after long hesitation over the rival claims of Oxford, had finally been accepted as a part of London university: London, though new, inexperienced and widely despised at the time, was not only conveniently closer to Egham, but far bolder in its attitude to new schools and branches of learning, and far better disposed towards women than Oxford (where, some twenty years later, the Vice-Chancellor still prayed daily that women might not be admitted to the degree: 'Lord, if it must be, let it not be in my time').[3] Moreover the Founder, taking note no doubt of the sad fact that at Oxford girls were too often a downtrodden company compared with their brothers, had declared it his 'express and earnest desire . . . that the College shall neither be considered nor conducted as a mere training college for teachers and governesses'. He had been perhaps over-optimistic, since Ivy herself was one of comparatively few in her year not destined to become a schoolmistress. Most of the others seem to have approached the higher education in much the same spirit as the girl in *Dolores*, who bettered her mind 'simply because I must earn my bread, or go to the workhouse'.[4]

There were fifty girls in Ivy's year, 137 altogether, and the students continued to increase in number throughout the four years she spent there. They lived in a magnificent pile built round two quadrangles in the fancy French style—steep mansard roofs, round pointed turrets, pavilions at the four corners rising to a flamboyant skyline—which had been especially popular in the 'eighties and 'nineties among the nouveaux riches. So charmed was Mr Holloway by the châteaux of the Loire that he had sent his architect to spend a summer measuring the exact dimensions of Chambord, which he then reproduced for sound commercial reasons on his Surrey hillside in 'flaming red brick which fairly scorched the eye'. Even now, when the walls have mellowed to a rich poppy colour against green English lawns and a blue sky, one can well understand the visitor who said nervously in 1908: 'My dear, you really musn't show it broadside on!' A few years later this astonishing building, with its courtyards and broad walks, its terraced gardens threaded by drives, its greenhouses, summerhouses, ponds, streams, swimming pool and elaborate system of ornamental statuary, was chosen in a film called *Alf's Button* 'to represent the bathing establishment conjured up by the djinn, when Alf asked for a bath'. It had been designed to provide generous accommodation for some 250 to 300 students, a corresponding number of staff and the hundred or more servants required to attend on them. The girls' bedrooms opened on to corridors one-tenth of a mile long, so that it was impossible for people at one end to recognize anyone walking in the far distance at the other. Whole floors were still uninhabited in Ivy's day (it was rumoured that the unexplored range of closets and bedrooms above the attics had been intended by the Founder to house the girls' individual lady's maids); there were about eight hundred rooms, some of them so far flung that a contemporary of hers who stayed on as a lecturer had still, after a lifetime spent in the college, never even seen them.

Ivy used memories of Holloway twice in her novels, as the basis of the women's college in *Dolores* and for the girls' boarding school in *More Women Than Men*: people are apt to get lost in both these 'great, rambling, complicated place[s]', to be confused by unfamiliar faces and by the din of girls bustling 'in a chattering stream' along 'perplexing corridors' to unknown destinations. Girls at Holloway, coming straight from home with little experience of the outside world and no notion what to expect of life in an academic community, must often have suffered from the sense of bewilderment and lost identity which overcomes Dolores on her first day at college: 'As other days followed . . . she found herself with a place and purposes in a passionless, ardent little world—a world of women's friendships; where there lived in a strange harmony the spirits of the medieval convent and modern growth.'[5] Other members of the college had also compared the enclosed atmosphere at Holloway—days spent moving between chapel and library, study and lecture room, according to a strict rule of decorum, silence and punctuality enforced by the ringing of bells—with the régime in a well endowed tenth- or eleventh-century convent where unmarried women pursued under close supervision a life devoted to religion, learning and the arts. Ivy's contemporaries prided themselves on their domestic appointments which were at once austere and comfortable, 'nicely feminine, yet learned'.

But the 'orderly, Christian household' enjoined in the Founder's trust deed was to be modelled on the standards of solid opulence brought to a high point in late Victorian country houses, vast establishments which sometimes housed as many as 150 people and maintained them by means of the latest technical devices: Holloway College had steam central heating installed from the first, and a tunnel built so that the sight of servants or their carts might not offend the resident ladies. The corridors were carpeted and the girls' studies—the 'narrow student chambers' of *Dolores*—each contained, besides the regulation set of severely plain dresser, two chairs and a table with brass fittings, a large looking glass (said to have been a stipulation of the Founder's will) and an open fire (rationed to one coal scuttle a day, which meant thrift and constant anxiety for those who, unlike Ivy, were not expert in the gentle art of lighting and tending coal fires). The college had been furnished throughout by Maples in massive mahogany, with carved oak, ornate plaster ceilings, oriental rugs and leather-backed chairs in the library. Maids swept and cleaned the rooms before breakfast. The Lady Housekeeper, a stern and fastidious martinet, was said to have been appointed by the Principal in 1891 on the strength of a sentence in her letter of application: 'I have been accustomed to keep a liberal table.'

Holloway, in sharp contrast to other impoverished and comfortless women's colleges of the day, was celebrated alike for its good living and excellent food. It had its own kitchen gardens, asparagus and strawberry beds, orchards and piggeries. Dinner in the great central dining hall was served by the butler and a line of starched maids off solid silver plate with specially woven monogrammed table linen. A procession in long dresses, often with trains on high nights, assembled every evening at seven o'clock and moved majestically in pairs from the drawing room through the library and museum under an avenue of candelabra along dangerously shining parquet floors (on which distinguished visitors slid and tripped, affording the students much simple pleasure) to the hall. The girls were expected to book their dinner partners beforehand, a precaution which Ivy generally neglected —several of her friends remembered her lurking with other latecomers at the back of the library, arriving sometimes so late that she was still doing up her buttons as she came, and a letter written in her third term to her cousin Katie Blackie perhaps explains why:

... The dramatic society are going to act a play.* The dress rehearsal is to be to-night, and to-night the first years are requested to attend. It is bad to be a first year; I am looking forward to next term, when I shall be a second year, & have about fifty whole first years to sit upon. I trust that you will be able to interpret this scrawl, writing it is only by courtesy; I am in a hurry, writing in the quarter of an hour in which I should be dressing for dinner. I have been intending to write to you for the last 3 months, & I trust that you have also been intending to write to me, for intentions, when they are good are better than nothing, & I have certainly seen no sign of anything more substantial. . . . I must say goodbye now, & go & endeavour, in the short space of 6 minutes and ¾ to arrange my wig, an operation which Mother declares should occupy every lady at least half an hour. (1 May 1903.)

Dinner was the serious ritual of the day but private social life revolved (as Ivy's continued to do for much of her life) round substantial tea parties—'A good hearty time was had by all from 4–4.45 p.m.'—held out of doors in the summer, in every bay of the terrace overlooking shaven lawns and flower beds in a formally laid-out parterre. Picnics might be taken on the river, or beyond the double row of pines which ran along the west side of the college bordered by beds of white roses. Nightingales sang here in the evenings, pheasants and gold-crested wrens nested in the grounds, primroses and wild orchids grew along the broad grass path to the south-east where the girls picked punnets of wild strawberries and, on a fine day, the whole of the south tower was reflected in the waters of the lower pond. Ivy, always particularly fond of wild flowers, would go for walks alone or with a friend and bring back tiny posies, arranged so that each separate petal showed. Others gathered blackberries and made jam with sugar from the college pantries—stealing sugar and being late for chapel were the chief, apparently the only vices regularly practised in what seems to have been an idyllic, if severely restricted and in some ways rumbustiously juvenile community.

The girls were narrowly supervised, forbidden to speak at all at certain hours, to walk without permission outside the grounds, to invite male partners to their dances, male spectators to their plays or men of any description to tea without a staff chaperone. In the seclusion thus jealously guarded, they called each other by their surnames in

* *The Rose and the Ring.*

imitation of their brothers, ran races in the corridors or tobogganned on college tea-trays in the gardens; and Ivy herself, though she joined in neither tennis nor hockey, cricket nor boating, did years afterwards recall with pleasure sliding on a tea-tray down the wide, carpeted stair-cases.[6] Enforced isolation (there were few trains to London and excursions, which were not in any case encouraged, could otherwise be undertaken only by horse-drawn cab, on foot or by bicycle) meant that energies left over from work were expended inside the college. There was intense religious and musical activity. The College Dramatic Society put on an annual play (including a performance of *Pride and Prejudice* in February 1904, which Ivy presumably saw and in which Lytton Strachey's sisters, Pernel and Marjorie, played respectively Mr Bennet—'exhibiting all the time a personification of slightly academic idleness'—and 'the oiliest possible Mr Collins').[7] Visiting celebrities* lectured regularly and there were at least a dozen clubs and debating societies which met in the evenings for literary, political, historical or scientific discussion. Ivy had certainly attended meetings of the Political Society, which was organized as a feminine replica of the House of Commons and hotly debated such issues as Mr Chamberlain's fiscal policy, alien immigration, the Licensing Act (on which the Conservative government inside the college was roundly defeated and fell in the Michaelmas Term of 1904) and women's suffrage (carried by a majority of 61). 'Everyone went to Political,' said Isabel Bremner, a friend and contemporary of Ivy (and often her partner at dinner). 'I know Miss Compton-Burnett did; when I made my maiden speech, they were very much amused.' Ivy, sitting among the back-benchers on this occasion, had called out, 'Let me have your notes,' which led to some ragging as 'we all thought she meant to put them in a book'. But when the Principal once warned her that she would never get used to speaking in public if she did not begin at college, Ivy had vehemently replied, 'Yes, I never shall, I never shall';[8] and, so far as I can make out from careful study of the minute books, Ivy took no active part in the transactions of any college society, spoke in no debates, acted in no plays, was neither elected nor volunteered to serve on any committee, and kept silence at both college and students' meetings—unless perhaps hers was the anonymous voice which asked (and received) permission to pick wild flowers at the students' meeting in May 1904.

* Ones who may have interested Ivy were Professor Sidgwick on Addison and Professor A. C. ('Shakespeare') Bradley on Shakespeare's Theatre in her first year; A. E. Housman on Robert Burns in her second; and Henry Newbolt on The Future of English Verse in the summer of 1906.

Ivy in these years seems to have left two distinct impressions on her contemporaries, neither difficult to reconcile with what little is known from elsewhere. On the one hand, there are those who remember her spending most of her time in her room, ill-dressed, unpopular, reserved and shy: 'Compton-Burnett had her study a few doors down from me on E III when we were students at R.H.C. I used to meet her in the corridor and we just exchanged greetings. . . . She never mixed with the other students, and we never met at tea, coffee or cocoa parties. She always wore black.'[9] Her friends, on the other hand, insist that she was neither diffident nor odd but 'pleasant and lively', excellent company— 'Oh, yes, she could make us laugh'—and a practised mimic:

> Miss Compton-Burnett's father was a doctor and she used to amuse us by telling us of the rapidly changing succession of page boys, thin boys, fat boys, tall boys, short boys—all had to wear the same uniform—the boy changed—the suit remained the same—with curious results [wrote Isabel Bremner]. Early in my stay at college, I had to ask permission to have a visit from a boy cousin. In fear and trembling, I knocked at the study door of the Vice-Principal (Miss Guinness). On entry I found Miss C-B. having a coaching. At dinner that night she described the interview, making the most of my faltering request—leading inevitably to refusal—followed by a demonstration of how I ought to have behaved to ensure success.

Miss Bremner's mother was the youngest of thirteen sisters, and the humorous doings of these aunts had greatly pleased Ivy: 'I remember her with a party of us—she wasn't shutting herself in her study *then*— when someone asked why we were laughing, she said: "All listening to stories about Miss Bremner's aunts."' Ivy's gaiety, and the malicious, quizzical wit recalled by her friends, are markedly absent from *Dolores* (in which a number of both staff and students at Holloway in her day are so faithfully drawn that the book was naturally read with attention inside the college, as well as by old Hollowegians). Miss Bremner herself, evidently expecting the kind of comical character sketches she remembered from Ivy's conversation. was disappointed and distinctly puzzled to find instead a moral tract concerned almost exclusively with the turbid emotional undercurrents of life in a women's college: 'I'm surprised it wasn't more humorous,' she said several times. 'I should've thought there would've been more fun in it.'

But Dolores' inner torments, which pervade that overwrought and joyless book, probably reflect a frame of mind that had little to do with

Ivy's early experience at Holloway, where a measure of social and intellectual freedom provided a welcome respite from the oppressive
atmosphere at Hove. By the time she came to write *Dolores*, her life at
home must have seemed bleaker and her prospects more hopeless than
anything she had known in her first three years at college. If she had
then endured undue emotional strain, it would undoubtedly have been
covered by her habitual reticence; but she had never made friends
easily, and there is no reason to suppose that her apparent reserve with
anyone outside her own particular circle amounted to anything more
than the sense of dislocation she had felt at school in the first shock of
separation from her brothers. All her contemporaries agreed that Ivy
had only one close companion at college, a girl named Daisy Harvey,
short, plumpish and rather pretty, whom she had known beforehand at
Howard College in Bedford. Miss Harvey, who was nine months older
than Ivy, arrived on the same day and remained, as Ivy did, for an extra
year. She lived in Lewisham, read science at college and once went to
stay with the Compton Burnetts at Hove where the family thought her
decidedly dull. She seems to have become a schoolmistress and died
unmarried in her seventies,[10] having long since lost touch with Ivy; and
it is at least possible that she provided the model for Perdita Kingsford,
the college friend whose frivolous charms give rise to so many of
Dolores' afflictions: 'There was that in Dolores which yielded to
womanhood's spells. She hardly judged of women as a woman amongst
them; but as something sterner and stronger, that owed them gentleness in judgment. From the first hour to the last of their years of friendship, she read Perdita as an open page; and loved her with a love that
grew, though its nurture was not in what she read.'[11] By all accounts
Miss Harvey, who was neither as clever nor as entertaining as Ivy
could be, shared something of Perdita's disingenuousness, her vanity,
her intellectual shallowness and the unscrupulous ease with which she
attempts to conceal it.* Perdita represents a type of pretty and predatory
feminine wilfulness which reappears several times in the novels, and

---

* Miss Bremner had read physics with Daisy Harvey, and remembered that she 'used
to come to my room night after night with difficult questions'; Miss Harvey, who
hated to acknowledge that she needed assistance, had a habit of sneaking across to
other people's benches in the lab. for surreptitious advice and was once painfully confused at being caught out by their tutor—behaviour not unlike Perdita's when Dolores
first meets her. (But the resemblance, if there was one, goes no further since Miss
Harvey neither married nor died before the novel—in which Perdita does both almost
straight from college—was published.)

perhaps one to which Ivy had always felt especially drawn. Miss Bremner at any rate thought that, of all their contemporaries at Holloway, 'Miss Harvey was the nearest to Perdita'.

It is perhaps worth noting that the two books which unmistakeably make use of Holloway College as their setting both deal, far more insistently than any of the other novels of I. Compton-Burnett, with strong currents of feeling between women. Miss Lemaître in *Dolores* (who was modelled on Marie Péchinet, the head of the French department at Holloway)[12] reappears in *More Women Than Men* as the teacher of modern languages, Maria Rosetti, and there are other points of resemblance between the staff common rooms of the two establishments. Feelings which, in *Dolores*, led to no more than a heady, platonic attachment take on, in *More Women Than Men*, physical expression described so plainly that, if the whole were not carried off with such studied lack of concern, one might well suspect the author of deliberately making a point. But the urbane homosexuality of the later novel, published in 1933 five years after the public furore which surrounded the prosecution of *The Well of Loneliness*, reflects the attitude of at least one section of Ivy's circle of friends in London when she wrote it; and her casual reminders of who sleeps where and with whom (matters invariably taken for granted elsewhere in her books) suggest a certain impatience with the mealy-mouthed euphemisms common at the time —as also perhaps a humorous contempt for the rabid denunciations in the popular press on the one hand and, on the other, for the absurdly high line taken in return by earnest propagandists on behalf of the Lesbian party. Whatever the explanation, *More Women Than Men* belongs far more to the comparatively sophisticated London society Ivy knew in the early 'thirties than to the 'passionless, ardent little world' of *Dolores*, which mirrors accurately enough the atmosphere of her girlhood before the first war.

Indeed, what seems to have happened at Holloway is that the more effusive aspects of communal life had led on Ivy's part to a guarded withdrawal. Hockey-playing stalwarts, strident feminists, impassioned high church ritualists or their stubborn low church opponents can have had little in common with Ivy though their exertions, and their disapproving, often indignant attitude to non-participants, may well have amused her. The domestic intimacy inevitable in so small a community, where first years were expected to know everyone by name within three weeks, was fostered by a system of 'College Families', groups of six or eight girls which 'coalesced under mutual attraction in a student's earliest days' and foregathered thereafter on every possible occasion, sitting together at breakfast and lunch, taking it in turns to hold tea-parties in each other's rooms and meeting again for evening sessions over coffee or cocoa. Ivy, who like Daisy Harvey and Miss Bremner had refrained from joining a family, 'once wrote an article making fun of R.H.C. cocoa parties. I believe she later on in her life was sorry to have been so contemptuous.'[13] 'Slackers' were constantly reproved for idleness, for lingering in one another's rooms at night, for staying up after the last bell at 10.30 p.m. or for walking the corridors in dressing-gowns with their hair down—all presumably attempts to discourage the kind of over-familiarity which led to 'long and hot discussion' at the democratic meetings held each term, when the students devoted much time and energy to remonstrating with one another. Privacy, let alone escape from the scrutiny of so many prying eyes at such close quarters, must have been almost impossible, though sternly enforced by the staff: '. . . bedrooms along one side of each of our main corridors did indeed require decorum to be observed; it was an object lesson in social behaviour to see Miss Block walking along the [ground floor corridors] and closing her eyes as she shut doors carelessly left open.' Ivy had closely observed Miss Block, had perhaps even attended her 'much-prized Sunday morning tea-parties' at which 'triviality or gossip just didn't arise', and later reproduced her characteristically lofty and repressive attitude in the person of Miss Cliff, who rules the staff common room in *Dolores* as her original had been accustomed to supervise the morals of both junior and senior personnel at Holloway.

Moral fervour among the lower orders ran at times uncomfortably high. 'When I entered the college, Uplift was the keynote,' wrote Marion Pick who had arrived in 1903 and who, though far more inclined to approve conventional observances than Ivy, nonetheless found something distasteful 'to a sober judgment' in the sort of 'excit-able, wayward emotionalism' which flourished among the college's various religious factions. The Society of the Annunciation, the R.H.C. Christian Union, the Bible and Foreign Missionary Circles ('a steady stream of recruits was drawn to the Mission Field') met regularly; there were daily Prayer Meetings, 'Lambeth teas', sewing bees, fund-raising gatherings, a Waif and Stray Society (which adopted, clothed and generally presided over a College Waif destined for domestic service) and numerous other cells performing good works for orphans and heathens at home and abroad. What Ivy made of these charitable activities is not hard to guess. Her attitude to the mission field had never been encouraging, and the various officious ladies who go about doing good in her books exhibit at best a harmless complacency, at worst a positively dangerous indifference to the feelings of the people they patronize. At a tea-party held some fifty years later, Ivy described a fellow student who (like Hamilton Grimstone in *The Last and the First*) could never feel comfortable about skipping prayers till she had made up the omission next morning: 'You know, Mr Eliot says that if he misses tea he doesn't feel quite the same till tea the following day,' she said later on the same occasion, and much enjoyed the discomfiture of her staider visitors when a friend[14] remarked on the likeness between the poet and the girl at college.

But it is as well to remember that the nervous excesses and the 'ring of inner tensions' described by Miss Pick were an inevitable reaction to the combination of social sneers and material hardship endured by Dolores, as by many of the girls at Holloway, in the struggle for independence. Miss Pick (who, like Dolores, had escaped the drab lot of a country parson's daughter only by means of a scholarship) vividly conveys the solemn sense of daring incumbent on a pioneering generation whose mothers had anxiously followed the progress of Mr Holloway's experiment, whose own hearts had bled 'for poor Ethel May' in *The Daisy Chain*, and who had been brought up to understand 'only too well that there was a vast surplus of women over men, and that spinster aunts were a depressed race'. Miss Pick's own first inkling of academic delights had come from a serial in the *Boy's Own Paper* which gave her, at the age of eleven, sharp sensations of 'relief that I could be independent, and was absolutely free of the need to marry'. Ivy, too, describes in *Dolores* the burden borne by 'the earnest academic novice' in a community so vulnerable to the slur of impropriety, and so severely conscious of its own rectitude.

There were seventeen resident staff in her day and three men—Messrs Cassie, Donkin and Loney—who kept house at a discreet distance just beyond the college gates. Teaching was conducted by lectures, delivered to groups so small that they must have been more like classes, in 'lecture-rooms which, with their rows of desks, large blackboards, charts and pictures'[15] closely resembled school class rooms. Ivy was one of five in her year reading classics in a school which, under a classical Principal, enjoyed several special privileges: classical students had their own club, their own walk in the grounds called Peripatos where they planted out bulbs from their studies, their own lecture room decorated by their predecessors in grey-green, gold and white, and regular 'Classical treats' devised by the Principal. Miss Penrose (later Dame Emily), who became in turn Principal of Bedford College, Holloway and Somerville, came of a learned and illustrious family. She was descended from Archbishop Cranmer, a great-niece of Dr Arnold of Rugby, second cousin to Matthew Arnold and daughter of an architect who, having criticized the pitch of the pediment as 'steeper than I quite like', had himself personally measured the Parthenon: Miss Penrose's lecture illustrated with lantern slides on his findings was an annual treat for her pupils. 'She had statesmanlike vision, fairness of judgement, devotion to learning, and imperturbable faith in the ends for which she worked. . . . Deeply religious, reserved in all personal matters, scrupulously careful in expressing opinion, she was difficult to know, and formidable to those who did not know her. . . .'[16] wrote Helen Darbishire, who was briefly a lecturer at Holloway in Ivy's day. 'Miss Penrose . . . inhabited a region where no student trod, from which she came down when her Office required,' wrote Miss Pick, whose views Ivy in her first year also had reason to share:

We have been having 'collections' at the beginning of the term. It is quite a new departure, and not altogether a pleasing one, for at the outset one's mind is painfully lacking in great ideas. After perusing my Roman History paper, which contained a map, shewing as I thought, considerable knowledge and artistic skill, the Principal impolitely informed me that it was evident that I had not much talent for drawing, would I do that map again please. I cannot say that she went up much in my estimation after that remark. To make matters worse, the only question she seemed to take satisfaction in, was one I had written in the exact words of the book. She praised my 'vivid description' & I discreetly refrained from telling her the sources of it. (1 May 1903)

Miss Penrose was not one of the six members of staff at Holloway whom Ivy later transferred to the senior common room of Dolores' college, and who are identified in a first edition at R.H.C. which contains at the back a pencilled key made by the distinguished mediaeval historian, Helen Cam (who came up in 1904, two years after Ivy). Neither was the Vice-Principal Miss Guinness, who had coached Ivy, nor the cheerful, absent-minded Professor Donkin who lived with his sister opposite the main gates, lectured on classics and occasionally entertained the college with dramatic burlesques written and performed by himself and his sister. But the head of the classics department, Margaret Taylor (known as Cato to her pupils because 'her standards were Roman'), reappears in *Dolores* as 'the lecturer in classics, Miss Butler . . . a small, straight woman . . . whose parted hair leaves the forehead fully shown, and whose hazel eyes have humour in their rapid glancing'.[17] Miss Butler resembles Miss Taylor not only in looks but also in the severity which frightens Dolores' more nervous companions, in her fastidious scholarship, her disapproval of all forms of slovenliness and her fierce championship of women's rights; it is an affectionate portrait and suggests that, as Dolores' appreciation of Miss Butler's exacting standards leads to the slow growth of mutual esteem, so Ivy had been on good terms with Miss Taylor.

The classical textbooks which Ivy had owned at Holloway, marked on the fly-leaf with her name and preserved to the end of her life, reveal little of her likes and dislikes, unless perhaps one may deduce from a note in Haigh's *The Tragic Drama of the Greeks* that she had imbibed something of Miss Taylor's feminism. Haigh sums up Euripides' 'conception of a model wife' as one who 'is careless of personal adornment when her husband is absent, and when he is present treats him with unreflecting reverence. . . . She humours his frailties, treats his mistresses with kindness, offers her own breast to his bastard children, and by such "virtuous conduct" wins and retains his affection.'[18] Ivy ended this passage with a small exclamation mark in pencil, and added her own laconic caption: 'An ancient Kipling'. But otherwise her markings are purely practical, consisting largely of underlinings, pencil strokes in the margin, useful sub-headings (as 'Soph. introduced third actor', 'Eurip. born 480 or 485', 'Aesch's disregard of probabilities') designed apparently to save herself the trouble of re-reading. Marks on the texts themselves are confined more or less to translations of hard words and phrases. Most of the *Iliad*, books I–V of Plato's *Republic* and the *Oedipus Tyrannus* in Jebb's seven volume edition of Sophocles are fairly copiously annotated. The rest of Jebb is almost untouched, the pages of *Electra* and *Trachinae* still uncut. *Antigone*— which was not one of Ivy's set books but which she must have seen, if not helped to stage, in an ambitious production by the classics department at Holloway on 5 May 1905*—has been read and lightly marked

* 'The stage was erected at one end of the College Picture Gallery and so admirably was it placed and arranged that even before a word had been spoken one seemed to breathe the very air of ancient Greece. . . . There was something in the quiet of this scene, with its comeliness of white stone and green boughs, which lent an added

throughout; a footnote on Eidothea, sister to Cadmus, a stepmother who hated her husband's first wife and cruelly persecuted her two stepsons, is heavily scored for no apparent reason save perhaps as an indication of the direction in which Ivy's own interests already lay. Some of the passages she has underlined in Haigh—on Aeschylus' concern for the dangers of wealth, 'often leading men into insolence and pride'; on Sophocles' use of conscious and unconscious irony; on the conflicting motives discernible in Euripides' tyrants; on Aristotle's view of crime ('the . . . most suitable for dramatic treatment are those committed against friends or relations'); and on the role of the chorus in ancient and modern hands—make interesting reading in the light of her own later development of all these themes. But careful study of her annotations adds nothing to her own statement, made some forty years later: 'The Greek dramatists I read as a girl, as I was classically educated, and read them with the attention to each line necessitated by the state of my scholarship; and it is difficult to say how much soaked in, but I should think very likely something. I have not read them for many years—another result of the state of my scholarship.'[19]

There were three seconds and two thirds in the London honours school among the classical students in Ivy's year. Her family had confidently expected a first for Ivy but, by the time she took finals, Guy had died and her sisters thought that afterwards she lost all interest in examinations. His last illness began on Easter Sunday, 23 April 1905, when he said to his mother that he 'wouldn't go to early service as he wasn't feeling himself'. Ivy went back to Holloway the same week for what was to have been her last term, leaving the whole family save her mother and Noel in bed with influenza. Colds, chest complaints and quinzies in one form or another were, as Ivy wrote later, 'a thing we are all very prone to',[20] and there probably seemed nothing especially alarming about the start of this particular epidemic. Minnie, who (with Daisy as under nurse) had charge of the sick rooms, 'never took her clothes off for weeks' and nursed Guy night and day: 'She was *incredibly* tough and incredibly devoted. Above all to Guy.' Guy, too weak to do more than lie still and listen, had asked for readings from the Bible.

---

poignancy to the horror and pity that filled the mind when human anger and remorse had driven away peace. . . .' (R.H.C. *College Letter* 1905.) Ivy was not in the cast but she must have found it hard to avoid helping in some capacity since the production, which was directed by Miss Taylor, had occupied the entire department for a whole term and was generally held to mark the final triumph of Classics over all other departments.

'One tires of all other books but never of the Bible' was one of his last reported sayings, and perhaps one of the reasons for Ivy's later bitterness towards the religion which had comforted her brothers but which left her without consolation. Variations on the same theme return throughout her books in conversation between brother and sister:

    'We may die at any moment.'
    'Not you and I. It is other people who may die young.'
    'Why should we be exceptions?'
    'I don't know. I wonder what the reasons are?'
    'You don't think you and I will have an eternity together?'
    'No, but we shall have until we are seventy. And there is no difference.'
    'Can you bear not to have the real thing?'
    'No,' said his sister.[21]

    The four youngest Compton Burnetts had been put to bed together in one room like a hospital ward and Topsy was feared to be dangerously ill, but it was Guy who developed double pneumonia, too swiftly for Ivy to be recalled in time from college. Before she reached home, he was dead. She spent the next four months at Hove, returned to Holloway that autumn, was awarded a Founder's scholarship[22] in April 1906, and took a second in finals the following summer. 'Guy and Ivy were everything to each other when they were young,' said their sister Juliet; and Julian Mitchell's tentative comment perhaps goes as far as anyone can on her life without him: 'Of the Latin poets, she liked Catullus best: I wonder if this might be because of the celebrated line "*Atque in perpetuum, frater, ave atque vale*".'[23]

2

'PEOPLE WHO WERE born too late to experience in boyhood and adolescence the intellectual and moral pressure of Victorianism have no idea of the feeling of fog and fetters which weighed one down,' wrote Leonard Woolf,[24] who was born in 1880. 'It was not a question of

unhappiness so much as of restriction and oppression—the subtle un-
perceived weight of the circumambient air,' wrote Lytton Strachey,[25]
born in the same year. Neither had suffered an especially unhappy
childhood, and both escaped earlier than most into the atmosphere of
spiritual, sexual and religious freedom beginning to flourish at Trinity
where, in the first few years of the century, both were regarded with
horrified loathing by their more conservative contemporaries at
Cambridge. No wonder if this sense of conscious revolt had not yet
touched Holloway. Girls had been their brothers' inferiors for too long,
and were too thankful to be educated at all, to care much for questioning the doctrines of patience, obedience and self-sacrifice which had
traditionally governed their sex. The cheerful scepticism prevalent at
Cambridge was something which does not seem to have reached Ivy
till much later, perceived and percolated through Noel at King's.

In the summer of 1906, when Ivy arrived home from college to help
teach the children and coach Noel for little-go, the feeling of fog and
fetters must have seemed to close round her on all sides. Her mother,
taking the practical view that talents so expensively polished should not
go to waste, had removed the four younger girls from school and Ivy
began without enthusiasm to supervise lessons in the schoolroom. Noel
had been working alone since Guy's death under a new tutor, a Mr
Bullick of whom neither his pupil nor Ivy thought highly. 'Noel always
had a very strong imaginative life, he did have that, but in a family
considered rather clever he was thought to be backward, or on the
backward side,' said his sister, Vera. At eighteen, his chances of getting
into King's were held to be touch-and-go: 'Well, candidly, Mrs
Compton Burnett, he has very poor ability,' said the despondent tutor,
who was master at a prep school up the road and had been retained to
teach Noel history since a classical discipline evidently suited neither his
tastes nor his capacities. But, whether in response to his mother's urgent
emotional pressure or because Ivy had taken his education firmly in
hand (Noel's friends at King's always afterwards believed that she had
coached him, a rumour confirmed by her sisters), Noel did somehow
scrape through little-go, later taking a double first and the Gladstone
prize, whereupon his mother, charmed by her son's success—'it is of
course a very great pleasure to us all, and I am particularly glad for him,
it will encourage him so much, having lost his father and elder brother
he stands very much alone, and he has always been so brave,' she wrote
to Noel's Cambridge mentor, Oscar Browning—fondly recalled that
the disobliging Mr Bullick had himself taken a second at Dublin.

What seems to have happened is that Noel, who had been 'quite satisfied until Guy died to be the inconspicuous one of the three', was a slow mover whose gifts, like his father's, developed late but to spectacular effect. As a child he had been bored by lessons, scarcely read a book, remained absorbed in his own private dream world, contentedly overshadowed by his brilliant elder brother and sister. His arrival at Cambridge coincided with a simultaneous emotional and intellectual awakening, when he suddenly found himself with energies untapped and whole new worlds unexplored. One of the reasons was no doubt his brother's death. This was the explanation he gave later for abandoning all extraneous pursuits under pressure of work in the term before his Tripos: 'I may perhaps say that it is not entirely for my own sake . . . I cannot forget the bitter disappointment caused to my mother by the death of my elder brother. Any small worldly success which I might gain would be to her perhaps the only recompense that would be still possible.'[26] Another was the stimulus of intellectual pleasures hitherto unknown, for which he had acquired already a voracious appetite in the year before he went up to King's. At his entrance examination in the autumn of 1906, he had met Oscar Browning, 'a man of bad character and European fame' according to Rupert Brooke[27] who had rooms that term (the same rooms as Noel two years later) on the landing opposite O.B. O.B., who boasted with some reason that he had single-handed reformed King's College itself not to mention the Cambridge history school, was then a few years short of enforced retirement. Vastly corpulent, prolix and obstinate, resembling in looks a degenerate Roman emperor and in unbounded egotism his hero Napoleon, accustomed to bathe naked in the Cam (he had once been bathed in his own bathroom by the Prince of Wales in person), to hold *levées* in his rooms *en déshabille*, to sleep through tutorials under a red handkerchief and to teach by inspiration rather than by formal precept or instruction, O.B.'s vocation and delight was the guidance of young men: 'His information might be erroneous, his method of conveying it intolerable, but he did lead them to discover themselves and to bring to birth what would have lain in embryo,' wrote E. M. Forster.[28] 'He took these young men and made them into young Fellows,' said Raisley Moorsom, a friend of Noel's at King's, 'and Noel was the last one he made'.

Mr Browning had picked up this latest protégé at the entrance examination (as was his habit—another nervous scholarship candidate has described O.B. stumping through the examination hall and enquiring in a fiendishly unsettling whisper, 'How do you like the paper? I set it'),[29] and by the following March Noel was writing diffidently from Hove to take up his promise of advice: '. . . as I realize what a privilege it would be, and what an advantage to me in the future, I venture to ask if I may come next Tuesday' (22 March 1907). O.B., who spent his vacations at Bexhill a few miles along the coast from Hove, duly granted this request and laid down a stiff programme of reading, beginning with Maine's *Ancient Law* and moving on to Gibbon's *Decline and Fall* on which Noel submitted a weekly report that summer and, having finished all six volumes in almost as many weeks, promptly re-read the whole on O.B.'s instructions. In the next few years the friendship prospered not only at Cambridge but on regular visits, swimming expeditions (O.B. had a beach hut at Bexhill named Tilsit, 'so-called from the floating pavilion on the Memel in which Napoleon had signed his treaty with Alexander of Russia') and reading parties in the vacation. O.B. lunched several times and once spent the night with the Compton Burnetts at Hove, where the younger girls entertained him with Mozart sonatas and their mother placed his photograph (sent in characteristically regal acknowledgement of her hospitality the month before Noel went up to King's) in the drawing-room. Noel's letters in these years are interspersed with references to Topsy's prowess on the fiddle, and to O.B.'s kind enquiries as to Ivy's progress on her novel.

Impossible to say what Ivy thought in return of this witty, celebrated, half fraudulent, half genuinely inspired and wholly worldly mountebank, so far removed from the academic manner—'a something of greater than the common earnestness and ease'[30]—which she had known at Holloway, and later described with admiration in *Dolores*. Ivy at this time is remembered by her sisters as generally silent, but 'when she was in the mood she had such wit and sparkle. She could hit off anyone, hit the nail on the head—it wasn't always very kind.' She had been allotted her own study or wrote at the schoolroom table, working already on her novel though not even Noel was allowed to read it. It is tempting to see traces of Ivy's own experience in Dolores' sad return from college to a peevish and disgruntled stepmother demanding that she teach the smaller children, a morose father and a disconsolate younger brother all depressingly unchanged in the setting she herself had left 'four years earlier, on the threshold of her womanhood. Now that womanhood seemed old. Those four bright, troubled years, which had left this early world the same! As she spoke and moved beneath the pressure of her pain, she found herself simply dwelling through a dream on their difference. . . .'[31]

Certainly Ivy's own lot in these years must have seemed, like Dolores', a straitened one. Distractions at Hove were few and limited. In the first week of May 1907, she had travelled up to London accompanied by her mother and Noel to receive her degree, a triumph let fall with modest pride by her brother in a letter to O.B. The following autumn Noel left home for Cambridge, becoming in his first term an active member of O.B.'s Political Society, speaking regularly at the Union, joining the curious and exclusive King's society of poetical revolutionaries called the Carbonari, and rapidly making friends for the first time in his life. The new world which absorbed her brother must have made Ivy's future—immured in a dull provincial town without friends or diversions (unless, as Mrs Elliott believed, she attended Miss Laura's literature class for old girls at Addiscombe College)—seem even drabber by comparison. Noel's weekly letters to his mother were read aloud to the assembled family at Hove, and his friends from King's came to stay in the vacations before Mrs Compton Burnett became too ill, and the house too wretched, to receive them. Otherwise breaks in the routine at home were confined to occasional visits from relations and to the family's annual holidays, when they spent six or eight weeks each summer at a different country vicarage: at Brythdir near Dolgelly in 1907 ('We are in a very wild district here. Mountains are on every side. The Welsh language is prevalent,' wrote Noel to O.B. 'I think I heard you say you were acquainted with thirty languages; I suppose Welsh is not of the number'); at Dent near Sedbergh the next year (this was the family's first visit to Yorkshire, and perhaps a clue to the setting of *Dolores* in a Yorkshire vicarage, since Ivy must then have been still at work on the novel which was finished by the following summer); and at Sourton on Dartmoor in 1909.

Noel was meanwhile immersed in the literary and intellectual ferment brought about, among the more adventurous members of his own and Ivy's generation, by the books of Henry James, Hardy, Butler, Swinburne, Meredith and Bernard Shaw. His circle at King's was largely non-athletic, anti-philistine and hotly concerned with modern literature. He himself was writing poetry, as was his closest friend Jack Beresford (second cousin to the novelist J. D. Beresford, who became a few years later a considerable arbiter of contemporary taste, lectured on such subjects as 'Experiment in the Novel' and was the first person to encourage Dorothy Richardson in whom he saw an English heir to Proust). Arthur Waley, whose visits were remembered by Ivy's sisters with especial pleasure ('We always knew we should have a very gay time when he came down'), was later a distinguished poet, and Rupert Brooke, a friend of Noel's and one year ahead of him at King's, read aloud his early verses at meetings of the Carbonari. Much of this excitement rubbed off at home, where Noel shared it with his younger sisters. It was Noel who introduced them to Ibsen and Strindberg, Masefield, 'any number of books', paintings, plays and new ideas: 'It affected us to the bottom of our souls. In our family that kind of culture didn't exist inside the home. Noll arrived on the scene with a whole new world of literature.' But what came as an astonishment and delight to Vera and Juliet in early adolescence was apparently received with less enthusiasm by Ivy. Perhaps the revelation had arrived too late to stir her as it stirred the others. She had stoutly resisted when Noel urged her to write verse not prose and her own tastes, always more scholarly than his, seem to have settled somewhat earlier in a rather different direction.

She had been reading Plato's *Timaeus* the year after she left college (her parallel Greek and English text is signed 'I. Compton-Burnett June 1907' and the first part, judging by her pencil marks in the margin which stop abruptly half way through, has been read with close attention) but 'she had abandoned classics—that was a chapter she had closed', said her sister Vera. 'I don't remember her working, or reading even, she was always writing.' For years before that she had been accustomed, like her sisters, to read and re-read the classic nineteenth-century novels which were practically the only books they owned. When she left college her mother had given her £50 ('or anyhow a sum') with which to found a library, and she spent it on her own complete editions of Jane Austen and George Eliot. These two, with Thackeray and Hardy, Charlotte Brontë, Richardson and Mrs Gaskell, remained her staple favourites to the end of her life. She was reading *Vanity Fair* a week or so before she died,[32] and both her sisters remembered the tart flavour she had given Becky Sharp ('She liked that sort of bite') when she read the book aloud to them after Sunday supper in the schoolroom more than sixty years before. Trollope had her guarded approval ('Yes, he is good. He is so good one wonders why he isn't better'), Dickens is several times firmly shown off in her early books and so is Henry James ('I hate people whose golden bowls are broken'),[33] whose achievements she invariably deprecated and whose influence she repeatedly denied. Samuel Butler had clearly acted on her, together with the sceptical humour peculiar to the Cambridge mind and more particularly to Noel's friend and tutor Goldsworthy Lowes Dickinson, by the time she came to write her second novel in the early 'twenties. But Butler's influence had not apparently reached her—or, if it had, her imagination remained untouched—in the years between the autumn of 1906 and the summer of 1909 when she wrote *Dolores*.

The book is saturated in notions of self-abnegation—the temptations of the spirit and the flesh set against the austere claims of conscience—common among the heroines of at least a generation earlier. Dolores' struggles begin at nineteen when she leaves home for college and end at thirty-three when she looks back on a life of useless sacrifice in which she has successively crushed her own aspirations, her hopes of independence and, on five separate occasions, her chances of love and marriage for the sake of 'service to her kin': 'Dolores' survey of a crisis in her own experience was primitive and stern. For others might be honest doubt, and blameless wavering at a parting of the ways: for herself there was one road to be taken, and another to be left. On the one side lay effort for strangers . . . on the other the claims of kindred, of her father and her father's children.'[34]

The book's tone is repellently extreme. Its moral doctrines are inhuman and its language the exalted terminology of religious passion and self-mortification: Dolores' voice is 'the voice of one taking a vow' and, although 'the sacrifice of her choice, lived day by day and silently, was hard to the brink of bending her will', she remains, regardless of the fact that 'her own experience was growing vexed to the utter clouding of her soul' as of the suffering she brings to others, 'faithful through all to her old religion of the duty she owed her kind'.

But Dolores' clenched hands, her trembling limbs, white lips, lined brow and face prematurely aged in nights of sleepless torment are by no means peculiar to herself. All these symptoms recur regularly in the novels of both lesser and greater lady novelists over the previous half century and more. Charlotte M. Yonge and Mrs Humphry Ward, to name but two, each of whom exerted immense influence in her day, deal in precisely the kind of anguished conflict between home and inclination, thankless spinsterhood and selfish freedom, which scourges Dolores as 'she wrestled along in the silent hours . . . neither weeping nor rising to pace the ground; but lying with dry eyes and worn face, and hands clutching the coverings tensely.' Ethel May in *The Daisy Chain* and its sequel (published in 1856 and 1864) and Catherine Leyburn in *Robert Elsmere* (published in 1888) are both sadly prone to nightly 'wrestles' ('But no wrestle had ever been as hard as this! And with what fierce suddenness had it come upon her! . . . She laid her head on her knees trembling').* Both shrink from the horrid tendency to free thought bred among their male contemporaries 'at the University' and both, like Dolores, renounce the love of an Oxford man for reasons which seem to the twentieth-century reader—above all to one acquainted with the later work of I. Compton-Burnett—quite preposterously perverse.

But Ivy in her early twenties was still, at any rate in her literary output, almost wholly unoriginal. There is the same imitative facility in the high solemnity of *Dolores* as in the set of album verses written 'To Vera on her sixteenth birthday, 23 September 1907, from her sister Ivy':

> Sixteen summers passing swiftly,
> Borne on childhood's fleeting wing,
> Have they taught you truly, Vera,
> Lessons from the early Spring? . . .
>
> Will you pause today to ponder
> What the years to come will yield?
> Will your eyes with wistful wonder
> Turn to chapters unrevealed? . . .
>
> Well has childhood done its duty,
> Steadfast at your side has stood;
> Faithfully its care has kept you,
> Clasped you closely while it could.
> Never may it break the spell,
> Never bid a last farewell,
> Ever may its voices reach you,
> Through your years of womanhood.

Among the 'lessons from the early Spring' which Ivy, as much as Vera, had learnt not to question was a stern sense, maintained to the end of her life, of her own and other people's obligation to their families. At Holloway she and Miss Harvey had remonstrated vainly with their friend Miss Bremner on what both saw as a clear dereliction of duty: 'They were of the opinion—they were very decided about it—that I

* *Robert Elsmere* by Mrs Humphry Ward, p.100. A similar battle is fought over the same ground to the same conclusion in *The Daisy Chain*, 'as Ethel tossed about listening to the perpetual striking of all the Oxford clocks, until daylight had begun to shine in. . .' (p.387).

oughtn't to have come to college. Because I was the eldest of the family and should have stayed at home.' Dolores' 'instinctive loyalty of service to that rigorous lofty thing, to which we give duty as a name' seems to have derived from Dr Burnett whose definition of 'Our Duty', laid down in a lecture to his medical students the year before Ivy was born, coincides (save only for his reference to 'our holy religion') exactly with his daughter's:

> It is duty that places me here today; duty it is that brings many of you here also . . . there is a beauty in duty peculiarly its own—that moral beauty which makes one like to roam alone in the stilly eve or sit by oneself in the dark. When a man has done his duty purely and simply, he has a serene satisfaction not afforded by mere honour or public applause. Indeed, in this life, next to our holy religion, nothing will stand us in such good stead as a sweet consciousness of having done our duty.[35]

This view of the moral beauty and imperative nature of duty, especially when associated with roaming in the gloaming, was of course George Eliot's;* and, though this kind of relationship between master and pupil is comparatively common among painters or composers, it is seldom that one finds one major author submerged so completely in the personality of another as I. Compton-Burnett, at the start of her career, in George Eliot.

It is not simply that the gaunt and angular Dolores possesses an uncomfortably large share of that 'strange impressiveness' with which George Eliot habitually endowed her outwardly plain ladies. Considering the number of more or less undistinguished copies strewn about the fiction of the period, there is nothing especially remarkable in a heroine who, plagued by a sense of duty keener and more casuistical even than Dorothea Casaubon's, set on a course of puritanical self-punishment

---

* See W. H. Myers' celebrated description of walking one evening in 1873 in the Fellows' Garden at Trinity, Cambridge, with George Eliot who, 'stirred somewhat beyond her wont, and taking as her text the three words which have been used so often as the inspiring trumpet-calls of men,—the words, *God, Immortality, Duty,*—pronounced, with terrible earnestness, how inconceivable was the *first,* how unbelievable the *second,* and yet how peremptory and absolute the *third.* Never, perhaps, have sterner accents affirmed the sovereignty of impersonal and unrecompensing Law. I listened and night fell; her grave, majestic countenance turned towards me like a sybil's in the gloom; it was as though she withdrew from my grasp, one by one, the two scrolls of promise, and left me the third scroll only, awful with inevitable fates.' (*George Eliot* by Gordon S. Haight, O.U.P. 1968, p.464.)

yet more dour than Maggie Tulliver's, lacks the independent life of either. Further borrowings in *Dolores* may readily be multiplied: the luckless Perdita is marked down by her creator for the kind of doom which inevitably awaits George Eliot's pretty, flighty feather-brains like Hetty Sorrel or Rosamond Lydgate; Dolores' hero and beloved, Sigismund Claverhouse, embodies in one person the unaccountable attractions of neglect, deformity, advancing age, poverty and other social drawbacks associated, in *The Mill on the Floss*, *Daniel Deronda* and *Middlemarch*, with artistic or creative yearnings; acrimonious scenes between Dolores' stepmother and her middle-aged sister recall the covert warfare waged throughout Maggie's childhood among the equally uncharitable sisters Tulliver, Deane, Glegg and Pullet. The author of *Dolores* is evidently happier in the vein of comical exuberance opened for her by the last than at the rhetorical sublime, where she is altogether clumsier and more turgid than George Eliot ever was. But her debt is also more specific. Dolores' home in a country village owing something perhaps to the summer of 1908 spent by the Compton Burnetts at Dent in Yorkshire, and rather more to the topography of Great Clacton where Ivy as a child had visited her Blackie cousins, seems to have been taken in the first place directly from a literary source. Actual details of life in Dolores' Millfield (the combination of church, brand-new Wesleyan chapel and disused barn made over into 'a meeting place at general disposal for religious ends' and based pre-sumably on the Coppins Hall barn used for Methodist gatherings at Clacton before Dr Burnett gave the land to build a chapel; the social awkwardness arising from collisions between church and chapel factions; the feuds tirelessly prosecuted among rival local preachers) were unmistakeably supplied by the doings of Ivy's own evangelical relations. But it is surely not coincidence that the opening sentence of *Dolores*—'It is a daily thing: a silent, unvisited church-yard; bordering the garden of the parsonage; and holding a church whose age and interest spare our words . . . and at some moment of its lying in sight an open grave with its mourners'—brings to mind another funeral scene, identical in tone and treatment as in personnel.

This is the open grave, in a church-yard also bordering the vicarage, which comes at the end of 'The Sad Fortunes of the Rev. Amos Barton', the first story in George Eliot's first book, *Scenes of Clerical Life*. The chief mourner in each case is the parson of the parish, attended by a congregation whose former disaffection towards their pastor is momen-tarily subdued in pity for the loss of his wife. Both widowers stand with heaving breasts in grief further harrowed by remorse, and each receives a pale consolation from his eldest child—the Rev. Amos Barton from the nine-year-old Patty who closely resembles her dead mother, the Rev. Cleveland Hutton from 'the nine-year-old Dolores, with her mother's voice, and her mother's face, and her fitting part in her mother's name of sorrows!' Points in common between George Eliot's Mr Barton and I. Compton-Burnett's Mr Hutton seem too many to be accidental: both have been affectionate husbands and conscientious pastors to an ungrateful flock, both were educated at Cambridge, both wait vainly in their mid-thirties for preferment, driven meanwhile through penury to debt, and both are recommended to the reader's attention in similarly off-hand terms:

> The Rev. Amos Barton, whose sad fortunes I have undertaken to relate, was, you perceive, in no respect an ideal or exceptional character, and perhaps I am doing a bold thing to bespeak your sympathy on behalf of a man who was so very far from remarkable. . . . Yet these commonplace people—many of them—bear a conscience, and have felt the sublime prompting to do the painful right; they have their unspoken sorrows, and their sacred joys; their hearts have perhaps gone out towards their firstborn, and they have mourned over the irreclaimable dead. Nay, is there not a pathos in their very insignificance,—in our comparison of their dim and narrow existence with the glorious possibilities of that human nature which they share?[36]

> No; there was nothing in the Rev. Cleveland Hutton to mark him a man apart. But it does not follow there was nothing about him to be written or read. Our deepest experience is not less deep, that it is common to our race. . . . There had been a strong, woman's heart to cleave to his own, through the struggles of the lingering unbeneficed time, the loss of his firstborn, and other things finding a place in his ordinary human lot. Standing by the open grave, dreading for the numbness of grief to pass, and leave him the facing of the future that was dark, he was as fitting a mark for compassion as if his name were to live.[37]

It is difficult to avoid the conclusion that Ivy intended a conscious tribute in choosing to take up the fortunes of her central character at precisely the point where George Eliot's concluding paragraph left off: 'Patty alone remains by her father's side, and makes the evening sunshine of his life.' This parting glimpse of Patty, prematurely lined at thirty and vowed like Dolores to spinsterhood for her parent's sake, is appended in the nature of a coda; just as the opening chapter of *Dolores* forms a pendant to the story proper which begins ten years later (with a second wife and stepchildren already installed at the parsonage by chapter two) and follows the process whereby Dolores' determination to make 'evening sunshine' is foiled at every turn. Both works are set back a quarter century or so from the time of writing—almost the only borrowing which (after a brief patch of indecision with *Pastors and Masters* and *Brothers and Sisters*) Ivy later kept, setting her novels to the end of her career in the same period as *Dolores*. Both writers start in the same slow focus ('If you had entered this straggling village at the time—somewhere in the latter half of the nineteenth century—when its parsonage was the home of the Reverend Cleveland Hutton . . .'), assume the same stiffish intimacy with the reader, and alternate between lugubrious solemnity and a vivid, mocking, generally patronizing gaiety at the expense of the lower orders. I. Compton-Burnett's Millfield, with its teeming clerical life, stand-offish clergy and jealous evangelists vying for attention from argumentative and sharply critical parishioners, might be George Eliot's Shepperton thirty or forty years on. Dissent had been the principal thorn in the side of the established church at Shepperton ('that notable plan of introducing anti-dissenting books into his Lending Library did not in the least appear to have bruised the head of Dissent, though it had certainly made Dissent strongly inclined to bite the Rev. Amos's heel');[38] drink and Roman Catholicism ('You ask me . . . whether I consider—the spread of Roman Catholicism—a *serious* thing. My answer is—that I consider it a *hopeless* thing, a damnable thing, a thing that is sucking the very life-blood of our religion') are held in equal loathing among the dissenting population of Millfield.

Prominence on Millfield platforms is anxiously disputed between the two ardent amateur preachers, Dr Cassell and Herbert Blackwood ('the art of oratory had become Mr Blackwood's second nature—it had been rather foreign to his first nature'), linked in an uneasy but indissoluble alliance by their identical views and the fondness of each for the sound of his own voice, the natural resignation each feels at the sound of the other's being tempered by their mutual reluctance to forego a potentially sympathetic audience. The originals of both may be easily identified among Ivy's own acquaintance. Just as George Eliot had drawn the plots and characters of her early stories from her country childhood, so Ivy's family background provided her with the more engaging absurdities of nonconformist antics in *Dolores*, with the complex series of intermarriages between Blackwoods and Huttons,* and with an intimate knowledge of the step-relationship which bedevils her heroine's home life. What she learnt from George Eliot† is the combination of minute observation and humorous assurance which informs all three stories in *Scenes of Clerical Life* as much as later scenes from low life in *The Mill on the Floss* or *Middlemarch*. The resemblance is at times uncannily close, so much so that the evening party given by the Blackwoods to introduce the new Methodist minister ('a wholesome little man of forty with smooth, red cheeks and twinkling little eyes, excellent both as a man and a Methodist, as his fathers had been before him, but falling short of them in not being excellent as a grocer as well') to the Huttons ('Mr Hutton shook hands with his host, gave a covered glance at the Wesleyan minister, observed to Dr Cassell that the evening was dry, and fell into silence; feeling that the initiative due from an ordained Churchman in Dissenting company was at an end') presents the weird spectacle of I. Compton-Burnett in George Eliot's skin, and on the point of shedding it.

For it is in these comic interludes—barely more than a sideline in the book's serious business—that the immature author of *Dolores* comes closest to the urbanity of her later novels, and more particularly in recriminations between the second Mrs Hutton and her sister Mrs Blackwood: 'They were sisters in the fullest sense. . . . They were, in a word, in that stage of affinity where, with human creatures as with other complex things, contact is another word for clashing . . . the sisters' dialogue was charged with hidden currents. It became a series of thrusts with verbal weapons seemingly innocent, but carrying each its poisoned point.'[39] What is here laboriously described is precisely the kind of concealed collision which, when once she had learnt to catch and pin it in the act, provided the material of her mature and often

---

* Herbert Blackwood in *Dolores* had married his fourth cousin whose sister Sophia later became the second Mrs Hutton; Ivy's uncle Robert Blackie had married his second cousin whose sister Katharine later became the second Mrs Compton Burnett. In the course of the book the young Blackwoods, Elsa and Herbert, marry their first cousins, Bertram and Evelyn Hutton—a connection suggested presumably by the dual marriage in 1875 of Ivy's uncle and aunt, Elizabeth and Charles Rees, to their second cousins, Robert and Esther Blackie (see family tree).

† Fifty years later Ivy told an interviewer that she had read a good deal of George Eliot round about 1911, and less since: 'I like her books very much—the fresh and lively part of them—not the instructive or moralising part. . . .' (*Review of Eng. Lit.*, October 1962.)

terrifying triumphs. Tiffs between the sisters in *Dolores*, each bringing
up her guns like generals who have spent a lifetime fighting over the
same ground, remind one on occasion of Jane Austen as much as of
George Eliot, and rather more of either than of I. Compton-Burnett's
later manner—but already by fits and starts, in the malicious small talk
tossed from hand to hand at the Blackwoods' party or in Mrs Hutton's
peevish efforts at domestic friction, one may catch glimpses if not of her
later passion, at any rate of her later coruscating wit.

The book contains several undeveloped instances of types later to be
fully explored. Dolores' stepmother is an obvious example; Perdita,
whose half-conscious falsity looks forward to the more sinister equivo-
cations practised by a long line of unscrupulous flirts from Sybil
Edgeworth in *A House and Its Head* to Verena Gray in *A Father and His
Fate*, is another; and Dolores' moody, deceitful, increasingly cynical
brother Bertram provides a first faint sketch of other spiteful and dissatisfied younger brothers like Clement Gaveston in *A Family and a
Fortune* or Esmond Donne in *Elders and Betters*. There are even occasional, faltering variations on favourite themes, such as the thorny
question of food and shelter on which conversation is apt to run in later
books: 'I have been so ashamed of being alive and well, and having to
be housed and clothed and fed and provided for. It really is not reasonable . . . when people have to be provided for, death is the only thing.'[40]
But the difference could hardly be more striking if one sets this kind of
casual irony, exchanged with an expertise born of long practice
between brother and sister in the later books, beside the awkwardness
caused in *Dolores* by Bertram's similar remark:

> 'Father takes credit to himself for having kept me sheltered and
> fed, while I should have starved or died of exposure, if he had not.'
> 'I suppose his income is really very much less,' said Dolores, in
> nervous uncertainty how to respond.[41]

Nervous uncertainty is marked on almost every page of a work
pieced together from a ragbag of styles, varying from epigrams as near
as this one on Dr Cassell—'He had so long interpreted a conversation
as a didactic utterance by himself, that argument on equal terms struck
him as deliberate baiting'—to his startling descent into fruity Irish
anecdote ('"Talking of the drink in connection with Irishmen," said
Dr Cassell . . . "have you heard of the Irishman in the barn and his
bottle of whisky?"'). Phrases like 'this oft-lived heart-throb', 'a

generous dower of brunette comeliness' or 'the prime knit with a nobler soul' suggest no more than a copious acquaintance with Victorian sentimental fiction, but elsewhere the author seems, like Samuel Beckett's Mrs Rooney, to be struggling with a dead language. The book reads at times as though she were alternately translating from the Latin—'From toil for her bread, unfitted for her tenderness, he had taken her to comfort unbought of weariness' (meaning that he had married a girl obliged to earn her own living)—and coining her own Homeric epithets, as 'smile-begetting naïveté', 'the outwardly genial, bread-winning woman', 'no power of hiding that which was within with lip-spoken words'.

This artificiality no doubt reflects Ivy's secluded background (her brother Noel was noted for the same stilted turns of phrase, marked in his case by a Gibbonian pomposity, when he first came up to King's) and academic training. Slovenliness in speech, lax grammar and colloquial usage had been heavily frowned upon at Holloway, notably by the Misses Taylor, Péchinet and Block (Miss Block had once reproved a colleague for using the expression 'jolly well': 'You know perfectly well, Miss X, there is nothing whatever jolly in your sentiments on this matter'), all three of whom provided models for women dons at Dolores' Oxford college. The atmosphere in this section of the book reflects Holloway as closely as life in and around the Millfield parsonage mirrors the world of Ivy's own relations at Hove and Clacton. One would guess, from her habit of peopling the novel with minor characters drawn from life, that her college friend Miss Bremner (who had 'been told I am "in it"' by other Hollowegians who had read *Dolores* and recognized the likeness) was the original for Dolores' astute and witty companion, Felicia Murray; and that Ivy had liked Miss Cunningham and Miss Frost, two of the staff at Holloway who reappear in *Dolores* as the amiable Miss Dorrington and the humorous Miss Greenlow.

But, apart from the heroine herself who evidently in some sense embodies her creator, the most intriguing of these portraits from a biographical point of view is the man who awakens Dolores' 'deeper heart-throbs', Sigismund Claverhouse, 'the creature who filled her heart and life, and on whom her lips were sealed.'[42] This is a hopeless, though not ultimately an unrequited love. Claverhouse, long revered from afar as a dramatist of genius, gives Dolores tutorials on the Greek drama ('she stood, with limbs that trembled, at the door behind which he awaited her alone') and later on his own plays, falls incongruously in love with her friend Perdita and, when Perdita dies in childbirth after a disastrous nine months' marriage, turns at last to Dolores who thrice cruelly rejects him in the name of family duty. The depth and bitterness of Dolores' protracted sufferings in this affair might suggest some underlying personal experience on her author's part but, of all the portraits in the book, Claverhouse is the hardest to identify. Helen Cam's key names him tentatively as: '? (looks only) T. Seccombe—visiting lecturer in History 1905–'. Thomas Seccombe was appointed visiting lecturer at Holloway in Ivy's last two years; he had been assistant editor to Leslie Stephen in the 'nineties on the *Dictionary of National Biography*, becoming thereafter author, editor, critic and a regular contributor to the *Bookman*—in short, a fairly typical Georgian man of letters whose heart, like Claverhouse's, does not seem to have lain in an academic career which culminated in his holding a chair of English literature first at the Royal Military Academy, Sandhurst, and later at Kingston in Canada. But Claverhouse, a taciturn and misanthropic recluse living alone in penury with his aged mother, cannot have borne more than the most superficial resemblance to Seccombe who was considerably younger, a genial host and a familiar figure at London literary gatherings, cheerful, sociable, expansive and already happily married with several children when he came to Holloway.*

Another possible model is Mr Salt, the tutor whom Ivy had shared with her brothers and who later coached her alone at Addiscombe College. Mr Salt, a cripple with 'an ethereal face, a look of great suffering and spirituality', seems to have had points in common with Claverhouse, whose 'aspect was grotesque at a glance; for his massive body and arms were at variance with stunted lower limbs, and his shoulders were twisted. His face was dark and rugged of feature; his eyes piercing, but unevenly set . . . his clothes and hair unkempt.'† Ivy's sisters both agreed that this description fitted Mr Salt, whom Ivy had evidently

---

* Seccombe (1866–1923) was, however, a generous talent-spotter among his youthful friends who met brother men-of-letters at his house (and sometimes worked off their own high spirits in boisterous games like 'Up Jenkins', see *The Early Life of Alec Waugh* by Himself, Cassell, 1962, p.90). It was he who introduced Frank Swinnerton to literary circles, and he who found a publisher for Alec Waugh's best-seller, *The Loom of Youth*, in 1917; and perhaps he encouraged Ivy, who was already known at college as one who meant to write.

† *Dolores*, p.111. Considering Claverhouse's evident staginess, one might well argue that he owes as much to Dorothea's lover, the elderly reclusive Mr Casaubon in *Middlemarch*—or for that matter to Maggie's, the crippled poet Phillip Wakem in *The Mill on the Floss*—as to either Salt or Seccombe.

admired: 'He *was* rather untidy. He was very crippled, and twisted in the shoulders, and he had a suffering face.' Further details of Claverhouse's strange ménage and stranger marriage may possibly have been supplied by a legend, current at Holloway in Ivy's day, concerning the elderly lecturer in physics who lived with his mother outside the college gates, had once been engaged to a girl at the college, and whose life was said to have been blighted tragically for love when his marriage was broken off in dramatic circumstances on the wedding morning. It seems likely that Ivy incorporated in Claverhouse elements taken from all these, and perhaps from other sources—from Salt her first introduction as a child to the heady pleasures of the mind and spirit, from Seccombe her first glimpse of a life lived outside domestic confines in the larger world of letters. But neither Mr Salt's private tuition nor Mr Seccombe's contacts with literary London, his seven hundred articles in the *D.N.B.* and his *'Bookman' History of English Literature* will provide a wholly satisfactory explanation of Dolores' attitude to 'the one, whom her young reverence had placed apart from the world, in the sphere which youth creates for those it sees as the world's great',[43] and whose lectures leave her pale, dazed and shaken with the effort to conceal 'tumult within her'. The most one can deduce is that Claverhouse's very existence points to a capacity in his creator at this stage in her career for ardent hero worship; and that, if Ivy had singled out at Holloway or Hove a particular object for her affections, she would scarcely have revealed it.

Probably in any case Claverhouse owed as much to her evidently vague but awe-inspiring notions of the nobility of the artist as to any factual model. His artistic genius provides, indeed, a curious comparison with what she herself long afterwards called 'my sort of dramatic novel, something between a novel and a play':[44] Claverhouse's plays are 'obscure' and 'very profound. Read as they should be read, they take one very deep.' They are not intended for the stage, ignored by all save a handful of readers and declaimed aloud by their author in a voice by turns swelling, trembling and tearful. They seem to be somewhat macabre chamber tragedies of a kind not uncommon in late Victorian literature, involving characters named Althea and Jannetta in sudden death or madness. What is interesting is that (if one discounts the romantic twitching fits which overtake the dramatist 'in the clutch of the creative spirit') Ivy seems already to have had some inkling of her own later working methods. Claverhouse draws his dramas from recollections of past sorrow, a gift which leaves him during the upheaval attendant on his marriage and returns only with the comparative tranquillity in which he writes his final play: 'His own deepest experience, which had lain covered from sympathy's touch, was bared to the probing of the world, which had shown itself unloving.'[45]

This seems a fairly accurate description of the frame of mind which produced the mature novels of I. Compton-Burnett. Two of her closest friends[46] in her last years recognized, when they came to read *Dolores*, more of Ivy's private character—her intense shyness, her shrinking from 'sympathy's touch', her tenderness and vulnerability beneath the defences erected against a 'world, which had shown itself unloving'—than in any of her other books. It is not that these traits are absent from her later work, rather that what has there been absorbed into the underlying emotional texture of the novels remains in *Dolores* raw and unassimilated—and therefore however distressing from a literary point of view, an open invitation to a more personal interpretation. One may see, for instance, something of Ivy's own habitual discretion in Dolores' unremitting effort to preserve the 'unreal' or 'surface life' from the sufferings which drive her in secret to distraction: 'She was living in two worlds; darkly groping in the one for a spot of solitude, that she might in the spirit live wholly in the other'.[47] Dolores' two worlds—her clandestine passion for Claverhouse on the one hand, the daily round of home or college on the other—may be said to correspond roughly to the incomparably subtler cracks and fissures of the later novels in which a bland, smooth, elegantly artificial surface is threatened, on occasion dangerously ripped and torn, by pressure from below. The dichotomy was evidently already apparent to the author of *Dolores*, though she is unable to present it except by crude statement and assertion: 'She was saved from darkness only by the suffering need of living the surface life'; 'Calmness and conscious courage went; and a life opened whose every day was a struggle—a life to which she clung with the grasp whose slackening speaks destruction'.

But Dolores' surface life is put at risk not so much by any palpable forces of darkness or destruction as by their sheer absurdity. As Dolores repeatedly renounces her career, her independence, her college salary, her love for Claverhouse and his for her, all to less and less purpose for the sake of friends and relations who prove indifferent or downright ungrateful, she causes abject misery at first only to herself but eventually to others—so much so that her self-immolation comes increasingly to look like cruelty, and the objects of her sacrifice more and more like victims. One dies as a direct result, and another indirectly. It is Dolores

who engineers the marriage of Claverhouse and Perdita (a marriage
which makes both wretched, kills Perdita and leaves her husband prey
to hideous remorse) at frightful cost to herself; and it is Dolores' triple
desertion which finally brings the blind, helpless and despairing Claverhouse down to a lonely grave. She had left him for the third time, again
at untold cost, to keep house for her father in his second widowhood: a
sacrifice promptly and perhaps wisely repudiated by Mr Hutton who,
seizing his chance while Dolores is briefly away at Claverhouse's
funeral, selects in self-defence a third wife who makes it very plain that
her stepdaughter's somewhat oppressive presence is no longer required
at home.

But tribulations which may well seem laughable to the reader are
bitter earnest to Dolores, and no less so to her creator. They are described in terms which, though evidently to some extent derived at
second hand from literary models, nonetheless suggest a sufficient
personal acquaintance with painful self-repression: 'It seemed to her . . .
that to suffer in secret daily, and lie in the night hours helpless under
agony below the easiness of tears, was the lot that was natural for her.'
This bleakness may, of course, reflect Ivy's own unhappiness from a
suppressed and one-sided love affair; or simply the background of her
life at Hove in the years after 1906 with a sick and fretful mother,
irritating sisters, no prospect of escape from duty to her family, her
unassuaged grief for Guy and her loneliness in Noel's absence; or it
may represent in part at least a kind of displaced emotion—the frustrations of struggling unsuccessfully with an intractable aesthetic form.

One may see much the same phenomenon in the painting of the
period or a little earlier: in, for instance, the dark, heavy, sometimes
even stiflingly Victorian interiors of Bonnard or Matisse which gave
way, after a brief, imitative apprenticeship, to canvases suffused with
light and colour. There is a similar sense of relief in turning from the
morbid atmosphere of *Dolores* to the exquisitely frivolous lucidity of
Pastors and Masters, published after a gap of fourteen years in 1925. The
comparison is perhaps closer if one considers the spectacular transition
from Mondrian's lowering, early landscapes, painted in the years
when I. Compton-Burnett was writing *Dolores*, or the lurid purple
tones and writhing forms of his paintings in 1910 and 1911, produced
in what was evidently a frenzied wrestling with convention, to the
clarity, simplicity and the delicate pale colours of his grid patterns
which followed a few years later. It is easy to see traces of the same
frantic, losing battle in I. Compton-Burnett's first novel: a battle which

led from the turgid, overblown naturalistic style, carried to a logical if ludicrous extreme in *Dolores*, to the austerity and concision of her mature novels and which meant, for both novelist and painter, that the emotional charge released by each increased in direct proportion as the superficial convulsions of the early work receded before a surface of increasing formal severity.

Whatever the reason, the curious point about *Dolores* is not so much that it is a startlingly bad novel as its peculiar kind of badness. It was plainly written at a time when, as one of Mrs Ward's characters says of Robert Elsmere, its author was 'more struck by the difficulty of being morally strong than by the difficulty of being intellectually clear'.[48] Hence presumably the presence of a whole gallery of perfectly solid, peripheral characters—Dolores' father, stepmother, brother and close college friend—whose presence is essential only as instruments of torture for the heroine. Dolores herself is at best negatively convincing. Her character, whether one considers her saint-like heroism or its monstrous results, is unsatisfactory and her stony selflessness wrought to a pitch which is neither probable nor possible. She becomes interesting only in so far as one asks why any novelist should need to create a character whose sole purpose shall be to receive unending punishment at her own hands and at the hands of fate—punishments in themselves so pitiless, so constant and severe that (though the very act of suffering them makes Dolores necessarily implausible) they suggest nonetheless the presence of emotion frighteningly strong. Whether one prefers to approach the question from a biographical or a literary point of view— to see the answer in purely personal or aesthetic terms, or as a combination of the two—there can be small doubt that powerful emotion continued to run underground throughout the life and work of I. Compton-Burnett. Or, as someone says of feelings in a later novel, 'One is not without them, because they are one's own affair.'[49]

3

IN 1884, THE year of her birth, Ivy's grandfather Rowland Rees had addressed some few pessimistic words to the youth of Dover on the perilous nature of novels: 'All books, he was sorry to say, were not healthy reading, and he would advise young men to beware of the mental poison, and to turn their attention to subjects which would afford real pleasure and improvement, such as history, geography, natural philosophy and the sciences. . . .' He went on to paint a grisly picture of any youth rash enough to discard the scriptures in favour of other forms of fiction: 'He could ruin his health and debase his intellect, he can deaden his conscience, fill his mind with debased ideas, and his mouth with impurity; he can break his father's heart and bring the blush of shame on the brows of his mother and sisters, and he can ruin his soul and bring it under the condemnation of God.'[50]

The Mayor of Dover's attitude was evidently not unlike Sabine Ponsonby's ominous reaction, on ferreting out the hidden manuscript of her granddaughter's first novel in *Daughters and Sons*: 'What is all this rubbish in your room, France?' Grandparents, in the work of I. Compton-Burnett, generally take a dubious view of literary activity: one thinks of Sir Michael Egerton ('It can't be so hard, or he could not write all those books. Long ones, too; I give him credit there') in *A God and His Gifts* or Jocasta Grimstone in *The Last and the First*. A curious, cancelled and unpublished incident in the draft of this last novel casts some light on what may perhaps have been Ivy's own experience as a child. The book itself, published posthumously in 1971, bears a suffi-cient likeness in point of plot and character to *Dolores* to suggest that Dame Ivy's thoughts, towards the end of her life, were running on things which had happened sixty or more years before, and the supposi-tion is confirmed by this particular episode in which Jocasta forces her terrified granddaughter ('standing . . . so aloof that she might have been unconscious, indeed almost was') to disclose the text of a school essay. Amy Grimstone's essay, like France Ponsonby's first novel or for that matter Dame Ivy's, concerns characters drawn from the author's own family circle. What is interesting is that the sentiments and stilted lan-guage of the essay* are unmistakeably a throwback to *Dolores*; and that Amy's feeling, as her grandmother reads her work aloud, is one of mortal trepidation:

* The manuscript contains an extract from this essay, which begins by describing a tyrannical grandmother attended by her nervous grandchildren, and continues:

> A day of leisure is our theme. But through the leisured hour thoughts made their way, and almost deprived it of the name.
> For before the younger eyes the future lay, its promise already dim, and before the failing ones there moved the past, with its joys and sorrows, its suffering and sin —for we deal with an ordinary human life—its progress to the grave.

Compare the opening chapter of *Dolores*, quoted on p.152 (a much briefer version of the episode in *The Last and the First* comes in chapter three of the published text).

. . . she suffered one of the extreme moments of her life. She sent up a prayer that it might pass, and a word of incredulous thanksgiving when it did. Jocasta let the paper fall from her hand . . . and Amy was enabled to retrieve it and move away.

She feared allusion to the matter, and lived in suspense for days; and the passing of the danger was a thing she could hardly believe, and was never to explain.

This atmosphere of secrecy and dread was well known to Ivy who, like France Ponsonby and practically all the budding authors in her books, refused to show her manuscript even to her brother. Years afterwards when she had long since disowned *Dolores*, consigning it presumably to the category of 'youthful agonies' ('I don't think anything in later life quite comes up to them, or makes one squirm as they did') so feelingly described by Miles Mowbray in *A Father and His Fate*, she even sought to shift the blame by claiming to several people that Noel had 'meddled in it': 'Yes, I did that piece of juvenilia, but my brother meddled with it, and I don't take any interest in it, because I can't remember how much I wrote and how much I didn't really. But people always *will* be prying into it, you know.'[51] Dame Ivy's memory must, as she suspected, have grown blurred with time since the inference that Noel collaborated on *Dolores* cannot have been strictly accurate. For one thing, his copy still survives inscribed on the fly-leaf in his sister's hand: 'Noël Compton-Burnett with the author's love'.[52] For another, her younger sisters well remember the book being written throughout the years at Hove when the girls sat round the schoolroom table, supposedly taught by Ivy but actually drawing, painting, reading, 'browsing at what we liked', while Ivy slowly filled a series of exercise books in a small, cramped hand, crossing out and re-writing as was her habit for the rest of her life, 'digging a very sharp-pointed pencil—I can see her now—into the notebook. She went over and over them.' Both agreed that it was '*quite* false' that Noel had helped write *Dolores*. They had watched Ivy writing day after day when Noel was away at Cambridge and, even in the vacation, Juliet Compton-Burnett thought it improbable that the two did more than share a study: 'This would have been where they would have had their intimate talks about earnest things—*if* they ever had any. I think it quite likely that they just sat side by side and worked.' Lastly, there is Noel's own evidence in a letter to O.B., dated 1 August 1909, that he had not been permitted a sight of the manuscript until it was finished:

You were kind enough in your last letter to ask about my sister's novel. When finished she sent it to Blackwood as a venture. But alas! it was returned with the enclosed letter, which on the whole was not entirely discouraging. Since then I have read the book. I do not think I was influenced by fraternal prejudice, but I will stake all my pretensions to critical acumen, and vow that the book is filled with literary and dramatic excellencies. However 'Unhistoric Acts' (that is the book's baptismal dower) still is on my sister's hands. Before taking a further step I have been wondering whether I might remind you of your own very good natured suggestion to give her a letter of introduction to a publisher. We know that your influence would count for much, and I need not say that we shall appreciate its exertion. I may say that in my view the quality of the work is such, that you might possibly come to feel some pleasure in having helped to let it take its chance. In any case I am sure you will excuse this quite absurd imposition on your good nature.[53]

The mysterious *Unhistoric Acts* was almost certainly an early draft of *Dolores* under another name, since it is hardly likely that Ivy had time to write a whole new novel in the fifteen months between receiving her first manuscript back from Blackwood and submitting her second (which was conditionally accepted) in October 1910. What O.B. thought of the novel is unknown, though either his good nature or Noel's shrewd appeal to his vanity as a patron prompted him to write to his own publisher John Lane, who apparently endorsed Blackwood's rejection. Neither publisher has preserved records of this correspondence which was conducted unbeknownst to Mrs Compton Burnett and her daughters so that Ivy's attempts to place her novel were kept, like France Ponsonby's, 'a dark secret' from her family and seem likely to remain one from posterity: 'People's first dealings with publishers are always secret and very dark. Especially when they come to nothing.'[54]

It seems probable that Ivy re-wrote the novel over the next year or so, perhaps with Noel's assistance, and perhaps incorporating advice contained in Blackwood's 'not entirely discouraging' letter (one cannot help speculating as to whether this might not have resembled the criticisms levelled against France's novel—that it was 'a string of beads' not welded into a whole, that it needed cutting, and that it was in parts so immature as to be unfit for publication). But these were also the months leading up to Mrs Compton Burnett's last illness, which fell heavily on both Noel and Ivy. Their mother had for years been afflicted by deafness which exacerbated her alarming nervous disposition and gave her terrible noises in the head. She was already gravely ill when, probably in the early summer of 1909, the family visited Clacton with the Blackies—and it was perhaps on this occasion that Robert Blackie, presumably not unaware of his eldest niece's dangerous tendency to fiction, prayed aloud before the two assembled families 'that his dear nieces might not be led into the sin of intellectual pride'. It was also this summer that Vera Compton-Burnett, at the age of seventeen, first realized the seriousness of their mother's condition. Ivy later accompanied her alone to Ryde in the Isle of Wight for a course of electrical treatment which lasted two weeks ('and they were hard weeks for Ivy'); Minnie nursed her, as she had nursed Guy, sitting up sometimes all night and running the household next day. Mrs Compton-Burnett would allow no one else near her for, like her eldest daughter, 'she had a horror of going to a hospital, a horror of going to a nurse'. Some time in the autumn of 1910 Dr Clarke, their father's friend to whom he had consigned his family before he died, took Noel aside and told him that she had cancer of the breast in an advanced and already fatal stage. Radium treatment was prescribed which produced fearful wounds and burns on the wrists; in July 1911, five months before her death, Noel accompanied his mother to London for a final radium cure.

In these last sombre years Noel's friends had long ceased to be invited to the house. Noel himself, who had spent industrious vacations 'reading six or so hours a day', taken a double first in 1910 and afterwards had 'little leisure owing to the very serious illness of my mother',[55] can have had no more time than Ivy for tinkering with her novel. By October 1910, the pair must have felt that time was running short if their mother were ever to see the book in print; and, after open family consultation since on this occasion money was involved, a new and more hopeful scheme was proposed to Blackwood, who replied to 'S. Compton-Burnett, Esq.' on 9 November:

Dear Sir,

We have now given our careful consideration to your MS. novel. We are willing to fall in with your wishes and to publish the story on the terms you suggest, viz:- at your own risk and expense. We would propose printing 1050 copies 6s fiction, allowing a sum of some £40 to be spent on advertising. The cost of production under these

conditions would be approximately £150, and before putting the
work in hand, we should like a payment to account of £75. . . .[56]

Jermyn Haslam in *Men and Wives* faced considerable domestic
opprobrium when, having dismally failed to place his first slim volume
of original verse, he was finally obliged to publish the book on payment
by his father of a suitably large sum to Messrs. Halibut and Froude.
Whether or not Ivy had had to contend with similar difficulties,
Dolores was duly published on 20 February 1911, and, as Mr Blackwood
(writing now to 'Miss I. Compton-Burnett') gracefully acknowledged,
it sold immediately and well: 480 copies had gone by the end of the
first month. The reviewers, conservative by nature then as now, were
markedly more enthusiastic over the old-fashioned virtues of this
eminently Victorian work than they were to be fourteen years later
over the same author's first genuinely original novel; even Ivy found
it barely necessary to conceal the pleasure with which she distributed
among her friends copies of the *Daily Mail* and the *Times Literary
Supplement* ('You must bear in mind for my benefit', she wrote
modestly to Katie, 'that it is something to be noticed in the Times at all.').
The *Mail*, dismissing Ada Leverson's *The Limit* and Constance
Smedley's *Mothers and Fathers* as second-rate efforts typical of lady
writers, singled out the author of *Dolores* ('Who Ivy Compton-
Burnett is, whether young or middle-aged, whether Mrs or Miss, I
know not') as one who might yet vindicate her sex by rising to the
dizzy heights scaled by Mr Wells, Mr Bennett, Mr Galsworthy and
Mr Robert Hichens: 'no one could call "The Limit" literature . . . But
"Dolores" is literature; of that no competent critic can have any
doubt'.[57]

The anonymous reviewer in the *T.L.S.* was Walter de la Mare who,
noting that Claverhouse 'is somehow suggestive of Victor Hugo,
whereas the rest of the characters have a just perceptible flavour of
Jane Austen,' proved quite as generous as the *Mail* if rather less effusive:
'Miss Compton-Burnett has written with intense seriousness, her book
lights up for the reader a serene and independent mind. . . .' Jane
Austen, George Eliot and even Henry James were invoked gratifyingly
often by, among others, Robert Ross (then 'rolling the Literary Log'
in a gossipy column between sport and fashion notes at the back of the
Bystander) who confidently predicted 'something really striking from
the young author' in the future. Altogether the young author had every

reason to feel satisfied with a début which seems to have left her with nothing but pleasant associations: Arnold Bennett's *The Card*, reviewed by de la Mare below *Dolores*, remained long afterwards a favourite with Ivy and, if she was struck by the possibilities of *Mothers and Fathers* as a title, she may also have noted and put by for future reference the name of another novel reviewed at the same time as her own: Mrs L. T. Meade's *Mother and Son*.

Ivy's mother was by this time too weak to resent, perhaps even to identify, the portrait of herself as Mrs Hutton. Whatever apprehensions Ivy may have entertained beforehand ended even more happily than Amy Grimstone's, for Mrs Compton Burnett was frankly jubilant at the book's reception. The staunchly Wesleyan Blackies were somewhat less so, and the Compton Burnetts' physician at Hove, a Dr Molson who recognized himself in Dr Cassell, was filled with such natural resentment that it became for some time a question as to whether he could bring himself to continue in attendance on the family. But, having once surmounted the dread of retribution at her mother's hands, Ivy treated querulous protests of this kind with characteristic insouciance. She freely admitted to her cousin Katie 'that I made use of your father and mother just to give a superficial touch to the person-alities. That I intended no resemblance in character I should have thought was clear. Surely there is no real likeness? Jimmie and Grandma could not even see the surface suggestion. If people will insist that a cap fits, and further insist upon wearing it, it is not to be laid to my account.' (23 May 1911)

She took meanwhile considerable pains to sell 'my little book', explaining that she could on no account distribute copies 'as it is against my publisher's interest for me to do anything at all that checks the sale', and urging her relations to purchase instead the 'special edition for the Colonies, bound in paper, and costing only 1s' (this last was disingenuous, since they cost in fact 1s 6d or 2s). Miss Bremner received an even thriftier suggestion on a postcard which simply said in Ivy's sprawling hand: 'Ask at your local library for *Dolores*.' Of the 1050 copies printed, 850 at six shillings and 200 in cheap colonial editions, all but 146 had been sold by 31 December 1911, whereupon demand abruptly ceased. On twelve out of every thirteen copies sold, Ivy had received three shillings and seven pence per copy, less a publish-ing commission of fifteen per cent to Blackwood. By December 1920, three more copies had been sold. The remaining 143 were probably then wasted. Six years before, Blackwood's had proposed to clear their warehouse by selling off the stock on hand, offering Ivy as many copies as she liked at threepence or fourpence each. Olivia Manning said long afterwards that Ivy kept a cupboardful of remaindered copies of *Dolores*, which had been delivered to her in a truck. The whole affair puts one strangely in mind of Samuel Beckett's Krapp, meditating on his own laborious rise to fame: 'Seventeen copies sold, of which eleven at trade price to free circulating libraries beyond the seas. Getting known.'[58]

VII

1911–1915

'Are we going to be broad and wicked?'

I

PHILIP NOEL-BAKER, then an undergraduate in his third year at King's, never forgot seeing Noel in May Week 1911, walking across the front court with a sister who 'knocked the college sideways'. This was Ivy, a few days after her twenty-seventh birthday, spending a week at Cambridge with her sister Judy to watch the races and perhaps to attend the King's Ball, which was held that year on Monday, 12 June.[1] Even allowing for the fact that women were rare at King's in those days (and, to say the least, not highly prized in what was still an almost exclusively celibate society), Ivy seems to have made a marked impression: 'She was stunning. Absolutely beautiful, and she had a wonderful figure.' Ivy had been justly proud of her figure ('a sort of well-covered slender', said her sister, 'and she dressed rather to show it'), as of her looks in general. 'I was a pretty piece, wasn't I?' she said of a studio portrait* that shows her looking, in 1929, still in her twenties. Mr Noel-Baker, watching appreciatively as she crossed the courtyard on her brother's arm and disappeared up the stair to his rooms, longed to meet her but never came near enough to manage an introduction.

Noel's rooms were in Wilkins Building, immediately to the left of the gateway as you enter the college, under the corner turret with what must be among the loveliest views even in Cambridge, looking directly across at the chapel from one window and down King's Parade from the other. O.B. lived until his retirement opposite on the same staircase, and seems generally to have selected a specially favoured under-

*To Madge Garland; the photograph is reproduced in the photo insert.

graduate to occupy this particular set of rooms in which Noel had succeeded Rupert Brooke. Judy, who was then eighteen and 'only half finished', was properly impressed not only by the beauty of the buildings and gardens in early summer but by the grandeur of Noel's domestic appointments, his gyp, his amazingly talkative friends, the luncheon served in his rooms of roast duck and green peas and asparagus —so very different from her own home life at Hove—and by the general air of consequence accorded to her brother in what seemed, to a schoolgirl up from the country, positively palatial surroundings. 'Inside the college by 1911, Noel was regarded as one of the brilliant people,' said Philip Noel-Baker who had first got to know him well on Noel's return from four months spent learning German at Munich and Göttingen in the summer of 1910. 'I suppose one could say he was shy. He was very quiet and gentle: I don't believe he ever said anything disagreeable to anyone in the whole of his life. He was so clever and so well-read that I was shy of saying anything in front of him for fear it was wrong.'

Noel had by this time developed his own peculiar style of eccentricity, affecting a stiff wing collar and a mock-pompous style of delivery derived from his favourite author. 'Edward Gibbon, Esq.' is the pen-name assigned to 'Mr N. Compton-Bannerman, B.A.' in an 'Index of Standard Authors' supplied by the *Basileon* (the college magazine, which favoured a brand of anonymous, personal, often highly obscure under-graduate humour) for June 1911. 'He had this curious manner—sort of huffing and puffing, and at the same time making fun of himself,' said Raisley Moorsom who had come up to King's that year. 'My chief memory is of him standing with a walking stick in the court and pontificating—on nothing at all—in that Gibbonian manner,' said William Haslam, another historian and an exact contemporary of Noel at King's. The manner which intrigued his friends at Cambridge had first taken hold of Noel in the spring and summer of 1907, when he sat in the schoolrooom at Hove with Ivy and raced through the *Decline and Fall* twice over. The raw and enthusiastic schoolboy who began sending weekly bulletins to O.B. ('I should think that there could be nothing in History more marvellous than the Crusades') rapidly made way for the budding pedant who, barely three months after he had read his first page of Gibbon, wrote to congratulate his mentor on a whirl of end-of-term activity: 'The Pageant at Oxford seems from all accounts to have been an almost worthy celebration of the past it recalled; while a subsequent attendance at the King's garden-party must, I should think, have afforded a contrast not less striking than delightful.' (2 June 1907)

Similarly balanced and sonorous, though this time rather more polished periods form the opening paragraphs of his thesis dissertation written five years later in the summer of 1912. It was presumably the combination of extreme seclusion and a highly developed inner life, the effect of an upbringing that had acted as a forcing house to the emotions but left the intelligence untouched, which had made Noel as susceptible to Gibbon as Ivy had been to George Eliot, and which meant that, again like his sister, he had early felt the need to adopt some form of protective covering. Outside his own immediate circle at King's, he seemed a stiff, shy, unworldly oddity. 'He was quite unlike any undergraduate. He gave the impression that he hadn't been to a public school—he hadn't had the raw edges rubbed off him,' said Raisley Moorsom. As a young Fellow cast in O.B.'s mould Noel was known as 'the C.B.' to his humorous juniors, who once proposed as a promising subject for debate: 'C.B. is B.C.'. It took years to wear out this witticism: 'Thank God I've lived down C-B at last. I'm called at discretion Jim & Noel,' he wrote to his Cambridge friend Elliott Felkin in July 1914. Criticisms of his awkward delivery when he first took part in debates at the Union suggest that Noel had had initially to overcome a dislike of public speaking much like Ivy's own. But years at home which had driven her to a fine point of concealment and self-control had left Noel at once more exuberant and gentler than his sister, though with the same singular ability to detach himself at will from his immediate surroundings, informed by the same extraordinary sense of humour. 'His very distinct personality had never been blurred by school,' wrote the economist John Clapham, who had succeeded O.B. as History Tutor at the end of 1908. 'Partly, no doubt, because he was the only surviving son in a large family which had lost its father, he seemed curiously mature. He could be either in or outside his generation, as suited his mood. He belonged to the once notorious little society at King's, "the Carbonari", to which Rupert Brooke read some of his earlier poems; and, while still an undergraduate, he would tell you about it as a man of thirty tells of such things in retrospect.'[2]

Noel had in some ways an easier lot than his sisters, who had no option but to remain for another eight years at Hove: 'The cloud lifted for Noel a little earlier, King's was a magic world for him. He made friends easily, though he'd never had any at all before.' Chief of these was Jack Beresford, to whom King's had also come as 'an almost magical release' from the strain of an intense, self-contained and often melancholy family life in an isolated country rectory. Jack was a frequent visitor at Hove and the two families saw a good deal of each other when, after Mrs Compton Burnett's death, the Burnett and Beresford sisters exchanged visits on Noel's engagement to one of the three beautiful Miss Beresfords. Jack's gay and impetuous disposition is nicely conveyed by, on the one hand, Noel's description of him to O.B. —'He is in a state of lyric enthusiasm over the flowers of the field. He is a charming fellow and the incarnation of the ingenuous; I like him much' (1 August 1909)—and, on the other, a curt riposte sent from Göttingen on 20 September 1910:

My dear Jack,
    I had your letter here, and more latterly your abusive postcard. Many thanks for the former. As to the latter I must warn you that should I receive any further missives from Wales breathing all the fervour of the Celtic temperament I shall avail myself in my reply of the German language and of German characters. I have not written because I have not had anything particular to say. . . .

The two had been inseparable at King's from their first term, always walking and talking together—'You remember our high Cambridge talk, so up in the clouds and so insincere according to the way of youth, and it's odd to consider how all of it is now brought to the rather sordid touch of practice,' wrote Noel at the end of 1915 in one of his last letters from the trenches.[3] His wartime letters are shot through with references to 'talk of literature and men' at Cambridge, Brighton and at O.T.C. training camp together, to 'our headshaking mighty exchange of argumentative broadsides' which had made Piccadilly reverberate on Noel's leaves in London, and with his longing to see his friend again: 'Oh! my excellent Jacobus if you were here, what should not we two veterans from the Cutlasses perform upon the Teuton. Alas! we are scurvily separated—a perpetual irritation to us both.' (4 October 1915)
    Arthur Waley (then called by his family name of Schloss, later changed to Waley in the war) also became a close friend in these years and remained one of Ivy's circle to the end of his life. The Schlosses had a country house in Sussex, not far from Hove, where Noel was often invited to lunch (sometimes with Ivy, and once with his mother), asking his friend back in return to spend weekends at Hove whence

they paid visits together to O.B. at Bexhill. 'Schloss ... came over some
time back for the day,' wrote Noel in his first long vacation. 'He always
seems to me a very remarkable personality. He is unfamiliar, and
perhaps for that reason attracts one. I can never quite satisfy myself
whether he is cleverer than he seems, or seems cleverer than he is, but
of his cleverness I have no doubt.' (3 August 1908) Noel's friends in those
days were as beautiful as they were clever, judging at any rate by a
moving account of the King's college pageant performed on the banks
of the Cam in their second year:

> The Queen of the May (Mr Beresford) is in the act of crowning her
> pupils with nosegays of incarnadined tulips, when enter, R, the
> Christian slave-girl, Granta (Mr Schloss), fleeing in terror from a
> fresh punt-load of Jutes and Picts ... who have surprised her washing
> her nightie on the bank. . . . Granta swoons and dies to Chopin's
> Funeral March (by request). . . . The whole of this tender yet stirring
> episode is the work of poor, dead, Robert Swithinbank, and copy-
> right by the Carbonari Society.[4]

The Carbonari, founded by Rupert Brooke and his Fabian friend
Hugh Dalton in their first term, was a fairly ferocious band of twelve
members who prided themselves on being intellectually superior to the
rest of the college, and who were regarded in return as an outrageously
odd lot. Brooke and Dalton, picking over the freshmen each year, had
singled out Noel for an invitation to join along with Arthur Schloss,
Philip Noel-Baker and Francis Birrell (first year in 1908, and remembered by Ivy's sisters as an occasional visitor at Hove). He read at least
two historical papers at the society's weekly meetings and certainly
attended the celebrated, ceremonial dinner held in Brooke's rooms on
5 February 1909, at which seven toasts were drunk including 'The
World, the Flesh and the Devil' and 'The King, God damn him'.
Unhappily Brooke's gyp, who had remained unobserved to witness
this incident, reported it next morning ('Well, they drank the King's
health, sir, but without much loyalty') whereupon, according to two
conflicting or perhaps complementary accounts, Dalton was debagged
and/or Frankie Birrell was chased round the courtyard by patriots who
wanted to duck him. The Carbonari were mostly Fabians, anti-
athletic, anti-philistine and ardently devoted to modern literature.
'There are only three good things in the world,' said Brooke according
to Dalton, 'one is to read poetry, another is to write poetry, and the

best of all is to live poetry!' A less exalted but perhaps rather more accurate view of their proceedings is suggested by Arthur Schloss in a programme note on promised delights at a Carbonari Ball: 'Finally, Mr Rupert Brooke will perform a dream-dance on tip toe.'

Noel's life at Cambridge seems to have been bounded almost entirely by college affairs: he had taken part in the second debate of his first term at the Union, speaking thereafter almost every other week until he was elected to the Committee in December 1908, and never spoke again. He had been from his first term a regular attendant at the King's Political Society which met in O.B's rooms, and became its secretary in his third year (reading a paper on 'The Soul of Our Age' at the 490th meeting and voting Aye, with Beresford, to the motion, 'Is there one?'). His withdrawal from outside pursuits was no doubt partly due to congenial company in King's, partly on account of his work which prospered exceedingly. 'Everyone knew at once he was a certain First,' said Leigh Farnell, another historian; and, on the constitutional history paper in part one of the Tripos, Noel is said to have answered only one question, writing fifteen pages on the hide, that most contro-versial unit of land measurement in Anglo-Saxon England—so learned and exhaustive was his treatment that he took a first by acclamation. The Gladstone prize was awarded 'for the excellence of C.B.'s work on the Special Period, Mediaeval History and Constitutional History,' wrote Clapham to O.B. who, in retirement at Bexhill, had also received a jubilant and characteristically consoling report from Noel: 'Out of the second year History people, Toulmin, Beresford, Forbes-Adam and myself are all scholars. That is pretty well for the last generation of the disciples of O.B.' (1 August 1909)

Geoffrey Toulmin, Jack Beresford and Eric Forbes-Adam all came down from Cambridge to stay with the Compton Burnetts at Hove, and were all well-known to Ivy. She herself paid visits to her brother at King's and was presumably already unconsciously absorbing the Cambridge attitudes which make her second novel so markedly different from her first. Friends of Noel who met Ivy before the first war remember her as giggly, cheerful, reserved in public but in private no less witty than her brother. What had seemed to their younger sister Judy a bewildering, bewitching glimpse of high life must have been for Ivy, observing it with eyes not so easily dazzled, quite as fascinating and almost as remote from anything she had previously known at home or college. But her own direct contacts with Cambridge, or with as much of it as was permitted to a woman,

Alderman Rees and his family at Dover in the 1860s. *Left to right:* Mr and Mrs Rowland Rees, Allen, Katharine, George, Elizabeth, Charles, Rowland, Lucy, John, Sophia

James Compton Burnett at the start of his career

Katharine Rees before her marriage

Ivy at three

Judy and Vera

Noel and Guy

Nellie Smith (Minnie) in her
mid-thirties at Hove.
' "You love Mummy and you love Daddy,"
said Mrs Compton Burnett,
to which Ivy replied:
"But I love Minnie best." '

The drawing room, Addiscombe College, for the Daughters of Gentlemen, Hove

Ivy (centre) in her first term at Holloway with Daisy Harvey (seated on the balustrade) and Isabel Bremner (in white blouse, far right)

Members of staff at Holloway who supplied models for *Dolores*.
Middle row standing left to right: Miss Pechinet (centre, in cap and gown),
Miss Hayes-Robinson, Miss Taylor, Miss Block, Miss Cunningham. *Seated left to right:*
Miss Frost, unidentified, Miss Guinness, the Principal (in centre)

The Compton-Burnett family with cousins in the summer of 1912.
Ivy in the centre with Topsy beside her on the left, Stephanie (Baby) standing behind on the right, and Noel on the right in front

The Family

i

I believe that more unhappiness comes from this source than from any other—I mean from the attempt to prolong family connection unduly and to make people hang together artificially who would never naturally do so. The mischief among the lower classes is not so great, but among the middle and upper classes it is killing a large number daily. And the old people do not really like it much better than the young.

'The Family' from Ivy's copy of *The Note-Books of Samuel Butler*, p.31

Dorothy and Tertia Beresford, 1914

Jack Beresford,
from a drawing by
Lucy Graham Smith, 1913

Noel as a young Fellow, from a drawing by
Kennard Bliss, in the *Basileon,* June 1914

First page of Noel's last letter to Ivy, written
from the Somme on Saturday, 1 July 1916

ii

The whole life of some people is a kind of partial death—
a long, lingering death-bed, so to speak, of stagnation and
nonentity on which death is but the seal, or solemn signing,
as the abnegation of all further act and deed on the part

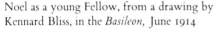

Note in Ivy's handwriting after Noel's death, from her copy of
The Note-Books of Samuel Butler, p.22

Margaret Jourdain on the steps of the Manor House, Broadwindsor, in 1910, at the time of her first success in London as poet, visionary and literary critic

Eleanor and Philip Jourdain

Ivy in the summer of her first success with *Brothers and Sisters,* 1929

Ivy as an established writer between the wars

Ivy and Margaret on the balcony
at Braemar Mansions, 1948

Ivy and Margaret taking tea in 1942 (previously unpublished photograph from a photographic
session with Lee Miller arranged by Jane Stockwood for *Vogue*)

were doubtless less revealing than the easy intimacy derived at second hand from the gossip of her brother and his friends. These high-spirited, intelligent young men who descended from time to time on Hove, turning the house upside down for bouts of table-tapping, dressing up and bathing parties, once even carrying off Ivy herself to the continent, must have provided in these years almost her sole window on the outside world. That she sat in it and watched with unremitting attention is suggested by the reflection of what she saw in her next novel, if not by the procession of high-spirited, intelligent young men following one another across the pages of almost all her later work. Certainly Noel and his friends, or rather their dealings with their tutors, contributed largely to *Pastors and Masters*. Perhaps even the scandalous machinations surrounding O.B. in his last years at Cambridge—machinations whose intricacies must have been familiar to Ivy, since her brother was among O.B.'s most valiant supporters—have a bearing on the atmosphere of academic intrigue and narrowly averted scandal hanging over that novel.

It was O.B. who had first placed the King's history school on a level with classics and mathematics and made it the envy of the university. But by 1907 his work had long since been completed and he himself, superseded in his seventies by a younger generation of historians, was well on the way to becoming an indignant, irascible and mortified old man. 'As he grew older his off days increased,' wrote his biographer and, when Noel first knew him, his conceit had already grown more alarming than endearing—'his inner voice supported him for he too, like Socrates, possessed a singularly encouraging *daimon*, thanks to whom he knew that what he did was good'—and his off days so frequent as to be almost insupportable. Twice disappointed in hopes (which he alone had entertained) of becoming first Regius Professor, then Provost of King's, he was finally obliged by what he regarded as a shocking manœuvre of his enemies to retire at the end of 1908 to Bexhill, where he morosely contemplated twin portraits in his dining room of Napoleon and himself. Noel, who became thereafter O.B.'s chief purveyor of college news, addressed himself in the next few years to the delicate business of condolence ('I think all those of my year have a right to feel sadly aggrieved' 3 August 1908), appreciation ('It was most good of you to let us come. Your talk I always look upon as an Educational advantage. Cambridge cannot be quite itself till you return to it' 5 October 1909) and reassurance ('I hope that Bexhill will not so win all your affection as to make your presence at King's too occasional. If we were to lose our chief celebrity the daughters of the Philistines at Trinity would rejoice past bearing. . . . I must plead guilty to a secret desire to see you the V.P.' 1 August 1909).

But, though Noel retained a vivid sense of gratitude to the end of his career at Cambridge, his early devotion to O.B. gave way to a growing respect and liking for John Clapham. Clapham's famous lectures on economic history (at which impassioned undergraduates stamped till the floor rang like a drum) had started the year after Noel came up to King's, just too late to fire him as they fired so many freshmen in the next twenty-five years and more. By the beginning of his second year, Noel was too firmly entrenched in O.B.'s camp—'I shall always think myself fortunate to have begun my study of history under you,' he wrote loyally in the long vacation. 'History studied as politics seems to me a vastly more important, not to say more attractive thing than history studied as economics or as anything else whatsoever' (3 August 1908)—to take readily to O.B.'s successor. It might have proved an awkward situation but any initial difficulties were resolved by tact on both sides. As President and Secretary of the Political Society at its five hundredth meeting in 1910, Clapham and Noel combined to organize the celebratory dinner which must have gone a fair way to mollify the society's founder, who was guest of honour. Clapham's own letters to O.B. suggest that he thought highly of Noel, and perhaps regretted losing him to a rival discipline ('You will be glad, I expect, to find him so well in the political tradition,' he wrote on 7 July 1911, of Noel's fellowship thesis, 'and not led astray by me into a study of the rural economy of the Godwin Sands as revealed in the Anglo-Saxon Chronicle or the origin of the two ways of dying wool'); and there can be small doubt that each thoroughly appreciated the other's combination of solidity with humour.

But stronger, or at any rate more lasting, than either of these relationships was Noel's affinity with Goldsworthy Lowes Dickinson, to whom he went for tutorials in his third year. 'Goldie admired Noel, and said he would have been a remarkable historian,' said Philip Noel-Baker; and it seems to have been from Dickinson that Noel absorbed not only the political and historical assumptions but also the underlying personal philosophy which, six years later in the trenches, were to sustain him in the bitterest months of his life. Not that there was anything especially remarkable about this friendship in its early stages, certainly nothing remotely comparable to Noel's dramatic schoolboy encounter with his first mentor. Dickinson was on every count the opposite of O.B.:

modest, gentle, unassertive, shy to distraction and often ludicrously unworldly, he imbued his pupils with his own dry wit and unfailing tolerance. When he was awarded a travelling bursary in 1912 for the widening of Fellows' minds, Rupert Brooke said: 'If they widen Goldie's mind any more, it'll break'. He was not at first sight attractive —'Well, you know, he looked like the carpenter in *Alice in Wonderland*,' said a former pupil long afterwards. 'You know what I mean— slightly seedy, badly dressed, dirty old grey flannel trousers, curious stoop and very curious walk with a long stride and threw his legs out in front of him; and he looked rather long-faced and gloomy, but I don't think one found him gloomy very long.'

'The hands were large,' wrote E. M. Forster, his pupil, friend and later his enthusiastic biographer. 'The clothes, except during his American visits, erred on the dowdy side—dark blue serge, shirts of indistinction, podgy ties. I dress like that myself, except for illogical flashinesses, and once when I invited him into one of these he replied that it is useless to dress well unless one's personal appearance corresponds.'6 What charmed his pupils was his disinterestedness and diffidence, his lack of self-importance and his extraordinary power of clarifying muddled or irrational views. His preference in civilizations was for the Greeks ('I am one of the few people who have studied Plotinus from cover to cover,' he said in a rare moment of self-congratulation of his thesis dissertation on Plato and Plotinus) and the Chinese. His reputation rests not so much on his contribution to the League of Nations, still less on any particular distinction as an historian, rather on his vast and (considering the more or less dismal failure of his practical aspirations) disproportionate influence on generations of young men at Cambridge.

Dickinson represents very nearly to perfection both the virtues and the drawbacks of what he called 'the Cambridge mind so rare, so exasperating to so many people, and as I think so precious and so indispensable'. Its effect on Noel was pronounced, and perhaps even more on Ivy. Its cast was rational, enquiring, scrupulously truthful, as far removed from passion as from bigotry or bias, its characteristic tone sceptical and ironic. There have been more dazzling Cambridge minds—Bertrand Russell and Maynard Keynes are obvious examples— but none so representative as Dickinson, and few more persuasive. His failings were a mild but resolute melancholy in which he took such satisfaction that it amounted at times to weakness, a naïveté whether in practical or ideal matters carried sometimes to disturbing lengths, and a maddening tendency to reserve judgement. Hard experience in later years taught Ivy the dangers inherent in this kind of passivity, which recurs again and again in onlookers helplessly watching tyranny triumph from the sidelines of her books. But at the time when she was writing *Dolores* or just afterwards, the impact of one who, in Forster's words, 'came down, perhaps rather too heavily, on the side of limpidity and logic' must have struck Ivy with particular force. 'One may almost say of him that he held nineteenth-century opinions in a twentieth-century way. For him, as for the Victorians, life was a pilgrimage, not an adventure, but he journeyed without donning their palmer's weeds.'[7]

The author of *Dolores* had held nineteenth-century opinions in an almost exaggeratedly nineteenth-century way; and, if it is impossible to say exactly when she changed (though it is not hard to adduce reasons as to why and how), it is evident that by the time she came to write her second novel in the early 'twenties she had imbibed not only the general scepticism prevalent at King's but even the mannerisms of Cambridge conversation:

'I think I have found myself at last,' said Herrick. 'I think that, God willing, I shall have done my little bit for my generation, done what every man ought to do before he dies.'. . .
'Assuming God, you wouldn't do much if he wasn't willing,' said Masson.[8]

The plot of *Pastors and Masters*, in so far as it can be said to have one, concerns nefarious doings among dons at the college of which Nicholas Herrick, aged seventy, is a retired Fellow and his two friends, William Masson and Richard Bumpus, still active members. The setting is an 'old university town' (evidently Cambridge since the author makes it very plain that the only other claimant to the name is Oxford, which she did not know), and the book contains at least one portrait drawn from Noel's acquaintanceship at King's: 'William Masson was a tall, large man in late middle age, with loose limbs and loose clothes, and a weather-beaten, high-boned face. He seemed an example of all the uneasinesses combined into ease.'[9] Masson's looks (his character seems to have been pure invention on his author's part) were borrowed from the Dean of King's, W. H. Macaulay, who, like Masson, was a mathematician and a bachelor from birth with the same handsome, high-boned features tortured by a shyness so devastating that he seldom spoke. Noel, wishing to reassure his future brother-in-law in June 1915, wrote a week or so before his marriage: 'Don't think of me as likely to be an unsympathetic, impossible person in your family. I'm only the characteristic don (though disfigured in khaki) with the nervous Macaulayisms of that tribe.'

Macaulay kept a horse in the meadow behind King's and is said to have ridden with Noel, who had learnt to ride like Ivy in the summer of 1912. Dickinson, who liked horses but frequently fell off them, also rode with Noel in his last two years at Cambridge. Both habitually kept well clear of women but Ivy had presumably seen them both (Macaulay, whose rooms were directly below Noel's in Wilkins Building, could hardly have avoided being seen, however adroitly he may have dodged an introduction) on her visits to King's. Whether or not she ever actually met Dickinson with Noel, she must have heard a good deal about him and she certainly knew him later. Her sisters remembered her visiting him at his sisters' house in Kensington after the war, when the two had a number of London friends (Arthur Waley and Noel's two younger contemporaries, Raisley Moorsom and Elliott Felkin, as well as Arthur's and Elliott's widowed mothers) in common. Dickinson in those days read Ivy's books as they came out, and 'said they were very queer stuff'.[10]

Considering that his tastes remained on many fronts notably unsophisticated, it is small wonder that Ivy's novels puzzled Dickinson, who had unwittingly contributed what was later to become a third strand—the type of detached and humorous observer who appears in almost every novel, perhaps most consummately as Mortimer Lamb in *Manservant and Maidservant*—quite as important as the theme of brother and sister or the archetypal tyrant to her books. This type is barely sketched in *Pastors and Masters* but already one may catch the characteristic tone. If one sets the book beside *Dolores*, the change in mood is very much that described by Forster in his comparison between Dickinson and Henry Sidgwick: 'Sidgwick wanted to believe in God and his inability to do so caused him a constant strain. Dickinson, equally conscientious, was somehow freer and less glum. It would never have occurred to him as it did to Sidgwick to compose his own funeral service. As soon as it came to the question of his own death, his own fate, he turned easy and modern, and one of the things which attracted the young to him was that he never gave them a sense of nursing a private destiny.'[11]

Ivy, too, had turned easy and modern by the early 'twenties ('"Are we going to be broad and wicked?" said Emily. "I like that, because I am not very educated, and so still young in my mind"'), and is plainly more at home in this atmosphere than she had been in the glum toils of *Dolores*. The difference is immediately apparent in a conversation—on God, and whether it is better to have Him or not—which pleasantly anticipates one of her favourite and most fruitful later themes:

'He always seems to me a pathetic figure, friendless and childless, and set up alone in a miserable way.'

'Yes, he has a touch of William in him,' said Emily. 'But you know he isn't childless. . . .'

'You can have him childless in these days,' said Bumpus. 'But if you have him, I like him really. I like him not childless, and grasping, and fond of praise. I like the human and family interest.'. . .

'And he had such a personality,' said Emily. 'Such a superior, vindictive and over-indulgent one. He is one of the best drawn characters in fiction.'[12]

Doubt and disbelief, which had led to desperate measures among an earlier generation of Cambridge dons, had become considerably less pressing by the turn of the century when O.B. kept a crucifix in his rooms 'to fwighten the agnoggers' and Dickinson was characteristically undecided. 'He hoped. He had no faith,' wrote Forster, and he had joined the Society for Psychical Research (which was known as the Ghost Club and met in O.B.'s rooms) just in case. At King's those who were not atheist or agnostic belonged to one of two parties. Floating voters were hotly contested between these parties, led on the one hand by the high church Father Waggett who lured likely undergraduates to his rooms with breakfast or luncheon invitations, and on the other by H. W. K. Mowll, a son of the Compton Burnetts' family solicitor and leader of the low church party. Howard Mowll, a fervent evangelical supporter of CICCU who had drummed up converts for a series of revivalist meetings in Noel's day at Cambridge and ultimately became the Anglican Bishop in Western China with a seat in Szechuan, appears on the *Basileon*'s index of standard authors for 1911 under the pen-name 'Aleister Crowley'. The general attitude seems to have been rather more relaxed than the 'ferocious agnosticism' practised a few years earlier up the road at Trinity ('"the College" is really enraged with us,' wrote

Leonard Woolf to Lytton Strachey in 1903. 'They think you are a witch and given up to the most abandoned and horrible practices and are quite ready to burn us alive at the slightest provocation.').[13] But even Woolf and Strachey had been advocates of truth and beauty, pursued with clandestine earnestness in what was still, for all their lurid talk—'The whole place seemed to me more depressed and more sodomitical than usual,' wrote Strachey on a visit to Cambridge in 1906—an optimistic and largely innocent society. 'We found ourselves living in the springtime of a conscious revolt against the social, political, religious, moral, intellectual and artistic institutions, beliefs and standards of our fathers and grandfathers . . .', wrote Woolf: 'The battle, which was against what for short one may call Victorianism, had not yet been won, and what was so exciting was our feeling that we ourselves were part of the revolution. . . .'

Noel's generation at King's shared this effervescence, combined with an agreeable sense of moral and material well-being. 'We prided ourselves on being less sophisticated than Oxford,' said William Haslam. Whisky, rumoured to be widely drunk by undergraduates at Oxford, was replaced at Cambridge by tea taken with walnut cake or anchovies on toast in each other's rooms at night, or at the discussion societies where:

> The young men seek truth rather than victory, they are willing to abjure an opinion when it is proved untenable, they do not try to score off one another, they do not feel diffidence too high a price to pay for integrity; and according to some observers that is why Cambridge has played, comparatively speaking, so small a part in the control of world affairs. Certainly these societies represent the very antithesis of the rotarian spirit. No one who has once felt their power will ever become a good mixer or a yes-man. Their influence, when it goes wrong, leads to self-consciousness and superciliousness; when it goes right, the mind is sharpened, the judgement is strengthened, and the heart becomes less selfish.[14]

Forster's glowing account well illustrates both what Ivy took from Cambridge and—perhaps rather more important—what she discarded. One might say that in a sense she spent a lifetime assessing the price of diffidence in her books among self-conscious, supercilious young men, whose flippancy is a measure of their own impotence in novel after novel against the forces of tyranny and oppression. But Forster's characteristically banal conclusion, on the mind, the judgement and the heart, reflects a lofty vagueness which he shared with Dickinson and with the Bloomsbury group in London (of which Dickinson was an honorary and Forster a founder member). This kind of spurious comfort, leading either to complacency or to an equally spurious nostalgic disillusionment, is something wholly alien to the world of I. Compton-Burnett where self-consciousness is an essential armour and superciliousness conceals a grasp of realities bleaker and more brutal than anything dreamt of in Forster's philosophy.

But these have as yet no place in the light fantastic vein of *Pastors and Masters*. The book is pervaded, as King's had been when Ivy knew it, by an incipient homosexuality which, according to a contemporary of Noel's, 'gave that golden glow. The college was suffused with it.' In the meadows beside the Cam the undergraduates 'ran quite naked in crowds over the green grass',[15] pairs of dons like Masson and Bumpus in *Pastors and Masters*—who 'had meant romance for each other in youth'—were common, and marriage (though permitted since the 1880s, and even indulged in by some few hardy Fellows) was beyond the pale. Scant sympathy was reserved for married dons like the one who, complaining to O.B. of his wife's coldness, said he might as well be living with a deal board: '"Take care," [O.B. replied], "or you'll find that you'll soon be living with someone a deal bawdier."' The general view is nicely represented by another mot of O.B.'s when someone consulted him as to whether or not the Venus in Botticelli's painting was out of drawing: '"It's no good asking me, my dear fellow," he answered blandly. "I've never seen a naked woman."' Women at King's were not so much disliked as simply disregarded, an attitude by no means unfamiliar to Emily Herrick in *Pastors and Masters* who, when her brother suggests that married women should be seen and not heard, cordially proposes that single women be exposed at birth ('"How would it be known at birth which of us were going to be single?" asked Delia. "That is really clever of you," said Emily. "Though people exposed at birth would be single, wouldn't they?"').

One can't help supposing that, however little Dickinson may otherwise have made of the novels of I. Compton-Burnett, he must surely have approved an outlook in Emily which coincided so exactly with his own. 'What I do mind rather is his [Dickinson's] quite unconsciously donnish attitude to women,' wrote one who did not share the spirit of affectionate indulgence extended by Emily to her brother and his friends. 'He never forgets that one is a woman, a woman who will presently leave the room, and whose remarks in the meantime must be listened to with pleasure if amusing, with civility if they are not.'[16] It might be a description of Nicholas Herrick's behaviour to his sister, who treats him in return with a tolerance which perfectly appreciates the nervous depredations brought about, on a delicate masculine sensibility, by feminine penetration. Quite apart from its first tentative inklings of formal innovation, *Pastors and Masters* is already an assured and humorous compendium of attitudes which must have given Ivy much quiet pleasure in the years when, like Emily Herrick, she too had sat discreetly listening to the conversation of her brother and his friends. The dampening effects of marriage are explained by Emily to her friend Theresa, who had broached the possibility of a proposal from William Masson:

'But he wants to marry you, doesn't he?'
'As much as he can want to marry anyone. Anyone who is a woman. And that is not very much.'
'Oh dear! These dons and people!' said Theresa.[17]

Pastors and Masters is the only one of the novels of I. Compton-Burnett which takes place wholly within a contemporary setting. For all its echoes of pre-war Cambridge, it was written and set after the first war, and published when its author was forty (which perhaps explains why all its main characters are well advanced into middle or old age). It contains therefore no hint either of undergraduate immaturity or of the sober optimism which prevailed in the Cambridge history circles Noel had frequented. Both dons and pupils held an encouraging belief in history as an active, beneficial, educative and pacific force. When this creed was contradicted by the outbreak of war, the effect on Dickinson was one of mortal shock—'The shock broke something in him which was never mended, and when at the close of his life he again functioned he had evolved a new apparatus, not repaired the old'.[18] Ivy, who had sustained a greater emotional loss and was to confront its implications throughout her later work, had perforce to abandon the illusion, to which Dickinson still clung, that passion might be prevailed upon by reason, or that the lessons of history might one day be learnt.

The effect of relinquishing so comforting a faith cannot have been made easier by the fact that her brother had himself subscribed to it.

'Noel believed in history, as people did in those days,' said Philip Noel-Baker. He and Noel had both belonged to a group which shared what their friend and fellow historian, Charles Webster, described as a 'sense of social duty higher than that of any of its predecessors and a greater belief that remedies could be found for the evils of the time'.[19] It was this sense of social duty—as sharply defined to Noel as family obligations were to Ivy—which lay behind the Fabian programme of the Carbonari, Rupert Brooke's socialist enthusiasms and O.B.'s tireless efforts to educate and entertain the working classes. It produced among young men at King's the strong and satisfactory feeling voiced by Nicholas Herrick, that each was required to do 'my little bit for my generation'; and they knew that this bit might be accomplished as much through the pursuit of history as through the holidays for working-class boys arranged on the King's barge at Rye, or the literary ambitions which preoccupied Brooke and appealed increasingly to Noel.

Webster's own monumental work on Castlereagh and European diplomacy had been undertaken at this time 'as a small contribution to preserve the world's peace' (though, as he afterwards ruefully remarked. 'I had underrated both the pace at which history would be made and the pace at which history could be written'). Webster, who had come up as a scholar in 1904 and was elected a Fellow of King's in 1910, three years before Noel, was one of the first among the coming young men at Cambridge to realize, at a time of considerable excitement on all historical fronts, that nineteenth-century foreign policy might be over-hauled and virtually re-written in the light of close study of the records. He himself set to work on Castlereagh at much the same time as his friend, Harold Temperley, on Canning, and the two books, published almost simultaneously some fifteen years later, subsequently became the standard works on their respective subjects. Noel, who in the spring of 1911 had been 'vaguely on the look out for something to make a thesis about' and applying to O.B. for suggestions as to 'something fairly modern, and if possible with human interest', eventually picked Palmerston, presumably in hopes of doing as much for him as his colleagues at King's for Castlereagh and Canning.

Webster in the years immediately before the war systematically combed the archives in London, Vienna, Paris, Berlin, Hanover, Warsaw, Cracow and St Petersburg. Noel, working meanwhile at Hove or on Foreign Office papers in London, corresponded regularly with Webster, reporting progress, thanking him for 'various tips', envying his trips abroad, noting that the Record Office and Chancery Lane were 'now quite desolate' in Webster's absence, even picturing him in verse—'In the city gay of Wien / There's a fellow to be seen / Long grey coat and Guy Fawkes hat /You'd wonder what they're staring at'*—and proposing in March 1912 to join Webster in Paris where he meant to examine the archives and learn French: 'thus shall enjoy at one and the same time the nimble flippancy of the Gallic intellect and the wholesome race of your English wit'. (31 March 1912) But, though he had applied for permission from M. Poincaré to consult the *Archive Nationale*, the Paris trip never materialized and Noel, already 'pretty despondent about the chase', grew steadily more bored with routine work ('Anything to go down must be *documenté* to the marrow,' he had written disconsolately to O.B. in June 1911) and more displeased with Palmerston. 'I think of him meanly enough, and I am inclined to quarrel with my lot of having to hoe with such a fellow for a twelve month,' he complained early in 1912 to O.B. He was also somewhat apprehensive when the popular candidate, Rupert Brooke, was passed over that spring in the Fellowship elections, which meant that Noel himself would have to compete with Brooke the following year: 'Still everything is in the lap of the Gods; I fancy—to adapt Fielding's saying, that the intrigues of the fellowship electors would not disgrace the conclave of Cardinals.' (24 March 1912)

In the event he got his Fellowship, tying thirteen votes on 8 March 1913, with Brooke. But notwithstanding his exuberant relief, his telegram to Jack Beresford—'Rupert and I elected to fellowships. Jim'—and his grateful message to O.B. ('I must write to you at once because to you I owe everything I have had at Cambridge'), Noel seems to have regarded a return to King's with small enthusiasm. His thesis dissertation, on 'Palmerston and Europe 1847–1850',[20] remained unfinished and, in his own view at least, unsatisfactory. 'There was a most distinctive, broad, kind, penetrating humanity of judgement in the finished parts, I well remember, which was the ripening fruit of his earlier idiosyncrasy,' wrote Clapham in Noel's obituary. But the whole, though eminently worthy, remained a far from brilliant piece of work. Noel's aim, as he explained with justified and engaging

---

* 21 January 1912. Professor Bindoff describes Webster's appearance nearly half a century later: 'his disdain for clothes was ducal, and in the decrepitude of his black hats he had no rival but Tawney'. ('Charles Kingsley Webster 1886–1961', PBA, vol. XLVIII.)

modesty, had been to institute a strictly limited comparison between received accounts of his brief chosen period and the records preserved in Foreign Office papers: an undertaking which, if pursued on Webster's massive scale, would have carried its author to all the major capitals of Europe and been measured in decades. Noel had spent instead one year at the London Record Office, and emerged with a study which he hoped might 'at least be held to possess a certain negative value'. Its findings were unexciting, its style (save for the Gibbonian opening paragraphs) pedestrian, its bibliography slipshod and its final chapters incomplete or given up for want of time. It reflects in short his own dissatisfaction in a letter dated 26 June 1912, to O.B.: 'I am writing my thesis—the business though is a bad one in so far as I have made no *discoveries*. Everything is known already. I am not going to degrade myself into a retailer of new *and unimportant* details. I am ready to take an independent view of Palmerston but I can't do any more for him.'

The college made Noel steward in the summer of 1914 'in order if possible to secure him for Cambridge', but by this time the chances of his staying had grown slim. 'I have left scholarship for the PRESENT and am sowing—prodigal the spirit but arduous the labour—certain literary wild oats,' he had written the previous December.[21] Exactly a year later, when he had already joined the army and was waiting to be posted, he wrote from Aldershot to Webster: 'You know Macaulay is stewarding for me? Very much confidentially, I doubt if I shall ever go back to Cambridge. I think I shall turn wholly to literature; and not *quite* impossibly get married or go round the world. All this of course when I get my discharge.' Even as he wrote it, the thesis seems to have represented the same kind of false start for Noel as *Dolores* a few years earlier for Ivy. What he would have done eventually— whether he would have turned in the same direction as his sister—whether indeed, if he had lived, she would have developed as she did—are unanswerable questions. 'I long to do something at literature but it will be a life of real hardship,' he wrote to Jack Beresford in March 1915, during his last spring in England. What is certain is that both Noel and his sister had thankfully abandoned the roads along which both had toiled with such forced and uncongenial effort in the im- mediate past—a break which seems to have come to Ivy as decisively, and for much the same reasons, as a similiar realization to Emily Herrick in *Pastors and Masters*: 'So I know for certain that I could never marry William. For I find that I only like wickedness and penetration.'[22]

2

'I THINK IVY observed everything that happened in everybody's life
and mind all the time she lived at Hove,' said her sister Juliet. The
household at Hove broke up in the autumn of 1915; and it was not
only Noel's friends, Arthur Waley and Elliott Felkin, who afterwards
claimed that Ivy's family at home had sounded exactly like the people
in her books. Harriet Cohen, at the start of her career as a pianist just
after the first war, drew the same conclusion from talking to Ivy's
younger sisters: 'Many were the tales they told of their extraordinary
doctor father and the fantastic conversations that took place in that
remarkable household. When I began reading Ivy Compton-Burnett's
books, I felt I recognized if not the people, the conversations.'[23]

Mrs Compton Burnett died on 5 October 1911. The rule of seclusion
imposed for years before that on her children ('We just had to live at
home really, concealing the family tragedy') had bred a nervous
resilience which must often have come close to exhaustion. She had
been mortally ill for a year, tormented by deafness, by acute rheumatism
and by sleepless nights which increased her weakness and pain. Only
Minnie was permitted to dress the wounds left on her wrists by radium
treatment, but there was little Minnie could do to lessen the strain of
constant attendance on the two elder children, and on Ivy alone in Noel's
terms at Cambridge. Even towards the end, when she had to be nursed
night and day, their mother refused to take to her bed. In the last week
of her life she would be carried downstairs in a chair to take the evening
air on the porch. Approaching death had done nothing to slacken the
force of a will bent, since her husband's death, on making time stand
still. She had been proud of installing a telephone at The Drive but it
was one of very few concessions made to the encroaching years after
1901. Her younger children could barely remember an existence not
governed by a morbid emotional intensity at home and an almost
complete withdrawal from life outside it. 'She was not progressive. She
couldn't have got used to a changing world. I remember on the day she
died Noel said: "Really we must regard it as a great mercy that she
hasn't lived to be old. Because she never could have faced it." And
she couldn't,' said Vera Compton-Burnett.

Their mother's death left the family listless, shocked and debilitated
—'for the first year one was almost stunned'—much like the young
Staces when Sophia died in *Brothers and Sisters*: 'The wave of emptiness
and release that came over them, held them silent. It seemed that a
weight had fallen, as a weight had lifted.'[24] The Compton-Burnetts
had spent so long in confinement that it is scarcely surprising if it took
another year for them to realize that the door was no longer locked,
and three more before they too escaped, like the Staces, to London. The
impulse, when it came, did not come from Ivy whose instincts seem to
have lain, with Samuel Butler's, against 'change of any sort . . . as
tending to unsettle men's minds'. She had discouraged all attempts to
soften the harsh daily routine at Hove ('It went on of itself, through a
kind of inertia,' said her sister Vera) and she resolutely opposed a
concerted attempt to abolish it altogether. A few years later, when her
tactics of resistance and delay had finally been worsted, she marked
with a thick pencil line in the margin a characteristic note of Butler's
against disrupting the established order ('. . . there is nothing so absolutely moral as stagnation') on grounds of strict moral economy: 'For
there will be an element of habitual and legitimate custom even in the
most unhabitual and detestable things that can be done at all.'[25]

The first few months of mourning were filled with family business,
hampered by colds and lingering quinzies, and further complicated by
the proofs of O.B.'s *General History of the World* which arrived from
the printers thick and fast by nearly every post that winter. Noel had
agreed to correct the proofs, issuing due warning ('I must tell you . . .
that I am a bad speller, know little about punctuation, and nothing
about names or facts' 11 July 1911) and, when neither his mother's
death with the mass of work it entailed on top of his own researches nor
his protracted influenza stemmed the flow, passing them to his younger
sisters. By 30 December Ivy was writing politely but firmly to O.B.
offering to return his proofs unread. Life at home meanwhile improved
slowly and slightly. Permission was occasionally given to miss lunch,
a thing unthinkable in their mother's lifetime, and friends could be
invited to the house as they never had been before ('It wasn't much of
a home to bring them to. It was so melancholy, and she was so
nervous.'). The whole family began to swim for the first time in June
—'a somewhat refrigerating experience,' wrote Noel to O.B. 'My progress in the art is very slow. You, who like Charlemagne and other
historical personages, have always been a great waterman, would laugh
at my preposterous marine evolutions.' The younger girls had bicycles

and Ivy and Noel took to riding on hired horses over the downs behind the town. Nearly half a century later, a friend happened to say that she, too, had once ridden with her brother on the beach:

'Oh, the horses like that,' said Ivy.
'Even walking was lovely,' she said, with a sort of mild ecstasy.
'Oh yes, bliss,' I agreed. 'Ambling along on an old horse, hedge-high. . . .'
For a few minutes we were away with our memories, with our brothers, and our horses.[26]

But, though Noel spent much of that spring and summer at home, he was also regularly away working at the Record Office in London and it had never entered anybody's head that he should settle at Hove, any more than it had as yet occurred to his sisters that they might settle elsewhere. Vera, who was just twenty when her mother died, and Judy, who was two years younger, had been for some time travelling up to take music lessons at the Matthay school in London; Topsy and Primrose, who were fifteen and twelve and who 'lived for each other' like the two older pairs, studied under music teachers in Hove. The gap in age and interest between these four and their eldest sister had always been wide, and now became unbridgeable. 'Ivy had inherited head of the household,' said her sister, 'and she was lost.'
'"Well, a house must have a head,"' says Miranda Hume in *Mother and Son*, listening in silence to the reply when her twelve-year-old nephew asks what it would be like without one: '"Someone would become the head," said his sister. "It is a natural law."'[27] Under the terms of their mother's will (a document which ignored the existence of her stepchildren as its author had never wholly succeeded in doing while she lived), Ivy and Noel became with Martyn Mowll trustees and guardians to their four sisters. Ivy at twenty-seven had already come into her money, Noel had a handsome allowance and would shortly take his full share, the others would neither inherit their portions nor be free of their guardians until they were twenty-four (which meant another twelve years for the youngest). They were to remain with Minnie as Lady Housekeeper in the house at Hove, where provision had been made for their upkeep and maintenance under an unbroken hierarchy—a point on which their mother, foreseeing perhaps a

possible source of contention, had left explicit instructions: 'and my said daughter Ivy shall so long as she remains unmarried be entitled to share the home . . . of my other children and take the head of it if she so wishes.' Ivy saw the injunction as her plain duty, and promptly set about eliciting from Mr Mowll the business secrets of a lifetime, for her father's estate had been joined to her mother's in the trust fund set up for their children and both largely consisted of property: farms, villas, building plots, whole streets full of working men's houses, each of which involved separate dealings with tenants. In September 1912, Ivy as landlord granted permission to the tenant of 40 Sackville Gardens, Hove, to attach a stop to her pier; a bulky envelope, dated April 1915, is endorsed 'Argument with Post Office in respect of telegraph pole and stay on land at Clacton'; and in the same year she paid the premium on eighty-nine fire insurance policies. Noel, whose interest in administrative detail was at best perfunctory, must have been glad to resign as much as he could to his sister. Another of her pencilled marks in the margin of Butler's *Note-Books* suggests that, before 1911, monetary transactions had been as darkly regarded among the Compton Burnetts as they were in most Victorian households: 'Next to sexual matters there are none upon which there is such complete reserve between parent and child as on those connected with money. The father keeps his affairs as closely as he can to himself and is most jealous of letting his children into a knowledge of how he manages money. . . .'[28]

Managing money became henceforward one of Ivy's strong points, and as head of the family she continued twice yearly to receive Martyn Mowll or Worsfold's son Rutley (or, when Rutley Mowll died, Worsfold's grandson) until the trust fund was wound up fifty years later. She had also taken over the housekeeping—sorting linen, ordering meals, engaging, supervising and dismissing maids—which remained her province to the end of her life. The rest of the family found themselves set apart from their two elders, who had moved from one side to the other of a traditional barrier which even Noel could not dismantle. The comical Gibbonian airs once assumed to conceal his crippling sense of weakness at home and shyness abroad had taken on an authority which, however much he might dislike it, was no longer simply a matter of make-believe and self-mockery. He was caught as much as Ivy in a system which proved stronger than either and remained—in spite of occasional forays into the twentieth century when friends from King's came visiting—frozen in all outward respects as it always had been since the year of Queen Victoria's death.

To the schoolroom party it seemed as though nothing had changed, except that Ivy had stepped into their mother's place. From now on she kept their accounts, inspected their property, oversaw their investments, arranged their education, interviewed their teachers, dealt out their allowances and generally assumed power over her sisters. One thinks of France Ponsonby's forecast in *Daughters and Sons*, when her brother says that it would be good to have power: '"No, we should use it," said France. "No one can stand it. None of us could: think of the stock we come of."'[29]

The overcast atmosphere which had briefly lifted settled again on the house at Hove. Music had meant freedom since earliest childhood for Ivy's sisters, and their one means of escape from a 'dark and loveless home'. Vera, who studied under Tobias Matthay and later under his pupil Myra Hess, had passed her L.R.A.M. ('She is very young to have four letters to her name,' wrote Ivy to their cousin Katie, '. . . and we are quite proud of her') a few months before her mother died, and Juliet a year or so later. Topsy, the most gifted of the four and the most like her father, promised already to follow her elder sisters. All four were accustomed to retire to the nursery, now renamed the music room and furnished with Botticelli prints handed down from Noel at Cambridge, where they shared a private world as remote as possible from their background and upbringing. Their only close friends in Hove were the children of Topsy's Wagnerian violin master, Siegfried, Isolde, Ludwig and Elfrieda Menges (two of whom later became professional musicians), who with their parents made a string orchestra to which Vera and Juliet contributed piano parts. The Menges opened a window on all that was most frowned upon in smug, respectable, philistine Hove; and the young Compton-Burnetts, who in their mother's lifetime had been forbidden to invite the Menges to their parties, 'half lived' at their house after her death. In the last summers before the war Vera would also walk over the downs to meet Myra Hess, in lodgings at Rottingdean, for a bathe and a practice. Ivy, whose respect for outward convention equalled her mother's, viewed these proceedings with misgiving: 'You see, music to her was a pure debit,' said her sister Juliet. 'You'd have thought she'd allow it was a recognized art—but she wouldn't, and she plainly said so.'

The practising which had distressed her for years steadily increased in volume until Ivy could stand it no longer. Piano playing was forbidden under her roof. The strings were still permitted to practise upstairs but the Bechstein grand—a gift to Vera from her mother, chosen by Mr Matthay when she passed her L.R.A.M.—was carried out of the house and round the corner to a hired music room in Church Road. Vera and Judy spent two hours there each morning, and were perhaps glad of the daily respite from their sister: 'We didn't develop as she would have chosen; she became very critical.' The three middle girls were by this time past saving, but it must still have seemed possible to retrieve the fourth from the hands of foreigners, artists, musicians, all equally undesirable influences in Ivy's eyes. After a bitter battle between Ivy and Topsy, which the elder and stronger inevitably won, their youngest sister was dispatched against her will to Cheltenham Ladies' College ('and it's *her* money that's being spent,' said Topsy furiously). Primrose had been 'Topsy's child' and devoted follower from birth, looking to her sister as Guy had once looked to Ivy for the protection and intimacy which were not to be had elsewhere; their mutual despair at parting led to a repetition of the miserable scenes enacted fourteen years before, when their elders had also been parted under duress. But Ivy remained as indifferent to tears and protests as her mother had been before her. After two terms at Cheltenham, just long enough for her to get over her first wretchedness and begin to accept her new life, the child was brought back—again without reference to her own wishes or Topsy's—and put to school at Addiscombe College. The episode was typical of Ivy's arbitrary dealings: 'There always *had* been a tyrant—she inherited the position, and she used it,' said her sister Vera.

Ivy, unlike her mother, never made scenes and was rarely seen to be angry. Her rule was quiet, orderly and cruel. Power seems to have been to her less an emotional gratification than a tactical advantage which she could no more help exploiting than her sisters could help but concede. 'Those were years in which Ivy wasn't master of herself— something was mastering her, and it wasn't the best part of her.' Her discomfited sisters found themselves put down and kept under, their proposals overruled and their attempts at retaliation hopelessly flattened by Ivy's sharp tongue. Asperity remained her habit to the end of her life, and so did a nerve-racking fondness for speaking aside, under her breath, like the characters who 'barely utter' in her books. Several of her friends in later life had much the same experience as Cicely Greig, who recalled that 'Ivy once "barely uttered" at me'. The two were sitting over dates and nuts at the end of lunch when Miss Greig, having ignored a suggestion that she use her finger bowl, heard her hostess say 'Wake up!' This was "barely uttered", a sort of sighing whisper which I pretended not to hear. I had only delayed movement by about half-a-minute, but the half-minute had been too long for Ivy.'[30]

Ivy's sisters had learnt submission from years of worse treatment than this, which came at first as a relief from more open methods of oppression. Vera had been nine when her father died, Primrose too small to remember him: 'Ivy had had a hard life, but what had ours been? *She* was away all those years.' But Ivy's four years at Holloway had given her perhaps grounds for a sharper grudge than her sisters, who had after all never known any alternative to life at Hove. If they had learnt to accept constant rebuffs, she had learnt a stoicism which went too deep for her ever again to attempt anything other than passive acquiescence. Their mother's death had come too late for Ivy to be able, probably even to want, to alter the system under which she had suffered herself. When her sisters foregathered in the music room, she sat alone downstairs in her father's study. She disapproved of their friends, mistrusted their ambitions, seldom joined in their activities, often scarcely saw them except at meals for weeks on end. When the others went bathing and practised fancy strokes or dived off the pier, Ivy would swim out at a steady breast stroke so far that her family 'used to wonder sometimes if she would ever come back'. Her sisters thought that she resented, and would have liked to prevent, their enjoying opportunities she had never so much as contemplated for herself. 'She had had just about as miserable and dull an existence as any young woman ever had—a neurotic mother, we never knew from one minute to the next what was going to happen—Ivy had to endure that,' said her sister Vera. 'She was twenty-seven. The iron entered into her soul. Left at home with four sisters younger—much younger—than herself. Schoolgirls. Noel was her *only* hope.'

But, as the future closed round Ivy, it was opening on all sides for Noel. By the autumn of 1911, Jack Beresford, Arthur Waley, Geoffrey Toulmin, Eric Forbes-Adam, 'almost all my contemporaries', as Noel wrote enviously to O.B. from Cambridge, had already 'gone into the great world', whither he himself meant shortly to follow them. He retained his rooms at King's as a Fellow from the spring of 1913 but he seems to have spent much of that year and the following summer in London, sowing his 'literary wild oats', visiting Jack in digs at Kew or calling for him at his office in Whitehall—'Last night I went out to examine our wire,' Noel wrote from the trenches in France in August 1915, 'and lying in the open under the stars I thought of you and of our foolish talks in St James last year.' Jack, who afterwards published

much pleasantly pastoral poetry besides his editions of Parson Wood-
forde and others, was already preparing his first slim volume of verse,*
and it seems likely that Noel was too. Both read, wrote and lived
poetry as Rupert Brooke had advised. Jack's wife Janet, to whom he
became engaged in 1914, was not a little disconcerted when her fiancé
would have no truck with boxes of chocolates but gave her a volume
of Wordsworth instead. Janet Beresford, later a close friend of Ivy's,
well remembered going to literary parties to meet H. G. Wells where
anyone as nicely brought up as she and Ivy had been was liable to end
up in a corner talking to the governess. Jack's cousin, J. D. Beresford,
was very much the coming man in these circles on the strength of his
first novel, *Jacob Stahl*, a somewhat earnest but fearlessly frank account
of its hero's social, sexual and sentimental education which rivalled Wells
as essential reading for the younger generation before the first war.
Jacob Stahl had been published in the same year as *Dolores*, and the
success of the one was as marked as the oblivion which had by now
overtaken the other.†

Not that Ivy in these years was by any means neglected. She and
Noel had spent a holiday with Toulmin and his sister in Austria (where
Ivy, greatly taken with the Tyrolean lakes, passed her evenings in the
hotel while her brother hobnobbed with German students), and Noel
was still much at home, frequently bringing one or other of his friends
to regale his sisters with tales of the great world. But to the inmates of
the unchanging household at Hove, Noel's accounts of amazing doings
in London must have seemed as remote as the dens of vice and sinks of
iniquity frequented by Robin Stace in *Brothers and Sisters*—dens and
sinks which prove such a disappointment to his family when they finally
decide to join him in town:

* *Poems by Two Brothers* by Richard and John Beresford, Erskine Macdonald, 1915.
Noel, who was already in France when the book came out, wrote to thank Jack for
the poems: 'yours very familiar to me and bringing back very many walks and talks. I
like them much and your brother's have a fresh beauty for me—these days they seem
to cling about the cannon's mouth safe because so frail and light.' (18 October
1915.)

† 'Dear Madam, We beg to enclose herewith statement showing the position of your
novel *Dolores* as at the end of 1913. There is, as you will see, no demand for the work,
and as our warehouse space is of value we think we should try to dispose of the stock
on hand as a remainder which would probably mean not more than 3d or 4d per
copy bound. If you wish any copies we would let you have them.

We would be glad to have your instructions regarding the matter. We are, Yours
faithfully. . . .' (Letter from Blackwood, 26 March 1914.)

'We find that Robin's London life has nothing to conceal.'

'Oh, and I have envied it so,' said Julian. 'I have wondered how it was I could do nothing with mine.'[31]

For years Jack and Noel (known as Jim to the Beresfords as he generally was to his sisters) had exchanged visits and, when Jack still travelled down from London almost every weekend to Easton Grey in Wiltshire where his father was rector, Noel often went with him and sometimes brought Ivy. 'I have not ever seen a brother and sister so devoted—so essential—to each other,' said Jack's sister Dorothy. They seemed uncomfortably solemn to the Beresfords' companion, Miss Fox, who as housekeeper and general helpmeet spent a good deal of time at the rectory and who found the Compton-Burnetts a difficult pair: 'I thought they took life very seriously'.

Perhaps their diffidence stood out among the Beresfords who were all voluble talkers, explosive, impetuous and erratic in temper, accustomed to fascinate by a desperate combination of the family magnetism with the family's startling good looks. The three girls—Dorothy, Tertia and Mary who were much of an age with Noel's sisters Ivy, Vera and Primrose—were individually dazzling, and together they must have seemed overpowering. It was always afterwards said that Jack had found husbands for all his sisters, and Noel on their walks early began to pair off with—was perhaps already writing poems to—Tertia, though they were not officially engaged till the beginning of 1915. Tertia was the third of the Rev. John Jervis Beresford's four daughters (one had died as a child) and the most retiring, with more than her share of the strain of melancholy and pessimism which ran through the whole family and a romantic disposition not belied by her white skin, green eyes and blue-black, raven's hair. 'A very beautiful, rather sultry, George-Eliotish character,' said one of her nieces long afterwards. Noel's sisters, who thought Tertia fey and none too bright, allowed that she led an intense inner life nourished, like all the Beresfords', on a passion for poetry. A painting of her by Margot Asquith's sister, Lucy Graham Smith, is so like the description of Ruth Giffard in *More Women Than Men*—' "I have hardly had my own news yet," said her daughter, in her husky, languid tones, turning to her mother her dark, unusual face, with its absent, indifferent eyes and curved and protruding lips'[32]—that one can only suppose Tertia sat for both portraits.

Ivy, who later shared a flat with both Tertia and Dorothy in turn, seems to have borrowed traits freely from each for characters in her books; and indeed all the Beresfords may be said to have left their mark on her work. They were the first family she knew well who belonged to that narrow pocket of the upper middle classes—'large gloomy moderately rich families in largish, though not immense, houses in the country, going as a matter of course to Oxford or Cambridge, interested in acquiring property or money, yet lacking almost all contact with an outer world, living in a state of almost hysterically inward-looking intensity' in Anthony Powell's definition[33]—which has nowhere been more minutely explored than in her next nineteen novels. The Beresfords boasted a pedigree going back to the Conquest[34] and a seat bearing their name in the Staffordshire dales; their mother was a Margaret Hollinsed descended, according to family legend, from the chronicler who provided Shakespeare with plots; Beresford sons had been sent since the sixteenth century to Cambridge, and afterwards put to the church or the learned professions. The rector's children had inherited intact their paramount sense of the family's importance but (the Beresford fortunes having passed to a collateral branch in the seventeenth century) they lived on their father's diminutive stipend making ends meet, like so many of the less prosperous families in the novels of I. Compton-Burnett, at the brink of financial disaster. Jack had been sent for tuition to a neighbouring clergyman and his sisters 'crazily educated' by their father at home. Mr Beresford was blind, a bard and, even by Compton-Burnett standards, a creditable autocrat. His daughters, like Milton's, had for years been obliged to take turns at reading to him in languages ancient and modern ('In the scene of misery which this mode of intellectual labour sets before our eyes,' wrote Dr Johnson of Milton's domestic arrangements, 'it is hard to determine whether the daughters or the father are most to be lamented')* or at writing down the poems he recited. His oratory seems to have

---

* *Lives of the Poets*, World's Classics, O.U.P., 1952, vol. 1, p.102. Mr Beresford's daughters were more fortunate than Milton's in that they had been taught at least the rudiments of Greek, Latin, French, German and Italian, but less so in the poems which resulted when their father wove what he called the Woof of Song. One may serve as an example:

'The Coming Woman' 16.1.95.

Time hath been a girl was blushing.
Hesitating, shamefaced, shy,

been as fierce as his will. Asquith, whose wife's sister was married to the squire of Easton Grey and who seldom gave his undivided attention to sermons, once confessed to Dorothy Beresford: 'I never read the collects when your father is preaching'.

Tart tongues and short tempers bred a high standard of wit at the rectory. The Beresfords lived in very nearly complete isolation, seeing no one save the few families in country houses round about, natural overlords in the village, revolving round an elderly tyrant at home—'an ancient Roman, man most excellent,' wrote Noel of Jack's father, 'though poles apart from me as such a man must be'—and preserving a fair crop of dark secrets in their past. Mr Beresford had been blinded in infancy by a twin brother who poked out his eye with a pair of scissors; the brother, dying young, was afterwards expunged from the family tree. Mrs Beresford—'a racehorse put to do carthorse work' according to her daughter Dorothy—had found family life too much for her and retired for good to a nursing home in Somerset soon after Mary was born; though she lived for another fifteen years, her daughters never saw her again, her name was not mentioned and there was no picture of her in the rectory. Jack's elder brother Dick, a King's choir scholar and a captivating child who had failed to live up to his promise, was finally dispatched round about this time to South Africa (as secretary to Lord Gladstone through the Asquiths' kind offices) and never came back. The whole family was given to freaks of temperament pricked on by an imagination which furiously coloured even their most humdrum transactions. 'They were a potent family to marry into,' said Jack's wife Janet, whose sisters-in-law must have proved on occasion a trial and who, though not often daunted, stood in considerable awe of old Mr Beresford.

It is not hard to see why the family made a lasting impression on both Noel and his sister: 'It was all observation with her,' said Juliet Compton-Burnett, who thought Ivy in these years spent her time watching and noting. 'If you came into a room, she would look you up and down in an instant, from head to foot.' Noel, less aloof than his sister and far

---

Time hath been: now she is crushing,
Or she will be by and by.
For she learns to play at Hockey
And at Hare and Hounds and Fives
Till, with hands and heart right rocky,
She will make the worst of wives.

more at home with the Beresfords, seems to have found in their company something of his father's boisterous spirits: Dorothy remembered him rising up with cries of 'My turn!' at one of Mrs Graham Smith's dinner parties, flagging his napkin in an attempt to shout down the assembled Tennants, Asquiths and Beresfords. It was not only their forcefulness which had impressed Noel since his first meeting with Jack at King's ('having my first friendly talk at Cambridge, and infinitely admiring your mastery of a very formidable landlady'). He liked also their extravagant vagueness, their indifference to shabby clothes and short commons, their habit of declaiming Matthew Arnold aloud at the hills or enthusing over 'the flowers of the field' with a fine rhapsodical buoyancy which matched his own. Ivy, though resilient enough if need be, took a firm line with people or facts she deplored: 'I daresay you are depressed. We most of us are that,' she wrote to her cousin Katie on 22 September 1914. 'Indeed, if long faces were of any help to anyone, it would be refreshing to reflect how much good we should some of us be doing. However, efforts in that line being no good, the other is the one to be taken. I suppose though economizing, & subscribing, & meeting folks with folks at the war, are things not to be welcomed by the most stoic.' Noel was as crisp as his sister but better disposed towards circumstances which might well have depressed him. 'There is a strong and very unexpected beauty about a camp,' he wrote in the spring of 1915, waiting for his posting to France under canvas in pouring rain on Salisbury Plain. 'There's a freedom about this swaying windy wet dwelling that more than makes up for not feeling comfortable . . . I would rather live in a tent than in a house for ever. But to that Tertia though she agrees to much, certainly will not agree so dont be alarmed. Its rather cold though. . . .'

3

ON THE OUTBREAK of war the Compton-Burnetts, who had finally decided to move as a family to London, had just taken a house in South Kensington. Noel had fixed on the first weekend in August to go down from Cambridge 'to pay a few visits, and then home' where his sisters were already preparing to shake the dust of No. 20 The Drive from their feet for good. Cambridge was no less surprised by the war than

Hove, or for that matter the British Cabinet, which had spent the better part of July urgently discussing the Irish question. On 28 July, exactly a week before war was declared, Noel wrote to Elliott Felkin from King's complaining how bored he was by 'dull dull English academicians' and proposing to spend the summer abroad. In the event, he spent the summer at an army training camp in Cambridge with Jack Beresford. Like most of his friends, Noel supported the anti-war movement hastily mounted by Dickinson and others, but by the end of August Cambridge had succumbed with the rest of the country to a violent fever of jingoism. Military hospitals were set up in college buildings, the O.T.C. installed at Pembroke and Corpus, boy scouts bearing messages buzzed about all over the town, railway bridges were guarded, telephone lines patrolled and troops so thickly billeted that, according to the *Cambridge Review*, 'you could hardly step in the streets without bumping into khaki'. Of the Fellows of King's, Maynard Keynes had been summoned posthaste by the Treasury to London, Rupert Brooke was negotiating with Churchill for a commission and Noel had been told by the local commanding officer 'that he thought I had very little chance of a commission. There are 50 very likely people in King's, all of whom have been refused. The doctor reported me as fit . . . but my chest measurement is absurdly small—not good enough for a private. Meanwhile I shall join the O.T.C. There is to be 3 hours drill daily.' (8 October 1914)

Noel, always pacific, was also like his sister a realist. He had voted No to the motion, 'Is war preventable?', at his first meeting of the Political Society in 1907 and, in a debate on conscription at the Union the following spring, 'Mr Compton-Burnett rose with loosened joints. If he had to serve in the army, he would be a demoralizing influence since he would be the last to advance and the first to retire. It was useless to force those to fight whose natures were against fighting. Mr Compton-Burnett has a neat, gentle way of putting things.'[35] Two years later Noel was describing local German manœuvres ('All looked very efficient and, to English eyes, regrettably formidable') to Jack from Göttingen. 'Personally I believe the war will be over in less than a year,' he wrote in October 1914; and in November he read a paper for the last time to the Political Society on 'Peace'. 'It was, as I remember it, a moving defence of the love of peace, because peace is life,' wrote John Clapham after Noel's death. 'He had already decided to take his risks in war.' The reasons underlying this decision are sufficiently clear in a letter written that autumn from King's:

Dear Charles Webster,

Your dissertation on college wine politics showed the grasp of the master. Many thanks. I won't trouble to get the Wine Committee to meet this term.

You are occupied indeed, and that is to the good if it prevents thought. Nothing comes of thinking of the good friends who have dropped out of our lives, whose death has done so little for the world they would have served so valuably with their lives. Nothing comes of thinking of it but one must think.

You want college news. Well of course there isn't any. We have no history but all the same we aren't happy. Various young men come up for a few days liberated from the front or from training camps. Stackard was in Hall tonight. How horrible *him* to be mentioned in dispatches and poor Freddie to be dead and done for, how horribly ironical and typical of war! . . .

I get more and more anti-war. I realise more completely how impossible it is to reconcile the intellectual attitude to the war with the popular politician's attitude. Ramsay Macdonald and the I.L.P. are my only hope in the home situation. The situation at the front seems uncertain enough.

N. C-B.*

Noel's attitude to the prevention of thought, and even his turns of phrase, bear an almost uncanny family likeness to the terse stoicism with which his sister in later years marked and mourned the loss of friends. He seems to have arrived early at that mood of uneasy resignation described by Robert Graves and others who, with few illusions as to their own heroism or the conduct and aims of the war, were driven to return again and again to the front by a sense of personal loyalty to their friends and their men which came to seem infinitely more real than the cloud of fraudulent emotion and dishonest propaganda covering political and military incompetence at home.

It was considered monstrous by his friends at Cambridge that Noel of all people, so dreamy, impractical and sweet-tempered, partly disabled since childhood and still in indifferent health, should be swept up and tossed away as a second lieutenant in the trenches. 'We thought it an outrage,' said Philip Noel-Baker. Elliott Felkin, who had written

* Freddie was F. M. Hardman who had come up to King's in 1909 and was killed in action on 27 October 1914; Dickinson shared Noel's contempt for all politicians 'with the exception of the I.L.P.' (*Goldsworthy Lowes Dickinson* by E. M. Forster, p.165.)

bluntly to ask why anyone should of his own accord abandon civilian life, received an answer which makes it clear that Noel stuck as firmly as his sister to their father's view of duty: 'The explanation of my soldiering is simple enough. Having searched my conscience very severely I decided that my main reason in not "rolling up" was personal aversion to doing so. That point having been reached for a man of my character my dear Sir the resulting action necessarily followed. Don't think tho' I'm a jingo. My view of the war remains. *Only* desiring as I do the defeat of Germany, or at least desiring Germany not to win, I couldn't stand out.'

This letter was one of the very few mementoes of her brother which Ivy afterwards kept to the end of her life. The two surviving letters from him to her, both written just before the battle of the Somme, suggest that the pair were so close, and so wholly at one in their view of the war, that they probably felt little need to discuss it. Noel's reasoning must have seemed self-evident to Ivy, whose whole adult existence had been a matter of submitting personal inclination to the severest search of conscience. It seems likely that she accepted from the start her brother's attitude to the wastefulness and futility of what seemed to so many of their contemporaries 'a war of defence and liberation'. It is almost impossible to over-estimate now the patriotic exaltation which then swept the country, a communal hysteria so powerful that, as casualties mounted to a point which still beggars belief, families at home took to placing cards in their windows proudly detailing their losses at the front. White feathers were distributed, and dachshunds stoned in the streets for German dogs. In October the Schlosses changed their name to Waley because, as Arthur told Raisley Moorsom, he was tired of being arrested six times in one month as an enemy spy. 'Thus do the mob and the idols of the market place reign in triumph,' wrote Noel to Elliott when he heard the news, 'all aesthetes and men of independent intellect palpably most prone before them.' (15 October 1914)

Noel embarked on a military career without rancour and without repining, though with a passionate sense of all he had already lost that autumn and of all that he still stood to lose. His sober estimate of the situation meant that he faced sooner than many of his more idealistic contemporaries the need to reconcile himself to his own extinction in a cause for which he felt no enthusiasm—' "for neither in law nor war is it right for any man to take every means of escaping death". Thus Socrates and also one's own inner mind,' he wrote to Jack the night before a raid which he did not expect to survive in October 1915. Two months in the front line had taught him to confront death with an equanimity which, though more solidly based, was not essentially different from the feeling with which he had first joined the army almost exactly a year before. People who entered the war without illusions in 1914 were at least protected from the bewildered disillusionment of those in whom an unsuspecting patriotism only gradually gave way to a proportionately bitter sense of betrayal till, as the war dragged on, 'its continuance seemed merely a sacrifice of the idealistic younger generation to the stupidity and self-protective alarm of the elder'.[36]

The practical uselessness of this kind of theoretic knowledge, and the impotence of a younger generation ruthlessly suppressed by its egotistical elders, are constant themes in the later novels of I. Compton-Burnett; and so is the vanity of struggling to achieve the independence which had eluded both her brother and herself. Otherwise there is little direct evidence, beyond one brisk, reproving letter to her cousin, as to how Ivy felt that autumn. The few people who discussed the '14-'18 war with her long afterwards were all considerably younger, and all agreed that it was a subject she still found almost intolerably painful. Nearly thirty years later, casual visitors in the second war were warned by her closest friend that the fighting must not be mentioned in Ivy's presence. The people who knew her well enough to talk about the first war at the time are nearly all dead now. Perhaps one of them was Lowes Dickinson, who certainly had Noel in mind after the war when Ivy knew him, though it is quite probable that neither overcame their mutual shyness sufficiently to say much about her brother. Dickinson had been appalled by a catastrophe which destroyed his whole basis for living: 'The outbreak of the Great War was an almost paralysing shock to Dickinson,' wrote Roger Fry. 'He had as it were staked everything on his belief that human beings were fundamentally reasonable, that the appeal to reason must find a response. . . .'[37] He had discussed matters with Noel at King's in the autumn of 1914; and, though Dickinson shrank all his life from giving advice, he did at least confirm Noel's feeling that there was nothing to be done but fight.*
Afterwards he seems to have felt Noel's death as an extra burden added

---

* Information from Raisley Moorsom; Dickinson was fifty-two when war broke out: 'there was for me no question of enlisting though I think I should have enlisted if I had been younger, for I was not "a conscientious objector", though I had no illusion about the war nor anything but despair in my heart.' (*Goldsworthy Lowes Dickinson* by E. M. Forster, p.156.)

to his general crushing discouragement: 'Goldie felt a mild sense of—not exactly remorse—a mild sense that perhaps he should have told him something different,' said Raisley Moorsom who knew Dickinson well between the wars. 'I remember so often his saying that, more than once to me, how he felt that about Noel and how sad he was.'

Whatever Noel's private struggle may have cost him, there is small trace of it in his wartime letters which suggest rather a cheerful confidence in his own adaptability. In spite of the forebodings of his friends he inclined to like the army, living 'in very passable comfort . . . at the nation's expense', growing 'more stupid and lazy with every day that passes' and agreeably impressed by the unfamiliar charms of white tents against the sky or, later, by 'old gold dawns' in the trenches. Ivy, as philosophical as her brother, watched his pleasure with indulgence and amusement: 'Jimmie was here with Jack Beresford for some days last week,' she wrote to Katie from Hove, where the pair had spent their leave from the Cambridge training camp on Royston Heath. 'He has so enjoyed his taste of soldiering, & looks so strong and well—with a *cropped* head, quite in military style!! Can you think of him?' By the late autumn the Compton-Burnetts had abandoned their move to London, Jack had returned reluctantly to his office at the Board of Education in Whitehall and Noel had become a member of Kitchener's vast new civilian army, receiving his commission on 23 November from the Leicestershire Regiment and his training at barracks in Aldershot, where he found little to console him among his brother officers: 'pleasant fellows enough—for them life and art being the latest musical comedy. I like and feel for the privates: they are just humanity, suffering and patient. I've just been inspecting their feet, 600 of the dirtiest, poor tortured feet you can think of. I felt my sympathy for them almost too much. It's this damned sentimentality that plays the dickens with a man's constitution.'

Jack and Janet Beresford were married on 11 February 1915, and settled in a flat on Queen's Road, Bayswater. Noel's letters at this time to Jack (who, with a new wife besides three sisters to support and an ailing, elderly father, had for the moment no choice but to remain at home) are unfailingly generous, showing no sign of envy or even despondency, only a persistent desire to reassure his friend which underlies any number of blithe and ingenious attempts to divert him. But Noel, marooned at Aldershot and later in billets at Andover, was increasingly caught up that spring in his feelings for Tertia, to whom he became engaged round about the time of Jack's wedding. 'I dread going back to Andover leaving behind all that I value. I wish I was settled with Tertia and that you and Janet were coming to stay with us. I feel a pleasant certainty that things—even small delightful things like that—are predestined,' he wrote at Easter, after a brief leave spent visiting the Rodin exhibition with Tertia from Jack's flat in Queen's Road. His letters turn constantly on their hurried, unsatisfactory meetings ('Tertia and I are getting one of our snatches next weekend . . .'), on their plans for the future ('Tertia and I will be lamentably poor . . . Still . . . my friends will stick to me and hers to her, both of them to us, so what does in the name of friendship money matter in any degree?') and on arrangements for procuring a ring from Liberty's ('a diamond to be set in silver . . . engraved inside "as rivers in the south" . . . this must be *slender*; very light and slight: see to that'). By the beginning of April he had made a will and moved to the transit camp at Perham Down, quoting nonchalantly from the Bible: 'The people complained in their tents'. From now on his letters become steadily more clouded by dread of the future, by news of Rupert Brooke's death at Gallipoli, by his anxiety for Tertia, the misgivings of her family, and ominous signs of his own impending departure: 'The report this morning is that we're going to Turkey in 6 weeks but I don't believe it . . . I trust and pray we don't go for poor Tertia. Oh Jack how terrible! I lie awake often and think of that till I'm as cold inside as out.' (11 April 1915)

Noel's preoccupation with Tertia can have left little time for his sisters, whose troubles meanwhile had multiplied. Their delight at the prospect of escaping from Hove had turned to desperate dismay when the war put a stop to their plans. 'For my part, I am quite dreading to see Mowll next week, & hear what effects the war may have on us,' wrote Ivy to her cousin in September. 'I have cut down the girls' musical expenses as far as I can, without really interfering with their progress. And they are all very good and sensible about it.' But Ivy's categorical directions were by this time more than her sisters could stand; and they were convinced that the household would have continued unchanged, with Ivy installed at its head in perpetuity, if she had not been faced with open revolt. She had written nothing since their mother's death, concentrating instead on home affairs and putting her manuscript, if she had one, in a drawer like the two novelists in *Mother and Son* whose youthful ambitions had likewise come to nothing ('"I wonder there is any drawer space left," said Miss Burke').[38] Domestic supremacy, combined perhaps with the stationary sales of

Dolores, had for the moment suspended her determination to write. But Ivy at thirty must still have aspired, like the authors in *Mother and Son,* to higher things—even apparently contemplating their pursuit at a fashionable establishment for young ladies in Kensington, which was another scheme scotched by the war. 'I don't think I must think of Amica's college while we are living in Brighton, though in some ways I should like very much to join the essay class. I daresay I shall, some time. . . . Both my nice maids leave this Saturday, and two more come,' wrote Ivy who, though she pinned no hopes on the efficacy of prayer herself, was not above asking her cousin to arrange 'public intercession at the after-breakfast ceremony, on my behalf, at this crisis'. The letter bears out her sisters' view, that Ivy at this time did indeed behave as though she were the only person on the premises: 'It was *my* servants, *my* house and not ever ours. . . . She was desperately holding on to my mother's place. She had no conceivable notion of equality between sisters.'

Myra Hess, who as the friend and teacher of Vera and Judy had been invited to stay at Hove, seems to have reacted with much the same startled incredulity as the Ponsonbys' visitors in *Daughters and Sons* ('"I rather wonder that your grandmother welcomes strangers in the house." "I can't think how she dares to," said Victor. "It is sheer impudence and dare-devilry. It comes of a lifetime of having her own way."'). Myra had pronounced that things could not go on. 'She couldn't believe the household she'd come into. She said, "You're all in fetters. You must get away."' The astonishment was mutual. 'When we saw other people who hadn't been brought up in that way,' said Vera Compton-Burnett, 'we perceived for the first time what an astonishing situation ours was.' Details of the struggle that followed—a struggle in which Ivy herself, unlike most of her tyrants, ultimately sustained defeat—are paralleled again and again in the state of simmering mutiny which pervades so many of the novels of I. Compton-Burnett. The Sullivans, discussing their governess in *Parents and Children,* give perhaps a sympathetic hint of the difficulties with which Ivy must have had to contend in these months at Hove:

'She still seems to me in her own way a person born to command,' said Luce. . . .

'I wonder if anyone is born to obey,' said Isabel. 'That may be why people command rather badly, that they have no suitable material to work on.'[39]

The Mowbrays speculate on similar lines about their father; and the Ponsonbys, Haslams and Edgeworths react to a brief respite from oppression with a mixture of uneasiness and relief not unlike the feelings of Ivy's sisters when, in the spring of 1915, she fell ill and was laid up for some weeks with bronchitis: 'Of course we went up to see her, there was no open breach at that time. But we felt so free—of her. There was no constraint at meals.'

The break was decisive. Ivy's sisters had been much moved by reading Emerson, and by a general stirring against the old order in the world at large which confirmed their own restiveness. Being still powerless to loosen Ivy's grip on the household, they determined to leave it. Minnie was consulted and took, as her descendants generally do in the novels, a pessimistic view: 'Minnie said, "You'll never manage it. We shall be here always, we can never change it."' But all four were now irretrievably bent on escape, led by Vera ('It became unendurable. One was twenty-three and one had had no life of any kind') who wrote to Noel at Perham Down saying she had urgent secret business to discuss. When Noel, suspecting a love affair, replied that this was neither the time nor the place for a visit, Vera delivered her ultimatum by post.

Noel's state of mind was by this time nearly desperate. 'Tertia and I have long had a plan which I think we will stick to,' he had written at the beginning of April to Jack: 'If all goes well and I am not sent to the wars we will wait for peace to be married, as in such things turmoil and haste, and waiting upon trains when one should wait only on the sun and moon, are all discords and hard to reconcile oneself to. If on the other hand the summons seems likely we will marry out of hand and get what comfort we can.'

In the meantime they had to make do with meeting uncomfortably at other people's houses in London for odd weekends before he returned to Perham Down and she to Easton Grey where old Mr Beresford, not best pleased by Jack's marriage, looked with open disfavour on Tertia's. Even Jack had his doubts about a match between two such highly excitable people. Tertia was by nature unstable, being prone like her mother to nervous trouble, and Noel himself, though calm enough to the outward eye, seemed to his friends to possess neither the robust temperament nor the physical stamina required to sustain prolonged emotional strain. Jack's mistrust must have been especially bitter to Noel. 'If I marry Tertia *now* it can only be a nominal marriage,' he wrote on 13 May in a letter which, though he felt it 'impossible [Jack]

should understand', makes a last, sad attempt to dispel his friend's
forebodings: 'I won't run the risk of anything else; and not being able
to live together, if we marry before I go it *must* be at the last minute. . . .'
Neither family can have been much reassured but no one could long
withstand Noel's urgency or, as rumours multiplied and it became clear
that his posting could not be much further delayed, his sound reasons
for snatching at happiness. By the end of May he was arranging details
with Jack:

> How speedy can the thing be done. I can only get four days so time is
> precious—the glass runs out sands of gold. Will you find out. I am
> so far from things here. Can one just go to a church and be married.
> . . . If ecclesiastical marriage is difficult, we will content ourselves
> (very willingly, and perhaps preferably) with the civil. You wouldn't
> mind would you. If you would that settles it for Tertia and me. We
> always call Janet and you our only friends—and neither of you can
> know the gratitude we have in our hearts. Write at once. I rather
> think I could get next Friday week—till Monday but I'm not sure.
> I've been practising with a pistol (leaving nothing to chance) Jim.

In the event, after some tactful negotiations on Jack's part, they were
married on 12 June by Tertia's father in the church at Easton Grey.
Jack was there but Ivy was not. On 16 June, after four days' privacy
and peace at a farmhouse in Wiltshire, her brother was back at Perham
Down still without knowing the date of his departure for France
(which came at short notice six weeks later). From Noel's point of view
his family could hardly have chosen a more wretched moment to
quarrel. Distracted by preparations for the front, by fears for Tertia, by
haste and uncertainty and the difficulty of conducting affairs through
the post at long distance, he had replied to Vera, defending Ivy and
upbraiding his younger sisters for what must have seemed an ill-judged
and mischievous squabble, erupting at the worst possible time. 'But for
us it was the *last second*. Flesh and blood couldn't stand it any longer. So
in a way there was a rift with Noel too,' said Vera Compton-Burnett.
'He took it very hard.'

What Ivy's reactions were at this point—what part Noel's marriage
or his dangerous future played in her feelings—one can only surmise. It
was years since the two had held all things in common but, though his
defection had been both gentle and gradual, one may perhaps suspect
that Ivy suffered as keenly as Noel from the isolation described in his

sombre letter of 13 May to Jack: 'I feel the profound loneliness of life, deepened and darkened, as I realise that only the heart knows its own weakness and bitterness.'* If Noel's engagement had come as a shock, perhaps a violent one, Ivy bore it in silence as she bore the prospect of his imminent departure, and the last phase of the long drawn struggle at Hove. 'It was a time of pain and difficulty, as it must be, like an abscess before it breaks,' said Vera Compton-Burnett. The four girls had agreed that, in spite of Noel's disapproval and no matter what Ivy might do, they would take their own house in London and share it with Myra Hess. They had calculated that they might 'live and pay for music lessons and get on quite well' on their combined allowances, eked out by the sale of their mother's jewellery ('She was very fond of diamonds. I remember I had a diamond pansy which I lived on for quite a while') which had been equally divided between her five daughters. They drew lots to decide who should break the news to Ivy.

'I never shall forget the day it had to be done. Or the meal at which I did it,' said Vera, who had drawn the shortest. 'I remember my voice dying away. And having to take a new breath to continue. And being kicked by one of the others under the table.' This was at an evening meal towards the middle of the summer. Ivy's only reply was to point out that both parties might conveniently live without meeting in a house with two staircases: 'One would be the servants', and the other would be hers—that was the way her mind worked.' For the next few weeks the matter was not mentioned again. Silence became Ivy's weapon. She might accept their decision but she would do nothing to implement it—'She would take no part. She took no steps'—though she did summon the family solicitor from Dover. 'He came to prevent it. A Victorian if ever there was one,' said Vera Compton-Burnett. But the girls' determination defeated even Martyn Mowll who said heavily, as he rose to go: 'Miss Vera, you have made your bed. And you must lie upon it.'

By the first week in August, Noel was reporting distant gunfire as he marched towards the western front. By the beginning of September, his younger sisters had signed the lease of the house in St John's Wood where for the next twenty years they lived with Myra Hess. By October they had left No. 20 The Drive, chosen what little of its contents

* 'The heart knoweth his own bitterness; and a stranger doth not intermeddle with his joy' (Proverbs 14:10). Violet Powell (*A Compton-Burnett Compendium*, Heinemann, 1973, p.85) points out that 'the heart knoweth' is a phrase Ivy later used twice, in much the same context as Noel, in her novels.

they wished to retain, and organized a sale of the rest which took place on the twelfth, thirteenth and fourteenth of that month. They spent the week of the sale at a boarding house in Holland Road and immediately afterwards followed their furniture to London, chaperoned by Minnie whose feelings—after thirty-three years spent serving the family with a devotion which had survived their father's death, Guy's, their mother's alteration in character and what seemed a similar change in Ivy's—may well have resembled Miss Patmore's at the end of *Brothers and Sisters*: '"Oh, well, things are over now," said Patty. "We shall be off to London, to start afresh. Well, anyhow, it will be a change." Her voice betrayed the craving of years, and the young faces fell and brightened at the thought of it, and its being satisfied.'[40]

Ivy, having accompanied her sisters to the boarding house and put her own furniture in store, had nothing to do and nowhere to go. Again, there is no clue to her feelings save that, after the publication of *Brothers and Sisters* in 1929, she continued to the end of her life to return to the situation in which she had first been oppressed and later become the oppressor herself. She had set her face resolutely against her sisters' departure but there is some evidence, in the copy of Butler's *Note-Books* which came into her hands at the end of the war, that her mind still dwelt on the dissolution of the household at Hove; and that, whatever her views at the time, she had moved in the interval very much closer to the attitude which afterwards prevailed in her books. A dozen of Butler's notes are variously underlined, annotated in Ivy's hand, marked with an ampersand or a pencil stroke at the side, but of these a single passage stands out, being scored with not one but six thick, heavy lines in the margin:

The Family

I believe that more unhappiness comes from this source than from any other—I mean from the attempt to prolong family connection unduly and to make people hang together artificially who would never naturally do so. The mischief among the lower classes is not so great, but among the middle and upper classes it is killing a large number daily. And the old people do not really like it much better than the young.[41]

VIII

1915–1919

'It quite smashed my life up'

I

'WE LEARN STRANGELY how to endure,' wrote Noel whose letters from the front quickly settled into that subdued and reticent tone which must have been familiar to anyone with a friend or brother in France. In the autumn of 1915, it was becoming increasingly clear that the war which was to have ended the Christmas before would not even be over by next Christmas. No hint of disaster reached the press but shrewder and more apprehensive readers were by this time schooled in a dreadful expertise to note the apologies and qualifications which monotonously followed each 'great victory' and each 'staggering blow', with nothing to show save a fresh row of deaths in a lunatic sum already beginning to be reckoned in millions. Conditions in the trenches could barely be guessed at between the lines of inadequate newspaper reports. Ivy seldom afterwards spoke of these months when, for people at home with nothing to do but watch the papers and wait for letters, the worst fate of all was to be cursed with an active imagination:

'We may as well imagine the scene.'
'No, my mind baulks at it.'
'Mine does worse. It constructs it.'[1]

Others have described how, after each new offensive, 'the awful sluggishness of the hours seemed a specially devised torture of hell',[2] how every knock at the door suggested a telegram, every telephone call might mean bad news, even the striking of a clock fell with shattering force on nerves strung up for days and weeks on end. There was small reassurance to be had from letters when the post took as much

as four days to reach England from France, and the writer had time to
be killed over and over again in the interval. 'I'm in for some danger in
the next few days, but if by the time you have this you hear nothing
all will be well,' wrote Noel, whose letters must often have been read
with a lurch of sickening apprehension. But even to Jack he never
mentioned a risk until it was over, and seldom referred to his own
safety at all. The curious detachment which he shared with his father
and Ivy was if anything sharpened by his first sight of the trenches
—'rather like a manufacturing district, only the smoke is white not
black'—or his first excursion by night into No Man's Land: 'As the
rockets went up from either trench I saw the cornflowers thick and tall
round me, covering with burial flowers so blue and hopeful the poor
crumpled form of some enemy, who had been there long dead, for
whom Ezekiel wrote an epitaph in the days past "Son of man, can these
bones live?".' (16 August 1915)

After a brief spell at the front in early August, he was sent back for a
course of instruction to Etaples where the archaic training in obsolete
open warfare manœuvres, and the homicidal ferocity of the bayonet
instructors, must have seemed as weirdly inappropriate to Noel as they
did to other incredulous young subalterns fresh from England. By the
beginning of September he was billeted just behind the line, engaged
on last-minute preparations for the forthcoming offensive at Loos, and
more amused than otherwise at the prospect of imminent death: '. . . we
have been told by the general in a most dramatic Boys' Own Paper
way, that the village is to be held at any cost. I wonder if you picture
how peaceful life is here with the Germans not a mile away. I am writing
at my table with roses and hollyhocks outside the window, and with
the church bells sounding as peacefully from the ruined tower as at
Easton Grey.' The incongruity of roses and hollyhocks, apple orchards
and lanes full of elderberries, of listening by night to an enemy in the
opposite trench whose 'guttural Bavarian talk' he had last heard as a
student in Munich, appealed strongly to Noel. In the last few days
before the battle, he still described a bombardment to Jack as sceptically
as he had once discussed the antics of the Carbonari with his tutor at
Cambridge:

> For one minute, lying alone together and close we seemed in the
> midst of a flaming fiery furnace, or like one of those immaculate
> heroes who stand in a perfect hail of missiles to advertise Dri-ped
> shoes or some military tailor. But really no shell came within 30 yds

and soon they got more distant. I feel something of the fascination of modern war—this strife of midgets who hurl the thunderbolt.

The noise is rather a bore. Will you get me the Mallock Armstrong Ear-Defender 4s. . . .

This letter is postmarked Thursday, 23 September. On Friday Noel moved back to the front line and sent Jack a sealed letter 'for Tertia in case I am killed', on Saturday the first offensive began and on Monday the London papers carried news of a 'splendid victory' at Loos. Noel survived that battle but, for his family and friends searching the terrifying casualty lists which followed, piecing together what had happened from laconic references in letters like this one, from sketchy accounts in the papers and from the wild rumours accompanying the wounded troops who filled the platforms at Victoria and Paddington for weeks afterwards, this must have been a war of attrition at home as it was on the western front. Nearly twenty years later Vera Brittain, whose brother and lover had both been killed in the war, wrote that she could still not work comfortably in a room from which it was possible to hear the front door bell. Ivy herself wrote in 1948 to Robert Liddell: 'I find I cannot read the news and do not do so. After living in mature awareness through two wars, that side of me is worn out and can do no more.'

In the autumn of 1915, Ivy was homeless. She had accepted her fall from power as dispassionately as she had earlier undertaken to wield it, and she wrote at the end of October proposing to stay at 8 Carlton Hill with her sisters, who flatly refused. They made no objection to her coming to tea, but any attempt to contain in one household two such formidable characters as Ivy and Myra Hess must have seemed tantamount to inviting disaster. There was one small spare room, known as the Developer because Ivy on a tour of inspection had said that in such a small house with no space to turn round her sisters would find no room to develop: it was at any rate abundantly clear that they could not hope to remain independent for long, once Ivy had taken up residence in the Developer. For the first time in her life she was free, through no choice of her own, from the family claims which had governed all her adult existence. One may perhaps suspect 'tumult within her' from the way in which her attitude to duty—'that rigorous lofty thing' which had meant mortal misery for Dolores—capsized between her first and second novels: '"The sight of duty does make one shiver," said Miss Herrick. "The actual doing of it would kill one, I think."'[3]

Probably the only person who could have appreciated Ivy's feelings at this time was Noel, whose departure had already snapped her last link with the past and whose future it was not safe to contemplate. That he perfectly understood her frame of mind is clear from one of the letters she afterwards kept. On 17 May 1915, when he believed that he had only three weeks left in England and was engaged in frantic preparations for his marriage, Noel still found time to write from Perham Down to Elliott Felkin:

> I wonder if you would ask your sister . . . whether she would put my sister Ivy up for her club. I should like my sister to know yours as I think they are rather kindred—at one in their contempt of the human race (tho' perhaps not quite primitive Christians for all that!) Ivy is often wandering about in town; the foxes have holes, the birds have nests, cabmen repose inside their hackneys, but my sister has not etc.
>   I wonder if yr sister wd write to Ivy 'if willin'.*

Elliott's sister Winifred had probably joined a club for the sake of some respite from a masterful, widowed mother (at whose house Ivy became a regular visitor after the war), and because it was by no means easy in those days for single women living at home to meet congenial company. Four years older than Elliott, without either his considerable charm or his Cambridge education, Winifred appeared to his young friends from King's a somewhat condescending blue-stocking in pince-nez with a habit of intellectual name-dropping. But it is small wonder if she found her spirits severely dampened in their presence. Her mother had been Henry Felkin's second wife and, as her stepbrothers and Elliott each in turn became independent and went, leaving Winifred alone at close quarters with their formidable parent, her nerve seems to have failed at the prospect (later it broke altogether when, after a miserable accident which cost her the sight of one eye, she could no longer support life at home). Ivy's sisters remembered Winifred being brought by her brother to spend a weekend at Hove, where she was no doubt drawn to her hostess by the sense of a blighted youth which had given both their sardonic attitude to the race at large (and perhaps to the

---

* 'The foxes have holes, and the birds of the air have nests; but the Son of Man hath not where to lay his head.' (Matthew 8 : 20) ' "When a man says he's willin'," said Mr Barkis . . . "It's as much as to say, that man's a-waitin' for a answer." ' (*David Copperfield*, chap. 8.)

younger members of the party in particular). Moreover Winifred's
mother was descended, like Ivy's, from an old farming family at
Clacton and had inherited in 1907 Lilly Farm,[4] which stands between
the Compton-Burnetts' Valley Farm and the sea. Both families spent
occasional holidays at Clacton and, if the link perhaps explains Noel's
interest when Elliott first came up to King's in 1911, it was certainly
the kind of thing calculated to appeal to Ivy, who had for years been
supervising her own family's property all round the Felkins' at Clacton.

Whatever the reason, the two took to each other as Noel had
predicted, and Ivy may well have stayed with the Felkins when, some
time in November or December, she finally left Hove for London.
Here, in spite of all her precautions, in spite of the policy of passive
resistance which she had pursued for so long and probably proposed to
pursue for the rest of her life, she was once again obliged to construct
a life of her own among strangers in that state of anonymous flux which
had so alarmed her at school and college; only this time the world to
which she had previously retreated was itself disintegrating under her
feet. People from all over England were 'running away', like the Staces
in *Brothers and Sisters*, 'and seeking cover in London, where it is easiest
to keep it'.[5] Single women who, even a year earlier, would have thought
it imprudent to travel unchaperoned were already beginning to elude
established controls, living alone, mixing without reference to their
parents or families, moving almost as freely as men, expending energies, which for years had been permitted no outlet, on war work of one
kind or another. In the circles to which Winifred introduced Ivy, even
the need to earn a living seemed less disreputable in the light of what
was happening to their male contemporaries at the front.

There were few of Noel's friends left in London, and those few
either, like Arthur Waley, immersed in the agonizing dilemma which
confronted men who could not join the army in wartime or, like
Jack Beresford, preparing that winter to join it. Ivy's relations with the
Beresfords were comparatively formal at this stage in the war: she
scarcely knew Jack's wife Janet as yet and Tertia, who was still living
at Easton Grey, was not on close terms with her sister-in-law. Tertia
was six years younger than Ivy and her opposite in almost everything:
graceful, dreamy, highly strung and easily upset, with a strong taste
for poetry but no intellectual leanings whatever and none of Ivy's scorn
for cultivating traditionally winning womanly ways. She had spent the
first months of her marriage furnishing a cottage for herself in the
village, 'she having much the home instinct,' as Noel wrote admiringly

to Jack. Apart from wide reading in the standard poets, Tertia's education had consisted solely of a short course at a domestic science college. The only things which linked the two—their deep mutual reserve, and the fact that Noel mattered more to both than anyone else in the world—were perhaps as likely to drive them apart as to draw them together. It cannot have been easy for Ivy to approach the girl for whom her brother waited 'only on the sun and moon' and with whom he felt himself 'almost mystically one'. Tertia for her part may well have found her first encounters with Noel's elder sister, who must have seemed in some ways to belong more to her parents' generation than her own, a fairly frightening experience.

In a motherless household, Tertia had grown up under the stern eye and firm thumb of her elder sister Dorothy, whose stormy temperament and scathing tongue were rather more to Ivy's taste. A lively dissatisfaction with their own affairs brought these two together at a time when they must have been pretty evenly matched, whether in point of sarcastic humour, strength of will or their wholesale 'contempt for the human race'. Perhaps, too, Dorothy's social success appealed to Ivy who, though she never shone in company herself, became in her middle years increasingly appreciative of the glittering as well as the seamier sides of London society. As a small girl Dorothy at the rectory in Easton Grey had been bosom friends with Violet Asquith at the manor* and afterwards became, as did several of his daughter's friends, one of the young ladies whom Mr Asquith enjoyed escorting and with whom he conducted a leisurely correspondence from 10 Downing Street. People who knew both the elder Miss Beresfords in those days found it hard to decide which was the lovelier but Tertia, persuaded of her own inferiority since childhood, believed that Dorothy was; and Dorothy possessed in any case a *savoir faire* far beyond her retiring younger sister. Tertia's marriage had not pleased Dorothy any more than it probably pleased Ivy: in the summer of 1915, Dorothy had gone so far as to become engaged herself from pique to a passing curate (she had done the same when Jack married, and the arrangement proved in each case a purely temporary expedient).

---

* After his marriage to Margot Tennant in 1894 Asquith and his family often stayed at Easton Grey with her sister, Lucy Graham Smith, who was 'a kind of fairy godmother' to the young Beresfords. When one was thirteen and the other fourteen, Violet Asquith and Dorothy Beresford held a joint Sunday school class in the village, shared Christmas parties, tobogganned, wrote poems, went for long walks together and corresponded regularly when apart.

Tertia, always inclined to feel herself misunderstood at home, had meanwhile left the rectory for the cottage which she shared with a friend from college whose husband was also away at the front (this was the Mrs Hilda Harrisson who, to Tertia's annoyance, followed Dorothy as one of the Prime Minister's young ladies, and subsequently published her correspondence with him in two stout volumes). But letters from France took even longer to reach Wiltshire than London, and an arrangement which had never been satisfactory must have seemed even less so as Noel's first leave approached. By the beginning of December, he had spent just over three months in the trenches and was nearing the point when, according to Robert Graves, an officer began 'gradually to decline in usefulness as neurasthenia developed in him'. Noel's part of the line had been out of the action that autumn but he several times described 'mighty narrow shaves' in his letters to Jack, and had already received a green card (three of which were believed by the troops to mean a decoration for gallantry) congratulating him on distinguished conduct in the field. On 3 December he wrote that he hoped to be in London on the seventeenth of that month: 'I shall be glad to get away because my nerves are getting a little shaky—nothing at all to speak of— but it's odd how tiring a hazardous life gets after a few months. You know the tag? "Skin for skin, yea all that a man has will he give for his life" and I've felt that rather too much in my bones lately.'

Tertia, who had taken a suite at the Savoy to celebrate the first time she had spent more than four days alone with her husband in six months of marriage, travelled up to London only to find that Noel's leave had been postponed for a week. Disaster was narrowly averted by Jack and Janet, who lent their Bayswater flat, spending Christmas night themselves at the Paddington Hotel and Boxing Day in their own spare room. After so long apart, this bare week together can scarcely have left Noel much time for seeing other friends, or even his sisters. On 31 December he left England again, with thoughts of a kind which were to preoccupy him increasingly in the next few months:

I saw the New Year in from the ship's deck. . . . Thank you dear Jack for the home you gave Tertia and me. We were happy, and wise enough to live for the day and the hour, and now we have what we had. We must be content. This you remember I expect from the Apology and school-days 'For so it is O Athenians in truth whatever is each man's post, chosen by himself as the better part, or appointed by his leader, there as I think he must stay in spite of danger, reckoning

not of death, nor of anything except of disgrace and of honour. . . .
For to fear death, O men of Athens, is to think oneself wise when
one is not so.' One remembers this too from earlier days and from a
profounder book 'And yet I am not alone because the Father is with
me.'

In years to come we shall perhaps look back not with horror to
this year when these thoughts are the most natural. . . .' (3 January
1916)

The prospect of returning alone to her cottage was too much for
Tertia. She found instead a flat in Queen's Road next door to her
brother (who had himself newly joined the Army Service Corps, and
by January was already in barracks at Aldershot) where Ivy joined her.
Ivy, seldom at ease under any roof but her own, seems to have accepted
this arrangement without any special enthusiasm as a means of combining practical advantage with family duty for the sake of her brother,
who certainly thought his wife too tender a plant to be left to struggle
untended. His letters to Jack are filled with solicitude for Tertia, requests
to cheer and console her, enquiries as to her health, her safety, her nerves
which bothered him far more than his own. Up to this time he had
carefully concealed from her any hint of his four months in the trenches:
'In my letters to her I say nothing of the war. I daren't. I beg you also
not to. . . .' What is striking, amid such constant concern for preserving
Tertia's peace of mind, is the absence of so much as a mention of Ivy's.
No doubt he rightly judged her to be self-sufficient, which Tertia
palpably was not; and perhaps he even counted on his sister's presence
to weather the shock when in February 1916, the month of Verdun, he
at last broke the truth to Tertia: 'I had to tell Tertia that I was actually at
the front, driven to this partly by a lonely feeling of my own, partly
by an idea that she would *wish* to know, and also by fear that she should
notice my battalion in the casualty lists; and that the cat suddenly
jumping out of the bag might terrify. She has been very brave about it,
and I hope will bear up, though its hard for her and I can't but feel
anxieties.' (14 February 1916)

It is a moot point whether, in these months when he wrote nearly
every week, sometimes oftener, to Jack and probably almost daily to
Tertia, Noel found time to keep up a third regular correspondence
with Ivy. Their sister Vera, who had seen some of Noel's letters and
poems to Tertia on a visit to Easton Grey in the summer of 1915, said
she would not have been surprised to learn that Ivy had few. Janet

Beresford had a similar impression: 'I somehow do not think Jim wrote regularly to Ivy though I do not really know—I think probably he meant much more to her than she to him though he definitely felt a responsibility for her. She was not a quick sensitive person anyhow on the surface as he was.' Ivy of course spoke of her own anxiety to no one. Once Noel was gone, she had indeed no one to whom she could speak freely. At a time when people dreaded the post as much as they longed for it, she must often have found it a trial to watch his letters coming for Tertia; and perhaps she felt that in sharing a flat she had shared enough with the person who meant life itself to her brother: 'having as I do' (he wrote to Jack) 'an assurance—so deep and faithful—that I shall come back to Tertia, for this is how it now solely seems—with no hair of my head harmed'. If this was how it solely seemed to Noel, then simple wisdom as well as the habit of years must have confirmed Ivy's inclination to keep her own counsel.

The two letters from Noel which Ivy afterwards kept suggest that brother and sister had preserved from infancy a tacit understanding free from the agitation of his feelings for Tertia, and probably almost as remote from the abstract speculations which became increasingly urgent in his letters to Jack. In practical matters he relied on his friend, sending a steady stream of requests for the various necessities of life at the front: a cholera belt and a canvas bucket, cigarettes, chocolate and copies of the *T.L.S.*, ear-plugs, 'wound stuff' and trench boots. These last arrived by return and proved, as heavy rain filled the trenches with liquid mud: 'a mighty comfort . . . and a symbol also of civilisation and artificiality, things it is good for one's nerves still to believe in. Do you know it's odd what courage is induced in the timid heart by respectable clothes. I'm sure anybody would face bullets with greater equanimity after putting on a new coat, than after reading the New Testament and Plato rolled into one.' (10 October 1915) Noel's respect for his boots goes some way towards explaining a similar outlook in Ivy who had set such store by preserving conventional appearances at Hove, and who later became a lifelong exponent of civilization and artificiality—things which provide a frail enough protection for the timid heart against the bullets ricocheting between the lines of her books.

But in the autumn of 1915 and the following spring Noel was evolving for himself a philosophy drawn directly from the *New Testament* and Plato; and it seems likely that he knew Ivy's views on the former too well to quote without scepticism from the Bible to her. Indeed, at the beginning of the war he could hardly have done so to Jack. 'Like you I pray now, and I pray for you,' he had written from Aldershot the week before Jack's marriage. But up to the time he left England his letters still mostly make fun of the future, and glance if at all only shyly at death: 'Tertia will be a weight on my heart when I go, if ever I do, but I fancy I shan't fear for myself, death being easily recognizable as the beautiful liberator. The sentimental subaltern thus writes to his friend. The brigade is indulging in a garden party this afternoon which accounts for this portentous gloom. How hateful such things are!' (13 July 1915)

Over the next few months Noel's style changed under the pressures which brought so many of his generation to a sudden maturity in the trenches until by December, when Jack proposed joining the army, it had shed all trace of self-mockery:

Dear Jack,

I was glad to have your letter and to know that you aren't doing anything militarily desperate. I think you intend what's right, and in this matter are choosing the better way. Life gets so obscure in its ends and means, and the common life of the world so heart-breakingly suicidal, that one thinks the best is to hold to what is nearest, the domestic responsibilities and affections. I feel these days that the only hope is the law of Christ, 'But I say unto you that ye resist not evil'. No doubt the world must go its way, and this is too hard a saying to be received—too spiritual and too intellectual. And again 'Blessed are the meek for they shall inherit the earth'. Personally I find this attitude the only satisfactory one so far as it touches the world, and for one's inner life its even more so. Religion, which is life, reaches its highest here 'Ye shall indeed drink of my cup, and be baptised with the baptism that I am baptised with, but to sit on my right hand and on my left is not mine to give but it shall be given to them for whom it is prepared of my father'. That's 'high as we shall go' with a vengeance, that promise of the suffering but not the reward. Quite a sabbath address. Goodbye. I shall turn up in London I think about a week today but dates aren't fixed. Yrs affectionately Jim.*

---

* Dickinson, still a follower of Socrates, was also beginning round about this time to turn to Christ, whose essential teaching came to seem to him 'sheer common sense and sanity, and not the paradox I used to think it'. (*Goldsworthy Lowes Dickinson* by E. M. Forster, p.160.)

Perhaps Noel was prevented from writing as freely to his sister for fear of her disapproval; more likely, he had fallen with Jack into a habit of abstract discussion which, beginning with life and art in their earliest days at King's, moved on as their friendship deepened to the pressing question of death. It is in any case impossible to say how far Ivy's unforgiving attitude to religion had already hardened, and how far it was shaped afterwards when she had to reconcile the knowledge that her brother had chosen the suffering with the certainty that there was no reward.

Noel's letters to Jack keep the nice balance between gaiety and gravity which both had practised at Cambridge. But a correspondence which, though it often mentions the tedium of the war, never refers to other more sordid, ugly or pitiful aspects probably gives a lopsided view of Noel's activities. It seems to have served as a safety valve, a means of discussing matters unmentionable in the trenches where cold, mud, exhaustion, misery, the constant spectacle of comrades mutilated or dying, the company of live rats and rotting corpses, the alternation of boredom with terror had bred a profound, quiet, deflationary cynicism. It must have been a considerable relief to Noel to be able to write in private to Jack of sensations better not broached in public:

> I've just come back to my dug-out, and have lit a candle to write to you. The first snow of the year is falling, and one's heart is quite heavy with its marvellous beauty. Our trenches and the Germans', the earth cast up irregularly and now white in the dawn, seem like a tempestuous sea of crumpled and curling waves; one waits for the crash as they break, and even when one has destroyed the illusion it recreates itself, and one wonders at the skeleton trees, marking the German positions and rooted as it seems in the surf. (Autumn 1915)

Poets were heartily despised at the front, along with staff and field officers, home service units and conscientious objectors in a carefully graded system of contempt which embraced all military and civilian forms of life from generals down to the detested ranks of journalist and politician. That Noel shared the general view is evident from an uncharacteristic tartness underlying his humorous reproaches when Jack joined the Army Service Corps, a race of notorious shirkers accustomed to feast on food meant for the troops who were 'scattered . . . to the right and left' by 'luxurious overpaid A.S.C. gentlemen' cruising about in large cars. Senior officers, whose contact with direct action at the front was largely confined to issuing unrealistic orders beforehand and compiling equally unrealistic reports afterwards, were especially loathed. 'In the army you *must* push yourself or you get nothing,' wrote Noel in another uncharacteristic spurt of resentment. 'Consider me, still a 2nd lieutenant though (as I say it who oughtn't) more militarily competent than the average field or staff officer.' He seems to have felt the same disgust as other supposedly incompetent poets who found themselves driven, through a combination of self-mistrust, despair of their superiors and sympathy with their men, to acts of conspicuous courage. Noel's fear was the common one, described by both Graves and Siegfried Sassoon, of cowardice when put to the test: 'This particular fear (certainly not the fear of death or wounds) is the burden of active service'. He sent Jack only one detailed description of a raid, set down next morning in the rush of relief at having lived to report on a mission from which there had been no survivors two nights before:

At 1 a.m. myself and a fellow subaltern from Trinity, with pistols, two desperate non-coms with bombs and bludgeons, all with faces blacked and wearing cap-comforters, got out of one of our listening posts and started on our voyage. . . . We went in pairs, the two timid officers in front, the two desperate sergeants five yards behind. We chose the clearest night we could—it was possible to read in the moonlight—so as to outwit the Boche who would surely think none likely to approach under such conditions. . . .

The result of this cheerful adventure was the capture of a flag marked 'Gott strafe England' from the German trenches ('The men want to keep the flag or else I would send it to you as a curiosity'); the general atmosphere of skulduggery confirms the remark of a fellow officer from Cambridge, reported by Professor Clapham, 'that it was hard to keep from laughing when on patrol with Burnett because of his whimsical comments'.

People who lived through the first war have described often enough the glazed eyes, lined faces and blank looks of troops returning from sights and sounds too raw and recent to be put into words. Noel himself had suspected this wall of incomprehension in the months when he waited at Perham Down for his own initiation in the trenches: 'It's odd how anxious we of Kitchener's army are to hear from those there, as if by much reading and hearsay we could guess at *it*', he wrote to

Elliott on 8 May 1915. Soldiers on leave were so bewildered by the spectacle of patriotic hysteria feeding on public gullibility that it was often a relief to get back to open madness at the front from what seemed a more shameful madness at home. Robert Graves found it 'all but impossible' to attempt anything but the most desultory small talk with his family and friends. Siegfried Sassoon had nothing to say to his. Vera Brittain, one of the few who described the shock of meeting this numbness from the other side, waited miserably for the war to divide her from her lover and brother, 'putting a barrier of indescribable experience between men and the women whom they loved, thrusting horror deeper and deeper inwards, linking the dread of spiritual death to the apprehension of physical disaster'.[6] Whether or not the barrier operated between Noel and Ivy, it was by his own choice impassable with Tertia; and it fell across much that he could not write about even to Jack, whose patient encouragement meant a brief, necessary oblivion from 'it'. 'It will be good and refreshing to see you, my Johannes,' wrote Noel just before his first leave, 'for these days sometimes I feel almost dotty, surely very pardonable to anyone living in this lunatic world.'

In a lunatic world the Beresfords stood for sanity, affection, continuity, all things which Noel knew well enough that he must almost certainly and probably very soon relinquish. His love for Tertia cemented his friendship with Jack and both drew him into a family circle which inevitably excluded Ivy. It was not that anyone meant to be unkind (though there must have been some constraint, if not a coldness between brother and sister over Tertia), only that the young Burnetts and the young Beresfords shared a whole new set of domestic pleasures which seemed especially precious in wartime, and in which Ivy played at best a peripheral part. 'Small delightful things', like the prospect of exchanging family visits, of owning a home of his own or the birth of his niece Rosemary Beresford in the spring of 1916, held a tantalizing charm for Noel, who had long since laid his plans for entertaining Jack's children 'with Othello-like stories of peril in the deadly breach, they being seated on the avuncular knee'. As it turned out one of them was dandled on Noel's knee, for the authorities were generous with leave in the months leading up to the battle of the Somme and, by the end of April, he was once again in London where Rosemary's mother remembered him 'looking very quizzically' and with unusual emotion at 'Jack's child'. Noel, unlike his sister, had always been fond of small children and this one must have seemed to give a kind of vicarious substance to his own hopes of a happiness he dared not yet contemplate with Tertia. He had already a ring, given him by Jack the summer before, which was destined for Rosemary: 'In the good future when I am godfather to a girl of yours and Janets, when she is ten years old, I shall produce it from the treasury of the past.'

There was a fastidious sharpness in Ivy that would have made it impossible for Noel to write unselfconsciously and optimistically to her, as he did to Jack, about the good future or the treasury of the past. He looked upon Jack as a brother to whom he confided raptures— 'Why, Tertia and I know each other to the end of things; probably as unreservedly as any two souls ever have'—which his sister could hardly have welcomed. But neither Jack nor Tertia had known him in more distant, comfortless times; and one cannot help wondering how much, in these desperate months, he turned to the permanent, perhaps almost silent consolation of an older intimacy with Ivy. The strains which drove him 'sometimes . . . almost dotty' were well known to his sister. These two after all had looked to each other before in fear and uncertainty, in grief for their father, in their desolation after Guy's death, as well as in years of dull daily endurance at Hove from which both derived a fund of stoicism drawn on still more deeply by the war. Ivy possessed little of Noel's spontaneity and none of his ability to keep open heart for his friends. Noel, in so far as one may judge from his letters and from his sister's borrowings from him for Robin Stace in *Brothers and Sisters*, had a smoother temperament than hers, sunnier, more direct, certainly more sociable, and one on which profound emotion left a shallower imprint. But if his straightforwardness made him more tender, it also made him if anything more vulnerable and apt in a crisis to depend on his sister's reserves of strength. However much his marriage had separated the two, one may suspect that it had not at bottom damaged a relationship based on unconditional sympathy and trust.

Much went without saying between Noel and Ivy, as it does between brother and sister in her books. This far at least one may go on the evidence of an unemotional letter, largely concerned with family business and written from behind the lines on Saturday, 24 June, the day on which the British artillery began its preliminary, supposedly lethal bombardment on the Somme. Bets had been laid on the date in the trenches for weeks beforehand, and the forthcoming 'Big Push' had been common knowledge all over England since the middle of June. The final seven days' bombardment could be heard from Kent and from the southern suburbs of London. But Ivy, who seems to have been unwell, had fled London (as, twenty-five years later, she frankly declared she had fled the bombs in the second war) with Dorothy for Wales. This letter was forwarded from Bayswater to Easton Grey, and on to a boarding house on the Mumbles near Swansea where it must have reached her the following Saturday, which was the first day of the battle of the Somme:

Saturday.
This letter will find you somewhere in the wild, and not too much bored I hope with life. You must have had an ill time,—yet we survive, such is the mercy(?) of Providence. These days that the locust devours, and an unappetising dish must he find them, shall according to the scriptures be returned to us again. I suppose the scriptures will be fulfilled when peace comes, which I truly think *will* be this year. The day and hour knoweth no man. I leave my school in a few days, so write to my old address. If you are with Dorothy, dont let her nerves get on your nerves.

I had the documents for the letting of No 20 and a Sackville mansion yesterday & have sent them back to Rutley. I think on the whole you do well, that is to say you couldn't do better, than accept the £150 for No 20, though it is enough to make our parents curse God to his face. 'Tis of a badness. I'm quite well and shall remain so, unless the Kaiser succeeds in his attempts upon me.

What are your permanent plans. I take it you return to your apartment in Queens Rd? I have nothing to say. I am your servant

N

This is the tone of voice of someone with no front to keep up, almost as though Noel were talking to himself or writing in a diary. The contrast is marked if one sets this letter beside a characteristic passage to Jack, in which he imagines being rudely wakened by a bullet to find himself a star. 'Do you know these endless days in the open, and even more these nights, looking at Jupiter flaming like a torch and the Pleiades like distant tiny candle points, fill me to bursting with the love of life and the desire for it? The thought that the lights would still shine for other eyes, if one slept, in some moods only chills. . . .' This was as far towards pessimism as he permitted himself to go in writing to Jack. Admittedly, Noel was perhaps not yet so deeply inured to horror in the months before Jack also left England for the front, but there is a resignation bleaker than anything he shared with his friend in his last, terse, flat letter to Ivy.

This was written on Saturday, 1 July, a day of blazing sunshine on which the British army suffered more casualties than on any other single day in its history. Noel's battalion was part of the 37th Division in the VII Corps detailed for a purely diversionary attack on the Gommecourt Salient at the northern tip of the line, probably the strongest point of a German system which, according to Winston Churchill, 'was undoubtedly the strongest and most perfectly defended position in the world'. The task of the VII Corps was peculiarly wretched: to attack without taking and with desperately inadequate resources an impregnable fortress under a German barrage which was fiercer on the first day of the battle than in any other sector of the Somme. Officers, batmen, even grooms in Noel's division had dug day and night for a week. The first line went over the top at 7.30 a.m. and by nightfall the VII Corps 'had lost 7000 men for no reason whatever'.[7] Observers like Noel, whose division was ordered simply to hold the line, watched wave upon wave of men mown down as they advanced shoulder to shoulder over the ranks of their dead and dying predecessors. By Saturday evening it was clear to the survivors, back where they had started from in their own trenches, that the battle was lost, though no thought of failure had reached Haig and his generals who, far from calling off the whole catastrophic attack, ordered a renewed offensive to begin at once. Noel's letter, which has neither superscription nor signature, was written in two parts and posted on Sunday. By 6 or 7 July, when it reached Ivy in Wales, the English papers were ecstatically celebrating a wholly illusory triumph:

Saturday.
This is a short letter written just on the fringe of the battle. So far as I know I shan't be in it; but in any case the ordeal can't last long. It must be 'too hot to last'. I wish I could finish the remark but the truth is I would give a thousand pounds *to* miss it. In any case its foolish to reckon up the gain and loss of Death. The comfort is that Death puts all one's arguments out of court. Its a hot day, and one pities the wounded jolting by in waggons. Lucky fellows really! I'm *not* depressed, only I defy anyone not to get a headache from the guns. The posts are likely to be irregular for the next few days but I'll write again as soon as I can.
    II/Should I by any chance get 'done in', I should like you to take any books of mine you like, & especially my Gladstone Prize[8] in pious memory of our Greekish youth. Oh! we *were* clever. I hasten to add I intend to attain a grand old age.

What Ivy did next is uncertain. Noel's battalion was shortly moved
down from Gommecourt to Mametz Wood near the point where, as
depressing reports gradually filtered back to the general staff, Haig
planned his second major assault to take place on 14 July. This was the
day on which, for the first and last time in the war, the cavalry, who
had waited in vain for the gap through which they were to gallop
against machine guns to victory, charged with lance and sabre across a
cornfield just beyond the two Bazentin villages which had been taken
with comparatively little fighting in the first surprise attack of the
morning. Noel was killed that day at Bazentin-le-Petit.*

2

TERTIA WAS THE first to hear of his death in a letter from his commanding officer commiserating with her on her loss. She ran out on the
street in her dressing-gown, beat on the next front door and implored
Janet to go at once for news to the Asquiths. Janet set out for 10 Downing Street and was shown upstairs where Margot Asquith, in bed with a
breakfast tray, was kind but not reassuring. She well understood what
Janet must have feared, that Tertia was 'more sensitive than Dorothy'
and might prove in despair the wilder of the two. But nothing could be

---

* Noel's battalion was the 7th Leicestershire in the 110th Brigade, deployed before
dawn just outside Mametz Wood: 'In the front line were to be the 6th and 7th
Leicestershires, each with a Stokes mortar attached. . . . The 6/Leicestershire moved up
via the eastern edge of Mametz Wood and the 7th and 8th by the light railway where
Lt.-Col. W. Drysdale of the 7th was wounded. By 2.35 a.m. in spite of shell-fire . . .
the battalions were formed in four lines on the tapes. . . . When the barrage lifted at
3.25 a.m. the leading companies [of among others the 7/Leicestershire] rose and
advanced through the ground mist at a steady pace . . . the enemy made but a feeble
and spasmodic resistance to the first onslaught. The leading British wave reached the
German line before a shot was fired. . . . The second line was taken without much
resistance, by 4 a.m. . . . and the Leicestershire battalions passed on to occupy Bazentin-
le-Petit Wood. The wood was taken with little fighting, except at the north-western
corner, where the Germans held out all day. . . .' (Official History of the War. France and
Belgium 1916, Macmillan, 1932, vol. 2, pp.75–81.)
    Noel was killed in the initial attack on the wood (this was to have been part of a
larger combined offensive which was first postponed and then abandoned in the course
of the afternoon because of heavy losses and a determined German counter attack;
some six hundred yards of ground were gained on 14 July at the cost of nine thousand
British casualties—'as brilliant a success as British arms have ever gained,' according to
that day's dispatch in The Times).

done or found out. Janet returned by way of Paddington to meet an old family friend who had been summoned first thing from the country. By the time they got back to Queen's Road, Tertia had swallowed what she hoped was a fatal dose of sleeping tablets.

Her suicide was impulsive and unsuccessful. The doctor who brought her round advised her to wait another three or four years when she would know her own mind better. Or, as someone says in *More Women Than Men*, people do not so easily let go of life: 'What kills them is their own death, and not the loss of anyone else at all.'9 It is a hard saying and a characteristic one. Ivy, in the days of Tertia's initial collapse, presented a granite front which supported her sister-in-law 'like a great rock'. The story that, on the day she heard of her brother's death, Ivy calmly discharged her duties as a V.A.D. nurse contains, like many of the legends which later sprang up around her, a basis of truth: its mistake lay not in assuming Ivy capable of carrying on business as usual but in the fundamentally misguided belief that it could ever have occurred to her to undertake war-work. She held the war, its works and the human race in contempt; and (even if her own early life had not given her a horror of nursing) she had endured too much at their hands to do anything but abhor public spirit.

Tertia in any case required attention. 'It is too sad to think that T's husband is killed,' wrote the Prime Minister on 25 July to Hilda Harrisson, 'but I am afraid it is so. I tremble to think what will happen to her. And his loss is a terrible waste. He was not chair à canon.'10 If Mr Asquith trembled for Tertia, so did her family who had to witness her first pitiful paroxysms of grief. Rumour got about that she was pregnant. Distracted and inconsolable, she could not endure the company of her family or friends or anyone save her father's faithful attendant, Eva Fox, who over the next eighteen months nursed her slowly towards recovery. 'Walking and talking and being with nature,' said Miss Fox, 'that seemed to bring her back more than anything.' It was Ivy who found the nursing home at Bexhill to which Tertia was dispatched with Miss Fox; Ivy who attended to winding up affairs in Queen's Road and at Easton Grey; Ivy who, as joint executor with Tertia, applied for probate of her brother's will;* and Ivy who paid

---

* The fact that probate was granted to Ivy alone means either that Tertia resigned as executor, or that she was declared unfit and incapable; Noel left her his personal belongings, the property inherited from his father, and the £200 a year provided for his widow under the terms of his mother's will (which meant virtually everything, since his estate came to £2,751), and the rest to Ivy.

regular visits to his widow in Bexhill, and a year or so later, at the cottage in Essex where Tertia was sufficiently restored to receive the attentions of another admirer. At the end of 1919, Ivy told her cousin that she still saw Tertia 'nearly every day'. Her attitude perhaps reflects the sympathy not untinged with distaste extended in her books to lovely, irresponsible egotists like Perdita Kingsford or Verena Gray who, helpless prey to their own emotions and perfectly impervious to other people's, are called to account less severely than their more stoical sisters for the consequences, always disastrous, of their own actions. Ivy's feeling for Tertia became, according to Vera Compton-Burnett, 'motherly almost'—a protective surveillance to which Tertia not unnaturally failed to respond. 'Tertia *didn't like* Ivy. She was not grateful to her at all.'

Nobody in the aftermath of Noel's death could do more than guess at his sister's grief: the more Tertia suffered, the less Ivy showed. Tertia's father had died a month before Noel on 11 June 1916, and it was again Ivy who went down with Dorothy to sort out and clear up at the rectory where, on 5 August, she too received a letter from one of Noel's fellow officers:

7th Bn Leicestershire Regt.,
B.E.F.
30 July 1916

Dear Miss Burnett,

How terrible it must be for you all at home. I'm sure we fellows in the midst of it all can't half realise what these losses mean to the people at home. From all the news I can gather Bumby fell in the greatest excitement of the attack, just as he and his wonderful platoon reached the German 1st line. He was hit in the head by a revolver bullet and passed away instantaneously, suffering no pain but falling like the wonderful hero he was. This was all just near the south edge of Bazentin-le-Petit wood and he would be buried on the battlefield by the chaplain and R.A.M.C. Do please write if I can do any little thing for you. . . . This is such a sad letter but please accept my deepest sympathy on your great terrible loss.

Yours very sincerely,
T. Cecil Howitt.[11]

A few days later Ivy wrote to her cousin Katie, on the black-edged mourning paper which had served for so many of her letters and Noel's in the fifteen years since their father's death:

Just a word to say that I *am* feeling braver, and that your letter *has* helped me to feel so.

It is a sorrow with a great pride in it—a terrible bitterness too, and a disappointment one cannot face as yet—but a great pride for—as the Provost of King's writes to me—the most complete and fullest sacrifice that any man has made.

Exact news has come to us too, and that is comforting. He was killed instantaneously, hit on the head by a revolver bullet, and had no pain. He had led his men right up to the German line, and secured it, and fell in the greatest excitement of the battle, and is buried on the battlefield. Well, one thinks how, as a little boy, he always said he would be a soldier.

It had haunted me to think that perhaps he had suffered, and longed for people who loved him, and now I am happier. Tertia is well again, but often very low spirited. What can one expect? No, there is no prospect of a child, dearest, I did not mean to give you that idea. There is no ordinary comfort, you see.

It will not do to build much on a letter written when Ivy was probably so stunned that she could barely apprehend the fact of her brother's death, far less deal rationally with it. But, even allowing for the conventional formulae of grief, her letter does suggest how far she still had to go before she reached the philosophy worked out in her books (where self-sacrifice is invariably, often criminally unwise, and its recipients neither proud nor grateful), and how difficult the journey must have been. Vera Brittain has described the mental inertia of people bereaved by the war who dared not look beyond the platitudes which stood between themselves and madness: 'My only hope now was to become the complete automaton. . . . Thought was too dangerous; if once I began to think out exactly why my friends had died . . . quite dreadful things might suddenly happen.'[12] More than a quarter of a million British soldiers were killed or maimed for a territorial gain of at most eight miles in the Battle of the Somme. Out of 12,500 Cambridge men who like Noel had joined the army, nearly a quarter were reported dead or wounded by October 1916. 'It was a terrible war,' said Ivy, 'it got into every life, it got into every home.' Private despair was multiplied on an inconceivable scale, and reflected in the public confusion which tried frantically to make sense in terms of sacrifice out of the loss of almost a whole generation. Long after the war people still clung to the 'perfect patriotism' of books like *Tell England* in which the country's population is likened to a Holy Family 'composed of fathers who so loved the world that they gave their sons', mothers similarly inclined and sons so ennobled by this parental generosity that they gladly died: 'To be eighteen in 1914 is to be the best thing in England. England's wealth used to be counted in other things. Nowadays . . . boys are the richest things she's got.'[13] It was not for another ten years and more that books like Robert Graves' began to put the case that England's boys had been squandered to no end save to pay for the complacent, callous stupidity of their elders.

'In these days we do not look forward,' wrote Ivy at Christmas 1916 to Katie. 'The hour is enough.' Since Noel's death she had lived with Dorothy who, though hardly a consoling companion, must have been a distracting and often a provoking one. People ignored Dorothy at their peril. Life at Easton Grey had cramped but not curbed her instinct for operating on the grand scale: 'Poor as church mice we may be,' said Dorothy, 'but proud as Lucifer'. Years later she compiled a list of the austere joys of her youth: almond blossom, bluebells, fine china, 'intense literature', days 'filled with plain living and high thinking'. 'Living vividly' was an article of faith with Dorothy who, as she said, had all her life 'a dread almost amounting to obsession of doing anything unless the Spirit moved'. It moved a great deal, always vehemently, and not always as harmlessly as the programme outlined above might suggest. But Dorothy's malevolence, brought on when the disobliging facts of plain living impinged too sharply on the raptures induced by high thinking, no doubt suited Ivy whose bitterness was not the less terrible for being shared. 'We were both witty women,' said Dorothy. 'I should think very few women have meant as much to each other as Ivy and me.' More than fifty years later Dorothy still had the exquisite carriage and the graceful, incisive gestures of a legendary Edwardian beauty; the classical perfection of her features, and the shyness carried off with such a high hand that few of her admirers can have had the nerve to suspect it, are nicely illustrated by her story of 'one of the greatest compliments I have ever received from a half-Russian dress maker who I had urged not to let me be too dowdy—"How can Madame ever hope to be fashionable with a face like that?"'

It was the combination of devastating looks with an equally devastating malice which appealed to Asquith (known as 'the Oracle' to Dorothy, who habitually annoyed her family and friends with often rather more opprobrious nicknames), and probably also to Ivy, who seems to have enjoyed the company of pretty women in something very like the Prime Minister's spirit of more or less platonic appreciation. One of the things which had irritated visitors to Easton Grey in the days when Dorothy was 'Queen of the rectory' was her ostentatious devotion to her father: 'Tertia did the housekeeping and Dorothy did her father's business,' said Miss Fox (who had herself copied out the whole of *Ecclesiastes* in braille on the rector's instructions). Dorothy had never forgiven her mother for, as she said, 'taking the easy way out of life at Easton Grey'. This was a kind of truculence which Ivy well understood and perhaps passed on to Tullia Calderon who, in *Elders and Betters*, retaliates against the defection of one parent by dedicating herself to the other: 'Father may spring a demand on me at any moment. I must turn a blind eye to general claims . . . my time, as you know, involves Father's . . . I can hardly leave my father for an hour, and must just submit to fate.'[14] One cannot help suspecting in Tullia's boastfulness echoes of much that must have amused her creator in Dorothy, who could on occasion show the same baleful candour as Tullia and who plumed herself on the same lofty indifference to practical affairs: 'She held it beneath her to talk or think of money, and assumed it was always there, which would indeed have disposed of its problems.'

Ivy's dryness was more than equal to Dorothy's condescension, and the two got along sufficiently well to contemplate setting up house together on Ivy's means. By December 1916, they were living temporarily at 30 Westbourne Terrace: 'The Christmas institution is truly a trial, and I have been in low spirits, I confess,' wrote Ivy. 'Dorothy too has been depressed—the many troubles of the year being enough to make her so—and the Asquith disturbance* has done what it could to worry people intimate with them . . . to be just and cheerier, a growing circle of congenial friends is doing a great deal for me.' One of these was Winifred Felkin and very likely another was Margaret Jourdain, whom Ivy met through Winifred or Elliott round about this time. A third was Alan Kidd whom she had encountered with Eric Forbes-Adam at a dinner party given that autumn by Janet for Ivy and Dorothy. Alan Kidd, a charming and eligible bachelor, comfortably off and strikingly handsome after the romantic Sherlock Holmes school of looks, was a friend of Jack's from Whitehall and promptly became a regular caller on Ivy and Dorothy, presenting each with identical bound volumes for Christmas. It was at first far from clear which of the

* Asquith resigned as Prime Minister on 5 December 1916.

two he was courting and Janet, well placed to observe the affair from the start, believed that Ivy would have been by no means displeased if his choice had lighted on her. But, as an unmistakable preference for Dorothy emerged, Ivy tactfully took to spending her evenings that winter in Queen's Road with Janet. Gallantry alone, according to Dorothy, prevented Alan from proposing until she and Ivy were settled in their new home. He had not wished her decision to be taken in haste or spoilt afterwards by hankerings for what Dorothy called 'the perfect rooftree', which was a flat at 59 Leinster Square taken by Ivy in the summer of 1917. Here the two entertained among others O.B. (on a visit from Rome where he had retired to an apartment largely furnished with revolving busts of himself) who, in spite of his vast bulk, insisted on being hoisted up to the roof to admire the Bayswater view laid out at his feet. Dorothy had confessed her engagement in some trepidation to Ivy—'I thought she'd think it weakminded of me'—but Ivy accepted the news as blandly as if she had planned it herself: 'That was her attitude to life, that what she chose went, so to speak. What it came to was it would keep me quiet and calm while she had more time for her writing, and she still had me there to say any wild thing that came into her head.' Dorothy was married from Ivy's flat on 31 August 1917; Asquith was witness to the wedding and Ivy dressed the bride who 'looked lovely', as Ivy complacently said.

It is of course possible that Ivy was writing again by this time but perhaps more likely that Dorothy, whose memory was not strong on facts, had confused this with a later period in her mind. 'One was a good deal cut up by the war; one's brother was killed, and one had family troubles' was Ivy's own 'masterly understatement'[15] when asked, as she often was afterwards, what had happened in the fourteen years between her first and second novels. By the summer of 1917 Tertia seemed well on the way to recovery, Ivy's sisters had apparently dropped out of her life and she herself presented a resolutely cheerful face to her friends. 'She was a creature of tremendous tenacity of feeling,' said Dorothy. But even Janet, who spent nearly every evening with Ivy when Jack was away for months on end at the front, was permitted scarcely a glimpse of anything below the surface of Ivy's inscrutable small talk. In the middle of July Janet returned for the birth of her second child to her parents' house in Lancaster Gate, where Ivy paid her a visit and kept the conversation as always to scraps of gossip and news: 'I remember thinking then that she was completely overcome,' said Janet. 'Jim meant the beginning and end of life to her.' A full year had passed since his death. One thinks of the bleak rejoinder in *Darkness and Day*, when someone says that time must help people get used to if not get over a loss:

> 'Time has too much credit,' said Bridget. 'I never agree with the compliments paid to it. It is not a great healer. It is an indifferent and perfunctory one. Sometimes it does not heal at all. And sometimes when it seems to, no healing has been necessary.'[16]

Janet had learnt a good deal that winter about the Compton-Burnetts in conversations from which she chiefly remembered how much Ivy had loved her father and how little her mother, to whom she had none-theless remained 'a dutiful daughter' at Hove. Her sisters were by this time a lost cause so far as Ivy was concerned: though she still stood guardian and punctually discharged their business affairs, they had forfeited all further claim on her sympathy. They can hardly have missed it, being by this time so taken up with hard work and friends of their own that it seemed small hardship to be 'kept rather tight' by their guardians. Freedom and the Bohemian life went far towards compensating for the rigid restraints of their childhood (though they were not yet sufficiently emancipated to realize that they might dispense with a boy for cleaning the knives, or manage without a maid who wore pink or blue print in the morning and white in the afternoon, and whose laundry placed a considerable strain on their slender finances). Other-wise their circle consisted largely of musicians and mystics, two callings which Ivy could never abide. She and her brothers had early abandoned religion on aesthetic and practical grounds; her sisters inclined rather to the spirit world, taking comfort in the life force, reincarnation, the mastery of mind over matter, the teachings of Mrs Besant and Emer-son's American disciples which, like a good many other quasi-religious, quasi-philosophical faiths, were much in vogue both before and after the war. Vera and Juliet later became lifelong followers of Rudolph Steiner and Anthroposophy. Topsy and Primrose were especially attracted by what was then called New Thought. Their music master had introduced them to *In Tune with the Infinite* by Ralph Waldo Trine, who writes with a fervent, higgledy-piggledy effusiveness not unlike Dr Compton Burnett's style of chat. It was perhaps Trine's rousing optimism, expressed with more vigour than clarity, which appealed to a similar strain in Dr Burnett's daughters; but it is hard to believe that the doctor would not have made short work of Trine's views on bodily health, or that he would have entertained Trine's general conclusions—on 'God-thoughts' inducing 'God-power' and eventually turning 'God-thinkers' into 'God-men'—with any more patience than Ivy. 'Mystical means muddle-headed'[17] was one of her sayings and her father, equally firm, had disposed of faith-healing as 'to my mind, rank nonsense'.

The gap in age and status had precluded much feeling between Ivy and her two youngest sisters, whose tiresomeness must have seemed not the least of her problems at Hove. From their point of view, Ivy meant trouble: 'Being held in the way they were, and being spoken to in the way that they were . . . that was unpalatable to them.' Primrose, who had been presented at birth to the infant Topsy as 'your baby', had scarcely had cause to feel herself much wanted afterwards by anyone else. She had been nearly two when their father died, Topsy five years old and so like him that he called her 'wee Daddy'. Their lives had been almost from the start so abnormal that the exchange of one tyrant for another on their mother's death had probably made little difference, though perhaps it increased their sense of their own helplessness. They turned to each other with an absorption which increased as they grew older to a point at which it involved a practically complete rejection of the outside world. By the summer of 1917 they had withdrawn into a dreamy, lethargic, secretive indifference which desperately worried their sisters. Veronal had been prescribed for Topsy's toothache before the family left Hove and, long before anyone suspected the reason, the drug which had provided at first a temporary oblivion, more soothing even than music, had become a permanent refuge. Topsy, once a passionate reader of Shakespeare, had not opened a book for months. Primrose had been an especially lively child, Topsy by common consent the brightest of the four and the one who was to have made a career as a concert violinist: she had played for O.B. at the age of eleven and given a public recital with Vera at Hove, but in London the two youngest sisters both gradually gave up practising.

The common front against interference which had been necessary in childhood had given all four girls a regard for privacy and a dread of intruding on one another which perhaps partly explains what happened next. Topsy and Primrose shared a bedroom and habitually kept the door locked. On 10 December 1917, they proposed spending a few days at a farm in West Wickham where they had gone for holidays before. Minnie, who left out a tray that night in the dining room, found the food eaten next day and the girls apparently gone. When, several days after they should have returned, she became sufficiently alarmed to make the journey to Wickham, the girls had not been seen at the farm. Their bedroom door remained locked. Iris, who had remained on friendly terms with her half-sisters, arrived from the Temperance Hospital and advised breaking down the door. On 27 December the lock was forced and the girls were found dead in bed, with five bottles of veronal, a water jug and a tumbler standing empty on the chest-of-drawers.

They were wearing dressing-gowns over their nightdresses, both lying on their right sides, Primrose's left hand clasping the dressing-gown of her sister. She had died first, twelve hours before Topsy, and both had been dead for at least two days. The two doctors who examined the bodies found it impossible to say whether the sisters had swallowed a lethal dose simultaneously, but they agreed that in spite of the cold it was almost inconceivable that either had been dead more than four days.* They were last seen alive on 10 December. What had happened in the interval behind their locked door never emerged. A copy of Trine's *In Tune with the Infinite* was found in the room, and adduced at the inquest by Rutley Mowll as evidence that the girls had not deliberately killed themselves. Certainly the book unequivocally discourages suicide which, since the spirit body coexists with and outlasts the physical, seemed to Trine not so much criminal as pointless. Evidence at the inquest showed that Primrose had bought the bottles of veronal one at a time from the same chemist over the past six months (and had said, in reply to his warnings, that she used it 'entirely to obtain sleep'). But the motives behind what *The Times* reported as 'Mystery in St John's Wood' remained uninvestigated, and the coroner recorded a verdict of death from an overdose of veronal with a rider for which the family was thankful: 'Under what circumstances such overdose was taken there is not sufficient evidence to show.'[18]

Ivy attended the inquest but was not called to give evidence. Having lost her father and both her brothers, settled her account with her mother and disowned her sisters, she seemed already so thoroughly detached from the past that Janet at least had supposed 'family troubles'

---

* It was at first assumed by the family (and by the local doctor) that the sisters had lain dead in bed for two and a half weeks before their bodies were found, but Dr (later Sir) Bernard Spilsbury, who carried out the post-mortems as Home Office pathologist, maintained that this was virtually impossible, and that they had almost certainly died on Christmas Day.

could never hurt her again. But even Ivy's reserve could not wholly conceal the effect of a tragedy for which no one had been prepared. She could not sleep afterwards and lay awake coughing night after night; insomnia was always an affliction with which she sympathized in her friends, and from which she suffered for the rest of her life. Pity for her sisters was perhaps compounded with pity for herself—one's own grounds for self-pity being, as Oliver Shelley says in *Two Worlds and Their Ways*, generally too deep for words: 'Mine are the knotted and tangled kind, that lie fallow in the day and rise up to torment people at night'.[19] The double death was too drastic, and its implications too grievous, to be explored much at the time. Drug addiction was not in any case a subject which could be readily discussed in 1918. Dorothy had her own highly characteristic explanation: 'They were bored with life—they lived vividly even at that age. They were very highly tuned, and they could bear it no longer.' Ivy at the very end of her life advanced another theory to Vera: 'You know, I think Topsy and Baby had too much music in their lives. I think it was all that music. John always thought so, I know.' (John had been Ivy's name for Noel, not used by the rest of the family.)

In later years, when wild rumours which she did not entirely discourage tended to circulate about I. Compton-Burnett, it was inevitably suggested that her sisters had killed themselves in despair at being detected in an illicit affair with one another. But the notion of Lesbianism, with or without incestuous connections, involves a misconception about what was and what was not accepted as normal behaviour in Victorian families, whose permissiveness in some directions seems often as startling as their prudishness in others. Caresses between girls, between men, between brother and sister were freely indulged as signs of a tenderness which might well now bear a more prurient interpretation. In Ivy's childhood it would have been considered incomparably more shocking that a respectable married woman should openly refer (as Ivy's mother apparently did) to sitting on her husband's knee than that two sisters should sleep together. Girls commonly shared a bedroom and often a bed. If Freud opened the door on much that was murky in family relations, he also put a stop to much that went on in perfect ignorance and innocence. People who grew up before the first war say that it is impossible today to conceive of the barbaric sexual darkness in which children of both sexes were brought up and expected to remain till they married. Ivy herself must have resented this suppression acutely, or so at least one would suppose from a note of Butler's in which he proposes that the facts of sex be fully and frankly explained to adolescents: 'There should be no mystery or reserve. None but the corrupt will wish to corrupt facts. . . .'[20] This was, even in 1918, a preposterously provocative suggestion, and meant to be so. Ivy marked the whole passage in her copy of the *Note-Books* with a stroke at the side, underlined the last sentence and added a pencilled note in the margin: 'Then what a mass of corruption is the average person!'

In this kind of atmosphere passionate attachments flourished as a matter of course. Novelettes of the period regularly contain brothers whose behaviour to their sisters is unashamedly 'lover-like'.* Such things could hardly have been encouraged in a society which less ruthlessly inhibited the discussion, let alone the practice, of sex or anything remotely connected with it; and, though it is tempting, it would be unwise to interpret Ivy's early life in the light of the relish with which she afterwards confronted all shades of homosexuality in fact and fiction. Habitual discretion among the Compton-Burnett children, reinforced perhaps by the havoc they had seen spread from their mother's love for their father, had bred if anything a more than usual delicacy in sexual matters. It was generally believed by their closest friends that Noel had never consummated his marriage to Tertia, and indeed he himself said as much in one of his letters to Jack; but, though one might ascribe this abstention to a vestige of what Noel called 'my old morbidities', it was more likely due to a characteristically generous resolve that, if he must leave a widow, he would at least avoid the additional suffering that his death would have brought to a fatherless child. The fact that neither Ivy nor any of her five surviving sisters and half-sisters married was the rule rather than the exception among their contemporaries. The slaughter of men of their own age was one of the privations Ivy's generation had had to endure, and she accepted it philosophically as part of the illimitable damage done by the war. She herself had for years relied for amusement at Hove on the company of Noel's friends from Cambridge; and Janet Beresford was positive that,

---

* E.g. the intense relationship between the chaste heroine of Maud Diver's *Captain Desmond, V.C.* (Blackwood, Popular Edition, 1925) and her favourite bachelor brother: 'He led her into the dining-room with more of lover-like than brother-like tenderness; for despite his forty years no woman had yet dethroned this beautiful sister of his from the foremost place in his heart.' (p.10) There is an excellent account of the physical relations considered perfectly proper between Victorian women to whom Lesbianism was unknown, whether in theory or practice, in John Fowles' *The French Lieutenant's Woman* (Cape, 1969, pp.154–6).

in spite of her shyness, 'Ivy wouldn't have minded at all' if Alan Kidd had asked her to marry him in 1917. Fifty years later there was even a hint that Ivy had been fond of, perhaps in love with, someone else who was killed in the war[21] which is possible though deeply improbable in the light of her character and circumstances. Both her sisters and Janet are certain that there was no truth in this rumour. If Ivy had suffered a further loss, it was in any case negligible compared to the pain of Noel's death which reinforced and brought back Guy's: '"Them both dying like that," she said many times, "quite smashed my life up, it quite smashed my life up." The violence of the phrase was most uncharacteristic, but she never varied it.'[22]

Her efforts to subdue and contain the long series of shocks culminating in the suicide of her sisters must have lowered Ivy's resistance for she was desperately ill in the influenza epidemic which ran through London like the plague in the late summer of 1918, raging with such virulence that by October the casualty lists from the front were matched by columns almost as long in the papers of people who had died from 'flu at home. Shortage of food, light, heat and domestic help, rising costs, frequent air raids and perpetual anxiety in the past four years had weakened the civilian population. The sickness struck mostly at young people and developed so swiftly into acute pneumonia that death followed often in a matter of days, sometimes hours. Ivy, who had remained alone in her flat at Leinster Square with a daily woman to clean it, declined to summon help or take to her bed and was found by chance almost unconscious in the empty flat. Nurses were not to be had for any money so for the next few weeks Minnie came over each day from St John's Wood and was replaced by Vera at night. 'We didn't have the antibiotics then,' said Ivy. 'One just fought for breath for about a month.'[23] She was often delirious and would struggle to climb out of bed.

Personal acquaintance no doubt accounts for the particular excellence of sickbeds and deathbeds in her books, and for her intimate knowledge of the pneumonia which draws Ruth Giffard 'down into depths of fear and suffering' and very nearly kills Dudley Gaveston. Dudley's illness, in *A Family and a Fortune*, closely follows the course of Ivy's own. His strength, like hers, had been undermined by what his family call 'the troubles', he too had gone away by himself and been discovered alone, barely conscious, close to delirium and fighting for breath: 'The crisis came, and Dudley sank to the point of death and just did not pass it. Then as he lived through the endless days, each one doubled by the night, he seemed to return to this first stage, and this time drained and shattered by the contest waged within him.'²⁴

Ivy lay for several months in this state of extreme debility, unable to read or write though she liked to be read to and gave specific instructions to Vera: 'Read, but don't put any expression into it. Read in a dull, monotonous voice.' Dudley Gaveston had made the same proviso, which is several times invoked in the novels among those who dread the excessive feeling and 'the beautiful self-conscious voice' displayed in reading aloud by Sophia Stace and other descendants of Ivy's mother.

As her strength slowly returned, Ivy began to see people again and to take more interest in books, though she herself said she could stand nothing stronger than Wilkie Collins. Margot Asquith came to visit her, and so did Arthur Waley who later maintained that for years after Noel's death Ivy refused to do anything but lie on a sofa all day eating chocolates: 'We all used to urge her to stop reading library books and write some of her own.'²⁵ He attributed the elaborate and, for a twentieth-century novelist, highly idiosyncratic machinery from which she eventually evolved her plots to her weakness for melodramas constructed around secret passion and sensational revelation, mistaken identity, misappropriated funds, missing wills, lost, stolen and always fatally compromising letters. 'That', according to Arthur, 'was Ivy's idea of a novel.' To help pass the time she had also taken to needlework, and covered the seats of her chairs: 'I couldn't do brainwork, you see,' said Ivy, 'but then my brain came back.'

3

THE TAPESTRY PATTERNS for Ivy's chairs were said to have been chosen for her by Winifred's friend, Margaret Jourdain, whose *History of English Secular Embroidery* had been published in 1910. Margaret was the youngest but two of the ten clever children* of the Rev. Francis Jourdain, who had been vicar of Ashbourne in Derbyshire and whose family was in its own way as remarkable, almost as indigent and quite

---

* Mrs Jourdain, on being told by a parishioner that a bus route had been opened between Jerusalem and Jericho, is said to have answered tartly: 'How I should like to fill it with all his clever children!' (*The Ghosts of Versailles* by Lucille Iremonger, Faber, 1957, p.65.)

as old as the Beresfords. The Jourdains descended from French Hugue-
nots (Raymond, Guillaume and Alphonse Jourdain had given distinguished service in the First and Third Crusades)[26] who crossed the
channel in two waves at the beginning of the sixteenth and end of the
seventeenth centuries. A John Jourdain was Mayor of Lyme Regis in
1584, his son a founder of the East India Company and his cousin
Sylvester was shipwrecked with Somers and Gates and one of Lytton
Strachey's forebears off the Bermudas in 1609 (accounts of this voyage
by Sylvester Jourdain and William Strachey are thought to have given
Shakespeare ideas for *The Tempest*). Another ancestor, Renatus Jourdain, was drowned off the Scillies with Sir Cloudesley Shovell in 1707,
several more rose to high command in the British army and the extra-
ordinarily varied achievements of the inmates of Ashbourne vicarage
suggest that by the late nineteenth century the family had by no means
lost its taste for adventure.

Two of the Rev. Jourdain's five sons travelled widely in Africa and
the arctic, three of his daughters were among the first women at
Oxford and, though he himself seems to have published nothing more
ambitious than a guide to his parish church, seven of his children wrote
books as easily and often as most people write letters. Margaret's eldest
brother was a pioneer and scholar as distinguished in ornithological
circles as she herself was to become on furniture and the decorative arts.
Her eldest sister was Principal of St Hugh's in Oxford, and something
of a celebrity outside it on account of having seen the ghost of Marie
Antoinette at Versailles; a second sister was governess to the Asquiths,
among others, and a third joined the community of the Sisters of Mercy
at Truro (a sisterhood which, some dozen years earlier, had been suspected of having designs on Lady Ottoline Morrell).[27] Her brothers
Arthur, Henry and Raymond had all fought in the war, the first two
commanding battalions: Raymond was wounded, Henry was the only
officer in his regiment to survive Gallipoli, and Arthur was killed in
France three months before the armistice. There is nothing to suggest
that Margaret had been especially attached to Arthur (who was considerably older, married, and had in any case spent the better part of
the past thirty years defending the empire in India, Ceylon and South
Africa), but the loss of a brother in the war must have deepened a
friendship already beginning to prosper with Ivy.

Stories about Margaret from childhood onwards suggest a shrewd,
self-reliant and singularly unorthodox character. Charlotte Jourdain's
decision to take the veil can hardly have met with any great sympathy

from a younger sister who, almost before she was out of the nursery, had understood and rejected her elders' exploitation of Christianity: 'Margaret saw that when she was a little girl,' said Ivy long afterwards to Elizabeth Taylor. 'She said to her governess, "I don't want to hear any more about that poor man," and walked out of the room.' Margaret in middle age, when Ivy first met her, seems to have had points in common with Emily Herrick in *Pastors and Masters*, including an attitude to religion which held that things might have gone better if the mediaeval church had kept the Bible chained up. She had freely declared herself an atheist for years before that (though she still sat on Sundays in the family pew, for much the same reasons as the civilized, tolerant atheists in Ivy's books). She had taken a third in classical Mods at Lady Margaret Hall in 1897, returning home afterwards to live with her widowed mother at Broadwindsor in Dorset and to found, with her younger brother and sister, what became almost a family industry.

Philip and Melicent Jourdain had been crippled from birth by an hereditary paralysis (Philip so severely that he could not hold a pen), but both contributed over the next decade and more to the steady stream of publications issuing from Broadwindsor Manor. Margaret and Melicent wrote poems; Philip, a Cambridge mathematician specializing in transfinite numbers, edited a couple of scientific and ethical journals; Melicent published an autobiography; Margaret and Philip produced between them fifteen books in the first sixteen years of the century (these included an English edition of Horace's *Odes*[28] in which Margaret, still in her twenties, placed her own translations side by side with renderings of the same lines from better known hands such as Milton, Ben Jonson and W. E. Gladstone). Margaret's output meanwhile had risen from three published articles in 1903 to nearly sixty in 1910, on anything from chintzes to Chinese wallpapers, stump work to samplers, card tables, knife cases, old grates and trunks, cradles, tea pots and royal gloves. These provided, if not an adequate income, at least a foothold in London and, by the beginning of the war, Margaret had taken rooms with a college friend engaged on relief work (which no doubt meant for them, as it did for so many women at the time, relief in more senses than one) in Trafalgar Square, Chelsea, where her scope widened to cover patriotic pieces on the Germans, on soldiers' letters from the front, on air raids for Philip's *International Journal of Ethics*, and a war-work series for *Country Life*.

Margaret belonged to the genre of New Woman which had once dismayed Dr Burnett, a small but growing band of unattached, self-assured, purposeful spinsters accustomed to make their own way in the world. By the end of 1918, she meant to make hers as a freelance from journalism, catalogues, handbooks and articles on the great country houses which she, being better connected and far more determined than many of her colleagues, was often the first professional to penetrate. Her tastes were rather more worldly than Ivy's on both social and literary fronts. She knew many of the writers and journalists who had revolved round literary hostesses like Violet Hunt before the war, and she had been a protégée of Lord Alfred Douglas during his short and stormy editorship of the *Academy*, when he took her about, lunched with her at the Café Royal, published her poems, encouraged her to write about nature or the French symbolist poets, sent her a weekly parcel of books to review and generally succeeded for almost two years in diverting her attention away from the decorative arts. Lord Alfred, cramped but not crestfallen after the Wilde trial, had prided himself on an eye for spotting young poets, publishing Rupert Brooke and Siegfried Sassoon as well as 'M. Jourdain' in the intervals between steering his paper on a fairly disastrous course of litigation. The *Academy* folded in 1910, but not before its editor had brought out Margaret's *Outdoor Breviary* (a set of pastoral prose pieces which appeared in the *Academy* throughout 1909) in the same format as his own *Sonnets*: Margaret had a copy of these inscribed 'To Miss Jourdain (author of so many good sonnets)—Alfred Douglas. 1909.' Her own *Poems*, published in the same year as *Dolores*, were dedicated 'To Janette'.

Margaret had shared rooms when she first came to London with Janette Ranken who, having gone down from Oxford after two years and pursued a brief career on the stage, left her companion in 1917 to marry the actor Ernest Thesiger—a marriage which astonished their friends, since neither bride nor groom had previously taken any great interest in the opposite sex. Ernest Thesiger became for Janette's sake a friend of Margaret and, for his own, a lifelong friend of Ivy. He was not only irresistibly fetching himself, but typical of much in Margaret's circle that greatly appealed to Ivy: a renegade from an impeccable family (his grandfather had been the first Lord Chelmsford and his father, as Ernest recorded with pleasure, 'knew nearly all the Peers of the Realm')[29] and an eccentric of the first water, a man who wore pearls next the skin and had told Réjane that her nose was even more ugly than his. His looks were extraordinary: he had been drawn by Sargent, caricatured by Max Beerbohm and painted on fans by

Charles Condor ('as Death, in black draperies, with a skull-mask wreathed in scarlet poppies'). He had enlisted as a private in 1915 and baffled his commanding officer by taking his needlework with him. Ernest Thesiger was the man who said, or is supposed to have said, when asked for a first-hand impression of Ypres, 'My dear, *the noise*!! and *the people*!!!'

All this must have come as a pleasant shock to Ivy, though it can scarcely have come all at once. Winifred had introduced her to Margaret before or just after Dorothy's marriage and for a time they formed a congenial trio, so much so that when Ivy and Margaret showed signs of becoming a pair Winifred was hard put to conceal her resentment at being left out. Ivy had probably proposed sharing her flat (though neither party can as yet have envisaged that the arrangement would work on a permanent basis) round about the end of 1918 when Margaret moved out of her old rooms in Trafalgar Square; an entry in Margaret's diary suggests that she was already staying at 59 Leinster Square by the following May. She was away for most of the summer, and on 1 October her brother Philip died. Of all her brothers Philip had always been closest to Margaret in interests as well as in age: the two had lived and worked together for years and, long after Margaret's departure and Philip's marriage in 1915, each had continued to put work in the way of the other—Margaret acting as Philip's editorial assistant, Philip putting forward her name for articles on anything from 'The Victorian Spirit' to 'What Bolshevism Is' for the *Daily Mail*. His death, fourteen months after Arthur's, must have been hard on his sister, and perhaps it provided a more intimate bond than anything else could have done when Margaret finally moved into Ivy's flat on 6 October 1919.

Margaret was forty-three that autumn, Ivy was thirty-five. Each had been at a loose end and each no doubt found in the other a convenient solution to their respective problems of where and with whom to live. Part of Margaret's attraction for Ivy lay perhaps in the fact that she had no connection whatever with the miseries and mistakes of the past; part also in her vitality, her formidable organizing powers, her decided opinions, multifarious interests and countless friends. But Ivy at this time was still 'drained and shattered' and in no state to cope with anything save a prolonged convalescence, which probably explains why Margaret fell into the habit of pampering her, fetching her book or her bag and saying indulgently, when Dorothy suggested that Ivy might fetch things herself, 'You see, she's like a child.' It was years since Ivy had mattered in this way to anyone, far less been able to depend on anyone as she had once done on her brothers; and it must have been under the reviving influence of Margaret's courage and humour and affection that Ivy's 'brain came back'.

One may also date from much the same time what seems to have been a crucial encounter with Samuel Butler. His *Note-Books* had been published posthumously in 1912 but Ivy's copy is a fourth impression of the second edition published in 1918. The first, and perhaps the most startling, of all her marks in the book was prompted by a passage on the life after death of great artists—on whom 'death confers a more living kind of life than they can ever possibly have enjoyed while to those about them they seemed to be alive'—in contrast to the death-in-life endured by their less ambitious contemporaries: 'The whole life of some people is a kind of partial death—a long, lingering death-bed, so to speak, of stagnation and nonentity on which death is but the seal, or solemn signing, as the abnegation of all further act and deed on the part of the signer. Death robs these people of even that little strength which they appeared to have and gives them nothing but repose.'[30] There is a note at the foot of the page in Ivy's hand, wild and sprawling and ill-spelt, as though forced from her at some moment when even she could no longer keep up her calm front of civilization and artificiality: 'I am a living witniss of this crushing lifless stagnation of the spirit.'

Ivy's was scarcely an excessive or even an uncommon reaction to a cataclysm which had taken all that she valued, smashed her private life and smashed with it the social and moral foundations on which the world had seemed so solidly built. People who emerged from the first war sore, angry, depleted and desperately in need of consolation suffered often enough from what Dr Compton Burnett called 'a kind of dead-all-over feeling' which simply increased the pain when their rational faculties returned. Many succumbed altogether to a mental and emotional numbness from which others only slowly or partly recovered. One of the hardest things for the survivors to bear, apart from their own personal losses, was the irretrievable collapse of standards and assumptions for which it seemed that their contemporaries had died in millions: '. . . my mind groped in a dark, foggy confusion, uncertain of what had happened to it or what was going to happen,' wrote Vera Brittain, whose experience is paralleled in a good many autobiographies of the period. 'Still partly dominated by old ideals, time-worn respectabilities and spasms of rebellious bitterness, it sometimes seized fleetingly the tail of an idea upon whose wings it was later to ascend into a clearer heaven of new convictions.'[31] For Miss Brittain, as for many others, wings were provided by the study of history and the new heaven meant campaigning for internationalism, the League of Nations and women's rights. For Ivy the quickening impulse apparently came from Butler, who provided her when she needed them with texts from which she was to work for the rest of her life. It was presumably at some time in the years when she lay on a sofa, tended by Margaret and teased by her friends, that she marked (with a recklessness quite unlike her usual caution) his passages on 'The Family'; on 'Religion'; on 'Change and Immorality'; on sex, money and the dangers of keeping young people from knowledge of either.

Butler had died in 1901, when he was known if at all as the eccentric author of *Erewhon* and various other more or less obscure and peculiar works, including one devoted to proving that a woman wrote the *Odyssey*. His vogue, which reached its height in the 'twenties, had been gathering strength since the publication of *The Way of All Flesh* in 1903. If Ivy had read Butler's novel before the war, it had made no impression or none that affected *Dolores*. The *Note-Books* contain a selection from the common-place books in which it was Butler's custom to pare down and polish reflections which, when they came out, were considered according to which way you looked at them either delightfully or dreadfully bold. The scored and pencilled pages of Ivy's copy suggest that she responded as readily as she had once submerged herself in George Eliot to a set of proposals for radical subversion laid down with Butler's most disarming and deceptive mildness. Both the subversive content and the sweetly reasonable manner are reflected in *Pastors and Masters*, and throughout Ivy's subsequent novels in which— though she retained her preoccupation with duty, self-sacrifice, power and its crippling effects on both those who wield and those who submit to it—she nonchalantly reversed the conclusions drawn in *Dolores*.

Up to 1911, and probably much later, Ivy had shown small sign of deviating from the conventional outlook of her class and age. Though she objected to society's blatant use of religion for highly dubious ends, she was not apparently inclined to cavil at its moral underpinning. One may at least suspect as much from a letter to Katie, dated 24 March 1913, expounding the improving power of sorrow—a theory Ivy afterwards had cause to revise, if not disown:

If you do not let it embitter you, as you are less inclined to do than I, and even if you cannot help its embittering you a little, it will make you larger in the long run. And as you grow larger, you grow more useful, to others anyhow, and in a way to yourself. No experience is ever wasted; and an experience like this will come to seem to you in years to come, to be the cause of the best of what you are—and will no doubt be the cause of much you would never have been without it. Real charity and a real ability never to condemn—the one real virtue—is so often the result of a waking experience that gives a glimpse of what lies beneath things.

The lesson Butler taught is easily seen if one compares this letter with Ivy's later views on real quality. It is not simply that the advantage in her novels seldom lies with people who aim at true success ('"The other kind of success is better," said France. "True success seems to be effort and achievement without any reward. It is as bad as true kindness or honest advice or anything else of that kind"')[32] or show true dignity ('"I always wonder if the true kinds of dignity, the dignity of toil and simplicity and frugal independence, are as good as the other kinds"'). This sort of thing might be dismissed, and indeed often has been, as a super-ficial playing on words, though one might as easily argue that a more fastidious use of words reflects a greater delicacy of feeling on Ivy's part than the conventional comfort handed out to her cousin in 1913. The unselfish conduct outlined in her letter had not proved a practical programme for Ivy in the years when she ruled her sisters at Hove. It is a short step, though a hard one, from tacitly condoning this gap between practice and precept to recognizing that the gap favours the powerful at the expense of the weak; that it promotes the worst excesses of hypocrisy and callousness; that it bedevils people's dealings with one another at all levels from international politics to the most humdrum transactions inside a family; and that it is not to be closed. What passes for cynicism in the novels of I. Compton-Burnett is more often than not a casual acceptance of these harsh facts, the last being generally the one people find hardest to stomach. Their justifica-tion is given in an unusually explicit discussion, from *Elders and Betters*, on unselfishness:

'Most things that are good, or called good, are founded on that,' said Thomas.
'And those things are very good indeed, too good to be possible. It comes of a foundation that must break down. Most people have tried to build on it. And they remember it, and respect themselves,

and are exacting with other people; and I think they are justified. A person who can really be called an unselfish person, has no place in life.'[33]

This is the philosophy implicit in all but the first of the novels of I. Compton-Burnett. It underlies her singularly persuasive portrayals of virtue as well as her sympathy with vice. And, though her readers must often have felt that it sprang fully armed from her head on to the pages of *Pastors and Masters*, its first inklings seem to have reached her from the following passages marked with her pencil in Butler's section on 'Elementary Morality'—passages which suggest that not the least of the things that pleased her about Butler was his fondness for speaking the truth with a thoroughly disingenuous air:

Vice and Virtue

i

Virtue is something which it would be impossible to over-rate if it had not been over-rated. The world can ill spare any vice which has obtained long and largely among civilized people. . . .

As a matter of private policy I doubt whether the moderately vicious are more unhappy than the moderately virtuous; 'Very vicious' is certainly less happy than 'Tolerably virtuous', but this is about all. *What pass muster as the extremes of virtue probably make people quite as unhappy as extremes of vice do.*

The truest virtue has ever inclined toward excess rather than asceticism; that she should do this is reasonable as well as observable, for virtue should be as nice a calculator of chances as other people and will make due allowance for the chance of not being found out. Virtue knows that it is impossible to get on without compromise, and tunes herself, as it were, a trifle sharp to allow for an inevitable fall in playing. So the Psalmist says, '*If thou, Lord, wilt be extreme to mark what is done amiss: O Lord who may abide it?*' and by this he admits that the highest conceivable form of virtue still leaves room for some compromise with vice. . . .

ii

The extremes of vice and virtue are alike detestable; absolute virtue is as sure to kill a man as absolute vice is, let alone the dullnesses of it and the pomposities of it.

vi

*Virtue has never yet been adequately represented by any who have had any claim to be considered virtuous. It is the sub-vicious who best understand virtue. Let the virtuous people stick to describing vice—which they can do well enough.**

It would be easy to find parallels for any or all of these passages in Ivy's books. Butler pointed her in a direction from which she never turned back, just as George Eliot had once misled her down tortuous paths to a dead end. What George Eliot blocked up, Butler unblocked, and there is evidence that Ivy retained her respect and affection for him long after she had discarded him as a pointer. Her fifth novel contains what I take to be a portrait of Butler himself, modelled so closely on material taken from Festing Jones' *Samuel Butler: A Memoir* that it is hard to believe it was not meant as a discreet but deliberate tribute. The *Memoir* came out in 1919, and was one of the library books that Ivy persisted in reading despite all Arthur Waley could say ('Have you seen the new life of Samuel Butler—by H. F. Jones?' she wrote to Katie in November 1919. 'Pleasant to get from the library—too dear to buy.'). From it she must have borrowed much that reappears, more or less thinly disguised and sometimes almost word for word, fourteen years later in *More Women Than Men.* Jones' book is immensely long, detailed and, as Asquith said, skipworthy; interesting at that time chiefly because it confirmed what a good many readers must have suspected, that *The Way of All Flesh* faithfully describes its author's own appalling childhood; and perhaps also, from Ivy's point of view, for a number of curious facts such as that Butler was a lifelong homoeopath and had once proposed becoming, if only to annoy his father, a homoeopathic physician himself. What he liked about homoeopathy, indeed what he liked about most things that appealed to him, was that 'It can't do you any harm'.[34]

The harm people do one another was an abiding horror to Butler. His own suffering at his father's hands had given him a driving sense of pain and punishment matched by the stoical conviction that, since people will inevitably inflict the one and suffer the other, the most one can do is limit one's power to hurt and to be hurt. He had escaped from

* *The Note-Books of Samuel Butler*, pp.27–8; the italics are mine throughout, and I have used them to mark the sentences singled out by Ivy's pencilled scorings in the margin of her copy.

his father at immense cost to his own emotional life. But the escape left him free to pursue, with unimpaired energy and greatly increased cheerfulness, his chosen rôle as a prophet—to spread alarm and despondency among all those who believed in religion, family life, the prospect of progress, innocence, charity, diligence, altruism or any other illusion whatever. He put his own faith where Ivy put hers, in material goods and very little else.

Hence no doubt the happy ending of *The Way of All Flesh*, whereby the woes of Ernest Pontifex are cancelled at a stroke on his coming suddenly into a suitably large fortune. The book, in some ways so like her own, perhaps showed Ivy what might be done with the past, if once one were sufficiently distanced from it; but here one treads on shaky ground, for Butler's novel belongs rather to the genre of satire or confessional than to imaginative fiction. Its characters are puppets deployed with a bland, judicious humour which is at once the measure of Butler's detachment from his childhood and the source of the book's controlled and savage power. His brilliance lies in extracting so much enjoyment, with so little bitterness, from his mother as a comic creation and, more subtly, from his father whose ferocity would be tragic were it not so humorous in the person of poor, fretful, hapless, hopeless, red-handed Canon Pontifex. Their brutality is the more atrocious for being dispassionately recorded; and the absurd dénouement, when Ernest returns home a rich man to confound his father, is all of a piece with the insouciance of the whole. There could be no atonement, not even the slow deaths in agony of both parents, in proportion to Ernest's suffering. Butler's tone is as light as his tale is dark, and the one fiercely illumines what in the other is shadowy, grim and fearful.

Butler preferred not to delve too deeply into horrors, whether in himself or his tormentors, which Ivy spent the greater part of her life probing. Beneath these opposite reactions one may detect a similar strength of will and a strong, though perhaps a superficial similarity of pattern: a tragic early life violently demolished and followed by a steadfast, stoical refusal ever again to put oneself emotionally at risk. Both, before they reached maturity, had survived a prolonged crisis or series of crises from which both emerged exhausted but intact. Butler made meagre use of the independence which he had so dearly bought, constructing for himself a routine of extreme and self-protective dullness pursued in drab surroundings with frugal pleasures, few excursions and fewer friends. His life became a matter of husbanding resources thriftily preserved from a struggle which left him in some directions permanently maimed, and which had intimate connections with the persistent 'knot of ideas' explored by P. N. Furbank in Butler's writings: 'the virtue of luck, the morality of health, the duty to be born of good ancestry, the reverence due to money'.[35] Ivy adopted this programme so naturally that the resigned and level voice of reason in her books might at times be Butler speaking:

> 'Have you never been taught about poverty not being a thing to be ashamed of?'
> 'I have always been ashamed of it. I would save anyone in my power from it. I have done so in the one case I could . . . things like poverty and old age and death are shameful. We cannot help them; but that is the humiliation. To accept conditions that would not be your choice must be a disgrace.'[36]

One may see also, in the apparent narrowness and sheltered regularity of Ivy's life with Margaret, something of the invalid sensibility detected by Furbank in Butler's dealings with his friends: 'It is the tone of the convalescent, and of the habitual rather than the temporary convalescent . . . Butler's life should be seen as a sharp and heroic resistance to a nearly mortal illness followed by a restoration to an inevitably low and never quite secure state of health.'* Ivy, on her own slow recovery from physical and nervous prostration, saw no reason to dismantle the camouflage of dullness remarked on in the 'twenties and 'thirties by Margaret's friends, most of whom incautiously dismissed her as the nondescript companion who poured tea and seldom spoke. After the precarious existence of the last few years, Ivy must have been relieved and thankful for this comparative oblivion. 'Relief is the keenest form of joy' is a characteristically guarded saying from *Brothers and Sisters* which recurs, in almost identical words, more than forty years later in the last of her novels.[37] But, though Ivy took much the same counter measures as Butler against unmanageable forces which threatened her with extinction, the resemblance goes no further. The difference lies in

---

* Dolores' experience in a dark hour suggests that Ivy well understood this state of mind long before Noel's death: 'She felt that her soul was dead. . . . She felt it was dead; and had a strange, dull gladness in feeling it; for that it might awaken was a petrifying thing.' (*Dolores*, pp.258–9.) I have relied heavily in the following on Furbank's *Samuel Butler*, which contains a brilliant analysis of Butler's intellectual and emotional evolution, and goes far towards explaining what seems to have been a parallel development in Ivy.

the degree of damage inflicted: self-imposed restrictions were essential to Butler's survival, dictating his scope as a writer as well as his plan for living, whereas for Ivy they seem to have been incidental, a convenient withdrawal which she exercised at will in her private life and which, far from inhibiting her work, enabled her to draw for the rest of her career on material stored at the deepest levels of consciousness.

As one turns the pages of her copy of the *Note-Books*, from the first terse confession to the last vigorous scrawl in the margin, one has the irresistible impression of watching her return to health and spirits. 'Then I got well, but I could do very little for some years, and then as my strength came back my mental strength came back too. But one did get very delayed,'[38] said Ivy. The delay must have been almost over by the time she finished Butler's book. He had restored her brain, sharpened her humour, improved her morals, confirmed her dislike of religion and, perhaps most potent tonic of all, shown her cause to congratulate herself on a good riddance from family life. A writer who touches on the emotions as reluctantly as Butler can have had little to do with reconciling her to the death of her brother. But as she settled into the security provided by Margaret's companionship, she had at least the consolation that, having insured her feelings as far as possible against damage or loss, she would never again be so mercilessly exposed to either. A programme of security, tranquillity, inactivity had much to recommend it after the '14–'18 war. It is the programme invariably adopted in the novels of I. Compton-Burnett by people who have seen and felt as much as they can stand: 'We have seen some real life, Roberta, a thing I have always wanted to see. But now I don't want to see any more as long as I live.'[39]

Ivy had reached the stage favoured by Sophia Stace in *Brothers and Sisters* 'when people have had experience, and are not quite in the dark about things'—though, as Sophia's son points out, darkness is what they might well prefer if given the choice: 'Every shedding of light has been a shock to me so far'.[40] The war had completed a process begun, for a nature as susceptible to shock as Ivy's, almost before she could think at all. From now on she looked clearly at things obscurely sensed in the past, chief among them that love of power which Butler had taught her to recognize in a domestic setting and which Lowes Dickinson called 'the most disastrous, if not the most evil, of the human passions.'[41] Perhaps Dickinson himself contributed something to the scheme which must have been beginning to take shape at the back of Ivy's mind in the years when she visited him after the war. The two had much in common, besides their memories of Noel. Dickinson minded as acutely about the disasters which afflict states and nations as most people mind about personal disaster. He had recovered from despair but not from the misery induced by a calamity whose causes he could dissect but not remedy. He still hoped that people might somehow be persuaded to abandon the urge to power both collectively and individually—indeed he spent the rest of his life working through the League of Nations to that end. But he seems to have been by this time more or less resigned to the defeat of hope by experience; and one cannot help suspecting that there was something deeply congenial to Ivy in Dickinson's imperturbability. He was, as one of his friends remarked, 'the sort of person you felt you could tell anything to, and he wouldn't be horrified or surprised, and he would say, "Oh well, my dear, I think we must just consider what's the best thing to be done if you've really killed this man."'[42]

This sort of person was later to become a familiar figure in Ivy's novels. Murder leaves him or her as unruffled as jealousy, incest, adultery, greed, rage or any other explosion of the aggressive and acquisitive instincts. These are the cynics and sceptics in her books, what Butler called 'the sub-vicious', people clever enough to be kind but too intimately acquainted with their own vices to admit of anything but a despairing acceptance of viciousness in others. They are gentle, humorous, melancholy, intensely curious and profoundly ineffectual. Mortimer Lamb or Dudley Gaveston serve admirably to represent the type but almost every book contains one or more examples of people who stand aside from the central conflict between parent and child, tyrant and victim, watching what the one does to the other; who see the abuse of power and recognize that the powerful can no more prevent themselves from exploiting their position than the weak can avoid being crushed; and who, understanding the tyrants, feeling for their victims, are helpless to intervene between the two. Dickinson's definition of the Cambridge outlook, set down in 1930 when he was sadly aware of another approaching war, provides as succinct an analysis as one may hope to find of the role played by this dispassionate spectator in the novels of I. Compton-Burnett:

> . . . there is, I think, a certain type, rare like all good things, which seems to be associated in some peculiar way with my alma mater. . . . It is a type unworldly without being saintly, unambitious without being inactive, warmhearted without being sentimental. Through

good report and ill such men work on, following the light of truth as they see it; able to be sceptical without being paralysed; content to know what is knowable and to reserve judgement on what is not. The world could never be driven by such men, for the springs of action lie deep in ignorance and madness. But it is they who are the beacon in the tempest, and they are more, not less, needed now than ever before.[43]

Ivy had no need to look further than the passionate will transmitted down three generations in her own family to find the submerged violence Dickinson describes. It was to become the central subject matter of her novels. All the ingredients lay ready to her hand. From Butler, she had learnt where to look and how to interpret what she saw. From Cambridge, she had learnt both the charm and the weakness of a sceptical intelligence: brothers and sisters in her books, mournfully contemplating their own lack of power, constantly echo Noel's last words to Ivy: 'Oh! we *were* clever'. From her mother, and from traces of her mother which she found and perhaps feared in herself, she knew well enough the dangers threatening a person ruled by the emotions, and to what desperate lengths that person might be driven. At all events, she never again attempted to recreate the position of authority thrust on her in her last four years at Hove. From now on her interest in the way people prey on one another was confined to the strictly intellectual pleasures of observation, speculation and deduction. The daily doings of her circle provided abundant material for all three; and her friendship with Margaret restored her emotional balance to the point at which she could begin to scrutinize the present through the mirror of the past. 'First the one brother dying like that—and then the other brother dying—put a full stop,' said her sister Juliet. 'And then she went into a retrospect.'

TWO

SECRETS OF A WOMAN'S

HEART

1920–1969

'I don't see why spinsters have any less success,' said Isabel.

'Well, they have no proof that they have been sought,' said Miss Mitford.

'Have you ever been sought?' said Venice . . .

'You must not probe the secrets of a woman's heart,' said Miss Mitford . . .

Parents and Children, p.86.

1920–1929

'Not one of those modern people'

I

WHEN IVY COMPTON-BURNETT published *Pastors and Masters* at the beginning of 1925, her friends reacted with varying degrees of shock, disbelief and dismay. Margaret Jourdain, who lived with her, said that the first she knew of the book's existence was one morning when Ivy, laid up with a chill, fished out a copy from under the bedclothes.[1] 'Margaret was horrified,' said Joan Evans, 'really horrified when that first novel was produced.' Joan herself was indignant. Other people, like Margaret's professional colleague Ralph Edwards and her old ally in the country Hester Pinney, were frankly incredulous. Hester Pinney's daughter, known as Little Hester, accepted the copy Ivy gave her without even bothering to open it: 'My mother, when I told her about the gift, said that as usual I'd got it all wrong. I ought to know by this time that Margaret was the one who wrote.'[2]

In Ivy's circle this was the general view. A friend who met both ladies some time in 1926 was astonished to find, when someone referred to one of the pair as 'the writer', that it wasn't Margaret he meant.[3] Ivy's lapse into authorship was something Margaret's friends found it best to ignore. People who visited their various flats in the 1920s and 1930s remember Ivy as drab, inconspicuous, inscrutable, generally mute: 'She was a rather stout, middle-class woman who poured out cups of tea for all the young men who came to see Margaret,' said Herman Schrijver (who was one of Margaret's young men himself in 1927). 'Ivy had no conversation of any sort or kind in those days . . .'[4] Herman, whose first move on meeting Ivy had been to go out and buy *Pastors and Masters*, maintained that for years he was her only reader, or at any rate the only one she knew.

Ivy's friends in the early 1920s had nearly all met her through Margaret, who was beginning by this time to be widely feared and respected as an authority on English furniture and interiors. She moved in a thoroughly conservative and quite unbookish, in some cases near-philistine world of collectors and country-house journalists, museum officials, dealers, decorators and their clients. From the start Margaret herself set the tone for furniture friends who boasted over the next forty years and more that they could make neither head nor tail of the writings of I. Compton-Burnett. 'Of course I never read Ivy's trash,' Margaret is said to have told Roger Hinks[5]; and the saying, by no means strictly truthful, well illustrates her characteristically brusque version of the Pinneys' offhandedness (the younger of the two Hesters did eventually get through her copy of *Pastors and Masters* but, though she remained a friend to the day Ivy died, this was the first and last time she read one of her books).

It was a state of affairs Ivy did nothing at all to discourage. The novelist David Garnett said that she looked like a schoolmistress and scarcely spoke when he first met her, at a lunch given for Margaret in 1923.[6] To the critic Raymond Mortimer, Ivy's earliest and most effective champion in the literary world, she seemed 'always more like the governess than the governess's employer'.[7] This was a common impression, and one she took pains to produce. Her highly stylized looks, the air of strange formal distinction she acquired in later life, grew from what had been in these years a form of the nondescript colouring adopted by the better type of governess in her books: meek, plaintive, underrated creatures, often queerly dressed in styles long since discarded by everyone else, always effectively sustained against pity or contempt by a rather startling degree of self-knowledge and an even more worrying understanding of other people.

Margaret and Ivy made an odd couple in their long skirts that neither rose nor fell with the switchback lunges of hemline in the 1920s, and hairstyles unchanged since their girlhood. But where Margaret (who was ugly and forceful and eight years older than Ivy[8]) wore lace jabots, dashing plumed and flowered hats, gold chains, feather boas, finery of all sorts with a watch in her belt and a dangling Regency spyglass, Ivy dressed like Miss Ridley, the governess in *The Present and the Past*, 'to make a whole that conformed to nothing and offended no one. She made no mistakes in her dress, merely carried out her intentions.'[9] Friends of Margaret visiting the flat for the first time barely noticed her ('*No one* ever went to see Ivy, or would ever have been asked by her,' said Raisley Moorsom who had known them both almost from the start of their association); and the few, like Herman, who tried to draw her out found it uphill work.

Like her own governesses, Ivy must have had much to put up with in these years by way of condescension from people who, in so far as they were aware of her at all, suspected that her social origins were a great deal humbler than Margaret's. But, like Miss Mitford, the governess in *Parents and Children*, she gave no quarter and expected none. Miss Mitford with her immediate successor, Miss Lacy in *Elders and Betters*, is among the most nearly contented characters in Ivy's books: a colourless exterior and constrained social manner mask, in each case, a curiosity too concentrated to operate without some sort of camouflage, since each shares with Ivy 'a knowledge of books which was held to be natural in her life, and a knowledge of people which would have been held to be impossible, and was really inevitable'.[10]

This was a side of Ivy not often glimpsed, unless perhaps by the brides or fiancées of Margaret's young men, several of whom found Ivy's silent scrutiny quite as unsettling as Margaret's tart comments. Juliet Compton-Burnett remembered from before the First World War her sister's habit of looking people over—their faces, their expressions, their hands as they took tea—'one might say to a degree that was hardly respectable'. Marjorie Edwards, Ralph's wife, produced for inspection soon after their marriage in the 1920s, found Ivy 'most alarming' at this first encounter. So did Viva Booth, whose engagement in 1926 to another gifted youth, Willie King of the British Museum, earned her Margaret's undisguised disapproval:

> She was an ugly, bosomy spinster with fluffy blonde hair and she used a spy-glass, the better to stare with. She was very clever . . . At that time [Ivy] was also plump and bosomy, with streaky grey-brown hair the shape of a mob-cap, kept in place with a string round her head—which colour and shape never varied

during the forty years I was to know her. She had written a book, *Dolores*, with no success and had attempted to call in the copies.

Dolores, published in 1911, had never been heard of in a circle still barely aware in 1926 of *Pastors and Masters*, but the general impression of novel-writing as a dim and faintly discreditable activity is accurate enough. 'Margaret's spy-glass and Ivy's hard stares, and the company of these intellectual women, were only for the strong.'[11]

But in those days it was only young women who found Ivy formidable. To Margaret's young men—for Margaret required, and saw that she got, a steady stream of young men to sit at her feet, pick her brains, join her for lunch, escort her round the sale rooms or on country-house visits—Ivy rated less attention than the chair she sat on. The celebrity was Margaret who had few rivals as an expert in a field cultivated until recently on a more or less haphazard basis by amateur antiquarians. Caustic and categorical, vehement, argumentative and often cuttingly funny, Margaret was capital company, centre of an energetic social life and a prime source of professional contacts not otherwise easily come by. Moreover, when they first set up house together in 1919, she had far better literary credentials than Ivy, who had published a single, forgotten and remaindered novel at her own expense before the war, and showed no sign of producing another.

Margaret was a published poet and prose poet, editor and essayist, translator and disciple of Baudelaire and the symbolists, as well as a regular reviewer for the literary weeklies on subjects ranging from Voltaire and the Greeks to Trollope, Samuel Butler and Henry James. Her reputation for painstaking scholarship had taken years to build up and, at the beginning of the 1920s, before Ivy's own routine of working at home was established, the two would spend mornings working together in the reading room at the British Museum. On the rare occasions when she could be brought to relax with people she knew well, Miss Jourdain's 'young friend'[12] seemed in those days the lightminded one of the two, gigglier and giddier than Margaret: 'Ivy was slightly silly. She was very young and sort of fluffy, and bubbling over with humour,' said her brother's old Cambridge friend, Raisley Moorsom. 'Everything that happened to her, and everything she said, was a great joke.' She herself always drew a sharp distinction between scholarship, or 'serious books', and her own kind of writing—the sort everyone reckons to be able to do because, as another novelist says sharply in *Daughters and Sons*, 'people think it needs brains and no training'.[13]

What one might call the running gag in Ivy's books about the superiority of scholars (as opposed to the intrinsic frivolity of novelists) has the wry, affectionate note of a private joke; and there is no shortage of evidence that, for all her disclaimers, Margaret did in fact read Ivy's books with understanding and pleasure. Like the learned Miss Marcon in *Daughters and Sons*, who also travelled regularly to the British Museum to research her next book in the reading room, Margaret in some moods took a genuine pride in her friend's success ('that wonderful child! To write like that, sitting at home, and not have to go by train to get it! I do look up to her!'[14]). Her asperity seems to have been, in part at least, a game played according to Ivy's rule of secrecy and discretion. 'I think people work at different levels of consciousness,' Ivy said long afterwards. 'I think I must work rather low down.'[15] Certainly there had never been any question, even in the days when she wrote *Dolores* sitting side by side with her brother Noel in the schoolroom at home, of anyone seeing a word she had written before the manuscript was completed.

Negotiations with publishers over that first book had been as darkly concealed as, by Margaret's account, they were for the second. Ivy placed *Pastors and Masters* in the autumn of 1924 with a small firm of 'vanity' publishers called Heath Cranton in Fleet Lane, paying for publication herself as she had paid for *Dolores*, and receiving in return the published price of 3s 6d per copy, less Cranton's commission of twenty per cent, or eightpence a volume.[16] Margaret's copy must have been produced from under the bedclothes early the following February; and, if it is clearly impossible for the two women to have lived at close quarters for more than five years without one suspecting that the other was writing a book (Margaret had published at least three in the time), the answer probably lies in a pact between them which Margaret described to Joan Evans: 'Ivy has written a book and I expect it's very bad. We have decided that I shan't read it, and then there'll be no trouble about it.'[17]

Part of the anticipated trouble was undoubtedly social. Margaret's upper-class friends seem to have felt that everything they deplored about Ivy—her drabness, isolation, lack of small talk, the fact that she came, socially speaking, from the wrong drawer—was compounded by her having written a novel ('It seems such a light sort of thing,' as Sir Michael Egerton says in *A God and His Gifts*. 'But of course people do earn by it, even more than by serious books they say'[18]). Even Ivy's maid felt (like the Egertons' butler) so ashamed when the butcher remarked on 'her lady' having written a novel that she drew herself up and said witheringly: 'My lady has no need'.*

Few people Ivy knew were likely to take the *New Statesman* which saluted *Pastors and Masters* that summer as 'a work of genius'.[19] *Vogue* was more in their line, and perhaps somebody spotted the young Raymond Mortimer recommending Ivy's novel ('The wit of it often, the acidity and quiet cynicism always, are a delight . . .') as a New Book for the Morning Room Table in April. But Margaret and most of her friends read or wrote for *Country Life*, where Ralph Edwards (who had begun his career on the staff just after the war, and ended it running the Victoria and Albert Museum's department of Furniture and Woodwork) reviewed Ivy's early work with no great enthusiasm strictly as a favour to Margaret.[20] His cautious reception of books that struck him as unhealthy, unsettling and too smart by half reflects widespread agreement in furniture circles that Ivy had much better stick to her place as Margaret's companion and housekeeper. 'I was more and more dazzled by Margaret's erudition. Ivy was always in the background,' wrote young Hester Pinney, whose first attempts to launch herself in London owed much to Margaret: 'The delightful company I met were Margaret's friends. The fine books on furniture and *Country Life* articles were Margaret's work. It was Margaret who told me Ivy was scribbling in little notebooks.'[21] By the end of the 1920s, and throughout the 1930s, when Ivy's growing reputation in the literary world could no longer be entirely discounted at home, Margaret's friends retaliated by referring to Ivy as 'Margaret Jourdain's Boswell', a nickname invented by Basil Marsden-Smedley (who had married young Hester in 1927) and widely

---

* This was Herman Schrijver's story (Burkhart 2, p.81), but Ivy told Nathalie Sarraute that it was the grocer who said to the maid how shocked he was to see a lady like Miss Compton-Burnett with her name in the newspapers. ' "But what could I do?" said she with a sigh. "I had to earn my living".' (Letter to H.S., 30 March 1973.)

circulated among people who took much the same view of the novelist's trade—'scratching and scribbling and shuffling papers!'[22] —as friends and relations generally do in Ivy's books.

Admittedly, there was a special stigma attached to the sort of books Ivy wrote. 'Mayfair murders I call them'* said Margaret who would declare, when Herman asked after Ivy, that she was 'writing one of her silly little books'.[23] Silliness in this context had a particular connotation for people of Margaret's background and generation. It went with lightness, brightness, irreverence, sophistication, and was a word often on the lips of indignant elders deploring the baffling, morbid, neurotic, unpleasant and unnatural tendencies of hardboiled modern youth. All these terms were applied to one or other of Ivy's four early novels by critics who found her tone indefinably suspect. Reviewers of the old school could never feel entirely happy with dapper, self-confident, irrepressibly flippant young men like Julian Wake in *Brothers and Sisters*, or Felix Bacon ('one thing about me is that limpness gives the effect of grace'[24]) in *More Women Than Men*: decadents (to use the contemporary term) who lay themselves out to tease with their sleek and frivolous wit, their passion for clothes and parties and gossip ('simple, candid probing of our friends' business'[25]), their profoundly sceptical view of their own and other people's motives. Even the most oppressed and downtrodden youths in the later novels of I. Compton-Burnett never quite lost the enthusiasm with which their predecessors, in the 1920s and early 1930s, repudiated duty, self-respect, usefulness, manliness and every other virtue the old and orthodox might be supposed to hold dear:

'Well, a man is a man,' said Mr. Bigwell.

'That is rather sweeping,' said Oliver. 'I am not.'

'Neither am I,' said Mr. Spode. 'And I should not think Cassidy is.'

'Of course not,' said Oliver, 'when he keeps a boys' school. And my meaning is simple, not sinister.'[26]

* Though they contain quite a few actual or attempted murders, none of Ivy's novels could be described as remotely connected with Mayfair (then a favourite setting with fashionable novelists like Evelyn Waugh, Aldous Huxley, Michael Arlen, Nancy Mitford, etc.). *Murder in Mayfair* by Ivor Novello opened at the Globe Theatre in 1934, but Margaret seems to have borrowed the phrase from a legal friend who claimed that undetected murder among the middle classes was by no means uncommon: 'He used to call them "Mayfair murders".' (Burkhart 1, p.26.)

This sort of thing was naturally hard to take for people whose standards of style, daring and wit had been set by Barrie, Wells and A. A. Milne. Equally naturally, it went down well with modern youth. 'It seemed absolutely wonderful, something quite, quite new,' said Rosamond Lehmann, who was in her mid-twenties (and already a best-selling author herself) when Raymond Mortimer introduced her to Ivy's writing: 'I was so dazzled by it, she became my favourite novelist immediately.' Word got round on the fringes of Bloomsbury, passed by people like Eddie Sackville-West, Henry Lamb and Margaret's friend Francis Birrell at the bookshop he ran with David Garnett: a good many lifelong readers of I. Compton-Burnett (Ivy always insisted on disclosing her initial only, never her full name, on her title pages) were originally recruited by Garnett's review of *More Women Than Men* in the *New Statesman*, published in 1933 round about the time Raymond Mortimer took over as literary editor.

It was the Compton-Burnetts' old family friend Arthur Waley who had first mentioned *Pastors and Masters* to Mortimer, then still in his twenties, a columnist on *Vogue* in its brief palmy period as an avant-garde organ, and already beginning to make a name for himself as a critic in stern pursuit of new and original talent. 'Was it possible that there could be a *bateau*, however *ivre*, moderner than himself?'[27] asked Harold Nicolson, whose own tastes, in literature at least, were decidedly more conventional (though both Harold and his wife, Vita Sackville-West, were shortly afterwards roped in to spread word of Mortimer's latest discovery). If Mortimer was one of the first to notice I. Compton-Burnett in 1925, ten years later he was also the first to point out that her strange, concentrated, almost abstract way of writing produced the same effect—an initial, often disturbing sense of unfamiliarity, followed by successive shocks of recognition—as the Post Impressionists had done on a public accustomed to Victorian naturalism in painting.

But when Ivy finished writing *Brothers and Sisters* at the end of 1928, she knew none of these people except Frankie Birrell, who had known her brother Noel at King's and turned up again afterwards as one of Margaret's liveliest, seediest and most amusing young men. Perhaps it was Birrell who persuaded her, directly or indirectly, to send the manuscript to the Hogarth Press where Leonard Woolf turned it down, together with J. B. Yeats' *Sligo* ('"She can't even write," he said . . . "At least this man, Yeats, knows how to write" '[28]). Ivy went back to Cranton who, having a good many copies of her last book still on hand, held out no great hope for the next which he took on the same terms as before.[29] *Brothers and Sisters* was published in April and, according to Hugh Walpole, 'would have been read by scarcely more than a dozen persons had not a group of professional critics connected with a literary journal made loud and violent outcry about it'.[30]

Mortimer was at the back of this outcry which culminated—to Cranton's astonishment and Woolf's consternation—in *Brothers and Sisters* becoming one of the year's minor publishing sensations. Walpole's 'professional critics' were part of the reviewing stable built up by Woolf himself as literary editor of the *Nation*, which had carried a review by Mortimer,[31] combining his accolade for Miss Compton-Burnett with a shrewd attack on the vulgar commercialism of Walpole's own newly founded Book Society. The Society, a controversial body already under attack from the book trade, capitulated handsomely by making *Brothers and Sisters* runner-up to its very next Book of the Month in May: a choice confirmed at the end of the month by a perceptive and characteristically generous puff in the London *Evening Standard* from Arnold Bennett.* Bennett had long since enthusiastically accepted the role assigned him by Virginia Woolf of philistine, materialist and literary reactionary number one; but, though he might grumble ('The novel has incurred the laudation of select highbrows—which of course put me against it'), it did him no harm with the trade or the reading public, who knew that Bennett meant business. *Brothers and Sisters* promptly went into a second edition which brought a fresh crop of

---

* According to Richard Kennedy's charming account in *A Boy at the Hogarth Press*, Bennett hailed *Brothers and Sisters* as A WORK OF GENIUS. What he actually said was rather more guarded, and seems to have been tacked on as an afterthought at the foot of a piece about making money from first editions:

> I am not sure but I think it quite possible that a work lying at the moment here . . . will one day be the cause of research, envy, covetousness and other vices: . . . *Brothers and Sisters* by I. Compton-Burnett . . . though by no means easy to read, it seems to me an original work, strong and incontestably true to life. I. Compton-Burnett may be a new star, low on the eastern horizon. (*Evening Standard*, 30 May 1929.)

The idea of the Book Society had been originally put forward by Bennett who proposed holding Walpole's post of chairman himself; and no doubt he watched its initial flounderings with a certain quiet satisfaction.

reviews in the middlebrow weeklies in June, all agreeing they had never read anything like it.

Ivy was taken up, talked about, asked to parties, pursued by photographers and gossip columnists (she posed for her picture but drew the line at reporters, being, as she told *Ideal Home* in October, 'a writer who will not have publicity at any price'). Frankie Birrell asked her to lunch on 9 April to meet Vita Sackville-West who took her the same afternoon to call on Virginia Woolf (describing Ivy in a letter next day to Harold Nicolson as a 'little spinster of at least 50, very shy, very nervous, very overwhelmed by the admiration we heaped on her, and at being carried off to see Virginia who wants the refusal of her next book'[32]). Birrell brought Raymond Mortimer to tea at Ivy's flat a week later, while Vita (who gave *Brothers and Sisters* one of its sharpest and most enthusiastic reviews on the B.B.C. on 2 May) dined alone with Ivy on the fourteenth and returned to a rather grander luncheon two days later. She and Mortimer were both entertained at parties composed otherwise entirely of Margaret's more presentable furniture friends like the Kings, together with a choice selection of her young men—Roger Hinks from the British Museum, Leigh Ashton (eventually head of the V&A), the architect Basil Ionides and the society painter Willie Ranken: a guest list calculated to leave envoys from Bloomsbury feeling almost as flummoxed as Ivy's own skilled impersonation of a governess of the old school.

But Ivy had become overnight a catch for literary hostesses as diverse as Mrs Robert Lynd (who regularly entertained high livers and plain thinkers, like the Victor Gollanczes and the J. B. Priestleys, to games, charades and singsongs at her Hampstead Friday nights), and the elderly but still furiously competitive Violet Hunt. Rose Macaulay, who sent a card for her party in July and dined at the flat the night after, became a close friend, and so did Mrs Hunt. For the first time in her life Ivy was courted by agents and publishers: she accepted the advances of Rose's and Vita's energetic young agent, David Higham of Curtis Brown, and had the gratification of turning down not only the Woolfs' Hogarth Press but also Sylvia Lynd with messages from Methuen in favour of a contract for her next three novels from Heinemann, topped off by hopeful overtures from Donald Brace of the American firm Harcourt, Brace (who brought out *Brothers and Sisters* that autumn in the U.S.).[33]

2

IVY WAS FORTY-FIVE. She had never been fêted like this before, never attracted attention, scarcely even had friends of her own, let alone parties: 'in a sense she had no youth,' as William Herrick says of his sister Emily in *Pastors and Masters*, 'just as in a way she will have no old age'.[34] At the end of the First World War, Ivy had drawn a line beneath everything that had happened in her first thirty-five years. She never again discussed her early life, indeed knew hardly anyone with whom she might have discussed it. Escape from the past, always a theme in I. Compton-Burnett, is nowhere more explicit than in *Brothers and Sisters* which, for all its melodramatic apparatus of missing documents and long-lost parents, contains at its core a faithful account of events in the Compton-Burnett household at Hove in the early years of the century. Like the young Staces running away to London at the end of that novel, Ivy had seen her youth wasted in Hove, her life several times blasted in it, her parents cut off in their prime.

Her own subsequent attempts to take cover in London in 1915 could hardly have been worse timed. When people asked afterwards about the gap between *Dolores*, published in 1911, and *Pastors and Masters* fourteen years later, Ivy put it down to 'family troubles and responsibilities and the loss of a brother in the war'.[35] The war itself, her brother Noel's death on the Somme, his wife's attempted suicide, the actual suicides of Ivy's two youngest sisters on Christmas Day, 1917, followed by her own nearly mortal illness: all these culminated in a period of prolonged mental and physical prostration, what Ivy herself described as a kind of death in life,[36] from which she only gradually recovered after Margaret moved into her flat in 1919.

It is the dislocation caused by this series of catastrophic upheavals that presumably explains why, though she was born in 1884 within a year or two of such giants of the Modern Movement as James Joyce, D. H. Lawrence and for that matter Virginia Woolf, I. Compton-Burnett can hardly be said to belong in their company. Membership of the Movement was not in any case a claim she would have cared to make, or see made on her behalf: her own view came closer to Felix Bacon's boast, in *More Women Than Men*, 'I am not one of those modern people; I try always to seem a survival from the old world.'[37] But in this characteristically misleading scheme she was only partly successful. Settings in the 1890s, plots which reminded her earliest reviewers of high Victorian tear-jerkers like *East Lynne* and *The Wide, Wide World* or the still more bizarre excesses of *Irene Iddesleigh*, none of these eccentric trappings could entirely conceal the boldness that struck her contemporaries as very far from old world.

Dolores, published in the same year as Lawrence's *The White Peacock*, respectively three and four years before Joyce's and Virginia Woolf's first books, had been a thoroughly misconceived homage to George Eliot (its original title, *Unhistoric Acts*, came from the last sentence of *Middlemarch* and its plot from *Scenes of Clerical Life*). Its very turgidity shows how fiercely Ivy had struggled, like the great moderns, with a dead form. 1911 was also the year in which Ivy's mother died, the year she found herself facing what must have seemed like life imprisonment inside the family, the year when (according to her sister Vera) 'the iron entered into her soul'.[38] Her writing career, in some sense her life itself, came to a standstill. For the next decade and more Ivy went underground. But the tide of destruction which, in her own phrase, 'quite smashed my life up'[39] also dismantled much that she relinquished without regret. By the time she took to scribbling again in the penny notebooks in which she had written *Dolores*, the assumptions and outlook underlying that false start had been drastically realigned. In the sense that Ivy's imagination was shaped and profoundly modified by the experiences of 1914 to 1918, she belongs essentially to the postwar generation of writers; and it is scarcely surprising that, when she eventually made her debut alongside the much younger novelists who surfaced towards the end of the 1920s, she had in some ways more in common with the young Evelyn Waugh or Anthony Powell than with her own contemporaries.

Ivy emerged from years of despair and stagnation with something of the survivor's elation, the gallows gaiety that overtakes Robin Stace in *Brothers and Sisters* when his family's fortunes touch rock bottom (' "You are not letting anything get the better of you, I know." "Things have done that, without any slackness of ours," said Robin'[40]). A heady sense of release and liberation runs through her early work, in the ebullient elderly novelists or would-be novelists of *Pastors and Masters* (' "Real books coming out of our own heads!" said Bumpus. "And not just printed unkindness to other people's" '[41]) as in the ceaseless party-giving and -going of *Brothers and Sisters*. No writer agreed more readily than Ivy with 'readers who demand of a novel that it should be light, malicious and high-spirited' in Peter Quennell's definition (the phrase comes from his *New Statesman* review of Powell's *Agents and Patients* but might as well have been applied to any one of Ivy's four early novels); and there is no mistaking the relief with which an earlier *New Statesman* reviewer switched, in June 1925, from a polite if faintly derisive account of Lawrence's *St. Mawr* to something decidedly less strenuous: 'As for *Pastors and Masters*, it is astonishing, alarming. It is like nothing else in the world. It is a work of genius. How to describe it—since there is nothing of which to take hold?'[42]

Much the same mixture of delight and bewilderment greeted Waugh's *Decline and Fall* three years later, together with the same charges of insubstantiality, brittleness and oddity. Indeed there is a marked affinity between Dr Fagan's famously shady establishment in *Decline and Fall* and the equally run-down prep school in *Pastors and Masters*★ with its watery marmalade, its alternately tearful and tittering small boys, its overworked and hopelessly underqualified staff, its indolent headmaster trading on the dubious services of a partner called Merry whose gift for ingratiating himself with parents amply compensates for his lack of any more palpable educational advantage (' "Isn't it generous of him to spend his life giving to others what he has not had himself?" "Why not hand over prayers to him, and retire, Herrick?" said Bumpus. "If he can read" '[43]).

The satirical exuberance of I. Compton-Burnett's first postwar novel never entirely left her though she never again let it play quite so freely as it does on dilapidated characters like Merry, or those quintessential poor relations, the Batemans (' "I wish it was us who

★ Both no doubt derive ultimately from Dickens' Dotheboys Hall, a debt freely acknowledged in Emily Herrick's account of the thirty-nine boarders filing out of their basement dining room in *Pastors and Masters* (p.48): 'There are those hundreds of helpless children, coming up from that cellar that we have never seen. I wish Dickens was alive to expose schools. Mr Merry has stopped to look back at Mrs Merry, as if she were a dumb pet that understood.'

had a party," said Tilly, who was an almost startling example of failure to rise above a lack of advantages'[44]) in *Brothers and Sisters*. It runs strongly to the last in the butlers whose aggressive feats of oneupmanship are recorded in an almost Wodehousian spirit of detached appreciation—one thinks of Bullivant, in *Manservant and Maidservant*, magnanimously clearing the dead jackdaw from a smoking chimney with the unction he might have reserved, in a better class of household, for dislodging champagne corks; or Buttermere in *Men and Wives*, first and perhaps most infuriating of all his tribe, showing the family solicitor where to wash his hands for luncheon: ' "The water is hot, sir," said Buttermere, standing by the open door and producing the impression that for many people he would have turned the tap'.[45] Anti-romanticism, always unremitting in I. Compton-Burnett, is implicit in the gaiety, malice and high surface polish of her literary, rather than her literal generation. It is the frame of mind responsible for a whole race of cynics like Theresa Fletcher in *Pastors and Masters* (' "It is unworthy of you to expect people to be prompt," said Bumpus. "Such a cold, self-esteeming thing to be." "I am cold and self-esteeming," said Theresa'[46]) as well as the urbane young men whose obstreperous wit was so highly prized in the 1920s. 'Given favourable conditions,' wrote the American critic O.J., reviewing *Brothers and Sisters* in the *New Republic*, 'a work such as this might conceivably, like a new *Euphues*, mould social talk for a decade'.[47]

Brothers and Sisters went down especially well in the U.S. where its author was several times contrasted with 'that other great master of conversation, Ernest Hemingway', and the 'coolness and candour' of her sexual deviants greatly preferred to the self-indulgence of a dozen other novels on 'problems of sexual abnormality' crossing the Atlantic in 1929 in the wake of Radclyffe Hall's *Well of Loneliness* trial the year before. Basil Davenport, voting incest theme of the year in the *Saturday Review*, compared Ivy's casual approach favourably with William Faulkner's Jacobean intensity in *The Sound and the Fury*—not, as Davenport explained, that he meant any disrespect to the latter, 'only to point out that Mr Faulkner writes of a decaying, old-world family with a heritage of insanity and Miss Compton-Burnett of some healthy moderns'.[48] The distinction is salutary, and perhaps it seemed so to Ivy at the time; at any rate, Davenport went on to discern in *Brothers and Sisters* the programme she was to follow for the rest of her career:

It is the only book where one can find implicit what every twentieth century reader of the *Oedipus Tyrannus* must have felt, that a prohibited marriage ignorantly contracted may be a calamity but is after all nothing to blind oneself about . . . One suddenly sees that she [Sophia Stace, prototype of Ivy's mother, who dominates the book] is all that is worst in the nineteenth century, and the young people with their forthrightness and independence, all that is best of the twentieth. Their modernity gives them almost the qualities of the children in *The Innocent Voyage*,* the ability to go through the fire and escape the burning. All other books on this theme are stories of the present defeated by the past; *Brothers and Sisters* is a story of the present hurt by the past, but not defeated.

Like so much else in the fiction of I. Compton-Burnett, *Brothers and Sisters* works by extracting its larger application from things that had happened in fact. In a sense, Ivy could never escape from the world that had ended with the First World War: in 1941, Margaret warned Francis Wyndham (who had posted a fan letter from school, and received in reply an invitation to visit) that 'Ivy lives in the past, and nothing after 1914 has any reality for her'.[49] To Anthony Powell, meeting her for the first time a few years later, she seemed 'a quite unmodified pre-1914 personality'.[50] New acquaintances often felt like this about Ivy, and the reaction goes back to the crucial years before 1919 when her violent slamming of doors on the past had entailed an equally harsh rejection of the present. *Pastors and Masters* marked a recovery consolidated four years later in *Brothers and Sisters*, where the incestuous complications provide a fictional gloss or counterpart to material supplied by Ivy's own unhappy family: here for the first time she turned back to her father's death and its disastrous effect on her despairing, despotic, hysterically unstable mother, the cat-and-mouse régime that followed, the children's helplessness in the ten years of steadily increasing strain that bound Ivy so intimately to her own two brothers. But, as Elizabeth Bowen pointed out, I. Compton-Burnett was 'not merely copying but actually continuing the

---

* The American title of Richard Hughes' *High Wind in Jamaica*, also first published in 1929 along with Hemingway's *A Farewell to Arms*, Henry Green's *Living*, J. B. Priestley's *The Good Companions* and Michael Arlen's *Lily Christine*.

Victorian novel',[51] and it was something that could only be done
from a firm stance in the present, in the light of that hard, frank,
pertinent stare her contemporaries found so essentially modern. Ivy
lived the rest of her life, in fact, on the principle that even a family
history as calamitous as Oedipus' was nothing to blind oneself
about. Perhaps she remembered Davenport's review when, twenty
years later, she made Bridget Chase confront precisely this situation
in fiction:

> 'People are so noble in trouble,' said Bridget. 'We forget how
> well they come out under a test. And we have been brave enough
> ourselves not to put out our eyes. Perhaps people are braver than
> they used to be.' . . .
> 'Perhaps we are fortunate,' said Selina, drily. 'Or perhaps
> fashions have changed. It does not seem that Oedipus was
> thought to have acted oddly under the circumstances.'[52]

3

PEOPLE DRIVEN to extremities of one sort or another were to be Ivy's
permanent preoccupation. But in the 1920s and 1930s she was still
sufficiently a child of her time to extract much entertainment from
the contemporary scene. *Pastors and Masters* takes place at the time it
was written, *Brothers and Sisters* has begun to move rather shakily
—and the next two books more firmly—back before the First
World War. But drinks before dinner together with the speed, ease
and frequency of divorce in *Men and Wives* (1931) make the period
setting a fairly hit-and-miss affair, as it still is in *More Women Than
Men* (1933) with its horse-drawn carriages and almost regal
widows' weeds ranged uneasily alongside talk of trades unions,
equal pay for women and telephone trunk calls. The high spirits
—what disgruntled reviewers took for cynicism—of Ivy's characters at this stage reflect an emancipation widespread after the First
World War. In all four early novels the pomposity and sentimental
rhetoric of overbearing elders are systematically undercut by 'frank
modern children'[53] like Ruth Giffard, defending her engagement in
More Women Than Men, or Griselda Haslam breaking hers off in
Men and Wives:

'It is Griselda, wild and sorrowing and burdened, whom I love, as I shall never love another woman.'

'If you think of me in that way, you do already love another woman.'[54]

Decor and dress sense, class and sex distinctions loom larger than ever again in these early books whose fictional world seems as often as not contiguous with Ivy's own circle at the time. Even Margaret's professional interests tend to spill over, most noticeably in the village of Moreton Edge in *Brothers and Sisters* with its commuters travelling up and down between London and their handsome, half-timbered or Queen Anne houses in the country, and its marked attention to furnishings—the Drydens' enforced economy at the rectory contrasting with the Staces' family portraits, or the Wakes' pursuit of expensive simplicity in a tumbledown cottage on the main street. At the beginning of the 1920s Margaret wrote a regular column for *Eve* on 'Furniture for the Country Cottage', urging the simple virtues of solid oak, recommending humble Georgian or Queen Anne pieces for the parlour with Toby jugs on the chimneypiece, generally promoting the fashionable taste for romantic rusticity embodied in the Wakes' cottage and its 'carefully cottage-like furnishings', its sitting room renamed the parlour, even its modest jug of columbines (' "I grew them, and cut them, and put them in that pot," said Julian. "Every little womanly touch in this cottage is mine" '[55]).

Julian himself is precisely the sort of escort regularly featured in gossip column or social calendar by illustrated papers like *Eve*. His ability to relieve his feelings by having a real tidy-up or a good cry, his gallantry towards older women, preference for his own sister's company, successive proposals to the sisters of two of his best friends on grounds that only marriage can excuse fading charm ('though of course I agree that nothing ought to excuse it'[56]): all unmistakably reflect the limp-wristed vogue endorsed by so many outrageously witty and talented men-about-town in the 1920s. Margaret's and Ivy's great friend Ernest Thesiger was one of them. Gossipy, acerbic, inquisitive and entertaining, Ernest was in his prime between the two world wars (and, to borrow Robin Stace's phrase from *Brothers and Sisters*, 'I can hardly tell you how utterly he was in it'[57]). In a decade of parties, he had figured on notable occasions from the Women's Ball at the Albert Hall in 1919—Lady Diana Manners and other Greek beauties led by Ernest as Pan, in a goatskin designed by Lady Lavery—to Norman Hartnell's circus party ten years later when Ernest, at fifty, came as a lion tamer in red tights and close-fitting black trunks. Like Julian, Ernest had married his best friend's sister (the friend, Willie Ranken—who had been a contemporary at the Slade and used to walk about town with Ernest, both wearing bouquets in their buttonholes—shaved off his hair at the news[58]). He collected rings and pink lustre, and, when his house in Montpelier Terrace was featured in *House and Garden*, made a point of demonstrating how he had marbled the bathroom himself, worked his own gros point carpets, painted his own Chinese wallpaper, appliquéed the curtains and frescoed a sky on his wife's bedroom ceiling.

Ernest's taste, according to *Eve*,[59] was the last word in wallpaper and white waistcoats. His face, as he said himself, was too queer to be caricaturable but, as a founder member of the Men's Dress Reform Society, he liked to show off his legs in pale moleskin shorts or a still more striking cerulean velvet pair, worn with matching silk blouse and muffler, in which he outshone even Shaw at the Malvern Festival in 1932. He designed his own clothes, painted in oils, learnt lace-making to run up a christening veil for a niece. It was Ernest who made the Aubusson carpet and dining room fire screens for Queen Mary's dolls' house (his aunt had been her mother's lady-in-waiting, and Queen Mary herself supplied the model for Ernest's own increasingly regal bearing in later life); Willie did the still life over the sideboard; they were both expert needlemen, apt to take out their embroidery and sit stitching on trains to the consternation or mirth of other incredulous passengers.

Ernest had been wounded in both hands as a private on the Western Front in 1915, and came home to make his name on the stage that autumn in *A Little Bit of Fluff*, playing the sort of stage dolt—'a lank, weedy, cadaverous, plaintive-eyed ninny with a nose as sharp as a pen—a kind of modern Slender'[60]—which afterwards became his speciality. His Bertram Tully was a wild success with the troops ('Mr. Ernest Thesiger is a scream'[61]), and was followed after the war by the boatman in Barrie's *Mary Rose*, a haunting Captain Hook and triumphant Dauphin in Shaw's *St. Joan*: perhaps his greatest hit in a long line of what the *Queen* called 'unhealthy parts'[62] like Bagoas the Eunuch in Bennett's *Judith* ('exquisite as a lady's lampshade with his swinging skirts and fringes, evil as the flash of a poisoned scimitar in an Eastern alley', wrote an appreciative Rebecca West[63]) or the catamite Piers Gaveston in Marlowe's *Edward II*. He left the cast of *St. Joan* in 1925 to do a Noël Coward number in drag with Douglas Byng for C. B. Cochrane's revue. He was Henry in *Gentlemen Prefer Blondes* at Blackpool and Miles Malpractice in Waugh's *Vile Bodies* at the Arts. Ernest once complained that Somerset Maugham never sent him anything: 'B-but, I am always writing p-parts for you, Ernest,' said Maugham. 'The trouble is that somebody called Gladys Cooper *will* insist on p-playing them.'[64]

Ernest represented, in short, everything that was silliest and most provoking in the social life of the time. He said, when he published his autobiography in 1927, that he charged people £50 for a mention and £75 to be left out.[65] A master of double, triple, even (according to Beverley Nichols) quadruple meaning, he had brought subversion to a fine and frivolous art. People thought him heartless, self-centred, cynical, but nobody questioned his nerve. For Ernest, who was a grandson of the first Lord Chelmsford and cousin to the Viceroy of India, to have become a professional painter and ended up on the stage was something unheard of. It was an extremist's version of his father's reaction to the tailor who suggested that a gentleman in his position ought not to carry his trousers about in a parcel: ' "A gentleman in my position can do *anything*," said my father indignantly. "That is the only point of being a gentleman in my position." '[66]

It enabled Ernest all his life to combine refusal or failure to conform with a front of unimpeachable moral and social rectitude. He delighted the children of Margaret's friend, Nelly Levy, by showing them his green-painted toenails,[67] and there are many stories (decidedly risqué in those days) of his unbuttoning at conventional dinner parties to fish out the pearls he wore under his shirt. Loyalty, independence, sensitivity, pluck were the qualities he liked best in himself, and he freely confessed himself a snob ('I have always maintained that the only way to make an impression on a celebrity is to insult them at sight'[68]), with a particular bias towards royalty and what he called 'gilded bounders'.

But Ernest was also irresistibly drawn to the obdurate, unfashionable and odd. He went out of his way to be attentive to social misfits like Mrs Arnold Bennett, the despised or neglected 'lesser halves of the great'* (a category for which Ivy certainly qualified among Margaret's friends when Ernest first knew her). He had long been a connoisseur of lady novelists, having built up quite a collection as a young man in the first decade of the century—Miss Mary Cholmondeley, Miss Florence Montgomery, Mrs Fuller-Maitland and Mrs Evan Nepean had all been courted by Ernest —and holding that all the best novels since the war had been written by women. He knew Ivy's friend Violet Hunt, and the redoubtable May Sinclair whom Ivy met at parties given by Hester's uncle, Alban Head, and who was one of the very few people capable of flustering Ernest:

> Even now that I know her well, I am careful what I say, when I am confronted with someone who looks more like a nursery-governess than a brilliant writer, and whose knowledge of the world and keen sense of humour are locked away behind a prim, pinched smile; and every time I read one of her books I wonder how anyone so reserved and conventional can know all the dreadful things she does. But appearances in writers, and especially women writers, are terribly deceptive![69]

Ernest's addiction to writers would have done him no good among Margaret's friends, many of whom in any case dismissed him as a snob and a rattle and worse, to be tolerated chiefly for his wife's sake: 'He was a sort of butterfly,' said one,[70] 'or more like a mosquito'. But Ivy liked him, more than Margaret did, precisely because of his rattling, his garrulity, irony, gregariousness, because nothing ever nonplussed him, and no doubt partly also because of the genuine sympathy that made him seek out Marguerite Bennett and get past the guard of May Sinclair. Ernest laid claim to clairvoyance, or at least to a knowledge of people that matched

---

* See his story of meeting Mrs Bennett at a party:

> Everyone was at that party—even I—and naturally everyone was in their gladdest of rags. Except one person. Seated in a conspicuous position was a somewhat grim-looking woman, strangely dressed, and wearing a large crimson jockey cap, adorned with a marabou! . . . 'I wore it,' she explained, 'so that everyone in the room should say, "Who on earth is that woman in the hat?" and then they would be told, "That is Mrs. Arnold Bennett." You see,' she added, 'no one seems to know that there *is* a Mrs. Arnold Bennett.' (*Practically True*, p. 129.)

Ivy's own and was based on the same strict professional habit of detailed observation:

> I have sometimes been asked whether it is not very awkward to know so much about people, but I have never found it so. '*Tout comprendre c'est tout pardonner*' is one of my favourite mottoes, . . . to know *everything* about a person, as I do when I know anything at all, puts one almost in the position of a benignant deity to whom everything can be confided without fear of blame or misunderstanding . . .[71]

He and Ivy would sit over their needlework together ('Nothing is more terrifying to me than to see Ernest Thesiger sitting under the lamplight doing his embroidery,' wrote the young Beverley Nichols[72]), sewing and talking in a spirit that was, by Ernest's own account, not unlike the Scropes' in *The Present and the Past*:

> 'I never feel disapproval,' said Elton. 'It is a feeling foreign to my nature. I hardly need to know all to forgive all. Considering the pleasure of knowing, that is only fair. I can hardly bear to know it, I forgive so much. I think people do such understandable things.'
>
> 'Yes,' said Ursula. 'I am often ashamed of understanding them.'[73]

Of all Margaret's friends Ernest was probably Ivy's ultimate favourite, together with the Dutchman Herman Schrijver who had been her first fan. Herman, another prime gossip and wit who, like Ivy, believed the worst of human beings, was making his way between the wars with fair success as an interior decorator. His clients among the wealthy and great eventually numbered Guinnesses and Keplers, financiers and socialites, Ernest Simpson and 'more than one of Ernest's wives',[74] and at the beginning of the 1930s he even had a hand in doing up Fort Belvedere for the future king. But his father, who managed a diamond-cutting-and-polishing works, had lost all his money in England after the war and returned to Amsterdam, leaving Herman to start his career in 1925, at the age of twenty-one, as a shop clerk at Peter Jones in Sloane Square on £5 a week.[75] A Jew and a foreigner, without money or connections, must have been open to innumerable slights in the world Herman was setting out to conquer. Even Margaret, who acknowledged no conventional prejudices against friends or clients ('She didn't mind if they were Jews or dagoes, provided they were rich enough'[76]), referred to Herman with her customary air of scorn as 'Ivy's Jewish friend'.

Although she had made the introduction herself, Margaret was not always best pleased to find Herman intrigued and attracted by something in Ivy to which other friends remained largely impervious; and perhaps Ivy for her part responded to Herman in the first place because she was, in some sense, a fellow outsider. She loved his flightiness, cheerfulness, unfailing pessimism, his wild overstatements and darting, allusive, fantastically embroidered accounts of his own and other people's professional and sexual manoeuvrings for power. More than that, she came eventually to depend on him for the unconditional, unspoken, mutual acceptance and understanding that had always been her essential emotional demand of other people. Not that their intimacy grew straight away. Ivy had been as constrained with him to start with as she was with everyone else. 'I found it very difficult to talk to her,' said Herman who required all his considerable powers of persuasion as well as heroic persistence to reach the stage at which he not only read her books but, by his own account, contributed to them as well. 'Ivy was really interested in people as material for her novels, in people's money, in their sex lives, particularly incest and servants'[77]: all subjects on which Herman spoke with authority and with an ingrained scepticism deeply congenial to Ivy.

It was Herman who reversed the tag, 'Kindness in another's trouble,/Courage in one's own.' 'Oh no, darling,' he said once to a friend[78] in distress, 'I've always thought it ought to be, "Courage in another's trouble,/Kindness in one's own."' No one delighted more fondly than he did in his friends' cleverness, beauty or wit; and no one could beat him at speaking evil behind people's backs, a talent Ivy admired as much as Hope Cranmer in *Parents and Children*: 'I like my friends when they are doing it. It makes them so zestful and observant. Original too, almost creative. You see, I am speaking good behind their backs . . .'[79] Herman believed, with Hope and most of the practical observers in Ivy's books, 'that every human being loves himself or herself best, and that for this very reason they prefer their own sex to the other.'[80] But, where characters like Hope (Rachel Hardistie in *Men and Wives* and Felix Bacon in *More Women Than Men* are parallel cases) combine this belief with notably successful marriages, Herman went further and held that all men were essentially homosexual. One of the games[81] he described playing with Ivy consisted in her attempting to name any heterosexual man they both knew while he refuted her claims so that (except for an early hit with Basil Marsden-Smedley) Ivy scored nil.

Exaggeration was a fixed principle, almost a mania with Herman ('Why make any statement unless you exaggerate?' he once blithely asked . . . 'What's wrong with too much?'[82]); and the game, if it took place at all, must have done so after the Second World War, almost certainly after Margaret's death, since Margaret would never have permitted such licence. 'She wasn't intolerant but she wouldn't have thought it *bon ton*,' said their friend Soame Jenyns of the British Museum, who maintained that Margaret was well aware of disreputable proclivities among some of her friends whereas Ivy took in nothing at all. But Ivy had always kept an eye on what she called 'homos' at a time when this, or any similar term, was unmentionable in polite society, let alone literature.★

It is not easy to reconstruct the taboos which prevented people from talking freely or writing about, sometimes even from recognizing, things we now accept as casually as Ivy did from the start in her books. The war had released what the literary elder statesmen of the day—people like Edmund Gosse and E. F. Benson, both of whom had ruthlessly suppressed unorthodox sexual leanings in their own lives—thought of as a 'flood of erotic fiction', in which for the first time 'sexual perversion' had become a legitimate, if still loathsome topic: 'Though all normal folk naturally regarded it [homosexuality] with disgust, it had to be recognised as a pathological deformity of the mind rather than a mark of unspeakable moral obliquity.'† In this heated atmosphere, it is no wonder if Ivy's attitude seemed at the time almost preposterously unemphatic.

★ According to Anthony Powell, excisions demanded by the apprehensive publishers (Chapman and Hall) of Waugh's *Decline and Fall* in 1928 included the remark that Captain Grimes did not like women, together with the phrase 'nothing happened' applied to his marriage ('boiler room' was also substituted for 'lavatory' where the boys smoked, and the Welsh station master was made to pimp for his sister-in-law, not his sister), *Messengers of Day* (Heinemann 1978), p.105.

† *As We Are Now* by E. F. Benson (Longmans, 1932), p.262. But high-mindedness did not prevent Benson inserting a good many steamy scenes in bathroom or swimming pool into his own popular prep school novel, *David Blaize* (Hodder and Stoughton, 1916): 'He was completely dishevelled and yet a very jolly object, and was quite altogether wet, his knickerbockers clinging like tights to his thighs, which showed pink through them . . .' (p.141).

Homosexuality, taken for granted among the dons in *Pastors and Masters*, crops up intermittently in her books thereafter with couples like the cook and parlourmaid in *Elders and Betters* ('If it was hinted that their devotion bordered on excess, Ethel would reply with quiet finality that they were first cousins'[83]). But it is most pervasive in *More Women Than Men* which came out in 1933 at the height of the vogue for deviant literature, and which dwells with quite uncharacteristic firmness on the mechanics of seduction among both homo- and heterosexuals, not forgetting shades in between (' "I cannot imagine any useful and self-respecting person of either sex wanting to belong to the other," said Josephine. "Neither can I, a person of that kind," said Felix'[84]). Faint but insistent signs of lesbian activity in the senior common room of the girls' school in which the book is set are complemented by the longstanding affair between the drawing master, Felix Bacon, and the headmistress's brother, the Rev. Jonathan Swift: a ménage disrupted after twenty years by Felix's engagement to one of the mistresses, whereupon Jonathan proposes setting up house with his son, brought up from infancy by his sister, on grounds that kinship is the natural tie ('Of course it is. But you wanted an unnatural one,' says Felix[85]).

Ivy's matter-of-factness is as different from the absurd high jinks of squibs like Compton Mackenzie's *Extraordinary Women* (1929) as from the no less extravagant, confessional earnestness of Radclyffe Hall and her followers. 'A most gentlemanly book' was Rose Macaulay's phrase for *The Well of Loneliness*;[86] and the point of Ivy's riposte is the thoroughly ungentlemanly spirit in which she deals with the way people actually behave, as opposed to the ways in which social and literary convention decreed that they ought. Ralph Edwards, who knew Ivy by this time well enough to feel rightly uneasy about *More Women Than Men*, warned *Country Life* readers that most of them would be well advised to steer clear of 'a study in morbid psychology,* the more extraordinary because the author is clearly unaware that her characters are beyond the pale of normal experience'.[87] Ralph Straus in the *Sunday Times* was not so much affronted as aggrieved, almost plaintive: 'Do men exist like . . . Jonathan, or the lady-like Felix, or Jonathan's son Gabriel—dim creatures who hardly seem to be male at all?'[88]

---

* 'Morbid' was the conventional codeword for homosexual: Felix describes Jonathan's feelings for himself as 'a morbid attachment'.

It was another thirty years and more before characters like Jonathan and Felix became commonplace in English fiction. In 1933 even David Garnett, who had also met Ivy and might have known better, was too puzzled by the flavour of 'this queer writer'[89] to register how accurately she reproduced the manners and mores described only long afterwards in his own and other people's memoirs of the period. Ivy's Victorian schoolmasters and -mistresses reminded him at the time of lavender and old silk, Meredith, Wilde and the Marx brothers. But anyone who has read recent accounts of what went on among the London intelligentsia in Bloomsbury and elsewhere between the wars will find something distinctly familiar about Ivy's portrait of a small, self-conscious and inward-looking society of intellectuals, waspish, hard-up and far from smart, almost all single and sexually on the make, fascinated by and madly curious about each other's ages, clothes, looks, incomes, sexual inclinations and changes of partner.

Ivy herself reacted with amusement and some complacency to charges of innocence or immodesty. Museum friends like Ralph Edwards and Soame Jenyns, who tended to doubt whether Margaret's unworldly, inexperienced companion understood quite what she was saying, might have taken a tip from the novelist Robert Liddell, who raised the question openly the first time he met Ivy and Margaret:

> Margaret picked up my suggestion that some of the good characters were not sexually irreproachable.
> 'The doubtful Felix?' she sad: 'Our landlady when we were staying in Cambridge said to me: "Miss Burnett must be a little naive. That young man sitting on an old man's knee: some people would think it improper."'
> 'I thought it was meant to be improper,' I said.
> 'Oh, it was meant to be improper, said Ivy, in a full, satisfied tone. She went on to say, 'One cut out a scene because one didn't want trouble.'[90]

Avoiding censorship trouble—the sort of thing frowned on by Jonathan's sister in 'some modern books I could mention'[91]—was not the least advantage of Ivy's old-world style. Far from inhibiting conversation or behaviour (the divorce and illegitimacy rates, not to mention general crime, being consistently high in Compton-

Burnett novels), it permitted a freedom by no means always inherent in 'the loose and easy realism of most novelists'. The point was taken at the time by another novelist, Alice Herbert (author of the bestselling *Heaven and Charing Cross* in 1922), who noted in her review of *More Women than Men* that I. Compton-Burtnett's Victorianism was barely skin deep:

> Her people 'converse' a little like Jane Austen's . . . Here non-modernity stops: for her sense of our own time is acute and very penetrating. The 'young' man Felix could never have been drawn in a novel of fifty years ago, nor the ethereally delicate hints given here and there of tendencies—not modern indeed, but unacknowledged in the old days.[92]

It is young men like Felix and Julian Wake who represent all that most appealed to Ivy in the contemporary scene. Their talk is what E. M. Forster called 'easy and modern',[93] as far removed from the shock and pioneering sexual excitement of Lawrence as from the Victorians' blanket inhibitions. But their homosexuality is incidental, or important only in so far as it enables them to remain detached from the scenes of family violence which, after *More Women Than Men*, occupied the foreground of Ivy's novels. Cool, clever, self-contained jokers like Felix remain steadfastly kind, if helpless, in the face of greed, lust, rage, jealousy, the explosive passions I. Compton-Burnett set herself to confront, in book after book, with the hard, dry, unblinking realism that puts her so utterly apart from her great romantic contemporaries like Lawrence and Virginia Woolf.

Virginia Woolf herself readily agreed with Vita's cousin, Eddie Sackville-West, that the Hogarth Press ought to have published *Brothers and Sisters* in 1929 but it was a blunder she could not bring herself to regret— 'There is something bleached about Miss Compton-Burnett: like hair that has never had any colour in it.'[94] As a shy, nervous 'little spinster', Ivy inevitably invited condescension from patricians like Vita and Virginia (the patronizing tone of Vita's description was not lost on Ivy, who startled the French novelist Nathalie Sarraute—coming to pay homage nearly forty years later to the two chief radical innovators in the English novel—by saying that Virginia Woolf was a terrible snob[95]). As a writer, she was too different and at the same time too formidable ever to make much headway with Virginia. Though there were only two years be-

tween them in age, Virginia was already in her professional prime at
their first meeting, and Ivy seems to have seen her as belonging in
some sense to an older generation—or at least to have regarded her
with that special ambivalence artists tend to feel for their immediate
predecessors. To the end of her life Ivy retained strong reservations
about Virginia Woolf's novels, combined with rather uncharacteristically high expectations of her as a person: 'She was a bit
malicious, you know—she'd say the most dreadful things about
people,' Ivy reported long afterwards to her friend Barbara Robinson. 'Of course, one does oneself. But one doesn't expect it of
Virginia Woolf.'[96]

For a few months in the summer of 1929 it looked as though Ivy
herself was well on the way to becoming a literary celebrity in her
own right. A steady stream of admirers called at the flat for the first
time to see Ivy, not Margaret, coming away often more mystified
than when they arrived. Lytton Strachey was said to admire her,
and so did 'that living index of printed books', J. F. Cox of the
London Library, who recommended all his customers to read her.[97]
I. Compton-Burnett was a name to conjure with by the early 1930s,
especially with the second wave of Bloomsbury intellectuals; so
much so that she seemed positively tainted to Anthony Powell,
then in his twenties, starting his career by working for Duckworths
(Waugh's former publishers who had lost Decline and Fall by
over-assiduous censorship) and vehemently rejecting all shades of
received opinion: 'my own generation regarding Bloomsbury as no
less elderly, stuffy, anxious to put the stopper on rising talent, than
the staunchly anti-avant-garde Duckworths.'[98] Ivy's growing fame
continued to keep Virginia Woolf awake at nights ('Dead and
disappointing . . . No life in it,' she wrote in her diary, contrasting
her own reviews for The Years in March, 1937, unfavourably with
Ivy's for Daughters and Sons: 'Much inferior to the bitter truth and
intense originality of Miss Compton-Burnett. Now this pain woke
me at 4 a.m. and I suffered acutely'[99]).

But, after the success of Brothers and Sisters, Ivy politely but
firmly turned down further overtures from the literary world. The
layers of protective camouflage so carefully built up in ten years as
Margaret's companion proved too convenient to be dismantled.
Though she preserved her press cuttings, kept an intermittent eye
on publicity and always remembered the gratitude due to her early
reviewers, Ivy never again made—or permitted Margaret to make

—the slightest move to mark, let alone celebrate, publication of one of her books. Intrigued or bewildered readers who wanted to know more about her had to make do with rumours circulating by word of mouth. Ivy herself sank comfortably back into her old role of spectator at Margaret's parties, ignored or dismissed by people who made a point of not reading her books: a choice perhaps best understood by analogy with the contented lives of her own governesses who also prefer to make their own terms among people who treat them at best with a certain indifferent respect. The image of the alarming Miss Mitford settling herself to her own satisfaction with her book and her box of sweets in *Parents and Children* is not unlike the picture passed on to Elizabeth Wiskemann when, as a young woman at the beginning of the 1930s, she first heard of I. Compton-Burnett from Bunny Garnett and other Bloomsbury friends: 'They said there was someone—a woman who lay all day on a sofa writing with a pencil in a notebook—and that she was the one to watch.'[100]

1930–1936

'Playing second fiddle'

I

FOR THE NEXT twenty years and more Ivy seems to have accepted her role in much the same spirit as Dudley Gaveston, in *A Family and a Fortune*, who indignantly rejected other people's assumption that he couldn't go on playing second fiddle all his life: ' "Yes I can," said Dudley . . . "It is a great art and I have mastered it." '[1] The centre of the stage suited Margaret as much as an onlooker's part suited Ivy, and middle age suited them both. They had arrived together, and for the first time in each case, at an orderly and highly agreeable existence designed to please nobody but themselves; and both agreed with Miss Mitford who said, when asked if she would have liked to be married, 'No. I never wanted a full normal life.'[2]

Few writers have celebrated the single state more cordially than Ivy, who did it with especial vigour in her early books. There is clearly something of her relationship with Margaret in the placid companionable intimacy of those two sceptical veterans, Emily Herrick and Theresa Fletcher in *Pastors and Masters*; the pleasures of spinsterhood, and even honorary spinsterhood, provide a theme nicely contrasted with the sombre tensions of family life in her next novel but one, *Men and Wives*; while the 'mature and settled spinsters'[3] of *More Women Than Men* have reached a state of such superlative satisfaction with themselves and their ways that even the intrepid Felix admits himself taken aback. All four early books are full of characters teetering on the brink of marriage, finding excuses for it, turning it down, or cheerfully making the best of it

like Rachel Hardistie who freely admits that her single years were
the happiest time of her life:

> 'Of course I see how civilised it is to be a spinster,' said Rachel.
> 'I shouldn't think savage countries have spinsters. I never know
> why marriage goes on in civilised countries, goes on openly.
> Think what would happen if it were really looked at, or regarded
> as impossible to look at. In the marriage service, where both are
> done, it does happen.'[4]

Civilized living for Ivy and Margaret meant reading, writing,
paying visits, travelling and the cultivation of friends. 'The life
those two led between the wars was very intelligently planned, and
very very pleasant,' said Hester Marsden-Smedley.[5] It approximated (in so far as life in a series of comparatively cramped London
flats ever could do) to the sober eighteenth-century pattern Margaret recommended to readers of *Eve*, in an article describing an
unfashionably small, plain Georgian house called Wandle Bank in
Surrey:

> It dates from a period of prosperity and comfort among middle
> class families, unspoiled by a passion for dimension and display.
> Here are rooms to live in, to write in, to dine in. Here is no
> suggestion of torture chambers in which crowds of semi-
> detached strangers trample on each other's gowns and
> reputations . . .[6]

Neither Margaret nor Ivy could ever abide a crowd but they
regularly entertained four or five friends at a time, often more, at
the tea parties they gave in the late afternoons for anyone who cared
to drop in ('Good many' is Ivy's complacent comment in her diary
when one of these occasions had been a success). Margaret liked to
lunch out with one or other of her young men, Ivy generally
lunched at home alone or with a friend. But there were people for
tea most days, others came to dine or stay at the flat, and 'Play at
night' is a frequent entry, sometimes as often as once or twice a
week in the winter, in Ivy's diaries. Husbands were invited if need
be without their wives, children only if kept well in hand. Young

couples might find themselves put into cold storage for five or ten years at a time ('After that, in their view, the marriage ought to be breaking up anyway,' said Elliott Felkin's daughter, Penelope Douglas, to whom this had happened), or tolerated on the sort of footing Hemingway described in his account of how he and his first wife made friends with Gertrude Stein and Alice B. Toklas in Paris in the early 1920s: 'They . . . treated us as though we were very good, well-mannered and promising children and I felt that they forgave us for being in love and being married—time would fix that . . .'[7]

Margaret and Ivy could put rather a strain on a young or inexperienced hostess who did not know them well or feared that her standards might fall short of theirs: they both had hearty appetites, 'fell to', then expected to be entertained by guests whose conversation might not always come up to scratch. But however scathing Margaret might be, she was always amusing; and she and Ivy made excellent hosts on their own ground, or on any of the countless excursions organized by Margaret, who had access to collections up and down the country at a time when none of the great country houses was yet open to the public. She was often on the move, sprinting about with Ivy, or Herman or Ralph or Basil Ionides, hiring a car to drive down to Hatfield or Knole for the day, staying at pubs near Chatsworth or Beaulieu, haring up by train to the Buccleuchs' and the Duke of Argyll's in Scotland for Chippendale.

Ivy, who never cared a button for furniture, china or the decorative arts, enjoyed these outings less for the homes than the gardens. Flowers were her delight, especially wild ones, and, if soft fruit were in season, she would make straight for the raspberry canes or strawberry beds, spending sometimes so much time under the nets on country-house weekends that Margaret declared she had been obliged to stop taking her altogether because of gardeners' complaints. Every year they went on a round of visits to Margaret's friends—the Marcons at Highclere in Berkshire, the Noyes sisters in Wiltshire, Lady Waechter at Ramsnest in Surrey and, later, Lord Bearsted's daughter, the Hon. Mrs Ionides, at Buxted Park in Sussex. Ivy would arrive punctually in the hall after breakfast, 'fully gloved and booted for her hour in the garden'[8] like the governess, Miss Ridley, in *The Present and the Past*, ready to be taken for a walk or a drive or once, when they came over from East Meon to call on

Raisley Moorsom at Ramsden End in Hampshire, for a bathe in the sea. Raisley drove them to West Wittering or Headingham where both ladies, highly delighted ('Ivy was terrifically excited, like a child'), put on old-fashioned, high-necked, long-sleeved bloomers and paddled about in the waves.

Summer meant a month in the country, generally by the seaside —they took rooms at Orford, Dunwich and Dymchurch on the east coast in successive years in the 1920s, as well as paying visits to Devon and Cornwall, and they were among the early guests in 1927 at Portmeirion in North Wales. This was Ivy's idea of a holiday, and was invariably followed by two or three weeks travelling on the Continent which was Margaret's: comfortable, leisurely journeys planned to take in museums and art galleries with flowers and patisseries for Ivy (one of her grudges against abroad was its dearth of tea shops) and, for Margaret, a visit to the Elliott Felkins in Geneva (Elliott, who had been a disciple of Lowes Dickinson at King's with Raisley and Noel Compton-Burnett, worked in the 1920s and 1930s for Dickinson's beloved League of Nations).

When Margaret stayed at the Felkins' small flat, Ivy went to an hotel up the road or sometimes stopped at home altogether, for she felt that a single annual trip abroad was as much as anyone could properly be asked to put up with. 'It was always nature Ivy spoke of,' said Vera Compton-Burnett, describing her sister's account of these travels, 'never castles or museums or Margaret's antiquarian things. But if there were wild narcissi on the mountain, she'd send a postcard about that.' Ivy in those days had not yet come to dislike 'abroad' as she was to do later, after Margaret's death, when she not only stopped going herself but kept a blacklist of people who lived there. But it is always a sinister spot in her books: abroad is where people go to forget the past, saddle themselves with unwanted bastards or attend to business affairs that generally end in false reports of their death (in some cases they might have been better dead since something fishy nearly always happens behind the backs of anyone rash enough—like Charlotte Lamb in *Manservant and Maidservant*, Fulbert Sullivan in *Parents and Children*, Ellen Mowbray in *A Father and His Fate*—to set foot abroad). It was not for nothing that Margaret wrote Ivy's name in her notes under a contemporary account of Lord Holland by someone who clearly shared Ivy's view of people going too far too often: 'He has already been long enough on the Continent for any reasonable end, either of curiosity or instruction, and his availing himself so immediately of this opportunity to go to a foreign country again looks a little too much like distaste for his own.'[9]

At home the housekeeping was Ivy's province, as it had been since she took over the household in Hove when her mother died in 1911. She ordered supplies, dealt with tradesmen, saw to the china and linen cupboards, carved at table (always the woman's part in Victorian families) and supervised the maid Jessie. 'My maid is a very pleasant creature and I trust will remain contented,' Ivy wrote after Jessie first arrived in November 1919. 'I am on the alert for any sign of dissatisfaction so that at any cost to myself it may be soothed. She calls me 'm, not miss. I suppose she thinks I have reached that time of life when it is suitable.'[10] Jessie who was tiny, not much taller than a circus dwarf, moved flats three times with 'her ladies', stopping in the end for nearly twenty years (the next maid stayed another ten which suggests that Ivy's soothing power must have been equal to her disreputable habit of getting her name in the newspapers). Like the knowledgeable and inquisitive Miranda Hume in *Mother and Son*, Ivy was keenly interested in every domestic process from plumbing to coffee-making or the price and quality of butchers' cuts—'Ivy used to say that she thought she would have been rather good below stairs herself'[11]—while Jessie had a gift for the sort of traditional English cooking Ivy liked: roast meat or fowls, great joints of boiled ham and bacon, steamed salmon with lavish helpings of parsley butter, followed by nursery puddings like junket, meringues and stone cream. 'Everything good and plentiful and in season,'[12] as the housekeeper says in *Mother and Son* of a meal specifically designed to impress Mrs Hume (Ivy's friends in the 1950s liked to speculate as to the exact nature of the dish singled out for praise at this luncheon: Roger Hinks wanted it to be Apple Charlotte, Robert Liddell backed the rum-flavoured blancmange which was one of Ivy's own favourites at the time[13]).

Ivy could never bring herself to taste caviare any more than she would drink champagne ('D'you heat it?' she asked plaintively when someone[14] brought her a bottle). Margaret, who had more sophisticated tastes in food though she scarcely set foot in the kitchen, chose the wine and collected what were in those days exotic, even faintly daring French recipes for lobster, sauces, meat cooked with herbs and wine. It was also Margaret who kept meticulous lists of their friends' preferences: 'Ernest Thesiger *likes* Indian tea. Dislikes eggs. Dislikes ices. Jane Thesiger likes vegetable soup. Ices. China tea without milk. Schrijver likes salt beef and dumplings; black coffee; Irish stews, plum pudding, ginger and celery stuffed with cheese.'[15] Food at Ivy's table was ample and excellent, by no means always the rule among the English intelligentsia then or now: 'Plain living and high thinking are best,' as somebody says in *Daughters and Sons*, 'but our standard of thinking is not high enough to warrant the living's being too plain.'[16]

The living was in fact so rich, both ladies so large and growing larger, that at the end of 1926 Margaret consulted 'an oddity among beauty doctors',[17] Laurence Lazarus Heyman ('*Viennese* . . . very foreign, gay . . . Probably a gambler . . . I put it on record that I think him quite trustworthy, and very intelligent, though I have not much illusions about beauty doctors generally; and the fee charged seems very high'). Dr Heyman's banting (or slimming) cure lasted five years, involving regular weighings, the consumption of vast quantities of mauve pills and cachets, and, from 1928 to 1933, weekly, bi-weekly, sometimes even daily trips to his consulting rooms in New Cavendish Street at a cost of £1,500 apiece, a staggering sum for people normally as prudent as Margaret and Ivy. It worked (these were the years in which both Margaret and Ivy acquired a trick of pulling out the loose folds of their bodices and looking complacently down to check that their dresses were indeed becoming several sizes too large). Dr Heyman's key point, worth any amount of trouble and expense in Margaret's view, was that patients might eat as much as they liked without fear of getting fat ever afterwards: both friends took full advantage of this dispensation for the rest of their lives, and Ivy at least never grew stout again.

Apart from holidays (and the banting régime) Ivy's own daily routine barely changed throughout the 1920s and 1930s: writing (which she did in an armchair in the sitting room,[18] keeping her current notebook stuffed under the cushions) was seldom permitted to encroach on more than one or two mornings a week, and there were long fallow periods between books. Shopping took up much time and attention. So did fittings for hats, shoes, corsets, coats-and-skirts (Ivy got her beautifully cut, severely simple black suits, like her furs, from Bradleys in Chepstow Place, Bayswater; Margaret's suits—also of the finest quality, and equally indifferent to fashion—were in grey gaberdine). Ivy's companion on these expeditions was usually one or other of the very few friends she had salvaged from the past. Her sister-in-law, Noel's widow, Tertia Burnett (who had married Horace Mann as her second husband in 1920), would come up generally at least once or twice a month from Potter's Bar, meeting Ivy at Smith's or Barkers or Boots, and going on for lunch to Tertia's club or the Case Café in Wimpole Street.

Tertia was then, perhaps in a sense always would be, still in mourning for Noel: their courtship had been so intense, the marriage so brief (it lasted thirteen months, all but two of which Noel spent in the trenches), his death such a crushing blow that nothing afterwards could ever quite match up to the past. Certainly not Horace Mann, who was another of her brother Jack Beresford's friends and thirteen years older than Tertia. Never a particularly forceful character, Horace worked for the Board of Education, read Chinese in his spare time, painted a little and rapidly resigned himself, like Emily Herrick's putative husband in *Pastors and Masters*, to having his predecessor installed 'as a sort of upper husband'[19] in a marriage that could never hope to be more than second best. Tertia remained childless and indefinably blighted, or at least nipped in the bud: always retiring, she became in later life something of a recluse and, though Ivy could be very funny at her sister-in-law's expense, she clearly always felt a protective duty towards her.

But Tertia had been eclipsed all her life by her elder sister Dorothy who had shared Ivy's top flat at 59, Leinster Square until she left to marry Alan Kidd in 1917. Dorothy, proprietary by nature, had a habit of annexing and renaming people or places she fancied: Asquith (who had paid marked attention to Dorothy as a young girl) was christened 'the Oracle', Ivy became 'Miss I' and Ivy's flat 'the perfect rooftree' so that, after Margaret moved in, the couple were known ever after as 'the Rooftreeites'.[20] Both Beresford sisters were beautiful, dreamy, unworldly and intensely competitive. But where Tertia's nervous energy turned inwards and tended to falter under the burden of early unhappiness, Dorothy was disposed to accept or exact tribute from a wider circle. The Beresfords, like the Burnetts, were a booky family and Dorothy, who had grown up transcribing her blind father's songs, sonnets and sermons for publication, had inherited his passionate devotion to literature, along with the family pride and the no less notorious family temper.

The novelist J. D. Beresford was her second cousin, and she herself came between brothers who had both published poems: the elder, Dick, had been shipped off to the colonies as a black sheep before the First World War, leaving Jack (who had always planned to write, like his best friend Noel Compton-Burnett) with more than his share of impecunious relatives to support, which he did by going into the Treasury. But, while Jack built up a substantial literary reputation on the side between the wars (as the editor and essayist J. B. Beresford), Dorothy held out against 'the urge to write'[21] with a determination for which she took credit, 'feeling all round me the fearful tyranny of the over-full inkpot and the unwanted word'. Quick, sensitive, acutely observant, widely read but otherwise uneducated save for what she had picked up from her father, Dorothy was one of those people—all too familiar in the novels of I. Compton-Burnett—who have brains but no training and cannot for the life of them see why writers make such a fuss about writing ('I always feel I could write a novel if I tried. But I am a bad person for trying and that is the truth,' as another of them says in *A God and His Gifts*[22]).

She had known Ivy since they were both dutiful daughters before the First World War, marooned at home in their mid-twenties, watching their younger brothers flourish at Cambridge and later in the larger literary world of London. Dorothy, who had the advantage in looks and was Ivy's equal in wit (she told T. S. Eliot that the three tall, pale, long-fingered Sitwells put her in mind of 'a stained glass window, hands joined in admiration of one another'), had never been prepared to let Ivy 'come the bluestocking' over her. But, when Jack and Noel both married within a few months of one another in 1915, Dorothy and Ivy were united by a disapproval exacerbated in each case by a family break-up that left the two elder sisters high and dry. If mutual displeasure at Noel's marriage to Tertia first drew Ivy and Dorothy together, the war further strengthened an alliance based perhaps as much on respect for each other's intensity of feeling as on their shared love of nature and still greater love of Jane Austen:

My mother and Ivy spoke together intimately [wrote Dorothy's son, Roger Kidd, who was born in 1923 and had grown up listening to these conversations from infancy]. My mother had a direct, unpremeditated approach to things which Ivy responded to: they were able to relax in each other's company. They appreciated each other's value for truth and spontaneity. Ivy was amused by my mother's remarks, and my mother laid store by Ivy's observations—one was never quite sure whether they were talking about relations, friends or characters from a novel.[23]

Dorothy was always ambivalent about Ivy's novels. 'You may impress others but you don't impress me,' she said, and remained perpetually on the alert to forestall any attempt at exploitation on Ivy's part ('Whatever you do, Ivy must never get to hear of this or it'll all come out in a novel,' she said once of a particularly juicy family scandal). She liked Keats, Wordsworth and the Romantics, Sir Thomas Browne, Thomas Traherne and J. D. Beresford's protégée Dorothy Richardson, what she called 'the Immensities' in life or literature; and she seems to have felt, like so many critics of Ivy's novels, that it was rash, if not wrong, to probe the seamier side of human endeavour: 'Too much analysis of our darker moments brings little help unless it leads to a stronger realisation that Beauty is Truth, Truth Beauty . . .'[24]

Ivy herself had learnt from the repeated shocks of her early life to welcome passivity as thankfully as the young Staces—'spotless dullness is what Andrew and I are so gifted at'[25]—looking forward to an uneventful middle age in *Brothers and Sisters*. But spotless dullness was emphatically not among Dorothy's gifts: 'You could describe Dorothy as wicked, as all sorts of things, but you could never describe her as dull,' said one of her nieces.[26] High-handed, strong-minded, by turns ecstatic and cutting but always 'utterly alive', as she herself said of a friend, Dorothy found an appreciative audience in Ivy whose grudge against 'people in life'[27]—as distinct from people in books—was precisely their lack of this sort of vitality and high definition.

However much it might rankle, Dorothy was inclined on the whole to accept Ivy's literary success as an asset: 'She was a very rare creature, one of the rarest of her generation,' said Dorothy who never got out of the habit of seeing Ivy regularly, even in the years when she was most taken up with running her own much larger household in Kensington, together with a nursery and husband ('I don't know how he bore Miss I always,' she said thoughtfully long afterwards). When Margaret spent a fortnight in Paris in the autumn of 1931 with a new friend, Lady Assheton-Smith, Dorothy, Tertia and Jack's wife, Janet, took it in turns to see Ivy nearly every day for lunch or tea; and, five years later, when Margaret was again away staying with the Felkins at Geneva, it was Dorothy who moved into the flat to keep Ivy company.

Alan Kidd had been another of the husbands Jack Beresford was always said to have brought home for his sisters. He was tall, dark and handsome, a successful civil servant with substantial private means and an equable nature that ideally complemented his wife's freaks of temperament. But he lost a good deal of money in the slump, and died suddenly of septicaemia after a family fishing holiday in Scotland in 1933 leaving Dorothy, with the ten-year-old Roger, his nurse (known as the 'Ancient Retainer') and a greatly reduced income, to join her sister in the ranks of affliction and grief. She was inconsolable; and though, unlike Tertia, Dorothy refused to succumb to straitened circumstances thereafter, she too turned for support to Ivy and Margaret. Outings with Roger and the Rooftreeites provided frequent distraction, and sometimes all four spent holidays together in the country, reading and walking and talking: 'We made constant visits to places, museums, galleries, these were always a delight to my mother and me,' wrote Roger. 'I remember no difficulties, only a sense of ease and pleasure. These expeditions were always planned by Margaret quietly and efficiently to give amusement to us all.'[28]

2

IN SO FAR as Ivy took any further part in family life after her own home had disintegrated, it was supplied by the Beresfords far more effectively than by her two sisters whom she scarcely saw from one year to the next, and then only on a strictly business footing. Under the terms of their mother's will Ivy had been appointed head of the family, a duty she punctually discharged to the end of her life since Vera and Juliet—for fifty years her sole surviving charges—were neither of them interested in managing money. Ivy's fellow trustees in the various trust funds set up by their parents had been Noel and the family solicitor, Martyn Mowll, both of whom died in 1916. From then on she presided alone at the quarterly meetings held in

Mowll's London office for which Martyn's nephew, Rutley Mowll, travelled up from Dover with his head clerk to submit the books and go through the accounts. 'She kept a tight eagle eye on her finances,' said the accountant who, like his father before him, had made a fourth at these meetings, and at the luncheons held afterwards in a nearby hotel. 'She scrutinised everything and demanded cogent reasons. There was never any question of her sisters being consulted.'[29]

Dr Compton Burnett's estate had been made up of almost a hundred properties, mostly round Clacton and Hove, any one of which might involve separate negotiations with tenants, rental agreements, mortgages, insurance policies, permission to erect a telegraph pole or a shed in the garden.[30] By the end of the First World War, Ivy and her sisters had sold the family home—Number 20, The Drive, Hove—which all three recalled with acute dislike. But they still possessed a string of houses up and down the country, marking the various stages of their father's rise to prosperity: his old home and consulting rooms at 17, Hamilton Square, Birkenhead; the larger house with its own stabling and gardens that he bought in Lee High Road, just beyond fashionable Blackheath, when he set about establishing a London practice in Wimpole Street; the highly desirable red brick villa in the country at Pinner where his first wife died and where his second wife came as a bride, nine months before Ivy was born in June 1884; and the first seaside home to which he moved his young family when Ivy was seven years old at 30, First Avenue, Hove.

But the bulk of their property consisted in shops and terraced houses on the outskirts of Hove, together with a number of more substantial establishments designed for the affluent middle classes, all put up on building plots bought by Dr Burnett as the town expanded westwards over fields by the sea towards Aldrington where he had once taken his Sunday walks, and where he now lay buried in St Leonard's graveyard with his second wife beneath a cross commemorating also their sons Guy and Noel, and their two youngest daughters Katharine and Primrose, who had died together of an overdose of veronal in 1917, aged twenty-two and eighteen. His growing estate had been a source of pride and pleasure to Dr Burnett, and after his death it remained dear to the heart of his wife who expressly stipulated in her will that no part of it should be sold. But filial piety was not proof against market forces, and by the early 1920s Ivy and Rutley Mowll were systematically getting rid of the family holdings, selling off whole streetsful at a time and investing the money instead: a state of affairs which, as Noel had once said to Ivy when property values slumped in 1916, was 'enough to make our parents curse God to his face'.[31]

Rutley Mowll (who would in due course be succeeded as Ivy's solicitor by his son Wilfred) was himself the son of Worsfold Mowll who had loomed over Ivy's childhood, paying regular visits to Hove to advise her father and, when Dr Burnett died, to regulate and control her mother's affairs. These Mowlls were a masterful race: sober, godly, righteous, physically commanding, each one overtopped—at any rate in the memory of people who knew them—only by his predecessor. Worsfold's father had been active, like Ivy's maternal grandfather, in the fierce public welfare battles that rocked Dover in the 1850s and 1860s. Worsfold himself, who had seemed to the little Compton-Burnetts a sombre embodiment of authority and repression, supplied the model for more than one of the tyrants in Ivy's books; Martyn was remembered by her sisters as 'only less Worsfold than Worsfold'; and Rutley came out of the same mould. 'He was a massive and awe-inspiring figure,' wrote the novelist Roy Fuller, who as a young solicitor in the late 1930s had several times appeared before Rutley Mowll in his capacity as coroner for East Kent. 'Can he still have worn a frock-coat? He certainly habitually wore one of those hats that start as a top-hat and finish as a bowler. I was terrified of him, but though severe he was always courteous and just.'[32]

Ivy herself, however circumspect she may have seemed to social acquaintances, left her professional advisers in no doubt that she was 'an exceedingly forceful woman'.[33] To her sisters, now that her power over them rested on consent not coercion, she remained inscrutable. The bitter struggles of the past were never mentioned between them, indeed they seldom talked about anything beyond what was for tea, or the sort of news that might as well go on a holiday postcard. 'Her manner was touch-me-not. So far and no further,' said Juliet. She and Vera had by this time found their own release from oppression and grief in theosophy, becoming disciples of Rudolf Steiner and turning the house they shared with Myra Hess in St John's Wood into an 'art house', filled with music, painting, modelling, eurhythmics, all activities that Ivy flatly deplored. She herself had once proposed moving into 8, Carlton Hill with her sisters, but that was in 1915 when she was still very far from the serene detachment with which Miss Mitford, in *Parents and Children*, overrides her pupils' objections to her own scheme for going to board with relations:

'You ought not to have to pay relations.'
'Well, the English have no family feelings. That is, none of the kind you mean. They have them, and one of them is that relations must cause no expense.' . . .
'Perhaps they are not near relations.'
'Yes, they are. It is near relations who have family feelings.'
'You might as well live with friends,' said Venice.
'Well, there is the tie of blood.'
'What difference does that make, if people forget it?'
'Other people remember it. That is another family feeling.'[34]

If Ivy had got out of the way of family feelings, so had her sisters. To outsiders, Mr Mowll and Miss Compton-Burnett ('the Oak and the Ivy' as they were known to people obliged to do business with them) made a formidable team, but Vera and Juliet were undeterred by their mentors' united if tacit disapproval of everything from their musical friends to their purchase of a supposedly impractical cottage on the hill above Berkhamsted at the beginning of the 1920s ('If you want my opinion, Miss Vera,' said Rutley Mowll, towering above her on the garden path during a disastrous tour of inspection, 'I think it's a *dreadful* property'). It was Margaret who had advised them to look for something in the country between Berkhamsted and Tring, but things were not much less sticky when she and Ivy came down from London to look over the cottage in turn: 'They arrived from the station by taxi—a good hour and a half before it was possible to have lunch,' said Vera. 'They sat there. I can see them now. Hatted and gloved. They didn't even take their gloves off. Hour after hour. And hour after hour. With rolled up umbrellas. They belonged to a different world.'

So did the five half-brothers and -sisters,[35] Dr Burnett's first family, whose very existence Ivy's mother had done what she could to deny. Olive, the eldest and the most unforgiving, earned some sort of living as a journalist and had set up house in 1919—the same year as Ivy with Margaret—with her friend Emily Pope. Iris, who was a nursing sister at the London Temperance Hospital in Hampstead, lived in Stanley Gardens a few streets away from Ivy's flat in Linden Gardens, though her reputation as an active churchwoman in the neighbourhood put her on the far side of an unbridgeable gulf. Daisy, the youngest, retired from the African mission field in the 1930s to run a home called Carfax for other retired missionaries in Bristol. Each received from her half-sisters, in recognition of past injustice, a voluntary allowance of a hundred pounds a year (Ivy's own income in the 1920s was roughly ten times as much). Beyond that the three sisters had dropped out of Ivy's life as completely as the two half-brothers her mother had shipped off to Canada before the First World War: Charlie prospered eventually as a fruit farmer in California but Dick, always considered a dull dog by his half-sisters, was done for by the stock market crash of 1929 which left him physically shattered, financially destitute and dependent on his brother for support, until he killed himself six years later by jumping off a bridge in Los Angeles.

'You would hardly believe about families. Or many people would not,'[36] as another governess, Miss Hallam, says in *Daughters and Sons*. Ivy's own escape from her family seems to have released, in her life with Margaret, a side her sisters had never seen in the strained and wary creature they had known from infancy. Ivy in middle age allowed herself a gaiety, an ebullience and a humorous teasing affection she had suppressed with everyone save her brothers, Guy and Noel, in her girlhood at Hove. Neither she nor Margaret had nephews or nieces (except for the two children of Margaret's eldest brother Frank, estranged from infancy and both in any case grown up by the late 1920s), but they made up for it with other people's children: there were tea parties for Molly Waechter's two boys and a girl, a trip to the circus for Hester's little brother John Pinney and, later, annual circus outings for Hester's own children at Christmas. It was Ivy who decorated the Christmas tree ('One always went to see Ivy's tree,' said Roger Kidd. 'It was loaded with decorations, like a little sort of flame'), and Ivy who could if she liked turn anything into a treat, from a sea bathe to tea in a café. Between the wars she was said to walk across the park every morning for the pleasure of eating cream buns at Buzzards in Oxford Street; and to the end of her life friends could still elicit a rapturous response, as one might from a child, with a present of chocolates, a pot of jam or a new sort of sweet.

Few novelists have written about children more perceptively than Ivy. They turn up in her books in increasing numbers after the first dim, downtrodden eleven-year-old (Muriel Ponsonby in *Daughters and Sons*), but she is always especially tender to lonely, backward or disabled children, oddities and misfits like Aubrey Gaveston in *A Family and a Fortune* or Reuben Donne in *Elders and Betters*; and Roger Kidd, himself a delicate only child, sensitive and highly strung, remembered being treated in much the same spirit in fact:

Ivy was like a favourite aunt. She showed interest and never patronised. She would often, rather surprisingly, level a direct question about one's life with a searching glance.

She took evident pleasure in things: relish in eating something in a restaurant, glowing fires, sunlight, flowers; I remember her bending over wild flowers in a Dorset wood and saying, 'Oh, you darlings!' She delighted in gossip but not maliciously, and always tempered with honesty. Looking back one is aware of a classical integrity—a dispassionate examination—and not of intellect so much as of perception. Sometimes she would laugh so much while recounting some absurdity that she wept.[37]

When asked if she would have liked children herself, Ivy said no, though she thought she might have managed them better than some mothers did,[38] which was roughly Miss Mitford's reaction in *Parents and Children* when Eleanor Sullivan complained of her children getting beyond her:

'I wish I understood children as you do. It would be such a help to me.'

Miss Mitford smiled in an absent manner, thinking of the shocks that Eleanor would sustain if this could be the case, and wondering if she had forgotten her own childhood or had an abnormal one.[39]

Family life remained Ivy's prime interest, one she pursued with curiosity and compassion like Miss Mitford ('She did not let pity for her employer or pupil mar her interest. Pity had come to be the normal background of her mind, and other feelings arose irrespective of it'[40]), and with sympathy above all. 'She was a friend of my family. Ivy liked families, and Ivy liked us,'[41] said the younger of the two Hesters who had been accustomed to turn to Margaret and Ivy for advice and support at all stages of her own, sometimes stormy married life. Pretty, breezy, rebellious, determined not to conform to the pattern of nice behaviour laid down for girls of her class and background, Hester had always found an ally in Margaret who helped her with odd jobs as a freelance journalist, and generally 'encouraged revolt against parental discipline'.

But Ivy, who never in all her life encouraged anyone to cast off his family (and almost certainly would never have done so herself if things had not got the better of her), was still more receptive. When Hester began walking out with Basil Marsden-Smedley —who came from a family decidedly better off and stuffier than her own—'Ivy used to ask us a lot about our relationship, and particularly the opposition on financial grounds of Basil's parents to me . . .'[42] For the next forty years and more Hester submitted to cross-examination by Ivy as to her job prospects, love affairs ('especially if they went wrong'), professional and marital problems, family conflicts: 'Margaret criticised. Ivy more often sympathised . . . she was always very understanding. Margaret found, quite rightly, many things in my life "regrettable". Ivy wanted to know more about them.'[43]

3

THIS IMPRESSION of Ivy—tolerant, affectionate, inquisitive and understanding—is borne out by practically everyone who knew her well in later life. Close friends after Margaret's death—George Furlong and Rex Brandreth, Barbara and Walter Robinson, Soame Jenyns, Elizabeth Taylor, Sonia Orwell, Madge Garland—all knew this side of Ivy; and even in the years when she most assiduously played second fiddle, there were always friends—some of whom had never opened her books—prepared to lay themselves out for her sake. People who found her perception alarming ('I am often ashamed of understanding them') seldom resented it, for Ivy, unlike Margaret, was not censorious. Reticent, aloof, often constrained in company herself, she could be an encouraging listener just as, when not bored or restive as she tended to be in the grander country houses Margaret frequented, she could be a gentle and ideally appreciative guest. Ivy was delighted with the smallest attention, a little walk down the lane or soft fruit for tea. 'She had to have strawberries from the moment she stepped inside the door until they could not be got for love or money,' said Janet Beresford, who did not care for Margaret at all ('Margaret definitely spoilt Ivy') but always took special trouble when Ivy came alone to stay at the Beresfords' country cottage at Ashwell in Hertfordshire.

So did Margaret's friends, Ella and Dora Noyes, who lived in a long, low, book-lined, wistaria-covered stone house at Sutton Veney, tucked under the Wiltshire downs and surrounded by a rambling, overgrown, secluded and sweet-smelling garden where Ivy spent hours at a time sitting in the shade of the mulberry tree. The Noyes sisters were among the few, perhaps the only people with whom Ivy discussed her books at all freely. Dora painted, Ella wrote and both, like Dorothy Kidd, set store by Ivy, who came to stay alone or with Margaret every summer between the wars. They would order a trap or a taxi to fetch her from the station, lay in the sort of food she enjoyed, turn her bed to the north, see that her room was just so: 'It was always a big thing when Miss Burnett was coming.'[44]

Margaret was an altogether tougher proposition, more energetic, more enterprising and far more willing to take the rough with the smooth ('I should have been inclined to reject the rough. I don't know why it always has to be included,' says Rosa Lindsay, echoing her creator in A God and His Gifts[45]). 'Margaret was determined to know people and make friends. She wasn't pretty and she wasn't rich but she worked away at it,' said Raisley. 'She was interested in one, she listened and she asked questions.' But she also toned people up with her sarcasm, her raised eyebrows, what Herman called 'the superior air, as if she knew more than most people, which I believe she certainly did; but also a certain contempt for human beings, as if she despised them'.[46] She was a famous debunker, adept at demolishing other people's pretensions whether they laid claim to fake Chippendale or to a veneer of gentility. Profoundly unconventional in some ways, she attached great importance to keeping up appearances which made her a potentially uncomfortable mentor to her young friends. Adultery or other irregularities might be tolerated but never condoned ('If Bridget has done what one has to do with a man to get a divorce,' she said to Hester when Bridget

D'Oyly Carte's marriage was dissolved in 1931, 'one will never feel the same towards her again'[47]). If Ivy hardly needed to know all before she forgave it, Margaret was straitlaced, unbending, apt to quote with approval Mrs Norris's saying, in Jane Austen's *Mansfield Park*, that it was 'a shocking thing for a young person to be always lolling on a sofa'.[48]

For a long time Margaret and Ivy possessed no sofa and when one was eventually purchased—after much teasing on Ivy's part, and reluctance on Margaret's—it was a straight-backed settee with nice legs but a hard, unyielding upholstered seat on which two, or at a pinch three, persons might perch but not loll. Ivy herself had a large, cushioned, black velvet armchair drawn up close to the fire, well stocked with chocolates and magazines. There was another, smaller armchair for a woman visitor but Margaret, who told Soame Jenyns that she had never sat in a comfortable chair made since the Reform Bill, preferred one of the handsome hard-backed uprights with which male guests had to make do. While Ivy worked at her ease with a notebook on her knee in the drawing room, Margaret wrote all her books in her tiny bedroom on a hard chair pulled up to the dressing table with a litter of notes, cuttings, jottings on old bills and the backs of used envelopes spread on the bed.

Her notions of taste and comfort derived from a time when, though Sheraton had recommended two for a drawing room, sofas were still widely regarded with suspicion: 'There would often be but one in a house, and in less luxurious households to lie down, or even to lean back, was a luxury permitted only to old persons or invalids,'[49] wrote Margaret, who furnished the flats she shared with Ivy according to her own characteristically vigorous interpretation of a whole generation's revolt against Victorian ostentation, fussiness and clutter. Margaret had been a pioneer long before she was recruited to pass on tips about 'modern design' to readers of *Eve*. Barely out of her twenties before she set about rehabilitating William Kent (on whom she wrote the first book nearly forty years later), she was one of the first to advocate the return to the eighteenth century promoted by neo-Georgians like Edwin Lutyens.

Her own highly idiosyncratic style of furnishing was based on few but fine pieces of Sheraton, Chippendale and Hepplewhite ranged round walls distempered pale grey (or green, unless the 'hospital green paint' recorded by James Lees-Milne[50] in the early

1940s was simply an illusion produced by the general effect of starkness and sparsity), and hung with mirrors to emphasize the sensation of space. Piles of magazines—*Tatler, Queen, Country Life, Eve*, all of which both ladies read avidly—stood about on occasional tables but, though two glass-fronted bookcases were installed later, there were few books to be seen in the 1920s. Ivy did not care for shop flowers, and Margaret shared Lord Chesterfield's distaste for building up a collection 'Knick-knackically'.[51] There were no carpets, no pictures, no colour, practically no soft furnishings. 'I could not give a house those unmistakable signs of a woman's presence,' says Ursula Scrope, explaining why she would not have liked to be married in *The Present and the Past*. 'I do not even recognise them.'[52]

Some visitors were exhilarated by the severity of Margaret's scheme ('very elegant with pale oyster walls and superb period furniture'[53]), others dismayed by its comfortlessness. At all events it never varied. Margaret had done up Ivy's Leinster Square flat at the beginning of 1921 and she supervised the decorations when they moved in July 1923 to 97, Linden Gardens—another small, dingy flat, in Bayswater, conveniently close to William Whiteley's emporium where Ivy did her shopping, but still on the unfashionable north side of Hyde Park—and when they eventually settled ten years later in Cornwall Gardens, South Kensington. After this last move nothing changed: 'The same furniture stood in the same positions, in the same rooms, and when the flat had to be redecorated . . . the colour scheme was simply repeated,'[54] said Herman whose own taste ran to artifice and opulence in decor and who found Margaret's 'Gloom Palace' depressing. So did Lady Colefax's partner, the young and afterwards highly influential decorator, John Fowler, when James Lees-Milne introduced him in the 1940s: 'John was amazed by the bareness and austerity of the flat, the uniform stark apple-green decoration and the floor linoleum against which the few nice Georgian pieces looked islanded and insignificant.'[55]

Partly perhaps this impression was a matter of economy ('Ivy wouldn't have thought of forking out money for furniture, and Margaret hadn't any to fork,' said Ralph Edwards). But the pieces islanded in Margaret's drawing room went back to the sparsely furnished interiors of painters like Arthur Devis (another artist Margaret had been among the first to rediscover) at a time when

Kent or Burlington could design a 'saloon, large enough to receive a
company of sixty or a hundred persons, furnished with six or eight
chairs, and a couple of tables'.[56] Even the mirrors were a decorative
trick of the Regency. Ivy and Margaret wasted no money on
modernization but they had knocked down a wall to transfer an
Adam fireplace from Linden Gardens to Braemar Mansions, where
another wall had to be demolished to receive it. The bleakness that
occasionally disconcerted guests—the linoleum floors, primitive
plumbing, unheated bedrooms—went back, according to Hester,
to the spartan upbringing of both friends: 'Good food and a warm
room with lovely things around were more important than the
actual physical comfort of sitting on a soft seat.'[57]

This was the pattern evolved by 'English middling people' in
their middling homes from the eighteenth century onwards: a
tradition of sobriety, understatement and what Horace Walpole
called 'snugness'[58] that went with plain cooking, hard chairs, coal
fires, and those other good things prescribed by the housekeeping
ladies in *Mother and Son*, 'fine old linen carefully darned'[59] and bone
china ('Cracked and mended, but rather rare! That strikes the exact
note'). Margaret's forthrightness and Ivy's unnerving honesty
belonged to the same tradition, and so did their refusal ever to be
carried away: 'I never heard, in forty years, either Ivy or Margaret
raise their voices,' said Herman. 'They were flat cultured voices,
and they never laughed out loud. Like Fontenelle, they never said
"Ha-ha-ha!" . . . I never heard Margaret call a piece of furniture
"superb" or "marvellous" or "fantastic" or even "beautiful". Her
highest praise was "jolly!" or "very jolly!" And that was that.'[60] By
the same token, 'regrettable' was as far as Margaret was prepared to
go in the opposite direction.

Naturally there were two schools of thought about the flats and
the food, just as there were about Ivy's books or for that matter the
ladies themselves. For old friends like the Kings, Beresfords or
Noyeses, dinner with Ivy and Margaret might be a tonic but there
were others for whom it was more of a trial. Raisley Moorsom
remembered a category of what Ivy called 'dripping dinners',
which consisted of hangers-on even humbler in the social scale than
Raisley and his friend Frankie Birrell, who had disgraced himself, in
a celebrated episode at Leinster Square, by falling asleep the first
time Margaret asked him to dinner and smashing the arm of his
chair:

I can quite clearly remember the soup . . . Then, I suppose, we must have had fish, because when I woke up there *was* a plate of fish, uneaten, in front of me. As a matter of fact, my left hand was in it, covered with sauce. I was alone in the dining-room; the lights were burning, and when I looked at my watch I saw that it was past midnight. The ladies seemed to have gone to bed.[61]

Birrell found his hat, let himself out and slunk home. There is a similar story told about Ezra Pound damaging a favourite chair on a visit to Gertrude Stein and Alice B. Toklas in Paris.[62] It is the sort of legend often defensively circulated about independent and strong-minded ladies in a position to suit themselves without reference to other people (' "Well, a selfish life is lovely, darling," said Rachel. "It is awful to be of use" '[63]); and it illustrates how completely, at the beginning of the 1920s, Miss Jourdain eclipsed 'her young friend' who had written nothing as yet, and whose presence Birrell barely registered. The next time a similar anecdote went the rounds, it was after the Second World War and the young man who passed out in the soup and woke to find himself alone was Philip Toynbee, invited as an admirer of Ivy's: 'The table, even down to the coffee cups, proved that the meal, as he sat bowed over his plate, had otherwise taken its natural and unperturbed course . . . He crept out from a dark and silent flat. It was Miss Compton-Burnett's habit to retire early to bed.'[64]

Thirty years or so separate these two stories, and it took at least that time for Margaret to recede into the background and Ivy to emerge as the one capable of petrifying apprehensive young men. But already by the early 1930s there were signs that the balance was beginning to shift. When the lease of the Linden Gardens flat ran out at the beginning of 1934, the two friends moved after weeks of energetic 'flatting' to 5, Braemar Mansions, Cornwall Gardens: a gaunt granite barracks ('You'll recognise the house, it looks like Balmoral,' was Margaret's instruction to visitors[65]) with a porter, lifts, a carpeted foyer and large high-ceilinged rooms, a great deal more spacious as well as an address in itself infinitely superior to their previous quarters on the wrong side of the park. Cornwall Gardens had been stuffily respectable when Terence Rattigan was born there in 1911, and it always retained a forbidding aspect although, by the middle of the 1930s, the young and fashionable like Cecil Beaton and Oliver Messel were just beginning to move to

South Kensington. T. S. Eliot took rooms in the vicarage opposite Cornwall Gardens the same year as Margaret and Ivy who, with their friends the Kings (established in Thurloe Square the year after), were part of a larger migration: 'Obviously they must have got more money, or inherited more money, for the change from Linden Gardens in Bayswater to Cornwall Gardens in Kensington was stupendous,' said Herman[66] on whom no social nuance was lost.

But in fact Margaret's income, never in any case large, hardly fluctuated during the 1920s and 1930s,[67] while Ivy's had fallen steadily from the beginning of the slump and was still falling at the time of the move. The change, in so far as their circumstances had altered at all, seems to have been moral rather than financial. Ivy's novels never sold in large numbers but by 1934 hers was a household name in households with any sort of literary or cultural pretensions.* She had moved for good out of the ranks of writers —always so feelingly described in her books—who find themselves obliged to pay for their work to be published or, losing hope of finding a publisher at all, to put their manuscripts away in a drawer for reading aloud to themselves in a low tone. 'The judgment of posterity is known to be the only true one. So there seems no point in getting any other. I wonder so many people do it,'[68] says Felix Bacon airily to Jonathan Swift, whose own works were too far ahead of contemporary taste for publication in *More Women Than Men*. It was not a consolation that appealed to Jonathan, or to any of the other aspiring writers in the works of I. Compton-Burnett, any more than it did to Ivy herself. She was, as she freely admitted, always a shrewd judge of property but even so it seems likely that, when she and Margaret held their flat-warming party at Braemar Mansions on 27 March—just over two months short of Ivy's fiftieth birthday—the move had less to do with her business acumen than with her arrival as a writer, or at any rate the satisfaction of knowing that posterity's judgment was not the only verdict she was ever likely to get.

* For instance, the Birrells' who received their copy of *Men and Wives* in April 1931, and spent the next few weeks 'snatching it out of each other's hands . . . We all *adored* it. And I thought that it was in some ways the *funniest* book I have ever read. I *howled* out loud . . . At meals we talk about Nothing But Matthew & Harriet & Godfrey and Spong. Your characters have just been added to our lives *en bloc* . . .' (Francis Birrell to I.C.-B., 29 April 1931.)

MARGARET JOURDAIN

'No point in being too Greek'

I

MARGARET OF COURSE was still the eminent one of the two, the only one most people they met had ever heard of, and by far the more prolific. Her *Regency Furniture*, published in 1934, brought her score to something like twenty titles since the turn of the century. Admittedly, this included translations, catalogues, collaborations and editions of other people's writings as well as her own original work but they were all indisputably what Ivy's characters call 'serious' books, the sort of thing that occupies Charity Marcon in *Daughters and Sons*:

> I have been up to London to get the book I am writing, out of the British Museum. I have got a lot of it out, and I shall go again presently to get some more; and when I have got it all, there will be another book . . . Mine ought to be quite a success. It will be just like the ones I am getting it out of, and they are standard books.[1]

Margaret was eventually responsible for a dozen or so of these standard books but it was not until the mid-1930s that she finally resigned a lingering desire to write fiction in favour of what Sir Michael Egerton, in *A God and His Gifts*, called 'something more solid and without the personal touch'.[2] Round about the time Ivy's first novels began to appear, Margaret narrowed down her own published output to articles in specialist journals like *Country Life*, the *Connoisseur* and *Architectural Review*, interspersed with scholarly volumes of a kind that need not make sensitive servants like the Egertons' butler (or, for that matter, Ivy's and Margaret's own Jessie) feel even mildly ashamed.

But she seems to have done it reluctantly and with no great conviction. While Ivy was writing *More Women Than Men*, Margaret was at work on a play, *Buchanan's Hotel*, which gives her own straightforwardly naturalistic and rather more detailed version of the circle they both moved in at the time; and, when Ivy's novels attracted attention, Margaret's reaction seems to have been that the sort of reviewer who could call Ivy a genius might surely be induced to do as much for herself. Raymond Mortimer certainly had the impression that she resented his admiration for Ivy,[3] and Rosamond Lehmann, who had published an enthusiastic tribute in the *Spectator* in 1937, actually received a letter from Ivy politely enlisting her help with theatrical managements on behalf of Margaret's play.[4]

Buchanan's Hotel[5] is a perfectly passable, three-act, West End comedy made up in roughly equal parts of topical chat—about the slump and the servant problem, Hitler's anti-Semitism, Mosley's British fascists, ominous developments abroad and the predicament of the dispossessed middle classes at home—personal gossip and fairly desultory social and sexual intrigue. Its themes are money and class. Its cast consists of professionally charming, generally well-connected, more or less penniless young men and their patrons, mostly wealthy and much older women: the new poor preying on the nouveaux riches, people with taste or breeding or both prepared to trade either for cash. What little action there is—a scheme for marrying money mooted by one of the young men, and another's attempts to secure lucrative contracts for doing up the local big houses—seems to have been largely borrowed from life. There are partial portraits of both Ivy and Margaret in the persons of Miss Wace and Miss Tunstall, indeed the nub of the play, in so far as it may be said to have one, is their mutual friendship with the cheerful, immodest, rising young decorator, Sigismund Siepel, who bears a striking resemblance to Herman Schrijver.

The hotel in which the play takes place has been recently opened in Cornwall by Jim Buchanan ('Before the war hotel-keeping wouldn't have been a possibility for our class'), a consumptive obliged to move south for the climate like Margaret's young friend Captain Colville. Invalided out of the army with damaged lungs

and advised by his doctors not to return to the family home in
Scotland, Norman Colville had settled instead at the beginning of
the 1920s on the ruined Tudor manor of Penheale in North Cornwall, which was rebuilt over the next decade by Lutyens, laid out
with gardens, courtyards, great hall, long gallery and servants'
quarters, and done up inside by the grandest of all London decorating firms, Lenygon and Morant. Margaret had worked for years as
Lenygon's adviser, and she rapidly made friends with Norman
Colville who was the soul of hospitality as well as an enthusiastic
collector (Margaret devoted a pair of *Country Life* articles to his
collections in 1923, and Ralph Edwards another pair to his house
two years later), and from now on a staunch admirer of Margaret,
who came to stay every summer in the 1920s and 1930s, and clearly
based her hotel on Penheale.

The select clientele at Buchanan's, when not absorbed in the
delicate art of sizing up one another's social standing ('We don't
know anything about Siepel. He's really rather bogus') or currying
favour with the local landowner, Lord Trevor, are inordinately
preoccupied with money. Camp followers like Buchanan himself,
and his unemployed, impecunious but otherwise presentable friend
Hugh Benton ('one knows his people: he's Trevor's cousin'),
discuss with great frankness ways and means of extracting funds
from unpresentables like Mrs Simonson:

> *Buchanan*: Simonson—good old non-Aryan name.
> *Benton*:   Who are they?
> *Buchanan*: Oh, nobody. Money from jute. She's a widow.

Naturally enough, after various manoeuvres of pursuit and evasion
on his part and Siepel's, Benton announces his engagement to the
widow in Act III, which calls for some mildly envious sniping from
Buchanan ('Well, Hugh, I'm glad you got the job . . . Mind you
hold out for your pin money'); and the curtain falls as Siepel is
publicly unmasked as a Jew.

The point of this ambivalent ending—whether it was meant to
endorse or expose the spectacle of the English upper classes ganging
up against a Jewish outsider—remains unclear, though the play
gives an accurate if unappealing impression of the manners and
assumptions current among Margaret's friends at the time. Certainly she was thoroughly familiar with this world of hard-up, ambi-

tious freelances whose careers depended on manipulating a complicated network of contacts. Her own reputation for disinterested
scholarship did not stop her working for dealers like Acton Surgey
or Phillips,[6] obtaining pieces on commission from the trade and
placing them with her own wealthy clients; and she seems, like so
many of her friends, to have had at least a passing connection with
interior decoration which, for a single woman of any social pretensions in those days, was often the sole practical alternative to a
well-heeled husband. Margaret's famous, encyclopaedic filing system covering all historical aspects of the domestic arts contains also
trade addresses ranging from Fabrics, Fringes and Floor Coverings
or Porcelain, Plywood and Paint to Glass Panelling for Ballrooms
(she had been working on an exhibition in March 1934, the month
she and Ivy moved into Braemar Mansions, for Philip Sassoon
whose glass ballroom in Park Lane was briefly the talk of Europe).

She generally relied on at least one steady client or patron whose
collections she helped build up and tend: in the 1920s it was the
Hon. Mrs Levy whose father had founded the Shell fortunes and
who was replaced, after her second marriage, by another rich
widow, Lady Assheton-Smith. Margaret also got smaller jobs for
and from decorating friends like Herman or Derek Patmore and the
architect Basil Ionides (architecture in those days covered anything
from garden trimmings to designing maids' uniforms), any one of
whom might put work in the way of another. It was Herman who
introduced Patmore to the ageing Edwardian beauty who subsequently became his protectress, Mrs Gwendolen Jefferson of High
Beech[7] (which Herman had decorated, and where Margaret too
was called in for a weekend in the summer of 1933). A few years
earlier Margaret had introduced Basil to Nelly Levy, herself by this
time a close friend and prodigal source not only of work (Margaret
had been employed on and off on the Levy collections in Lowndes
Square, and later Berkeley Square, since 1922) but also of gossip,
company, entertainment, splendid parties and no less splendid
stories like the one of her saying, when someone admired her
necklace in the garden at Buxted Park, 'My dear, these are my
gardening pearls.'[8]

Basil found himself summoned one day to build a bow window
in Berkeley Square, and shortly afterwards married his client. He
and Nelly dined on 23 May 1930, the night before the wedding,
with Margaret and Ivy who for once both warmly approved Basil's

scheme for hanging up his hat in his wife's hall ('I always think that sounds so comfortable,' says Joanna in *A God and His Gifts*. 'And then you will go in to her fire'[9]). Even so, the Ionides' and others among Margaret's friends could scarcely have been best pleased to see themselves even faintly reflected in *Buchanan's Hotel*, supposing it had ever reached the stage in the 1930s.

Not that Margaret would have minded. 'Margaret had a wonderful quality of indifference, the same quality which made Boucher call his picture *Le bel indifférent*,' said Herman. 'It was a kind of I-couldn't-care-less; she was so independent, obviously, in spite of her financial poverty, of what people thought or did, and in many ways she was really a French *epicurienne* . . .'[10] None of the Jourdains had means of their own, a fact which if anything reinforced their contempt for trade and their faith in the family's impeccable Huguenot pedigree. Even at the height of her powers in the 1930s, Margaret had small prospect of earning enough to make her comfortably off, indeed for most of her working life she had no regular income at all. 'I can't do collar work,' she would say (meaning the work collar worn by plough or dray horses) to Ralph Edwards, who remembered her in her fifties and sixties still 'stumping about for £5 for an article'. After 1923 her financial position had been somewhat eased by a steady arrangement with *Country Life* as secondary sales room correspondent, a post not unfairly summed up, in Ivy's phrase, as choosing 'to behave in an undignified manner for a pittance' ('That is the best definition of work I have heard,' says Felix Bacon in *More Women Than Men*[11]).

Before that Margaret had been accustomed to get by on very little more—in a bad year decidedly less—than Emily Herrick in *Pastors and Masters* who would 'have had to go on the streets, or even be a governess' if her brother had left her to support herself on her own income (' "A hundred a year," said Emily. "Nicholas is kind and without a true dignity. He calls that on the streets" '[12]). Emily is the first of those shrewd, humorous, sceptical spinsters who were to become one of I. Compton-Burnett's specialities. She is not exactly a portrait of Margaret, more the product of a profound alteration in Ivy articulated, as it were, in the light of Margaret's peculiar personality and outlook. A good many of Emily's views were also Margaret's, not least the horror of teaching that was a natural reaction among women born into a world where even penniless boys, like the five Jourdain brothers, went into the church, the professions or the army as a matter of course, while girls had no choice (failing Nicholas Herrick's alternative) save to marry or teach.

2

MARGARET was the eighth child of the vicar of Ashbourne in Derbyshire, 'a man of little force but considerable charm',[13] who did not believe in education for girls and possessed neither funds nor connections, which put marriage out of the question for his five plain daughters. His wife was Emily Clay, a daughter of the distinguished Manchester surgeon Charles Clay who pioneered ovariotomy and died, embittered by lack of recognition, in 1893 when Margaret was seventeen. What little schooling she and her sisters received had been provided by these Manchester grandparents, who also paid for the two eldest girls, Eleanor and Charlotte, to join the first generation of women at Oxford. Margaret's first name was Emily after her mother:

'I believe their mother, Mrs Jourdain, was a charming woman,' [said Ivy to Rosamond Lehmann]. 'Eleven children altogether,* the first six almost simultaneously and all the same size. She dressed them all alike and of course it is scarcely surprising that she could scarcely tell them apart. Eleanor was the eldest. Eleanor would have to say, "Mother, I am now twelve: should not my skirt be let down an inch?"—that sort of thing, you know. She was not at all an intellectual type, the mother, so Margaret told me. She would have preferred something less serious and academic in the way of six daughters—something with more of social grace and lightness. She did not feel at home with them. They were ambitious girls . . .'[14]

---

* The family tree compiled by Margaret's brother, Lt.-Col. Henry Jourdain, gives the number of the Rev. Francis and Emily Jourdain's children as ten, of whom the first six (Eleanor, Francis, Charlotte, Maria Lucy called May, Arthur and Raymond) certainly arrived within seven years, 1863–70; Henry was born two years later and the three youngest—Margaret, Philip and Melicent—were separated from the rest by a gap of four years so, unless Ivy mistook the number, perhaps there was an eleventh child in this gap who died young or was deliberately expunged (like Philip's wife Laura) for some other reason.

The boys attended Ashbourne grammar school and the four able-bodied ones (Philip and Melicent, the two youngest Jourdains, were cripples) did at least dance at the Okeovers' balls, which gave them some contact with county society, while the girls were taught at home and asked nowhere. Reticent, tenacious, self-sufficient and starved in childhood of intellectual contact, Margaret and her two celebrated brothers, Francis (called Frank) and Philip, were all afterwards known as much for their personal austerity and biting tongues as for encyclopaedic knowledge in their respective scholarly fields of furniture, ornithology and mathematics. All their lives they referred to themselves and one another by initials, as 'M.J.' (this was what Margaret was called, even after half a century, by all her closest friends except Ivy), 'F.C.R.J.', 'P.E.B.J.', so that family letters read as impersonally as office memos. A self-contained and critical habit must have been learnt early in the vicarage nursery. 'It was not a very happy household,' said Joan Evans whose mother had gone up to Oxford in 1888 with Charlotte Jourdain, and who had herself been educated by Eleanor and later befriended by Margaret. 'Margaret had no backing at home. Her mother couldn't conceive what intellectual work was; and her father wouldn't have bothered about it in his daughters.' The vicar was remembered by parishioners as 'dangerously high',[15] his wife as uncomfortably prickly, both as too stand-offish to be popular in the village. When the eldest son, another Rev. Francis Jourdain (later the founding father of British birdwatching), became vicar of Clifton-by-Ashbourne and married the squire's beautiful daughter, Frances Smith, in 1896, the Jourdains disowned the bride on the grounds that her family fortunes had been founded by a Smith in the grocery business. Other Jourdain wives were not much more welcome: 'The Jourdains were a very strange family—very brainy, but they lacked other things, such as family affection', wrote Frank's daughter, Violet Clifton-Smith[16] (who took her mother's name in adult life by way of repudiation).

Chronically hard up and short of friends in the neighbourhood, the family 'tended to be centrifugal' in Joan Evans' phrase, and the tendency applied emotionally as well as physically speaking. But, if life under a withdrawn, ineffectual father and a sardonic mother worn down by genteel poverty and twenty years' childbearing inhibited fondness or intimacy between the children, most of them flourished on the family's ruthlessly competitive, sink-or-swim policy of self-help, self-control and self-determination. Margaret's upbringing, in some ways bleak and chilly as the vicarage itself, left her implacably anti-Christian, independent and determined at all costs to avoid the humiliating moral and intellectual compromises involved in being a teacher like her three older sisters. Charlotte and May began life as governesses: May went east with a diplomatic family and died at the age of twenty-six in Persia in 1894; Charlotte ended up in an Anglican sisterhood in Truro (and, again by Joan Evans' account, 'if she'd gone on the streets it couldn't have put her outside the family any more than being a nun, so far as Margaret was concerned'). Their eldest sister Eleanor (called Nelly) became a schoolmistress and eventually Principal of St Hugh's College, Oxford, as well as a bestselling author on account of *An Adventure* which she wrote with her predecessor as Principal, the Bishop of Salisbury's daughter Miss Moberly, describing their encounter with Marie Antoinette and her ghostly court at Versailles in 1901. The book ('My sister's folly' was Margaret's phrase for it[17]) was published under pseudonyms in 1911, causing a good deal of what Miss Mitford called family feeling partly because of its sensational reception in the popular press, partly perhaps because of the faint but perceptible odour of high-minded fishiness analysed by Mrs Henry Sidgwick in the journal of the Society for Psychical Research.* Ivy (who claimed to know Eleanor well, and even once put her into a book) said she could not think of anyone more likely to delude herself into believing *An Adventure*.[18]

Eleanor was thirteen years older than Margaret. She was romantic and not in the least intellectual, a pious, orthodox High Anglican with mystical leanings and scant respect for the sterner exigencies of scholarship: on all these counts the opposite of her sister (though even that unbending sceptic could on occasion be brought to admit that Eleanor had second sight). Both were energetic, ambitious,

---

* The Society, having dismissed *An Adventure* in 1901 as not worth investigating from a scientific point of view, remained unconvinced by further evidence adduced in 1911 ('I imagine she really understood at the bottom of her heart that she had done a rather fishy thing, and was determined that it should not be exposed,' wrote the Society's officer sent down to interview Miss Moberly, *The Ghosts of Versailles* by Lucille Iremonger, p.203). Mrs Sidgwick's review was bitterly resented by both authors; what they actually saw at Versailles in 1901 is now generally supposed to have been preparations for a fancy dress party given by Robert de Montesquioux (see 'An End to An Adventure' by Joan Evans, *Encounter*, October 1976).

determined, perhaps faintly French, with the same 'superior air' and the same fondness for feathers and finery. But on fundamentals they were always at loggerheads. Eleanor had gone up to Lady Margaret Hall as a scholar in 1883, five years after it opened, and, when her grandfather died, it was Eleanor (by this time running a small private school of her own called Corran at Watford) who helped subsidize Margaret on a Hall scholarship at the same college in 1894. Their principal was the witty and worldly Elizabeth Wordsworth who publicly subscribed to much the same view of woman's role as Mrs Jourdain (and practically the entire Oxford establishment, from dons to the humblest male undergraduate): 'My ideal woman is always graceful and beautiful, better with her hands than with her head, and best of all with her heart,' wrote Miss Wordsworth. 'She is not a bore because she has never overworked her brain . . . She has an income, if a lady, of from £500 to £1,000 a year; if a poor woman, from twenty shillings to thirty shillings a week . . .'[19]

It was an equivocator's ideal to which Eleanor Jourdain had no difficulty in subscribing, but Margaret rejected out of hand the implicit disparagement of learning itself, as well as of girls without a pretty face and a small fortune. 'The education of my generation, especially of girls, was too often fogged and darkened by doctrines of self-sacrifice for the taught, that marked a want of respect for the individual in the teacher,' wrote Joan Evans,[20] whose own education—supervised throughout by Eleanor, first at the Watford School then at St Hugh's—might have been abandoned altogether if it had not been for Margaret. Joan was the youngest child of the archaeologist Sir John Evans, half-sister to his still more celebrated son Sir Arthur Evans, discoverer of Cnossos, who was forty-two years Joan's senior. She had had a difficult childhood: neglected by scholarly parents (her mother was Maria Lathbury, a ruthlessly dedicated intellectual in her own right), wholly dependent for company and affection on her beloved nanny, she had lost confidence in herself so badly by 1910, at the age of seventeen, that she begged her mother with tears to let her off going to Oxford.

Margaret took her in hand, commissioned her while still a schoolgirl to write a book on jewellery, and generally restored her nerve to the point at which she could face going up to St Hugh's in the autumn of 1914; and Joan was only one among a whole series of young people encouraged to flower by Margaret, who took infinite pains to train them up in ways not only of erudition but of self-reliance, scepticism and irreligion (even Joan, reluctant to follow Margaret too far towards atheism, never forgot being helped to shed crushing burdens of guilt and piety in adolescence). Anyone young and in difficulties—especially anyone struggling for independence—could always rely on Margaret's sympathy and practical advice. Joan, at the end of a long and distinguished professional career, felt she had been launched on it by Margaret. So did young Hester Pinney, and perhaps the traveller Freya Stark (who stayed with Margaret and Ivy in London in the 1920s while planning her own rather more drastic escape from the dull, futile, self-denying round of a daughter at home), not to mention any number of rising young men in the furniture world. In a sense Ivy herself was the most spectacular success of a system first evolved to help Margaret's sister Melicent (called Milly), the youngest of all the Jourdains and the only one ever described as having a sweet disposition.

Milly, like Philip, was crippled by a hereditary disease called Friedrich's ataxia, a kind of multiple sclerosis that declares itself generally round about the tenth year and grows worse so rapidly that it is rare for sufferers to survive into their twenties. As children, she and Philip had spent their days roaming the country together, playing horses or shipwrecks, building tree houses, all pastimes that had to be successively abandoned as they found it harder to keep their balance, to walk, eventually even to stand without help. Philip, perhaps the most remarkable member of a remarkable family, so deformed he could scarcely hold a pen, had achieved an international reputation as a mathematician and mathematical historian before he was thirty, while Milly—shy, nervous, imaginative, more than content to stick to the shadows cast by her brilliant next brother and sister—grew up to write two notably original books of her own. The first was *A Childhood* by 'Joan Arden' which came out in 1913 (Eleanor had published *An Adventure* two years earlier under the name of 'Francis Lamont'), with a preface by Professor Gilbert Murray who admired the book both for its own sake 'and because it somehow reads like the proem to something sterner and sadder'. The stern, sad sequel was *Unfulfilment*, a slim volume of verse published in 1924 which records with singular terseness and clarity its author's decline into paralysis and death:

The Sea Fog

The fields below me are sodden and grey and the fog has
                            blurred the line of the hills.
I sit by the hedge and think that every year the darkness
                            will grow closer round me.
The fog has crept up and all is a sea of whiteness;
My face is wet with its gentle touch and I can only see a
                      few steps in front of me on the road.

Self-pity was an emotion foreign to the Jourdains. Milly's two short books are unsentimental, unsparing, quite free of imitative or second-hand reactions. There is no mention of her illness in *A Childhood* which describes skating, tobogganing, haymaking and exploring the dales round Ashbourne with an intensity which is the only indication that the writer could herself no longer run or climb or move at all. The scrupulous accuracy that turned so many of the Jourdains towards scholarship combined with feeling and great sensitivity in Milly to give a piercing sharpness to even the simplest recollections: terror of bogeys under the stairs, the solemn rapture of being lifted on to a drayhorse or allowed to feed worms to the hens by the vicarage gardener (a comforting character called William who was borrowed, along with the hens, by Ivy fifty years later for the opening chapter of *The Present and the Past*).

Margaret, who was six years older than Milly, is called Judith in *A Childhood* and emerges as the figure who counted more to the child than her nurse, her benign distant mother or any of her other sisters and brothers except Philip (called by his middle name of Bertrand in the book). Some of the vividest passages describe her pride and pleasure at being detailed by the daredevil Judith to climb the tallest beech tree, or take part in illicit expeditions up the steep gabled roof, crawling after Judith and clinging to her foot. It is Judith who spurs the child on, always Judith she strives to impress, Judith whose scorn is more dreaded than any adult reproof: 'Judith said contemptuously, "If you are *afraid*, the beech tree will throw you down, but if you climb to the top and are not frightened, he will hold you and not let you fall." I climbed to the top with no fear . . .'[21] The reward for feats like this one was an invitation back up the beech tree to listen to stories of ghosts, devils, tree-spirits, clandestine battles between the noble beeches and the demonic yews ('all evergreens were wicked') whose roots reached down to hell beyond the kitchen garden. This bracing relationship—between the bold, exacting, self-confident elder sister and the younger one, always timid and easily tired—persisted throughout their adult life. When Milly first realized the hopelessness of her condition, it was Margaret who persuaded her to fight despair by attending art classes in Cambridge[22] and, when Milly's hands grew too twisted even to draw, it was Margaret's example that made her turn to writing instead.

But Margaret was always more of a goad than a comforter. According to Joan Evans, Margaret's debunking instincts—the scornfulness that eventually extended to practically every person or subject she mentioned—went back to earliest childhood when an innate sense of beauty combined with a horror of sham made her reject piety, complacency, insularity, philistinism, all the unthinking orthodoxies for which her family (*'Oh* her family!' said Joan Evans bitterly) stood. Mockery had early provided relief from a harsh and demanding home life for Margaret and Philip whose revolt against the moral opportunism of their vicarage upbringing made both despise religion as unequivocally as Ivy and her own two brothers were to do a few years later in Hove. 'No good can come of it,' said Ivy long afterwards, discussing Christianity with the novelist Elizabeth Taylor. 'Its foundations are laid in fostering guilt in people—well, that obviously makes it easier for our Pastors and Masters when we are young. Margaret saw that when she was a little girl. She said to her governess, "I don't want to hear any more about that poor man," and walked out of the room.'[23]

The presence of two such cool, humorous, pacifist, atheistical (in Philip's case, downright anti-clerical) rationalists made for tension at home. Never a demonstrative family, tending always to reserve their strongest feelings for things or abstractions rather than people, the Jourdains took no small pride in virtuoso displays of grudge-bearing, will-dangling and the patient tending of feuds. Margaret and her elder brothers and sisters ('She couldn't stand any of them,' said Joan Evans) retained to the end of their lives an outstanding knack of rubbing one another up the wrong way, and Philip, too, quarrelled in the end with them all.

By all accounts it would have been hard to find two more stoutly conservative characters than Colonels Arthur and Henry Jourdain, but they were if anything outclassed by Eleanor, who put paid to attempts to impeach her own and Miss Moberly's testimony in *An*

Adventure with the ringing declaration: 'We belong to no new schools of thought: we are the daughters of English clergymen, and heartily hold and teach the faith of our fathers.' Margaret had no more patience with this sort of simple faith than Ivy's characters have with honest worth or true kindness or any other convenient formula appropriated by people attempting to put something over on others (' "Being cruel to be kind is just ordinary cruelty with an excuse made for it," said Evelyn. "And it is right that it should be more resented, as it is" '[24]). Margaret's directness from girlhood onwards had attracted a great many people besides Ivy who, constitutionally circumspect herself, delighted in stories of her friend's reckless disregard for cant or pomposity. 'There's no buckram about it' was one of Margaret's sayings,[25] denoting approval of anything plain, simple and unpretentious. 'Margaret was certainly completely unaffected,' said Herman, 'she would never affect anything; she was herself, standing, as she did, with legs slightly apart and her strange clothes, her hats with feathers, her eyeglass, and raising one eyebrow in that peculiar and inimitable manner.'[26]

It was a stance by no means easy to maintain in the last years of the nineteenth century at Oxford where girls, admitted on sufferance, were expected to keep their heads and voices well down. Conformity, humility, gratitude, hard work and juvenile meekness formed the programme enthusiastically endorsed by Eleanor Jourdain when she reached St Hugh's as Vice Principal in 1901. But Margaret as an undergraduate had insisted on following her own road rather than anyone else's. She read classics, like Ivy, but what chiefly preoccupied her—most unlike Ivy at this stage—was the latest thing in modern literature which, in the 1890s, meant the French symbolist poets. Her closest friend at Lady Margaret Hall was Janette Ranken, a statuesque beauty from a well-to-do Edinburgh family with leanings towards the arts and the theatre. They were both passionately interested in contemporary poetry ('which people weren't at Oxford in those days,' said Joan Evans, who had herself suffered throughout her career from Oxford's traditionally disparaging view of the arts). It seems likely that Margaret was not only reading but already translating Baudelaire, José de Herédia, Villiers de l'Isle-Adam and others whose work she interspersed with her own *Poems* in 1911.

She was almost certainly at work on the calendar of nature

writings eventually published by Lord Alfred Douglas as *An Out-door Breviary* in 1909; and it is noticeable that, though the most striking parts of the *Breviary* celebrate monochrome wintry land-scapes—bare downland, clear or colourless skies, grey-limbed leafless trees—in the Oxford passages it is always spring or high summer. There are uncharacteristically luxuriant descriptions of the city's towers gleaming through green leaves in Christchurch meadow on May Day, a great spendthrift red hawthorn blooming beside the Cherwell, hedgerows festooned with elder, meadow-sweet and dogroses at Iffley where Margaret found, like so many hopeful undergraduates loafing beside the river in June, that 'the passage of the long summer days seems gradually to attune the mind to expect something unusual, to wait for "that expression of hope which is called beauty".' The *Breviary*, which owes as much to mystical English nature writers like Blake or Traherne as to the French decadents, preaches the contemplation of beauty, es-pecially beauty in its more ephemeral and random aspects:

> The art of life is to accept; to notice without ever going out to see. For the strain of any purpose defeats itself and clouds the charmed moment. But purposeless, in a little we become one with the great and smooth current of existence, and undistracted. It is only in the course of aimless and repetitive sauntering that we can be permeated with the charm of light, and the secret beauty of small things.[27]

It is perhaps scarcely surprising that Eleanor Jourdain disapproved of her sister's conduct at Oxford. The cult of purposelessness, expressed in aimless and repetitive sauntering, was not likely to appeal to one who could imagine no higher goal for a woman than the education of others. Perhaps Eleanor had hoped to recruit a new member for her own school staff at Watford. At all events she took umbrage when Margaret left college in 1897 with a third class degree in classical mods, and obstinately refused to teach. Their father's death the following summer left Mrs Jourdain impover-ished and homeless, with two disabled children on her hands as well as three older, unmarried daughters. Eleanor, keeping her own head above water with difficulty and burdened for the rest of her life with the need to make provision for Milly, could hardly be ex-pected to do anything further for Margaret, who seemed to have picked the worst possible moment at which to embark on a literary career.

But none of the elder Jourdains was prepared to abandon all hope of independence, as Margaret did for nearly half her adult life, in order to live at home with the two invalids, their nurses and their elderly mother. The household moved in the autumn of 1898 to lodgings in Cambridge so that Philip might read mathematics as an undergraduate under what Norbert Wiener called the Mad Hatter's Tea Party of Trinity: Bertrand Russell (whose pronounced likeness to Tenniel's Mad Hatter was later shrewdly exploited in Philip's *The Philosophy of Mr. B*rtr*nd R*ss*ll*),* Ellis McTaggart, and the philosopher who afterwards exerted a magnetic pull on the Bloomsbury group, G. E. Moore.

Intellectually the most brilliant of all the Jourdains, Philip was also the most outgoing. To the timid and retiring Milly he seemed, like Margaret, always enviably self-assured, 'sociable and talkative and never shy'.[28] He had been an enchanting child, delicate, precocious, bright-eyed, and, by Russell's account, he had lost none of his charm when they first met during a course of lectures on mathematical logic in the winter of 1902:

> He is very ill, partially paralysed, and at first sight almost half-witted. But as soon as he begins to talk of mathematics his face shines, his eyes sparkle, he speaks with fire and ability, one forgets that he is ill, or remembers it only in passionate admiration of the triumph of mind . . . I saw his mother for a moment: she pressed my hand, I loved her, and she seemed deeply grateful to me for encouraging her son: it was a deep moment of intimacy, though not a single word was said by either of us, and I had never met her before.[29]

Philip's early years at Cambridge had been shadowed by disappointment and false starts, interrupted by an electrical cure at Heidelberg that cost him his chance of a fellowship at Trinity and quashed all hope of recovery, forcing both Philip and his sister to

---

* According to Russell, this absurd booklet with its text from the White Knight, frequent acknowledgements to Tweedledee, and set of twenty appendices pointing out correspondences between Russell's philosophy and Lewis Carroll's, was a faithful account of his conversations with Jourdain at Cambridge and afterwards. (*Autobiography of Bertrand Russell*, vol. 1, p.217.)

realize at last that their illness could only get worse. Philip failed his Tripos in 1901, settling instead for a pass degree and thereafter slowly regaining intellectual confidence, becoming runner-up for the coveted Smith's prize in 1904 and winner of the university's Allen studentship two years later. The turning point had been his meeting with Russell who sponsored him for the scholarship, guided his research into analytical mechanics and the Cantorian theory of transfinite numbers, discussed the problems of Russell's own *Principia Mathematica* and, from 1902 to 1910, traced the slow, painful growth of that magnum opus in an extraordinary series of long, close, technically detailed letters exchanged with Philip after he left Cambridge.

But Russell's revolutionary mathematical and philosophical discoveries were only part of that intense intellectual ferment at Cambridge at the turn of the century which profoundly affected Margaret, and proved a formative influence on Ivy, captivated by the same heady atmosphere a few years later through her own brother at King's. Philip became the particular friend of Sidney Waterlow (afterwards turned down by Virginia Stephen in favour of Leonard Woolf) who was dazzled, as people commonly were, by the 'vivid, brilliant, boiling over mind'[30] that impressed Philip's sisters' friends as much as his own. He was Woolf's and Lytton Strachey's contemporary at Trinity, and responded as eagerly as they did to the political, social and moral iconoclasm beginning to stir inside the college. 'Margaret was rather on the fringe of the Bloomsbury group,' said Joan Evans. 'Cambridge always counted far more for her than Oxford.' Women were only just beginning to put in a first tentative appearance on the university scene but Philip shared more than most with his mother and sisters ('Philip was so happy in the bit of life he had got, though he must have known how incomplete it was, that he simply overflowed to us'[31]), and in spite, or perhaps because of the effort entailed in coming to terms with the grim future awaiting the two youngest Jourdains, this was a time of achievement, even liberation for all of them. Milly, roused from her initial trance of black misery by Margaret, was absorbed more happily than ever again in her drawing class and her friendship with Charles Darwin's grand-daughter, Frances (who later married a Fellow of Trinity and became famous as the poet, Frances Cornford). Margaret herself took up with dons' families such as the daughters of Professor ('Dictionary') Skeat, published her first three books as editor and translator ('No one would have been more surprised than M.J. to find herself in print,' said Janette Ranken long afterwards[32]), and, by the time the family left Cambridge in September 1903, had assumed for ever the sceptical, ironic, characteristically Cambridge frame of mind—so marked in her later that friends found it hard to believe she had been at Oxford—that Ivy found irresistible.

The Jourdains settled eventually at Broadwindsor in Dorset where this strange, shabby, scholarly household was received with sympathetic amazement by the local inhabitants: 'Their view of. . . mathematical work was expressed by an old woman who used to come and work in the house sometimes: "Mr. Jardeen do and be allus writin': I s'pose it pleases he".'[33] But Broadwindsor, though small, remote, backward and not apt to change its ways for outsiders, was less inaccessible than Ashbourne, and Cambridge ties remained strong. Russell himself stopped off regularly on bicycling tours in the summer for lunch and tea, or to spend the night and sit up talking with Philip. Milly's best friend, Frances Cornford, was also a frequent guest, collaborating on various projects for which she supplied the text and Milly the illustrations (Frances' *Poems* beat *A Childhood* into print by three years, though Milly had already slipped past the post in 1906 with line drawings for Philip's *Topsy-Turvy Fairy Tales* by Somebody-or-Other with Three Illustrations by Somebody-Else). But in these years when Milly's only means of leaving the house was a donkey cart supplied by the Darwins, while Philip chugged round the village in a mechanical wheelchair, Margaret became their chief link with the outside world, undertaking commissions in London, bringing back gossip and news, suggesting outlets, helping Milly place poems with periodicals on which she herself had a foothold such as the *Nation* and *Country Life*. 'Margaret was always very good to Milly,' said Joan Evans; and Margaret seems to have accepted her role in much the same dry, disparaging, eminently practical spirit as France Ponsonby in *Daughters and Sons*, who also chose to sink her own personal resources in the family pool: 'People want some reason for not doing good. Or they would have to do it, as I have to.'[34]

It was precisely this note of contrariness in Margaret that had always infuriated her sister Eleanor, though it found a more sympathetic response in their mother who was musical and cultivated, if not intellectual, and clearly relished the teasing of her three youngest children: they called her 'Mrs Mouse' (she was tiny) and formed an alliance that was, at any rate after their father's death, far closer and more relaxed than anything their elders had known. Philip contributed a stream of comical and cautionary poems, skits and satires to the Cambridge undergraduate magazine *Granta* (including a popular series, 'Some Unconscious Humourists of the Nineteenth Century', featuring Carlyle, Wordsworth and Mrs Humphry Ward). Margaret, who never made jokes in print, pronounced magisterially in favour of prophets like Shaw and Samuel Butler (whose posthumous rehabilitation she attributed largely to a speech by the President of the British Association, Frances Cornford's father, Francis Darwin).[35] Even the devout and peaceable Milly followed the others' iconoclasm far enough to develop socialist tendencies ('The Red Flag will soon be flying over Broadwindsor at this rate,' wrote Frances approvingly in 1910).

When assorted Darwins, Cornfords, Murrays and Will Rothenstein invented a plan for dividing the entire human race according to outlook and temperament into pinks and blues, Philip instantly appropriated the system, becoming expert at spotting rare subspecies and expounding his general principles in *Granta*: nearly all artists were blue, along with all dissidents, sceptics and anyone inclined to line up behind Shaw or Butler, 'while Miss Marie Corelli and most curates are indelibly pink'.[36] Except that subsequent opinion has reversed the colour scheme, assigning pink to the radical party and blue to conservatives, the classification holds good to this day; and with it went what sounds like a useful adjunct to the novels of I. Compton-Burnett, 'a Dictionary of Received Opinions for the use of blue people who find it a tactical necessity to learn the language of the pink'.

There was no shortage of disapproving, even scandalized pinks in Broadwindsor when Margaret and Philip set about mounting their joint assault on Fleet Street and the London publishing houses. The household income had been drastically reduced in 1904 when the trust fund set up by their father for his two youngest children was wound up and his capital divided. Money was something the Jourdains begrudged one another more fiercely than anything else: Frank fell out with his family once again over it, Philip afterwards maintained that he and Milly had been landed with dud investments, Raymond (a schoolmaster who seems, like Frank, to have withdrawn from the family under some sort of cloud) was specifically cut off with nothing under the terms of his father's will. Funds, always tight, now became desperate. Eleanor Jourdain in her youth is said to have tried living for a time on a working woman's income of one pound a week, and, up till 1911 (when a year's retainer from Lenygon provided her for the first time with something approaching a living wage), Margaret scarcely earned more. Philip assessed his earnings in 1914 as £200 ('and my total private income £12'[37]); Margaret's for the same year were £83 8s 1d.

Both sums represented a vast amount of work: on Philip's part, historical, philosophical and mathematical papers in learned journals, a voluminous scientific correspondence, time-consuming duties as English editor of *The Monist* and (after 1915, when he took over from Waterlow on the editorial board) *The International Journal of Ethics*. Margaret (who wrote regularly for both Philip's periodicals, and later succeeded him briefly in both his editorial posts) was steadily acquiring a name as a translator, poet and literary critic as well as expert on decoration. But her best efforts brought in little more than enough to pay for railway fares, and family resentment (which on Eleanor's part at least was intense) must have pressed hard in the twenty years it took her, after leaving Oxford, before she could work up a sufficient income on which to leave home.

3

SUPPORT AND ENCOURAGEMENT came from friends like Janette, and Alice Dryden with whom Margaret collaborated on a revised edition of Mrs Palliser's *History of Lace* in 1902.[38] Alice, who was ten years older than Margaret, generous, witty, warm-hearted, high-spirited, fond of racing and riding to hounds, was the only child of the Northamptonshire antiquary, Sir Henry Dryden of Canons Ashby, of whom it was said that 'next only to the poet' (John Dryden had died ten years too soon to inherit Canons Ashby, which went instead to his son Erasmus in 1710), 'he was the most famous of the Drydens'.[39] A popular and notably eccentric High Sheriff, an entertaining and controversial lecturer ('he liked to shock people: by him, indeed, they rather liked to be shocked'), Sir Henry was also a learned historian, immensely knowledgeable about his own home and hospitable to interested visitors such as

Margaret. Her own expertise seems to have grown, in the wake of the lace book, from a handful of articles on lace extending into stumpwork, whitework, samplers, and so on, via embroidered hangings and Chinese wallpapers to teapots, andirons, card tables and knife cases; and, though she can hardly have envisaged her future as a furniture historian at this stage, it seems likely that, in John Cornforth's phrase, she 'started to get her eye in at Canons Ashby in the 1890s'.[40]

Sir Henry died the year after Margaret's father and Alice, forced to uproot herself from the home she had known for thirty-three years, settled eventually on Boar's Hill outside Oxford, in a house called Orchard Lee which became a convenient research base for Margaret as well as herself. The lace book proved a success, and the following year they put together an anthology, *Memorials of Old Northamptonshire*, based on Sir Henry's papers and illustrated from the pioneering photographic archive Alice had built up, driving herself and her camera round the country in a dogcart. One of Alice's cousins wrote the chapter on Dryden, leaving Margaret (who was called in on the literary side as a regular thing, whenever Alice edited further volumes in the same series) to cover lesser fry like Thomas Fuller, the historian of *England's Worthies*, a Northamptonshire man who had begun his career as a royalist divine in Broadwindsor vicarage and found himself ousted, during the civil war, by a John Pinney.

Fuller, according to Virginia Woolf's father Leslie Stephen, 'was apparently one of the first authors to make a living by the pen':[41] a point that can hardly have been lost on Margaret, starting out on the same uphill path in the same village with the same Pinney family for neighbours. The Jourdains rented Broadwindsor manor house and insisted on sitting on Sundays in the manor pew on purpose to aggravate the rightful lord of the manor, Lieutenant-Colonel (later General Sir Reginald) Pinney, who had himself taken a house in the village while waiting for tenants to vacate his family home at Racedown. But his wife was not in the least put out: Lady Pinney (born Hester Head and descended from Quaker merchant stock) was a powerful personality in her own right* and agreeably sur-

---

* Lady Pinney is said to have told her husband on their marriage that theirs should be a partnership: 'A partnership—my money shall be yours—or let us say rather, a limited company. Six months later, I had to say to him: "When I said a limited company, I did *not* make you managing director." '

prised to find a kindred spirit on her doorstep. 'She found in Margaret Jourdain a companion in mind, probably the first and only intimate woman friend she ever made,' said her daughter, young Hester, who was as impressed as her mother by 'Margaret's keen interest in everything, so different from what you might expect to find in a spinster daughter in a small country village, and even more different from the regimental wives who had been the main companions of my mother's married life'.[42]

When Colonel Pinney was posted for four years to Egypt in 1909, Margaret volunteered to keep an eye on the children—eight-year-old Hester, her younger brother Bernard and the baby Rachel —who were charmed with the arrangement. She invented new games, wrote verse plays for them to act, taught them to make up stories, read the tombstones and dance on the graves to the horror of their governess, a Miss Partridge, who complained that Margaret was bad for discipline, unseemly, irreverent, a downright unwholesome influence. The jolly, horsey, hunting Pinneys were, by Jourdain's law, as indelibly pink as Marie Corelli: Margaret and Philip Jourdain were the first professed atheists young Hester had ever encountered, and they retained for her ever afterwards a special aura of pleasure and wickedness. Margaret in particular stood for everything bold, dashing and free: 'Ask Margaret Jourdain' became a Pinney slogan. It was Margaret who supervised the decoration and furnishing when the family moved to Racedown in 1911 or 1912; Margaret who urged the elder of the two Hesters ('who, she said, was the only intelligent Pinney, and that by marriage') to take custody of the family papers; Margaret who chose a boarding school, kept by one of her old Cambridge friends, the Miss Skeats, for young Hester.

Professor Skeat was one of the eminent contributors recruited by Lord Alfred Douglas to write for the *Academy* alongside rising talent in the shape of Margaret herself, Frederick Rolfe, Siegfried Sassoon and Noel Compton-Burnett's friend and rival at King's, Rupert Brooke. Margaret's first, decidedly mannered but not undistinguished sonnet, 'Seleucis of Lesbos', was published in the *Academy* on 16 May 1908, and from then on she contributed a rapidly increasing number of poems, French translations and weekly book reviews, covering everything from Hardy's poetry to *Papuan Fairy Tales*. *An Outdoor Breviary* began serial instalments the following February, and was published by the Academy Press as a book (bound in pale blue buckram with gilt decorations, which suggests that Margaret's taste in her giddy youth was not yet as severe as it was to be later) that autumn, together with Lord Alfred Douglas' own *Sonnets* and his wife's *Poems*.

The *Academy* had been bought for Douglas in 1907 by friends vainly hoping to divert his litigious instincts, for his reputation was still highly unsavoury, though his part in the Wilde trial remained so utterly unspeakable that it is quite likely none of Margaret's neighbours in the village knew exactly what sort of a cloud he was under.* She herself was often in London, sharing Janette's rooms in Chelsea, and already more than equal to keeping her editor's disreputable proclivities sternly in check (Lady Pinney's brother, Alban Head, remembered Margaret being accosted in the Café Royal by Douglas with a potentially libellous document from his latest lawsuit which she refused to read, to her companion's lasting regret). Her own unconventionality was always strictly functional, and she disapproved then as later of sexual impropriety and the desire to shock for its own sake. But General Pinney was not alone in harbouring misgivings. Margaret's mocking air, her poetry (if not her Wildean connections) and her trips to London, her evident penury and complete failure to apologize for it, her irregular behaviour in the graveyard and still more irregular attendance at church: all these nettled pink people like the Pinneys' Miss Partridge and the vicar's daughter, Dorothy Hutchings, who reacted as ungraciously as the neighbours do in *More Women Than Men* to the spectacle of a penniless, unmarried, Oxford-educated girl obliged to work for her living:

> 'Neighbours don't seem to hold the Greek view of the nobility of suffering.'
> 'Neighbours are English,' said Felix.
> 'There is no disgrace in honest poverty.'
> 'You can't really think that. There is no point in being too Greek.'[43]

---

* Lord Alfred's editorial secretary, the young Alice Head (afterwards editor of *Woman at Home* and *Good Housekeeping*, eventually a director of *Country Life*), told me that neither she nor her mother could make out the exact nature of the scandal surrounding her editor, with whom she herself remained on excellent terms: 'They didn't tell women anything in those days,' said Miss Head.

Margaret afterwards said that Ivy had never known what it was to be poor, something she herself had known only too well 'as the hard-up-daughter of a hard-up country parson'. Her output, though not her income, had increased fivefold under Douglas who persuaded her in 1908 to turn almost wholly to literature. Margaret in these years was following in the footsteps of William and Dorothy Wordsworth whom she described scouring the country-side round Broadwindsor for subjects to write about, tramping the roads to keep warm, growing their own food ('no doubt for motives of economy almost all the meals consisted of vegetables'[44]), and generally giving rise to gossip in the village. The poet and his sister had lived in the 1790s in the Pinneys' house at Racedown on the slopes of Pilsden Hill where, just over a century later, Margaret and Milly must have spent hours, even whole days at a time, together or more likely alone, immersed in the Dorset countryside both knew and wrote about intimately, especially in its harsher and more frugal aspects. It is always the drab and the dun-coloured that please Margaret best, from the threadbare copses and luminous floodwaters of February to the last shabby garland of an autumn hedgerow ('a tattered and dusty embroidery of humble and graceless flowers, flesh-coloured hemp agrimony, flat-faced yarrow, and ragwort'[45]). The height of delight in Milly's poems is a single celandine or crocus in the grass, the feel of cold stream water, thin sunlight on glittering frost-covered hills. Perhaps she had learnt from Hardy or Wordsworth, perhaps simply from her own constricted life, the deceptive simplicity that matches an unobtrusive verse form with an equally unassuming truthful-ness:

> And still I see how clearly shines the light
> On winter branches, and how the dripping rain
> Deepens the colour on the hills, and how
> To draw those horses plodding up the lane.
>
> I know too late; my hands can do no more;
> All powerless upon my lap they lie.
> Only my sense of colour and of smell,
> And biting pain, increases till I die.[46]

There is no way of dating Milly's poems. Some clearly gather intensity from being written in retrospect, after the Jourdains had

left Dorset in 1919, but all of them have a musicality, a concentration of thought and feeling, a desolate clarity well beyond the scope
of Margaret's *Poems* (published two years before *A Childhood*).
Milly's voice, low and faint but true, belongs to an authentic poet;
Margaret's verses are accomplished but impersonal by comparison,
mannered in the contemporary aesthetic style and heavily dependent on classical or symbolist originals. Her prose in the *Breviary* is
another matter: Margaret in those days could hear Pan piping on
Pilsden Hill and take messages from the 'vague and speechless
voices of leaves', but her most nearly authentic visionary effects
come from intent, exultant, minute observation of sun, rain, cloud
or the track of the wind rushing up a dry hill pasture. She was to be
all her life a byword for scrupulous accuracy but anyone familiar
with the relentlessly prosaic style of her later writings will find it
hard to account for the fire of, say, this characteristic description of
a day on the downs:

> Towards the late afternoon, the blue has dropped away from the
> lower sky, as a dyed cloth bleaches in keen air, until a pale
> glass-like colour is left—like the very pale green panes that filled
> the church windows half a century ago—through which the huge
> sun soars downward to the shining edge of the pale-coloured
> world. It is here, in the empty Downs that Richard Jefferies'
> worship of the great sun in the heaven becomes fitly
> explicable . . .[47]

Other entries in the *Breviary* reflect the diarist's knowledge of
hangings, embroidery or jewels as clearly as her distaste for Victorian stained glass. But Margaret's habit of comparing the sky to
church windows, or autumn leaves to tapestry pictures framed and
hung up on hooks, makes it hard to pin down exactly when she
switched from being a poetical nature-lover interested in interior
decoration to a furniture historian with all mystic tendencies rigor-
ously suppressed; and it is harder still to say whether, if things had
not so drastically got the better of her, she would have changed in
any case of her own accord. Douglas sold the *Academy* at the end of
1910 which meant that Margaret's contributions abruptly ceased.
She scraped together the money for her *Poems* to come out (in a
plain paper binding this time) the following year, but a characteris-

tically bracing note from Philip points out that 'M.J.'s greatest possible net gain on this edition of 500 copies, supposing all sold . . . would be about £3'[48] (in fact Philip had failed to allow for the cost of paper covers, estimated by Hatchard at precisely £3 and 'not to be materially reduced by using cheaper paper').

It must have been abundantly clear that poetry would not pay; also, that practically anyone who could hold a pen was capable of turning out the sort of hackwork—pieces on 'Street Noises', 'England As She Is Seen', 'Literature and the Snob'—Margaret produced from time to time for papers like the London *Evening Standard*; whereas there was little competition to meet the increasing demand from periodicals like the *Connoisseur*, *Queen* and *Country Life* for the knowledgeable pieces on samplers and stumpwork that rapidly became her stock-in-trade. Margaret's services were snapped up in May, 1911, by the enterprising young decorator Francis Lenygon (who had just opened his first New York branch —eventually responsible for the Georgian craze in America—and was currently negotiating to buy Morant & Co., cabinet-makers since the reign of George IV).[49] It was a shrewd move on Lenygon's part: his subsequent reputation for expensive simplicity, purveyed with a unique combination of fashionable and historical acumen, owed much to Margaret's work in cataloguing the contents of the firm's premises at 31, Burlington Street in a pioneering book, *Furniture in England, 1660–1760*, which came out with a parallel volume on decoration in 1914. The originality of the Lenygon books lay in their recognizing, long before anyone else did, the importance of English Palladian design while insisting, again for the first time, that furniture should be studied in its decorative context.

Margaret's standing at this stage was still that of a cultivated amateur, called in 'to tidy things up on the literary side' (in Ralph Edwards' phrase) by craftsmen like Lenygon and his colleague, Colonel Mulliner, a bottle-nosed Birmingham coachbuilder whose book, *Decorative Arts in England (1760–1880)*, was also written for him by Margaret. Most of her early work was published under men's names, her own ('Mr M. Jourdain' was the translator of F. Gusman's *Pompei* in 1900 and editor of Horace in 1904 as well as author of the *Breviary* in 1909) or other people's, for Margaret, who was singularly free from personal vanity, saw no objection to Lenygon and Mulliner taking the credit for books they had hired her to write. They taught her things about cabinet-making that she could have learnt nowhere else, while she supplied them with the cachet essential in a trade so rapidly expanding and so intimately connected with intangibles like taste and class.

In the furniture field, from museums and the great auction houses down to the shadier undergrowth of dealing and faking, much depends on the sort of jockeying for position described in *Buchanan's Hotel*. Mulliner operated from rooms in the Albany on fairly bogus social credentials but he had the sixth sense that can tell a fake from the genuine article by something like divination, which was more than could be said for Margaret's other employer, Edward Hudson of *Country Life* ('the Hudson idiot' was Mulliner's phrase for him in characteristically irascible letters to Margaret[50]). Son of a printer, 'indifferently educated but avid of culture',[51] gruff, inarticulate, outwardly unprepossessing but profoundly romantic at heart, Hudson had evolved the *Country Life* formula from *Racing Illustrated* at the turn of the century when a photographer sent to take pictures of the brood mares at Sledmere is said to have come back with a photograph of the Sledmere library as well. Hudson was the first to exploit a popular craving for glamour and the picturesque that coincided exactly with his own lifelong passion for 'princely mansions and quaint old houses of long-lineaged householders'.[52] He was notoriously churlish towards employees but, though neither he nor Mulliner had any scruples about treating Margaret as a dogsbody, both knew well enough that they were on to a good thing. Her combination of erudition and integrity was a crucial factor in *Country Life*'s development from relatively naive beginnings before the First World War into what Walter Runciman called 'the keeper of the architectural conscience of the nation'.

Though the war effectively suspended Margaret's career as an all-purpose freelance, it gave her a living wage, for she was employed with Janette on government war work in London, submitting for the first and last time in her life to an office routine and staying at Janette's Chelsea boarding house (where they took up with another independent, unmarried blue-stocking, Winifred Felkin, sister to Noel Compton-Burnett's friend Elliott, who eventually introduced Margaret to Ivy). Margaret's attitude to the war was, so far as her family was concerned, a thoroughly provoking detachment. Frank was too old but Arthur, Raymond and Henry Jourdain all fought on the Western front. Margaret and Philip inclined to share Russell's unpopular pacificism,* or at least that prophetic sense of waste and destruction felt by so many Cambridge intellectuals, including Noel Compton-Burnett whose position in October 1914, outlined in letters from King's was neatly summed up by a jingle of Philip's doing the rounds from Trinity:

'Gott strafe England!' 'God save the King!'
  'God this!' 'God that!' the warring nations shout.
'Good God!' says God,
'I've got my work cut out.'[53]

But a rational response, strengthened by revulsion from jingoism, only made things harder in wartime for intellectuals not prepared to rate their own safety or comfort higher than anyone else's. Philip's initial reaction in the opening weeks of the war had been to offer his two typists, and his own services as telephonist, to the Cambridge Officers' Training Corps (to which Noel also reported with a heavy heart for military training that autumn). The rejection of both offers, together with a subsequent attempt to give skin for wounded soldiers, plunged him into a depression so black that, even eleven months later, he could still scarcely bear to read a historical account of the outbreak of hostilities in August, 1914, because 'it brought back the emotional stir-up'.[54]

Humour and an iron reticence had always been Philip's chosen armour, as they were Margaret's. Brother and sister were perhaps at their closest, professionally and intellectually if not emotionally speaking, in the war, when Philip was estranged from the rest of the family, even in some sense from Milly, whose letters after 1914 were more and more shadowed by suffering, sadness and dread. She and Philip were by now virtually helpless and the Christian submission with which she had struggled for years to contain her illness was beginning to seem to her more like spiritual defeat. But

* Philip, who published Russell's paper on 'The Ethics of War' in the *International Journal of Ethics* for January 1915 (also Margaret's account of proposals for a prospective League of Nations in October 1918), sympathized with Russell when he was first imprisoned as a pacifist and later attacked by a jingo, and sent him a set of encouragingly unpatriotic, anti-clerical and non-belligerent verses on 'The War and Christianity'. But Philip and Margaret themselves defended British war aims in strictly rational, anti-jingoist terms in *The Open Court* (January and February 1915).

the physical torpor that drove Milly towards a despairing indifference had the opposite effect on Philip, who all his life resisted each fresh depredation with a heroic refusal to dilute or diminish intellectual output combined, at times of particular stress, with a passionate outpouring of feelings he could no longer hold back. All Jourdains suppressed emotion on principle: 'You wouldn't have *scenes* in that family. It was just silence,' said Joan Evans, who had suffered more than most from the obstinacy of hostile and taciturn Jourdains.

A set of melancholy poems written when the family left Cambridge records Philip's attempts to stifle an unhappy love affair; a later attachment to a girl called Eva Loudrun at Broadwindsor in 1911 roused the united opposition of his family, including his mother whose 'unsympathetic shockedness'[55] sounds much like Margaret's reaction in middle life to any hint of sexual self-indulgence. Margaret was away that spring, working for Lenygon's in London and no doubt distancing herself so far as possible from an episode that gave the village more than its usual quota of gossip and ended, after a great many painful, sometimes explosive confrontations, with Philip moving out of his mother's house in July, to set up for himself with an attendant called Fred just outside Cambridge at Girton. The forebodings of friends like Waterlow and the Cornfords were as nothing to the commotion three years later when Philip announced his engagement to a beautiful, serious, spirited girl ten years younger than himself, Laura Insull (called 'Queen' because of her regal carriage and bearing).

Sne was a clergyman's daughter, orphaned, penniless, but not in the least daunted by onlookers like General Pinney who freely declared it was monstrous for a healthy girl and potential mother of sons to shackle herself to a tragic wreck like Philip: the outraged pink party was not mollified by her declaration that patriots who applauded the brides of wounded heroes shipped back from the trenches could hardly object to her choosing a man of brilliant intellect maimed by heredity rather than war. She and Philip met in August 1914, and fell in love almost on sight: they were married the following June in spite of threats, inducements, moral blackmail (Laura's employer, the botanist Ethel Sargant, offered her an allowance of £100 a year together with provision in her will if she would give up the marriage), and stony silence from the Jourdains: 'the absurd meanness of most of my family does make me feel that I have only you,' wrote Philip to Laura on 4 July 1915, eight days after the wedding. 'Except my mother, Milly and Margaret, who have been nice, not a single one has given me a present or even written to me about my marriage . . .'

The marriage proved a success, a source of great happiness and strength on both sides as even Miss Sargant grudgingly conceded, though Philip's family could never bring themselves to acknowledge Laura's existence. The sheer obstructionism that made them object to one another's marriages as a matter of course was sharpened, in this case, by financial anxiety, and a no less pronounced family prudishness. 'I see she is good,' wrote Milly of Laura during the engagement, 'but it shocks me more and more that he should think of marriage. Well, don't bother. I am rather glad there are people like Margaret and me who don't marry.' Margaret explained the position to young Hester: 'Margaret once told me that she had never had any desire whatever for marriage or motherhood . . . She thought this "neuter" feeling might have been a safeguard as the genes of this sad family were probably hidden in her.'[56] Raymond said the same ('Raymond was very embittered towards the end of his life and told me that the Jourdains were meant to die out,' wrote Frank's daughter Violet[57]), and Milly found marriage in general frankly baffling ('I can't really understand it except for the sake of the children, but that isn't enough, do you think?'). Margaret died, like her four sisters, unmarried, and though the five brothers each took a wife—Henry took two—only Frank had children: they were born before the disease affecting Philip and Milly had declared itself fully, and all three died (the eldest as a boy at school) without issue, so that by the middle of the century it was clear that the Jourdains, like the Compton-Burnetts—families of ten and thirteen children respectively—drew the line at reproducing themselves.

Margaret herself sided emphatically with the spinsters in Ivy's books who are apt to reply to any suggestion that marriage might mean a fuller life: 'I don't want the things it would be full of.'[58] But her *Outdoor Breviary* shows signs of a struggle much like Philip's to subdue unruly feelings in the many passages calling for strength, stoicism and self-denial, or—almost continuously in the Broadwindsor sections—celebrating the 'bare and sterile' consolations of age and autumn. The *Poems*, which appeared in 1911, are dedicated 'To Janette' who is said to have paid for them to be published, and an undated note, from Broadwindsor—'My dear Jane, Here are a few last desperate violets laid at your feet. M.J.'[59]—might possibly point to a more passionate attachment. Certainly Janette was generally agreed to have found women more attractive than men, except for her younger brother Willie who was the love of her life as he had been, at one stage, of Ernest Thesiger's: she and Ernest apparently married on the strength of their mutual adoration of Willie and, after the marriage (which was never consummated[60]), Janette ranked high on the list of Margaret's women friends whom Ivy mistrusted.

But, whether or not the *Breviary* records a specific emotional crisis, it clearly reflects the precautionary withdrawal and distancing in Margaret that made Milly and Frances grumble about her heartlessness, her mockery, the strain her presence imposed on Milly's gentler, more pliable temperament. Every withdrawal of stimulus—leaving Cambridge, Frances' marriage, Philip's removal and, still more painful, his subsequent absorption in Laura—had meant a marked physical deterioration in Milly. She had supported Philip's departure in 1911 on the grounds that, as he grew more and more hopelessly dependent, burial alive at Broadwindsor must be unendurable for his adventurous spirit; but she seems to have resigned herself to her own living death by the summer of 1915 when Philip paid his last visit to the family.

She had put away her drawing things for ever the year before and would shortly give up driving her donkey cart. 'My body is triumphing over my spirit,' she wrote to Frances when Henry left England for the Dardanelles in 1915 and, after Rupert Brooke's death at Gallipoli, 'This is a wretched letter but what can you expect from a degenerate mind? Only write to me. Your C.M.J.' Her loneliness, despair and increasing physical pain were met thereafter with a passive endurance that Margaret also fought hard to achieve in the years spent watching her sister slowly turn to stone. Milly felt her spirit shrivel within her, lamenting 'the dried-up state of my mind and body' in her very last letter in 1926 to Frances. Margaret had described the same process in the *Breviary* nearly twenty years earlier in terms that seem by comparison the height of youthful romanticism: 'What a reducing quality there is in subjecting oneself to the open air, until some quality of the spirit seems to die, as a little water dies in the sand, and one becomes passive with a wise passivity.'[61]

4

A SANDY, GRITTY DRYNESS was one of the first things people noticed about Margaret in middle age when, for all her gaiety and vigour, she struck most of her friends as embittered. So were all the Jourdains more or less, including even Philip who had for most of his life no alternative save to stifle personal feelings in work. Henry did the same when his beloved Connaught Rangers were disbanded,* and so did Frank ('My Father . . . sacrificed his family life and also his priesthood to ornithology,' wrote Violet Clifton-Smith[62]), whose monumental five-volume *Handbook of British Birds* set standards of scientific breadth and accuracy that have scarcely yet been superseded. As for Margaret, she set out quite consciously to eradicate in herself all trace of the romantic girl who had wandered the hills round Broadwindsor, seeing visions and hearing voices, communing with 'Pan of the promontories' on Pilsden Hill and fancying that birds were 'the loosened souls of a tree'. 'She made herself work at documentation,' said Joan Evans, describing the years before the First World War when Margaret had insisted on the need to cultivate flatness and factual precision. 'She trained me. She made me translate French sonnets, and so on.'

Hence presumably Margaret's own French and German translations, her editions of Horace and Diderot, the gradual ruthless elimination from her own style of any flicker of individuality or ornament. Her actual writing in the pioneering books that made her name between the wars is painfully skimpy and dull (most of them consist of a brief introductory chapter or two followed by little more than catalogue lists). Margaret frankly despised the frailty and potential fallibility involved in offering to assess or draw conclusions from original research. Her furniture articles eventually grew so desiccated—'like dry seed cake' said Dorothy Stroud, who began her career as an editorial secretary on *Country Life*—that Christopher Hussey was obliged to ginger them up in the office. He was also called in to add a graceful, explanatory preface to what ought to have been her magnum opus, *The Work of William Kent* in 1948. But

---

* As the Rangers' last commanding officer, Henry subsequently published a history of the regiment, followed by numerous pamphlets itemizing its medals, decorations, mess plate, etc.

Margaret's text consists of sixty pages in all, stitching together the admittedly meagre documentation with no attempt to interpret Kent's revolution in taste, or relate it to any historical context: one has only to compare the pedestrian prose of this official rehabilitation with the fire and indignation of her original defence of Kent, written almost forty years earlier in the first of the Lenygon books, ★ to see how far the process of suppression had gone.

It is the process Ivy described in *Daughters and Sons* when Miss Marcon, encouraging France Ponsonby to take her first faltering steps as an author, ruefully compares her own scholarly achievement with the sort of writing that is done by brains and not training:

> I have trained myself to be accurate and industrious and other low things; trained myself; that is the pity of it, for I began by being as untrained as anyone. I am not one of those people who are born trained.[63]

No more was Margaret born trained. By the time she met Ivy, she had pretty well got the better of the side of herself that survives only feebly and drily in *Buchanan's Hotel*. Twenty years of research and grinding hackwork had turned her into a pundit much in demand to sustain the growing vogue for Georgian furniture and decoration. But it was clearly impossible for Margaret to survive without patronage of one sort or another, perhaps especially in the years immediately after the First World War when she found herself for the first time, in her forties, released from family ties. For a decade and more before that she had relied on Alice and Janette for encouragement, commissions, introductions, somewhere to stay and, especially from Janette, a good deal of financial help 'delicately and unobtrusively given'.[64] But Alice married John Marcon in 1913 and went to live at Highclere near Newbury, while Janette's marriage to Ernest four years later meant that Margaret no longer possessed any fixed foothold in London. She still paid visits and

---

★ 'Had Kent worked in France, instead of England, his name would have been world-wide and examples of his craft would have been almost priceless . . . At the present day Kent is ignored by the many and harshly criticised by the few; one or two modern writers have embellished their pages with illustrations of his work, while at the same time they timidly abuse him for no apparent reason beyond lack of authority for praising him . . .' (*The Decoration and Furniture of English Mansions during the Seventeenth and Eighteenth Centuries* by Francis Lenygon, pp.36, 43 and 46.)

came up on business but her permanent base was Broadwindsor until, in 1919, her mother moved out of the manor house leaving Margaret high and dry—'*sur le pavé*', in Joan Evans' phrase—with nowhere to go and a lasting grudge against her sister Eleanor for the high-handed way in which she had broken up the family home.

What seems to have happened is that Eleanor, always autocratic and growing more so after she succeeded Miss Moberly in 1915 as Principal of St Hugh's, decided without consulting, or even telling, her sister that it would suit her personal convenience to settle the family at Oxford. She had always detested her obligatory, half-yearly visits to Broadwindsor, resenting especially the indignity of being fetched from the station in a farmer's gig, and no doubt depressed by the state of the household she found when she got there. Old Mrs Jourdain was seventy-seven in 1919, Milly by now wholly dependent on her nurse Elsie Barton. They were in no position to protest at whatever plans might be made on their behalf, being largely supported by Eleanor (well off by Jourdain standards on account of *An Adventure*), and by whatever contribution could be extracted from Frank, Raymond and Henry (Arthur, Milly's favourite brother, had been killed in France in 1918, when the family's miserly behaviour towards his widow added yet another black mark to the tally of Jourdain scandal in the village). Eleanor seized the opportunity of one of Margaret's trips to London to persuade Henry, now their mother's sole surviving trustee—classed by Margaret with Frank as the most disagreeable of all their brothers—that it was high time to transfer the family to somewhere smaller and more accessible where they might be kept more easily under her eye. They settled on 24, St Margaret's Road, Oxford, almost next door to St Hugh's: a mean little house only just big enough for Milly, her mother and the nurse with a spare room for Eleanor but none left over for Margaret.

Philip, who might have sympathized, was immersed in trouble of his own that summer. As he lay clenched ever more closely in the tightening grip of paralysis, he had started a wretched feud with Russell that began with editorial misunderstandings over money and escalated when Russell remained unconvinced by a new proof of the multiplicative axiom on which Philip had been working since 1916. The proof (since shown to be faulty) became an obsession. Driven nearly frantic by pain and by the knowledge that he lay dying with what he saw as the crown of his life's work unrecog-

nized, Philip begged Russell to visit him in September 1919, to hear
the latest addition to his proof. Russell refused (on the grounds that,
even for the sake of a dying man, it could never be right to entertain
arguments incompatible with mathematical truth), then relented
too late: Philip, who had somehow hung on all summer in hopes of
convincing Russell, was already unconscious by the time Russell's
telegram arrived and he died five days later on 1 October.[65]

Margaret, who had taken over a good deal of Philip's editorial
work in the past year, spent part of the summer travelling between
his home at Fleet in Hampshire and her mother's in St Margaret's
Road. She must have understood, perhaps shared, the 'speechless
desolation of pain' that his death meant to Milly, who was already
installed in the narrow room in North Oxford where she was to
spend the rest of her life. Many of Milly's poems describe this
suburban exile, sleepless nights of waiting for the dawn, days spent
gazing through brick walls at the imagined hills and fields of
memory. Some are prayers for death, others passionate evocations
of the countryside, still others combine both themes:

> 'Death, like a narrow stream, divides
>   That heavenly land from ours.'
>
> O only once to loose my hold, and slip
> Down the familiar bank, and feel the chill
> Of water lapping round my feet, and hear
> The sounds of distant music in the wind.
>
> And yet in dreams I know the growing fear
> Of living waves that rise and rise around,
> That grip my throat, and make it hard to bow
> My head and know what I have never known.
>
> And then I cry that I may see again
> The crocus in the grass of early Spring.

What Margaret felt is impossible to say. Though his comprehensive
History of Mathematical Thought remained unfinished, and his proof
was eventually discredited, Philip had achieved a personal fulfilment and public recognition that neither of his closest sisters had
known. For nearly a quarter of a century Margaret stood firm,

putting duty before inclination, and now the rug had been pulled from under her feet. She told Hester how deeply she disapproved of handicapped people being shut away, as Milly now was, in concealment and isolation. But Eleanor's intervention meant that Margaret could do no more for Milly; and there are indications that Milly herself found Margaret's unremitting scepticism too hard to take at the end of her life and transferred her allegiance to Eleanor. At all events, Milly's future was now out of Margaret's hands; and though in a sense it must have been a relief to be free, she was also for the first time unwanted, besides being wholly reliant on what she could earn to keep herself off the streets. It meant that she was emotionally as well as practically at a loose end when she travelled up to London in the week of Philip's funeral to move into Ivy's flat.

In so far as the various flats they shared always belonged to Ivy (whose income remained until the slump between four and five times the size of Margaret's), their alliance clearly had practical advantages, like all the other close relationships with comparatively wealthy women who were far more important to Margaret than men in both private and professional life. There was never any shortage of admirers more than happy to finance Margaret in return for what she herself (describing Kent's relationship with his patrons) called 'companionship and services'.[66] One of them even went so far as to make her an allowance of a hundred pounds a year, paid quarterly from the end of 1924, on condition that she made no attempt whatsoever to discover its source.[67] She never did, though rumour variously identified the anonymous donor as one or other of the generous and affectionate friends of whom she probably saw more between the wars than anyone else except Ivy—Lady Waechter, Lady Assheton-Smith and the Hon. Mrs Levy.

Molly Waechter was Irish, large, cheerful, expansive, somewhat disorganized but often extravagantly kind, a skilled embroidress and châtelaine of Ramsnest in Surrey where Margaret frequently stayed before the Waechter divorce in 1924; after which Molly (who moved to Buckingham Gate and was often at the Linden or Braemar Gardens flats with one or more of her three children, for whom Margaret and Ivy organized playgoing and tea parties) was in no position to make provision for others. Sybil Assheton-Smith was the childless third wife and widow of the baronet Sir Charles Assheton-Smith, stepmother of Robin and Lady Juliet Duff, owner of an exquisitely appointed house in Queen Anne's Gate (where meals were served off gilt dishes and even the cushions were medieval): a remote, even regal figure highly esteemed by the furniture trade and genuinely devoted to Margaret, who catalogued her collections, located new pieces for her, accompanied her on visits to Paris and lunched with her generally two or three times a week in the 1930s. Sybil had begun to monopolize Margaret after Nelly Levy married Basil Ionides in 1930. Before that, Margaret had been in the habit of dropping in most days at the large, convivial Lowndes Square luncheon parties served by butler and footman, after which a chauffeur would call to take Nelly on her afternoon rounds of sales rooms and dealers with Margaret, who seemed to the Levy children almost a fixture at home in the 1920s: 'She was always there. A jolly old schoolmistress, frightfully dowdy, hair in a little cowpat—part of the family really. A nice old bun.'[68] Herman claimed that Margaret told him the money came 'from dear Sybil', but in fact her secret benefactor was almost certainly Nelly Levy* attempting with characteristic generosity to lessen the financial discrepancy which seemed to furniture friends to constitute Ivy's sole hold over Margaret.

Not that Ivy's indifference to furniture necessarily precluded her taking a professional interest in Margaret: the frictions and deepening gloom of the Jourdains at home—the tensions surrounding Philip's deathbed and later erupting far more publicly round Eleanor at the close of her life—held something of the lure and lustre of a collector's item for anyone with a connoisseur's interest in families. The Jourdains moreover belonged to the world Ivy wrote about—the isolated, impoverished, small country gentry —as the Compton-Burnetts never had done. In this sense, collaboration with Margaret might be said to have proved in the end as useful to Ivy as Margaret's expertise in another field ever was to Lenygon or Hudson, Nelly or Sybil.

But Ivy, who was two years younger than Milly, belonged in many ways with the much younger girls who had always touched Margaret's heart in time of stress or discouragement. Margaret said

---

* The cheques started arriving in September 1924, before Margaret had met Lady Assheton-Smith, and they continued after her death in 1943, coming via Mrs Levy's solicitors (Raisley Moorsom thought the money came from Lady Waechter, who was said by others to have left Margaret an annuity of £100, but Lady Waechter died four years after Margaret whose annuity—which was £25—came in fact from Lady Assheton-Smith).

afterwards that Ivy looked so ill when they first met it seemed as though she could scarcely survive.[69] Ivy in 1919 had reached probably the lowest ebb of her life. She had recovered from the pneumonia of the year before but was still fast in the grip of that mental and spiritual lethargy Margaret had resisted so hard in Milly; and her invalid state—in the months, even years when she lay about the flat eating sweets, reading Wilkie Collins and silently watching Margaret's callers—certainly puzzled old friends like Janet Beresford and Arthur Waley. It sounds the sort of condition Ivy's father had once diagnosed in her mother when she, too, collapsed in her youth after prolonged strain brought on by 'family trouble' ('People could not think what had come over her. She is one of those human high-breds who will not cave in, but, if duty calls, will go on till they drop: till then, existing on their "go" rather than on their physique . . .'[70]); and something in Margaret clearly responded to Ivy's distress much as James Compton-Burnett had done to his wife's.

In later life when they had settled into the comfortable, often captious intimacy of an old married couple, Margaret always remained the active partner, the forceful, enterprising, in some ways masculine one of the two, though—in a circle much given to well-informed speculation as to its members' sex lives—their oldest friends agreed that it was frankly preposterous to picture Ivy and Margaret as lovers.* Margaret's censoriousness ruled out homosexuality as much as heterosexual frailty. 'She belonged to what my mother used to call the army of unenjoyed women,' said James Lees-Milne: 'Margaret had a very unenjoyed look about her.' If her early life had, as she said, extinguished the faintest twinge of sexual desire, her tastes, as soon as she was in a position to suit herself, ran to feather boas, pretty hats and the attentions of charming young men like Lees-Milne who (as their ranks were thinned by marriage or postings abroad) continued to the end of her life to succeed one another in waves.

But her feeling for Ivy was deep, constant and grounded in that

---

* Even Willie King, who was adept at coupling the most improbable sleeping partners, admitted that in this case it was out of the question; the only dissenting voice among Ivy's intimate friends came from Herman who tended, at any rate towards the end of his life, to see homosexuality as an almost universal condition ('The women he knew who he asserted were lesbians, Wembley Stadium would not hold,' Burkhart 2, p.44).

rush of fierce, anxious tenderness that any sign of strain in Ivy
—exhaustion after finishing a book, or a return to earlier hurts
brought back by the Second World War—could always evoke in
her friend. It explains Ivy's unexpected dependence on Margaret as
well as the dominance over her noted by so many of their visitors:
the fact that, though Ivy was the housekeeper, the one who poured
tea and dealt with the tradespeople, she was also the one who
needed to be looked after, indulged, even humoured. The protective element in their relationship was strong from the start and still
uppermost in Roger Kidd's memories of Margaret twenty years
later: 'Her consideration for Ivy was remarkable; tender, self-
denying and dignified. When Ivy was demanding, Margaret would
say, "She's like a child". She encouraged Ivy to meet new people
and introduced her to many of her museum friends.'[71]

Work was always Margaret's remedy for people in trouble. It
was presumably at Margaret's suggestion round about 1919 that
Ivy first read Samuel Butler, whose *Note-Books* affected her so
strongly that she wrote in her copy, underneath Butler's description
of people whose life is a partial death ('a long, living death-bed, so
to speak, of stagnation and nonentity'), her own terse confession: 'I
am a living witniss of this crushing lifless stagnation of the spirit'
(sic).[72] Margaret heartily endorsed Butler's exposure, in *The Way of
All Flesh*, of 'the glooms and deceptions of the English upper and
middle-class households'; and the prescription worked for Ivy as
effectively as research into jewellery had once done for Joan Evans,
or drawing classes for Milly.

Margaret gave Ivy confidence, and perhaps something more that
surfaced in the books she began writing again in the 1920s when, as
she put it, 'my brain came back'. Uncharitable characters like Emily
Herrick and Theresa Fletcher in *Pastors and Masters*, or their immediate successors Sarah Wake and Caroline Lang in *Brothers and
Sisters*, belong unmistakably to Philip Jourdain's blue party. They
make short work of received opinion; they vet themselves and each
other unmercifully for the least trace of smugness or falsity; they are
dab hands at debunking their friends; and they do it in Margaret's
voice. 'Margaret talked like a character out of Ivy's books,' said
Raisley Moorsom, who had known both ladies before they ever set
eyes on each other, and who recognized a familiar tone in *Pastors and
Masters*: 'Ivy couldn't do it then. In the end she learnt to talk like one
of her own characters.'

Their friends in the 1920s and 1930s all agreed that Margaret's 'quiet biting sparkle of wit'[73] could be far more ruthless than Ivy's. 'She was a very acid type,' said Ralph Edwards. 'Ivy wasn't bad at acidity, but Margaret was rather better.' There could be no more persuasive refutation of Ivy's first novel, *Dolores*, with its almost hysterical insistence on the cardinal importance of sacrificing one's own life to others, than the amiable selfishness first propounded in *Pastors and Masters* (' "Egotism is a gift, like anything else," said Herrick'[74]). Thereafter Margaret's doctrine of self-reliance is elaborated in every single one of Ivy's 'silly little books' as an alternative to the tyrannical excesses of far more dangerous egotists like Hetta Ponsonby in *Daughters and Sons* (or for that matter Ivy herself, in the years when she too had tried to impose her will on her younger sisters at Hove):

'Why is Aunt Hetta getting so much worse?'
'She tried to live for others,' said France, 'and people try to improve what they live for, and that is the end.'[75]

One of the best descriptions of the relationship Margaret eventually arrived at with Ivy came from Rosamond Lehmann, who had not yet met either of them when she set about analysing the work of I. Compton-Burnett in 1937: 'In each novel . . . good is embodied in the persons of independent, shrewd, rather donnish women past their youth: Nature's spinsters, if not actually unwed: for Miss Compton-Burnett does not believe in marriage. An unambiguous respect is accorded to friendships between such women.'[76] Marriage in Ivy's books provides scope above all for the love of power and the horrors that flow from it, a side of family life about which Margaret thought the less said the better. 'It cannot be said strongly enough that Ivy had *genius*, and of course Margaret had erudition —two entirely different things,' said Herman.[77]

It was a verdict Margaret could never accept without some faint sense of grievance ('*That* Mr Mortimer says Ivy's a genius . . .'[78]). Her teasing, her scorn for things in general and 'Ivy's trash' in particular, gave some indication of the price she herself had paid for her own victory over imagination and feeling, for she came after all of a long line of first-rate raconteurs. Eleanor (who owned to 'psychical gifts' descended from the family's much vaunted Huguenot stock[79]) made what amounted to a professional speciality out of tales of the supernatural; Henry's memoirs are full of tall stories (including several told by their grandfather, a friend of Walter Scott, who claimed to have seen the face of Robert the Bruce before it crumbled to dust when his tomb was opened in 1819, and once to have escaped by the skin of his teeth from an army of homicidal rats); Philip turned out a steady stream of 'Cynical Ballads', 'Dorset Stories', fairy tales and fables like 'The Fate of the Pragmatic Cock' and 'The Bergsonian Hen'. Margaret when young had once peddled a highly superior line in fantasy, rhyming nonsense and ghost stories, and no doubt the family tendency towards romancing reinforced her subsequent determination to stifle all trace of the fanciful in herself.

Certainly Eleanor's inability to distinguish very sharply between reality and illusion twice brought her to grief. *An Adventure* had made her famous, but demands by some few disobliging critics for more scientific standards of evidence had come as a nasty shock (and Mrs Sidgwick's review remained a sore point with both authors to the end of their lives). Far more damaging was the public scandal that terminated her regime at St Hugh's in 1924. She had dismissed a young history tutor, Cecilia Ady, on charges of disloyalty which boiled down to the fact that the two had never got on, whereupon half the college council resigned, together with a number of dons. Accusations of lying, spying, victimization and emotional blackmail were freely bandied about; pupils from St Hugh's were boycotted by other colleges; and, after successive interventions from parents, old students, and the university authorities, the matter was adjudicated by the Chancellor, Lord Curzon, who exonerated Miss Ady while confidently anticipating constitutional reform and 'changes in personnel' at St Hugh's. A friendly don, coming to warn Eleanor of the news, is said to have been greeted with the words: 'We've won, haven't we?'[80]. The report was dated 31 March 1924. Eleanor died of heart failure six days later, Miss Moberly maintained that she had been murdered and the *Oxford Magazine* reported her death with the tag from Tacitus, '*Felix opportunitate mortis*' (which might be roughly translated: 'Lucky for her she is dead').

Milly and her mother shared Miss Moberly's bitterness. Feelings ran high on both sides at St Hugh's, and for Milly—impotent, immobilized, tormented by physical pain as well as by grief and loss and the misery of having watched her sister publicly hounded down—the only consolation was that Eleanor had 'died fighting for what she thought right'. Laura Jourdain had used almost identical words about Philip and, whatever else the family may have felt, they might surely take pride in the invincible courage and stubbornness that had sustained both Jourdains to the end. Even Margaret, who had suffered all her life from Eleanor's domineering instincts, remained loyal in public (Miss Ady once stayed in the same hotel as Margaret and Ivy with whom there was a definite awkwardness, according to Nancy Mitford[81]), though invariably caustic in private about her sister's disasters. There was no open breach but Margaret's 'disapproving detachment' seems to have been too much for Milly, watching her own life drain away as Margaret's caught the full tide: she dedicated her poems in 1924 'To E.F.J.' and made a typically Jourdainian will two years later, distributing her minute capital with scrupulous fairness in legacies of £5 or £10 to all her surviving brothers, sister and sisters-in-law with the sole exception of Margaret. She died on 23 December 1926, aged forty-four, after a life that for all its suffering and struggle leaves an impression of singular sweetness, like the robin's song in her own poem, 'September Dawn':

> The pure chill air of dawn blows on my face,
> And in the room the sheets grow white again.
> A robin's song drops in the quiet air
> So sad and fresh and incomplete.

When her mother died, a month to the day after Milly, Margaret had long since cut her losses so far as the past was concerned. It is a moot point if Margaret talked much with Ivy, or in any but the most glancing terms, about her peculiarly sour and rancorous family life; but, if the St Hugh's affair epitomized everything she had always disliked and rejected in Eleanor, it must have confirmed her own decision to come down heavily on the side of objective, verifiable fact. Margaret's mistrust of fiction became thereafter a standing joke between herself and Ivy: 'She said none of Ivy's books made sense,' said James Lees-Milne who maintained that Margaret's powers of observation were even more frightening than Ivy's. Margaret herself seems to have admitted something of the sort to John Bush, who joined the firm of Victor Gollancz at the end of the 1940s and was reading one of Ivy's novels on top of a bus when a fellow passenger leant over and said: 'I write all her books.'[82] The stranger was Margaret Jourdain. When Hester once asked Margaret if she minded seeing her books published under the names of Lenygon and Mulliner, she said that it never mattered to her whose name was given as author. But presumably just for once, anonymously, to someone she did not know and had no expectation of meeting again, Margaret could not resist claiming credit for having made Ivy—or at least for having set her on the path towards achieving the twin goals admired by Emily Herrick: ' "I grow prouder and prouder of you, darling," said Emily. "An author and an egotist, and both of them such lovely things." '[83]

IVY

'A woman of blameless character'

I

THERE IS NO specific portrait of Margaret in Ivy's books, save perhaps for touches of her manner and looks bestowed on Maria Shelley (in *Two Worlds and Their Ways*), who is affectionately known as 'my pretty' by her husband, Sir Roderick: 'With her broad, massive frame, her crumpled weather beaten face, her prominent, greenish eyes and the signs of fifty-three years, she was no one's pretty but Sir Roderick's . . .'[1] Blunt-spoken, good-natured, able, ambitious, industrious, an altogether higher type than her husband (though often too immersed in her work to pay him more than perfunctory attention), Maria, like Margaret, is given to making notes on the backs of old envelopes and turning the table into a haystack with her papers. Nearly all the happiest marriages in Ivy's books started out, like the Shelleys', on a practical rather than romantic footing (romance being generally reserved by the husband exclusively for a first wife who died young): relaxed and restful affairs between non-combatants—sometimes more nearly refugees—who look on, often aghast, at the upheaval and wreckage of other, more strenuous lives. This was very much the case with Margaret and Ivy in the thirty years and more when, though their professional spheres remained sharply distinct, they were otherwise scarcely separated, even at parties. However querulous each might seem on occasion (and there are many stories of Ivy's bossiness, Margaret's boredom and irritation), there can be no doubt that what had begun by all accounts as a marriage of convenience became for both the central feeling of their lives.

But memories of Ivy's first love for her brother Noel remained to the end of her life so strong that few of her friends had the nerve to mention his name, let alone talk freely about him in her presence; she herself could sometimes hardly speak of him at the end of her life without tears welling up. 'Ivy very rarely put into words what was her real feeling,' said Vera Compton-Burnett. 'She put herself into her books and she was a secret otherwise, known only to herself,' said her sister Juliet. What is certain is that Ivy, who struck sensitive friends like Janet Beresford as more enigmatic but also far more emotional than Margaret, had inherited something of her mother's passionate and demanding temperament. In later life, after Margaret's death, when she would very occasionally discuss such things with a woman friend, she talked to Sonia Orwell about sexual passion with a depth, thoroughness and intimacy that left her ostensibly more experienced interlocutor greatly shaken.[2] Ivy made it clear to Sonia that she had never actually made love; and she discussed with another young married friend, Barbara Robinson,[3] the cost of the First World War in sexual frustration and deprivation for a whole generation of women: ' "Men can't do without it, you know," Ivy said with a bleak look. "Women have to" .'*

Of the two great affairs of her life, the first had ended tragically with Noel's marriage and death while the second, for all its apparent smooth running, seems to have involved some sort of initial explosion that left a residue still smouldering half a century later. When Margaret first moved in with Ivy, their mutual attachment had been keenly resented by Winifred Felkin (who seems never to have recovered entirely from her sense of exclusion), and also perhaps by Janette, whose devotion to Margaret remained unimpaired by a marriage so unexacting on both sides that a great many of Ernest's friends never suspected him of having a wife at all. But the friendship was still more trying for Joan Evans, who would dearly have liked the privilege of providing a flat for Margaret herself at the end of the First World War. Newly down from Oxford, far better off than Ivy and still deeply under Margaret's

* 'In judging Ivy's sexual proclivities, I should at once make a distinction between homoerotic and homophile . . . ,' wrote her friend, the novelist Francis King (who put Ivy in the second category): 'All this would not be worth probing were it not that Ivy wrote about sexual passion so convincingly—far better than D. H. Lawrence. This is one of the miracles of her art: she was writing about something which she herself had never experienced except (where novelists often experience things most intensely) in her imagination.' (Letter to H.S., 26 June 1983.)

spell, Joan was miserably lonely in her mother's large, grand, unfriendly house in North Kensington. With her big black hats, her celebrated brother and scholarly father, her aura of intellectual as well as material riches, she seemed wonderfully dashing in those days to Margaret's other protégée, the schoolgirl Hester Pinney; and perhaps she seemed something of a menace to Ivy who shared neither her professional interest in Margaret's fields of decoration and jewellery, nor her close links with the Jourdain family.

Joan for her part thought Ivy common, nowhere near Margaret's equal in brains let alone breeding, and almost criminally indifferent to the beautiful things Margaret prized above all else ('That was the basis of what I am bound to call the tragedy between them,' said Joan, who put Margaret's coldness and dryness in later life down solely to Ivy's stranglehold on her spirit). For a time the three got on well enough. But Joan, who prided herself on being probably the only person ever to have made friends with both Margaret and Eleanor Jourdain, began spending more and more time at St Hugh's as one of the makeshift tutorial staff hastily assembled at the end of 1923 to tide the college over when reputable dons withdrew their services (a stink bomb[4] let off in Miss Evans' room signified the students' indignant rejection of this arrangement).

Always the Principal's staunch supporter, Joan herself came to think that 'the balance of Miss Jourdain's mind was disturbed' and tried desperately to persuade her to resign, even providing her in secret with a substantial sum of money on which to do so. It proved an unwise move for, when Eleanor died on 6 April 1924, she was found to have left everything (except her shares which went to Henry as executor, with instructions to hold them in reserve for her mother and Milly) to Joan, including the family jewellery. Margaret was outraged: the Jourdain pieces, though pretty, were not particularly valuable (unlike Joan's own extensive collection which Margaret had written up in *Queen* that April and which eventually formed the nucleus of the V&A's holdings) but Margaret, never inclined to concede Eleanor's superior claims as the eldest daughter, had always been especially fond of jewellery. 'And this was where Ivy was so clever—Ivy said I had nabbed the lot. She persuaded Margaret to write to my mother,' said Joan, who felt herself hopelessly outmanoeuvred ('I was a sitting bird') by what seemed masterly tactics on Ivy's part. Harassed, isolated, worn down by the strain of the St Hugh's debacle, Joan had no one in whom to confide her own case (which was that the solicitor, having drawn the will 'in an old-fashioned way', had provided her with a list of recipients among whom Eleanor had meant her possessions to be distributed), except Henry Jourdain who first agreed to explain matters to Margaret but afterwards thought better of his offer without telling Joan.

Margaret refused to see her; Lady Evans (whose horror of drawing on capital made it impossible for her daughter to explain what she had done to put Eleanor under an obligation) took Margaret's part; Milly and her mother were unbudgeable on Eleanor's side, and in any case so distraught by this time as to be past intervening with anyone. Margaret was implacable. She never spoke to Joan again, went out of her way to give a hostile review twenty-five years later to her mediaeval volume of the Oxford history of art, and generally saw to it that the feud remained undimmed to the last. Joan detested Ivy—'poison Ivy'—to the end of her life. As for Ivy, her feelings, though never overt, were still palpable long after Margaret's death when Madge Garland inadvertently mentioned a book by Joan Evans: 'Ivy said nothing. But I knew that I had stubbed my toe. I knew I must never, never mention that name again. The temperature dropped to freezing point.'[5]

Ivy's jealousy of Margaret was always intense, and quite distinct from envy (far from resenting Margaret's fame, Ivy went to considerable lengths to play down her own as soon as it gave signs of becoming a sore point with her friend). It showed itself rather in her evident unhappiness whenever a new admirer made a dead set at Margaret, her dread at being left out (hence Ivy's invariable inclusion in all but the most tedious, technical furniture visits), the inner trepidation that made the prospect of even a brief separation from Margaret seem almost insupportable. She made no attempt to conceal her feelings from close friends like Herman, who said Ivy always insisted that jealousy was the dominant motive in human behaviour. He backed vanity himself; and the two would sit together on winter evenings after tea, with the lamps unlit in the bare, high-ceilinged Braemar Mansions drawing room, dissecting their friends in the light of their respective theories and sternly contradicting one another's diagnoses: 'We would sit there like the fates with their scissors, Ivy saying "Jealousy!" and I would say "Vanity!"'[6] It sounds a melancholy scene, borne out by the many other friends who were also well aware by involuntary signs and promptings of the jealous nature Ivy kept firmly in check. It was presumably what Ivy meant when she said that the character in fiction with whom she most strongly identified was Charlotte Mullen,[7] the jealous, tyrannical, eventually murderous heroine of that strange and powerful novel, *The Real Charlotte* (1894) by O. Œ. Somerville and Martin Ross.

It is at first sight a disconcerting claim. Charlotte Mullen is a jolly old Irish eccentric—drab, squat, grasping and almost grotesquely plain, famous in the Lismoyle neighbourhood for her cutting tongue and racy stories, but otherwise widely regarded as a thoroughly amiable stout party: a view shared even by the few who, like Charlotte's pretty young cousin Francie, are uneasily, indeed subconsciously aware of 'the weight of the real Charlotte's will and the terror of her personality'.[8] The book shows how, without in the least disturbing her reputation for harmless goodwill, Charlotte very nearly kills Francie (for marrying the man Miss Mullen had in mind for herself), and actually brings off the death of a previous rival in a scene strikingly like the one in which Josephine Napier also gets away with murder in *More Women Than Men*.

More Women Than Men (last of the four high-spirited early novels, after which Ivy set about coming more seriously to grips with the infinite varieties of human aggression that preoccupied her for the rest of her life) is a work of transition and something of a freak, the jerkiest and in some ways the least satisfactory of all Ivy's novels. For all its rather startling modernity of tone, the plot turns on the machinery of Victorian melodrama—one sub-plot revolving round a tall, dark, veiled stranger coming out of the night to revive memories of an ancient wrong, another round an illegitimate son reunited after twenty years with his long-lost mother ('Oscar Wilde is not so much borrowed from as contributed to,' wrote Asquith's daughter, Elizabeth Bibesco, at the time[9]). It also served as a convenient depository for various still more disparate oddments: its central character, Josephine Napier, for instance, clearly owes much to Eleanor Jourdain. Both are exceptionally efficient headmistresses of flourishing girls' schools worked up from scratch entirely by the prodigious industry of their respective founders (both had started modestly on capital borrowed from a friend, Josephine with twelve pupils, Eleanor at Corran with six[10]). Each attaches supreme, self-congratulatory importance to the education of girls (and hence to her own solemn, even semi-sacred role as its guardian and dispenser), and each is apt to make short work of facts that contradict or interfere with her own sovereign rule. Each functions in her middle fifties on the same inflammable mixture of vanity, touchiness, genuine concern for others shading into authoritarian control, and an appetite for flattery fed shamelessly by the more sycophantic members of her staff: Josephine's wheedling manner, covering a ruthlessness she barely troubles to conceal in private, closely corresponds to first-hand accounts of the almost hypnotic hold Eleanor Jourdain established over her own 'favourites' like Joan Evans.

But, however much Ivy may have amused herself at Eleanor's expense, she did it for fun, in the same casual spirit as she had once by her own account 'made use of' her Uncle Robert and Aunt Lizzie Blackie in *Dolores*, 'just to give a superficial touch to the personalities'.[11] Borrowing so much from Eleanor seems to have been, like the mock Victorian setting, yet another device to distract attention from undercurrents in *More Women Than Men* that remain too close for comfort to its author's own home life. For, at a deeper level and perhaps more directly than any of the other tyrants, Josephine derives ultimately from Ivy herself. The core of the book is its exploration—part humorous, part painfully explicit—of Josephine's passionate, possessive love for her nephew and adopted son, Gabriel Swift, who rouses in his formidable relative a disconcerting girlishness expressed in her constant complacent daydreaming of his masterfulness ('He does not let me forget it. He is my masculine companion, my protector'[12]), his jealousy, her own submission to his lover-like caprices:

> 'You will find it a change when he marries,' said Miss Rosetti.
> 'I must recognise that I have no prospect of such a change. His attitude towards me must keep me a prisoner: I don't know what any young woman would say to it. Well, I must remember that the tie of blood between us is not of the deepest kind. Anyhow, it is put aside by my young gentleman, in determining the basis of our intercourse. I am not his aunt any more than any other woman.'[13]

It is the sort of fatal boast bound, in literature at least, to be taken up by fate. Gabriel's prompt announcement of his engagement to the young Ruth Giffard turns Josephine—with her careful smile and hands trembling beneath her desk—into a monster at once pitiless and pitiful in her successive attempts to bully, override and ridicule the young couple, followed by her resolute refusal to acknowledge or discuss their marriage plans. Bottled-up emotion makes her pick a wretched quarrel with Gabriel on his wedding morning which, in Josephine's subsequent account of the affair to her senior staff, somehow re-emerges as a triumph for herself, with Gabriel ('he . . . fussed and fumed, and almost forgot to go to his own wedding'[14]) cast once again in his old role as jealous lover: 'I might have been the bride instead of her imminent aunt-in-law.' As so often with Ivy's tyrants, there is something irresistible about the sheer impudence of this reversal, whereby Josephine's humiliation is not so much accepted as abolished and her raging jealousy reconstrued as a fond, maternal indulgence towards the luckless Ruth: 'I daresay she found me a great rock to come up against; a formidable bulwark, built out of lifelong feelings; offered to her as an allurement, poor child, when she could only see it as a menace.'[15]

2

PEOPLE WHO KNEW IVY well in the First World War, when her younger brother Noel became engaged to Tertia Beresford, used similar terms to describe what happened. 'Tertia found Ivy like a great rock,' said her sister-in-law Janet Beresford; and according to Vera Compton-Burnett, 'Tertia *didn't like* Ivy at all.'[16] 'So far as I remember Ivy made no mention of it [the future],' said Vera, discussing the unhappy months leading up to Noel's marriage and his posting to France in 1915: 'Silence was a weapon.' But Ivy, who played no part in Noel's hurried wedding preparations and did not attend the ceremony, afterwards made the best of a bad job, providing a home for Tertia in London, steadying her alarmingly susceptible nerves, and generally keeping an eye on her for Noel's sake in the dreadful winter and spring of 1916 which he spent in the trenches. Vera described Ivy's attitude to Tertia in these months and later as 'motherly almost'. 'Ivy helped them all through the marriage time,' said the Beresfords' old friend, Eva Fox; and, when Tertia swallowed sleeping tablets on learning of Noel's death, Ivy naturally took charge, finding a nursing home for the half-demented Tertia, sitting with her almost every day for well over a year, gradually pulling her through the breakdown that followed her unsuccessful suicide by an exertion of will for which her sister-in-law 'was not grateful . . . at all'.

When Ruth collapses in *More Women Than Men*, taking to her bed soon after the honeymoon under the strain of a renewed 'contest with Josephine',[17] it is Josephine who assumes control, calls a truce to the hostilities, sends Gabriel away and nurses his wife through pneumonia with tireless strength and devotion, sitting up night after night by her bedside and listening to her 'delirious murmurs' ('I cannot go to meet him now I am ill; but when I am well, I will go to him; and nobody shall watch us. We will tell her not to watch us'[18]). This is the scene in which Josephine, yielding like Charlotte Mullen to a sudden murderous impulse, lifts her half-conscious patient into the icy draught from an open window, relenting —again like Charlotte—almost at once in response to the girl's helpless appeal. In each case the victim dies,* leaving her tormentor appalled, grief-stricken (both Josephine and Charlotte weep copiously at the respective funerals), and rather rapidly reconciled to what comes to seem an unexpected stroke of luck. Neither at any point betrays the faintest sign of either guilt or satisfaction: 'The movements of Charlotte's character . . . were akin to those of some amphibious thing, whose strong, darting course under the water is only marked by a bubble or two, and it required an animal instinct to note them.'[19]

This sort of character movement, caught and pinned in its most intimate, infinitesimal workings, was what interested Ivy above all, though she approached it by very different methods from Somer-ville and Ross's comparatively conventional, if assured and subtle treatment: where they note the bubbles, Ivy learnt eventually to reproduce the darting course of the subconscious mind itself in the strange, supple, highly-charged and passionate dialogue of her mature writing. But the direct authorial intervention and explana-tion she later almost entirely discarded is still occasionally invoked in *More Women Than Men*, at moments of crisis such as the one towards the end of the book where Felix Bacon (who has by this time supplanted Gabriel in Josephine's affections) comes in his turn to tell her of his own impending marriage: 'Josephine looked from

---

* Charlotte's rival is a semi-invalid with a weak heart who dies of a heart attack because Charlotte denied her the medicinal drops that would have saved her life. (*The Real Charlotte*, chapter 32.)

him to Helen, as if she hardly followed his words. Afterwards she seemed to remember hearing her own voice, coming after a crash and through the ensuing din.'[20]

News of the engagement of a brother or close relative (Josephine calls herself Gabriel's 'aunt-sister'[21]), falling out of the blue with shattering force, is a recurrent motif in Ivy's books. In the next novel but one, *Daughters and Sons* (1937), it destroys the close relationship between the middle-aged brother and sister, John and Hetta Ponsonby: John's unexpected engagement to a comparative stranger drives Hetta (who has held out against the match in stubborn silence like Josephine) to stage a fake suicide in a last, vain attempt to teach her brother a lesson. In the novel after that, *A Family and a Fortune* (1939), Edgar and Dudley Gaveston find the mutual devotion of a lifetime shattered by Dudley's violent reaction to his brother's marriage to Maria Sloane ('Dudley looked at her and met her eyes, and in a moment they seemed to be ranged on opposite sides, contending for Edgar'[22]). Dudley, who had first proposed marrying Maria himself, had ceded her quite amicably to Edgar. It is the spectacle of his brother's love directed to another that turns Dudley from a tolerant, calm, sceptical observer into a raging fury:

> Maria stood apart, feeling she had nothing to do with the scene, that she must grope for its cause in a depth where different beings moved and breathed in a different air. The present seemed a surface scene, acted over a seething life, which had been calmed but never dead. She saw herself treading with care lest the surface break and release the hidden flood, felt that she learned at that moment how to do it, and would ever afterwards know. She did not turn to her husband, did not move or touch him. The tumult in his soul must die, the life behind him sink back into the depths, before they could meet on the level they were to know . . .[23]

This uncharacteristically explicit passage, describing the emotional shambles of the human heart that was to become Ivy's especial province, is perhaps the nearest she ever came to a manifesto (its language and imagery are closely paralleled in the actual manifesto issued on her behalf in 1956 by that doyenne of the French *nouveau roman*, Nathalie Sarraute[24]); and it sprang from a knot of ideas intimately associated with her own personal experience. The scene between the two Gavestons ends with Dudley leaving the house alone on a suicidal flight through the snow, contracting 'trouble with the lungs'[25] and very nearly dying in an episode based on Ivy's own critical illness in the winter of 1918. The course and circumstances of her pneumonia—the bitterly cold weather, the coughing, fever, delirium, weakness, the frantic attempts to get out of bed, the final crisis following a seemingly endless struggle for breath—are repeated in both Ruth's and Dudley's illnesses, and again in Horace Lamb's at the end of *Manservant and Maidservant* in 1947 (a collapse also precipitated by a jealous contest over a near-sibling*); and there can be no doubt that Ivy's return to health was a matter of emotional as much as physical recovery, as it is for Horace Lamb, and still more for Dudley Gaveston:

> The change was more rapid in his mind than his body . . . The threat of death with its lesson of what he had to lose, had shown him that life as he had lived it was enough. He asked no more than he had, chose to have only this. His own personality, free of the strain and effort of the last months, was as full and natural as it had been in his youth . . .[26]

Ivy's illness, too, marked a kind of release or abdication, the point at which she split her life in two, finally disclaiming any further attempt at domination in that clash of desire and will that had proved so ruinous for all the Compton-Burnetts at Hove. She had loved Noel with the passion and tenacity of an intensely emotional nature that had been denied all other outlet. He never failed her throughout the bleakest period of her adult life, the years of tyranny and isolation that had set in for the whole family with their father's death and closed over them completely when Guy died, a week before Ivy's twenty-first birthday in 1905. For the next ten years Noel had been her only comfort; but however hard it may have been to bear the news of his engagement—harder still to witness, as Ivy did 'all through the marriage time', his exclusive absorption in Tertia—nothing could in the end destroy a relationship far closer at bottom to the mutual security and trust taken for granted, in almost

---

* The outsider who comes between Horace and Mortimer Lamb (first cousins, born in the same house and brought up together from infancy) is Horace's wife Charlotte, whose proposed elopement with Mortimer eventually comes to nothing to the undisguised relief of both cousins, each having by this time realized (M & M, pp.174 and 212) that losing the other is what he minds most of all.

every single one of her books, between brother and sister than to the bullying, rivalrous, overtly sexual domination Josephine attempts to establish over Gabriel.

Whatever her own choice might have been in the matter, circumstances had ensured that Ivy's love for Noel approximated less to the Wordsworthian model (Ivy herself stoutly maintained that William and his sister Dorothy had been lovers[27]) than to the Byronic, or at any rate to the valedictory mood of Byron's letter to his sister Augusta after their final parting in 1816:

> What a fool I was to marry, and *you* not very wise, my dear. We might have lived so single and so happy as old maids and bachelors. I shall never find anyone like you, nor you (vain as it may seem) like me . . . Had you but been a Nun, and I a Monk, that we might have talked through a grating instead of across the sea—no matter. My voice and my heart are ever thine . . .[28]

Incest remained always a welcome topic for discussion in Ivy's drawing room along with other forms of sexual obsession, transvestism and homosexuality. Lust in her books is glimpsed generally in incestuous or other furtive, illicit couplings—one thinks of Grant Edgeworth seducing his uncle's young wife by moonlight in *A House and Its Head*, Teresa Calderon locked in her father's embrace in *Elders and Betters*—or, among the relaxed and tolerant intellectuals of *More Women Than Men*, in Felix Bacon's sitting on Jonathan's knee, Maria Rosetti nuzzling Miss Luke in the corridor on her way to Helen Keats' bedroom, before finding at last a less casual gratification in Josephine's arms:

> 'I think we might call you masculine, Miss Rosetti,' said Mrs Chattaway . . .
> Miss Rosetti was silent.
> 'Miss Munday and I can only claim to be neuter,' said Miss Luke.[29]

Miss Munday, the senior English mistress at Josephine Napier's school, is the origin of all the shrewd, watchful, funny-looking governesses in Ivy's later books, a pattern her creator evidently approved in life as well as art; indeed Ivy used Margaret's phrase and Miss Munday's—'We are neutrals'[30]—when discussing sex in connection with herself and Margaret. She explained that a neutral stance gave her greatly increased objectivity, as it does to so many alarmingly observant spectators in her books:

> 'I have a great knowledge of life,' said Miss Munday.
> 'If I may say so, I have noticed it,' said Josephine. 'And again if I may say so, I have noticed it increasing.'
> 'You may say so again,' said Miss Munday.[31]

The drawback to the blameless and contented life of anyone whose interest in human affairs is largely confined to observation and deduction is of course its dullness; and there was perpetual grumbling among Margaret's visitors (and later Ivy's own fans) about Ivy's relentless small talk, her insularity, domesticity, and insistence on a routine unbroken by anything more exciting than a banting programme. Tameness and insipidity are part of the price willingly paid by people in her books who have opted out of, or been worsted in, the power struggle: bystanders like the Scropes in *The Present and the Past* ('We have had such a dear little, narrow life. Will Catherine broaden and enrich it? I couldn't bear a wealth of experience'[32]), or strained and wary survivors unexpectedly released from a tyrant's orbit like the Ponsonbys who find themselves, after Sabine's death in *Daughters and Sons*, contemplating with something not unlike dismay 'a future flat, dim, smooth, without extremes'.[33] The vitality and recklessness of unscrupulous egotists like Sabine Ponsonby or Josephine Napier have a certain splendour acknowledged even by their victims: hence Ivy's own considerable respect and sympathy for her tyrants, her defensive loyalty when horrified reviewers complained that their behaviour was exacerbated by her own apparent readiness to condone it: 'The *New Statesman* wanted wickedness to be punished, but my point is that it is not punished, and that is why it is natural to be guilty of it. When it is likely to be punished, most of us avoid it.'[34]

'People say that things don't happen like they do in my books,' said Ivy, discussing family life with Janet Beresford: 'Believe me, Janet, *they do*.'[35] By 1933, when she finished *More Women Than Men*, Ivy had taken steps to see that things—at any rate unmanageable, explosive things—no longer happened to her; but, if she herself had settled for the flat, dim, smooth future of non-participants like Miss Munday, it was no doubt because she recognized in herself so much of Josephine. *More Women Than Men* is the novel in which she first broached a particularly sharp-edged set of associations—possessive attachment to a brother or other close relative giving rise, when thwarted, to murderous or suicidal impulses followed by a dangerous bout of pneumonia; and it is also the only one that propounds, in its cheerful, comical dénouement, something very like Ivy's own eventual solution to her life.

' "Josephine is built on a large scale," said Gabriel. "She is powerful for both good and bad." '[36] Her dealings with Gabriel and Ruth show her at her worst: passionate, rapacious, grasping, fatally ignorant of the true nature of the predatory instincts that make her a liability to herself and others. The most she will admit, in response to Felix Bacon's shamelessly inquisitive probing on the wedding day, is that people might be pardoned for thinking Gabriel's bride unworthy of him (Felix's reply is characteristically extreme: 'I don't think we ought to be pardoned. My feelings, when I think about it, are quite unpardonable.'[37]) Practically every one of Ivy's books revolves around a protagonist of ferocious energy operating sub- or half-consciously with catastrophic consequences for the weaker or dependent members of his or her household; but none of the later tyrants is put through anything quite like the obstacle course devised for Josephine whose heroics are baulked at every turn by the persistent frivolity of Felix (and, to a lesser extent, Maria).

Felix's brazen curiosity and bland comments, Maria's forthrightness, their evident admiration and no less evident grasp of the squalid tangle of emotions Josephine tries frantically to keep even from herself: all these combine to steer Josephine away from her state of perilous innocence, in which suppressed tensions are always apt to break out in violence, towards the relaxed and conscious concealment practised, in Ivy's books, by those only too well acquainted with their own unpardonable feelings. The change in Josephine is signalled by her reaction to a second crisis that parallels the first in everything except its ending. When Felix (who has consoled her for the loss of Gabriel) himself in turn eludes her grasp by marrying another, the dazed and shaken Josephine for the first time deliberately confronts her inner turmoil, curbing her retaliatory instincts and gracefully relinquishing all claim to Felix in a practical demonstration of his own theory, put forward long before when he followed her out of the school staff room on Gabriel's wedding day:

> I could not stay with women who have no sorrow to hide, and not enough to hide of anything else. I am ill at ease with people whose lives are an open book. There is so much in me that must at all costs be hidden.[38]

Josephine was from the start an open book to Felix: his triumph is to make her read it too. Ivy's moral, in so far as she can be said to teach one, is always the same: that anyone who reads him or herself as clearly as Felix and Maria remains thereafter, to other people's prying eyes, a closed book. The division runs invariably between prying eyes—her bystanders, and open books—her tyrants; and the reason *More Women Than Men* is finally a comedy is that Josephine, unlike so many of the later tyrants, is brought to read what in herself must at all costs be hidden.

In so far as any single person might be held responsible for enabling Ivy to do the same, it was Samuel Butler; and the similarities between Butler and Felix Bacon—in their views, circumstances and family background—are too many and too striking to be accidental. Ivy's debt to Butler was immense and, judging by her pencilled markings in the margins of his *Note-Books*,[39] it had been in the first instance personal rather than literary. He had taught her at least as much about her family and herself as about how both might be exploited in her books, and his influence is nowhere so specifically acknowledged as in her humorous variation—in the persons of Felix and his father in *More Women Than Men*—on Butler's relationship with his own notoriously despotic, huffy and resentful father, Canon Butler, the original of Theodore Pontifex in *The Way of All Flesh*.

Felix Bacon, like Samuel Butler, is supported by his father under constant threat of having his allowance cut down or withdrawn altogether:

> 'My father has written to me for my birthday,' said Felix . . . 'He congratulates me on completing my fortieth year . . . He says it is absurd to be doing nothing at that age . . . Do I realise that he has paid for every meal that I have eaten? I had not actually realised it, meal by meal; he must be always thinking about food. That I

have been a daily expense to him? Of course, it is a daily expense to pay for a person's meals; but he does not really consider them; it is a false implication. I don't know anyone who thinks less about his child's meals.'[40]

For twenty-two years Felix has in turn kept his friend Jonathan Napier (the fact that the unscrupulous Charles Pauli lived off Butler for more than twice that long was one of the Canon's many grievances against his son). Sir Robert Bacon, Felix's father, might almost be said to make a third in this ménage with Jonathan, an invisible but far from silent presence registering permanent protest in the name of backwoods conservatism, intolerance and religious decency. Felix's lack of occupation or earnings, his supposed effeminacy and epicurean extravagance in the matter of food and tailor's bills, his thoroughly suspect morals all serve as a constant irritation to Sir Robert who is not above the sort of emotional blackmail the Canon regularly applied to Sam.* It is Felix's successful application for the post of drawing master at Josephine's school that proves the last straw for his father, just as Sam's proposal to adopt drawing as a profession had done for his.†

But the Bacons' likeness to the Butlers sustains a severe jolt when Sir Robert, putting in his first actual appearance at the school speech day, turns out to be more than a match for his son in point of humour, gallantry and charm. Felix's and his father's mutual pride in one another is as fetching as their mutual disparagement (' "He says that in your view he might be a woman," said Miss Munday in a plaintive tone. "A father is disposed to take a hopeful view of his son," said Sir Robert, bowing as he turned away'[41]); and both are

---

* Both fathers, for instance, make a point of blaming their wives' deaths on inconsiderate or downright callous behaviour by their respective sons (MWTM, p.25 and *Samuel Butler. A Memoir* by H. F. Jones, Macmillan, 1919. Vol. 1, p.188).

† 'Dear Sam, If you chose to act in utter contradiction of our judgement and wishes and that before having acquired the slightest knowledge of your powers which I see you overrate in other points, you can of course act as you like. But I think it right to say that not one penny will you receive from me after your Michaelmas payment till you come to your senses . . .' (Letter from Canon Butler, 9 May 1859.)

Compare the strikingly similar threatening letter and telephone call from Sir Robert Bacon to his own erring son in the second and third chapters of *More Women Than Men.*

rooted in an affection that surfaces quite openly during Sir Robert's
last illness, making their final parting—with its mixture of genuine
grief, surprise, tenderness and habitual reticence—among the
finest deathbed scenes Ivy ever wrote. Its function, in this most
schematic of all her novels, was perhaps partly valedictory (Butler
after all had struggled for much of his life in vain to elicit from his
father some sign of the fondness and goodwill Felix ultimately finds
in his), partly experimental: a practical application of Butler's
theory (which Ivy marked with a pencil in the margin of her copy of
his *Note-Books*) that 'Virtue has never yet been adequately represented by any who have had any claim to be considered virtuous. It
is the sub-vicious who best understand virtue . . .'

Felix, along with his many collateral descendants in Ivy's books,
provides a pretty fair working model of what Ivy and Butler
understood by virtue. For all his flippancy, shallowness and affecta-
tion, his vanity and showing off ('But, seriously, do you not think
him a very brilliant and polished man?' 'We could not think it more
seriously than we do'[42]), Felix's influence on Josephine is wholly
good. His inquisitiveness—the poking and prying that gradually
drain off her pent-up vehemence—is a form of tact. His fascination
with his own and his friends' appearance, age, tastes and dress
(none of Ivy's other novels is anywhere near so clothes-conscious as
More Women Than Men) helps Josephine evolve a cover as impenetrable as his own, a manner far removed from the reproving
stiffness of her very first interview with Felix:

> 'Shall we have a gossip about your staff?'
> 'No!' said Josephine. 'When you have known me a little
> longer, you will know that my mistresses, in their presence and
> in their absence, are safe with me. I hope I could say that of all my
> friends.'
> 'I hoped you could not. But it is interesting that they would not
> be safe, if we had the gossip. They must have treated you fully as
> a friend. I almost feel we have had it.'[43]

3

'SOMETIMES ONE TAKES a real person for a mounting block. Only for a
mounting block, that is all,' said Ivy when asked where she got her
material;[44] and clearly Samuel Butler provided the same sort of

mounting block for Felix as Eleanor Jourdain for Josephine. But if in a deeper sense Ivy herself stands behind Josephine, then behind Felix stands her friend Herman Schrijver. It is not simply that Felix reproduces many of Herman's turns of phrase and mannerisms, his dancing gait, green eyes and penchant for formal Savile Row suits. Herman also gave his gregariousness, social poise and sunny temper, his gallantry to older women (almost a professional qualification in the decorator's trade), the relaxed, teasing, flattering approach that goes so far to disarm Josephine, calming her inner turmoil as effectively as it thaws her external constraint by making her laugh, and let him off small things like going home to dress for dinner:

'Stay by all means. Your clothes do not matter at all.'
'I noticed that you thought that about clothes; and I see that your clothes did not matter; but I don't think mine can be dismissed like that.'[45]

Exchanges like this one catch the tone of Ivy's London drawing room between the wars much as discussions between the three young Staces in *Brothers and Sisters* (published four years earlier) had drawn on memories of Ivy talking with her two brothers about their mother's tyrannical excesses at Hove. The original in each case supplied what was to become one of the basic patterns of Ivy's fiction. Felix is less an individual portrait ('People are too flat in life to go straight into a book,' said Ivy[46]) than a distillation of all that Herman, and people like him, stood for in Ivy's life by way of diversion, consolation, sympathy and understanding. She prized especially their captivating frankness, and the corresponding skill at side-stepping emotional entanglements that enables Felix to give Josephine the slip as soon as her feeling for him shows signs of heading for the rocks.

He represents perhaps more directly than any other single character in Ivy's books the discreetly homosexual element among her friends and Margaret's, the shrewd, uncharitable, high camp contingent always to the fore among connoisseurs and collectors, dealers and decorators, people who attach the utmost importance to style and artifice ('"I never think about people's age," said Josephine. "I often think about it," said Felix; "and hope they show it more often than I do, and wonder if they can guess mine" '[47]).

Herman held that 'narcissism was the basis of homosexuality'[48] just as, in decoration at all times and places, the supreme element was in his view human vanity. He shared Ernest Thesiger's passion for *trompe l'œil* and, though Ivy may not have cared greatly in practice for Ernest's handpainted marble bathrooms or Herman's mania for mirrors ('The eye cannot be deceived too much or too often in a house,' he said[49]), she belonged, like Anthony Powell's Lady Warminster, to a generation that fully appreciated the strategic importance of an indirect approach:

> Layer upon layer of wrapping, box after box revealing in the Chinese manner yet another box, must conceal all doubtful secrets; only the discipline of infinite obliquity made it lawful to examine the seamy side of life. If these mysteries were observed, everything might be contemplated: however unsavoury, however unspeakable.[50]

Neither Ivy nor Margaret was under any illusion as to the seamy side of Herman's life. Nazi anti-Semitism, and its polite equivalent on this side of the Channel, provide a central theme of *Buchanan's Hotel*, culminating in the denunciation of Sigismund Siepel: 'He's just a dirty Polack, a Jew'. Siepel at curtainfall faces the sort of social and professional ostracism still occasionally incurred, in the stuffier reaches of English public life, by anyone unlucky enough to be unmasked as a homosexual rather than a Jew. Any attempt to deal openly with homosexuality in a play aimed at the West End stage between the wars would, of course, have been out of the question. Margaret belonged to a world where it went without saying that marriages like the Thesigers' involved some sort of precautionary element or that a foreigner like Herman, without means or family connections, was particularly vulnerable to prosecution and deportation. He shared a flat when Ivy first knew him with his sister Elka in Montpelier Terrace: 'We went about everywhere together. Herman took me almost everywhere, and we shared friends to a great extent,' said Elka (who was working for the advertising agency, J. Walter Thompson, while Herman had by 1927 moved on from soft furnishings and second-hand furniture at Peter Jones to an antique shop in Brook Street). 'He told me to be very careful about strange men coming to the door and asking for him. He was *terrified* of being blackmailed. All his life.'

It was only after Elka returned to Holland at the end of 1931 that Herman began moving—by infinitely slow gradations spread over the next twenty years—closer to Ivy. Before that he and his sister had never been parted (except by Elka's three years at a Dutch university) and, after her departure, he sent her regular weekly bulletins interrupted only by the war until he died. He was twenty-seven in 1931, Elka four years older. They came from a frugal, philistine, stiflingly narrow middle-class background in Amsterdam where, being enterprising, inquisitive children in a rigidly conventional and not especially happy family, they had been accustomed from earliest years to turn to one another rather than to either of their parents: 'Herman and I were always great friends from the day he was born,' said Elka. 'We were a great deal together.' Both had detested their father who was something of a martinet at home, perhaps because he cut comparatively little ice outside it: as general manager of M. A. Rozelaar and Zoonen, a fair-sized Amsterdam diamond-polishing works, he had had trouble making ends meet when the diamond market stood still in the First World War, and landed himself in a worse fix at the beginning of the 1920s when he lost his entire capital in a fraudulent enterprise called the National Diamond Company,[51] set up under British government auspices to employ war veterans in Brighton by swindlers supposedly representing de Beers. The factory, which he had agreed against his better judgment to take over in 1920, closed down two years later, the company went bankrupt and, after a brief, unsuccessful venture as a diamond broker in London, Herman's father returned to Holland where he never fully recovered from the shock of having been ruined.

Herman, whose only training had been in the diamond business, set about supporting himself and subsidizing his parents thereafter with characteristic energy and brio, educating himself as he went along from books, museums, sale rooms and friends like Margaret. He rapidly built up a reputation as a talented and amusing youth ('See Maples and die', though often attributed elsewhere, was originally a pun of Herman's), much in demand among hostesses and a growing circle of faithful clients, many of whom went back to his days on the trimmings counter at Peter Jones. In 1932 he took over the prestigious but badly run-down decorating firm of Elden's in Duke Street (when his bid was accepted, Herman, who banked on a gambler's luck and no capital, borrowed the entire purchase price from the Thornton Smith brothers who owned Fortnums); and it was a commission from Mrs Simpson, followed by work for the Prince of Wales, that made his name and gave him for the first time the solid prospect of a comfortable living.

But insecurity could never be kept entirely at bay. For all his luxurious tastes and frequent generosity, Herman was seldom extravagant with money and remained in private life discreet to the point of obsession. Recurrent fever in childhood, followed by a serious bout of diphtheria leading to rheumatism and other complications at Brighton, meant that he seldom felt completely well and, if his infectious gaiety and good humour made his company a tonic to others, their society was for him an essential stimulant. To his sister, his temperament seemed fundamentally melancholy, and his vanity compensatory: he was haunted by the prospect of want as well as the threat of prosecution, 'and he had a terrible fear of the future'. His homosexuality had declared itself very early, round about the time of his father's first financial crisis, when Herman as a child of ten or eleven had begun picking up men in the local park. As a small boy kept short of funds by thrifty Dutch parents on principle, he always had money to buy presents or flowers for his mother whom he adored. He had inherited her inclination to worry and fret but, where his mother was apt to meet disaster with lamentation and tears, Herman kept his own counsel. Stoicism had set in very young, along with the evasiveness Ivy understood so well, and a flair for the sort of gossip that made Boswell say of a friend: 'Lord Lucan tells a very good story which, if not precisely exact, is certainly characteristical.'[52]

This submerged self—unscrupulous, unprincipled and easily dismayed—was a side of Herman familiar to his sister from infancy (Elka had first realized with shock that her little brother told lies to make things more interesting when he announced, at the age of four, that his teacher had told him a pineapple was an animal, not a vegetable, and that it hunted its prey with what people mistakenly thought of as its leaves). Self-reliant like Herman, Elka was always the more dependable, shyer and less wilful of the two. She seems to have regarded him from childhood with something of the admiring, indulgent, protective pride that had coloured Ivy's relationship with her younger brother; and Ivy, like Elka, became expert at detecting how far Herman might or might not be trusted. 'I don't know what Herman had told Ivy. But quite obviously the stories he told her, she hadn't believed. She knew, just as I did, when he was telling the truth.'

Elka, who first met Ivy soon after the war (most of which she had spent interned in Nazi prisons for her part in the Dutch resistance), never forgot being invited alone—in spite of Herman's indignant remonstrances—to Braemar Mansions where Ivy made it quite clear that she wished to know everything about Herman's childhood, upbringing and family background: 'During this solo teaparty, Ivy cross-questioned me, really a kind of third-degree examination, except that it was done in a (to me) fascinating manner and not at all as any SS or MI6 man would have done (I've experienced both). It took her a couple of hours before she was satisfied.'[53] Several other young women have left similar, often rather more unnerving accounts of the interrogation technique Ivy herself described in *Daughters and Sons*:

'But if we ask no questions, we have no lies told us. I have subtler ways of finding out the truth.'

'You mean you have subtler ways of asking questions. If you ask no questions, you have no truth told you either. It is surprising how much truth people tell: I would not, if I were they. And you can get a lot of truth from the falsehoods they tell, when you ask them questions. I admire them so much for telling them so awkwardly: I have a great respect for people.'[54]

Elka never read Ivy's books, never met her again, and certainly never suspected that, in Ivy's life too, the person who had meant most in her formative years had been a beloved younger brother. Herman meanwhile came more and more to fill the role, if not of brother, then of favourite nephew to both Ivy and Margaret. He was infinitely obliging, always on hand to fetch or carry, provide chocolates and flowers, taxis and travelling rugs for a trip to the theatre ('All expense has been spared' was Herman's *mot* on a shoddy West End production[55]) or a stately home in the country. 'Margaret certainly was one of the most remarkable women I have ever come across, and what was fortunate for me was that I liked both Margaret and Ivy immensely,' said Herman;[56] and, whatever her reservations, Margaret for her part appreciated his qualities as keenly as Ivy.

There are clearly recognizable touches of Herman in the easy, unstrained, semi-flirtatious relationship established with the two ladies in *Buchanan's Hotel* by Sigismund Siepel, with his hard-headed determination to make a success in the decorating trade, his endearingly naive delight at having apparently pulled it off, his insistence on rolling up his trousers to prove to Alexia Tunstall that he can at last afford the very best silk underpants, his equally unselfconscious, un-English and over-familiar generosity towards Elizabeth Wace ('Your bag is *almost* bald. I'll get you another with your name in large stones on the snap'). He is the soul of chivalry with both ladies—affectionate, considerate and encouraging towards Miss Wace, a shade more deferential towards the know-ledgeable Miss Tunstall who shows him Wyatt's original sketch for her family home, together with correspondence about the new wing in the reign of George II, and receives in return a confidential account of his own misgivings about the English upper classes ('You think me a sort of adventurer? You think me a sort of bum? Quite outside the people you have heard of? You see, I'm a worker. I can be on terms with a moulder or a plumber, anyone with a trade or calling. But *those* people make me uncomfortable, and I can't pass the time of day with them. *Alexia: I'm* one of those people. *Siepel:* You? You're different . . .').*

Herman shared a world of professional concerns exclusively with Margaret, who was in any case inclined to discourage his more irresponsible side, the fibs and rumours he spread in the interests of making life more exciting. Ivy on the other hand led him on to make up more and more outrageous stories: he appealed to her reckless, games-playing instincts—the part of her that sided so strongly with her tyrants—and the private games they played together tended to start from the fact that, in any gathering of Margaret's upper-class friends, Herman was often the only person to have penetrated Ivy's cover as the mousy, innocuous, insignificant governess or companion. Their tacit mutual understanding if anything increased their mutual respect and, as each came increasingly to rely on the other, Ivy grew with time in some ways more intimate with Herman than with anyone else except Margaret. He had recognized her as unique from the start:

---

* Though the resemblance to Ivy and Margaret is unmistakable, it will not be pushed too far: Miss Wace, in her seventies, lives alone with a dog in rooms in Ealing and lays regular bets on the horses, while Miss Tunstall is a local landowner of marriageable age and respectable private means.

My great attraction to Ivy was that she was perhaps the only human being who made me feel that whatever I said she understood perfectly—unlike so many other friends who gave me the feeling that they had no idea what I was trying to say. Sometimes I would complain to Ivy that I understood nothing about nothing —which is true; and Ivy would look at me and say, 'And I understand everything about everything'. She did not say this once; she said it several times; and I wonder what she meant.[57]

Herman was thinking of a time after Margaret's death, towards the end of Ivy's life, when her changed status could hardly have failed to register with even the least observant furniture friends, while her literary admirers—at any rate those apt to write Ivy off as hopelessly out of touch with the modern world—were frequently taken aback by her sharp, disconcertingly well-informed judgments on, say, the contemporary novel or the Wolfenden Report. She would still put on her governess manner from time to time, almost as a matter of form, to amuse herself and her friends; and what she meant by the saying that puzzled Herman seems clear enough from similar claims made by the governesses in her books, for instance Miss Lacy in *Elders and Betters*:

> 'You really know a good deal, don't you?' said Julius.
> 'Yes,' said Miss Lacy in a simple, deliberate tone, keeping her eye on the child, perhaps in compensation for her thoughts being on other people. 'On my own rather narrow line, and in my own way, and according to the standard of human knowledge, I know a good deal.'[58]

Power in the form of knowledge is the compensation awaiting the bystanders and onlookers in Ivy's books, all those who never had, or have preferred to pass up (as in some sense Ivy did herself), any more active opportunity to control or manipulate other people. Ivy, who had switched camps midway through her life, held that circumstances may modify but not change the essence of a personality; and nearly everyone who knew her long enough was struck by the effects of what must have been a drastic modification in her own. 'When I think of the dim woman who poured out cups of tea in 1927 in the Linden Gardens flat, and the delicate, spirit-like creature whom I saw before she died in 1969,' said Herman, 'it is difficult to believe it was the same human being.'[59]

All her life Ivy made a point of misleading people bold enough to inquire about her past, like Herman ('I could never get it straight, because Ivy obviously never wanted to tell the truth'[60]), or Kay Dick, to whom she explained that she had not the faintest intention of giving anything away: 'Well, I think if I wrote an autobiography, a really good one, and put myself into it, I think it would be very interesting, and I think I should do it very well. But I'm not thinking of doing it.'[61] In so far as Ivy ever did touch directly on her own inner secrets, it was via Josephine Napier, who learns to subdue her essential nature, controlling her destructive impulses and beating a retreat thereafter towards the calm, unruffled surface where people like Felix Bacon and Dudley Gaveston lead such pleasant, civilized and entertaining lives.

When Ivy agreed at the end of her life to talk about herself to Kay Dick in the most intimate interview she ever recorded, they discussed whether or not 'people in civilised life'[62] actually do 'real deeds' like the characters in Ivy's books. Kay had recently tried to kill herself, which was what Ivy meant by a real deed ('I think there are a good many more deeds done than some people know. You've done a deed, haven't you?'). Ivy herself cheerfully insisted that she had never done one ('I haven't been at all deedy. Not at all'). But perhaps something akin to the temptation Josephine had failed to resist lay behind Ivy's further mysterious claim to be 'a woman of blameless character', by which she said she meant 'quite perfect morally'. If the springs of action lie, where Ivy's friend Lowes Dickinson located them, 'deep in ignorance and madness',[63] Ivy might be said to have spent the second half of her life exploring those depths in fiction and steering clear of them in fact.

1937–1939

'Well, and in Swaffham Bulbeck!'

I

'I HAVE HAD a publisher's account and although I did not look for much from it, I looked for more than is forthcoming,' says the novelist John Ponsonby,[1] beginning to feel the pinch of falling sales in *Daughters and Sons*. The book which came out in March 1937 —Ivy's first to be published by Victor Gollancz—contains much gloomy talk of retrenchment, economy, dwindling royalties, mounting expenses and the impossibility of earning a living by the pen. Ivy could count, like John Ponsonby, on a fairly substantial private income though hers had shrunk in the slump from a comfortable thousand a year to about £750 throughout the 1930s: she told Hester's husband, Basil Marsden-Smedley, that she was ashamed to be so poor. Retrenchment does not seem to have entailed any very drastic cutting back on Ivy's part (she and Margaret replaced Jessie with a grander, starchier and altogether superior maid, Gray, round about 1937, as well as adding an annual winter holiday abroad to their regular travels on the Continent in the late summer), but disappointing sales were said to have been her reason for leaving Heinemann when her three-novel contract ran out with *A House and Its Head* in 1935. Years later she described being accosted at a publisher's party by a man from Heinemann's who claimed that his firm had once had the honour of publishing her: 'Honour?' said Ivy. 'No one would have known it at the time.'[2]

David Higham had by this time left Curtis Brown to set up his own agency, taking many of his best clients with him; but, though he tried to dissuade her,[3] Ivy stayed put which meant that her affairs

were from now on in the hands of Albert Curtis Brown's son
Spencer, fresh from Cambridge and as yet wholly inexperienced in
the ways of the book trade. It was the newly promoted Spencer
who got rid of Higham in July 1935, the month in which *A House
and Its Head* was published, and, when Rose Macaulay attracted
Gollancz's attention by lending him her copy of *Brothers and Sisters*,[4]
Ivy presumably made her own decision to accept his offer for the
next three novels. After less than ten years in the business, Gollancz
had a reputation for being able to sell virtually anything by what
struck staider competitors as hair-raisingly unconventional tactics.
Lavish use of advertising space was his trade mark together with
gaudy yellow jackets, intensive promotion campaigns and an inim-
itably flashy line in publicity ('For years the cognoscenti have
considered Miss Compton-Burnett one of the finest living novelists
. . . Will "the public" now show that it is not without taste and
discrimination?' ran one of his advertisements for *Daughters and
Sons*, ending on a characteristically scolding note: 'Probably not').
Gollancz raised such a dust in the spring of 1937 that 'the London
success',[5] *Daughters and Sons*, was promptly snapped up by the
American publisher W. W. Norton, who is said to have confessed
years later ('strong men at Norton's still blench at the thought'[6]) to
some confusion between I. Compton-Burnett and the highly
sought-after writer of Chicago gangsterland thrillers, W. R. Burnett. The bestseller lists that April featured 'Mrs Virginia Woolf's
The Years, Miss Agatha Christie's *Murder in the Mews*, Miss I.
Compton-Burnett's *Daughters and Sons*' (of the three, only Ivy
figured at the end of the year in the *Bookseller*'s Glass Slipper awards
for novels that deserved better sales than they got). Reviewers
invoked Congreve, Jane Austen, Emily Brontë; and Gollancz went
to town with the *News Chronicle*'s obliging claim that Mr Bernard
Shaw was the only other maker of comedy in the same class as Miss
Compton-Burnett.[7]

Gollancz was the sort of enthusiast who works best by establishing a close personal contact with his authors. Autocratic, didactic, self-confident, forceful and shrewd rather than subtle, he got on
famously with Daphne du Maurier and Dorothy L. Sayers, twin
mainstays of the firm's fiction list; but it would have been hard to
find anyone less likely to hit it off with Ivy, who had so far had no
cause to feel much confidence in her dealings with publishers ('I
have always thought of Cape as such a good one, and wished I

belonged there,' she wrote sadly long afterwards to Robert Liddell. 'But I believe they are all alike in a way, only just different from any other business firm'[8]). Gollancz for his part cannot have relished being ranked by his new client with the accountants and lawyers who still called twice yearly for instructions as they had done in her father's day. He was always a soundly commercial publisher and, when Ivy's sales nearly doubled (from about a thousand copies of each novel to eighteen hundred[9]) but failed for the moment to budge any further, his initial enthusiasm was damped. His loyalty never wavered but in a sense he and Ivy had been at cross purposes from the start. I. Compton-Burnett represented a catch in 1937, at any rate for anyone with an eye on the sort of fiction list being built up by Jonathan Cape, or for that matter by Charles Evans at Heinemann ('They each could spot quality, and Victor only success,' wrote Higham. 'The other two could spot success as well, and that made it the more galling'[10]). Gollancz, having caught the tide the year before with his immensely successful Left Book Club, was very much in the market for new novels; and perhaps the fact that his proselytizing socialism made him almost house publisher to the front, or political half of the *New Statesman* attracted him to an author so highly prized by the paper's literary back parts.

But Gollancz's spectacular coups came from anticipating a popular trend almost before anyone else was aware of it, a brand of originality—eye-catching and effective if relatively ephemeral—that had nothing in common with Ivy's. Both of them clearly hoped for quick returns which perhaps explains why, when 'the public' paid scant attention to Gollancz's blandishments, each tended to blame the other. Ivy was naturally anxious to see her early books back in print to which Gollancz could not agree while he still had unsold copies of those already in hand. She complained that he failed to advertise her sufficiently widely, he parried with her fatal lack of mass market appeal. Ivy grumbled to her friends, Gollancz dined out on his story of Margaret Jourdain turning up out of the blue at the office with a typescript which she plonked on his desk, saying flatly, 'Here's some more of Ivy's twaddle'.[11] The story may well be apocryphal (Ivy's manuscripts tended to arrive, unaccompanied and without warning, by taxi at Curtis Brown) but it gives a fairly accurate impression of their mutual disgruntlement in later years when Ivy's mounting distress continued to be met with waning interest from Gollancz.

But, though it baffled their friends and Ivy herself made at least one attempt to dissolve it, the partnership had its points for both parties. On the one hand, from Gollancz's point of view, I. Compton-Burnett was a name that brought tone to the list (as well as a steady if not sensational profit) while, on the other hand, a hard-headed commercial firm with a rapid turnover and an almost legendary flair for publicity must have seemed the obvious choice for someone who never entirely got over her hankering to write a bestseller. It remained all her life a source of grief and vexation to Ivy that her novels failed to sell in their tens of thousands ('D'you know, I don't think she takes more trouble with her books than I do?' she said once of Daphne du Maurier[12] and, in another conversation about Agatha Christie's worldwide circulation, 'Think of the pleasure she must give—think of the pleasure'[13]). Writers in her books who find themselves forced to appeal to a small but discriminating readership over the heads of 'the public' generally do so as regretfully as Ivy herself: 'Much of the pleasure of making a book would go, if it held nothing to be shared by other people. I would write for a few dozen people; and it sometimes seems that I do; but I would not write for no one.'[14]

Ivy's readers—the sort of readership her characters disparagingly describe as 'the few'—could hardly have been more appreciative. 'I can't resist writing to tell you how I have revelled in every page, every line, every word of your *Daughters and Sons*,' wrote Vita Sackville-West from Sissinghurst on 1 April 1937, in the same week as a letter from the flower arranger Constance Spry (two names carrying so much weight in *Country Life* circles must have given even Margaret pause) hoping it would not seem impertinent or fulsome to say she had taken such delight in the book that 'I am spoiled for anything else for a long time'.[15] If a number of more conservative critics and novelists—especially among Ivy's own generation, like Virginia Woolf—still found her work hard to take, there was no difficulty with the rising generation of writers: Rosamond Lehmann, L. P. Hartley, Desmond Shawe-Taylor, Elizabeth Bowen and Sybille Bedford all wrote about I. Compton-Burnett at the end of the 1930s as one of the most original writers alive. Her growing reputation (and the difficulty of reconciling it with her absurdly incongruous appearance) is nicely illustrated by James Lees-Milne's account of inviting Ivy and Margaret to tea at the end of the war with the young James Pope-Hennessy who brought a French friend, Maurice Gendron: 'Maurice spoke not a word until they left, and then asked in his French English, "Who are these impossible governesses?" J. explained that one of them was the foremost novelist of our time.'[16]

'My books won't live. Yours may, Ivy,' said Rose Macaulay[17] who was the only bestselling author—indeed for a long time almost the only novelist of any description—among Ivy's close friends. Rose herself tended to deprecate the light, bright, astringent, topical novels that, from *Potterism* onwards, had made her name in the 1920s. She had been serialized in *Eve*, featured in any number of women's magazines and employed regularly to write for the popular papers but, by 1929 when Ivy first met her, she was already beginning to turn to the more serious, scholarly books on seventeenth-century poetry, or the pleasures of travel and ruins, about which there was no need to feel defensive before even her cleverest friends. Rose's misgivings about her own huge and highly successful output recall Hereward Egerton (in *A God and His Gifts*), another popular novelist inclined to worry about whose books will live and whose won't and apt to need consolation from his family and friends for being despised by the few: 'Well, I am glad you write for the many too. It is natural that I should be. I am one of the many myself. And it gives the whole thing its meaning. The few have too much done for them. To serve the many is the larger aim . . .'[18]

Modesty was an essential part of Rose's charm, together with a deceptive spinsterish primness that Ivy must have understood very well. The two brought out the best in one another from the start; indeed it was typical of Rose that she set about straight away providing practical advice about agents, contracts and terms, recruiting Ivy for Curtis Brown in 1929, as well as eight years later for Gollancz (who, whatever his difficulties with Ivy, remained always Rose's devoted admirer). They were almost the same age and, though Rose's curiosity about human nature found far more active expression than Ivy's, they shared the same delicately derisive view of themselves and their friends. Always eccentric, abstemious and frugal, very detached, very Cambridge (Rose's uncle, W. H. Macaulay, had been dean of King's in Noel Compton-Burnett's day, and afterwards modelled for one of the dons in *Pastors and Masters*), Rose was by all accounts incapable of doing a mean thing or saying a dull one and, for all her austerity, possessed an innate sense of style that made her Herman's favourite of all Ivy's friends:

'I simply adored her,' he said. 'I loved her appearance, her delicious speaking voice, her little curls which covered her rather skeleton-like head, her elegance of movement and her wit.'[19] Ivy too loved Rose's vitality, gaiety, audacity—what Rosamond Lehmann called her 'wit and crackle'—her fearlessness, and above all her integrity ('If, before she died, I had been asked to define integrity to some moral moron . . . or to a man from Mars,' wrote her publisher, Mark Bonham-Carter, 'I would have arranged for him to meet Rose Macaulay'[20]).

Ivy called her 'the most prominent spinster in England'[21] and said she delighted to see her 'bubble over with high spirits' teasing Ernest Thesiger, or another of their mutual friends.[22] Ivy herself, generally so sparing of repartee in company, would sometimes rise to Rose's challenge and put on a sort of cross-fire double act in which, both parties being evenly matched, neither got the upper hand for long and one or other always ended by bringing up religion (Rose who, after a bumpy start, eventually regained her firm faith in the Church of England, returned with interest Ivy's frank incredulity at an intelligent woman allowing herself to be so sadly deluded). Both were sociable, if to vastly different degrees. 'Rose adored parties,' wrote Gollancz, 'she was one of the best party-goers in London. She liked the glamour and the noise: she liked the talk: but what above all she liked was that parties . . . implied people, and people meant even more to her . . . than words.'[23] Ivy, though never in quite the same class as Rose, had a fair share of parties herself in those days. Her diary for the summer season of 1934, for instance, lists between the end of May and mid-July 'Rosie's party [this was Rosie Bruce, a friend of Margaret's], Pakingtons' party, Herman S.'s party, Nelly's regatta [the Ionides always had a military band on the lawn for summer parties at their house by the river at Twickenham], Soame Jenyns' party, Mary's party, Lady Sprigge's party, Nelly's party [this was a tamer affair in Berkeley Square], Raymond M.'s party', not counting the regular tea, sherry and dinner parties she and Margaret gave at least once or twice a week on their own account.

These gatherings, heavily weighted in favour of furniture friends —scholars, connoisseurs, collectors and a congenial selection of Margaret's wealthy clients—were already beginning to be infiltrated by Ivy's admirers. But, apart from Rose and perhaps Francis Birrell (who died unexpectedly in 1935 to the great grief and shock of his friends), no one on the literary side penetrated anywhere near what remained an intensely private area of Ivy's life. 'She would talk to me about her writing, but always in a mysterious way,' said Herman: 'she would say, "I am writing again" and look happy; or she would say, "I'm not getting on with my writing," and look unhappy . . .'[24] Probably only Margaret realized what writing cost Ivy who was no stranger to the sense of failure, exhaustion and deprivation described by Hereward Egerton on finishing a novel (' "Well, the book is ended," said Hereward. ". . . I am in a strange solitude. I seem to move in a void. I am without my foothold, my stake in life. I have suffered it before and it is never different. I have had and done what I wanted. But I pay the price" '[25]).

Each of the two professional novelists in Ivy's books has his privacy guaranteed by a devoted sister standing ready to repel intruders from the outside world; and possibly some kind of jealously guarded nervous strain connected with her work might account, in part at least, for the rather startling altercations that blew up between the two friends when Ivy insisted on things being fetched for her, or on ticking Margaret off in public. 'We ate lentil soup, white fish with sauce and steamed potatoes, a rhubarb and ginger tart, Morecambe shrimps and biscuits,' wrote James Lees-Milne, describing a memorable luncheon at Braemar Mansions in wartime. 'Margaret Jourdain opened a large bottle of Cidrax, poured out Thesiger's and my glasses and was about to pour her own when Miss Compton-Burnett shouted, "Margaret! Remember at breakfast it was decided that you were to finish the open bottle of flat Cidrax." '[26] This was at the end of May 1942, when Ivy was having difficulty with the early stages of *Elders and Betters*. She herself said she felt drained by the time a manuscript was ready to be typed, 'and she even used the stock phrase—not a habit of hers —that virtue had gone out of her'[27] (another novelist uses the same cliché after a family row about writing in *A God and His Gifts*: ' "Virtue has gone out of me." "It has," said Reuben. "We saw and heard it going out" '[28]).

Ivy felt that producing a book entitled her to a holiday and throughout the 1930s, as soon as she had packed off a manuscript to Curtis Brown (which she did punctually every two years round about Christmas time), she and Margaret crossed the Channel—for two weeks at an English pension in the Swiss Alps in February 1933 (*More Women Than Men*), Rome, Naples and Paris in February 1935

(*A House and Its Head*), and Italy again at the end of January 1937 (*Daughters and Sons*). In between there were countless trips to the country, generally a week at Easter and another at Whitsun in rooms in Dorset or Cornwall or once at a farmhouse near Keswick in the Lake District, and any number of weekends with friends in the country like Nelly at Buxted Park or Soame Jenyns at Bottisham Hall.

2

BUT, OF ALL THEIR FRIENDS' country places, the only one to which Ivy went regularly alone, and where she clearly felt entirely at home, was the Noyeses' in Wiltshire. Ella and Dora prided themselves on providing complete recuperation and change from her crowded London life, and Ivy at Sutton Veney made a point of doing 'no paperwork at all'. She would rest in her room or under the mulberry tree, picking raspberries or blackcurrants and sitting for hours at a time in the shady garden which seemed, to the neighbours' children who played in it, a magical place: romantic, mysterious, sweet-scented—'Miss Jekyll's sort of a garden'[29]—full of hiding places and secret corners, with a fish pond, grassy plots divided by yew hedges, masses of flowers growing higgledy-piggledy and lavender spilling out between the paving stones. Beyond the garden lay the downs which always suited Ivy better than any other countryside: her father had been born and brought up forty miles away at Redlynch on the far side of Salisbury Plain, and, though her grandfather died before Ivy was born (and her mother had in any case severed all connection with the family's numerous humble Wiltshire and Hampshire relations), generations of Comptons and Burnetts had been labourers, farmers and tradesmen on the eastern side of the county and over the border in Hampshire. Ivy had inherited her father's love of growing things ('It's no good going for more than a week without sticking your fingers in the earth,' she said once to Sonia Orwell in London), and villagers at Sutton Veney still remember Miss Burnett's knowledgeable interest in garden plants. But all her life Ivy loved best of all the small, frail, fine flowers bred by the keen air and thin soil of the high downland and described so vividly in Ella Noyes' *Salisbury Plain*:

The slender cowslips, nodding all down the slopes in the sharp wind in April, the blue and white and pink inlay of the milkwort a little later, the purple thyme fitting itself closely to the ground of the molehills, the bright gold of the bird's-foot trefoil creeping along the ground, the yellow rock rose and tiny tormentil . . . Knapweed and hawkweed in miniature, starring the ground with purple and yellow, and the scabious which spreads an airy blue mist over the whole down in autumn; all flowers and herbs up here are humble and lowly, with a vigour and sweetness bred of repression. Only the harebells, of all mortal things the most bodiless, ghosts of blue, swaying upon gossamer threads, inviolable even by the roughest gales, belong to the high downs, and have no grosser selves below.[30]

Harebells had been Ivy's favourite flower from earliest years, perhaps for the same reasons that made her write so feelingly of the 'vigour and sweetness bred of repression' among the children and young people in her books. Certainly Ella and Dora found no difficulty in Ivy's writing: 'They read her books and talked to her about them, definitely they did,' said Margaret Hawkins, who had been in and out of the Noyeses' house from childhood on, and whose education had largely come from their bookshelves. 'That was their life, books. They talked books. They lived books.'

The three sisters (Minna, the eldest, lived rather apart from the other two, cut off by deafness and a preference for music rather than literature) read or worked in the mornings, gardened in the afternoons, and read again or sewed in the evenings over the fire in the drawing room. Ella and Dora were twenty years older than Ivy, already well into their sixties when she first knew them (Minna was eighty in 1936) and somewhat withdrawn from the outside world. They wore strange, beautiful, patched and faded silk blouses and dresses, all at least fifty years out of date. They lived the traditionally busy, orderly, disciplined lives of English country gentlewomen except that—highly unusual in a small village—each was an accomplished amateur in her own particular art. Minna played the piano. Ella had published several historical-cum-topographical books about Italy as well as her much admired *Salisbury Plain*, all written in a fine, firm, clear prose style that has the same unpretentious distinction as her younger sister's delicate, Sargentesque portraits and

landscapes. Dora, who painted all the local children from the Sutton
Veney baker's son to the future Marquess of Bath as a boy, had also
exhibited in London and even contributed, like so many of Margaret's friends, to the dolls' house Lutyens designed for Queen
Mary.

She had been roped in to do dolls' house water colours by
Lutyens' friend, the painter Sir William Nicholson who lived in
some state at Sutton Veney manor house with his second wife and
relays of children, stepchildren and grandchildren, the youngest of
whom ran wild all over the Noyeses' house and garden, next door
to their own except for an orchard. 'Their house was idyllic inside,'
wrote Nicholson's stepdaughter, Anne Northcroft: 'I remember a
lot of light-coloured oak and old furniture and floors gleaming with
polish . . .'[31] There were collections of china and 'fine old linen
carefully darned', books everywhere, and texts from the psalms
painted on the drawing room rafters in gothic letters on green. 'The
whole room had a green feeling,' said Nicholson's youngest daughter Liza, who remembered the Noyeses providing throughout her
childhood a refuge from the comparative formality of home life at
the manor. She and her four nephews and nieces—children of her
half-sister Nancy Nicholson's marriage to the poet Robert Graves,
who lived in the old school house in the village—spent whole days
at the Noyeses', climbing their trees, fishing in their pond, squirt-
ing one another with water or rifling the dressing-up chest in the
attics. 'They really liked children,' said Liza Banks. 'And they were
very, very tolerant. It was such a relief to go there—no sense of
strain—no imprisonment. There was a spiritual wholeness going
there, very much so.'

As they grew older, the sisters were not often seen outside their
own garden; but they welcomed the Nicholsons' many visitors,
especially the younger generation of poets and painters who regularly crossed the orchard to call on the Noyeses for tea or supper.
Graves was often at Sutton Veney until, after a notorious scandal at
the end of the 1920s, Nancy left him to set up house in the village
with another poet, Geoffrey Taylor (with whom Ella discussed
modern poetry as equably as if nothing had happened, to the
consternation of more prurient neighbours). The young Ben
Nicolson also spent holidays with his father, and seems to have got
on well with the Noyeses who owned several landscapes (their
'Foothills in Cumberland' was eventually left to the Tate) done at a

time when his work already verged on abstraction. They had no family life of their own, being almost the last survivors of a long, largely clerical and by no means undistinguished Wiltshire line (the poet Alfred Noyes was a connection,[32] and so was the academic painter Henry James Noyes; a Noyes had been burnt at the stake under Mary Tudor and two more sailed for America with the pilgrim fathers; in 1798 there was even a Robert John Noyes appointed curate of Barton Stacey where Ivy's Burnett great-grandfather lived till he left to marry a blacksmith's daughter named Compton in 1803).

Their father and at least two of their brothers had been London solicitors but Ella and Dora had returned to Wiltshire some time after their father's death in 1890, in time to record a world of ancient rural isolation and self-sufficiency already beginning to break up even before the First World War. Dora painted the great haywains, the men in smock frocks wielding scythes and sickles, the lines of women harvesters in their pink and blue skirts, white aprons and cotton sunbonnets, whose passing Ella deplored in *Salisbury Plain*. The book is full of laments for the damage done by 'telephones and newspapers and bicycles', for the fencing in of Stonehenge and, far worse, the raising of the monument's great central stone, fixed upright in 1901 by 'the violent intrusion of modern science'. The Noyeses were notably free from prejudice when it came to modern poetry, painting and novels; they were progressive in politics with socialist and Fabian leanings considered eccentric, if not downright dangerous, by the retired admirals and colonels who constituted the Sutton Veney gentry; and they were remembered by everyone who knew them as inexhaustibly tolerant, whether towards the rackety Graves and Nicholson children or their elders openly living in sin in the village. But they looked, dressed and spoke in the 1930s and 1940s as though they belonged to an era nearly half a century earlier; and part of their charm for Ivy clearly lay in the fact that a visit to Sutton Veney brought her as near as it was possible to get to the world of the 1890s in which her books were set.

The Noyeses lived with the utmost simplicity, tending their own garden, baking their own bread, making jam, doing their own darning and mending. Minna collected sheep's wool from the hedgerows for spinning into shawls and seaboot stockings. They had a maid, Mrs Pink, replaced later by a series of girls who came in from the village, but, though all their friends remembered the

house as enchanting, its arrangements were spartan and its rooms
often perishing cold ('always rugs on your knees—they had blue
hands from the cold, blue hands and red noses'). Ivy, whose
standards of comfort were exacting if never exorbitant, must have
had much to put up with in the way of plain living, and she seems to
have borne it in something very like Hope Cranmer's spirit of ever
so faintly disparaging forbearance towards the Marlowe sisters in
Parents and Children:

> 'I always feel that being here is a lesson,' said Hope.
> 'In rising above disadvantages, do you mean?' said Susan.[33]

The three Marlowes (Susan and Priscilla have a brother, Lester,
who lives at home writing books that don't sell) were Ivy's tribute
to the three Noyeses and, among all her many partial portraits of
friends, theirs was apparently the only one she freely acknowledged, indeed explicitly intended as a compliment to the sitters.
'They knew she was writing about them,' said Mrs Hawkins who
was already working for the Noyes sisters when *Parents and Children*
came out in May 1941, and vividly remembered their pleasure on
receiving a copy from Ivy. 'They talked about that—that it would
be them—and they were very happy with it.' Ella and Dora read
Parents and Children aloud to one another over the fire in the
evenings, and congratulated Ivy on the likeness when she came to
stay.

The Marlowes lead lives of great seclusion and contentment,
making do in a modest country cottage ('low cramped rooms', 'thin
walls and no damp course'[34]) with meagre financial resources, an
inadequate coal ration and an elderly Mrs Morris who comes in to
do for them. They seldom go out save to gather firewood—after
dusk so as not to be seen—in the park belonging to their neighbour
at the big house, Sir Jesse Sullivan, a regular benefactor whose rare
visits to the cottage are a source of memorable embarrassment (' "I
wish he would not keep gazing at the fire," said Priscilla aside to the
others. "People are supposed to see faces in it, but I am so afraid he
will see wood" '[35]). Like the Noyeses, they have no family besides
themselves, no interest in charity outside the home (' "We are the
last people to support orphanages," said Susan. "They are fortunate
in not having to support us" '[36]), and no desire for any company

except their own. Parties made up of the older Sullivan children, or the Sullivans' visitors, slip across the park on more or less surreptitious visits to the cottage, much as the young Nicholsons called on the Noyeses, for a brief respite from the constraints of the big house. But the Marlowes themselves are adept at inventing excuses for not returning these visits ('"We don't wear their kind of clothes," said Susan . . . "We should have to look like other people," said Priscilla, "and that costs money" '[37]), and for turning down Hope Cranmer's repeated advances:

'Books and a fire,' said Priscilla, looking at these things. 'What more could we have?'

'I see you haven't any more,' said Hope with some exasperation. 'But does that prevent your having dinner with a friend? You could have that as well.'[38]

Ella was the only one of the three Noyeses who could on occasion be lured up to London alone, or very occasionally with Dora, to spend a few nights at Braemar Mansions. They had little in common with Margaret's circle, and so little contact with Ivy's that none of her London friends in later life had so much as heard of the Noyeses. No doubt the sisters preferred to keep their distance, and no doubt they enjoyed the note of asperity running through Hope's dealings in *Parents and Children* with the infuriatingly unworldly Marlowes. Hope herself is one of Ivy's most charming variations on a type that recurs constantly in her books, the wry, humorous, observant middle-aged woman whose invariable kindness and tolerance are matched by an insatiable curiosity. Comfortably off herself, and tolerably satisfied with her own domestic arrangements, Hope is consumed by the need to get to the bottom of the Sullivans' family frictions and the Marlowes' no less baffling satisfaction with themselves and their lives. Much of her time is spent cross-examining Susan and Priscilla who answer her questions as frankly as they discuss her shortcomings—her streak of vulgarity ('there is something second-rate going through Hope'[39]), and her very nearly successful attempts to make it seem better by joking about it—behind her back.

One of the many bones Hope finds to pick with the Marlowes is their contempt for frivolities like 'cushions and flowers and things

that shimmer in the firelight' (' "We like the firelight better by
itself," said Priscilla. "I can see you do," said Hope. "And I like the
things that go with it. I don't even want a mind above material
things; I enjoy having one on their level" '[40]). Another is the
unmistakable air of serenity which, with their high-mindedness and
eccentricity, was always the first thing people noticed about the
Noyeses. 'I think they were very, very unusual,' said Liza Banks,
which was no more than the Marlowes thought of themselves ('No,
but we are unusual. It is no good to say we are not'[41]). Ivy invented a
scandalous secret in the family background (it is noticeable that the
Marlowes treat the plot's romantic revelations about their past with
a fair-sized pinch of salt); but, given that she intended the Marlowes
expressly to amuse the Noyeses, they must surely have recognized
another of Ivy's private jokes at her own expense in Hope's
inquisitiveness, intrusiveness, humorous self-deprecation, her love
of comfort and material possessions coupled with a sneaking sense
of her own inferiority when set beside the Marlowes' lofty indifference to either:

> 'If you liked me a little better, I should not be so petty,' said
> Hope. 'What is the good of striving to be worthy of your
> friendship, when I have no chance of it? You know how I long for
> your affection; people always know the things that add to
> themselves; I expect you exaggerate my desire for it. Of course I
> don't show it in public, when you are so neglected and
> eccentric . . .'[42]

Hope's friendship with Priscilla and Susan is riddled with this sort
of fretfulness: part of the strength and subtlety of Ivy's treatment of
friendship in general lies precisely in her never assuming that
mutual comprehension and sympathy necessarily rule out a quota
of what Hope calls 'normal human discontent'.[43] Ivy herself, secure
in the Noyeses' affection, confident of their understanding, had not
the faintest intention of abating one jot of her social round of
parties, theatres, holidays, foreign travel and visits to friends, nor
for that matter her and Margaret's frank predilection for 'things that
shimmer in the firelight'.

3

PARENTS AND CHILDREN came out in 1941, by which time the life of
ease and plenty had already receded into the past: in retrospect the
decade that had opened for Ivy with the publication of *Brothers and
Sisters* in 1929, and ended in war, had brought her more settled
happiness than any other in her whole life, except perhaps the first.
She and Margaret, in their respective fifties and sixties, had
achieved a degree of emotional and intellectual as well as material
prosperity that neither could have anticipated in her bleak and
unpromising youth. 'Well, anyway, we have nothing to dread
now,' says the ten-year-old Sefton Shelley, looking back on a
peculiarly wretched school term at the end of *Two Worlds and Their
Ways*: 'Everything seems to be over.'[44] It is a child's dramatically
nihilistic view ('Nothing good, nothing bad, nothing to dread,
nothing to hope for. Nothing') of the cheerful adult resignation and
self-reliance practised in *Parents and Children* by the Marlowes who,
like Margaret and Ivy, 'lived in their interests and their anxieties and
each other, with as much satisfaction as most people and more
enjoyment'.[45]

For Ivy especially the strain and horror of the past meant always
that relief was the keenest form of joy. If she was still vexed at not
having brought off a bestseller, she could count on a gratifying
amount of attention, especially from the young ('All Ivy's fans are
under eighteen, you know,' said Margaret sourly at the beginning
of the war when the bookseller Heywood Hill produced yet another
young man anxious to meet or hear more about Ivy[46]); and she must
have been pleasantly conscious that as a writer she had at last come
into her prime. She was steadily deepening and darkening her range
with the series of irresistibly entertaining, unsparing and profoundly unsettling family novels that started in 1935 with *A House and Its
Head* and continued thereafter, with only a brief hiccup in wartime,
at two yearly intervals. In a sense the stable, unchanging, pre-1910
world that became from now on the permanent setting of her
novels ('When an age is ended, you see it as it is'[47]) provided a retreat
from the perils and uncertainties of the depression, rearmament,
Mussolini's Abyssinian invasion, civil war in Spain, and the rise of
Hitler's National Socialism. In another sense, the collapse of civil-

ized values was Ivy's especial subject: 'In the age of the concentration camp when, from 1935 or so to 1947, she wrote her very best
novels, no writer did more to illumine the springs of human
cruelty, suffering and bravery,' wrote Angus Wilson when she
died.[48]

A Family and a Fortune, published in February 1939, had been
finished towards the end of the previous November,[49] two months
after the Munich crisis. Herman had a story that on the day war was
declared Ivy, alone in the flat at Braemar Mansions, telephoned to
say she was terrified and beg him to come at once and sit with her.[50]
In fact this happened a year earlier on Wednesday, 28 September
1938, the day on which a declaration of war was widely expected
and only narrowly averted in the late afternoon by Chamberlain's
announcement of plans for his last-minute dash to Munich. The first
air raids on London were confidently anticipated that night. Margaret had been away all week with a newly acquired young man,
Peter Wilson (afterwards chairman of Sotheby's), touring stately
houses in Leicester, Derby and Chesterfield. 'That *was* a dismal
time,' said Sir Peter who remembered Margaret's sardonic reply,
when asked what her brother Frank might be doing: 'Burying his
great auk's egg, I should think' (if Frank's marrying money still
rankled with his family, worse still was the frivolous way he chose
to disburse it on birdwatching expeditions and his celebrated egg
collection). When Herman reached Cornwall Gardens, Ivy, who
had washed her hair, was sitting in front of the fire with a towel over
her shoulders looking 'really quite yellow with horror'.

It was a widespread reaction. Herman had Jewish parents and a
sister in Holland; Ivy's maid Erna Gray was German (widow of an
English husband, she decided to throw in her lot with 'her ladies'
and later supplied the English war office, via Margaret's friend
Soame Jenyns, with maps and details of factories in her German
home town). People all over the country were trenching their
orchards, laying in supplies, and blacking out windows. Ivy and
Margaret must have known, when they spent a week in Provence at
Easter 1938 and another fortnight just over the Channel in Normandy at the beginning of September, that this was likely to be
their last glimpse of abroad for some time. 'I am perfectly convinced,' said Hester, 'that these two non-political, rather apart
women, living in their comfortable flat with their good maid, their
good food, their fascinating work, were quite certain that Munich

was not the end of war threats, but the end of life as they had known it for ever.'[51]

Arrangements were put in hand for evacuation and storage. Gas masks had to be fitted ('The girl said to Margaret: "Don't you write? Didn't you have *The Adventure?*" ' reported Ivy, describing the scene at the depot. 'And Margaret said no, it was her sister, but she also wrote. Then she came to me and said, "I think you write?" I felt thankful that the maid didn't write'[52]). The V&A was in turmoil throughout the following year, even Kensington Gardens, where Ivy walked as she worked on scenes from her current plot, had men digging trenches against bombardment. When the war did eventually break out, Ivy and Margaret were staying at Lyme Regis in Dorset ('I don't think that they were in the country to run away from the bombs,' said Hester, who was herself hoping to be posted as a war correspondent to Holland, 'but because they went to the country in August and early September'[53]). On Sunday, 3 September 1939, they took a bus along the coast road to Seatown near Chideock, where Basil and the three little Marsden-Smedleys were staying in a row of black-painted coastguards' cottages known as the Watch House, arriving just in time for family Bible-reading and hymns in the garden overlooking the sea before Chamberlain's broadcast at 11.15. Official evacuation of London refugees began that afternoon and once again the first air raids were expected that night. Ivy and Margaret stayed on in their lodgings for a week or so and, by the end of the month, were installed with their maid as paying guests of Soame Jenyns' widowed mother at Bottisham Hall just outside Cambridge.

It was a rash and, as it turned out, unsatisfactory arrangement on both sides, but there was ample room at the hall for two maiden ladies with their own maid, and no doubt Soame's highbrow friends struck his mother as a more hopeful proposition than the parties of unwilling, unwanted and often completely unhousetrained London evacuees liable to be billeted on anyone with room to spare in the country. There had been Jenynses at Bottisham ever since 1700 when it belonged to the father of the first Soame Jenyns, the writer, theologian and M.P. for Cambridge who never forgave Dr Johnson for laughing at his pretensions to serious scholarship ('What Soame Jenyns says upon this subject is not to be minded,' said the doctor when someone brought up Jenyns' belief in disinterested benevolence: 'he is a wit'[54]). Margaret's friend Soame was considered an odd fish in the village on account of his London job and literary leanings; but he cut quite a dash in a generation of memorable eccentrics at the British Museum by deliberately cultivating something not unlike his namesake's reputation as a country squire dabbling in matters a gentleman would hardly take seriously. He specialized in Japanese ceramics, and claimed to be frightened of Ivy's old friend Arthur Waley who would lie in wait in the museum's corridors and courtyards to jump out and stun him with learning, much as Dr Johnson had stunned his ancestor.

Soame got on better with Margaret's other friend, Willie King (the two were connected through Bulwer Lytton on the Jenyns' side whose grandson married Byron's daughter Ada, wife to the eighth Baron King), another celebrated wit who looked like a defrocked eighteenth-century abbé and was, from a very different standpoint, as great an expert as Ivy on the ravages caused by the struggle for power down several generations in an English upper-class family. Willie's unexpectedly successful union with the lovely but decidedly raffish Viva ('As if a Daumier drawing had married a Toulouse-Lautrec,' said Margaret with disapproval to Soame[55]) had been so strenuously opposed—and Viva so contemptuously treated—by his parents that the young Kings relieved their feelings (like Horace Lamb's wretched children in *Manservant and Maidservant*) by sticking used gramophone needles into a wax effigy of Willie's father who died, shortly followed by his wife, 'one happy day in 1934'.[56] Whereupon the pair ran through Willie's inheritance with phenomenal speed, fury and splendour, leaving Willie once again rich only in the fund of anecdote he supplied to colleagues like Soame, and the young Angus Wilson, who shared air-raid duties with him at the museum (' "Oh God," groaned Willie, stumbling about with Angus one night in the blackout through a sculpture gallery of Great Assyrians, "Why *do* they let the public in here?" '[57]). He walked to work every day from Thurloe Square via Piccadilly Circus to Bloomsbury, and said when the amiable Soame proposed an alternative route: 'Walk across Hyde Park? My dear Soame, I *hate* the country.'

Ivy and Margaret, though nowhere near so extreme as Willie, took the Londoners' view of the country as all very well for holidays so long as you were not expected to live in it. But they were both fond of Soame who returned their liking, admiring especially Margaret's habit of speaking her mind no matter whose toes she trod on, and seeing straight through Ivy's small talk: 'She was one of the very few women I've ever met, whom one just used to sit and listen to.' Even with Soame, Ivy never discussed anything much beyond housekeeping—the vagaries of refrigerators and the new gas boiler, varieties of biscuit and gentleman's relish—but 'the things she said were strange, mysterious, illuminating'. Though still very much one of Margaret's young men, Soame came eventually to see Ivy as by far the more remarkable of the two, and the seeds of a lifelong affection were sown during the three months she spent at Bottisham in the autumn of 1939. This was her first and only stay of any length in the kind of country house she generally wrote about, and Bottisham was everything she and Margaret liked best: a severely simple, small, elegantly proportioned Georgian brick house with a flagged hall and a lovely square stairwell, pierced by long windows which give the hall and the principal rooms that sensation of light and space so perennially dear to East Anglian builders.

The hall stands in its own park, approached by a long, curving gravel drive, backed by stable yards and service wings, encircled by lawns, glades and woods, formal walks and alleys full of daffodils and violets in spring, as well as two great walled gardens (where Ivy in happier times picked soft fruit, and apricots trained round the walls with roses, japonica and a border of espaliered apples). Bottisham, like Sir Roderick Shelley's ancestral home in *Two Worlds and Their Ways*, is surrounded by trees sighing in the wind and by 'flat green land'[58] stretching as far as the eye can see. Like Horace Lamb's house in *Manservant and Maidservant*, it is 'fifty miles from the east coast of England'[59] with the same 'wide bleak rooms' where water froze on the windowpanes (the winter of 1939–40 was the coldest for more than forty years), and the same once despised Georgian furniture newly restored to fashion. Like so many of the impoverished estates in Ivy's books, the place was no longer self-supporting (there had been an indoor staff of six, including a boy whose time was almost entirely spent trimming lamps, before death duties when Soame's father died in the 1930s had entailed drastic cutting back); and its occupants suffered, like the Lambs and the Shelleys, from the difficulty of heating, maintaining and repairing the fabric in time of fuel restriction and staff shortage.

Admittedly, Ivy's country houses are as artificial and inconsistent as her arbitrary period settings: their primary purpose is to provide a sealed environment as isolated and enclosed as Kafka's castle or Beckett's dumping grounds, another sector of the twentieth-century no-man's-land designed for exploring man's inhumanity, inadequacy and infinite resilience in face of both. As a writer, Ivy was no more interested in nuances of class than in other inessentials like her characters' looks, clothes or taste in furniture. In so far as she bothered about domestic detail at all, she drew on the comparatively rootless, suburban, rising professional or self-made middle classes to which she herself belonged (Andrew Stace and Godfrey Haslam, the first two landowning squires in her books, share her own family background of nonconformism and trade respectively) as much as on the quite different ethos of the landed gentry. Supposed country squires like Duncan Edgeworth, Horace Lamb, Cassius Clare and Miles Mowbray—or for that matter John Ponsonby with his goatee beard and his life of 'service to the pen'[60] —would all ring a great deal more true as masters of the grander sort of residential villa, standing in its own shrubbery instead of a park, and staffed by servants recruited from the local employment agency rather than from a village dependent for generations on its big house. What is missing is any sense of continuity, of the network of responsibilities and obligations binding the manor to its surrounding community: it is a discrepancy easily overlooked since the upper classes, never in any case great readers, were almost by definition debarred from tackling any writer as unorthodox as Ivy, while her admirers were generally not much concerned with social niceties. 'Margaret showed her the first butler she ever saw,' said Willie King,[61] who was one of the few (Hester's cousin, Michael Pinney, was another) in a position to note that Ivy was not in fact writing at all accurately about his own, largely obsolete social caste.

Nonetheless it is noticeable that, after her visit to Bottisham, a slightly more practical note creeps into her writing on the rare occasions when it touches on the routines of estate management (' "Bailiffs, tenants, gardeners," said Cassius . . . "Accounts," he said in a just audible voice'[62]), or the successive stages by which people's grounds go to pot (' "Your gravel wants attention, Chase," said Gaunt . . . "And the road through the park needs repair" '[63]). Ivy always had pleasant memories of Bottisham: she found the low-lying, windswept countryside sad, but the park with its sheltered gardens and walks was a consolation, and, since she kept all her life the knack she had learnt as a child in the schoolroom of being able to work anywhere in spite of distractions, she was almost certainly beginning to think about her next novel. 'We would often see her about the village, usually too absorbed in her thoughts to notice us,' wrote Dulcie Pendred,[64] who had read Ivy's books and been invited to meet her at the hall by Mrs Jenyns (whose attempts to amuse her guests were not always so well received).

Soame, working for the Admiralty in London, came down only at weekends, leaving his mother, who was wholly without intellectual or artistic leanings, to cope as best she might with what was proving a trying visit. Several people noticed at the time that old Mrs Jenyns—a kind and punctiliously attentive hostess, devout churchwoman and solid subscriber to the conventional morality of her generation—was rather puzzled by Ivy, and remained puzzled until out of politeness she read one of her books, when she was appalled. The book was thought to be *Pastors and Masters* which takes Dr Johnson's line, rather than the first Soame Jenyns', on doing good (' "The sight of duty does make one shiver," said Miss Herrick. "The actual doing of it would kill one, I think" '[65]). Soame's mother, who came of Quaker stock (she was one of the formidable Yorkshire Peases, descended from the Gurneys and Elizabeth Fry), had the ingrained Quaker horror of passing judgment though she could not help complaining, to Ivy herself as well as to Soame and Mrs Pendred, about the wickedness and oddity of the people in Ivy's books.

But, if she was flustered by Ivy's characters, she had far more to put up with from Margaret who did not trouble to hide the fact that for her there were no compensations at Bottisham: her friends were nearly all scattered, called up or seconded, social life was a desert, the sale rooms were out of reach, professional outlets were drying up, even the long-postponed book on William Kent seemed uninviting at close quarters. Mrs Jenyns had hoped that having Margaret in the house would help loosen her hold on Soame, or at least increase his mother's share in the professional, intellectual and social side of his life which Margaret at the end of the 1930s had looked like monopolizing; but in fact, far from making headway with his London contacts, Soame's mother found her position in her own house made steadily more uncomfortable by Margaret's critical looks, scornful laughter and mocking tongue. Bored and restless, Margaret disapproved of practically everything her hostess did, disliking especially the sight of Mrs Jenyns setting off down the drive on her regular rounds of the cottages, to distribute largesse in the village and see to the school.

Mrs Jenyns for her part had always taken her duties as the squire's lady seriously. She was well-liked on the whole by the villagers who relied on her support, helped themselves to her services, applied to her with their problems and knew all about her own troubles at home ('To some extent she was a brass serpent,' said Ivy's friend Anna Browne, meaning that, like Moses' followers in the Temple, the local people found it handy to have someone set up on show as a figurehead: 'There was a lot of brass-serpenting in those days'). When Mrs Jenyns had first come as a bride to the hall there had been soup at the lodge gates for the poor, and to the end of her life the schoolchildren still touched their caps; before the war, some of them even wore the Jenyns' charity clothes—green suits for the boys, and purple frocks for the girls.

It was all too much for Margaret, who had always drawn the line at organizing anything beyond Shakespeare readings for the Broad-windsor villagers. Perhaps this whole encounter with a way of life that struck her as intolerably overbearing and interfering brought back painful memories of conflict in the schoolroom at Ashbourne; certainly her friends were astonished when news leaked back to London that Margaret and Ivy throughout their visit to Bottisham had been obliged, by the sheer force of Mrs Jenyns' personality, to become regular churchgoers for the first and last time in their life together. The visit lasted in mounting mutual uneasiness ('I don't know if Ivy had ever been inside a church before,' said Soame, marvelling with mixed consternation and pride at his intrepid parent) until Christmas, when Mrs Jenyns thankfully packed her bags and left to stay with another son for the holiday: Ivy and Margaret went back to London and wrote, no less thankfully, cancelling plans to return on 8 January.

Churchgoing had been one difficulty, bearing the burdens of the village was another, the dogs made a third (Margaret, who, like all the Jourdains, loathed domestic animals, had not hesitated to object to the Jenyns' dogs coming to be fed by their mistress after meals in the dining room instead of being kept, if at all, out of sight in the servants' quarters). An already exasperating state of affairs was not improved, from Margaret's point of view, by the fact that Ivy had fans in the neighbourhood. Young Mrs Pendred, married to a carver teaching at Bottisham Village College and living a mile away in Swaffham Bulbeck, vividly remembered being tackled by Margaret in private after tea on the first day they met: ' "You haven't really read her books, have you?" she said brusquely. "Almost nobody reads them, and she only sells about 250 copies." ' Mrs Pendred, who had worked for the *New Statesman* and 'dutifully followed the avant-garde tastes of the literary editor', replied firmly that she had, and could if required prove it by producing her copy of *More Women Than Men*. 'Miss Jourdain was silenced. Then she said, "*Well*, and in Swaffham Bulbeck!" '[66]

1940–1945

'When war casts its shadow, I find that I recoil'

I

MARGARET BEGAN THE new year, January 1940, with a tag from Spinoza at the front of her diary: 'A free man thinks of death least of all things, and his wisdom is a meditation not of death but of life.' The war having apparently got off to a false start, evacuees had been steadily trickling back all that winter to London. 'Ivy had no courage, I mean no physical courage at all,' said Herman. 'Margaret on the other hand was splendidly brave.'[1] It was Ivy who had insisted on fleeing the bombs in the first place and, when none fell, presumably Margaret who determined that the time had come to return. It meant that she could work again, and go back to lunching with Soame, Willie, Herman or Sybil Assheton-Smith; while for Ivy there was a new admirer, the young novelist Robert Liddell, who had sent her a critical essay on her work and was invited to tea in April to collect his manuscript. He was one of the small army of readers recruited by the *New Statesman*, having first heard of Ivy five years before when Raymond Mortimer identified her as the single most powerful force at work in the English novel in the generation following James Joyce and Virginia Woolf:

At first sight her work strikes you as clumsy and heavy-fisted; her figures, though solid, are not what is called 'life-like', and she composes her books on highly defined and artificial designs. In fact, she is open to all the reproaches laid upon the founders of post-impressionism. And it is still as useless, I think, to put her work before the general public as it was to put that of Cézanne a quarter of a century ago . . .[2]

Robert had immediately ordered a copy of the book under review which was *A House and Its Head*: 'It filled a weekend when I was alone . . . I read it twice, my hair (like that of Henry Tilney in *Northanger Abbey*) standing on end . . . I thought I should go mad if my brother did not come home at the appointed hour, for I longed to thrust it into his hands.'[3] Robert and his younger brother Donald were themselves only slowly recovering from damage inflicted in their formative years by a tyrannical stepmother. Robert, having got away from home to go up to Oxford, had been joined by Donald in rooms in the Banbury Road where, to their own content and their relatives' considerable annoyance, they set about leading the peaceful, unmolested life of seclusion and self-sufficiency so often enjoyed by survivors or non-participants in Ivy's books. Her novels (Robert sent for the four early books as well as writing to Blackwoods for a copy of the 1911 edition of *Dolores*) supplied them with a map of a landscape which they already knew intimately. It was a double shock of recognition and revelation: the two brothers spoke and wrote to one another thereafter in the manner of Ivy's books.

Robert, who worked in the manuscript department of the Bodleian Library, hunted in vain for traces of Compton-Burnett family history in directories, Burke, Crockford's and back copies of *The Times* (which yielded only Noel's obituary, and a cursory report of the inquest on Ivy's two youngest sisters); and the search was not much helped by Spencer Curtis Brown, who became Robert's literary agent in 1937 and justified Ivy's dim view of anyone connected with publishing by saying, quite untruthfully, that she was 'very deaf and very slow'. The Liddells' curiosity remained unappeased and their admiration intense. Their own experience of persecution and cruelty in a thoroughly respectable, upper-middle-class household in South Kensington, only a few streets away from Cornwall Gardens ('my brother and I were her predestined readers. And so often we passed under the windows of that Sibyl who knew everything'[4]), meant that they grasped sooner than most that Ivy's apparent clumsiness was not so much unlifelike as, on the contrary, an attempt to pursue reality itself well beyond the currently accepted limits of literary realism.

A friendship sprang up at once on Robert's first visit to Braemar Mansions: 'Ivy opened the door to me; she was small, neatly dressed in black, and rather surprisingly jewelled; her greying corn-coloured hair a little reminded me of the "blond head" in the Acropolis museum in Athens.' Robert had hopes of placing his article on Ivy with Cyril Connolly's highly fashionable *Horizon* (in the event Connolly published long essays by Mortimer and Eddie Sackville-West, so Robert's was published as an appendix to his *Treatise on the Novel* in 1947). Ivy was pleased and grateful. No one else had yet attempted to assess her work at anything like this length, or for that matter had the nerve to submit a manuscript beforehand for inspection; and, though she often met and some-times made friends with people who had written appreciatively about her work—Mortimer himself, Rosamond Lehmann, Vita and Eddie Sackville-West, Elizabeth Bowen and Mario Praz are obvious examples—she treated none of them as frankly, and with as little constraint, as she talked that afternoon to Robert about her books.

> I was seated on a hard sort of sofa covered with worn black velvet, and tea (as in *More Women Than Men*) went 'through all its stages'. 'Water-cress? Very wholesome,' offered Ivy. 'Home-made gingerbread, very good. Cheese straws.'

She asked him to emphasize the goodness of her characters, espe-cially the sensitivity and generosity evinced on occasion by her tyrants ('"It's because they were intelligent," she said, and for her there was no greater virtue than intelligence'). Before, during and for two or three hours after tea they discussed tyranny, virtue and sex in her novels, the influence of Greek tragedy and the gap in her career after *Dolores*, before moving on to the strengths and failings of other authors in a long, comfortable talk about books interrupted only when conversation got on to Margaret's sister's *Adventure* (one of Robert's jobs at the Bodleian had been to cata-logue the contents of the box—'Miss Jourdain's baby'—contain-ing all the original documents), and 'would not easily get off it'.

A few weeks later Robert was up again in London, bringing his brother on 4 May for a hasty tea before all four left to catch the 4.45 p.m. train at Paddington, for Margaret and Ivy were on their way to spend a week at the Bear in Woodstock, just beyond Oxford, with Herman who had eagerly accepted Margaret's invitation to go over the furniture at Blenheim Palace. Apart from the food—even more frightful than usual in English pubs in wartime because it came out of tins—the visit was a success, especially for Ivy who cheerfully consumed her own and the others' daily dose of stewed prunes and never so much as set foot in the palace, giving her attention instead to the bluebells carpeting the grass and woods in the great park: 'Ivy was in her heaven. She would walk among the bluebells and sit down and look at them and admire them and was altogether very happy.'[5] Ivy saw to it that the stay included an excursion down the Banbury Road for tea with the Liddells, another hurried occasion (the ladies were en route for Margaret's brother Henry, also settled in North Oxford) when Margaret, whose social manner was a good deal more impressive than Ivy's, monopolized the conversation.

> Donald afterwards a little reproached me (and justly); he felt Ivy wanted to be more intimate, and that I held her off, and let Margaret dominate [wrote Robert]. He liked Margaret, but loved Ivy. I think it was when I took him to Braemar Mansions to tea that Ivy tapped on Margaret's head with the teapot, to stop her talk, and get down to tea.[6]

Nothing was said, then or later, about either party's family background. But Robert had sent Ivy a copy of his second novel, *Kind Relations* (1939), based on his own and his brother's experience as bewildered and unhappy small boys after their mother's death: 'You mean to go on?' she asked at their first meeting,[7] and at their next two she certainly saw enough to understand very well what the brothers meant to one another, and why. When Robert himself came to write about these years in a second autobiographical novel, *The Last Enchantments*, he described something very close to the special bond of intimacy and affection common between siblings in Ivy's novels.

Books and a fire—the Marlowes' refrain in *Parents and Children*—are also the sign and embodiment of happiness, blocking off the outside world, sealing in everything pleasant and companionable, in *The Last Enchantments*. The book was published in 1948, four years after Donald's death, and celebrates the two brothers' brief, peaceful respite together in Oxford between leaving home and being engulfed by a war that, in the spring of 1940, barely seemed to have started. 'None of us spoke of the War, in which (I think) none of us much believed; but it was there all the time, like a nagging pain,' Robert wrote afterwards of this afternoon in the Banbury Road, which neither he nor Ivy ever forgot. 'Soon, my brother and I knew, it must separate us, and we lived these last months together in the mutual kindness that (I hope and imagine) commonly exists between deeply attached people of whom one has been condemned by the doctors—but we might both be condemned. Such a time seems happier than it was in recollection, for anxiety, its chief torment, is over. Anxiety may be replaced by loss and intolerable grief, but at least it does not in itself last forever—not even in Hell, where there is no hope.'

Ivy and Margaret returned with Herman to London on 10 May, the day on which Hitler invaded Holland and Belgium. Hester, stranded as a press correspondent in the Netherlands, caught the last boat home three days later with help from Herman's sister Elka in Amsterdam, arriving in time to be struck by Margaret's courage in the terrifying weeks leading up at the end of the month to the fall of France and the evacuation of Dunkirk ('I remember Basil telling me he had never seen her so moved as by the invasion of the Low Countries and France . . .'). Herman's parents, who had gone into hiding when the Nazis reached Amsterdam, were persuaded like many other Dutch Jews to give themselves up of their own free will to the Germans, and both died in Auschwitz; Elka joined the resistance, was arrested and disappeared into German prisons; Herman himself, called up to join a contingent of the exiled Dutch army in Wales, suffered some kind of breakdown and was discharged as unfit to serve. Ivy and Margaret spent the summer in London, apart from a fortnight at the Marsden-Smedleys' seaside cottage in July, just before the first waves of German bombers began daily flights across the Channel. The London blitz started in earnest in the first week of September and, by the twenty-eighth of the month, Ivy and Margaret had left for the country just as Ivy had fled from the sound of guns on the Somme nearly twenty-five years earlier in the First World War.

This time they returned to the Noyes sisters in Wiltshire, putting up briefly at the Manor House Hotel in Warminster before taking refuge on 15 October with the Noyeses' niece, Joan Hadden, on Calves Hill at Chedworth in Gloucestershire. It was an experiment that turned out in its own way quite as badly as Bottisham. Miss Hadden was between the two friends in age, an old-fashioned gentlewoman with a pleasant, grey stone Cotswold house and a garden which she cultivated with that flair for colour and design —amounting in her case almost to genius—no other art so readily brings out in the English. But she was not popular in the neighbour-hood (according to Ivy, who told this story 'laughing so much that she could barely get the words out',[8] their hostess's only social intercourse with the local colonels, vicars and doctors took place at innumerable blood transfusion parties where 'they all lie prone on sofas and the floor in most intimate positions, and are publicly "cupped" in turn, and refreshed with tea afterwards'); and she was not kind to her aunts. Minna was by now eighty-four, Ella and Dora fast approaching their eighties. All three had made wills leaving everything to Joan, who was for all practical purposes their sole surviving relative, and who made no secret of finding them a burden. Her apparent heartlessness, both behind the aunts' backs and on visits to Sutton Veney, disturbed others besides Ivy and Margaret who reacted, as the helpless, horrified bystanders do in Ivy's books, by covering pity with humour. 'The two were very entertaining about their refugeeing with the niece of an old friend near Chedworth,' wrote James Lees-Milne, describing in his diary the first time he met Ivy and Margaret in 1942. 'They hated the niece, who tactlessly referred to her aunt's impending demise from senility, and let them know what she would do with her aunt's furniture and belongings.'[9]

Asked afterwards what she had made of her visitors, 'Miss Hadden was a bit reticent about them but she did say that Miss Jourdain had been difficult about her food.'[10] Food was by no means the only difficulty, and Margaret got away whenever she could, making trips to London or Oxford, fetching clothes, posses-sions and papers from the flat for disposal in parcels up and down the country—a mahogany occasional table with Henry in North Oxford, silk dresses and manuscript files with Alice Marcon (who had settled there too, after her husband's death in 1929), a fur coat with Elliston and Cavell in St Giles, and a hatbox full of oddments with Frank's son Seymour at Worth. War news grew worse, air raids heavier, future prospects more disheartening and, at the beginning of February 1941, Margaret came up to Braemar Mansions to supervise the storage of furniture at Frank Partridge's depository in South Mimms. Homelessness, falling incomes, food shortages, fuel and petrol rationing, uncertainty about where or how to get through the next year—the general physical and mental dislocations of War—all posed in acute form the problem, so vividly brought home to dependents in Compton-Burnett novels, of 'having to be housed and clothed and fed and provided for' ('When people have to be provided for, death is the only thing').[11]

Work became increasingly difficult, either to do or to manage without. 'As you say, it was an effort to write it in these days,' Ivy admitted to Robert about her next novel, 'but my reluctance to disappoint the few hundred people who were looking for it, held me to my purpose.'[12] She must have put in much time at Chedworth on the final stages of *Parents and Children* (' "Sir Jesse says we must continue to practise economy," said Priscilla Marlowe . . . "He says it need not interfere with our comfort. I could see he knew it prevented it" '[13]). Ella and Dora knew she was writing about them and, if Ivy disliked her hostess's bullying, grasping attitude to the Sutton Veney household, she could hardly have chosen a more delicate or cheering consolation than the portrait of the three Marlowes, which gave such particular satisfaction to both artist and sitters in the bleak spring of 1941.

The manuscript was acknowledged by Curtis Brown, writing to Ivy at Chedworth on 18 March,[14] but by the time Gollancz published the book two months later, the friends had packed up and moved on, as thankfully as they had left Bottisham, to stay with the Marsden-Smedleys at Hartley Court near Reading. This was a large house with its own staff and grounds, poultry yard and kitchen garden (priceless assets in wartime), which Hester had taken on the autumn before from her uncle, the neurologist Henry Head, and promptly turned into a sorting house and transit camp for friends and relations, their children and nannies. Margaret and Ivy, staying there for a few days at the New Year, had been relieved to find the Thames valley full of evacuees like Janette Thesiger (living with her sister at Farley Hill Place, Reading), and the Graham Rawsons with whom they had dined regularly in London. Basil, always a particular favourite with Margaret, found her company more of a comfort than ever at weekends when he left the Ministry of Economic

Warfare in London to join his wife's cheerful but noisy household with its floating population, improvised meals and miscellaneous collection of extras. Hospitable by nature, loving bustle and change, Hester had even found a new and appreciative young man for Margaret in the shape of her cousin, Michael Pinney, billeted with his family at Hartley while serving as a gunner nearby. But it says much for Ivy's relationship with the Marsden-Smedleys—or rather for the way in which, with old friends, she was still completely overshadowed by Margaret—that *Parents and Children* was published on 19 May, and reviewed at length with considerable enthusiasm in all the national newspapers, without anyone at Hartley Court taking the faintest notice. 'We knew absolutely nothing about it till long afterwards,' said Hester[15] who, like Basil, never entirely saw the point of all the fuss people later made about Ivy.

Ivy herself worked or read in her bedroom at Hartley, emerging to walk in the garden or compete for oranges at meal times ('I don't know if you remember Ivy eating an orange,' said Hester. 'She would attack it almost fiercely, but very neatly and sometimes eat several after quite a big meal'). Ivy's craving for fruit (hardly ever obtainable in wartime, even for ready money) grew sometimes so sharp that she told Michael Pinney she had once been reduced to raiding the larder for raw rhubarb, and her insistence that, when oranges were in short supply, she needed her share at least as much as the children rankled for years with Michael's wife, Betty. Margaret, too, found the little Marsden-Smedleys (the eldest, Luke, was her godson), their cousins, second cousins and small hangers-on hard to put up with en masse. There was a dispute over oranges, another about the discipline and upbringing of children. The children themselves looked on Margaret as a fixture, part of the furniture, the sort of honorary aunt who could always be relied on to throw up a sandcastle or, when you got older, sympathize about school and propose a holiday outing; while Ivy was still very much 'the poor relation', assigned in their minds to that vast army of dim, depressed spinsters tagging along in the wake of more fortunate relatives.

The friends spent the month of May at Hartley, searching meanwhile for a roof of their own which they finally found by the twenty-third and to which they moved ten days later. 'Our war-time activities compare most unfavourably with yours,' wrote Ivy

to Robert in Egypt. 'We are lurking ignobly in a little furnished
bungalow at Thatcham, three miles from Newbury, and about ten
miles from Reading, for the simple reason that we are afraid of
bombs.'[16] The bungalow, called 'Zealand', stood on the Elmhurst
housing estate, conveniently close both to the Pinney headquarters
and to Janette, who seems to have relied a good deal on Margaret
when Willie (also sharing their sister's house at Farley Hill) died
suddenly of a stroke on a trip to London in March. Rose Macaulay,
whose flat had been reduced to rubble in the last great raid on
London in May, paid them a visit at Thatcham, and so did Elizabeth
Bowen, one of the reviewers who found *Parents and Children* more
than a match for the enormities of life itself that spring ('. . . an icy
sharpness prevails in the dialogue. In fact, to read in these days a
page of Compton-Burnett dialogue is to think of the sound of glass
being swept up one of these London mornings after a blitz'[17]).
Marion Rawson took them to call on Louis and Mary Behrends
who had commissioned the painted chapel at Burghclere from
Stanley Spencer, kept open house for friends like Benjamin Britten
and generally cultivated the contemporary arts with an enthusiasm
that cut no ice with Ivy and Margaret, who would have preferred
more conventional country-house comforts.

Heywood Hill came down from London with his wife, Lady
Anne, both enthusiastic admirers of Ivy's, already beginning to
recruit a steady stream of new readers at their bookshop in Curzon
Street. Soame also brought his wife, Anne, soon after their wedding in April, so that Margaret might help them choose chairs.
Herman arrived, aggrieved and affronted to find Ivy, Margaret and
Gray carrying on business as usual in a modern 'monstrosity'
furnished with fumed oak, frightful paintings, reproduction dining
and living room 'suites', but otherwise greatly reassured by their
comforting air of serene and resolute triviality:

> I don't think that on the whole, and apart from fearing the
> dropping of bombs, the last World War meant a thing to either
> Margaret or Ivy. They simply looked upon it as unspeakable, and
> it did force them to change their habits and live in various and
> different forms of discomfort until it was over and they could
> resume their pre-war way of life, and that was all it meant to
> them.[18]

2

CERTAINLY THIS WAS the effect Ivy desired at all costs to produce, though there are indications that it was not always easy to preserve a calm front over what people in her books call 'inner tumult'.[19] When the seventeen-year-old Francis Wyndham (who had sent Ivy a fan letter from Eton) came to tea at Thatcham in the critical period after the German invasion of Russia in June, he was intercepted at the bus stop by Margaret who warned him that neither the bombing, nor the fighting on the Russian front, must on any account be mentioned in Ivy's presence.[20] War brought out the protective instinct always uppermost in Margaret when Ivy struck other people as being, however obscurely, in distress. Ivy herself told Robert a few years later that her ability to read the news had been exhausted by the shock and strain of two world wars ('I turn my eyes from the reconstruction of 1914,' she wrote to another friend when a spate of war memoirs flooded the papers in the 1960s: 'I have had enough'[21]). At the time she did not discuss her own state of mind in this war any more freely than she had in the first. When Jack Beresford was killed on duty with the Home Guard in the autumn of 1940, Ivy resorted to the same formal, guarded tone she had used to contain her desperation after Noel's death in 1916:

October 22, 1940

Dearest Dorothy,
    There is so much courage about us today, and so much feeling that any demand upon it must simply be met, that the normal thoughts and feelings seem out of place. And yet I can't help seeing it all as tragedy. It is a rough piece of road for you. May you be able to push on. Let me have a word to say how you are.
                With all my love and sympathy,
                                Ivy.

Jack was the person to whom Noel had confided his hopes and fears without reserve, as he never could to Ivy, from the trenches in the First World War. His death brought back feelings reinforced a year later when Hester's closest brother, Bernard Pinney, was killed in

Libya at Christmas 1941. Hester, supported as always by Margaret (who had first known Bernard as a small boy jumping on the gravestones in Broadwindsor churchyard), found great gentleness in Ivy at this time as well as strength and practical realism. Matter-of-factness was always Ivy's strategy against grief. 'I hope that your brother is quite well and not in any danger, a thing I can't help hoping about my friends,' she wrote on 5 January 1942, ten days after news came of Bernard's death, to Robert whose brother was serving in Bomb Disposal: 'I am a very bad war-time subject.'

She and Margaret had decided once again to return to London, encouraged by the respite from bombing and constrained by shortage of funds (Margaret's bank, more than usually restive about her permanent overdraft which now stood at £316—as much as she had earned in any one year even in her palmy prewar period—had written ominously in December to remind her 'that the Bank is now only lending money for essential War purposes'[22]).

> The problem of meeting two rents on an income sunk below the level of one, has proved impossible of solution, and we are soon returning to Kensington and whatever risks there must be— many less than there were, I should think [wrote Ivy in her letter to Robert]. We are looking forward to rescuing our poor flat from its plight of shattered windows and fallen ceilings and deluge of water from a burst cistern on the roof. The enemy attentions stopped short of an actual hit with a bomb, but bestowed this on so many adjacent houses that we got a good share of the results, and on more than one occasion it was a good thing we were not at home . . . we shall be glad to be back in sad and battered London, and among the stoic and battered friends who are held to it by work or poverty or sheer liking for the city in all her moods.

They returned on 17 February. Braemar Mansions remained intact ('Well, Miss, we had a bomb drop in Cornwall Gardens and broke nearly every window in the Gardens. There was only one in your dinner-room so do not worry as I have had it fix', wrote Gray,[23] who seems to have gone on ahead at Christmas to clear up). But the porter of the Thesigers' block of flats just round the corner from

Cornwall Gardens had been killed in the street while Ernest him-self, hanging out of his window one Sunday morning, had watched a dogfight over the mansions which ended with one plane shot down in flames; another time a house almost next door disappeared in front of his eyes, carrying with it a friend who had run out to help.[24] Ernest, having sent Janette to the country, was one of the friends held to the city by work throughout the blitz: he spent evenings at the theatre, days making a comprehensive record in water colour of London's bombed churches, nights camped out under the stairwell with the only other two remaining occupants of the flats. Ivy and Margaret took to this makeshift version of London life with alacrity and relief. Gaps left by friends evacuated, bombed out or posted abroad were filled by newcomers like James Lees-Milne, invited to join the Hills after luncheon at Braemar Mansions on Saturday, 28 May 1942:

I arrived for coffee. This is a great occasion. Margaret Jourdain is patently jealous of Ivy Compton-Burnett, whom she keeps unapproachable except through herself, and even when approached, guards with anxious care. This is evident from the way in which the former diverts one's attention if she thinks one is talking too much to the latter. It is a selfish kind of affection, to say the least. The two have lived together for years and are never parted. They are an Edwardian and remarkably acidulated pair. The coiffures of both look like wigs. The hair is bound with a thin fillet across the forehead and over a bun at the back. Thin pads of hair hang down their foreheads unconvincingly. Miss C.-B., whom I consider to be the greatest living novelist, is upright, starchy, forthright and about fifty-seven to sixty. There is a bubbling undercurrent of humour in every observation she makes, and she makes a good many, apparently hackneyed and usually sharp, in a rapid, choppy, rather old-fashioned upper-middle-class manner, clipping her breathless words. She enunci-ates clearly and faultlessly, saying slightly shocking things in a matter-of-fact tone, following up her sentences with a lot of 'dontcherknows', and then smiling perceptibly. She has a low, breasty chuckle. She has not unpleasing, sharp features, and her profile is almost beautiful. But she is not the kind of woman who cares tuppence for appearances, and wears a simple, unrememberable black dress (I guess all her clothes are unrememberable), which she smooths down with long fingers.

. . . We talked chiefly of country houses. Miss Jourdain looks rather wicked and frightening, when she peers through her quizzing glass. Miss C.-B. says that Miss J. has too little occasion to use it these days, now that there are so few houses available with furniture to be debunked; that she lost a lens in the train, and it has hardly mattered.[25]

James Lees-Milne, historic buildings secretary to the infant National Trust (it had a staff of six in those days, and about half a dozen historic houses open to the public), had been recently invalided out of the army and was to spend the rest of the war inspecting properties that eventually formed the basis of the Trust's collection ('I knew at once he was the sort of young man you would rope in,' said Ernest Thesiger to Margaret, who cordially agreed: 'He is quite a new acquisition'[26]). But it must have been disconcerting to find someone who might legitimately have been supposed to fall well within Margaret's sphere of influence regarding her as scarcely more than an adjunct to Ivy. Michael Pinney, charmed and flattered by Margaret's interest in him as a young man, had the impression from the start that Margaret felt herself cold-shouldered by the literary admirers who did not bother to conceal their low opinion of the furniture faction. The war had reduced Margaret's income to vanishing point and severely cramped her professional scope: she had not even found a publisher for her last book, an anthology called *Fantasy and Nonsense*[27] which she had spent much time compiling at Chedworth and Thatcham. Ivy's sales meanwhile were beginning to increase sharply, and so were her letters from fans ('I think I should hardly have ventured to write to you but for the war,' wrote one who thought 'the wit, the restraint, the balance' of *Parents and Children* 'almost perfect: superior even, if I may say so without impertinence, to the wit, the restraint, the balance of Jane Austen'[28]). Her critical reputation had never stood higher, and she herself enjoyed on occasion playing something other than second fiddle. Accounts of Ivy in the early 1940s show her as generally more forthcoming, talkative, even assertive than ever before: these were the years when for the first time people who met her—Robert Liddell, James Lees-Milne, Anne Hill, Robin Fedden—began noting down things Ivy had said as soon as they got home:

She makes very acid comments in a prim, clipped manner, enunciating sharply and clearly every syllable while casting at one sidelong glances full of mischief [wrote Jim Lees-Milne in his diary on 28 May 1942]. We talked about servants. She agreed that today fewer servants managed to get through double the work, doubly efficiently, to what a greater number did a generation ago. They are better fed and housed, she said. Her parents took care to have excellent food themselves, whereas their children were thrown the scraps . . . For supper she used to be given the crusts cut from her parents' toast. She has an insatiable appetite for chocolates, and Ernest Thesiger told her she was intemperate in some of her habits. Miss Jourdain gave us cherry brandy, but did not offer any to Miss C.-B., who took some for herself. She swigged it all in one gulp instead of sipping, declaring that it was excellent and she would have some more. Miss J. intervened and would not allow it.[29]

Clearly some sort of realignment was going on between the two friends now that Ivy's subsidiary status was no longer a matter of course. She still went nowhere alone, but it was not always easy to tell who was whose consort, at any rate for onlookers faced for the first time with this majestic and arresting couple, sitting side by side bolt upright on a sofa at somebody's party, or arriving for dinner dressed in their full prewar fig of long satin evening dresses with matinée coats ('Look, Margaret, do you see?' said Ivy one night at the Kings when Viva, who had been cooking, wore a Viyella frock and Anne Hill came straight from working all day at the bookshop in a shirt and skirt: 'When we get home we shall have to chop a foot off our dresses'[30]). When they went out these days, it was as likely to be to a literary as a furniture function. They were among the notables assembled at the Aeolian Hall for the Sitwells' celebrated poetry reading on 14 April, along with the Queen and the two princesses and the poet Dorothy Wellesley, who was tipsy and had to be forcibly restrained from reciting by Vita Sackville-West and the programme seller, Beatrice Lillie. 'Ivy Compton-Burnett ate half a pot of raspberry jam, and I was shocked to see her surreptitiously wipe her sticky fingers upon the cover of my sofa,' wrote Jim Lees-Milne, with whom Ivy seems to have behaved at times less like the governess than the naughtiest girl in the school: 'Both she and Margaret ate like horses. This time Miss C.-B. talked a great deal more than Margaret. Her description of the Poetry Reading and Lady Gerald Wellesley's antics was very funny. They are a wicked pair.'[31]

They dined with Jim and John Pope-Hennessy before a charity concert given in Whistler's house by the young Peter Pears and Benjamin Britten in November. Ivy still kept herself to herself so far as the literary establishment was concerned, presenting an impregnable front more often than not to other writers like Lytton Strachey's niece, Julia, at a christening party for the Hills' baby daughter on 2 December 1943:

> Miss Compton-Burnett looked handsome, not unlike Elinor Glyn. She stood, a solid blockbuster or blockhouse whichever way you look at it, in a navy Bradley's coat embroidered with winding strips of astrakhan like the carefully-designed paths in a municipal garden. Her portcullis, drawbridge and visor were all down too. After an hour's hard work, I elicited only two things from her that interested me, one that she never felt guilty about anything, and the other that she had no set working hours—'Oh no, nothing like *that*.'[32]

But in this shifting, erratic, oddly mixed wartime social scene, Ivy and Margaret belonged undeniably as they never had before to the London intelligentsia, or, in Ivy's phrase, what there was of it ('Let us shut the door to keep the heat in. What there is of it,' was one of her sayings, part of the ritual recorded by John Pope-Hennessy of 'going in to lunch on a freezing draught ridden day' at Braemar Mansions[33]). They saw a good deal of Richard Aldington's ex-wife, the poet Hilda Doolittle (always 'Mrs Aldington' to Ivy as Rosamond Lehmann was 'Mrs Philipps' and Elizabeth Bowen 'Mrs Cameron'), and her friend Bryher in Lowndes Square; also of John's austere and erudite mother, Dame Una Pope-Hennessy, who lived with her two clever sons at 48 Ladbroke Grove in North Kensington (opposite St John's church which Ivy's half-sister Iris attended, on the wrong or north side of the park). Dame Una's was one of the houses where Margaret found herself underrated, now that Ivy was beginning to cut a figure in her own right and clearly enjoying it no end. 'I went to tea with Ivy Compton-Burnett and Margaret Jourdain. Anne Hill was there; also Dame Una and Rose Macaulay. Again I was the only man among blue-stockings,' wrote

Jim, who must have felt he took his life in his hands in the highly competitive atmosphere engendered whenever Dame Una began trading intellectual snubs with Margaret: 'Ivy C.-B., I noticed, when she did condescend to speak, shouted everyone else down.'[34] Chitchat about the weather, prices, or servants was out of the question at Ladbroke Grove—'Dame Una wouldn't countenance small talk to a degree that was really terrifying'[35]—where Ivy politely discussed Greek tragedy instead with her hostess.

When they first met round about the winter or spring of 1943, Dame Una was writing her life of Dickens, John (the art historian, later head of the V&A) was at work on a book about Domenichino while his younger brother, the brilliant and wayward James, had just finished his *West Indian Summer*. 'Can't you write a book and join us?' said Dame Una to John's and Jamesey's friend Jim, who felt he would need more than a book to his name as a passport to this hopelessly exclusive, united and mutually protective society of three.[36] If Ivy's literary credentials were by this time unimpeachable, Margaret's barely passed muster:

> My mother was not much interested by Margaret Jourdain, but admired Ivy's books and was fascinated by her whole identity [wrote Sir John Pope-Hennessy]. For me Ivy was an acquired taste, but the more often one saw her and the better one got to know her the fonder of her one became . . . Sometimes I think the most important thing in life is how one tends one's talent, and she tended hers with marvellous disinterest and conviction and consistency. B.B. [Benjamin Britten] once said that if Giacometti sculptures could talk, they would speak like the characters in her books, but face to face one was conscious of a great wealth of humanity which was never, or scarcely ever, articulated.[37]

People who met Ivy in the 1940s or later were often aware of the unspoken sympathy and understanding flourishing alongside the rocklike endurance that had carried her through what had seemed unendurable in the First World War. Her attitude to the second was resigned, and thoroughly practical: the worst that could happen might dismay but could not surprise her and, in the meantime, she took the only available precaution which was flight ('We are such cowards. We both hate air raids and are frightened to death of bombs' were her opening words to Eddie Sackville-West on a visit to the National Trust's headquarters at West Wickham in June 1942[38]). But if Ivy had learnt early to count on nothing, she had also developed to a fine point the survivor's art of extracting pleasure from small things: a dish of prunes or an illicit lump of sugar in wartime, little tins of blackcurrant purée hoarded to give to her friends at Christmas 1942, a sunny afternoon spent with Dorothy Kidd in deckchairs in Regent's Park or exploring a country garden. 'The day with I. C.-B. and M.J. in the country was full of Visions Spiritual and Physical, we spent much time in Arabian Fruit and Flower Gardens, ripe Raspberries literally dropping about our feet—' wrote Dorothy on 18 July 1943, when Ivy and Margaret were staying for ten days at Uckfield in Sussex. The three saw much of one another that year when Roger Kidd was up at Cambridge: 'What a good vacation it was—Hampton Court in blazing sun, Kew Gardens, the Rooftreeites, all the readings behind these "magic casements", the list is endless but to be run through often if a dismayed moment comes,' wrote Dorothy to Roger on 8 October ('Another Keats like day after our rather gunfired night'), and again two days later: 'So glad I pulled myself together to meet the Rooftreeites in the Orangery [Wren's orangery in Kensington Gardens] this morning—M.J. and I sat warmly in the sun while Miss I. prowled about the Round Pond—Walpole is tiresome but the saying of one of his characters "It isn't life, it's the Courage you bring to it" rings in my head—certainly M.J. has a goodly stock'.

Margaret's courage buoyed Ivy up, perhaps especially in the long, hot, gunfire-ridden summer and autumn of 1943 which the two spent in London, until a warning from Elliott Felkin that the Germans had invented some kind of flying bomb made them pack up once again just after Christmas to take refuge in Dorset. But Margaret had none of the gift Ivy was beginning to cultivate for cherishing her friends, and making them feel how much they meant to her. Raisley Moorsom remembered Ivy, some time in the 1920s, contradicting Elliott when he looked forward to escaping from all human claims in a shamelessly selfish old age: 'Nonsense, my dear Elliott, you will need all the love and affection you can get.' The saying—so unlike the cheerful cynicism Ivy generally conveyed in those days when she seemed neither to ask nor expect anything from anyone—startled Raisley so much that, even fifty years later, he remained at a loss to account for it. But it explains much about Ivy's own old age when she drew more and more on a side of herself she had long and severely suppressed in life, though never in her writing. Bertrand Russell describes a comparable readjustment when he summed up his position, in June 1931, by saying that he had always 'believed in the value of two things: kindness and clear thinking'[39] and that as he grew older he found the two things almost impossible to separate.* It is the philosophy invariably adopted in Ivy's books by characters like Dudley Gaveston who explained, when asked what he meant by saying it was always a mistake for people to try to see themselves as others see them:

> 'I think I only mean . . . that human beings ought always to be judged very tenderly, and that no one will be as tender as themselves. "Remember what you owe yourself" is another piece of superfluous advice.'
> 'But better than most advice,' said Aubrey, lowering his voice as he ended. 'More tender.'[40]

The fourteen-year-old Aubrey in *A Family and a Fortune* (1939) was the first of those enchanting, mercurial, tender-hearted and hard-headed children whose strangeness corresponds (as one reviewer remarked of the pair in *Elders and Betters*[41]) more to what it was actually like being a child than to any conventional, external, grown-up's eye view of childhood. After Aubrey, there were nine young Sullivans—including the tyrannical three-year-old Neville, surely one of the most accurately observed infants in literature—in

---

* At first these two remained more or less distinct; when I felt triumphant I believed most in clear thinking, and in the opposite mood I believed most in kindness. Gradually, the two have come more and more together in my feelings. I find that much unclear thought exists as an excuse for cruelty, and that much cruelty is prompted by superstitious beliefs. The War made me vividly aware of the cruelty in human nature, but I hoped for a reaction when the War was over. Russia made me feel that little was to be hoped from revolt against existing governments in the way of an increase in kindness in the world . . . I have not found in the post-war world any attainable ideals to replace those which I have come to think unattainable. So far as things I have cared for are concerned, the world seems to me to be entering upon a period of darkness. (*Autobiography of Bertrand Russell*, Vol. II, p.158.)

Russell, spurred by personal unhappiness in 1931 to articulate a pessimism widespread among people of his and Ivy's generation, was appalled by the 'very sober philosophy' she took for granted: what interested her was not the metaphysician's unending search for attainable ideals but the ways in which people actually function without them.

Parents and Children, two Calderons and a Donne in *Elders and Betters*, six little Lambs in *Manservant and Maidservant*: dependent, vulnerable, alert and unsentimental, they live precariously in an unpredictable, often violent world which seemed perhaps more readily recognizable in wartime than before or since, as Elizabeth Bowen was the first to point out, reviewing *Parents and Children* in the *New Statesman* on 24 May 1941:

> Miss Compton-Burnett, as ever, makes few concessions; she has not, like some of our writers, been scared or moralised into attempting to converge on the 'real' in life. But possibly life has converged on her.

Ivy never wrote directly about wartime conditions, unless you count the austerity regime imposed on the household in *Manservant and Maidservant* (published in 1947, when food, fuel and clothes rationing became, if anything, stricter than ever) by Horace Lamb who skimps on his children's shabby, frayed, shrunken and handed-down clothes, docks them of sweets and toys, doles out economy rations to the adults (' "Six cutlets would have been enough," said Horace. "They know we do not eat seven" '[42]) and prowls the house snatching live coals from the grates (' "Fire piled right up the chimney! Who is responsible?" said Horace'[43]). When *Parents and Children* came out in May 1941, Ivy told Douglas Muir (a young R.A.F. officer invited as an admirer to meet her at Hartley Court) that she did not think she would be able to write anything more during the war.[44] Eighteen months later she complained to Jim Lees-Milne that she could not get on with her book because the war was drying her up, and *Elders and Betters* was indeed a year behind schedule when it finally appeared in January 1944. 'Not a cheerful tome,' wrote Dorothy, who was staying with Ivy and Margaret at Lyme Regis when *Elders and Betters* was published. 'Reviews of Ivy's book are too good, encouraging this devastating analysis of the evil in human nature.'[45]

Dorothy's was the common complaint of romantics defending down the ages the importance of being ignorant ('Of all his lovable qualities there was none so nobly potent . . . as David's white innocence, his utter want of curiosity about all that was filthy,' wrote E. F. Benson[46] who had fought to the last against the novelist's right to deal openly with matters much better kept dark, like homosexuality). But it was an attitude less prevalent in wartime when Ivy's hard line seemed on the whole as exhilarating as it was alarming. Vita Sackville-West told Ivy that reading *Elders and Betters* was like sucking a lemon ('She writes that she often felt inclined to hurl the lemon to the far end of the room but was aware that she would have to get up and pick it up again!' reported Margaret from Lyme to Heywood Hill[47]); and for once Ivy's astringency appealed to a public accustomed by this time to fear and privation, unable any longer to bank on the future, unimpressed by official evasiveness or easy sentiment, increasingly inclined to feel with Vita that the only answer was a lemon. Ivy's sales had risen steeply with *Parents and Children* in the early part of the war; Gollancz started with an initial three thousand copies of *Elders and Betters* on 24 January 1944, followed by two thousand more, then another thousand, all of which had sold out by April without satisfying the demand (the eventual print run came to more than double that amount[48]). 'The effect out here is quite astonishing,' wrote Captain Muir, whose copy reached him that summer on a posting in Malaysia with South East Asia command. 'If it has been difficult to write in wartime, I assure you that the extra effort has at least brought an extra reward to us.'[49]

What might be called the moral economy of Ivy's books had always been organized on a war footing. The rigorous honesty and irony that so often strike detractors as heartless, uncalled-for and cold will be familiar to anyone acquainted with soldiers' letters from the front in both world wars. The frame of mind underlying Noel Compton-Burnett's letters to Ivy and Jack in the first war was analysed in the second by the poet Keith Douglas, explaining his own lost innocence as a writer shortly before he was killed in Normandy in 1943:

I suppose I reflect the cynicism and the careful absence of expecta-tion (it is not quite the same as apathy) with which I view the world. As many others to whom I have spoken, not only civilians and British soldiers, but Germans and Italians, are in the same state of mind, it is a true reflection . . . To be sentimental or emotional now is dangerous to oneself and to others. To trust anyone or to admit any hope of a better world is criminally foolish, as foolish as it is to stop looking for it. It sounds silly to say work without hope, but it can be done; it's only a form of insurance; it doesn't mean work hopelessly.[50]

This form of insurance, too costly and painful to be generally recommended for long, was essential to Ivy whose humanity had grown from the complete lack of illusion with which she had emerged from the First World War. It was a policy that paid handsomely in the second, as L. P. Hartley reluctantly acknowledged, reviewing *Elders and Betters* for the *Sketch* on 23 February 1944: 'Anti-realistic, careless and even defiant of probability as it is, Miss Compton-Burnett's work sometimes seems nearer to reality than that of any living novelist.'

3

AT THE BEGINNING OF 1944 when *Elders and Betters* came out, Ivy once again turned her back on the war, embarking with Margaret on a final period of what she always called 'exile' at Lyme Regis where they had often spent holidays before the war. Lyme lies a few miles along the coast from the Marsden-Smedleys' cottage at Seatown, within easy reach of Pinneys at Racedown and Michael's family home at Bettiscombe as well as Margaret's old haunts at Broadwindsor, but low spirits, high prices and petrol restrictions made for isolation. Dorothy and Roger had travelled down with them at the New Year ('How lovely it is to feel that we know this place of Peace to be found with Persian Carpet ease—unfettered sea and coast'[51]) for five days spent exploring the precipitous little town with its harbour, cliffs, Tudor tea shops and sheltered sea walks, its prospect of sky and sea which Ivy and Margaret admired from deckchairs in wintry sunshine or, more often, from behind the bow windows of the Royal Lion overlooking the front. The Lion ranked high on Margaret's list of 'possible pubs'[52] for its '*ample* food' and willing service, but cramped quarters and fairly hit-or-miss housekeeping meant that, by the middle of the month, when heavy regular bombing had begun again on London, the two friends were looking for cheaper rooms of their own.

Yesterday M.J. and I turned to Lyme (Upper) as I have on one or two evenings after tea, having walks along lanes where the evening birds seemed certain of primroses and white and purple violets [wrote Dorothy on 18 January to Roger (who had started his Cambridge term while his mother returned for a further week to the Lion)], but yesterday we just called on a delightful old lady who'd apartments and a bureau like the one Anne received the letter from (here I went off for your *Persuasion* to find that Captain Wentworth was seated at a table so it was only in the room, *how* inaccurate one's mind is even about Jane Austen . . .) How grateful I am to you and the Rooftreeites for making me return to this unbelievably blissful place.

Jane Austen was always much in mind at Lyme, where she herself had stayed with her family and where she set parts of *Persuasion*. Hester remembered once driving Ivy to the far end of the sea front for a walk along the famous breakwater called the Cobb: 'I can see Ivy standing on the Cobb with her gloves on, her hair neat, but a rather flimsy scarf blowing in the wind, which is never very far off at Lyme Regis.' When they reached the place where Louisa Musgrave slipped in *Persuasion*, Ivy looked down, 'saying how much more important in the long run was the twisted ankle of a young girl than all the clamouring of leaders in far off countries . . .'[53] This, or something very like it, was Jane Austen's response when urged to turn her attention to foreign affairs;* and she crops up repeatedly in the dialogue Ivy and Margaret composed in the spring of 1944 for *Orion*. This was a new literary magazine founded by Edwin Muir (long an admirer of Ivy's), Denys Kilham Roberts, Cecil Day Lewis, and Rosamond Lehmann who had boldly asked Ivy to explain her astonishing technique and received a rather dubious response ('She said she had not known she possessed a technique "until I looked and found that it was so" '[54]). 'In the end we compromised by writing together a "Conversation in Lyme Regis" in the manner of George Moore's *Conversations in Ebury Street*,' wrote Margaret on 22 June 1944 to Heywood Hill. 'I rake up all the absurdities of criticism and she answers them, and tells us

---

* By the Prince Regent's librarian (*Jane Austen's Letters*, ed. R. W. Chapman, O.U.P. 1952, pp.451–2). Ivy, pressed by John Bowen in a radio interview in 1960 to explain why her characters steered clear of politics and the Irish question, replied that public affairs never bore on their lives in the same way as personal experience: 'and I think that must always be so with everyone in all countries and at all times, and in every case—don't you think so?' (Burkhart 3, p.168.)

why she writes as she does—It has its points.' This 'Conversation' was the nearest Ivy ever came to a considered public statement about her work, and for once it was Margaret who gracefully played second fiddle:

M.J. I should like to ask you one or two questions; partly my own and partly what several friends have asked. There is time enough and to spare in Lyme Regis, which is a town well-known to novelists. Jane Austen was here, and Miss Mitford.
I.C.-B. And now we are here, though our presence does not seem to be equally felt. No notice marks our lodging. And we also differ from Jane Austen and Miss Mitford in being birds of passage, fleeing from bombs. I have a feeling that they would both have fled, and felt it proper to do so, and wish that we could really feel it equally proper.[55]

Apart from this brief aside, apologetic but firm, current events hardly enter the 'Conversation': 'When war casts its shadow,' Ivy said, when asked why she never wrote about modern life, 'I find that I recoil.'[56] So do the bystanders in her books whose civilized, restraining voices prove so ineffectual against the explosions of primitive feeling that grew if anything fiercer as she steadily reduced overt contact with the contemporary world. Her four early novels, each in some sense experimental, had each maintained at least a nodding acquaintance with the life of the 1920s and 1930s, culminating in the cheerful modernity of tone, stylistic jerkiness and loose, gossipy structure of *More Women Than Men*. Thereafter, from *A House and Its Head* (1935) onwards, she narrowed her focus on the self-contained, heavily controlled and monitored, closed society of the high Victorian family. 'You write of the family as being a destructive unit,' said the novelist John Bowen in his 1960 radio interview with Ivy, who answered austerely: 'I write of power being destructive and parents had absolute power over children in those days. One or the other had.'[57] Concentration brought greater technical control, and with it the greater emotional pressure banked up, in *A House and Its Head*, behind Duncan Edgeworth's repressed and withering rages or, with *Manservant and Maidservant* (1947), the nervous tension licking out of control round the edges of Horace Lamb's voice in repeated, hysterical attacks on his two defenceless small sons. Nothing in the early books matches the great family gatherings in *A Family and a Fortune* (1939) where passion seems to swell between the lines, scenes which are closer to a play than a novel in their surge and beat of feeling, the tumult of voices juxtaposed and interwoven so that the reader is successively aware of up to eight or nine characters reacting, collectively and individually, in a richly orchestrated whole.

The political aspect of Ivy's novels was not lost on contemporaries: 'Apart from physical violence and starvation, there is no feature of the totalitarian régime which has not its counterpart in the atrocious families depicted in these books,' wrote Edward Sackville-West immediately after the war.[58] But less was said about the emotional generosity always present and, as her plots grew harsher and more constricted, increasingly prevalent in her work. Admiration and pity—mixed feelings evoked as much by those who inflict suffering as by those who endure it—came in this middle period of her life as a writer to be the normal background of her mind, as they were of Miss Mitford's in *Parents and Children*. Ivy's tyrants, by their very destructiveness, breed little pockets of resistance. Courage, tolerance, sweetness, sanity and understanding spring up everywhere in holes and corners of nursery, schoolroom and servants' hall. Romantic love may be outside her compass (though never the misdeeds committed for love's sake). But no writer has made more of the affections that bind people across the generations in the same family (children, grandparents, quite often one or other parent as well as sympathetic uncles and stepmothers), young or middle-aged friends, and the convivial old married couples who flourish so cheerfully behind the front lines—or beyond the closed front doors—of her 'atrocious families'. Persecution is not the less palpable because its victims are adept in the ancient and honourable British tradition of bearing the unbearable by joking about it ('"It is true that tragedy arouses pity and terror," said Nance. "In me, terror is getting the upper hand"'[59]). *A House and Its Head* and *Daughters and Sons*, two chilling tales of domestic oppression and exploitation, contain between them half a dozen of the funniest proposals in fiction; and, if comic relief was always a speciality, so is the long, slow return to equilibrium after havoc and ruin at the end of books like *A House and Its Head* and *A Family and a Fortune*, or the knack of extracting sympathy even for monsters like Horace in *Manservant and Maidservant*:

'Is there something in Horace that twines itself about the heart? Perhaps it is his being his own worst enemy. That seems to be thought an appealing attribute.'

'The trouble with people who have it,' said Charlotte, 'is that they are bad enemies to other people, even if not the worst.'[60]

Elders and Betters, the book Ivy and Margaret discussed in 'A Conversation', has less of these grace notes than most ('In no other novel does Compton-Burnett allow such a consistently low standard of behaviour to prevail among the principal characters,' was Violet Powell's verdict in *A Compton-Burnett Compendium*[61]), perhaps because it was conceived, written and published in wartime. But neither Ivy nor Margaret felt inclined to raise the wider implications of this or any other book (Margaret had still not got round to reading *Elders and Betters* the month after publication,[62] though she had mastered the plot by the time they came to write 'A Conversation' in March). Their dialogue stuck firmly to the concrete and particular. Ivy began by politely and airily endorsing Margaret's belief in the intrinsic absurdity of critical theorizing: 'I cannot tell you why I write as I do, as I do not know. I have even tried not to do it, but find myself falling back into my own way.'[63] Questioned about sources, she declined to acknowledge any debt to other writers, saying no most emphatically to Henry James and the Russian novelists, less so to the Greek dramatists, least of all to Jane Austen ('I have read Jane Austen so much, and with such enjoyment and admiration, that I may have absorbed things from her unconsciously. I do not think myself that my books have any real likeness to hers. I think that there is possibly some likeness between our minds').

Margaret's prosaic style of questioning clearly suited Ivy better than the more formal, literary approaches of later interviewers. Margaret was accustomed to treat a novel much like any other historical source, itemizing points of interest[64] like the little modern tables cluttering an old-fashioned parlour in *Persuasion*, the sybaritic sofas in *Mansfield Park*, the mahogany wardrobe in *Northanger Abbey*, the Pembroke tables in *Emma* and Jane Austen's unfinished fragment called *The Watsons* ('Once I thought I should go mad because I couldn't finish *The Watsons*,' Ivy told Robert Liddell at their first meeting[65]); and Margaret's professional eye for incidentals perhaps pushed Ivy further than she might otherwise have gone towards defining and defending her own condensed and abstracted kind of reality ('I hardly see why the date and style of the Gavestons' house should be given,' she said, faintly nettled by Margaret's only comment on *A Family and a Fortune*, 'as I did not think of them as giving their attention to it, and a house of a different date and style would have done for them equally well'). Though she would not waste her time or Margaret's on questions of novelistic innovation and theory, Ivy's part of 'A Conversation' returned explicitly, again and again, to her preoccupation with those mysterious, submerged, subconscious depths where human beings function without inhibition well below any visible, external level, which was why people in general gave her no help at all: 'They do not say or do things that are of any good. They are too indefinite and too much alike and are seldom living on any but the surface of their lives. Think how rarely we should ourselves say or do anything that would throw light on our characters or experience.'

Certainly Ivy and Margaret gave nothing away, either publicly or to their oldest and most intimate friends. 'Dear I. C.-B. and M.J. I *am* so thankful we bring cheer to an, at the moment, rather overcast existence for them though I don't exactly know why,' wrote Dorothy to Roger on 18 January 1944, when advance copies of *Elders and Betters* reached the Royal Lion from Gollancz. Ivy had been especially edgy and tiresome that week, as she so often was when she had finished or was on the point of bringing out a book, while Margaret found herself probably for the first time in her life at a loose end with no work on hand save a single French furniture article, Ivy's 'Conversation' and the Kent book (a prospect beginning to look up at last with the discovery of various Massingberd and other papers, including five unpublished letters from Alexander Pope). The last two were projects she would never have undertaken, as she told Heywood Hill, if it had not been for 'the breakdown of our ordinary life'.[66] Margaret was getting on for seventy in the spring of 1944, Ivy would be sixty in June, and neither welcomed the thought of living hand-to-mouth out of suitcases again, very likely for months on end. Exile seemed drearier than ever the second time round. Both missed London sadly, and their friends even more. 'I. C.-B.'s letter this morning is most amusing,' wrote Dorothy, back in London on 19 April, 'a description of the party from Bettiscombe; a criticism of her and

M.J.'s dialogue from *Orion*; saying they miss you and me! and ending "May we soon all gather on the pavements"—'

They had hoped to return to London themselves with the slackening of air raids at the end of March but Elliott's warnings of secret weapons meant that they were still in Lyme ('It isn't amusing but it is safe'[67]) when the new and terrifying V1s began falling in June, after the allied fleet landed in Normandy. Ernest, playing Malvolio in Regent's Park, reported flying bombs several times cutting out overhead, once so close that he was blown off the stage by the blast. 'I hope you have got Anne and the baby away?' wrote Margaret anxiously to Heywood on 22 June. '. . . It sounds unpleasant writing from a safe place to anyone in London and I feel apologetic about it. I hope this chaos won't last long.' Left to herself, Margaret might perhaps have settled, like Rose Macaulay, for braving the destruction in London, though she admitted that flying bombs —and later the even more alarming V2s or explosive rockets —made the capital 'impossible for the moment to idle people like ourselves, who are so used to safety that we feel like soft-shelled crabs!'[68]

Not that Lyme proved an ideal refuge. Money was a problem (they split the proceeds when Heywood sold one of Ivy's letters, supplied by Margaret in response to a request for manuscripts: 'Many thanks for the £1 which Ivy and I divided,' wrote Margaret, 'It will encourage her to write more letters'[69]). Where to stay was another problem. They moved at least half a dozen times at Lyme—from the Royal Lion to rooms at 'Cliff Bank' on the Sidmouth road in February, and on a month later to the Victoria Hotel, where they were staying when their Braemar Mansions flat 'had all its main windows blown in, so that it is a cave of the winds and uninhabitable'.[70] Margaret went up at the end of May to inspect the damage ('She says Ivy will not come back to London, she is so afraid of bombs'[71]), followed briefly a month later by Ivy: 'Our flat is blasted but the structure stands,' she wrote to Heywood on 3 August from the Victoria Hotel. Forced to pack up again, when the Victoria closed for a staff holiday in November, they shuttled to and fro for the next few months between the Royal Lion ('dearer and worse'[72]), the Clarence ('a smaller and cheaper hotel') and their old rooms at Cliff Bank. 'It is awfully harassing being driven from pillar to post, and it develops an acute longing for London,' wrote Margaret in an afterthought on the back of a letter to Jim Lees-

Milne on 5 November 1944, and again, in another muddled, uncharacteristically wistful postscript five months later, 'I wish I was in London, and could see one's friends again.'

Friends were supremely important in these years to both Margaret and Ivy. Margaret made her will at Lyme in 1944, leaving everything to Ivy and, after Ivy's death, to her godson Luke Marsden-Smedley, in spite of Basil's best efforts on behalf of Frank Jourdain's son Seymour (cut off with £100). Seymour was by this time, with her brother Henry, Margaret's sole surviving relation. Frank had died at the beginning of the war (a will-dangler to the last, he too had explicitly disinherited Seymour, leaving his still considerable fortune to his daughter Violet, who promptly seized her chance to drop the hated name 'Jourdain'). Iris Compton-Burnett died in November 1944: 'It is sad news indeed. My sister was only sixty-three, and did a great deal for other people, and will be missed by many,' wrote Ivy diplomatically on the twenty-second to Mr Mowll: 'I had not seen her for over a year, as I have seen no one.' Family feelings had by this time ceased to trouble either Ivy or Margaret but, of all the deprivations of exile, the loss of friends was perhaps the hardest part.

Margaret was once again bored and restless, making plans that autumn to move nearer London ('for Dorset is a barren and dry land'[73]), to settle in Alton, Oxford, Winchester, anywhere within reach of a library, at the very least to get away from the seaside with its bad train service and dearth of congenial company, its want of any furniture to speak of, its stubborn resistance to diversions like the architectural exhibition put on by a friend 'to enlighten the people of Weymouth (who are a tough and refractory lot)'. Her *Georgian Cabinet-makers* sold out, like *Elders and Betters*, on publication in November ('I certainly did not think it was the book the world was waiting for!' reported Margaret fondly[74]), and the long-postponed first number of *Orion* was enthusiastically reviewed in the New Year. War news grew steadily more encouraging. By March, Ivy and Margaret were beginning to contemplate going home; on 4 April they left Lyme for the Swan at Alton (afterwards a favourite pub), and on the twenty-seventh they left Alton for London. 'We are returned from exile,' wrote Ivy triumphantly summoning the Hills to tea on 4 May, three days before peace was formally declared.

The tea party to which the Hills were invited was the first of many, for Ivy and Margaret had no notion of surrendering to postwar austerity which—in a phrase Margaret quoted in *Regency Furniture* about the Napoleonic campaigns—had 'doubled the cost and trebled the difficulty of genteel living'. Her diary shows that they spent the spring and summer of 1945 seeing their friends, renewing contacts, exchanging visits and generally picking up where they had been obliged to leave off. They scarcely left London save for a few days with Alice Marcon at Oxford and a weekend at Cambridge in June, followed by brief sorties later to Lyme Park, Kelmscott and Shillingford. Robert Liddell was back in England in August to dismantle the Oxford flat he had shared with his brother:

> I went to tea with 'the ladies' (as their maid called them). 'Marge?' said Ivy, in a frank, open tone.
>
>   She asked after Donald, and I had to tell her that he had died of wounds in the Normandy invasion.
>
>   Ivy knew that it was the worst thing that could have happened to me, but she was, rather nicely, awkward. 'Oh, that is bad news; I didn't know, I hadn't heard.' Margaret was far more socially adequate. She helped us both. Ivy (I now know) minded too much.[75]

Nothing more was said. They changed the subject, swapping literary gossip, discussing Robert's new book, *The Watering Place*, and his efforts to help an elderly aunt, the sole survivor of his mother's family, who was giving up her house in Tunbridge Wells after losing her sister as well as her nephew the year before, and who kept addressing Robert by his brother's name as 'Don':

> I mentioned that my mother, having died young, was canonized by her. 'And you are canonized too,' said Margaret.
>
>   'But she wants to live,' I said—it seemed extraordinary to me. 'You lack imagination,' said Ivy sternly. 'Death is the end.'[76]

This was as far as Ivy was prepared to go, then or later, with Robert or anyone else, towards deliberately breaching the surface of life which, in her view, afforded such precarious protection against what lay below. But she had read *Kind Relations* in which Robert and Donald reappear in the persons of Andrew and Stephen Faringdon; and, though she never mentioned her own brother, she knew that Donald had been to Robert what Noel had once been to herself, 'the beginning and end of life'.[77] Robert left England at the end of the summer, returning for the last time in August 1947, when he called again at Braemar Mansions and found Ivy briefly alone. Margaret arrived late for tea, bringing ice cream ('for which Ivy and I were insufficiently grateful I am afraid'[78]) and the latest news of Dame Una's dissatisfaction with a reviewer who had cast doubt on her qualifications for writing a book about jade ('"I don't know about jade," said Ivy. "Except that it's that green stuff you get from China." "I know a lot more about it than that," said Margaret in a full, satisfied tone.'[79]) They talked about religion and relations and whether or not Edith Sitwell ought to sue a critic whose views might damage her sales ('we thought it had merely been his duty to his readers to discourage them from buying a book he thought bad'[80]). Margaret, with her scornful air, her superior poise, her unstoppable flow of wickedly funny gossip, had again taken charge, steering all three of them over deep waters which Ivy, for once, was determined not to ignore: 'Ivy caught me alone in the passage to say how much I must miss Donald. "Dreadfully" I said, and it was very much worse when I was in England. This she well understood, though she did not think much of "Abroad".'[81]

Robert was one of the very few people Ivy freely forgave for settling abroad; and, though they never met again, they continued to share a side of her life firmly closed to friends who still saw her regularly at home. His book on the novel was published just before he left England for good in 1947, and she wrote on 14 October to thank him in Cairo 'for the part about myself', ending with a gentle reminder: 'I am still hoping for another book about the two boys, but know that your time must be full.' A year later he sent her *The Last Enchantments* which tells how Andrew's and Stephen's story ended in Oxford (called Christminster in the novel):

July 9, 1948

Dear Mr. Liddell,

I returned from a month abroad to find *The Last Enchantments*.

And I was indeed enchanted, and find it a great pleasure to tell you how *much* I shall like to carry it with me as a companion.

It recalled to me the day when the two of us had tea with the two of you in your flat in North Christminster, and it even gave me the measure of what you have had, and what you have lost, and of the courage you must have needed to press on.

And there is still the gap in the history of Andrew and Stephen, that I want to be filled, though it is indeed ungrateful to ask for any more at the moment.

Yours very sincerely and gratefully,
Ivy Compton-Burnett.

Over the next twenty years and more, Ivy kept a close, benign, almost motherly eye on Robert and his activities through letters and reports from mutual friends, asking after his work, urging him not to write too fast, not to move house, not to draw on capital or tamper with his domestic arrangements (all problems with which Ivy found herself forced to contend in the 1950s and 1960s), always maintaining her delicate, insistent pressure on him to write what she called '*my book*'—'the further enchantments, and my especial ones'.[82] This was to be the middle instalment of the story of Andrew and Stephen, describing what happened after their father's second marriage when, under their new stepmother's rule, the two had no one but each other to turn to for comfort or affection. Robert's experience had been essentially Ivy's own and, for all their mutual reticence, it drew them together as nothing else could have done. In the aftermath of Donald's death, she offered what help and encouragement she could: 'We were sorry to hear that you are not thinking of coming to England for some time,' she wrote on 26 July 1950. 'But I see that the past must become the past and leave the present before you can wish to do so, and in your place I should feel the same. I hope you are writing, or will do so when the mood returns. It is subject to fits of wandering . . .'

Another ten years were to pass before 'my book' was written (whereupon publication was delayed for almost a further ten): years in which the two grew steadily more at home with one another's work, writing appreciatively whenever a new novel appeared, exchanging consolation when one was held up, discussing the contents of Robert's *The Novels of I. Compton-Burnett* ('I should be grateful indeed for this book to see the light'[83]). *The Last Enchantments* had contained an implicit tribute to Ivy,[84] and *Stepsons* (when it eventually appeared in 1969, after the second Mrs Liddell's death and only a few months before Ivy's own) brought them—as Ivy said—'very near'.[85] Robert wrote directly about an experience that

Ivy had broached with no one, probably not even with Margaret, though it acquired in her work, in distilled and abstracted form, a universal application not accessible to a more strictly naturalistic novelist. Their literary methods could hardly have been more different but morally, emotionally and intellectually they were at one as Ivy had not been with anyone since Noel died. Both before and after the 'Conversation at Lyme Regis', Margaret in private scarcely let up in her derisive attitude to Ivy's (and by this time practically everybody else's) books; and, after Margaret's death, Ivy looked to Robert for a sympathy and comprehension that grew stronger with time.

> I feel that in many ways I was closer to her mind than anyone [he wrote after Ivy's death]. I am told she never gave a hint of this, and that does not alter my view. We started off with a similar (though no doubt different) experience of family life, and an adoration of Jane Austen, and . . . a profound feeling for Samuel Butler. And we knew a similar love and loss. It was a tragic accident that the pattern of our lives should have so followed each other. Of her goodness to me, if I tried (ineffectually) to fill the gap and her charity, I don't wish to speak . . .[86]

1946–1951

'Truth is so impossible. Something has to be done for it.'

I

MANSERVANT AND MAIDSERVANT was finished at the beginning of
March 1946,[1] which means that it must have been written over the
previous year, in London, after the end of the war. It was one of the
books Ivy most enjoyed writing ('I quite missed it when it left my
hands,' she wrote to the novelist Elizabeth Taylor[2]), and the one she
afterwards singled out whenever anyone asked for her favourite. Its
publication marked a high point in her reputation with reviewers on
both sides of the Atlantic who responded to the richness, complexity and emotional warmth of her mature work, set off by a return to
something very like the buoyancy and high spirits of twenty years
before in humorous, hopeless Mortimer Lamb (variously interpreted by Ivy's friends as Elliott Felkin and/or Ernest Thesiger,
mixed on a base supplied by Goldsworthy Lowes Dickinson and
topped off perhaps with an astringent dash of Roger Hinks), and his
friend, the magisterial butler Bullivant. The book is unsparing on
Horace Lamb's cruelty to his deprived and defenceless small children ('I am so glad you think I am a compassionate writer,' wrote
Ivy in another letter to Elizabeth Taylor when *Manservant and
Maidservant* came out, 'as I always feel myself so very pitiful'[3]). But
it ends leniently all round, and the general impression is light, gay,
airy, full of energy and good humour, a marked relief after the
cramped and wintry world of *Elders and Betters*. 'It is as if the author
has turned a corner in a dark tunnel and emerged into a brighter
landscape,' wrote Violet Powell in her *Compton-Burnett
Compendium*.[4]

This was very much how Ivy felt at the time. She and Margaret had emerged intact from a second round of violence and upheaval ('After living in mature awareness through two wars,' she wrote to Robert Liddell a few years later, 'that side of me is worn out, and can do no more'[5]); and both were only too thankful to settle back with their maid, their flat and their friends into the 'dear, little, narrow life' so highly prized by Elton Scrope and his sister in *The Present and the Past*. 'I tolerate nothing that looms ahead,' says Ursula Scrope, explaining why she preferred at thirty-two to take no further active part in human affairs: 'I will not be threatened by life.'[6] Ivy, who had been not so much threatened as systematically assaulted by life between her seventeenth and thirty-second birthdays, wholeheartedly endorsed the Scrope plan thereafter; and she managed to make the most of it again for a few years after the Second World War.

An abundance of gossip and visits made up for much that was missing from bombed and blackened London. The flat had been restored, its furniture retrieved and ranged round the walls again between the tall windows of the bare, high-ceilinged drawing room instantly recognizable, to a visitor seeing it for the first time, from Ivy's description in *Manservant and Maidservant*: 'large and light and chill, and furnished with few and stately things . . . good to look at, less good to live in'[7] (a rather gloomier view was taken by Raymond Mortimer, whose memories of Ivy's various London flats clearly lay behind his impression of her fictional country houses: 'We feel that the rooms are sombre, the furniture massive, the food too plentiful and too plain'[8]). Entertaining was possible again with the help of food parcels sent from abroad by friends like Robert: it was round about this time that cucumbers, bowls of lettuce and radishes with home-made curd cheese and white and brown loaves began to appear on Ivy's tea table in place of the buns, cakes and enormous sugary meringues no longer obtainable in time of shortage and sweet coupons.

Rationing is a running joke in *Manservant and Maidservant* where scones, puddings, stale cake and lamb cutlets are all parsimoniously counted out, the children steal sweets and raid store cupboards, while the servants pass disparaging remarks in private about 'labour-saving', mass-produced 'factory stuff' and substandard redcurrant jam (' "I prefer jam that is not all pips; that is all," said George, routing in the pot as though for some substance distinct from these'[9]). The stern line taken below stairs in the Lamb household was by and large Ivy's own in an age of austerity. Sonia Brownell (Cyril Connolly's very young and extremely pretty assistant on *Horizon*, afterwards George Orwell's second wife) came to tea for the first time immediately after the war, when Margaret apologized for having run away to the country—'You must have suffered a great deal, my child, in London during the bombing'—and was teased for it by Ivy: 'Nonsense, Margaret, you remember how we suffered from that butcher!'[10]

Sonia belonged to a younger generation of Ivy's admirers with whom it was Margaret's turn to register, if at all, as the funny old companion who kept the conversation going, fielding awkward questions and plugging gaps with social protocol of the most banal kind. At this first meeting, when Margaret asked after 'dear Mr Connolly', Sonia replied without thinking: 'Oh, he's getting frightfully boring—only interested in *furniture*'. Even before the publication of *Manservant and Maidservant*, life at Braemar Mansions was beginning to fall into the postwar pattern set by increasing numbers of newcomers who found Margaret affable enough but officious, interfering and, by comparison with Ivy, decidedly dull. Of course there was still a furniture faction, generally friends of much longer standing who continued to write Ivy off to the end: 'If you went to their flat, you'd never have thought she had anything to do with the world of letters,' said Ralph Edwards. 'Literature was a topic you hardly raised. She was very strong on charwomen. And patum peperium and radishes and whether this was a good biscuit. She hadn't read *anything*. If Ivy didn't wish to be communicative' (and in his experience she never did) 'you couldn't do anything with her.'

Ivy had always adopted a protective carapace with people like Ralph Edwards but it changed a good deal after the war. For one thing she was no longer inconspicuous. Her unfashionably long dark dresses had ceased to serve their original purpose of deflecting attention, and she wore her delicate, Georgian diamond brooch and ear-rings (chosen by Margaret, when Ivy—who had inherited her mother's love of diamonds—lost all her jewellery in a burglary at Christmas, 1945[11]) with simplicity and distinction.

Her jewellery managed never to look like jewellery but, on her, seemed hieratic insignia [wrote Robin Fedden, describing their

Ivy photographed by Cecil Beaton after the Second World War, a portrait that went far towards establishing her austere public image in the last two decades of her life

Herman Schrijver after the war: 'But, seriously, do you not think him a very brilliant and polished man?' 'We could not think it more seriously than we do.'

'Nothing is more terrifying to me than to see Ernest Thesiger sitting under the lamplight doing this embroidery . . .'

Rose Macaulay: 'My books won't live. Yours may, Ivy.'

Madge Garland about the time Ivy first met her at the beginning of the 1950s, photographed by Cecil Beaton in the ballroom at Londonderry House

Victor Gollancz at a meeting of the Left Book Club

Elizabeth Taylor drawn by
Rodrigo Moynihan in the early
1950s at the beginning of her
long triangular friendship
with Ivy and Robert

The Liddell family at tea. *Left to right:* step-aunt with dog, Robert, Donald, their
half-sister Betty, their father, step-grandmother and the step-mother
in whom Ivy took such particular interest

Ivy with Vita Sackville-West (previously unpublished photograph by Vita's friend, Edith Lamont) in the white garden at Sissinghurst on the day of the expedition described by Madge Garland: 'Once Vita received us wearing a Persian coat in vivid colours and crimson silk pants . . .'

Ivy requested to pose at her writing desk, though in fact she wrote all her novels on her knee in a comfortable chair by the fire

Ivy photographed by John Vere Brown in a characteristic pose that seemed to her friends to express both her stoicism and her loneliness at the end of her life in the empty flat

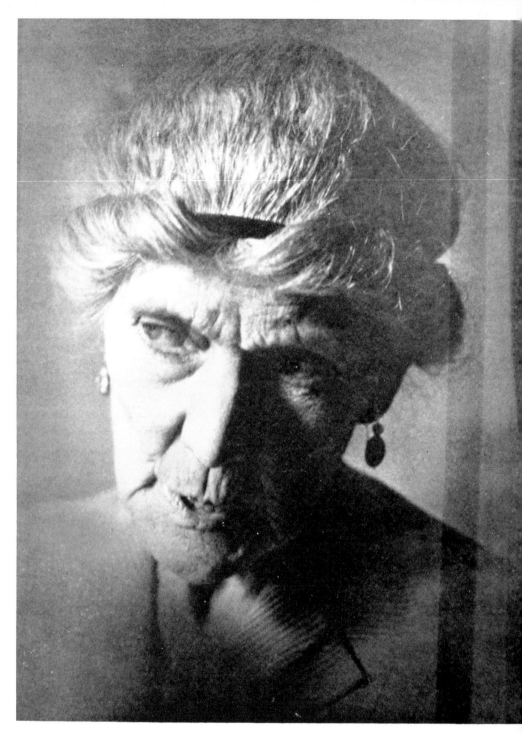

Ivy photographed at the end of her life by Hans Beacham: 'I am old. I have seen and heard. I know that things are done.'

first meeting at tea in 1946]. I do not recall seeing her out of black.
She wore it like a uniform, with care but with the disregard for
mode proper to uniform. A sense positively of the Services
attached to a black tricorne, vaguely reminiscent of an
eighteenth-century quarter-deck. There was also the long black
umbrella. This she would carry to dinner a mere two hundred
yards from Braemar Mansions on a halcyon evening . . .[12]

Strangers like Fedden, who had read Ivy's books with astonished
delight since the 1930s, seldom had much difficulty in recognizing
the classic integrity of her writing in Ivy's erect carriage, firm
features and humorous expression:

> For me, the physical impression was recurrently of a Roman
> head, a soldier-emperor, perhaps Galba. The rolled hair and the
> ribbon sometimes seemed like a laurel wreath.
> The moral impression was of sanity and principle. Level-
> headed, in the best sense of the word, was an adjective that she
> evoked. If I have met a human being whose values were not
> blurred, it was Miss Compton-Burnett.

Others found both the author and her books altogether more
off-putting. Several observers remembered the striking figure she
made in her black tricorne town hat (she had a brown straw, with
brown coat and gloves, for the country, and a parasol for sunny
days instead of the umbrella) at a party given by the Edwardses a
few years after the war to watch the Oxford and Cambridge boat
race from their house on the Thames in Chiswick Mall. 'She looked
formidably severe. I think she was severe,' wrote Anthony Powell,
whose introduction to her at this party induced 'the sort of constraint experienced as a child talking to an older person, whom one
suspected could never understand the complexity of one's own
childish problems'.[13] She produced the same reaction in a good
many people of Powell's generation, and it grew more pronounced
with age:

> I think the explanation of my sense of unease was no more and no
> less than what has been said; Ivy Compton-Burnett embodied in
> herself a quite unmodified pre-1914 personality, so that one was,

in truth, meeting what one *had* encountered as a child . . . No
writer was ever so completely of her books, and her books of her.

Ivy's 'pre-1914 personality' was, as Powell went on to point out, an
illusion or rather an invention, as artificial in its way as her period
settings and providing, like them, a formal context which could
preclude or permit intimacy at will. There are many accounts of the
consternation Ivy caused by hitching up her long dress far above the
knee and splaying her legs as she sat down to table (a habit left over,
according to Fedden, from days when the legs of both table and
diners would have been modestly concealed by a floor-length
damask cloth), sitting back afterwards with her legs comfortably
stuck out in front of her like a man, or—most disconcerting of all to
nervous subjects—rummaging around under her capacious skirts
in a slow, methodical search for the handkerchief tucked in her
knickers ('I always stuff mine in the elastic of my breeks,' she
explained frankly to Elizabeth Taylor[14]). She shared with Margaret
a trick of ducking her head to look down the front of her bodice, 'as
though she had detected something surprising there, and not
altogether pleasant'[15] (Margaret blew down hers as well, so often
that friends used to wonder what on earth she kept in her bosom
—Herman suggested perhaps a white mouse). For all her insistence
on propriety and manners, Ivy's conventionality was never more
than skin deep: 'In her life as in her novels,' wrote Fedden, 'she used
the framework of her Victorian–Edwardian background as a convenience to be discarded when it suited her.'
    Powell and Fedden had both been formally presented to Ivy and
both remained afterwards on decorous, dinner-party terms, but
1946 brought another admirer who scrutinized her with great
affection and shrewdness from a quite different angle. Ivy marked
the completion of *Manservant and Maidservant* by spending a fortnight in Cornwall with Margaret, returning on Tuesday, 26 March
1946, in good time for the Edwardses' first postwar boat race party
the following Saturday, and sending on the twenty-seventh for a
new typist to replace the agencies who had typed her manuscripts
up till now. This was Cicely Greig, who had discovered Ivy's books
at a very early age through David Garnett in the *New Statesman* and
knew them by this time well enough to recognize almost immediately the rules by which she was expected to play: 'I was of the

governess class, I decided. Once I had solved this little problem of our relationship I was quite happy and content to "keep my place" . . . I enjoyed my part, and our relationship was always a smooth one.'[16]

Cicely, starting out on a freelance career after the war, with ambitions as a writer herself, had simply sent postcards care of their publishers to favourite authors, including Rose Macaulay and I. Compton-Burnett ('I would love to type one of your novels. I have read *A House and Its Head* seven times'), and thought no more about it until Ivy's summons, arriving out of the blue many months later, filled her with amazement and disbelief. Ivy saw to it that their first interview kept to a strictly business footing. Effusiveness was in any case ruled out under the terms of their tacit agreement but Cicely was rapidly accepted as a regular visitor at Braemar Mansions—'To Ivy and Margaret I was a creature from another world: I worked for my living'—becoming something of a favourite with both ladies, and one of their principal informants on strange, new postwar anomalies like the welfare state and the National Health Service.

She typed for them both, dropping in at least every two or three months, often stopping for tea or coffee after lunch when she called to fetch or deliver work. Ivy's manuscripts came in batches of cheap school exercise books, neatly written in pencil, twelve or fourteen to a novel, with red or blue covers and multiplication tables on the back ('I remember thinking this last detail quite a fitting decoration for a book of Ivy's'). Margaret's articles, or later the loose chapters of her book on William Kent, were stuffed into bulging untidy parcels and had to be pieced together from scribblings on the backs of old coal bills, circulars, used Christmas cards, letters and their flattened-out envelopes (these were naturally read with care on both sides by Cicely, who found her employers' lives as fascinating and as hard to imagine as they found hers). From 1946 onwards, Cicely was the first person to set eyes on each fresh novel as it left Ivy's hands and, though she had started with no intention of being Ivy's permanent typist, it became a satisfaction she could not give up:

Her writing never changed. And her wit remained sharp, the knock of her sentences as powerful, the same strong beat and rhythm throughout. And the pleasure I got from typing those sentences can't be put into words. Their beauty slowed me down. I would read the sentence I had just typed again, and stare at the finished page.

Cicely's enthusiasm, however carefully subdued and ineffusive, made a change from the comparatively blank if deferential reception Ivy's manuscripts got elsewhere. She tried for the last time to change publishers in 1946 when the novelist Graham Greene, then working for Eyre and Spottiswoode, persuaded her to let his firm republish the three Heinemann novels together with *A Family and a Fortune*, [17] the second to come out from Gollancz who had sold two thousand copies and let the book go out of print—to Ivy's surprise and chagrin—less than four months after publication. She had remonstrated at the time, holding that Gollancz should have either printed a larger edition in the first place or preserved the type long enough to meet the demand for another impression. Gollancz remained adamant, preferring in the end to relinquish rights over *A Family and a Fortune* sooner than agree to reprint it or any other of her novels. Ivy saw no alternative save to accept Greene's proposal, promising him her next new novel but one when Gollancz's second three-novel contract ran out with the book after *Manservant and Maidservant* (her confidence in publishers was so shaky that she seems to have taken it for granted Gollancz, like Heinemann, would drop her at the end of the first contract, and had been pleased and taken aback by his prompt acceptance when Curtis Brown's wife Jean offered him refusal of *Elders and Betters* in 1943).

But nobody mentioned the shadier side of this deal to Gollancz, who was first alerted two years later by Eyre and Spottiswoode's advertisement for the first volumes of their handsome new Compton-Burnett *Collected Works*. A telephone call to Douglas Jerrold, the firm's managing director and Gollancz's longstanding publishing rival, erupted into heated accusation and recrimination, sharpened on Gollancz's part by an acute if not wholly justified sense of personal betrayal. By this time—the beginning of September 1948—the two-year period stipulated for Eyre and Spottiswoode's republication had expired which meant that their contract was technically cancelled: Graham Greene wrote at once to Ivy, explaining that all four novels were already at the printers and apologizing for the delay ('You know my own feelings about your work, and that there is no living English novelist whom I would rather publish'[18]). Spencer Curtis Brown washed his hands of the whole affair, disclaiming any further responsibility to Ivy and executing a rapid volte-face in favour of Gollancz. Ivy herself sent Gollancz a series of letters in her loopy, black, illegible handwriting setting out her own position from the start: her anxiety to see her books in print, her repeated discouragement at his hands, her reluctance to leave him ('I have never had a wish to make a change of publisher, only a very strong one that my books should be made available'), and her current disappointment with Eyre and Spottiswoode, ending with a confession of helplessness and a still more disarming apology ('I am sorry indeed to have discussed the matter on a wrong basis. But you will see that I am more sinned against than sinning').

The upshot was that Gollancz, who had apparently published Ivy's books for over a decade without ever meeting her, took her out to lunch on 6 October 1948, when they settled that Eyre and Spottiswoode should go ahead with the four old novels while Gollancz got the new ones on condition he republished *Daughters and Sons* and *Brothers and Sisters* (which left only *Pastors and Masters* outstanding). Both parties emerged from this affray with mingled relief and dissatisfaction: Ivy cannot have felt entirely sanguine about forcibly extracting Gollancz's consent to an arrangement he roundly denounced as bad publishing while, though Gollancz had held on to his author, he must have felt her behaviour legitimately discharged him from any further pretence at enthusiasm. He turned down Jerrold's last offer to take Ivy off his hands altogether or, failing that, take over her back titles in April 1951; but he never shared Jerrold's view that each new novel built up overall sales or that her reputation might be enhanced by keeping her books in print. His correspondence with Ivy settled over the next two decades into routine complaints from her about the handling of her current book, automatically parried by his insistence that prominent advertising would damage her sales while the reissues to which he had so reluctantly agreed were in his view pretty well bound to prove a glut on the market.

But relations, though cool, were still cordial when *Manservant and Maidservant* came out on 11 February 1947, after Ivy had decided to leave Gollancz and before he suspected her intentions. Publication was celebrated by a party in Ivy's honour given by the Hills with Robin McDouall (gourmet, bon vivant and later a convivial secretary to the Travellers' Club) who had met her through Heywood and remained ever afterwards a faithful friend. The critics were almost uniformly appreciative, and mostly a good deal more discriminating than Ivy was inclined to allow ('I have never had such superficial reviews on the whole as I have had this time, or had so far,' she wrote ungratefully to Elizabeth Taylor on 28 June). Other novelists—Elizabeth Bowen, P. H. Newby, L. P. Hartley, Anthony Powell ('this new one is in the top class'[19]) and Pamela Hansford Johnson—were especially generous; Daniel George went so far as to lay a public curse in *Tribune* on 21 March on Compton-Burnett fans—'I hope their water freezes again'—who made off with his first editions; and several writers recommended her to the redoubtable Blanche Knopf of New York, making her first publishing sortie after the war in search of fresh talent in Europe that summer.

'My books do not take in America, and this one will need all the help it can get,' said Ivy,[20] writing to thank Elizabeth Taylor for negotiating on her behalf while she was abroad, spending June with Margaret in France. *Manservant and Maidservant* sold nearly five thousand copies in six weeks, easily overcoming the token resistance put up by Mrs Knopf—'I daren't take home any more prestige'[21]—whose firm became the third (after Harcourt, Brace and Norton) to try to get Ivy to take with the American public. Knopf published her next three novels, beginning with *Manservant and Maidservant* which came out as *Bullivant and the Lambs* in 1948, and was generally felt by reviewers to have won the season's New York novel stakes by a short head from Norman Mailer's *The Naked and the Dead* ('Miss Compton-Burnett is increasingly unfair to most other contemporary British novelists . . .' reported the *New York Times*. 'They seem to be breathing too hard by comparison'[22]).

2

THE TIDE OF CELEBRITY showed signs of washing over Ivy again as it had done twenty years earlier and this time, though she did not ask it in, she made no move to shut it out either. Cecil Beaton, arriving to take her portrait for *Vogue*, found his wheedling professional charm assessed by an eye as stonily expert as his own: 'He was more interested in the furniture, I think,' Ivy reported to Cicely. 'He asked me to sit in that chair . . . I told him it was broken, and might give way. He just said, "Yes, but you will sit in it for *me*, won't you?" '[23] According to Jim Lees-Milne, it was Margaret rather than Ivy whose vigilance rivalled Beaton's own ('I don't know anyone who approached Cecil Beaton for being observant. His eyes were fixed on every blemish. Margaret wasn't quite like that, but she came damned close'); but he and Ivy summed one another up pretty well. He photographed her in black with a diamond brooch and a touch of white at the neck, enthroned on the rickety chair, gazing squarely at her photographer with hands clasped and eyes level, framed beneath a gilt mirror by two small, ornate, fan-shaped eighteenth-century firescreens on tall, slender stands. Between them, she and Beaton had arrived at an image—formal, hieratic, the extreme simplicity, severity and firmness of the pose emphasized by the delicate straight lines and curves of the furniture—that did much to fix the impression Ivy and her work were from now on to make on the public.

Beaton's pictures were of course specifically designed as public portraits, which did not please people like Cicely who thought he made Ivy look old, sinister, unlike herself and uncomfortably close to her own tyrants. But what Beaton saw is borne out by another trained observer, Cecil Gould of the National Gallery, who also met Ivy for the first time in 1948 or 1949 when he wrote about the paintings in Sir Malcolm Stuart's collection which Margaret was cataloguing:

She was something which I hadn't met before, and haven't since. Her attitude to life was that of an intellectual, but she had the minimum intellectual interests in the academic sense. Almost the only one was contemporary English fiction—of which she had read, and immediately on publication, everything that anybody ever claimed might be any good, and of which she was a penetrating and never wholly favourable critic . . .

The object of her intellectual curiosity was almost exclusively people's behaviour, their habits of life, their reactions under temptation, and particularly the minutiae of their lives. The latter linked with the only material thing which really did interest her—money. She was passionately interested in the price of everything, particularly of indispensable things, food, domestic appliances, rents, rates and servants' wages. She was also much interested in sexual aberrations. 'He's getting married, like so many homos one knows,' she remarked once in my hearing . . .

She had very little overt vanity to the extent that she never led the conversation to her writing, and tended to kill it quickly if anyone else did. Some of this may have been due to another kind of vanity—the idea that no one was equipped to give her work its due. She undoubtedly thought highly of it herself. She took a very low view of people in general, always imputing the worst and most selfish motives until the contrary was proved . . .

She seemed with all this very cold. Hard—but not impossible —to be fond of, and hard—but not impossible—to have her fond of one. Most people in addition were a little frightened of her. She depended on her friends to constitute a circle and much resented it if they defected. Undoubtedly some of them were drawn to her by her celebrity value. To me the attraction initially was as a survival of a very interesting form of life—a Victorian intellectual of an unusual kind. And of course entertainment value. Though the cracks were not nearly as thick off the ground as in her books, one was not bored.[24]

This is a retrospective portrait, based on a friendship of twenty years during which Ivy changed a great deal in private as well as becoming to the public one of the legends of literary London. Even so, estimates of her coldness varied wildly, generally corresponding quite closely to what the observer found in her books ('One had a gruesome feeling that, for the moment, one had *become* one of her characters, and not a favourite one at that,' wrote Pamela Hansford Johnson, whose first nightmare visit to Braemar Mansions in 1951 bore out her view of the novels as on the whole brilliant but heartless[25]). Ivy was, as she said, always pitiful in her books to the maltreated and weak, young or old, from the elderly Miss Griffin brutalized by her employer in *A Family and a Fortune* to the seven-year-old Avery Lamb who can't sleep in *Manservant and Maidservant* for fear of his father ('"Is Father gone now?" said Avery. "I don't want him to come here. He is always in all the places. I don't want him to come where I sleep. I don't like to think he might look at me in the night"'[26]). But she was scarcely less sorry for their tormentors, caught in a situation they can no more control or resist than their victims; and what made people nervous of Ivy was often this impartial distribution of feeling, coming from someone who hardly needed to know all before she forgave it. If her friends preferred on occasion to avoid exposing their problems to Ivy, it was not so much for fear of what she might do, or even what she might say, rather for fear of how much she might understand ('I wonder people are not afraid of the truth,' says Charity Marcon in *Daughters and Sons*, discussing death with her brother who answers: 'They are afraid of it, terrified, as you are. You have put their fears into words. You are much bolder than most people; I think you are too bold'[27]).

'Where everyone says what he thinks, and thinks much, it is as if everyone were clairvoyant,' as an American reviewer said of *Bullivant and the Lambs*[28]; and visitors to Braemar Mansions—at any rate those who had read her books attentively—were often painfully aware of Ivy's clairvoyance. It explains her insistence on talking about prices and plumbing, which grew steadily more perverse after Margaret died when Ivy, who could not say what she did not think, was seriously short of innocuous small talk. 'To me Ivy and her books were inseparable,' wrote Cicely. 'If you loved one you loved the other, and you understood Ivy from reading her books and enjoyed her books more from having met her.'[29] But even for Cicely—easily flustered by Ivy, and too close to the workings of her inner mind ever entirely to shake off an initial trepidation—it was often a relief to be relegated to the governess class. Though Margaret's casual, friendly manner eased the strain, Cicely remained acutely aware of how much a slow or insensitive reaction grated on Ivy who marked her displeasure with withering silence or a cutting aside, very rarely an open rebuke: 'At such times Ivy's grey-green eyes could take on a fierce, cold glint, and she made me think of some of her old tyrants . . .' But Cicely bore Ivy's occasional sharpness ('and even her sharpness was worth having') meekly in silence; and no one has left a more persuasive picture of Ivy's private face, the hospitable and encouraging side of her nature that played no part in her public image:

Photographers like line and bone structure, and wanting this they made her tilt her head upwards, some of them, so that her chin appeared to jut menacingly. She had a strong face, but her chin was not at all the jutting kind, and there was no hardness in the lines of her mouth. Her small, arched nose was not arrogant but suggested the classic austerity of her thought. Her mouth, on the other hand, showed a great sweetness and gentleness of character. Her humour was in her eyes, wonderfully expressive green-grey eyes. I never heard her laugh, but I have often seen laughter in her eyes. At other times they were watchful, wary, sometimes hostile . . .

Probably only Margaret knew Ivy well enough to understand what lay behind her wariness, and Margaret to the end of her life protected, even pampered Ivy as she had done since they first met more than thirty years earlier. Cicely describes a curious incident in the summer of 1948 when Margaret was so stirred by a review of *Bullivant and the Lambs* in *Time* magazine, fixing her eyes on Ivy's face with an expression of such rapt pride and intimacy, that Cicely made an excuse and left ('there was an urgency in her look that fairly drove me away'[30]). Certainly the general impression was that things were going well between the two, now that Margaret was also securely back in the top class as a pundit. Vere Watson-Gandy, a contemporary and close friend with whom they often stayed at Buckland Newton in Dorset after the war, remembered Margaret treating Ivy with the sort of indulgent, amused affection a man might keep for a silly little wife, especially the 'wonderful snort' with which she greeted each fresh absurdity of Ivy's, like not knowing which end of a train was the front or how to fix stamps and string to a parcel. Mrs Watson-Gandy's son, Jim Brandreth (the name was changed to comply with a relative's will), arranged a visit to the Marquess of Blandford's place in the country where Ivy infuriated her hostess by first politely declining to admire the magnificent formal borders and beds, then being captivated by a stray daisy the gardener had failed to pluck from the lawn. On a second trip with Jim to Maple Durham (unknown and generally inaccessible even to connoisseurs in those days), Ivy mesmerized the entire party, when four o'clock came and there was no tea, by retreating once again to the centre of the lawn, sitting down and refusing to budge, a small mutinous black dot ('she was the very picture of revolt') in matching coat, hat and gloves.[31]

To people like the Pinneys and the Watson-Gandys—members of old county families, descendants of hunting squires, the last generation still clinging to the pleasant, well-appointed lives of the cultivated country gentry in a world that knew nothing of the novels of I. Compton-Burnett—Ivy remained always 'Margaret's shadow': retiring, inconspicuous, comical, even derisive, but more than content for all her teasing to follow where Margaret led. Ivy's constant complaint in these years was of being abandoned in London while Margaret flitted round the country escorted by one or other of a fresh supply of young men ('Bobbie' and 'Robin' and 'Keith'—Bobbie Heath, Robin Ironside, Keith Miller-Jones—had replaced the married men, Soame and Peter Wilson, in Margaret's postwar diaries) on furniture jaunts or lucrative consultation jobs at fifty guineas a time. Being left alone was what Ivy dreaded more than anything. She was, as she said, 'a very sociable person'[32] but, apart from a handful of old familiars—Rose, Herman, Ernest, Roger Hinks when he was at home, the Kidds and the Marsden-Smedleys—she could never feel entirely comfortable in company without Margaret to bear the brunt.

> Margaret was quite unselfconscious [wrote Elizabeth Taylor, who met Ivy for the first time through Robert in 1947]. Would stand stock-still in a restaurant surveying the tables through lorgnettes. Had bitter feuds, bore rancour, took umbrage (*her* phrases). She stuck out her legs in theatres, so that people who had annoyed her couldn't pass, & prevented some poor creature from pursuing his studies at the V&A because they seemed to encroach on her territory.[33]

If Margaret struck most people as the man of the party, there were others who found something essentially masculine in Ivy's strength and reserve; while, to young women like Cicely and Dorothy Stroud, Margaret (who had given generous encouragement to both in the early stages of their respective careers after the war) seemed the embodiment of feminine charm and warmth, all feather boas, pretty hats and voluminous Edwardian drapery. 'I remember seeing her once in the Library of the Victoria and Albert Museum,' wrote Cicely. 'She rustled and flowed between the bookshelves, a harmony of soft pinks and greys and E flat, so that heads were turned . . . Margaret was languorous-seeming, with a charming graciousness.'[34] The fact is that Margaret and Ivy were both, as Ralph Edwards said, *sui generis*, unique, outside ordinary categories. 'Their drawing room might have been a man's room,' said

Soame Jenyns. 'If you'd gone into that flat, you wouldn't have known it was inhabited by women.' 'Yes,' said his wife, 'but then, on the other hand, you wouldn't have thought it was lived in by men either.'

At all events, Ivy and Margaret in those years were both at the height of their form. The young writer Kay Dick, commissioned by the B.B.C. French service to write a script about Ivy, met them for the first time at tea in October 1950:

> Ivy welcomed me with grace and some amusement. I felt at ease—this was a trap—because physically she reminded me of a patrician step-aunt I had known in childhood. She was tiny, yet unequivocally imposing. Her physical quality was neat and precise. Her eyes were beautiful, and most appealing. They reminded me of someone I loved, who had a similar perceptiveness. Her ringed hands were small, delicate, sprightly and suggested gentleness . . . So enthralled was I with my experience of tea with Miss Compton-Burnett, that at first I failed to notice that I was the one who was being questioned. In fact, with a sparse directness I was soon to recognise as her forte, Ivy was fast discovering everything about me, and I was lamentably failing to discover anything about her.[35]

It was not till much later that Kay Dick, who had not then read any of Ivy's novels, realized her mistake in thinking she had concealed the fact from her hostess. But her growing confidence at the time was strengthened when Margaret, arriving late, brought her own charm to bear alongside Ivy's:

> I felt quite stunned as I sat between the two ladies and was amiably interrogated by both of them—about my reading, not, happily, about Ivy's novels. 'What would you advise us to read?' they innocently asked. I fell right into it, and gave my act of young, up-to-date reader advising two quiet elderly spinsters what titles they should add to their library lists. I was being quizzed and had not the wit to appreciate it until I was outside the flat. Their smiling faces and dutiful nods impressed me—with my own knowledge . . . 'You must come and see us again,' they said, I feel certain, in chorus.

Margaret was by no means always so benevolent to Ivy's callers; but on a good day in the right company when she and Ivy were both in the mood, they were expert at tending, coaxing and firing a conversation much as others might stoke coals in a grate. They capped one another's witticisms with a vigour and skill that made their perpetual scoring off one another almost a spectator sport for their friends, and they had a very funny antiphonal style of telling stories, taking it in turns, for instance, to describe the frightful fix they found themselves in at a French convent (Ivy always strongly recommended convents for holidays, as being cheap, quiet, clean and free from strong drink), when they set out along a cloister, making for the bathroom with soap and sponge bags, only to be met head on by a procession bearing the mass.

After the tedium, isolation and hardship of England in wartime, even Ivy admitted that abroad had its points ('We had a perfect month in France,' she wrote on 16 July 1947, explaining to Elizabeth Taylor that people who didn't drink could manage quite well on the government's meagre £75 travel allowance: 'Of course, *Paris* is ruinous'). They spent June 1948 in the Savoy, returning the year after for another month at St Gervais within easy reach of Elliott who came over from Geneva to walk, talk and explore with Margaret while Ivy gave her full attention to the Alpine flowers. It was probably on one of these holidays that Joan Evans, sitting in a slow train from St Moritz in the Alps down to Macon, saw Margaret standing with Ivy on the platform at Bride-les-Bains (one of only three treasured glimpses of Margaret after the breach in 1924—once Joan caught sight of her from the top of a bus in Sloane Street, and once they were in the same room but did not speak on the day women were admitted to the Society of Antiquaries[36]). Later plans for a holiday in Greece, to see Robert Liddell and admire the wild flowers, were successfully scotched by Roger Hinks who said there was nothing to look at and nothing to eat except things cooked in oil. Roger's career at the British Museum had been abruptly terminated before the war by a notorious scandal over cleaning the Elgin Marbles, and a subsequent stint as British Council Representative in Athens had given him no cause to revise his low opinion of Greece. He looked like the National Portrait Gallery's bust of the poet Gray and excelled at the quick, dry, glancing wit Ivy practised herself: 'He and Ivy were made for each other,' said Cecil Gould to whom Roger once said, when told about a ski resort with the great attraction for bored or indifferent skiers of easy access to Innsbruck: 'Rather a homoeopathic cure, I should have thought.'

These Alpine visits were as it turned out Ivy's last sight of abroad since she and Margaret settled on a Yorkshire tour in the summer of 1950, taking in various great houses, stopping at Leeds and the Watson-Gandys' old family home, Heaves, by then run as a luxurious ('though too expensive') hotel near Clitheroe. Here they listened to themselves reading their old 'Conversation in Lyme Regis' (recorded for the B.B.C. Third Programme the previous February and broadcast in June): 'The bangs and bursts caused by the disturbance from the hills in Yorkshire rendered our hopes of hearing our own voices null and void,' wrote Ivy, back in London, to Vere on 4 July. 'In London the talk seems to have come through fairly well, though some people heard Margaret's voice better than mine. One critic, favourable otherwise, complained that my voice was too high and light, as though I had purposely ordered the wrong one . . .'

There were country weekends with old friends like the Ionides' and new ones like the Watson-Gandys and the infinitely hospitable Charlotte Bonham-Carter ('She never will say a single disagreeable thing about anyone,' reported Margaret. 'A most tiresome woman to be with'[37]). People with gardens invited Ivy down to raid the soft fruit, but people with pets kept them dark if possible on pain of both ladies' disfavour (Ivy's dislike of cats was so pronounced that their owners—several of whom had seen her push, if not kick, an offending animal out of her path with a small, firm, neatly-shod foot—found it hard to credit her intently observed and by no means unfeeling portrait of the cat Plautus when she came to write *Mother and Son*). Ivy spent a few days each summer in the strawberry season with Janet Beresford at her cottage near Ashwell, while Margaret went to Alice Marcon at Oxford, and they paid separate visits to Sutton Veney again after the war, though the three Noyes sisters were growing increasingly frail: Ella, always closest to Ivy, died in 1949 within a few months of Minna, leaving Dora alone, too old and infirm either to pay or receive further visits.

Life at Braemar Mansions ran smoothly in spite of minor vexations—'a change of landlord, a dishonest porter who made away with all the coal in the mansions, a painter to do over the kitchen, all sorts of irritating household jobs,' wrote Margaret to James Lees-

Milne on 29 May 1948—and an accelerating postwar turnover of maids:

> Frightfulness has fallen on us in the shape of the loss of our valuable Jayne, who is taking a long-wished-for chance of leaving 'sleeping-in service' and going out to work from a home of her own. She has found good quarters in a horrid, coal-mining place called Pontefract in Yorkshire, and I expect will be miserable [wrote Ivy gloomily to Vere] . . . We have engaged an elderly superior woman for the simple reason that we could get her, as 'her lady' had died, and hope for the best . . . Jayne, on hearing of our prompt action and its outcome, broke into tears.
>
> Did she expect us to keep her place sacred to her and look after ourselves?[38]

Ivy, who could no more cook or clean than work a typewriter or drive a car, continued to get on well with her housekeepers long after the last of the stern, starched maids who kept visitors at arm's length and spoke only when spoken to (Gray had left after the war and Henrietta Day, Jayne's successor, belonged to a breed already almost extinct), and who were in turn replaced by a procession of untrained helps and companions in coloured nylon overalls only too pleased to pass the time of day. Both Ivy and Margaret also depended increasingly on Basil Marsden-Smedley, a tall, thin, dry, patient, immensely kind man chiefly devoted all his life to good works and municipal affairs in Chelsea (it was Basil who, as mayor of Chelsea at the end of the 1950s, insisted on trees in the streets and a fountain in Sloane Square). Basil was generally invited alone ('he used to say he appreciated being "a loose man" at their parties,' said Hester), having long since been adopted by both ladies as a cross between father-figure and favourite nephew: 'Ask Basil,' 'Ring Basil,' 'Send for Basil' was always their cry in time of trouble. His mistrust of Ivy's writing was balanced by a boundless admiration for Margaret whose company he enjoyed, according to Hester, more than anyone else's not excluding her own: after the war the two had a craze for exploring golf clubs together, buzzing about all over the Home Counties at weekends, casting a critical eye over the greens, sampling amenities, quizzing the members and lunching quite irregularly in the club houses.

The nearest Ivy came to these country jaunts was wooding, or 'faggoting', with Margaret in Kensington Gardens, expeditions for which she wore thick brogues, an ancient Burberry and a battered pork pie hat (these were her casual clothes, for rough or heavy work, and she put them on again whenever she stepped out to water the flowers in her balcony window boxes at Braemar Mansions). Marketing in the Gloucester Road occupied part of every morning, and Ivy took pride in the frugal art of stretching and saving three sets of 'points', or ration coupons: 'I was brought up to think it was wrong to waste anything,' she said. 'And what was worse, it was vulgar.'[39] Food at Braemar Mansions was once again, points permitting, good and plentiful and in season (too plentiful for fastidious visitors like James Lees-Milne who was regularly taken aback by the staggering quantities of depressingly plain cooking put away by his hostesses). Both Margaret and Ivy ate hugely, but they also enjoyed themselves hugely and saw to it that others did too: 'I dined with Margaret and Ivy,' wrote James on 2 December 1947. 'Charlotte Bonham-Carter and Soame Jenyns the other guests. It was the greatest fun, although there was only cider to drink, and it was perishing cold. Ivy and Margaret were at their best, playing up to each other and making strikingly pertinent and lively observations . . .'[40]

Ivy had been approached about writing her memoirs by Knopf's English agent that autumn, but claimed (as she invariably did to pokers and priers) that it was out of the question because a life as uneventful as hers supplied no biographical material ('There just is none'[41]). She was working instead on *Two Worlds and Their Ways* in which Cicely (who typed the manuscript in the summer of 1948) recognized touches of Margaret in the large, plain, cheerful person of Maria Shelley with her great good nature, untidiness, industry and habit of jotting things down on the backs of old envelopes. *Two Worlds and Their Ways*, published in June 1949, while Ivy was on holiday at St Gervais, was also the first and only one of her novels centred on a happy family (the tolerant, loving and united Shelleys find their days darkened only by the parents' decision—taken reluctantly, and for purely disinterested motives—to send their children to boarding school). Work was going well for Margaret too. *The Work of William Kent* came out in 1948, together with a highly successful revised edition of *Regency Furniture* and, in the intervals of journalism, she was running up a history of interior decoration for Batsford, revising another seminal furniture hand-book by the cabinet-maker, John C. Rogers, and collaborating with Soame on *Chinese Export Art*. Ivy, unlike Margaret, liked to let each book settle for nearly a year before starting another, as she told an interviewer from *Books of Today* in April 1950:

'And then,' she says, 'I do not go so slowly as you might think.'

'It flows?' I said.

'I do not think it comes more slowly than it has to,' she corrected. 'I do believe it seldom flows for anyone.'

3

THE BOOK that was flowing as fast as it could at the beginning of 1950 was *Darkness and Day*. 'I did some work in the winter and spring and am now giving the book a rest, as it needed it,' Ivy wrote to Robert Liddell on 26 July. 'London is pleasant and peopled again; and food is easier, but life grows in expense.' In fact Cicely had already collected the manuscript (which Ivy feared might prove too short, though it turned out to be the usual length and in no need of what she called 'interpolations') three weeks before this letter was written, on 3 July, when the signs of strain Ivy generally showed on finishing a novel were more marked than usual. She had barely spoken ('Now and then a slight whispering sound escaped her, as though she was talking to herself'[42]), seeming withdrawn, ex-hausted and so frail that she could not walk properly and had to be helped to stand.

It was Margaret who kept the conversation going over glasses of sherry and escorted Cicely to the front door, reacting sharply to a polite hope that Ivy might feel better after a holiday:

'I thought she seemed not very well,' I said.

To my surprise Margaret looked at me with a sort of anguish, and cried: 'She's *very well*,' with bitter emphasis on each word.

She turned and rushed back into the sitting room.

It was the last time I saw her. She died the following April.[43]

Since the war Margaret had had what she called a smoker's cough without smoking, and her heart was tired ('This was a medical description and she said it was a very apt one'[44]). She consulted various doctors but otherwise carried on much as before, though Cicely was by no means the only person aware of fierce undercurrents between the two friends in the last year or two of Margaret's life, when Ivy was preoccupied with *Darkness and Day*. This was her variation on an Oedipal theme (in which Bridget Lovat, having caused her mother's death and supposedly married her father, stops short at putting out her eyes to her family's great relief—'Anything like that would make it very public'[45]); and the absurd, outrageous, tragi-comic inventiveness of the plot, combined with its strictly classical machinery of reversal and revelation, to some extent distracts attention from a more mundane, secondary theme of old age, infirmity and death.

Sir Ransom Chase, a widower of eighty-eight, spends much of the book anticipating with various degrees of gloom and reluctance the death that finally claims him in the last chapter; while his neighbour, Selina Lovat, refuses out of hand to admit the possibility that she will not live for ever though even her small grandchildren feel pretty confident that her days are numbered:

> 'Could anyone be older than Grandma?'
> 'Yes, of course,' said Rose. 'She is only seventy-eight. People can be ninety and a hundred.'
> 'But then their days are but labour and sorrow. Are her days like that?'
> 'No, I shouldn't think so. Other people's may be, when they are with her.'[46]

Other people's days were often labour and sorrow at Braemar Mansions during and after the writing of *Darkness and Day*. Pamela Hansford Johnson, invited to dinner in the winter of 1950–1 when she was working on her British Council pamphlet about Ivy, mistook the time out of nerves and spent thirty minutes walking round the square, arriving frozen cold on the doorstep only to be told that she was half an hour late and the others had started without her. She was shown into the dank, dark dining room and narrowly cross-examined as to her unpunctuality by Ivy—'ivorine, sharp-featured, with eyes green as peeled grapes'[47]—before being offered a chair on which she sat in mutinous silence for the rest of the meal ('I do not think the dinner could have been utterly spoiled since the main course was corned beef'), while her hostesses talked to one another and a nameless third party without addressing a further word to their reprobate guest. Robert Liddell had another hair-raising report from his friend, Peter Duval-Smith, who went to tea armed with an introduction and a big box of Turkish delight from Robert, and ended up making sticky conversation with Margaret about Rose Macaulay's *Pleasure of Ruins*:

> Ivy said: 'She's writing not only about ruins, but about things people built to look like ruins. I don't know what she sees in them.' Margaret developed the theme and Peter (a South African) did his best. Then suddenly Ivy began talking to herself aloud. 'I can't think why Margaret is showing off like that; she can't think how silly she sounds. And this young man obviously knows nothing about it whatever.'
>
> Margaret showed him out, and helped him to find his umbrella or what not. At the door she said: 'What do you think about Edith Sitwell's poems? We think they're bosh.'
>
> Peter said that was much his own opinion. Margaret then called: 'Ivy, Ivy, come here! This young man says Edith Sitwell's poems are bosh!'[48]

There were similar incidents with other visitors, several of whom realized unhappily that something was up. The last winter of Margaret's life was bitterly cold, and she would sit crouched over an oil stove supplied by Hester, or quite often take to her bed. Altercations with Ivy grew sharper, and not funny at all. Elizabeth Taylor remembered a tea party at which the two nagged one another about fetching the jam ('Margaret, there's no gooseberry jam.' 'There isn't any apricot, either.' 'If you fetch the apricot, I'll fetch the gooseberry'[49]) for what felt like hours while the guests hung their heads and stared at their plates. Margaret's cough grew worse. She suffered from catarrh and had such difficulty in breathing that, at the beginning of December, she had X-rays taken of her heart and throat.[50] Ivy, always delicate, accustomed from childhood to taking care and wrapping up warm, accepted bad throats, chest complaints, bouts of quinsy or influenza as a matter of course in the winter. But Margaret had never needed nursing before, and Ivy reacted with panic-stricken protest, misery and rage. She could not stand the sound of Margaret's cough, or stop herself punishing Margaret for it. Friends grew increasingly worried, strange stories began to circulate, a rumour reached even Joan Evans about a distinguished colleague who had dropped in at the flat to find Ivy engaged in teasing Margaret till she cried. Things got so bad in the end that—after another distressing public scene over jam, with Ivy refusing to pass the pot unless Margaret first submitted by fetching a handkerchief from Ivy's bedroom—Herman and Peter Wilson of Sotheby's decided to tackle Ivy together in private but, courage failing, applied instead to Basil Marsden-Smedley who said there was nothing to be done.[51]

Trouble was apparent even to comparative strangers: the Jungian psychotherapist Margaret Branch, meeting the pair at a party, heard Ivy turn on Margaret with such oblique, wounding cruelty that she could hardly believe her ears and consulted the friend who had introduced her, the poet Stevie Smith, who explained that Ivy was beside herself at times with terror of being abandoned.[52] Ivy's behaviour went back to the years immediately after the First World War when old friends, seeing the two together for the first time, were embarrassed at the way Margaret gave in to the much younger Ivy, fetching her bag or her book or her handkerchief, and saying mildly when Janet Beresford protested: 'You see, she's like a child.'[53] What seems to have happened is that the tyrannical streak that had dropped from Ivy completely in time of mutual happiness surfaced again after the Second World War, when Margaret first showed signs of failing her, and mastered her more and more as ill health wore Margaret down. 'Margaret wanted to go, and she didn't want to go,' said Margaret Branch who thought that Margaret fought against encroaching weakness less for herself than because she, too, was appalled at the prospect of Ivy being left on her own: 'But I think she had had enough.' Certainly Margaret responded generously for as long as she could to Ivy in trouble, bearing her thrusts in silence, setting aside her own jealousy ('Ivy had always been in the background of her fame, as it were, but she was only on the outskirts of Ivy's,' said Hester loyally), coping with the literary admirers who otherwise got short shrift in those days at Braemar Mansions. Margaret took to escorting Ivy's ruffled or indignant visitors to the front door so as to mollify their feelings with a change of subject or, for Pamela Hansford Johnson after that disastrous dinner party, an outright apology: 'She said to me kindly, "You mustn't mind. Ivy isn't at her best tonight" '[54] (Miss Hansford Johnson was by her own account more graciously received at a later visit for tea on 26 February 1951, the afternoon before the two friends left for a few days at the Eardsley House Hotel, Worthing, in the vain hope that sea air might do Margaret good).

It was not simply that Ivy, like her mother before her, needed someone permanently on hand to smooth her path, to support and shield her from 'a world which' (in Ivy's phrase from *Dolores*) 'had shown itself unloving'.[55] More than that, by enabling Ivy to remain in some part of herself 'like a child'—with a child's uncontrolled egotism, helplessness, fear, resentment and anger—Margaret had also enabled her in another sense to grow up. Perhaps Ivy's childishness was the price she paid for her rare and discomforting maturity. Margaret after all had not only made it possible in the first place for Ivy to write, she had supplied the tone of voice that allowed Ivy's characters to comprehend, if not master or modify, their own and other people's emotions in the light of that 'great wealth of humanity' that many friends sensed in Ivy's presence, though it was fully articulated only in her books.

Margaret's death and the reactions it provoked provide perhaps the clearest and strangest example of the two levels on which Ivy worked. As Margaret's illness gradually declared itself, Ivy began talking more and more under her breath, a habit Cicely first noticed on the day she came to collect the manuscript of *Darkness and Day*. Cicely wondered at the time whether Ivy might be repeating snatches of conversation from her novel, and perhaps she was, for—whatever sort of mess Ivy and Margaret made, or seemed to their friends to be making, of their last months together—their general predicament is explored with great delicacy and feeling in a series of conversations running through *Darkness and Day* between the dying Sir Ransom Chase and his much younger friend, Gaunt Lovat. The pair cover the ground pretty thoroughly, ranging from practical details like the reading of Sir Ransom's will after his funeral (a gathering pictured by Gaunt with disobliging alacrity: '"You can imagine me sitting there, having my curiosity satisfied . . ." "I shall do no such thing. I shall imagine you weighed down by grief" '[56]) to the metaphysical question of which of the two deserves the more pity:

'I never see why people should have it for being old,' said
Gaunt.
'Everyone else does. You want some reason for not giving it.'
'We are supposed to like to pity people.'
'We only like to look down on them for needing pity.'
'Well, why should I not do that?'
'You are too attached to me. It would have to be real pity, and
people do not like that. They are not equal to it.'[57]

Darkness and Day begins with this tentative exploration and ends,
after the more spectacular upheavals of the main plot have subsided,
with the eventual acceptance by these two deeply attached friends of
the elder's forthcoming death. They start in the first chapter
discussing, to Sir Ransom's steadily mounting irritation, his failing
powers, his will, his well-spent life and his determination at all costs
to hang on to it. The same themes crop up repeatedly—the
disparity in their ages, the empty place Sir Ransom will leave, the
annoying way Gaunt keeps harping on the future—and are majestically resolved in two long, lucid deathbed conversations in the last
chapter:

'You cannot have much to regret.'
'There is not much that I do regret. I have done much that I
ought to have done. Much that I ought not to have done, I would
do again . . .'
'You will leave a great blank. I shall never find things quite the
same.'
'But you will find them nearly the same? Life will not be over
for you?'
'I do not believe in not taking people on equal terms until the
end. Your mind is not failing. You are as much a man as I am.
You would know if I distorted the truth.'
'Truth is so impossible. Something has to be done for it. If you
had said you would find life quite different, I should have
believed it. I think I do believe it.'
'I think I do too,' said Gaunt, in another tone. 'I shall be a lonely
man when you are gone.'[58]

Of the two, Gaunt is perhaps the more touching, certainly the more
ignoble, his genuine grief tinged with the insatiable curiosity and

the deferential, self-deprecating, ill-concealed confidence of the survivor. Sir Ransom on the brink of the grave is a model of stoic composure: humorous, sober, regretful, even faintly tetchy but dry-eyed, issuing instructions, directing the mourners, and still with his last breath firmly proclaiming his irreligion (' "I believe I shall be as I was before I was born." "It is interesting to see that a man can face that, when he is actually confronted by it." "It does not sound as if he had much choice," said Sir Ransom'[59]).

Margaret of course cannot have read *Darkness and Day* which was published ten days after she died. Her cough and catarrh had eased a little after Christmas, though her breathing was no better, and she kept up the usual round of luncheon and tea parties until well into the New Year, 1951. But entries in her diary peter out towards the end of January, leaving a blank that suggests she scarcely saw anyone or went anywhere in February save for four days' sea air (Dr Compton-Burnett's sovereign remedy for bronchial trouble) at the end of the month. She and Ivy were back in London on 2 March, and on the thirteenth Ivy's doctor, Stephen Pasmore, arranged for Margaret to be admitted for a five-day course of drug treatment to a nursing home in Knaresborough Place. Dr Pasmore, called in because Margaret's own Dr Landor was not available, thought her condition ominous—'I didn't like the look of her at all'[60]—and Ivy's evident distress almost equally worrying. Margaret, exhausted by pain and anxiety and attempts to conceal both from Ivy, seemed by this time to have accepted the end, perhaps even welcomed it ('She feared Ivy might come to a full stop,' said Margaret Branch. 'But I think she herself was glad enough to go. And no wonder'). Whether or not she talked openly to Ivy, Margaret's mind was certainly moving in the same direction as Sir Ransom's. 'People do not always run consistently true to form,' wrote Ralph Edwards, describing the only time in their long and close association that the formidable M.J. showed him another side of her character: 'That staunch atheist was badly rattled by the fear of death . . . & told me shortly before her end that she thought the odds are on personal survival!'[61] But Margaret was still quite sufficiently herself to make a Roman exit: her last words (widely circulated later in a variety of versions among her friends) as she left by ambulance for the nursing home were, 'Ivy, don't let Day eat all the Elvas plums.'[62]

This flash of the old scathing Margaret served perhaps in some sort as a signal to Ivy, in much the same way as Sir Ransom's tart pronouncements forestall any possible inclination on Gaunt's part to lapse into self-indulgence or sentimentality. Ivy had refused, almost to the end, to acknowledge a catastrophe she was powerless to prevent. She had suffered, and watched Margaret suffer, and made things worse for them both; but, with another part of herself, she had been preparing for the worst, exploring and charting the process of mourning, at least since the end of 1949 when she started writing *Darkness and Day*. From now on she retreated again into her old resolute courage, dignity and reserve ('I had to follow my nature,' said Dudley Gaveston, explaining his own iron restraint after an emotional explosion in *A Family and a Fortune*: 'It may be my second nature in this case. It would be best to hide a first nature quickly, and I was very quick . . .'[63]).

Ivy visited Margaret in Knaresborough Place, complaining freely about having to go up and down in a narrow, box-shaped lift designed in her view for coffins. Margaret came home the week before Easter on 17 March (two days before *Darkness and Day* was published in America by Knopf), and seems to have rallied briefly, judging by a final entry in her diary on 27 March—Easter Tuesday —recording the various heart treatments prescribed since December in a memorandum at the front, and marking the day itself, 'End of fortnight bedridden'. Ivy clung to hope and disbelief even now: 'Margaret was certainly better on the Sunday,' she wrote later to Robin McDouall, 'and the doctor had no idea she was in any danger.'[64] But Joyce Felkin, Elliott's wife, who had a flat round the corner and called every day for news, reported that Margaret was seeing imaginary people at the foot of her bed.[65] On 3 April she collapsed, and was taken to the Charing Cross Hospital where she died of a blood clot on the lungs on Friday, 6 April.

Joyce, ringing the bell on her way to work that morning, learned what had happened from Day who opened the door and brought a message from Ivy asking her to come in. They sat together, saying very little, and later drove to the crematorium at Golders Green, to make funeral arrangements. Ivy was not demonstrative, then or later, with Joyce or anyone else, but she did need company. An old friend of Margaret's, Helen Rolleston, stayed for a while at the flat, and Basil Marsden-Smedley also came, bringing his two teenage children, Luke and Henrietta, to whom Ivy gave tea ('I don't think she was in such a state then,' said Henrietta, who remembered Ivy calmly passing plates and filling cups), while Basil, as executor, hunted in Margaret's room for her will. 'I have never been in Margaret's bedroom,' Ivy said, when Basil suggested she might find the will there, 'and I don't mean to start now.'[66]

Ivy sent a great bunch of Margaret's favourite violets, but did not herself attend the funeral which was large and well-patronized and not without the sort of incident that might have appealed to its chief protagonist. 'This is the happiest day of my life,' a distinguished museum official was heard to say to a colleague, 'Margaret Jourdain is dead, and you've got the sack.' Margaret's nephew, Colonel Seymour Jourdain, who presided (his offer to escort Ivy as chief mourner having been turned down), amused the Marsden-Smedleys by rashly 'doing the relative' without knowing—as they did by now—that his claim as the last of the Jourdains had been passed over in favour of Luke's as heir. Herman hurried home by taxi to give Ivy lunch at his flat in Mulberry Walk, claiming that he heard her say under her breath, as she struggled up his stairs, in her clearly audible triple aside: 'I have lost my man, I have lost my man, I have lost my man.'[67]

Certainly she struck a great many people at this time, and for months, even as much as a year afterwards, as lost, depleted, physically and morally shrunk. 'Ivy seemed to wither. She shrivelled,' said Vere Watson-Gandy. 'We thought she was going to die.' To the many friends who wrote in condolence, Ivy replied at once, tersely and often in a variant of the same phrase: 'I feel that my life has been torn away, and do not try to face the future.'[68] She made no attempt to conceal a misery that appalled her friends ('I was so upset by Ivy Compton-Burnett's letter that I wrote again saying that if she wanted a refuge she could come here for some days,' Vita Sackville-West wrote from Sissinghurst to her husband on 16 April. 'I really cannot bear to think of people's sorrow and grief and loneliness. I cannot bear it . . .'[69]). But Ivy had shut herself up, seeing hardly anyone and refusing invitations, offers of help, suggestions, advice and proposed visits with the same polite formula. 'You are kind indeed, and some day I would like to,' she wrote on 5 May to Elizabeth Taylor, and to Robin McDouall on 14 April: 'I am going to the country for a week on Tuesday, and a little later I should like to see you. I shall have to depend on my friends.' Like people dreadfully bereaved in her books—the widowed Sophia Stace and Duncan Edgeworth, both of whom demand constant reassurance on the score of their own dealings with the dead—Ivy turned in the first few weeks to friends prepared to talk about Margaret, people who had loved her like Basil and the New Zealander, Helen Rolleston, whose visit was not a success. 'Ivy said she was "horrible" to her [Helen], because she could not forgive her for not being Margaret. Nor could she forgive herself for ever having been impatient with the latter—she really suffered from remorse—but most of all she could not forgive Margaret for having left her.'[70] To the end of her life, Ivy could never be reconciled to living alone. 'Every minute of every day,' she said fifteen years later to James Lees-Milne, who had asked if she still missed Margaret, and to Olivia Manning: 'I miss her more with every day that passes.'[71] For nearly twenty years, Ivy mourned Margaret in the phrases she had used at the end of *Darkness and Day*, when Gaunt first learns of his own loss:

> 'I shall miss him day by day. Not an hour will pass, but I shall miss him . . . I see for the first time the place he held in my life.'
> 'He always saw it. Do not fear. There is nothing for you to regret.'
> 'I can only regret being myself. I suppose all regret comes to that.'
> 'It is the last thing that he regretted. It was always a refreshment to him, your difference from other people.'[72]

For a while 'the various duties incident to these times' took, as Ivy said, all her energy.[73] With Basil she set about winding up Margaret's affairs ('The letters about everything are almost too much for me'), answering queries, dealing with publishers, sorting belongings, going through the vast jumble of papers that had somehow to be raked into sheaves and stacks, crammed into folders and files, stuffed into tea chests and hat boxes for eventual dispatch to the V&A. Ivy had no talent whatsoever in practical matters: 'Her helplessness in a crisis was truly pitiful,' wrote Cicely, who found her, well over a year later, still defeated by even the simplest domestic chore which seemed to rear up against her in token of how much she missed Margaret (' "She did so many things I find difficult to do—like doing up a parcel, for instance," Ivy told me . . . pointing to an arrangement of brown paper and string she had been struggling with when I arrived'[74]). Ivy learnt in time to cope with the Post Office, receive admirers, give interviews, go to parties, even travel on her own, but she never got over the great trouble ('the greatest I could have had'[75]) symbolized by these lesser ones: 'Three years after she [Margaret] died, as we parted one evening, she [Ivy] said: "I begin to get a little organised, but it is very difficult being alone." '[76]

It is perhaps scarcely surprising if her disorientation in those first months resulted in various uncharacteristically impulsive gestures, all of which were more or less promptly withdrawn. Ivy, always derisive about the scientific pretensions of psychiatry, many of whose secrets seemed to her an open book, nonetheless made—or seemed, at this time of desolation and overwhelming defeat, to make—tentative, indirect inquiries as to the possibility of therapeutic help from Margaret Branch[77] (who replied that, on the contrary, she advised her students to consult Ivy's novels as practical textbooks—a compliment Ivy accepted with some small satisfaction). She retreated while Day was on holiday for three weeks in June to a country hotel in Tilgate Forest, near Pease Pottage in Sussex, from where she sent an equally startling suggestion to the Principal of Somerville College, Oxford:

> June 11th, 1951
>
> Dear Madam,
>   I hope you will forgive my broaching a personal matter.
>   I have lately lost a friend who had lived with me for many years, and I now have accommodation in my flat for another woman, and should like to meet one who would like to live at a moderate cost in London, and who would up to a point share my life and interests.
>   I am myself in the sixties, and am a novelist, in so far as I have a profession; and I thought the arrangement might perhaps suit some don who is retiring, and does not want living expenses on a large scale. I would make the expenses about £3 10. 0 a week, for anyone who would take the life in my flat as it is.
>   Yours sincerely,
>   Ivy Compton-Burnett
> My own friends are settled in homes of their own.[78]

Ivy thought better of this rash proposal almost before any answer could reach her ('Dear Dr Vaughan,' she replied on 20 June to the

Principal, '. . . I am afraid I have made the mistake of solving my problem along too many lines, and have become rather involved at the moment. But I hope I may write to Mlle Aline Lion later, if my way is clear. And thank you so very much'). In the end she gave up hope of filling Margaret's place because, as she said to a decorating friend, Ivo Pakenham (who moved in briefly with Ivy himself a few years later, while his own flat was being refurbished), it was no good settling for less, 'once you've lived with someone with a first-class brain'.[79]

Ivy was made a C.B.E.—along with Peggy Ashcroft, Margot Fonteyn and the soprano Isobel Baillie—in the Birthday Honours on 7 June 1951, but the congratulations forwarded to her at the Tilgate Forest Hotel came, as she wrote to her cousin Katie Blackie on 14 June, 'at a time when things have little meaning for me'. Critical acclaim must also have seemed a painful irrelevance when *Darkness and Day* was published in April. All that spring and summer reviewers took particular pains to emphasize that the glittering sharp points and cutting edges of I. Compton-Burnett's dialogue ('Within the last few days one has counted rapiers, axes, stilettos, knives and grenades,' wrote Elizabeth Taylor, reviewing Ivy's reviewers in the July *Vogue*) should not make the reader overlook the glitter of tears between the lines of her talk. Stevie Smith, in the June *World Review*, insisted on the power and truth of Ivy's tragic vision; and so did Francis Wyndham, defending her in the *Observer* on 6 May against the old charge of being too cold and too clever by pointing out that the sole aim of her dazzling, destructive wit was to clear a way to the naked feeling beneath —'for the writer's air of detachment covers a sensibility to suffering that responds to the subtlest social embarrassment as well as to deep passion and pain'. Ivy herself copied out in her own hand Raymond Mortimer's magisterial accolade in the *Sunday Times* on 15 April, nine days after Margaret's death, which began by comparing her to Sophocles and Plato ('Though often she makes me laugh aloud, she must be read with the same unhurrying vigilance as these pithy, formidable Ancients'), and ended by declaring her immortal.

All these people knew Ivy (the acquaintance being based in each case on admiration for her books), and all of them knew what had happened to her. It is hardly possible at this stage to establish how far what they wrote reflected a new profundity and compressed feeling in *Darkness and Day*; how far her admirers had simply got used to a way of writing that seems difficult only when it is unfamiliar; or whether their understanding was quickened, with this particular book, by a sense of personal pity. Probably the answer lies in some mixture of all three elements. But, whatever the reason and whether the effect was intended or not, there can be no doubt that Raymond Mortimer's tribute to *Darkness and Day* may be applied equally well to what its author had recently gone through in fact:

> Everyone in it is either protecting himself from the truth or unearthing it. 'What we ought to be is not what we are.' If all the characters blaze with wit, this is in order to illuminate the most unlovely recesses of the human heart: in none of the fashionable prophets of despair do we find a blacker view of human nature. Yet here the reader is exhilarated—by the author's iron courage and by her austere diction, which can rise to poetic grandeur . . .

XVI

1952–1959

'The English secret'

I

'I KNOW THAT you, if anyone, can measure my loss, and understand how hard it is to look forward. And it is true indeed that work is the last thing that can be done,' Ivy wrote to Robert Liddell on 28 April 1951, three weeks after Margaret's death. 'I find I can only live from day to day, and do not look forward; and concentration of any kind seems impossible . . .' she wrote a month later to Cicely (who had recently moved to Sussex). 'I am glad that you like the country, and that your work progresses. I must try to get back to mine before long, but so far the effort seems too much.' Visitors to Braemar Mansions privately feared that Ivy might never be equal to the effort again, for her loneliness that autumn was dreadful to see. Furniture friends, never for the most part enthusiastic about Ivy, still less so about her books, stayed away in large numbers. People who had put up with her for years as Margaret's appendage naturally looked on Ivy alone as a liability, while others who were genuinely fond of her hesitated to intrude on a grief that even outsiders could see was literally crushing. Ivy relied on old friends and neighbours like Herman, Basil, the Thesigers and Kidds, and a few persistent new ones like Carol Rygate who had first met her with Margaret and afterwards spotted her one day in Kensington High Street, dressed all in black, looking so small and so sad that she went up and asked her to tea. The flat itself seemed as mournful as its mistress: 'When the maid opened the door on the dark brown hall, one felt "Oh, help," ' said Sonia Orwell, who also said that in all the years after Margaret's death her only moments of comfort or intimacy with Ivy came when two or three friends, gathered round the fire, could turn their backs on the high, chill, dismally empty drawing room beyond.

Ivy confided in no one and nothing, unless perhaps in the novel she was writing that winter. *The Present and the Past* was finished on schedule the following summer, two years to the day after *Darkness and Day*, and it, too, begins and ends with death. Chapter One starts with the Clare children watching a dying hen tormented and trampled by its companions in the hen run (something Ivy said she had seen herself when she and Margaret kept poultry at Zealand in the war[1]), which leads to a long, unflinching discussion as to whether or not the sick bird will be better off dead (' "It won't go to another world," said Henry. "It was ill and pecked in this one, and it won't have any other" '[2]). The same theme is taken up later in the funeral service for a dead mole conducted by the three-year-old Toby ('Dearly beloved brethren. Let us pray. Ashes and ashes. Dust and dust. This our brother. Poor little mole! Until he rise again. Prayers of the congregation. Amen'[3]). Toby's foibles—his captivating self-confidence and bids for attention—are less endearing when they reappear, barely modified, in his father, the jealous, demanding and highly competitive Cassius Clare who is the book's tyrant. The second half is given over to Cassius' fake suicide, staged in a bid to pay out his family who retaliate with an uncomfortably acute analysis of his motives, only to be overtaken by genuine compunction when the book ends with Cassius actually dying ('I wish he had been happier. I wish he had had more. I wish I had given it to him. I had the opportunity day by day. I had it only a few hours ago, and to the end of my life I shall wish it'[4]). It is a plot expressly designed to give death a second thorough going over in all the aspects that currently interested Ivy—its squalid physical reality and posthumous ennobling effect, its finality for the deceased and mixed effect on the survivors. The children's ruthlessly logical speculations—frightening to both themselves and their elders, whose own reactions are clouded by pain and pity—are developed on a more detached level by the bystanders, Elton Scrope and his sisters, who pick up where Gaunt Lovat and Sir Ransom left off discussing immortality, religious faith or the lack of it, parting, grief, loss and extinction:

'Cassius was not of an age to die,' said Catherine.
'What is the age?' said her sister.

'About seventy,' said Elton, 'when we have had our span, and people have not begun to think the less of us.'[5]

Ivy was sixty-eight in June 1952, the month when she finished *The Present and the Past*. She wrote asking Cicely to type the manuscript on 2 July, and turned to reading Robert's new novel, *Unreal City*, which is the story of Charles Harbord, teaching in Caesarea (Robert himself taught at the universities of Cairo and Alexandria) and learning slowly to live with his grief at the death of a beloved sister.

> I have just come to the end of *Unreal City*, and though I do not think it suits either you or me quite as well as the real one, I wanted to tell you what great pleasure it has given me, and how I look forward to reading it again [wrote Ivy on 1 August]. Its unrealness is of course its real nature, and it could not be better given. And Charles's situation, essentially yours and mine, gives me the sense of fellow-feeling that perhaps one should not welcome as much as one does . . .

Ivy by this time seems to have been ready to surface again from the long seclusion and unreality of mourning; also perhaps to note with satisfaction that, though she was only two years short of her span, people clearly thought more and more of her.

She was known as 'the English Secret', a phrase coined by the aesthete Brian Howard on account of the fact that, though I. Compton-Burnett had been a name freely bandied for years by the literati of London, New York and Paris, precious few had actually set eyes on her.[6] But Ivy in the mid and late 1950s became steadily less of a secret. She gave interviews, sat for photographers, attended functions, appeared on television; and she might be said to have marked a fresh start in the spring of 1952 by readily agreeing to help with the radio adaptation of *A Family and a Fortune*, which was broadcast by the B.B.C. in November ('They are giving me £90,' she said flatly, 'so naturally I accepted'[7]). This was the first of a good many radio, stage and television plays about which Ivy took a characteristically deprecatory line to her friends, though people who worked with her found her a cooperative and surprisingly flexible colleague. She got on at once with the young radio adaptor,

Peter Mellors; and the producer, Christopher Sykes (who made later adaptations himself, when Mellors moved to Canada after his highly successful, pioneering versions of *A Father and His Fate, Men and Wives* and *Pastors and Masters*), found her from the first a pleasure to do business with: 'Of all distinguished writers with whom I worked in radio, this severe character was the most harmonious collaborator. The reason was simple. She had no vanity. Absolutely none.'[8] She was practical, easy, encouraging, never moody or shy, and flustered—to the point almost of 'panic rather than embarrassment'[9]—only when Sykes made the mistake of saying how much he admired her work. This remained always tricky ground for Ivy, now that she entertained increasing numbers of admirers herself and could no longer ward off any mention of her books by an automatic reference to Margaret's. But she grew more resourceful at negotiating the difficulty, chiefly by a technique of diplomatic forestalling: 'People always say the wrong thing about the books,' she said sweetly to a young painter, Barbara Robinson, who had invited her to a private view, 'so I shan't say anything about the paintings.'[10]

She used similar tactics when Sybille Bedford sent her a fan letter in the shape of a long, subtle, highly polished and knowledgeable survey of her work and its revelatory effect on the writer over the past fifteen years. The letter is dated Rome, 3 July–10 August 1952. It was prompted by the excitement of reading *Pastors and Masters*, available for the first time in nearly thirty years in Gollancz's reissue that spring; and perhaps parts of it too vividly evoked memories of the start of Ivy's career, when her early happiness with Margaret leaked over into her writing in the persons of Theresa Fletcher and Emily Herrick whose company cuts—in Sybille Bedford's phrase —'like a breath of air' across the rancorous, claustrophobic confusions of self-deception, greed and desire ('Theresa and Emily are admirable women, perhaps they are great, with their minds, their honesty, their sadness, their deprecations and their wit. And how agreeable they are, how well-bred, how articulate. There are not many of their kind'). Ivy's laconic response to a tribute that had taken nearly six weeks and ten thousand words to compose ran simply: 'Dear Mrs Bedford, Thank you so much for your letter. I shall treasure it always as a possession. Yours sincerely, Ivy Compton-Burnett.'[11] She used the identical formula four years later when writing to thank for Sybille's novel, *A Legacy*. Her polite

reserve, maintained for years after Herman arranged an introduction, cracked only once, when Sybille was working on her life of
Aldous Huxley at the end of the 1960s, and Ivy—who had never
before permitted conversation to stray beyond trivialities—gave
her 'a straight look' as they sat together in the twilight after tea at
Braemar Mansions: 'She knew what he was, and what he'd been,
and what I saw. And she said, "You love virtue, don't you?".'

Other young writers who made less daunting approaches to Ivy
after the war, and more easily made friends—who might indeed be
said in due course to have constituted a kind of court round her after
Margaret's death—were Olivia Manning, Francis King, Kay Dick
and Kathleen Farrell. Nancy Spain (who had never heard of Ivy in
those days, nor Cyril Connolly either) heard Elizabeth Bowen
complain mysteriously at a literary party: 'It's really too bad of
Cyril to say that Ivy is the only one of us all that will live.'[12]
Readers, would-be acolytes, devotees and prospective hangers-on
had comparatively little trouble finding people prepared to point
out, or even present them to the English Secret who was herself to
be seen on occasion, looking memorably fine in her black velvet and
diamonds, at select London parties. Madge Garland, an admirer
ever since her days as a junior on *Vogue* when its readers were first
alerted by Raymond Mortimer to *Pastors and Masters*, met her at the
beginning of the 1950s at a Christmas luncheon party given by the
Vere Pilkingtons in Hamilton Terrace (Vere was chairman of
Sotheby's but generally rated, at least by Ivy's friends, rather lower
than his wife, the brilliant and fascinating Honor, who said she had
only to think of *Pastors and Masters* to shake with laughter).

Ivy unwrapped Honor's presents so enthusiastically, clearly
giving herself and others such a good time, that Madge rashly
invited her a few years later to another Christmas party at which
Nancy Cunard was a rival guest of honour. Nancy, whose stylistic
allegiance to the 1920s and 1930s was as intransigent in its way as
Ivy's own to a period thirty years earlier, was another of the
extraordinary women to whom Herman paid homage ('Please,
darling, please; no Compton-Burnettry for me,' Nancy would say
firmly whenever he showed signs of wanting to mix his two great
devotions[13]), but only Madge ever attempted to bring them
together: 'Nancy Cunard decked out in all her corals, with spit-
curls on her cheeks, together on a sofa with Ivy in black velvet was
quite a sight.'[14] Ivy was mesmerized, Nancy scarcely less so by

every detail from the conspicuous tea-cosy hairdo to the neat bows on Ivy's black, pointed shoes, and, like ships in the night, they passed and parted in silence: 'I don't suppose they exchanged a word all evening,' said Madge. 'The only thing I could do as hostess was go into the kitchen and get drunk.' Angus Wilson witnessed a similar confrontation a few years earlier at a party given by another intrepid London hostess, Cara Harris, and presided over—this time on strategically placed separate sofas—by Ivy and Norman Douglas (a close friend of the Kings, then staying near them in Thurloe Square and enjoying the kind of social amnesty conferred by great age on even the most scandalous of prodigal sons). He and Ivy seemed to divide the drawing room, 'like a lion and a hippo sharing space at the zoo',[15] each well aware of and perfectly impervious to the other's existence. The only acknowledgment either made was when Douglas recited from time to time an obscene or irreligious limerick: 'Ivy would perk up and send one of her young men "to see what that old gentleman is saying"—she'd a sense that something blasphemous was being said at the far end of the room.'

Ivy had always sensed undercurrents as anyone who ever met her gaze will confirm ('it was a very peculiar gaze, round-eyed, reptilian, she might be talking and seem to be thinking of prices,' said Sybille Bedford, 'but not when you saw her eyes'). But it was only after Margaret's death that she found she could also negotiate quite well for herself, socially speaking, on the surface as well. Within her own strict limits, Ivy in her seventies would go anywhere, see anyone, fall in readily with any suggestion whether it was for a quiet tea-shop lunch with a woman friend or to go on after dinner to a party of Lord Kinross's at which Ivy (who had been dissuaded by Madge at the last moment from going home to bed) put on a star turn with Rose Macaulay: 'She and Ivy had one of their heated arguments with a circle of admirers egging them on . . .'[16] Ivy spoke evil of Rose to her face as easily as behind her back, and she was often sardonic in private about celebrities like Douglas ('They always said he was up to snuff,' she told Angus, 'but he *wasn't quite up to it*, that was the trouble'), but in public, with people she did not know or disliked, she was almost unscrupulously loyal. Though she held no great opinion herself of Virginia Woolf as a novelist, Robin Fedden was struck by her indignation when Angus Wilson argued (in a notably fair and sensitive review of *A Writer's Diary* in the *Observer* of 1 November 1953) that Mrs Woolf's reputation had been overestimated—'Ugly behaviour,' said Ivy, 'I trust it will do him some harm':

> In the previous year she had been hardly less incensed by Harold Nicolson's paragraphs in the *Spectator* at the time of Norman Douglas's death, with their allusions to noisy drinking and boasts of sexual triumphs. 'A most improbable thing,' she said. 'I do not recall that he boasted of his sexual triumphs to me.' She was not well-disposed to Harold Nicolson and found in him a streak of conformity and a tendency to go along with the times, a tendency which she saw reflected in his Labour sympathies. 'I dislike progress,' she said. Thereby meaning, I believe, the thoughtless acceptance of contemporary ideas and attitudes.[17]

Ivy's own judgments, at least on literary matters, were always informed and unorthodox. 'Dr. Leavis's bad criticism, which is so very bad, takes from the value of his good criticism, which is so very good,' she wrote to Robert Liddell at the beginning of the 1950s, when the literary establishment was seething and splitting under the impact of Leavis and his critical crack troops: 'One feels the truth is not in him, and anyhow the whole truth is not.'[18] She held no brief for Leavis' popular opponent, Charles Snow ('I am wading through the C. P. Snow novel, *The Affair*,' she wrote to Barbara Robinson on 26 April 1960: 'It is able only in a way, and I hardly recommend it'), who rose to fame in the great imagination v. science debate that raged at the start of the next decade: 'I can see Ivy now,' said Herman, 'chuckling as she read out a bit where Dr Leavis said that some people had feet of clay, but Mr. Snow . . . was entirely made of clay, particularly his head.'[19] Snow's wife, Pamela Hansford Johnson, had given Ivy no cause to revise her unfavourable initial impression: 'She works in such haste that her words cease to have a meaning, and a mind seems to be going to waste,'[20] Ivy wrote of Miss Hansford Johnson's British Council pamphlet, which turned out a dashing affair, full of enthusiasm if at times inaccurate and understandably nervous in tone.

Ivy herself, in the opinion of a good many friends, would have written trenchant criticism, and she certainly never slackened her scrutiny of current intellectual trends. She thought Rupert Brooke as unjustly neglected after the second war as he had been overrated after the first;[21] she greatly preferred Charlotte to Emily Brontë, sharing Anthony Powell's unfashionably moderate estimate of the latter ('Posterity has paid its debt to her too generously,' she wrote to him, 'and with too little understanding'[22]); she granted E. M. Forster a pleasing talent but no genius long before the general verdict supported her;[23] and she found Henry James' revaluation by Leavis and others exaggerated, even exasperating, perhaps because her work was so often compared to his ('Of course Henry James had talent, but he makes one work too hard for such a small result,' she said to Barbara Robinson, and to Lettice Cooper: 'A curious talent. One has to respect him. But how one would like to give him a push'). Shakespeare was, with Jane Austen, her comfort and joy: 'I should say that I have heard her talk about Shakespeare more than any other writer,' wrote Anne Hill, 'I think she must go to nearly all his plays that are performed, and read him constantly.'[24]

She told Robin Fedden in 1953, when *The Confidential Clerk* had its premiere at the Edinburgh Festival, that naturally she admired T. S. Eliot, 'but perhaps not as much as one is expected to do', and, when Dylan Thomas died in the same year, she said how much she had enjoyed his poetry ('At the time the qualification on the one hand, and the appreciation on the other struck me as unexpected').[25] Among contemporary novelists, she rated Anthony Powell and Henry Green highly, also Elizabeth Bowen, though again perhaps not quite so highly as other admirers did ('People are always writing to tell her about the death of their hearts,' said Ivy sarcastically when *The Death of the Heart* proved yet another of Gollancz's bestsellers: 'I suppose her publisher sends her peaches'[26]). Elizabeth Bowen was one of the friends who seems to have dropped out of Ivy's life after 1951, perhaps because each found the other's growing celebrity hard to take, or simply because Ivy made heavier weather than ever after Margaret's death of the more penetrating critics of her own work. But she saw more and more of many younger novelists, all of whom regularly sent her their books, which she generally acknowledged by return in the encouraging but noncommittal formula used to Sybille Bedford, for even—perhaps especially—with friends she came to cherish greatly, such as Olivia Manning and Rosamond Lehmann, Ivy could not write or say the word she did not think. She mystified Rosamond, when they first met at the publisher's party for *The Echoing Grove*, by saying kindly: 'I've read your book, oh yes, I've read your book, and I've decided that one of us cannot be a woman.'[27] But she could not resist being more explicit when Cecil Gould asked afterwards what she had thought of the novel: 'If it had been half as long—which would have done no harm—and if she had taken out half the characters—which would have been an improvement—' Pause. 'Well, there wouldn't have been much left, would there?'

Ivy's friends in the 1950s and 1960s relied on her implicitly in the matter of literary merit. 'Ivy educated me,' said Madge Garland. 'For seventeen years she was my guide. I read what she read; and she read *everything*. And that is why I have never come to grips with the contemporary novel since she died.' But Ivy would only discuss other writers freely, or even at all, with people whose judgment and discretion she could trust: 'One remembers . . . those rare discussions about the contemporary novel,' wrote Sir John Pope-Hennessy, 'when one would ask whether it was worth reading a new novel by Iris Murdoch, and she would reply: "I don't think you need trouble".'[28] Ivy made short work of anyone classifiable as a literary snob or a bore, or simply too keen on her own work for comfort, and admirers who begged to meet her were apt to find the introduction going disastrously wrong. There was the famous wartime encounter arranged by James Lees-Milne when Ivy successfully baffled Eddie Sackville-West with 'Do you know Manchester?' and, when he hesitated, 'You get excellent teas there.'[29] At the very first tea party to which Madge invited her, the unfortunate admirer—a charming and up-to-date lady, intellectually fashion-conscious to a fault—chatted civilly about the latest reviews, plays, modern novels ('Nothing Ivy liked better than talking about modern novels,' said another old friend,[30] 'but not with someone who hadn't read any'), until cut short and left gasping by Ivy politely but coldly asking after her weekly butcher's bill, and what she made of the shocking price of meat.

Invited by the editor of the *Times Literary Supplement*, Alan Pryce-Jones, to meet the Duchess of Buccleuch (later apocryphal versions of this popular story substituted the Duchess of Devonshire), Ivy obstinately refused to volunteer information about anything except her window box and her new refrigerator, saying plaintively when Herman reproached her afterwards: 'I wish people would *tell* me when they want me to be literary. I don't think it was a great success.'[31] But perhaps the most memorable of all the parties reduced, at any rate in the host's view, to a shambles by Ivy was an intimate luncheon given for the French ambassadress in the early

1960s at which 'Ivy pretended—I think I may say pretended—that she had forgotten who Mme de Courcel was . . .'[32] Offended as always by Herman's exquisitely un-English food ('Ivy . . . despised a *cuisine raffinée*,'[33] said Herman, who was used to her pointedly scraping off sauces and leaving her wineglass untouched), further affronted by his lapsing momentarily into French, Ivy cross-examined her fellow guest severely and in impertinent detail on the running of the embassy in Kensington Palace Gardens, popularly known as Millionaire's Row ('Aren't they rather large houses? . . . How do you get staff? Don't you find it difficult to get someone to clean the front doorsteps?'). But the ambassadress, who later melted Herman's heart by calling him '*notre M. Swann*', proved socially quite equal to the crankiness of eminent old British authors: 'A *déjeuner*,' she said, 'with Miss Compton-Burnett . . . is rather like a *déjeuner avec le général de Gaulle.*' Silence. '*Ce n'est pas facile.*'

With Herman Ivy was always at liberty to behave as irresponsibly as she liked, and she saw no reason to oblige strangers who came to marvel at her like sightseers at a monument. But with people who lacked social confidence, anyone diffident or at a disadvantage, Ivy was altogether different: 'She had charming manners, she was the perfect guest,' said Olivia Manning, meaning that Ivy could be counted on to take her fair share in the conversation and—unlike some literary lions who turned up only to be admired—would always help out in a sticky patch. She loved style in friends like Madge Garland (who became the first Professor of Fashion at the Royal College of Art after the war), and the novelist Theodora Benson, a 1920ish figure of great charm, chic and dramatic, angular beauty whom Ivy came to love dearly after Margaret's death. Theodora and Madge would always dress up for Ivy's tea parties —'And what fun we have all had in that Stygianly gloomy dining room,' wrote James Lees-Milne,[34] remembering the years when tea at Braemar Mansions turned into a ritual rather far removed from the constrained and conventional occasion it had been in Margaret's day.

The tea table drawn up between the drawing-room windows was abandoned in favour of a more substantial meal announced by a handbell—'school-room tea' said Angus Wilson—with everyone sitting up to table in the dim, cheerless dining room, lit only by a curtainless window opening on a fire escape and a single electric light bulb dangling on the end of a wire, absurdly out of scale and character with its pretty little fancy shade of blue Bristol glass and crystal teardrops. These occasions—'Braemar gatherings' in Roger Hinks's phrase—might not be cosy but they were often uproarious, with gossip rising and flying round the table alongside clouds of white sugar as the guests bit into outsize meringues specially supplied by a local bakery. 'The fare, as tea goes, was perfect,' wrote Robin Fedden. 'Everything was home-made: the oat cakes, the large iced cake, the jams, the cheese and cress, or cucumber, sandwiches, and not least the brandy snaps which were referred to as "jumbles".'[35] There was always something hot—muffins, crumpets, at worst toast—generally a loaf of bread with a honeycomb or gentleman's relish, possibly potted shrimps as well, and 'once,' said Robin McDouall, 'there was ice cream on glass plates.'

The company was mixed, old and new, the sharper or more tenacious of Margaret's upper-class friends eyeing and eyed by the literary contingent, recent acquisitions jumbled up with old standbys like Rose and Roger Hinks, even one or two who, like Arthur Waley, had first known their hostess in the Compton-Burnetts' original, shabby schoolroom at Hove half a century earlier. Anyone might be invited since Ivy, unlike Margaret, seldom if ever dropped people on grounds that they were too dim or too dull (some who found the conversational standard too high or the going too strenuous fell out of their own accord); and anything might be discussed, especially friends ('I like to hear about them,' as Hope Cranmer says in *Parents and Children*, 'and the different ways in which they have gone downhill'[36]). Ivy looked on smiling as she used to do at Margaret's parties, only now she took a more active part, stirring up the talk from time to time with a fresh subject, putting in a word or a story, occasionally convulsing the table with laughter but mostly watching and listening, as amused as her guests, who went home often exhausted but always amply entertained. 'Ivy's parties were totally unlike other people's,' said James Lees-Milne. 'Walking away from Braemar Mansions one had so much to think about. *What* had she meant by that?'

People who knew Ivy before and after Margaret's death all agree that she emerged transformed from her period of mourning. 'She changed and flowered,' said Carol Rygate, 'she became enchanting to her friends.' 'She began to blossom,' said Vere Watson-Gandy, 'she seemed a different person.' The change was obvious even to newcomers like Olivia Manning who had been very young, nervous and practically unknown when she first set eyes on Ivy standing with Margaret at a party of Rose Macaulay's, observing everyone, talking to no one—'As a pair they gave me the impression of close self-sufficiency'[37]—and looking so forbidding that, when Olivia actually met her a few years later, 'she seemed totally different from the Ivy I had seen at Rose's party'. They made friends at once though Olivia remained always faintly dubious, like Rosamond Lehmann, about Ivy's cryptic compliments on her own novels. 'It's an organic book,' Ivy said approvingly of *Friends and Heroes* and, when Olivia complained of her reviews, 'The trouble with you, Olivia, is that you *deserve too much.*' To Olivia, who suffered more than most from unfriendly criticism, Ivy was always consoling, affectionate and understanding. 'Once you pick up a Compton-Burnett, it is hard not to put it down again,' Ivy said encouragingly; and another time, when Olivia stormed out of a tea party at Braemar Mansions, infuriated by 'Ivy's rich friends' lamenting the plight of one of their number obliged for tax reasons to retire in idleness to the South of France, she overheard her hostess explaining that she was a writer. 'Has she had much success?' someone asked coldly as Olivia trod noisily down the passage. 'Oh yes, indeed,' said Ivy enthusiastically, 'yes indeed, she has had *much success.*' Even in private with the discreetest of confidantes Ivy's loyalty scarcely faltered: 'It really is full of *very* good descriptions. Quite excellent descriptions,' she said when Elizabeth Taylor asked about Olivia's latest novel. 'I don't know if you care for descriptions? I don't.'[38]

The B.B.C. producer, Norman Wright, was another who approached Ivy in some trepidation and was surprised to find how easily she dispelled his constraint. He met her at dinner at Theodora Benson's flat in Sloane Square where he found himself scrutinized, interrogated and so shrewdly summed up that he was beginning to wonder how he would get through the evening when Ivy abruptly changed and took charge of the conversation, producing, pursuing and switching topics—religion, life, art, sex (this last being the only one that dismayed her: 'She said she could not understand it, had nothing to say about it, she got quite worked up about it'). It was a brilliant display, 'as though, every so often when enough had been said, she tossed in a firework or threw up a whole lot of coloured balls', and the whole party sat up talking till two in the morning when Ivy—who had by this time closed up again as suddenly as she had opened out—stoutly refused to allow anyone to escort her home.[39]

This sociable, expansive side of Ivy recalls her father, and still more her brother Noel who would also sometimes startle his Cambridge contemporaries by abandoning his habitual ironic reserve to dominate a whole dinner table with irresistible energy and wit. Accounts of Ivy in the last two decades of her life suggest that she came closer than ever before to disclosing something very like the sensitive, responsive, deeply emotional nature that Noel had always shown to his friends. 'She was ruled by her heart,' said Vere Watson-Gandy who, like a great many others, came to love Ivy and know her intimately only after Margaret's death when old friends realized for the first time how much she craved their affection, and how surprised and glad she was to find she had it. Both Watson-Gandys thought it was realizing she had not in fact been abandoned that changed Ivy, who made an art at the end of her life out of cultivating her friends. 'Why did we love her so much? She had a gift for friendship,' said Carol Rygate. 'After Margaret's death I learned to love Ivy, for she was lovable, like a child is lovable,' said Herman. 'She would look up at me, and her eyes would twinkle, and she looked so mischievous, and you felt that she had done something that she shouldn't . . .'[40]

Ivy never lost her mischievous air, nor the infectious pleasure she got like a child from a treat or an outing, but the tyrannical childish urge to hurt or wound dropped from her again after Margaret died. To people who knew her well in those years, she was gentle, considerate, patient, often protective:

I remember . . . thinking as I went to sleep that night that really everything had passed off quite well [wrote Madge, describing her first encounter with Ivy], when, with a blinding flash of insight, I saw a remark of mine pinpointed by a counter-remark from Ivy—but too politely said, too understated, to be immediately apparent . . . Yet, in spite of her famed wit and repartee, I never, in all our seventeen years of friendship, left her presence feeling diminished, or with any barb planted in my sub-conscious. Her generosity of friendship was extraordinary, her interest in one's life and surroundings never-failing. She was the most tender of friends.[41]

No one has left a more intimate portrait of this private Ivy than Elizabeth Taylor, who saw her only intermittently on trips up to town from the country but described each meeting to Robert Liddell in letters often written the same night from notes made on the train going home to Buckinghamshire. It was Robert who had given her an introduction to Ivy in the spring of 1947: they shared the same initial delight and amazement over her books, and Elizabeth came gradually to feel as deeply attached as Robert to Ivy herself. From the start the two speculated furiously—as Compton-Burnett readers commonly did—about mysteries on which no one had the nerve to probe Ivy herself: who she was, where she came from, what dark secrets had lain 'through long lives and on death-beds'[42] concealed in her past, above all who had supplied her with first-hand experience of the cruel patterns of tyranny and exploitation in her books. Elizabeth was inclined to rule out Ivy's mother, if only on the grounds that someone had certainly mothered Ivy, who sensed Elizabeth's nervousness and 'knew what to do' ('She wouldn't have known if someone hadn't done the same for her'[43]).

Robert pooled his researches. Elizabeth put in a little light detective work on a fruitless visit to the village of Compton in Wiltshire with her husband John (a manufacturer of fine chocolates who greatly appealed to Ivy). Both acknowledged themselves hopelessly outclassed as investigators by Ivy, who serenely asked questions and gave advice, eliciting all she needed to know about Elizabeth's domestic affairs, making occasional tantalizingly casual references to her own family and still airier pronouncements about families in general. 'What about that murder?' she asked suddenly one day in 1955, when a neighbour of the Taylors was shot dead (killed by Ruth Ellis, afterwards notorious as the last woman to be hanged in England): 'I saw the young man came from Penn. Did you know the family?' Elizabeth admitted that she did: ' "Such dreadful things happen in families nowadays," she said. (I liked "nowadays").'

Elizabeth's writing is at its very best—clear, pure, almost transparent on the surface, full of ambiguities of humour and feeling below—in this correspondence from one novelist to another about a third regarded by both recipient and sender with admiration bordering on awe. 'The dialogue is as fresh as a water-ice . . . ,' V. S. Pritchett had written of Elizabeth's fourth novel, *A Wreath of*

Roses, in 1949, 'a water-ice from those brilliant refrigerators of family utterance, Virginia Woolf and Miss Compton-Burnett.'[44] In a sense Elizabeth's position at the time parallelled Ivy's own twenty years earlier, when she was introduced at the start of her career to Virginia Woolf on the peak of hers. Though the letters to Robert show a relationship that grew steadily warmer and more relaxed, it had begun formally enough with constraint on both sides, quickened on Elizabeth's part by apprehension and pity in the early 1950s when Ivy had only recently emerged from grief and isolation. The first letter describes a luncheon on 9 June 1953, a week after Elizabeth II's coronation, three months after Ivy and Elizabeth had respectively published in March *The Present and the Past* and *The Sleeping Beauty*, while Robert, having just brought out *Some Principles of Fiction*, had also sent Ivy five draft chapters of his forthcoming book on her novels:

10 June

Dear Robert,

I think this will be a long letter. I even think you may wish it to be, for it is Reporting Back. (I need not say for you alone.) I was in a fine state of disintegration when I arrived for luncheon. It is impossible in these Coronation days to judge how long it will take to get from place to place and I asked the taxi-driver not to be too early. He put me down in the Brompton Road—very kind & understanding—saying 'If you walk from here you'll keep him waiting just a minute like all you ladies do.' I made him take me on a bit further at the risk of him thinking I lacked the right sexual tactics. Then I was afraid I was late & began to run, with my arms full of flowers from the garden—people stared. 'The Servant' looked me over contemptuously. *She* was reading *The Daily Telegraph*. The room looked the same. She was pleased with the flowers & said, as I remembered her saying before—'Before I do anything I will give them a drink'.

She looked smaller but not much changed. Do you remember the dusty black velvet chairs and the sofa with too many cushions? There were no Coronation decorations. ('We seem to have been crowning her for a whole year. I was bored with it long ago, and so relieved to know it is really done at last.') We were alone. The longest time I have ever been alone with her. We had sherry ('Do have some more. There is only a bottle of beer in the dining room'). She obviously waited for me to prove myself an old toper, but I did not. She talked incessantly, her head averted towards the window boxes. She seemed much gayer, much less strange, younger (but not in appearance), rather mischievous. We could talk about anything, but not the Five Chapters. This was made clear.

Luncheon: Hot gammon, cabbage, sauté potatoes. Raspberry fool—with dollops of cream. And then, oh dear, a Camembert of mahogany colour. I do not know how I ate it. It had gone through all its stages. Not helped by: 'So delicious to eat, but it makes the whole flat smell as if the drains were wrong.' She was wonderfully kind & maternal to me, as she has once or twice been before. She gave me all the blobs of cream on the raspberry fool, as if I were a child.

We discussed you—'Robert'—and your works. How once she & Margaret had tea in Oxford with you & your brother and —again—how cut up you were at his death. She was very nice about this. Of your books—'I liked the last novel [*Unreal City*] very much. That old homosexual really *was* one—not like Angus Wilson's—he just says they are and we must take his word for it.'

'I wish writers would not write such annoying letters to me. Joyce Cary wrote a very kind letter . . . I was quite glad to have it . . . sending a copy of my book to be signed, & saying he would like to have it back quickly, as at least a dozen people were waiting to borrow it . . . such a dreadfully stupid thing for one author to say to another. I always write my friends' books on my Harrods list, even if they give me a copy, and then I keep it out for quite a time so that other people can't have it. Another thing is the way others think they can have free copies. One has to pay two thirds, and Mr. Gollancz only gives me six (How many does Mr. Davies give you? Exactly!). One has one or two friends who must be given a copy, and there it must end. And of course, one must keep one or two clear copies for an emergency.' (I loved this.)

(I hope I remember her words correctly. I am not a good Boswell.)

We talked about horses quite a lot. How they always love her and keep nudging her. ('Of course, one falls over, unless one is standing against a wall.') 'I used to ride but I can't afford it now, naturally.' Cats she hates—all domestic animals—cannot bear a house where there is a dog—'Parrots are jealous'. She loves pigs. (A wonderful categorical conversation.)

Literary: Reading life of Gorki—all Russians are brutal, except Tchekov. 'People dislike his plays as they are all about nothing. *I* like them very much.' She also likes Aksakov—& that beautiful Chronicles of a Russian Family.

Rosamond's novel[45]—(She called her Rosamond but was only introduced to her once at a party). 'Little bits of it very well-written.' Over coffee we discussed Blanche Knopf. 'I went to see her at Claridge's . . . they are always so obsequious when one asks for her . . . I think I caught her on the hop for she was wearing trousers and sandals and . . . no, I cannot remember what else . . . whatever one wears with trousers . . . she must have worn something . . . a blouse, do you think, or a jumper? Yes, I think I caught her on the hop. I imagine she was resting and over-ran her time. I do not understand Americans, and she is a Jewess as well, so there you are. She said: "I think I am making a mistake about Liz Taylor (her name for you, not mine). Do *you* think I am making a mistake?" I told her she must make her own mistakes in her own way. She said: "I would never ask *you* or Elizabeth Bowen to alter a comma, but Liz Taylor's only a baby." ' (This amused her very much.)

All this time, she was staring at my legs, & suddenly asked: 'Are those nylons you are wearing, or are you wearing no stockings at all?' I said they were the last pair of nylons, memorial to my relationship with Blanche. 'Oh, she didn't ever give me nylons. I daresay she thought I was too frumpish' . . .

Blanche had summoned her to Claridge's to make impossible suggestions about *The Present and the Past.* Either she didn't want to publish it this year, or not at all, but wanted her not to go to another publisher all the same. 'I could not understand what she was trying to say, because it was too preposterous *for* her to say.' She has followed my example (which she kindly applauded), & gone to another publisher.

She remembers her reviews and quotes them, knowing long passages by heart . . .

I hope I have remembered the things she said. I am writing almost at once, in case I forget. I am glad she was so alert and gay. She only mentioned Margaret twice—once tenderly—'the beautiful curtains Margaret and I chose together'—and once tartly—'Margaret would never prepare her lectures . . . just gather a few notes together and wonder why she was nervous at the last moment. In the end I urged her not to do it.'

It seems a grim, uncosy life there, but it appeared (yesterday at least) not to be having that effect upon her. She is thinking of her new novel ('letting it germinate for a period') and seems busy and hungry. She wasn't quite as neat as she used to be. Hair the same grey tea-cosy streaked still with gold. The same diamond earrings. The same interest in money. Knowing the price of everything. That intense love of flowers—a window box with flax and fuchsias. 'People say the earth must be sour, but it has been there eighteen years & still grows plants. What *is* sour earth?'

I was not quite sure, though confessed to having used the expression. 'Then very honest of you to say so.' 'I love,' she said, 'to see a seed push out of the earth & crack in two. That is quite enough for me. I should not want many flowers.'

She gave me much advice about the children, whose ages she remembered precisely . . .

She took some old flowers out of a vase—'You can see what a poor way we were in'—to make room for the new ones. When she had gone to get water I put this one in my handbag for you. The only one not dead.

Do not bother to answer this. I hope you are having a nice holiday.

Aren't you glad you are not Joyce Cary?
                    With love,
                         Elizabeth.

She asked why Blanche did not like my book and kindly suggested that perhaps it was the woman being scarred from a motor accident which she didn't like. (It was really the book itself.) 'But a very real modern problem it is, as being injured in war is, too.' She said this with energy and emphasis and I was astonished ('When war casts its shadow I find that I recoil', etc.). She kept her eyes lowered to make sure she did not look at me at this moment, at my own quite irrelevant scars.[46] I kept my hands tightly clasped, to avoid the habitual gesture of hiding myself from sight. The room froze with self-control. I wished I could say: 'This is nothing to do with my book. Definitely not.' I so dreadfully wanted her to know that, although I am sure it is not really important either way. I think she felt awkward, because she quickly helped me to more raspberry fool. The hand shook and she spilt a bit into my glass.

Mrs Knopf, who gave Ivy flowers done up in cellophane ('I thought she was going to give me a doll,' Ivy reported to Angus Wilson, 'and of course, I was very fond of dolls. She'd put them into a—what should I say?—a receptacle. Strange, wasn't it?'[47]), had in fact written the previous December declining to publish *The Present and the Past*, on the grounds that Ivy's sales—satisfactory to start with—had failed once again to rise in America in spite of consistently enthusiastic reviews.[48] The book was published instead by Julian Messner of New York, and Ivy much enjoyed describing the various prevarications advanced by Mrs Knopf who thanked her, according to Ivy, for behaving like a lady ('What did she expect me to do?' said Ivy tersely to Francis King. 'Hit her?').

The new book that was germinating in the summer of 1953 was *Mother and Son* in which a brisk plot (comprising missing documents, long-lost parents, a strong line in discreditable personal revelations) is constantly held up by a placid, leisurely flow of talk about housekeeping, and more particularly hospitality: food, drink, menus, what to order and how to serve it, all the domestic minutiae that fascinated Ivy are discussed in detail, down to the finer points of laying a table, getting out special china and opening wine only for guests. Rose's *Pleasure of Ruins* was finally published in 1953, the year in which Ivy signalled her return to vigour and spirits with *Mother and Son* which is, incidentally, the closest she came to compiling her own *Pleasure of Entertaining*. More to the point perhaps is the book's main theme of companionship: the two neighbouring households in *Mother and Son* are both largely preoccupied by questions of how and on what terms to live with other people, whether or not to stay single, the vexations of sharing a home with strangers, and the impossibility of managing alone. Companions of various sorts are engaged under more or less gloomy auspices (' "Are you proof against insult, Miss Wolsey?" asked Francis. "Because, if not, this is no place for you" '),[49] though all but one of these rash engagements, marital and otherwise, are broken off in the end. There is a congenial couple of spinsters running an eminently civilized ménage together, and Miranda Hume, the mother of the title, dies of heart failure, leaving her unprepossessing, unmarried, elderly son plaintive and, as he says, partnerless. But in so far as the book gives an authentic glimpse of its author at all, it is in Miranda herself, who probes candidates for the post of companion with such shameless personal questions about their age, sexual aspirations and financial circumstances that the rest of her family are appalled:

> 'Where is Miss Wolsey, Mother?' . . .
> 'Well, where is she?' said Francis. 'Not fled the house so soon?'
> 'Gone to her room,' said Rosebery. 'A most natural thing to do.'
> 'In a state of collapse?' said his cousin.
> 'Why, what should be the reason for that?'
> 'I thought she had had a talk with Aunt Miranda.'
> 'You will have one yourself, if you are not careful,' said his aunt.[50]

Young women commonly emerged shaken, if not in a state of collapse, from cross-examination at Ivy's hands. 'Had I known what it would be like I should *never*, *never* have attempted to see her again,' said Elliott Felkin's daughter, Penelope Douglas, who emerged from cold storage after her marriage some time in the 1950s and wrote to Ivy only to find herself invited alone to Braemar Mansions, seated facing the light and interrogated at length about her own and her family's affairs: 'I remember being jolly well looked over and gone into. She was very fierce. And I know that I was determined never again to have a tête à tête with Ivy (though of course I did).' Ivy had known Penelope's parents, her unlucky Aunt Winifred and both her grandmothers; and there was an impersonal intensity about her curiosity that impressed Penelope, as it had done Herman's sister Elka, but not everyone had the stamina to stand it. 'Though she lacked Margaret Jourdain's eye for works of art, nothing where human beings were concerned escaped her,' wrote Robin Fedden. 'There the eye and the intelligence never slept. She sometimes seemed to watch people as intently as a predator watches its prey.'

This was precisely the impression Ivy produced over the next decade or so on strong men as diverse and distinguished as Lord Goodman (who claimed to have found her so daunting that he would leave any house sooner than risk being placed next to her at dinner[51]), and Tom Matthews of *Time* magazine (a man unaccustomed to fear but said to have been visibly cowed nonetheless by a simple enquiry from Ivy as to how many pairs of shoes he possessed[52]). The philosopher A. J. Ayer, finding himself seated beside her at table, could think of nothing to say until he nerved himself to ask if she minded people discussing her books, and was reduced to silence again by her civil reply: 'Not if they have something interesting to say.'[53] But Professor Ayer, nerving himself a second time, said something interesting about the immorality of her characters, after which the two got on splendidly for, however short she might be with over-confidence or pretentiousness, Ivy was seldom discourteous. 'I was always surprised when someone whom I was taking to meet her admitted to fear, because there was nothing formidable about her . . .' wrote Kay Dick. 'To anyone who was inordinately shy Ivy was enormously kind, and took great pains to put him at his ease.'[54]

Now that Ivy's life was no longer shaped and run by Margaret, she laid herself out to comfort and amuse her friends who looked out for anything that might please her in return, whether it was a scrap of gossip, a cutting from the *Spectator* about the Sitwells' latest raid on its letter columns or the first spring violets packed in moss and posted straight from the country. She went often to the theatre with Herman or Madge or Carol Rygate, preferably meeting for lunch and going on to a matinée. She kept an eye on her friends' books, and an equally sharp lookout on their children: the Braemar Mansions Christmas tree was given up after Margaret's death, its decorations packed away and given to the Hills' small daughters (who were charmed one tea time, as they were saying goodbye, when Ivy ran them up and down several times for fun in her lift), but Ivy, who never forgot names or ages, always asked affectionately after other people's children and got on exceedingly well with quite a few of them, sympathizing particularly strongly with anyone in trouble at boarding school. She made a spontaneous hit with Rosamond Lehmann's teenage daughter Sally who found Ivy's jokes killingly funny (pressed to another slice of Fuller's walnut cake, Ivy said it was so good 'it might almost be said to eat itself', whereupon she and Sally collapsed in giggles on the sofa), and she surprised the Feddens by asking specially to see their small children ('To what depths I wondered, as she considered my own children, was she penetrating? The disturbing children in her novels provide the answer . . .').

Gardening was another great pleasure. Besides her own balcony window boxes—running the whole length of the flat on two sides, stocked with flowering thrift and thyme, old-fashioned granny pinks, petunias, little roses and fuchsias, even a tiny hydrangea —she helped plan and plant the neglected, junk-filled wilderness that eventually became an exquisitely groomed town garden at the back of Madge's new house on Clarendon Road in North Kensington. Ivy sat on the grass to make a daisy chain the first time she visited Madge's prospective property, and later the two made expeditions to choose flowers and shrubs, striped grasses, lilies of the valley, spring bulbs, roses, viburnums and clematis, always single and simple, as far removed as possible from the frilly, fancy florist's blooms that Ivy deplored ('She particularly disliked chrysanthemums with their heavy towelled heads and heavy, damp smell, but liked dahlias if they were single,' wrote Madge,[55] who even agreed to reprieve a few daisies in her lawn on Ivy's account). If museums and the great country houses no longer detained her, gardens remained Ivy's delight. She and Madge would meet at the bus stop in Kensington High Street for a trip to Kew Gardens (once with lunch at the pub on Kew Green), and they made annual outings to Vita's magical garden at Sissinghurst Castle, choosing a different season each year, hiring a car and driving down for lunch, first at the Royal Oak in Sevenoaks which Ivy approved for its plain cooking, rambling garden, and the photograph in the hall of Lord and Lady Sackville entertaining royalty, with Vita as a little girl in a frilly dress, lace hat and black boots:

Only the boots (brown riding ones, not black buttoned) were visible when we met the adult Vita who, in her mannish clothes and with her dark, cropped head was the antithesis of the small Ivy, dressed in brown tweed, matching brimmed hat, and brown lace-up shoes and gloves to tone. Vita did not usually bother much about tea but she always took special care that a large and proper meal was offered to Ivy, beginning with toasted buns and a cake made specially by the cook . . . Once Vita received us wearing a Persian coat in vivid colours and crimson silk pants —her exotic appearance was marvellous in the all-white garden, sitting at the end of a path lined with lilies, with Ivy, small, neat and darkly-clad beside her.[56]

There were still regular country visits each spring and summer to friends such as Janet Beresford at Ashwell, the Kidds (Roger was now married with small daughters of his own) at Eastbourne, the Jenynses at Bottisham (Soame had fallen into the habit of calling at the flat every three weeks or so after Margaret died, for lunch or tea and a talk) and the Watson-Gandys at Buckland Newton in Dorset (where Vere drove her all round the country, stopping now and then to admire the cowslips or buttercups or for Ivy—who loved riding about in a car—to go behind a hedge and be cheerfully and expeditiously sick). She had become a notably easy guest, quite free from the stiffness and boredom that used to afflict her on furniture visits, entertaining, appreciative, always ready to amuse herself with a flower or a book or a little light brain work: *Mother and Son* was finished at the beginning of June 1954, and typed ('It is short, but it will want some care, as it is rather smudged and interrupted by interpolations'[57]) by Cicely at once so that Ivy might take it away with her to correct in the country. 'I had a happy summer with a good many country changes in the houses of my friends, the kind of holiday I like best, now I am alone,' she wrote on 20 October to Robert whose *The Novels of I. Compton-Burnett* was scheduled for publication by Gollancz with *Mother and Son* the following spring. 'It was good news that your book and mine were to appear on the same day, and I wish the novel was good enough to hold its place at the moment, and that there were four of us, instead of two, to await it.'

One of Ivy's favourite stopping places for work or rest in the country was Broome Park in Kent, a large, plain but palatial, pink brick house between Dover and Canterbury, built in the reign of Charles I and done up by Lord Kitchener ('He was a bachelor *or something*, wasn't he?' Ivy said sweetly to Robin McDouall), who ransacked the empire to furnish it but died in 1916 before finding time to move in. It was acquired between the wars and opened after the second as a retreat—part country house, part hotel—by Dennis Jell and his wife, the painter Pauline Jell (née Konody), who provided precisely the sort of surroundings that suited Ivy: good plain food, pleasant service, spacious rooms, a secluded untidy garden and wild grounds where she might pick tiny posies of the inconspicuous woodland and hedgerow flowers she had loved best from girlhood. 'Cowslips are out in front of my window, and the blackthorn, my favourite of the prunuses—or is it pruni?—is out in clouds,' wrote Ivy[58] who made a point of going each year 'to Broome to see the spring', as well as spending two or three weeks there each summer. There were long drives, short walks and huge fires on a hearth big enough to burn whole branches of trees on a great mound of white wood ash, with a tea trolley drawn up in front and a fireside armchair reserved specially for Ivy.

She had first come to Broome in the mid 1950s with Helen Rolleston for Christmas (a festival increasingly hard to bear without Margaret in London), and sometimes she invited another friend—Carol Rygate, Vere or Madge—with whom she would explore the park and the deep flowery lanes round about that had once been smugglers' tracks, or catch a bus at the end of the drive to ride into Hastings for a blow on the front. She questioned Dennis Jell closely on the management of the estate, helped choose a riding school—interviewing the owners, going over the curriculum, inspecting the bedrooms—for Madge's teenage Parisian goddaughter, and once she took Madge to lunch with Mr Mowll at his house in a pretty village outside Dover (Ivy told Pauline Jell that the original Mowll, her parents' solicitor, had been the tyrant who darkened the days in her childhood).

But mostly she was alone, walking by herself, reading or working in her room: 'She had a staggering power of concentration,' wrote Mrs Jell. 'She would go on writing, without any feeling of irritation, while the chambermaid made her bed and tidied up her room.'[59] Other guests noticed her talking incessantly even at her table for one in the dining room—'apparently she was rehearsing a couple of sentences over and over again, rearranging the order of the words until she got it right'[60]—and so did Mrs Jell:

> Sometimes one would find oneself walking behind her along the main corridor, and would overhear a lively dialogue as she was on her way to the bathroom, which one could hear continuing in full spate through the closed door. Occasionally this oral trying out would break into ordinary conversation between us; she would slip in a sentence that had nothing to do with what she was saying, but was obviously something that had come up in connection with her current book—this without any change of

voice or expression. She would then resume the conversation as if nothing had happened.[61]

Other people reported strange behaviour in Ivy when she seemed, like Charlotte Brontë, to be what Mrs Gaskell called 'possessed' by her novel. Charlotte Brontë, too, was adept at putting up with interruptions, carrying on with her ordinary domestic routine 'even at those times when the "possession" was on her', only hurrying through the housework 'so as to obtain leisure to sit down and write out the incidents and consequent thoughts, which were, in fact, more present to her mind at such times than her actual life itself'.[62] Mrs Gaskell's description sounds very like Hereward Egerton, the last of Ivy's novelists (in *A God and His Gifts*), emerging from his room 'dazed and dumb and vacant-eyed'[63] to find his actual family vague and insubstantial compared to the fictional characters 'who have lived with me and made my world. More deeply than mere flesh and blood.' Ivy seldom discussed her own methods, and then only with fellow professionals like Christopher Sykes or the painter Barbara Robinson ('I get an idea and start writing and the book seems to have a life of its own, and takes twists and turns I hadn't foreseen,' she told Barbara. 'The characters develop and change and then the beginning has to be altered'). But she did once say to Kay Dick that writers were hard pressed for material to work on—'We have to dig it out of our insides'—compared with painters who have theirs laid out before them: 'I think I feel on the whole that something's there trying to get out . . . It's sort of trying to get out and wants help.'[64]

She also said what so many other writers have said about the difficulty or impossibility of writing, the impossibility of not writing ('What a difficult kind of work to choose! But of course one did not choose it. There was no choice'[65]), and how much easier life would have been as an interior decorator or a furniture expert, 'because their artistic instincts are satisfied without too much effort. Producing something is rather an effort.'[66] Cicely Greig has described how coming to the end of a book drained Ivy, so that lunching with her to collect a newly finished manuscript was always a strained and edgy affair compared with the convivial occasion a month later when she called to deliver the typescript. 'They are hard matters and take their toll,' Ivy warned Robert when he contemplated a travel book at the same time as a novel.[67] She herself left comfortable gaps—'at least they seemed comfortable to her'[68]—between books, insisting sternly to Barbara that any artist must learn to endure what she called 'a blank time', which might in any case produce results in the long run.

Ivy had met Barbara and her husband Walter Robinson through Arthur Waley, who brought them to tea at Braemar Mansions in 1956. Walter was charming: a classical scholar and orientalist specializing in fourth-century Japan because it possessed, or so he said, 'no human interest', he was also a devoted and exceedingly knowledgeable admirer of Ivy's books which suited his own subtle, complex, profoundly ironic temperament so well that he might have stepped out of one himself. Both Robinsons were presently adopted as part of the growing circle of honorary nephews and nieces whose doings in the 1950s and 1960s Ivy followed with inexhaustible interest, pleasure and concern. Walter touched her intellectually, Barbara (brave, forthright, determined, until comparatively recently an art student at the Slade School) stirred the generous sympathy Ivy felt increasingly for young women struggling to make an independent career in the arts: by way of encouragement she talked a great deal to Barbara about technical problems common to both writing and painting, such as composition ('The plot is not very important to me, though a novel must have one, of course. It's just a line to hang the washing on'[69]), and pruning ('One must do it,' she said emphatically, many times).

With other novelists, she tended to stick to the drab, concrete, mercenary terms in which writers generally discuss their work among themselves, swapping hard luck stories, girding at publishers, grumbling about sales, commiserating over reviewers ('Their verdicts are always so incalculable that it is best to take them as amongst the vagaries of the spring,' she wrote to Robert on 6 March 1955, when their books came out together). She was invariably a comfort to writers in trouble, urging them on, sympathizing in blank times, enquiring solicitously whenever there was too long a gap between books, tending her own talent meanwhile as steadily as she tended her garden ('Ivy was strict about dead-heading, weeding, watering and general tidying-up. All had to be done regularly. She disliked disorder'[70]). 'Writing is not breaking stones,' as somebody says in *A God and His Gifts*, and one can almost hear Ivy's voice behind Hereward's, answering that the saying is only partly true: 'Everything is breaking stones up to a point.'[71]

2

ALL THIS was of course far removed from Ivy's normal conversational method which was to round up and head off her guests until she had reduced the most unlikely people to discussing the price of refrigerators at the Army and Navy stores, whereupon she would say with mild surprise: 'Here we are—some of the best-educated people in England, I suppose—and all we can talk about is the price of refrigerators at the Army and Navy.'[72] An outstanding partner in this particular game of skill was T. S. Eliot, who moved into a house round the corner from Cornwall Gardens with his new wife in 1957, and met Ivy at a party in Knightsbridge. She came home with the Eliots in a famous taxi ride when—according to Alan Pryce-Jones and Christopher Sykes as well as to various enthusiastic accounts put about by Ivy herself—they talked about nothing but the forthcoming Rent Act, cake shops, fishmongers, greengrocers in the Gloucester Road and where to go for the best fillet steak. 'Ivy roared with laughter at this visit from one of the leading literary figures alive at the time,' said Herman. 'Somehow it rather emphasised her poor opinion of married life.'[73] The Eliots for their part had been chiefly 'tickled by the fact that she was complaining bitterly both at the party and in the taxi at having to pay the porter five shillings for bringing up her coals!'[74]

But observers could not help suspecting that behind their respective impenetrable façades, the two illustrious neighbours were by no means displeased to display their critical expertise in debate over shopping lists and scones rather than literary theory. They continued to glimpse one another on their rounds of the Gloucester Road ('I don't see very much of him, you know,' Ivy told Barbara, 'but I like to know he's there'), while 'Mr Eliot's bride' remained a source of much friendly and fruitful speculation in Ivy's drawing room:

Apparently she's always adored him, although she was his secretary for years. I am sure if I had been his secretary for a

fortnight I should have wanted to poison him, not marry him
. . . [Ivy said to Elizabeth Taylor]. Yes, I should have run round
to the chemist's for threepennyworth of poison after a very short
time. John Hayward, with whom he used to live, is keeping on
the old flat, and Eliot has apparently paid up the rest for another
two years. There was a great deal of talk about that . . . no, I
don't think there was really much talk. I think I just asked a lot of
impertinent questions. People say that if you don't ask, you get
told more, but I have never found that to be true. I have found
that one gets told nothing at all.[75]★

Ivy's idea of an impertinent question naturally varied according to
whether it was put to or by her. She might question her younger
friends singly and in private as to their family or financial circumstances ('There is no point in discussing furniture if you don't know
how much it cost,' as she said to a couple of collectors, 'and no point
in discussing incomes if they won't tell you how much theirs is'[76]).
But she gave no quarter herself to pokers and priers like the
Frenchman who, having come to England expressly to meet her
and prevailed on the Hills to arrange it, rashly raised the question of
stylization in her work: 'She said a little severely, as if he was
blaming her: "One can't help *that*. One talks in a certain way, and
one writes in a certain way; one certainly can't *help* it." '[77]
   Ivy's standing among intellectuals in Paris in the 1950s was high if
still somewhat mysterious. Five of her novels had been published
by Gallimard and hailed with enthusiasm by those manning the
barricades of novelistic theory in places like *Critique* and *Les Lettres
Nouvelles*. For Sartre's contemporaries, immersed on the literary
front in the upheaval that issued in the *nouveau roman*, Ivy seemed to
have surmounted precisely the difficulties with which they were

★ Compare Ivy's comments on the Eliot marriage in 1957 with the neighbours'
reaction to the Ponsonby marriage in *Daughters and Sons* (1937), p.182:

   'You are not going into the house?'
   'Yes, of course I am going in. But we can't arrive in a body to ask questions.'
   'No, no, not in a body, no. But we want to ask some questions; yes, I think we
do.'
   'To find out about the marriage we have seen in the papers. How else are we to
know about it? It is a wonderful and startling thing and fraught with bitterness
for others . . .'

themselves still struggling.* Where English critics have tended to
see her achievement in painterly terms, mostly French—she has
been variously compared with the Post Impressionists, Cézanne
and the Cubists, Bonnard, Picasso, even Mondrian, all radical
innovators who changed the face of painting this century—for
Nathalie Sarraute, Ivy plainly stood in direct line of descent from
Proust, Joyce, Kafka and Virginia Woolf. Ivy's writing became the
central framework round which Mme Sarraute erected her own
theory of the novel: if Ivy's originality struck readers on the far side
of the Channel as heroic, so did her courage, stamina and clarity of
purpose ('For nothing could be . . . more astonishing than . . . the
monotonous obstinacy with which, during forty years of labour,
and throughout twenty books, she has posed and solved in an
identical manner the same problems'[78]).

Ivy for her part received their homage with a majestic, indulgent,
ironic indifference which suggests that, though she had no intention
of mentioning it, she did not entirely reject their conclusions ('I am
sometimes rather complacent about my writing,' she said once to
Robin Fedden). Mme Sarraute was taken to tea at Braemar Mansions by Sonia Orwell (which vexed others among Sonia's Parisian
intellectual circle, who saw no reason to underestimate their own
claims to be presented to 'cette Ivy'): 'She did not seem to have the
slightest idea as to what I might be doing in life. Neither did she
seem to know that I had written anything about her books. I believe
that if she had known, she would not have cared,' wrote Mme
Sarraute,[79] who was enchanted by her visit and everything about it
from the hostess's long black dress and velvet hairband to the coal
fire and the maid in cap-and-apron, the buttered buns and the silver
teapot, the demure conversation about rising prices, and not least
by Ivy's parting shot: 'Do you girls want to go down the passage?'

Literature was a topic not raised at all, or only far enough for Ivy
to slip in a complacent account of the Eliot encounter and to
describe Virginia Woolf as a snob. Mme Sarraute went away feeling
much like Alice waking up after her trip down the rabbit hole
—'maybe all this was just one of my delightful dreams about
England?' Ivy must have made a similar impression on the French-

---

* 'La solution absolument originale, à la fois élégante et forte, qu'elle a su leur donner,
suffirait pour lui faire mériter la place qui lui est attribuée depuis quelques années par la
critique anglaise unanime . . . : celle d'un des plus grands romanciers que l'Angleterre ait
jamais eus.' (Nathalie Sarraute, L'Ere du Soupçon, p.119.)

man, Roland Cailleux, invited to meet her by the Hills at a luncheon when their mutual imperviousness so impressed their hostess that she made notes afterwards, describing how M. Cailleux doggedly developed his views on the novel ('The Frenchman said that Ivy, Céline and some South American writer whose name I've forgotten [presumably Jorge Luis Borges] were the only really modern writers quite uninfluenced by Jam Jars. We were surprised and puzzled until he referred to Jam Jars' *Ulysses*') which Ivy, primarily interested in the food on her plate, doggedly countered with remarks about her maid, her rent and her holiday plans, how to patch holes in a carpet and 'the devotedness, as parents, of swans'.

What struck Mme Sarraute and other visitors to Braemar Mansions was the sensation of stepping into a Victorian novel, much the same misleading impression Ivy had long since perfected in her books: 'The old-world atmosphere is so important, and I pay it strict attention', as Felix Bacon said in *More Women Than Men*.[80] As the 1950s wore on, Ivy complained fiercely about the accelerating winds of change which she disliked even more than ordinary winds ('Death to me draughts, death to me draughts, death to me draughts,' she said once under her breath when Janet Beresford asked if she minded an open window at Ashwell). ' "Don't speak to me," she would say, "about the 'age of affluence'. How I loathe the age of affluence." '[81] She made no attempt to fathom the workings of socialism or the welfare state, steadfastly blaming all ills on a Labour government even when Labour was not the party in power. 'I don't know *what* Margaret would have said,' became her standard response to rising rents, rates, bills and wages, falling standards of service, tall buildings, increased immigrants and thickening traffic ('The roads are like a dangerous sea,' she wrote to a cousin[82] as old and infirm as herself at Christmas 1959). She seemed at times so cut off from the modern world that her younger, naturally leftish, intellectual friends were constantly taken aback by her vigorous approval of changes like the liberalization of the censorship laws, and the Wolfenden Report which so greatly eased the lives of friends like Herman in 1957. 'I remember her also saying that it made her smile to see what ridiculous precautions young people took when they spoke to her about homosexuals,' wrote Mme Sarraute, 'as if that could have shocked her . . .'[83] It was Rose who had been shocked when Ivy said of an old friend's marriage eleven years earlier: 'He's homosexual, so of course he had to get married.'

'*Ivy*,' said Rose, 'you really can't say things like that—think of all our friends.'[84]

1957 was also the year of the Rent Restriction Act, a prospect which filled Ivy with gloom and foreboding for months beforehand. 'I feel nervous, too, about the new, short BBC novel,' wrote Elizabeth Taylor to Robert (the novel was *A Father and His Fate*, due to be broadcast in Christopher Sykes' adaptation on the Third Programme in June before publication in August). 'She has to have the money, though, because goodness knows what her rent will be, & Rose Macaulay says *she* will not pay a penny more but Rose will do exactly what everyone will have to do, & pay what she is told. Ah, naughty, headstrong Rose.' Tea parties at Braemar Mansions grew loud with the sound of protest, alarm, appeal and lament. 'I live under the sword of Damocles in that my rent may soar after the revision of the Rent Act in the autumn,' Ivy wrote on 12 July to her cousin Katie Blackie, and on 17 September to Robert: 'The Rent Act is looming over everything here, and it has fallen on me with thunderous force.' Her friends were disturbed and full of advice. Robin McDouall suggested they might buy a house together and share it: Ivy had always had a soft spot for Robin because, as she said, he would have made such a wonderful butler—'I suppose you mean I look as though I'd been at the port,' said Robin. 'No. I don't mean you've been at the port,' said Ivy laughing, 'but you look as though you knew about the port.'[85] But she had long since discarded the notion of living with anyone ('It is a kind idea, and might be such a useful one, if I were not past the age for moving and moving alone . . . ,' she wrote on 21 August, adding prudently: 'If you are not providing for possible marriage, would not a flat be better than a house? Houses produce so many unforeseen expenses, and have roofs and drains and outside painting and dry rot, and people never know where they are').

In the event Ivy's rent was almost tripled to a stupendous £512 a year, which she paid with incredulous outrage ('It would be of little good to move as the same thing is happening everywhere and there is nothing to be done but suffer it, though in my case not in silence,' she told Robert on 25 June 1958). Ivy responded to what struck her as a shocking piece of opportunism on the part of her Polish landlord by breaking her generation's ingrained taboo against drawing on capital, arranging for herself and her sisters each to receive £3,000 from trust funds[86] and confessing the deed ('I've done something wicked') to Jim Brandreth. 'These are hard days and we are the doomed class,' Ivy wrote grimly to Katie. Tea parties grew stormier—'We all in London talk only of Rents'[87] —servants harder to come by and their wages steeper as their services became more essential to Ivy, whose last maid went mad[88] in the mid 1950s and had to be taken to hospital:

Poor Ivy alone in the house with her & sudden strange conversations about spiritualism & the stars [Elizabeth reported to Robert] . . . Ivy found 'a very strange library' in her room. 'So very peculiar. I didn't know that kind of book existed, but I have since learnt there is quite a demand for them. Horribly unpleasant. Quite a shock to me.' I hope I didn't look too anticipatory, or too disappointed when she said they were all about horoscopes & 'Find Yourself Through the Stars', etc. 'A very unhealthy lot. When she recovered, I advised her to get rid of them & so she did. It was distressing to hear her talking like that. When people are upset I always say I have a headache & that takes their mind off their troubles. But she only said, "I *knew* you had. I always know about you, because we are both under the same star."' This is carrying the democratic attitude too far. I said in a careless laughing way: 'What star is that?' 'I am afraid I don't remember,' she said coldly.

Towards the end of the 1950s more and more friends with private incomes left the country to lead a roving life in continental hotels like Jim Brandreth, or settle like the Robinsons in the South of France. Ivy, whose horror of dislodgement and dispersal went back at least to the time when her sisters had dismantled the household at Hove nearly half a century earlier, was deeply indignant. She refused to accept or even listen to the Robinsons' reasons for going, and they felt themselves disgraced ever afterwards. 'I am sorry you have gone to make a corner of a foreign field for ever England,' she wrote on 9 April 1958, to Barbara and Walter, who grew accustomed over the next decade to the mixture of disapproval, grief and reproach in Ivy's letters which grew wilder and sadder as she neared the close of her life: 'Yes, it is long since we met, but not, I think, longer than it tends to be, when people live under different skies,' she wrote to Barbara on 3 December 1968. 'I have quite a number in my life; and expect long partings and unfamiliar young faces . . .

When you barter your heritage, you will have great wealth, but perhaps cannot even think you need it.'

Ivy spoke often and openly to London friends of her loneliness ('Living alone is unspeakable' was another regular refrain), to which she was by this time resigned. 'My life goes on in the same groove since Margaret Jourdain died, always with its roots in the past,' she wrote to Peter Mellors (who had emigrated to Canada by this time, in spite of all Ivy could say): 'I wish you had met her, and so met more of me.'[89] She still missed Margaret constantly, at times—on what Cicely called her 'Margaret days'—with palpable, angry vehemence. Cicely describes a dreadful occasion when she and her sister with a woman friend entertained Ivy to lunch at the National Book League in Albemarle Street where, the Regency staircase having first called Margaret to mind, Ivy retreated into herself with freezing dignity, Cicely referred to her as 'Miss Jourdain' by mistake, the rest of the party seized up with nerves and, all through the meal, 'Margaret seemed to come like a ghost between us'.[90] This was 12 January 1956, when Ivy was working on *A Father and His Fate* which perhaps had something to do with her state of strain. A year later Margaret's spirit presided in altogether more sardonic and humorous mood over the tea party Ivy gave for Lucille Iremonger whose latest book, *The Ghosts of Versailles*, attempted to get to the bottom of the various adventures of Eleanor Jourdain and Miss Moberly, beginning with their respective upbringings and ending with the public debacle at St Hugh's. Though Margaret is nowhere mentioned by name, the book's patronizing and somewhat inaccurate account of the Jourdain family—especially its unfairness to Eleanor ('She was, in sum, a sneak and a spy, with uncanny powers to boot')[91]—made Ivy feel that family loyalty on Margaret's behalf, together with curiosity on her own, might be served by meeting the author:

She asked me to a cocktail party to which I didn't want to go . . . And then I thought I would write and suggest that she should suggest herself to tea one day & not only did she have the effrontery to do so ['Gave me pause to think myself', Elizabeth wrote in the margin of her letter reporting Ivy's words to Robert], but she brought her husband. As soon as Rose knew that she was coming, she said that she must come too, & challenge her statements about Margaret's sister. For so much was untrue,

& Margaret never had doubted her sister's integrity; they really believed, poor things, that what they said was true, & Miss Ironside or whatever her name is seems to have had some grudge against her. Then everybody wanted to come to tea. They swarmed in, & I had to have a cup which didn't match the saucer. Lots of people had to be refused. I couldn't just have them standing up at the back. It became out-of-hand & I had to stop Rose, for after all Miss Ironside was my guest & she was getting very angry & upset. I believe she has written other books, you know, though I am sure I don't know what they are.

But Ivy, for whom the art of conversation was always a matter of drama, movement and friction rather than academic discussion, had organized this affair with rather more care than her casual account to Elizabeth suggests. She had taken pains with the guest list—besides Rose, there was Carol Rygate who had been an active undergraduate member of the anti-Jourdain faction at St Hugh's in 1924, together with a strong detachment of Margaret Jourdain's supporters: Cecil Gould, Ivo Pakenham, Jim Brandreth and Basil Marsden-Smedley (Hester had begged to come too but been forbidden by Basil—'we had the worst row of our married life over this'[92]—on grounds that she knew too much about the Jourdains and was bound to get over-excited). All had been primed beforehand with copies of the book—'Have you done your homework yet?' Ivy wrote on a postcard to Jim Brandreth—and required to come armed with pertinent questions. The general verdict was that in the event the party had been spoilt by Rose's heckling, but retrieved after the Iremongers left by Ivy saying expectantly: 'Now, let's all say what we think of them,' which they did, to everybody's satisfaction. But it casts an interesting light on Ivy's stance as neutral observer that—whatever her other guests may have supposed to the contrary—she had privately contrived to give Mrs Iremonger the impression beforehand that she fully endorsed her view of Eleanor Jourdain[93] (and the Iremongers remained on Ivy's visiting list for years afterwards).

Ivy had a revenant of her own from the past round about this time in the shape of her long-lost cousin, Anthony Compton-Burnett, a distinguished amateur cricketer and science master at Eton, whose parents made contact by chance in 1957 with Ivy's sisters (they shared a radio repairer in Watford), and who subsequently turned up himself at the flat of his illustrious relative. His great-grandfather, William Compton-Burnett, had been the brother of Ivy's grandfather Charles; the first inkling either set of descendants had of the other's existence had been when Ivy's half-sister, Olive, herself a cricketing enthusiast, came across Anthony playing for his prep school on the south coast between the wars; and, though the connection was distant, both sisters must have been struck by the family likeness, for Anthony had the broad open brow, massive frame, curly hair and square-set eyes they had known in their father and their brother Noel. Ivy naturally warmed to him at once, and continued to see him regularly, asking in due course after his children (Anthony's sons, Richard and Nicholas, were, after all, the last of the Compton-Burnetts in a position to pass on the name), and enjoying his company on a much less impersonal footing than her sisters', or the Blackie cousins' who were her only other surviving relations.

These Blackies were the children of Ivy's Aunt Lizzie, her mother's favourite sister; and the strenuous rivalry between the two forceful sisters that had loomed large in Ivy's childhood might be said to have found a peaceful solution at last in herself and her cousin, Margery Blackie, who was by this time well on the way to succeeding Ivy's father as the country's leading homoeopathic physician (the official recognition of homoeopathy for which James Compton Burnett fought all his life was eventually achieved under the new National Health Service in 1948, thanks largely to a campaign organized by Dr Blackie who followed her uncle as senior consultant at the London Homoeopathic Hospital in 1957, afterwards becoming dean of the Homoeopathic Faculty and personal physician to the Queen). Dr Blackie practised in Kensington but, being profoundly religious, exceedingly busy and in any case twenty years younger than Ivy, left contact with their cousin chiefly to her older sister Katie.* Another devout churchwoman (Ivy's relations clung to religion as staunchly as she repudiated it), Katie had been as a girl the closest of all the Blackies to Ivy, who found

---

* The late Katharine Blackie insisted, when I wrote *Ivy When Young*, on being identified only as 'Katie' for fear of possible damage to her own and her sister's reputation if the family's Wesleyan background ever became common knowledge ('It must never come out, oh no,' she told me Dr Blackie had said, in dismay at the thought of her connection with Ivy being made public: 'Even the Queen—*even the Queen* who has done so much for homoeopathy—would think the less of me').

cordial conversation about parish activity hard to sustain in later life ('My congratulations on the church garden,' was a characteristically truthful compromise, 'I think it is a very good work'[94]).

But Ivy was growing less strict about keeping people in separate compartments. 'My own circle seems to come from several different worlds, one of them hardly literate,' she wrote to Robert ('Perhaps *we* . . . are really her hardly literate world,' wrote Elizabeth darkly on hearing about this letter) on 20 February 1962, at a time when she was beginning to let her friends edge open the door so firmly slammed on her past after the First World War. She invited Herman (always faintly resentful about her family having been, as he said, 'deliberately kept from him') to tea to help be nice to Katie: 'She believes,' Ivy said by way of warning, 'and'—another of her favourite sayings—'people who believe in the resurrection will believe in anything'.[95] She responded generously out of the blue after fifty years' silence to a fund-raising appeal from her old college, Royal Holloway; and, when Basil was elected mayor of Chelsea in 1957, the two set off on a jaunt in the mayoral car to call on his friend, the principal, Edith Batho (Miss Batho apparently had happier memories of this occasion than her guest, who was frankly appalled: 'The library crowded, the dining hall also, the roses gone, the principal housed in a first floor flat instead of the ground floor rooms that were rightly her own . . .' Ivy reported gloomily long afterwards to a long-lost college contemporary[96]). She produced Elliott Felkin, by this time almost her oldest friend, also out of the blue one day at tea with Madge, who was charmed and disconcerted by his evidently extensive but unexplained links with Ivy. Elliott's daughter, Penelope Douglas, went to some trouble to bring about a reunion with Raisley Moorsom which —since neither he nor Ivy was prepared to stand host to the other—took place in a tea shop, and turned out a great success: 'I have never seen her so relaxed with anyone as with Raisley.'

Though never exactly forthcoming on the subject of her early years, Ivy talked more freely about her family in the last decade of her life than ever before. *A Father and His Fate*, published in September 1957, contains incidentally Ivy's first direct portrait of her mother since *Brothers and Sisters*,[97] but its central concern is a fuller working out of the theme of the present and the past already propounded in the novel of that name. In each case, a missing wife (divorced and supposed dead, respectively) returns home to confound a disgruntled husband anxious to exchange the drab reality of unromantic middle age and an unappreciative family for a more glamorous role (an heroic fake suicide for Cassius Clare and, for Miles Mowbray, a clandestine affair with his son's fiancée); both husbands find themselves back where they started from, only appreciably worse off; and both try with the same dauntless ingenuity to carry off the impossible. But, where *The Present and the Past* ends painfully with death and recrimination, *A Father and His Fate* closes on something very like victory for the jaunty, unscrupulous, irrepressible life force embodied in Miles Mowbray (it is not for nothing that Miles' first grandchild, expected at the end of the book, is in fact his own bastard), and subsequently taken a great deal further in Hereward Egerton, hero of the next novel but two. *A Father and His Fate* is full of energy, vigour and the determination not to look back:

> 'It is the future we must look to,' said Constance. 'It is useless to pursue the past.'
> 'It is needless,' said Audrey. 'It will pursue us.'[98]

The book might also be said to have the last word on that wave of feeling flowing like a receding tide through Ivy's work since Margaret died, in a passage where the orphaned Verena Gray talks about the death of her mother:

> 'Do you miss her very much?' said Audrey.
> 'I miss my life with her, and am still strange in the new one.'
> 'Do you not enjoy your freedom at all?' said Ursula.
> 'I might, if I had it. But I do not enjoy the things that go with it, the homelessness and the feeling that I matter to no one.'
> 'You can have that feeling no longer.'
> 'No, I have lost it. I can be myself. I have ceased to be a leaf tossed on the wind. I can look to the future.'[99]

Ivy too could look to the future by this time. She abandoned the strict black she had worn for years in favour of occasional grey, and even a touch of pale colour, with advice and encouragement from Madge (who had once been asked by Virginia Woolf to choose clothes for her, when success as an author in 1925 was followed by a greatly increased social life[100]). Though Ivy said that her fame meant little without Margaret, and even the most enthusiastic reviewers seldom earned a kind word ('I have had on the whole "a good press", but many of the comments were, as usual, incomprehensible,' she wrote on 17 September 1957, to Robert), she clearly enjoyed the wider recognition that came in the 1950s. *Mother and Son* won the James Tait Black prize in 1955 and throughout the decade her name was a household word increasingly popular with cartoonists and the compilers of literary competitions. Interviewers came thick and fast (one of Roger Hinks' favourite pastimes was enumerating 'the delicacies and indelicacies with which journalists would say that Ivy's tea table was "literally" groaning'[101]). Entertaining grew more and more lavish: 'Wine crept in, and sherry, especially in the evenings,' said Robin McDouall, though drink at Braemar Mansions remained for the most part deplorable, supplied in job lots by admirers, served too cold or too warm, and frequently corked in spite of remonstrances from Robin himself and Ernest Thesiger ('He was most impertinent about my wine,' said Ivy, dropping lumps of ice into her glass of sweet Graves overheated in front of the electric fire: 'I am not very wine-wise, you know'[102]). But the food was copious in time of austerity, and generally good (though not everyone cared for the rum-flavoured blancmange —'cornflour shape with hair-oil'—to which Ivy herself was so partial). Soame looked in often with a box of chocolates or occasionally a brace of pheasants, Robin could be relied on for 'a rich gift'[103] of butter, the Robinsons sent supplies of quince paste, friends in the country brought fresh eggs, soft fruit and garden flowers.

Ivy made probably more friends on her own account in the 1950s than she had ever had before, and her old friends drew closer. She saw Herman at least once a week at his house or hers: 'He flirts with her & flatters her. It is rather like being at the court of Elizabeth I,' wrote Elizabeth to Robert. 'He teases her. She answers him sternly and literally, but talks a great deal more, and more fluently, than usual. "And you will not repeat what I have said, Herman"'. Ernest was always on hand for shopping or sewing, sorely missed when he left to play Jaques in *As You Like It* ('Ernest Thesiger is back from America, successful and in funds, but looking absolutely worn out. What a bad thing work is'[104]), or Polonius to Paul Scofield's Hamlet in Moscow in 1955 (when Ernest borrowed a pencil at a party to write on the pristine wall of a Muscovite gents: 'Burgess loves

Maclean'[105]). Roger Hinks returned from running the British
Council in Athens in 1957 to Ivy's great pleasure ('I am sorry you
have lost him,' she wrote generously to Robert: 'It is hopeless the
way life has to change and become less than life. It just has to be
accepted'). She had always loved Roger's charm, erudition, his
inability to tolerate humbugs (to whom he could be immensely and
wittily rude), and, best of all, his fantastical, far-fetched stories like
the one about a Roman Catholic friend who said, when asked if that
morning's mass had been quite as she liked: 'Well, not exactly
perhaps, it was rather Hail-Mary-well-met.'[106] Roger immediately
joined the Braemar Mansions regulars, keeping Robert posted by
letter and becoming indispensable to Ivy until he annoyed her again
by a posting to Paris two years later.

Basil was her standby in all practical matters, supplying advice,
assistance, invitations to mayoral parties (Basil said 'Ivy was the
best thing that happened in Kensington'[107]), and support at her
Saturdays—'it isn't as if the others have a wife to leave behind'
—from which Hester was banned, as she freely admitted, for
talking too much. As often as not, in these years of fame and
self-confidence, Ivy's parties consisted of men only ('her attention
in any group was always for the men,' said Rosalie Mander, another
of the young writers Ivy met and made friends with after the war).
Her closest women friends were probably Madge, Theodora and
most of all Rose, whom she had known on and off, through thick
and thin, good reviews and bad, for nearly thirty years ('Once at
lunch with Ivy Rose Macaulay said, "I'm reviewing your book for
Sunday." "That will be very nice," Ivy said complacently'[108]).
They still teased one another with great delight and vivacity, and
Ivy was not above shamelessly misrepresenting Rose when it suited
her ('quite sane friends of mine whose opinions I respect over other
things, believe in this terrible religion,' she told Elizabeth Taylor.
'Well, it is something I can't understand, and Rose Macaulay can't
either'). Their perennial debate was if anything more heated, as each
grew older and more set in her allegiance:

Almost the last time I saw her [Rose] [wrote Alan Pryce-Jones],
we were both sitting in Ivy Compton-Burnett's dining room and
she was carrying out a firm inquisition on her hostess's beliefs. 'I
cannot understand you, Ivy, a clever woman like you. You have

never got the hang of it. Of course, you may perfectly well be right. There may be nothing to believe *in*. Though I don't lose hope.'[109]

Rose died in October 1958. 'She was a unique person, and I feel a light has gone out, and that the world gets more and more grey,'[110] wrote Ivy, perhaps unconsciously echoing the butler who prides himself on his pessimism in her current novel ('Yes, ma'am, it adds a touch of darkness to the greyness of life'[111]). 'I shall miss Rose Macaulay to the end,' she wrote to Katie that Christmas, and to Cecil Gould: 'I am utterly deprived by losing Rose.'[112] Ivy's grief at the deaths of friends was always sharpened by indignation. Life without Margaret, whatever its compensations, could never be acknowledged as anything but a poor substitute. 'I never thought to enjoy a book about a foreign country so much, as I am an insular person, and essentially at home only in my own land, and perhaps chiefly in the past in that,' Ivy wrote on 2 June 1959 to Robert, thanking him for *The Rivers of Babylon*. '. . . I have enjoyed having Roger in England, and wish you were coming, though it is empty to you now, as indeed it is to me, though it is the only foot-hold I have and can have at my age.' She still urged Robert to write about his brother, talking often about him to Elizabeth ('He was very much cut up about Stephen dying. They were so happy together'), responding enthusiastically when the book was at last begun in 1955, unwillingly resigned two years later to further delay ('It must not be spoilt by being adapted to the sensibilities of living persons . . . It may live beyond their lives, and it should not suffer from them'[113]). She herself came in some ways close to the position taken up in *A Heritage and Its History*, the novel she was writing in 1958, by Walter Challoner who barely exists save in his capacity as intellectual observer: a character disabled by early misfortune ('"I am grateful for the compulsions of my boyhood." "I am not," said Walter. "They rise up before me in the night. I might have been a less bitter poet without them"'[114]), but unresentful, indeed thoroughly appreciative of the past, and in any case amply compensated by interest in the present: '"I wish Shakespeare were here," said Walter, to lessen the tension. "I mean, I wish I was he. I could make so much of this scene . . ."'

A Heritage and Its History was finished at the end of October and published the following September (Julian Messner, who had

Ivy in the drawing room at Braemar
Mansions by Feliks Topolski
(see p. 511)

brought out Ivy's last three books in America, now handed her in
turn to Simon and Schuster, who published this and the next two).
Ivy agreed to be interviewed by Alan Pryce-Jones who arrived on
8 September 1959 with a television crew and cameras at Braemar
Mansions. She herself missed the programme on television, 'as
even my friends who had it had not the Independent, and the only
person who saw it seemed to be the greengrocer, who naturally had
everything'.[115] But Elizabeth watched it, and described what she
saw to Robert:

> My heart was knocking wildly. The camera hovered in a sinister
> way over Cornwall Gardens, the grim outside. It looked like the
> beginning of a murder film. Then, once inside, I felt better. The
> high, light, pretty voice, the mouth pursed yet smiling. The eyes
> . . . sometimes looking bewildered, even desperate, but I think it
> was the horrible bright lights which are the worst part of all . . .
> She was most amusing, & described how much she had been
> abused by reviewers & how one man wrote to her asking her to
> explain what on earth her books were all about, & enclosed a

stamped and addressed envelope for her reply—'I used it when I was paying a bill'. When asked which was her favourite of her books she said: 'Well, I do really rather like *Manservant and Maidservant.*' 'I'm very fond of *A House and Its Head,*' said Mr. Pryce-Jones. 'Yes, I like that very much, too,' she said enthusiastically. 'I rather like them all, in fact. After all, they are mine.' . . .

I feel now more that it was her *father.* You know what I mean. Mothers would never speak of workhouses. And someone has. I almost dare suggest myself again and take a stiff brandy and ask a lot of questions we want to know the answers to. Stake everything. She would at once understand the motive and, however coldly she dealt with me, she would understand the necessity.

1960–1969

'One of nature's Dames'

I

THE FIRST PERSON to come anywhere near asking the questions Elizabeth and Robert wanted answered was probably Kay Dick, who had felt thoroughly at home with Ivy from the day they first met:

> I felt that I was somehow established as one of those near-impossible children in her novels who might do and say anything. She assumed a favourite maiden-aunt quality for me, and vaguely, I felt adopted. In fact, I suspect, she regarded all my generation as children, and she watched our antics with a sort of measured anticipation. She expected us to behave as we did, and indeed, she was not slow to encourage us in our behaviour.[1]

Kay had recently emerged from hospital after a very nearly successful attempt at suicide when Ivy agreed to an afternoon of what she called 'note-taking' on 9 October 1963. The interview, intended ultimately to form part of a book of conversations with writers, was in the nature of a consolation prize for Kay—'it was her present to me'[2]—with compensatory advantages for Ivy, who was intensely curious about what had happened ('I was her raw material, she was sniffing me out'), as well as deeply sympathetic.

Her manner was gentle, cooperative, even eager throughout: the tape-recording of their conversation is punctuated by little exclamatory flurries of encouragement from Ivy and the involuntary low laugh she gave, almost under her breath, whenever things were being said that generally go without saying. She answered clearly and copiously, interrupting every so often to ask for a question to be put more definitely, held back apparently less by her own reticence than by the nervous delicacy that prevented her interrogator from probing too hard in what might have proved sensitive areas. Ivy talked freely about the process of writing itself, about her observation of people, her view of human nature in general and, in particular, her own childhood, upbringing and early life. She protested emphatically, with a great deal of humorous, deprecatory umming and erring, only when asked about her own reputation for wisdom: 'Wise, in what way? Well yes, perhaps one does think one is wise. One thinks one knows, of course. Perhaps that is thinking one is wise?'[3] When Kay admitted that she herself hardly ever thought she knew, Ivy rapped back in a flash, laughing at herself, with impeccable comic timing and intonation: 'Then perhaps I think I'm wiser than you think you are.'

The interview changed their relationship. 'Ivy grew fonder,' said Kay, 'after the interview, really—you felt her affection when you went in. She was so pleased to see you.' Always interested in her friends' private lives and prepared, as she said, to give any human problem her full attention ('Some people don't. They give it a very casual attention, and then tell you about an antique they've bought'), Ivy had questioned other people closely about Kay's present crisis. But it was characteristic of both her tact and her generosity that she mentioned it only once—'You've done a deed, haven't you?'—submitting instead to being questioned herself about matters she had scarcely permitted an interviewer to touch on before. The information she volunteered about her family was matter-of-fact, and perfectly accurate so far as it went (spreading confusion among inquisitive friends had always been a pleasure to Ivy, who made no move whatever to contradict the belief— almost universal by this time in her literary circle—in a mythical Compton-Burnett family 'place' in the country). Clearly the afternoon spent 'note-taking' with Kay was part of a general relaxation and loosening in Ivy towards the end of her life; and she went a good deal further a few years later with the writer Julian Mitchell, who pressed her as no one else had dared to do on tricky points like her feeling for her mother, her attachment to the nurse who had been 'the real mother', the influence of her peremptory and tyrannical maternal grandfather, and her love for her brothers. These conversations were probably the closest Ivy ever came to broaching the compulsions of her own childhood: 'She knew what she wanted known,' wrote Julian after her death, '. . . and no biographer is ever going to be able to explain what Ivy didn't want explained.'[4]

Julian was half a century younger than Ivy ('I'm afraid I may once or twice have come into her category of "a gaping boy" '), who had been all her life peculiarly susceptible to the sort of charming, sensitive, intelligent, humorous young men she had first met in Noel's company at Cambridge. In her books, they occupy what even Pamela Hansford Johnson recognized as a soft spot ('It was the adolescent boys who touched her heart the most'[5]), and she grew fonder than ever in her eighties of what she called 'a nice lad'. Ivy by this time was apt to make fairly arbitrary age distinctions, referring airily to anyone under fifty as 'young'. She entertained Herman's guests like an elderly aunt unbending in spite of herself to a hopelessly flighty younger generation ('She was at her best and talking as she writes, and trying not to smile when she made us laugh,' wrote Elizabeth Taylor of a luncheon in 1963 at which the other guest was Lesley Blanch: 'We kiss now. Even in the Brompton Road, saying goodbye'); and she treated Herman himself on occasion as a delinquent youth—'Herman, how can you stand there telling me such lies?' To which he stoutly replied, 'I can, and I do.'[6]

But Ivy always knew who was lying, and who not. 'People have a way of not coming out well in a temptation. They generally behave quite as ill as they can, don't they?' she said to Kay. 'Well, not any worse than I should expect them to behave. I mean, people have to consider themselves before anyone else, don't they, and one wonders what would happen to them if they didn't.'[7] Her comprehension came from self-knowledge—'I don't think there is such a thing as self-deception'[8]—and it made her inexhaustibly lenient. Ivy's friends at the end of her life felt very much what Noel and Rupert Brooke had once felt about Lowes Dickinson, that nothing they might do—no matter how shameful, squalid or actually criminal—could ever be too much for such patience, humour and tolerance. Her support was unfailing, though often ironic. 'She asked me about your novel,' wrote Elizabeth to Robert (who had posted her the manuscript of *Stepsons*—the book for which Ivy had waited so long—in the summer of 1960): ' "It's all about his stepmother, isn't it?" And then she made a noise that sounded like Ho-Hum.' Sonia Orwell, grumbling one day about the drudgery involved in her meticulously documented, four-volume edition of George's letters and journalism, was surprised by Ivy's reaction: 'It's your plain duty,' she said gently but firmly.[9]

Ivy congratulated the Robinsons on news of an impending first baby, advising Barbara to make the most of her last few months to herself ('You will never be so much your own person again'[10]), recommending a second child a year later which was the interval between herself and Guy (the Robinsons took Ivy's advice and stopped short at two), and later sending her sympathy to the supplanted elder child ('You will have to show great tact, and continually asseverate your preference for him in open words. "Love me best" he will say, and you will say it'[11]). She gave Barbara much domestic as well as professional advice in these years ('It is much better to have only one maid. More than one either hate each other or hate *you*. And anyhow they have tea together all day, cementing one hatred on the other'[12]). She treated Elizabeth, for all her two children and lengthening list of successful novels, as an irresponsible girl, urging her to wear warm underclothes, eat more ('I think she is trying to console me with food for not being a very good writer. When she fills up my glass with water—for there is not always wine—it is a protective and consoling gesture'), and avoid unnecessary risks, especially in the perilous winters when Ivy herself suffered more severely each year. 'I had a letter from her [Ivy] this morning in which she said she had a bronchial chill and hoped I fared better. "But still take care. The evil days are on us. I hope we will meet when they are over." It is like the Ides of March and we had better all stay indoors . . .'

When Herman asked Ivy on her eightieth birthday—5 June 1964—what she had learnt from life, 'she thought for a long time, and then said: "That people are morally the same, and intellectually different."'[13] Now that she herself was no longer sufficiently attached to a single person to be emotionally in anyone's power, Ivy watched her friends with a truly disinterested affection. 'That marriage won't last,' she said, after a somewhat sticky luncheon given by Herman to meet Sonia Orwell's prospective second husband, Michael Pitt-Rivers (who had only comparatively recently emerged from prison after one of the most notorious homosexual scandals of the 1950s): 'That young man won't like all this bookish talk.'[14] For Sonia, installed as châtelaine of the Pitt-Rivers family home in Dorset, one of the memorable disasters of her short married life was an evening at the Watson-Gandys, with Michael loudly expounding the folly and misery of marriage to Jim, while Ivy (on one of her annual summer visits to Vere) carried on stolidly passing the potatoes and saying that a little more cauliflower would be acceptable. It is the attitude philosophically explained by Oliver Shelley in *Two Worlds and Their Ways*:

'We have done our best, and must leave it. No one can do more.'

'We have done nothing,' said Maria.

'Well, that is usually people's best,' said her stepson. 'Their worst is something quite different.'[15]

Ivy made no comment to Sonia, beyond making her welcome again when the marriage was over ('I can't imagine her in a country life,' Ivy wrote diplomatically to the Robinsons on 15 September 1962: 'I am sure London is her home'). She had taken much the same line nearly ten years earlier over the equally painful and public collapse of Madge's brief marriage to Sir Leigh Ashton, then head of the V&A. 'After the break with Leigh, when I was once again alone in the little house, Ivy came to tea,' wrote Madge, 'and, as soon as she entered, went directly to the glass doors which opened on to the garden, turned to me and said, "You have the garden, you have the house, there are worse things than loneliness." And never spoke of the matter again.'[16] The certainty that Ivy, who understood everything, could be relied on to say nothing was often a comfort: 'You know, I think that my friendship with Ivy was one of the happiest things in a long and troubled life,' said Madge. 'It was because nothing was said. *Nothing*. We didn't have to say anything. There was complete trust on both sides.'[17] Ivy seldom gave advice unless on practical, tangible matters like which novel to read, or where to go for the best brand of stockings ('I always swear by Harvey Nichols'). But her general policy is clearly formulated by the aged Selina Middleton in *The Mighty and Their Fall*, comforting her grand-daughter Lavinia at a moment of crisis, despair and public humiliation:

'What am I to do?'

'What people do, who have been found out. Wait for the trouble to subside. Suffer it when it arises. Fight it, if it is too much. There is nothing else for you. And the worst is behind. You have little more to dread.'[18]

A hard person to surprise, Selina, like Ivy, is grimly disillusioned about both human and religious affairs ('I don't believe in a future life, or want to. I should not like any form of it I know. I don't want to be a spirit or to return to the earth as someone else. I could never like anyone else enough for that'[19]). She is watchful, unyielding, a tartar to her grandchildren, who find themselves unaccountably fond of her, and no less unaccountably consoled to discover how well she knows them: 'I am old. I have seen and heard. I know that things are done. Temptation is too much for us. We are not always unwilling for it to be.'[20]

The Mighty and Their Fall was begun in the autumn of 1959, finished by 10 February 1961, and published on 18 September.[21] The Robinsons and others were immediately struck by the twenty-year-old Lavinia's likeness in looks and character—she is described as an 'autocrat' and an 'intellectual'[22]—to the young Ivy; and certainly Lavinia belongs with the many brave, spirited, vulnerable girls, more or less ruthlessly exploited by their elders, who might be said, from Dinah Stace onwards (*Brothers and Sisters*, 1929) to contain a touch of Ivy—more than a touch in the case of France Ponsonby (*Daughters and Sons*, 1937) and the eleven-year-old Clemence Shelley (*Two Worlds and Their Ways*, 1949). But Selina represents an older, less innocent Ivy. Admittedly, there are repressive, tyrannical grandmothers elsewhere in her books—Sabine Ponsonby in *Daughters and Sons* is the first of a line that ends only with Jocasta Grimstone in the posthumously published *The Last and the First*. It is a type that owes something to stories of Ivy's own maternal grandmother—Sophia Sabine Rees—and great-grandmother, more perhaps to a number of fierce, domineering, big-chinned old women she and Katie Blackie had known as children among their Rees and Pudney relations in the Methodist connection round Clacton, most of all no doubt to the stubborn Rees will passed down by both Ivy's mother and Katie's.

But Selina combines an autocratic temper with for the first time another side of Ivy—the alert, neutral intelligence previously embodied in governesses like Miss Mitford, outsiders like Hope Cranmer, non-participants like the Scropes or Walter Challoner. This is Ivy in her professional aspect, so to speak, and there could hardly be a clearer definition of the writer's relationship with society than Selina's account of herself: 'my presence makes no difference. I am on no one's side. I see with the eyes of all of you. It is as if no one was here.'[23] Selina is eighty-seven, ten years older than her creator when *The Mighty and Their Fall* was published, and strongly reminiscent of the sardonic, self-contained, grimly humorous spirit of *The Real Charlotte*. But Selina's influence, unlike Charlotte Mullen's, is wholly benevolent (as she herself readily concedes when told that her grandchildren consider her bark worse than her bite: 'That is an empty saying. There is no opportunity to bite. I have wished there was'[24]). As a self-portrait, this is far from flattering though perhaps not wholly dissatisfied, since anyone as familiar with her own faults and as frank about them as Selina is clearly on reasonable terms with herself. 'I think people know themselves. I am sure I know myself,' Ivy said to Kay,[25] and the knowledge brought with it—as it always does in her books—a kind of peace, or at least release from the intensity of feeling that had caused such misery in the past.

Ivy in her seventies and eighties had many close friendships with women, quite a few of them lesbians ('Come to tea on Saturday,' she would say encouragingly, *'my lesbians are coming'*[26]). Margaret's death had laid her open for a while to anyone anxious to establish a larger stake in her life, but even in what she called 'the difficult days' Ivy made short work of unwelcome advances ('And weren't they surprised young women,' said Margaret Branch, who had watched several of Ivy's more proprietorial friends firmly shown off at this time). She herself told a funny story about an unknown woman who sent long and persuasive fan letters, backed up by rich gifts of butter and eggs and invitations so pressing that in the end Ivy agreed to a rendezvous on Brighton Pier. She told Madge that she thought it best to avoid inviting her new admirer to the flat; and she told Renée Fedden that, when she eventually spotted the lady bearing down behind a huge bunch of red roses, evidently less interested in Ivy's work than her person, it had seemed better still to leave her standing and flee. Even Herman, who delighted in arranging his friends' affairs as much as in fixing their flats, could not persuade her to reconsider this decision, though he never entirely abandoned his hopeful view of her lesbian proclivities.[27] If Ivy got on better with women, in the sense of being generally more relaxed in their company, it was in much the same spirit as Hope Cranmer, who also preferred her own sex: 'Most people do. It is a thing that has not been noticed. People know too much about their own sex to think it possible to prefer it, when really they find it familiar and congenial.'[28]

But Ivy, like Hope, was strikingly partial to men, and not only nice lads. 'We've got a bit of your mother, all of us, in us,' she said once to Kay, who was the illegitimate child of a dashing and romantic parent—'my mother was a very feminine woman, adored by men, a great flirt and a great liar'—with no very obvious likeness to Ivy. If Margaret had settled for celibacy by choice (and seems in any case always to have found her emotional fulfilment in women), Ivy liked to imply that it had been forced on her by the war that had taken Noel and so many of his friends, who were the only young men she had known as a girl. She often said she belonged to a generation that had had to do without marriage; and she was clearly thinking of herself when she explained to Kay about the preponderance of women novelists between the wars:

Well, I expect that's because the men were dead, you see, and the women didn't marry so much because there was no one for them to marry, and so they had leisure, and, I think, in a good many cases they had money, because their brothers were dead, and all that would tend to writing, wouldn't it, being single, and having some money, and having the time—having no men, you see.[29]

Not that Ivy in later life ever slackened her mistrust of married couples, however much she might like each partner singly:

The same food *of course*—the boiled bacon and parsley sauce and white pudding [wrote Elizabeth in the autumn of 1962, of a luncheon at Braemar Mansions with Herman and John Pope-Hennessy]. She carved up Muriel Spark and Iris Murdoch at the same time as the bacon. Marriage and religion were discussed and deplored. I felt guilty to be married and to have stayed married so long, and was almost thankful not to be religious. Rose Macaulay has never been forgiven. To have such a thing happen—when for a lifetime she had been a perfectly sound agnostic like everybody else.

Marriage was a blight for anyone who prized her friends' company as highly as Ivy. If she and Margaret had once consigned newly wedded couples to cold storage, it was for much the same reason that made her so stern with expatriates like the Robinsons and Jim Brandreth. Marriage, which removed people, was a malign influence, like 'abroad', and must be as stoutly resisted. 'So dangerous, these fusions of personality, don't you think?' she said softly one day at tea,[30] when Hester arrived late from a wedding at the House of Lords; and she strongly advised another woman friend[31] against accepting a late, last proposal: 'Don't ever get married, unless you absolutely have to.' Naturally, as her fame spread, people labelled Ivy a lesbian or even an androgyne just as others liked to think she had had a lover killed in the First World War, or that she had been all her life incestuously in thrall to her brother. A façade as impenetrable as Ivy's, coupled with writings so violent, bred a rich crop of rumours ranging from Sybille Bedford's story that Ivy's father had burnt the manuscript of her first novel to the legends proliferating about her two youngest sisters, who were said to have been found drowned in a pool or hanged in a cupboard, to have been murdered, or surprised illicitly in bed together by their parents—alternatively, accused of being lovers by a half-brother —and to have killed themselves from remorse (being discovered, in one version, hanged at intervals in the same room). All these stories, all false, were circulated in her lifetime (and several printed after her death) by friends driven wild by Ivy's inscrutability.

The truth behind an image as imposing and unusual as Ivy's can perhaps only percolate slowly. Her public face, in the last decade of her life, was itself something of a legend. She seemed austere, unapproachable, positively regal when she travelled up to Leeds University to receive an honorary doctorate on 19 May 1960: 'Ivy and the Princess Royal (who was Chancellor of the university) got on splendidly,' wrote Madge, who went too as companion. 'They sat beside each other at tea, after the ceremony, and there was something about the basic honesty of those two women which made them immediately sympathetic to each other. Luckily for me the Princess's lady-in-waiting was now Mrs Seaton Dearden, the wife of a friend, so that the real and the make-believe ladies-in-waiting got on just as well as their superiors.'[32] Ivy, who had been dissuaded by Arthur Waley from her initial 'idea of having flu instead of Leeds',[33] afterwards confessed to Robert that, in spite of the ruinous expense (hotel charges of £3.10s a day), 'actually I rather enjoyed it'. Actors presented to Ivy during radio or stage adaptations of her work—'She came like a queen with Rosamond Lehmann as lady-in-waiting'[34]—found the experience very much like being lined up to meet royalty. Photographers, following Beaton's example, show her majestically composed, often enthroned, though she emerges from the characteristic birds'-nest tangle of Feliks Topolski's drawing in the early 1960s as a slightly hunched, pensive, sad but not at all stern, and very old sibyl.

Herman was her escort on a first visit to Topolski's studio, recorded in a passage that nicely catches his own and Ivy's respective brands of vagueness and obstinacy: 'One day at tea time she said, "Do you know Krassovsky, the painter?" I said, "Yes, Ivy, but he isn't called Krassovsky; he is called Balthus." "No," she said, "he is called Krassovsky." She meant, of course, Feliks Topolski.'[35] As she grew older and frailer, Ivy seldom went anywhere without a faithful attendant, very often Herman or Madge, with an extra supporter for serious occasions such as the matinée of Samuel Beckett's *Happy Days* at the Royal Court Theatre in November 1962 (Ivy had enjoyed Nicholas Bentley's cartoon, in the wake of *Waiting for Godot*, of one tramp saying to another as he fished a dilapidated book out of a dustbin, 'Look! An Ivy Compton-Burnett!'[36]). 'This should be a rather unusual outing,' wrote Elizabeth, and so it proved in her detailed report to Robert:

Well, then, we went to the theatre. (I am sorry to make such a letter of it, but is it not like going to one of the Basingstoke Assemblies with Jane Austen?) It was a sparse audience, & Ivy took a great interest in it. 'Would you call this an *intellectual* audience, Herman?' (Too distinct voice in an empty auditorium.) 'One or two look that way inclined,' he whispered. 'Do you think they are staring at us, because they think *we* are intellectuals?' 'Of course they don't think that,' she said scornfully. 'We are far too well dressed.' 'Would it help if I took off my tie?' he asked. 'Not very much,' she—I think I will say 'retorted' for the first time in my life, 'for I daresay Elizabeth will have to take off everything.' So much for my intellectual underwear. The play —just the middle-aged woman buried in a mound—was to me quite unexpectedly wonderful. I went for Ivy, & found myself forgetting her. She watched it keenly, through opera glasses, from the third row of the empty stalls, & I don't know how that poor actress carried on under the circumstances. 'Not a play to miss,' she said in the interval, while Herman had gone running round Sloane Square to buy her a box of chocolates. He had dozed off in the first act, but always does after luncheon wherever he is, he explained. But I am sorry to say that, however alert Ivy's attention was & no matter how much Herman admired Brenda Bruce, they both seemed to miss the point. It is really devastating, & as much as one can bear—a middle-aged woman's gallantry (I see so much of it) signifying the human tragedy—the terrifying attempts at optimism & the Molly Bloom nostalgia —heart rendering! [A word coined by Robert's Oxford servant.] 'Now is the crucial moment,' Ivy said, her hand wavering over the opened box of chocolates. 'One hopes for a ginger one.' 'I wish your husband would make some good, cheap sweets,' she said, & then said—almost tenderly—'he was very good to me in the difficult days.'

I am glad—as you must be—that she has her adoring courtier, to take care of her in old age, to give her gallantry & flattery & sweets. Not many women reach her years & have as much—for everything he can imagine her wanting, he hastens to provide; & it is bestowed as if she were a young & lovely creature at her first ball, & when he helps her down the stairs or into a taxi—for she is getting frail—he turns her into Gloriana.

If Herman brought with him the atmosphere of a court—at any rate, something of a court's bustle and intrigue—so in his own way did Ernest, growing at the end of his life more and more like Queen Mary with his pursed lips and bolt upright bearing, his censorious dowager's air and crushing line in regal retorts. He would startle his colleagues by turning up at rehearsal in the drab 1950s wearing a pink linen coatee, and was once reproached for extolling the past glories of the stage by a young actor who said that sort of thing was considered by modern standards distinctly ham: 'I am well aware of it,' said Ernest grandly, 'but you may as well know that I consider the type of acting that you advocate as definitely "spam".'[37] Ernest was five years older than Ivy who had for years been aware of his growing exhaustion, though he showed no obvious sign of it. He died without warning in his sleep on 14 January 1961, to her great distress ('He was a very old friend and his loss is a real grief, and I feel I have had enough,' she wrote to the Robinsons on 21 January. 'And the suddenness made it a shock, though it was good fortune for him'). His death left Janette blind and bedridden, confined to the flat with her housekeeper, but it was years since Ernest had been able to offer her consolation, or even company. Her form of stoicism, a certain massive simplicity and nobility of nature, was altogether foreign to her husband who—like Mortimer Lamb and other unreliable jokers in Ivy's books—had always given more to people who needed less: he is aptly commemorated, as his obituary in the *Journal of the Embroiderers' Guild* pointed out that spring, on one of two kneelers he stitched for Chelsea Old Church in honour of 'Henry Patenson, Sir Thomas More's Jester, "a man of special wit", pictured in the costume of the time with cap and bells . . .'

Ivy was also by this time a performer in her own right. Alone with one other person, or with at most two or three old friends ('She was always an *intimiste*,' said the publisher George Weidenfeld who often made the third at Herman's luncheons), Ivy made absurd, inimitable play with her murmured asides, her flat throaty chuckle and the impossible truth that occasionally shot past her guard. 'Dreadful, absolutely dreadful,' she said once when Ivo Pakenham asked her what she thought of his latest fake-Adam interior; and, when Ivo protested that she ought not to say such things to his face, Ivy said sternly: 'You asked a question and I gave you the answer. If a question is asked and no answer is given, no communication of thought is possible and all conversation ceases.'[38]

Ivy had spent the great part of her life devising stratagems —inconspicuousness, evasiveness, unstoppable small talk or an equally impregnable stonewalling—to cope with the truthfulness that made her writing so startling, and her life at times quite impossible. She deplored other writers' compromises—'I read *Prelude and Fugue*, Joan Evans' autobiography' (which makes barely a reference to the St Hugh's affair, and no mention of Ivy), 'and enjoyed it, but found it too discreet,' she wrote to Barbara Robinson on 21 November 1964. 'It is no good to write about things, and then *not* write about them.' Her own books of course were widely held to go too far in the opposite direction; and conversation at Braemar Mansions, on occasions when Ivy spoke her mind, could take on a hair-raising edge—'part prize-giving, part disciplinary hearing', as Proust's illustrator, Phillippe Jullian, wrote in *Les Nouvelles Littéraires*,[39] describing a tea party with

Robin McDouall, Francis Wyndham and Arthur Waley. M. Jullian had been suitably primed beforehand by Robin ('*Il vaut mieux être voltairean que religieux, réservé que banal*'), who was horrified after-wards—as Ivy was too—to find his friend publishing without permission this uncensored sample of her deft, backhanded disposal of the various writers put forward in turn by her guests. Asked what she thought of Lawrence Durrell—invariably the first ques-tion put by a Frenchman discussing the English novel in the early 1960s—Ivy said she had not read him: 'Is it essential nowadays to turn a novel into a travel book?—He is greatly admired in France.—But then, you admire Charles Morgan in France, don't you?—Angus Wilson?—I like him very much. Especially the short stories you find tucked away in his great long novels.' Ivy used a more scarifying technique on Rebecca West, who had told her friends she could make nothing of Ivy's books, and whose request for an introduction had been wisely turned down by Elizabeth Taylor:

Madge Garland, however, fell for it and, although scared, invited them both to lunch. Rebecca was apparently at her most scintil-lating—brilliant talker as she has the reputation of being. She put everything into it, and Ivy simply lopped off everything she said and left it lying there, dead. Feverishly she went on, and coldly Ivy felled her. Gaps grew in the conversation—unimaginable in Rebecca's presence. Poor hostess! She should have known how it would be . . .[40]

2

THIS FORMIDABLE STREAK had long been familiar to Victor Gollancz,[41] who confessed to the novelist Lettice Cooper in the 1960s that he was afraid of Ivy. Perhaps Spencer Curtis Brown was too, for the pair spoke and wrote of 'the Compton-Burnett' behind her back in much the same terms as the ill-used younger generation banding together to bait one of the tyrants in her books. 'Dear V.G., I hope you have taken Ede's advice [Chuter Ede, Home Secretary in the postwar Labour government] and not destroyed your air-raid shelter for I have heard from Compton-Burnett . . .' wrote Curtis

Brown on 25 July 1949, when Ivy protested as usual about Gollancz's failure to advertise *Two Worlds and Their Ways* ('Will you ask him what his reasons are for not wanting my books to sell?'). Curtis Brown's procedure, on receiving a confidential complaint from his client, was to forward her letter with a request for instructions as to what sort of reply Gollancz would like sent. 'I know you realise as well as I do that whatever arrangement is mutually satisfactory to you or Douglas will be equally satisfactory to me,' he wrote on 1 May 1951, enclosing Jerrold's last, unsuccessful proposal that Eyre and Spottiswoode should take over all the back titles that were proving such a burden to Gollancz, 'but it is extremely unlikely that it will be satisfactory to Miss Compton-Burnett. As you know, her aim is to have all her books published every day.'

Spencer Curtis Brown was nearly thirty years younger than Ivy, who seems to have cast him from the start as a sort of solicitor's clerk—an inexperienced and not particularly promising junior in constant need of reproof and supervision—a role he apparently accepted, making little effort to protect Ivy's interests and tending to side against her, or wash his hands of the affair altogether, whenever a fresh altercation blew up with Gollancz. From Curtis Brown's point of view, Ivy meant trouble—'Curtis Brown is indeed sadly in need of the goad,' she wrote when *Manservant and Maidservant* was published[42] and his letters to her are understandably cautious and wary in tone. Gollancz for his part threatened to retire and write a novel in the Compton-Burnett style, with Ivy herself as the central character. Admittedly, others doing business with Ivy also found her on occasion a trial: she behaved with peremptory, high-handed courtesy to her accountant who was not in the least put out, rather amused than otherwise, at being kept in his place in the 1960s exactly like his father and grandfather who had served her father before him; and, though she scrutinized every transaction in detail, Ivy in return approved and generally accepted his professional advice about stocks and shares. But the handling of her books was another matter. Dealings with Curtis Brown and Gollancz had none of the pleasant air of family tradition and mutual respect that enlivened the twice-yearly luncheons with the accountant and Mr Mowll ('She talked like her characters, you know—we had great fun, the three of us'[43]). But, if Ivy acted tyrannically, she got as good as she gave for the scolding note in her letters bred, in both agent and publisher, a stubborn resistance to even her most reasonable demands.

Much of Ivy's grumbling went no further than the normal dissatisfaction of authors with publishers ('Their ways are not as our ways,' she wrote to Barbara[44]), disappointment over sales being after all an almost universal grievance. Ivy was more open than most about her feeling that she had done all that could be expected towards producing bestsellers ('good plots, interesting characters and plenty of sex,' as she explained encouragingly to Curtis Brown[45]), and been let down by others. 'Nowadays one's agent, and one's solicitor, and one's bank manager only do the irreducible minimum,' she said to Lettice Cooper, 'but unfortunately it is the minimum one cannot do oneself.'[46] Commercial success fascinated Ivy. 'I have always wanted a portrait of a real, bestselling novelist, done honestly and ably and with understanding,' she wrote on 9 June 1957, describing her *great* and *lasting* pleasure' in Elizabeth's new novel, *Angel*: 'You have served your theme well, and to my mind it was a theme that both needed and deserved the service' ('I should love to read a reference written by her for a maid leaving her employment,' wrote Elizabeth, complacently forwarding this testimonial to Robert). A few years later she met a real bestseller when Soame bravely arranged a dinner for Ivy and Angela Thirkell, which turned out a great success (one of the college books Ivy kept all her life was her *Epigrams from the Greek Anthology*, edited by Angela's father, Professor Mackail): 'She's got plenty of go,' Ivy said admiringly afterwards, 'plenty of go'.[47] She attended the celebrations for James Pope-Hennessy's life of Queen Mary, which included a film of the royal progress: 'At the stage of the funeral procession there was hardly a dry eye in the audience of publishers and other sinister men!' Ivy reported to Barbara. 'He is reaping a fortune.'[48] Rose's fortune (assessed when the will was published at almost £90,000) became a source of extreme chagrin to Ivy, who was only partially mollified by repeated assurances that the money had not come from books. 'She had some bestsellers,' said Ivy gloomily. 'I have never had bestsellers. I don't sell.'[49]

Her sales figures after the war remained steady, at about seven thousand copies for each new novel[50] with back titles also in regular demand, though Gollancz's thrifty reissues of never more than a thousand at a time were perpetually running out. It was seldom easy to obtain any given Compton-Burnett, and readers' confidence was further diminished by the fact that even the new novels, with their cheap paper, garish wrappers and drab bindings, were got up—as Raymond Mortimer pointed out[51]—to look like school textbooks (reviewers were almost unanimous in congratulating Eyre and Spottiswoode on the good looks of their abortive Collected Works). Gollancz had never believed in spending money on appearances, and his advances were generally frugal. 'My last book brought in £60, and it took two years to write,' said Lester Marlowe in *Parents and Children* (1941);[52] Ivy's last book at the time of writing was *A Family and a Fortune* (1939) which had netted her £62 (including £50 advance on royalties[53]) in the four months before it went out of print. Her first novel issued by Gollancz in 1937 had apparently failed to cover its £50 advance in the year of publication, and at that time Ivy had no other income from writing ('It is awkward that I am assumed to earn so much more than I do,' says Lester. '. . . I am ashamed to confess how poorly my work is paid'). It was only with *Darkness and Day* in 1951 that Ivy's advances went up to £200 on publication, and her contracts stipulated that earlier titles be returned to circulation.

But money was never Ivy's prime complaint of her publisher, nor did she mind much what her books looked like. What she wanted always, more than anything, was for her books to be read; and, though there can be no doubt that Gollancz was in his way proud of her, it was not only Ivy who noticed the contrast between his lavish advertising of authors in whom he believed, and the brief box announcements of her novels. Publicity in her case was in his view, as he frequently assured her, worse than useless just as reissuing old novels would almost certainly damage her sales. He was consistently disparaging about the 'highbrows' who had been 'wildly praising her for years'; he was among the first to detect a potential falling off in praise from the rising, resentful, young generation of critics in the early 1950s; and he was always as acutely aware as Ivy herself that she never could or would sell like Daphne du Maurier. He never discussed her books with her, before or after publication (doubtless she would have made it impossible, if he had tried). Her manuscripts continued to arrive unannounced at Curtis Brown who forwarded them without comment to Gollancz's office, where Ivy had the reputation of being the only author nobody bothered to read before she went to the printers.

In due course a cheque would be dispatched, the books reached the shops, Ivy's complaints would be parried and dealings would be over for another two years in a relationship which was always, even on strictly business terms, abnormally bleak. Gollancz was or could be a man of extraordinary generosity, warmth, flair, humane and social concern, but he was also arrogant and obdurate, a prince of prevaricators and impossible to worst in a bargain. He and Ivy were perhaps too alike to bring out anything but the worst in one another: he must have realized he had given her grounds to speak disparagingly of him as a Jew, she surely might have recognized the folly of treating him like a tradesman who failed to give satisfaction. Their first meeting in 1948 had not helped matters, and worse was to follow at a second lunch proposed by Gollancz in the early 1960s when Ivy requested a collected edition of her works. She was eighty, and he had published thirteen of her novels to great critical acclaim. Lunch began badly with Ivy declining a drink: 'No, I don't drink. But you have one, if you feel you must.' 'I feel I must,' he said. His polite attempts at making conversation about music and travel were summarily lopped off by Ivy ('No, I know very little about music. I don't care for abroad'), who insisted on getting down to business, whereupon Gollancz asked if she meant that she wanted every single one of her books reprinted. 'Yes,' said Ivy. 'Well, that would ruin you, and ruin me,' said Gollancz. 'I can't do it.' After a pause, Ivy declined his offer of coffee or pudding, said she must go home and went, leaving Gollancz to order two stiff brandies;[54] and (except for a single chance encounter in hospital when they found themselves for once in agreement about institutional food) they never saw or spoke to one another again.

It was a preposterous way to treat an author of Ivy's great age and distinction, but perhaps in a way she left him no alternative. Though her friends tended to blame Gollancz for Ivy's virtual exclusion from London literary life, she herself undoubtedly preferred her fame on terms which included a fair measure of withdrawal and privacy. Gollancz combined the negative merit of non-interference with what was in her eyes the inestimable boon of permanence. 'I am too old to change' was her invariable response to people who urged her to switch to a more appreciative publisher, find a less incompetent maid or move to a pleasanter flat. At the beginning of 1963, Ivy's Polish landlord had hopes of letting her flat to the Dominican Embassy which occupied the other half of the first floor at Braemar Mansions: 'A nice thing if an English gentlewoman is to be turned out by Poles to make room for South Americans,' Elizabeth reported to Robert, though both knew perfectly well that this was no joke for Ivy, whose old terror of disruption and dispersal returned with a force that dismayed her friends. The flat was not simply a place to live in, nor even the home she had shared with Margaret: it contained the whole precious, narrow, intricate, orderly existence the two had built up together inside it, and the prospect of losing it unnerved Ivy, always acutely aware of the precariousness of civilized life.

For two months she could talk and write to her friends of little else. Herman, Madge, and Herman's Dutch friend Riemke Zouthout trudged all over Chelsea and South Kensington in search of more comfortable, convenient and cheaper flats, all of which Ivy rejected out of hand. By the beginning of April, she had forced herself to contemplate moving to a place in Kensington Square, but her trepidation worried everyone who saw it. Cicely, coming to collect the manuscript of *A God and His Gifts* at a more than usually strained luncheon on 5 April, feared some sort of nervous collapse, and so did Vera Compton-Burnett, who well understood the enormity of Ivy's capitulation when the landlord finally agreed at the end of the month to settle for what struck her as a second, exorbitant rent increase. 'I am thankful to stay in my flat, though the rent is vast and will mean resorting to capital which at my age is after all a reasonable thing,' Ivy wrote sombrely to Robert on 5 July. 'Don't follow the example at yours. And stay in your flat. A move is a dreadful thing. And other flats are always worse.' None of Ivy's friends in those days knew how she was placed financially, but the experience had evidently been a great shock. 'I am immensely relieved,' wrote Elizabeth, 'she had a terrible anxiety feeling, and the move might have killed her altogether, and must have as a writer, I think.' Ivy herself felt ever afterwards that she had only narrowly and perhaps temporarily escaped being sucked under by the tide that engulfed so many apparently secure, even affluent old people on fixed incomes in the genteel, residential areas of London in the early 1960s. 'You are the fifth friend of mine to be turned out of her house!' she wrote to her cousin Katie Blackie, that Christmas. 'The threat came on me, but I hope it has passed.'

It left Ivy seeming older, with a sharply renewed sense of the world as a shaky place. Roger Hinks, who had planned to return to London for good in the autumn of 1963, died suddenly that summer: 'It is hard to think of a more wretched misfortune . . .' she wrote to Robert on 5 July. 'I knew him as a very young man, and in the time when he was back in London, got quite dependent on him. And I was so looking forward to having him settle here, and seeing him fulfil himself at last. At 59, he should have had a future before him, and he had not been too fortunate in the past . . .' Helen Rolleston also died at much the same time, and Ivy, who had recovered from her regular winter bout of bronchitis, succumbed to one of her 'old bad throats',[55] brought on she thought by grief and shock. In the past five years she had lost Rose, Ernest, Roger and Helen. Basil Marsden-Smedley fell ill that summer and was surprised and touched to find a case of his favourite burgundy waiting in his hospital room, ordered by Ivy who seldom gave presents and had never shown the faintest interest in his taste in wine.

He died in 1964 (killed, according to Ivy's more cynical friends, by the enforced union between the boroughs of Chelsea and Kensington), followed by the earliest of all her friends, Arthur Waley, two years later. 'I have lost more than one old friend of late, and the world grows emptier,' she wrote to Robert. 'There are many left, and new ones come, but the space is never filled. It is to be expected, but that is no help.'[56] She herself was warned in 1965 by Dr Pasmore that she had a weak heart and must rest, which she did ('Anno Domini really, and tedious!'[57]), amazing Herman by the determination with which she clung to life—'Remember, it's all we've got; remember, it's all we've got,' said Ivy,[58] always strictly practical when it came to mortality. Ten years earlier she had impressed Anne Hill by her matter-of-fact reaction to news of the death of another old acquaintance, who had died of a stroke in her sleep: 'Of a stroke?' said Ivy. 'Good, good. And she had her maid to the last? Good.'[59]

Ivy's nineteenth novel, *A God and His Gifts*, finished at the height of the crisis in March 1963, had by her own account 'suffered from my months of flat-hunting and threatened upheaval',[60] though its author's distress had by no means damped the spirits of the hero, Hereward Egerton, the god of the title, a novelist of prodigious energy and egotism. The book's period setting is sufficiently elastic to permit an unusually high proportion of characters earning a living, including a working wife ('I thought I would have a change this time', Ivy said[61]), also a notably casual attitude to sex which somewhat modifies Herman's assertion that Ivy was baffled in the

1960s by the permissive society: 'It was perfectly in vain for me to try to tell Ivy that nobody thought anything of anybody sleeping with anybody, it was just part of daily routine, and that one could not say it was immoral for people to have promiscuous love affairs: she simply couldn't understand it.'[62] Admittedly, Ivy had always insisted that taking a by-blow into a family to be brought up alongside its legitimate brothers and sisters (as the Egertons do in *A God and His Gifts*) had been standard practice in her own youth.[63] What sounds much more like Herman's account of the swinging Sixties is the open, uncensorious, wholly businesslike spirit in which this supposedly Victorian family accepts as the eldest son's bride a girl who turns out to be pregnant not by her fiancé but by an unidentified married man. The seducer is revealed in due course as her father-in-law, the godlike Hereward himself, a potent figure unique among Ivy's tyrants in that, far from bottling up his energies as the repressive head of a totalitarian household, he has expended them generously over thirty years by helping himself to every young girl in sight as well as churning out a steady flow of lucrative popular novels.

Hereward is placed in many ways like that other popular author, John Ponsonby in *Daughters and Sons* (1937), who also had a child determined to write something less ephemeral than the trashy bestsellers that bring in enough to support the family and subsidize the ancestral estates. But Hereward's self-centred and coldly contemptuous son Merton is a markedly less sympathetic portrait of an ambitious young writer than France Ponsonby; and the contrast is part of a general shift, for Ivy, drawing closer to old age herself over the past twenty-five years, had grown steadily more cordial towards the older generation in her books, represented here by an irresistibly flighty, amusing, broadminded and soft-hearted couple of grandparents. Sir Michael Egerton and his wife Joanna are both the same age as Ivy herself when *A God and His Gifts* came out. ('"Seventy-nine is not what it is," said Joanna. "Or it would be old age." "Neither is it," said Sir Michael. "I feel as young as I ever did"'[64]). Both are harassed, like their author, by worry over money and property, the catastrophic consequences of drawing on capital, the dread prospect of being obliged by looming debts and pitiless creditors to move, leaving their shabby but beloved old home to the tender mercy of strangers ('I was glad we could keep it. Because what would happen to us without it, I am at a loss to say. It would be the end of our world'[65]). Both end by doting, like every other member of his large and complicated family, on the three-year-old Henry Egerton who is—more than any of his contemporaries, except perhaps Neville Sullivan in *Parents and Children* (and even he had an anxious and tyrannical streak largely foreign to Henry) —Ivy's purest celebration of infancy. Her friends were delighted and even Gollancz, noting that the reviews were more mixed than usual, went so far as to predict record sales for *A God and His Gifts* ('An odd thing about this new novel . . . ,' he wrote to Herbert van Thal on 29 November 1963, a week after publication: 'Quite a little run on it has been started').

If Ivy's central theme in *A God and His Gifts* is one of indiscriminate, explosive, creative vitality, she also attended in a minor key to unfinished business from the past. Hereward has an unmarried sister, Zillah, who, like John Ponsonby's sister Hetta, has willingly submerged her own adult life in his. They represent the final working-out in Ivy's books of the relationship between a brother and sister whose consuming, exclusive love for one another goes back to her own successive absorption in each of her two brothers. The book, which covers a time span of three decades, starts with the lusty young Hereward confessing to Zillah that, since irresistible urges force him to marry, he has selected a wife too humble and dim to pose any threat to his sister ('She may hardly be a friend to you, but she will leave us our friendship. That is a condition I must make, and could not make with every woman. We are not asking nothing, Zillah. We can hardly ask more'[66]). Hereward is equally frank in his proposal to the unfortunate Ada, who meekly endorses his view that her desires must take second place to Zillah's in a marriage designed from the start as a ménage à trois: 'It is safe and open and sound. It carries no doubt and no risk. It will not separate Zillah and me.'[67]

In fact the marriage proves neither safe nor open and, though it does not separate Hereward from Zillah, it reduces her to a self-effacing, spinsterly shadow who barely speaks save in praise or defence of her brother. Her original scheme for collaborating in his work boils down in practice to mounting guard over his door, intercepting his callers and seeing that his meals are sent up on trays, as well as covering up for his love affairs, since both brother and sister openly acknowledge that the satisfaction of Hereward's sexual needs is crucial to their life together:

'Zillah, we are brother and sister. If we were not, what could we be?'

'Nothing that was nearer. It stands first among the relations. There is nothing before it, nothing to follow it. It reaches from the beginning to the end.'[68]

Hetta Ponsonby at a similar junction had pretended to kill herself sooner than accept her brother's marriage. But, whatever Ivy's own feelings may once have been, there is nothing personal about her rueful, humorous, conclusive demonstration in *A God and His Gifts* that 'the brother and sister relation'—at any rate Hereward's idyllic, self-deceiving version of it—is a thoroughly inadequate emotional solution to adult life. Hetta is humiliated and embittered by her attempts to prolong it, Zillah gives in gracefully, each is crushed in the end by her inability to find fulfilment in anyone but her brother. For children and young people the love between brother and sister is often the one wholly satisfactory aspect of family life in Ivy's books. But in middle age it works only for people prepared to settle for the passive, constricted, asexual existence—'the dear little narrow life'—beloved by Elton and Ursula Scrope. Zillah's predicament is not particularly important, or presented in any great detail, but it is Ivy's ironic last word on what had been the major catastrophe of her own early life. It gives *A God and His Gifts* that sense of completion she herself got from Robert's *Stepsons* when (though she had fully intended waiting till the book was in print) she finally read it in manuscript a few years earlier: 'I could not wait any longer. It fulfilled my highest hopes, and they were very high. And I am enjoying the sense of peace that comes from the feeling of gaps filled and curiosity satisfied.'[69]

Robert's book on Jane Austen, also published in 1963, was dedicated to Ivy which made her feel, as she said, highly complacent: 'I agreed with most of it, and got new light on a great deal. I seem rather by myself in thinking the Portsmouth picture a great success'[70] (Portsmouth is the home of the Price family in *Mansfield Park*, always a favourite with Ivy—'I can't understand why people call it *static*. It is so full of movement and life. Even her dull scraps are music to me'[71]). She and Robert exchanged news via go-betweens—Olivia Manning, Kathleen Farrell, and Elizabeth all visited him in Athens—and Ivy (who never gossiped by post) wrote probably more freely to him than to anyone else about the problems and sorrows of mutual friends, and even about her own troubles: 'Yes, Roger's empty place is very empty, and so many of them yawn about me now,' she wrote that Christmas. 'But it is hardly your time to begin to face them yet.'[72]

She still made her annual round of country friends in spring and summer but she was beginning to think twice about accepting invitations in cold or wet weather, to evening gatherings, flats with stairs (climbing was bad for her heart) or houses in outlying parts ('I think if people live in Hampstead, they ought to come to one, don't you?' she said to Barbara Robinson, 'not expect one to go to them'). She missed Julian Mitchell's adaptation of *A Heritage and Its History*, directed by Frank Hauser at the Oxford Playhouse in April 1965,[73] and put off seeing it even when it transferred briefly to the West End ('I have not yet seen the play, as I can't do stairs at the time, and they are *everywhere*,' she wrote to Cicely on 25 May. 'And in a way I shrank from seeing it! I felt that a book should be left as it was written. The notices are good . . . Though the *Evening Standard* gave it a fortnight! And some insults!'). Ivy eventually attended a matinée at the Phoenix Theatre, sitting with Julian in the front of the circle, watching through opera glasses and taking tea in a box afterwards with the cast to whom she was polite and congratulatory but diplomatically vague, commenting specifically only on the costumes.

Expeditions were becoming increasingly tiring, for both guest and host, since a formal visit from Ivy in those days was no light matter: taxis had to be called, dogs shut up, the cat put out and the table properly laid, with butter scraped thin on the cucumber sandwiches, crisp toast (Ivy deplored what she called hotel toast as much as bought flowers and shop sponge cake), weak tea and rich cakes (once, at a friend's, when someone complained of a diet that restricted eggs and butter, Ivy said with an encouraging glance at the slice on her plate: 'I don't think you would have any trouble with *this* cake'[74]). Old age made her imperious and sometimes forgetful, but so fond and attentive to her friends that a great many grudged neither time nor trouble to please her. She was growing smaller: after her eightieth birthday, Herman said that there seemed less of Ivy every time he saw her.[75] When vexed or distressed, she would complain under her breath just loud enough to be overheard, like Sabine Ponsonby in *Daughters and Sons*, and people made allowances for her as they had done for Sabine (' "Stephen, of course she is wonderful. People over eighty always are." "It is what they are not. They are more wonderful at any other age . . . Unless you mean they are not blind or deaf, or actually dead, which is what you do mean" '[76]). Ivy had always talked in muttered asides, more and more since Margaret's death, but now her exchanges with imaginary characters slipped over fairly often into conversation with real ones: 'The first time it happened, one stopped politely, and she gave you a sort of blank look, as if nothing had happened. But when you got used to it, you learnt to carry on,' said Kay who found the habit not so much macabre as companionable. 'Of course Herman loves her whisperings,' wrote Elizabeth, '—for he is always convinced that he will catch a word or two—but all he has ever heard was when she was going from the dining room to the drawing room after lunch with him, and she whispered, "I hate sauces, I hate sauces, I hate sauces." "And that I am sure I was meant to hear," he said.'

Ivy's Irish housekeeper, Peggy, told Herman she could never get used to hearing her employer talk all day alone. Peggy (who came in 1959 and stayed nearly six years) was herself the most talkative and friendliest of all Ivy's maids: she wore a cap 'as a concession'[77] and was a competent plain cook, what Ivy called a factotum, warm-hearted and willing but untrained, without the habit or discipline that might have enabled her to bear the dismally lonely, ill-paid, uneventful life of a Victorian servant more than fifty years out of date. Ivy, in many ways a considerate employer, could never be induced to offer any advance on what would have been by prewar standards the princely wage of £6 a week, and she sternly discouraged Peggy's sociable custom of waylaying visitors for a chat in the kitchen, offering them drinks without being asked, and making up little gifts for her favourites. But, though Peggy was already talking of leaving at Christmas 1963, she stayed on to see Ivy through the coughs and quinsies of another two winters before she finally returned to Ireland at the beginning of April 1965.

Peggy's successor was a ladylike platinum blonde ('an elderly companion who does everything but is at meals,' Ivy wrote glumly on 6 April to Cecil Gould. 'Thought I should warn you'), chiefly memorable for her reaction to a ribald conversation among Ivy's lunch guests one day about Viva King's latest young man. Willie had died two years earlier and Viva, in her sixties, had opened an antique shop with help from a charming young sailor called Mat, who was systematically rooking his benefactress, filching her china, making off with her etchings and gradually stripping her shelves. The companion had been a buyer in Barkers' eminently respectable department store in Kensington High Street where nothing had prepared her for this sort of depravity. She was incredulous, appealing to each guest in vain before turning in desperation to Ivy: 'Oh, Miss Burnett, won't *you* call the police?' 'Not,' said Ivy politely, 'until I have seen how much Mrs King is enjoying the situation.'[78] The companion lasted two months and was followed by a widowed Mrs Lamin, 'an elderly working woman'[79] who was herself replaced a year later by Mary Maguire. Mary was another Irishwoman, stout, plain, bespectacled, dim, even childlike, and so rough that visitors often complained. But she suited Ivy who relied on her physical strength, understood the need to humour her moods, and found her simplicity such a relief that, when Ivo Pakenham protested about her rudeness, he received a box of sweets with a consolatory note from Ivy explaining that, from the point of view of survival, Mary was far more important to her than any of her friends.

Ivo, who always had the knack of provoking Ivy to frankness, was the person who asked her what quality she valued most in her friends (modestly hoping she might say 'charm', 'affection', 'loyalty such as yours, Ivo'), and got the famous reply: 'Availability'.[80] Footloose friends like Madge, who wintered abroad, lived under a cloud only less dark than expatriates like the Robinsons, who did what they could with letters and visits to show Ivy they knew how much she missed them. She grieved now quite unaffectedly over her friends' defection, though her grief had a stoical nip to it:

'I like growing old,' said Herman Schrijver.
'One goes on living and everyone else is dead,' Ivy remarked, spooning up lovingly late strawberries in a sabayon sauce.[81]

Lettice Cooper, introduced by Ivo round about this time, said that her classical education was the thing that made Ivy proudest: 'It was the only thing I ever heard her boast about. She was very Greek, you know. She didn't like trimmings. She liked bare facts and bare lines and brief sentences.'

3

On 29 November 1965 Ivy caught her foot in a rug on the polished linoleum of her drawing room floor: 'I seemed to run forward and I couldn't stop myself, and then I fell and I thought I had died. Then I found I hadn't died, but I could not get up.'[82] When the maid came to look for her and summoned Dr Pasmore, Ivy was found to have broken the neck of her right femur. She was admitted for an operation on 2 December to the private wing of University College Hospital where she stayed for the next six weeks. Her room was filled with fruit, flowers and streams of visitors bearing delicacies of all sorts, sweets, honeycombs, home-made cakes and fresh produce in such quantities that much of it had to be redistributed in the wards. Victor Gollancz (who had reluctantly resigned from the firm that year on grounds of ill health and was also in hospital) sent flowers—'Ivy, somebody very rich has bunched you,' said Herman inquisitively[83]—and commiserated about the food, which drew them together as nothing else ever had (though Ivy would not adopt Gollancz's solution of having all meals sent in from a decent hotel—'but then,' as she said, 'I'm not a socialist'[84]).

'I was too badly hurt & helpless to want much for the first few weeks,' Ivy wrote long afterwards in a comforting letter to Sonia Orwell, also recovering from an operation in hospital, 'but later I felt like a schoolboy writing to his mother for supplies, & when I got home I enjoyed the simplest things, a baked potato, a milk pudding, a welsh rarebit, etc, cooked so that they could be put to their proper use.'[85] The nurses treated Ivy with a boldness and disrespect that startled her visitors, giving her a Christmas stocking, calling her 'poppet' and 'sweetie pie' ('I always thought nurses were a tough crowd', Elizabeth reported to Robert), wheeling her off on Christmas Day to sing carols and be entertained along with the rest by doctors in funny hats, all of which she described sardonically enough to Herman and others. But her account to Elizabeth was amused and accommodating: 'It was very tiring, and I believe that one or two of the patients took a sharp turn for the worse afterwards. But I think the nurses enjoyed it; and, after all, it was for *them*'.[86]

The operation was a success though it was months before Ivy's strength began to come back. In the first few months she was 'dragged daily to a chair' and imprisoned there ('I found it a terrifying experience at first, and always dreaded it'[87]), helpless, immobilized, afraid to stir for fear of jarring her hip. She could not read in hospital, let alone write, and, though she did not complain, the sister told Francis King that she was in great pain.[88] She left hospital on 12 January—'I am at home with nurses, but *at home!* There is still tediousness ahead but the worst is past,' she wrote to the Robinsons next day. She was visited the day after by Cicely who had not seen her since before the accident and found her sadly changed: 'Her face was gaunt, haggard and had a ravaged look. The neat, strong features were puffy; her cheeks sunken, her skin colourless. Even her hair, always so tidily folded away, had an abandoned look. Her dignity, the "iron dignity" critics wrote about, had suffered outrage. I nearly wept at the sight of her.'[89] Two weeks later Ivy was walking feebly with crutches, by March she looked more herself though much older ('The ordeal of all she had been through, and the worry of the expense, and the fear of those jarring pains had left her with a look of weary anxiety'), the following month she had left off night nurses and 'progressed from crutches to sticks, an advance!'[90]

> I went to see Ivy [wrote Elizabeth that spring]. She has bronchitis now, and her breathing is laboured. It was a great shock to me to see her. I felt that I had never seen anyone so old. Her hair is in two little plaits, and she was wearing a rather dashing pink nylon night-gown. Quite a surprise, that. Her eyes look enormous —pale milky blue. She was in marvellous form—exactly the same Ivy, talking a great deal about money. And food. Though one would think not a morsel had passed her lips for months. She took my hand and played with my bracelet—and her fingers, her wrist were just bones. But the same pursed smile and mis-chievous sideways glance, as if she really must not laugh at her own jokes.[91]

As her health returned, Ivy's friends were increasingly worried by her evident distress over money. The rent increase was now overshadowed by hospital bills, surgeon's fees, the cost of day and night nurses at home. When Ivy had protested at Christmas that she could not afford to stay much longer in hospital, Herman immediately sent a cheque for one hundred pounds, while Lettice Cooper went straight home to telephone John Lehmann on the committee of the Royal Literary Fund which promptly responded, on the recommendation of Francis King and Osbert Lancaster, with an emergency grant of £500. But, when Ivy applied for further relief three months later, the intrepid committee sent its secretary, John Broadbent, to investigate her financial resources: 'He came to see me, you know,' she told Lettice, 'but he found I was too rich.' An application for a Civil List pension was turned down on the same grounds, to her friends' indignation. No one in those days suspected that Ivy's frugality, like Rose's and Arthur Waley's (all three were apt to strike strangers as having trouble in making ends meet), had less to do with actual poverty than with the ingrained, almost superstitious prohibition laid on their class and generation against disbursing capital. For Ivy, the taboo remained unbreakable long after the family trust had been wound up in 1961, and she herself discharged after half a century as her sisters' trustee. People had gone out of their way for years to save Ivy the price of a cab fare and, at a time when even Herman accepted her view of herself as perilously close to destitution ('she had me completely foxed'[92]), nobody could be quite sure she was joking when she said with her pursed smile at tea: 'Soon I may have to ask you all to bring your own buns.'[93]

In January 1967, Ivy slipped backwards in the bathroom and broke her other hip ('She would have broken a third, had she got it,' wrote Viva King tartly[94]), which meant another six weeks in hospital, followed by nurses again at the flat, and a walking frame which she used for the rest of her life. 'Considering my age, my frail bones and lack of muscle, I wondered I had survived, and I suppose the surgeon did too,' she wrote to Cicely a year later, on 25 January 1968. From now on she referred to herself as a cripple, and she seemed to others besides Herman to shrink, sometimes from one month to the next. Several of her friends had suspected after her first fall that she did not mean to go out again and, after the second, she never did. Her world narrowed to the flat with its balcony garden (she was greatly disturbed in the last year of her life when the block of flats opposite her was raised by two storeys, cutting off part of her sky), and nothing anyone could do would persuade her to leave it. Even in spring she contented herself with the bulbs in her window boxes and the constantly replenished pots of snowdrops, violets, primroses, bluebells and cyclamen that she kept drawn up on the floor in front of her chair.

The flat itself, never especially inviting, grew less so. The rooms seemed bare, shabby and dark to Mario Praz, coming to pay tribute in the summer of 1967 (Lady Mander had once proposed lecturing in the 1950s on 'I. Compton-Burnett' in Rome—'We must find a subject that Mario Praz doesn't know more about than any English person,' said Roger Hinks at the British Council, only to find that Signor Praz had already delivered his lecture of the same title).[95] Elizabeth was not the only regular visitor to find herself almost unutterably depressed by a first glimpse each time of what seemed a moral rather than actual dustiness and neglect. The fact was that Ivy's indifference to material surroundings had been growing steadily more pronounced since Margaret's death. Flowers mattered much to her but flower arrangement meant nothing: she would watch in silence while Sonia or Cicely hunted in vain for a pretty pot, or set about tweaking and fussing over the bunches jammed into the ugly, chimney-pot vases ranged three or four in a row at her feet. She infuriated Herman by allowing Mary to replace Margaret's delicate, striped Coalport cups and saucers—'Cracked and mended and rather rare!'—with cheap, thick crockery from Woolworths. 'To me a room is just a space,' she once said to the music critic, Andrew Porter; and even friends undeterred by the flat's bleakness—'Oh no, it was cosy,' said Lettice Cooper, 'you just sat in front of the fire and talked'—admitted that the only source of comfort and warmth was Ivy's little igloo by the hearth (or later, when laying a coal fire became too much for Mary, where she sat toasting between two electric fires), barricaded by cushions, and chocolate boxes, and a waist-high pile of new novels.

But Ivy herself could still radiate an energy, amusement, humour and sympathy that captivated strangers. 'Her head is lively and finely chiselled; her grey hair is gathered together in the form of a helmet; she has not at all the look of a witch as she appears in many of her photos,' Mario Praz wrote in his diary on 9 June 1967. Herman, who brought him, claimed to have forbidden Ivy beforehand to mention servants or seedlings, 'and for an hour and a half I sat there pouring out cups of tea and listening to the most brilliant lecture on Thackeray'[96] (according to Signor Praz, though they discussed Jean Rhys, Muriel Spark, Joe Ackerley's death and the Sitwells' bad temper, 'Thackeray was not even mentioned'). To the end of her life Ivy read everything anyone ever claimed might be worth reading—'Of all the autumn and spring books I have enjoyed yours the most,' she wrote to Elizabeth on 2 May 1968, when *The Wedding Group* was published—and, second only to gossip and prices, she liked talking about the contemporary novel. 'She never wrote a word of literary criticism, but it was with unerring precision that she would indicate the defects in the latest work of this or that admired author of the day,' wrote Francis King when she died. 'Yet few people whose literary standards were so exacting have found so much to enjoy in even the most ephemeral of books.'[97]

She admired Francis' own technical skill and confidence but not what she called his 'murkiness',[98] deplored Iris Murdoch's symbolism ('added on top like a layer of thick, hard icing on a cake'[99]), Joyce Cary's facility (Cary once asked her if she didn't find herself thinking of ten or twelve plots at a time: 'I said, "No, I don't," and it would be better for him if he didn't, one must keep an eye on that sort of thing'[100]), and the sentimental side of Evelyn Waugh ('one must not ask people to do more than they can'[101]). 'He has so little talent, so little talent,' she said sadly to Soame of a friend whose novels grew progressively longer, 'but we should be grateful, my dear Soame, because there is so little talent altogether in the world.' Among her literary friends, she loved Rosamond's beauty ('Oh, a water lily,' she told Lettice Cooper), and Olivia's plaintive, funny, faintly waspish style of self-deprecation, which laid her open to much gentle teasing from Ivy ('I always felt she saw Olivia as one of her characters,' said Kay, 'one of her *favourite* characters'), though she was still not entirely happy about Olivia's writing: 'A great many novels nowadays are just travel books disguised, just travel books really. Olivia has just published one about Bulgaria,' she said to Barbara. 'And it is all about Bulgaria, really.' The only travel books for which Ivy regularly made an exception were Robert's; and she thanked him for his novel, *The Deep End*, on 21 May 1968, with perhaps the finest compliment one author can pay another: 'I admired your book very much, not so much because I sometimes felt I had written it myself, as for the deep & subtle treatment of Deadly Nightshade's rise to power & exposure of the theory that honesty is the best policy.'

Ivy depended more than ever in these years of confinement on her friends, especially neighbouring friends like George Furlong, former head of the Irish National Gallery, and Rex Britcher, who shared a tall, thin house in Thurloe Street crammed with furniture, pictures and objets d'art: Ivy laughed a lot about their five crowded drawing rooms, advising them to fit in two more by building on an extra storey, and mischievously aggravating the problem herself by leaving them two each of a set of four grey-painted armchairs in her will. They came frequently to weed, water and restock Ivy's balcony garden. Rex baked her cakes, and so did Lettice Cooper who took it in turn with Carol Rygate and Elizabeth Sprigge to make tea on Sunday which was Mary's day off. Ivo came in on Saturdays, Madge on Thursdays, Herman was constantly there, and Soame dropped in every few weeks to catch up on new novels—'There are far too many books about sex, my dear Soame, and far too few about money'—and run through the latest gossip. Country friends came when they could: people like Kathleen Farrell (who had moved, in spite of pleas and remonstrance, to Brighton —'Oh, *don't* go to Brighton,' Ivy said, and, with positive horror, '*Not Hove?*') and Cicely Greig would be asked to come again soon, or pressed to stay behind when everyone else had left for a gossip or to share a companionable silence, 'just sitting in front of her fire chewing chocolates with her'.[102]

Being cheated of this sort of intimacy was what Ivy minded most about exiles like the Robinsons, and the fonder she was, the more unforgiving. Barbara and Walter found themselves punished for living abroad by constant small teases like, for instance, her flat refusal to explain or comment when Arthur Waley died and was found, to the stupefaction of nearly all his old friends, to have left a widow. Arthur had lived for most of his life with Beryl de Zoete (who died in 1962)—'The trouble was they loved, honoured and obeyed each other for thirty years,' said Ivy, 'but whenever one wanted to marry, the other didn't.'[103] But six weeks before he died he had married Alison Grant Robinson, a second lifelong companion whose existence even Ivy had never so much as suspected. Arthur, who had seen Ivy through a lifetime of painful, sometimes catastrophic upheavals as well as two world wars, turned out to have been her match in the art of giving nothing away ('It was no good again today,' he said after one of Ivy's Saturdays,[104] which he attended without fail and often in silence, barely uttering save to say 'Hello, Ivy, hello, Madge,' and, when he got up to go, 'Goodbye, Ivy, goodbye, Madge'). Alison, his faithful chauffeur on these trips to Braemar Mansions, met Ivy for the first time as his widow when the two talked a great deal about Arthur whose life had been in some ways as strangely suppressed as Ivy's own. 'I am seeing a certain amount of his widow . . .' she wrote tantalizingly to the mystified Robinsons, 'and find I know our side of him well but not much of the other . . .'

All but the boldest of Ivy's friends had learnt to go carefully when approaching her past, to register inexplicable changes of temperature, sudden comings forth and drawings back indicating the presence of a hidden knot she would not untie or, in Madge's phrase, a stone against which one stubbed one's toe. But at the end of her life Ivy was demonstrative as she had never been in her youth, and she took great pains to help or comfort anyone in trouble. When Carol Rygate fell ill in the summer of 1968, Ivy, who loathed telephoning but knew very well what it meant to be cooped up alone all day in low spirits, rang her every night at six o'clock to talk ('Dearest Carol, I rejoiced much to hear you were on the water, & so on smooth waters at last,' she wrote on 18 December when Carol was convalescing on board ship for Christmas: 'It is a long time of buffeting behind you. I congratulate you on all of it, heat, paucity of fellowship, scope for gluttony and pudding in prospect . . .').

She had done what she could to console Sonia in hospital the winter before, and she wrote copiously several times a week when Madge, too, broke her hip and wrist in a fall in June 1968: 'I felt I had had my third accident, I minded so much. And I mind more & more as I can't get to you & can do nothing . . . I have never been so angry at my own helplessness.'[105] She applied to the Royal Literary Fund (an appeal rejected on Madge's behalf for the same reason as Ivy's) and, when Madge left hospital, arranged for her to be looked after by the nurse, Sister Hallet, who had come to tide Ivy over Mary's summer holiday:

10 July, 1968

Dearest Madge,
    . . . Sister H. will go to you on the day you have fixed. She is kind & reliable & equal to all that has to be done; nervous about her cooking, but manages quite well for warm weather & strawberries for pudding . . . 'Sister' is violently interested in meeting titled people, & no doubt you will oblige her in the matter. She talks & talks & seems always to be everywhere, but is

much above the average, & I shall be easy about you in her
care . . .

All my love. I wish I were not such a helpless friend. Fate has
not considered us.

Ivy

Julian Mitchell brought Lady Diana Cooper & her son, Lord
Norwich to tea last week, & Sister almost expired.

It was a gloomy summer, but of all the misfortunes Ivy dreaded for
her friends—'friends are away, & ill, & injured, & domestically
harassed & financially oppressed'[106]—loneliness was the worst. Dr
Pasmore dropped in often (Ivy told him that summer that, after
reading and re-reading Jane Austen for seventy years, she knew the
novels so well that she no longer needed to read them[107]). He said
that rest and isolation in her flat prolonged Ivy's life by lessening the
strain on her heart; and perhaps her seclusion provided a physical
equivalent to the moral aloofness that had for most of her life
protected perceptions so acute as to be, in her sister's view, almost
indecent. Certainly she was loved by more people than ever before
in these years of her final retreat from the world when Ivy, who had
never seen a hippie or tasted frozen food, never touched a typewriter or entered a tall building, seemed almost infinitely remote
from London in the swinging Sixties. 'She cut herself off, and she
lived in the past,' said Kathleen Farrell. 'And then she was thinking.' As her world closed in, as material things fell away, as she
herself grew bodily more helpless, Ivy put her faith in gossip and
visits, the compensations of the contemplative life—'people will
not realise that the pleasure in being well-informed should be
intellectual; they make it social.'[108] But above all else she prized the
affection of her friends, who were often taken aback in these last
years by her energy, constancy and generosity of feeling: 'This zest
for life was the counterpart of her dread of death,' wrote Francis
King, 'so that, even when she was in the greatest pain and discomfort, one never felt, as often with the extremely old and ailing, that
the end would be a mercy.'[109] Selina Middleton had said the same of
herself in *The Mighty and Their Fall*: 'I would rather be alive than
dead. When I die, people will say it is the best thing for me. It is
because they know it is the worst. They want to avoid the feeling of
pity. As though they were the people most concerned!'[110]

Ivy was made a Dame—'one of nature's Dames' according to the London *Evening Standard*—in the Queen's Birthday Honours the day after Mario Praz's visit in June 1967, receiving the palace envoy alone at home and keeping the insignia ('some little contraption of silk and ribbon, spelt "riband" in the directions . . .'[111]) in a drawer for favoured visitors to take out and play with. She asked Dr Furlong to represent her at the Royal Society of Literature's reception the following year, when she was elected one of their twelve Companions of Literature, along with Dame Rebecca West, Sir Compton Mackenzie and John Betjeman ('quite a nice little honour,' she said to Cicely,[112] though to Madge she was less enthusiastic: 'It is an empty and inconvenient honour, and I am not grateful for it'[113]). These public tributes gave her on the whole much satisfaction and so, for all her misgivings, did seeing versions of her books in the theatre and on television (she missed Julian Mitchell's *A Family and a Fortune* at the Yvonne Arnaud Theatre, Guildford, in July 1966, but watched *A Heritage and Its History* with him in 1968 on Mary's television—'It was a very good play, Dame Ivy,' said Mary afterwards, 'but a tiring play'[114]).

> I was surprised and pleased to be a Dame . . . [she wrote on 27 June 1968, to Robert]. I am just beginning to write again—the elaboration is a true one—but the days, which I should find so long, pass by so fast. Being disabled takes time in itself, & I have rather a heavy post . . . The one I miss most, Margaret Jourdain, has now been dead sixteen years; and I still have to tell her things, as you had to, and may still have to tell your brother. I am not fully a Dame, as she does not know about it.

Ivy's last novel had been giving trouble long before illness forced her to lay it aside ('My next novel is in a lamentable state and belongs to the future. I am sorry it is so,' she wrote to Victor Gollancz on 21 August 1964, when delivery should have been nearly due according to her biennial schedule unbroken since the war). Well before her first fall, she told several people that, though she had got the characters, she did not yet know what was going to happen to them and that she had never found a plot so elusive before.[115] She kept her 'little book'—or rather the growing pile of flimsy, tattered school exercise books, thirty in all by the end —stuffed under a cushion with chocolate boxes and newspapers at

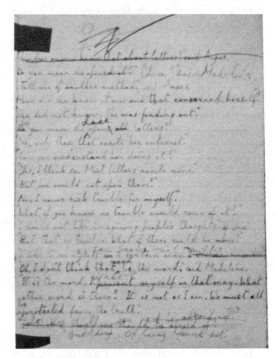

Pages from the manuscript of *The Last and the First*, showing Ivy's two different handwritings.

A fair copy (printed with minor alterations on p. 132 of the published text) in the neat school-girl's hand she kept for the final version of her manuscripts.

the end of the sofa (where the pile was discovered the day after she died by Elizabeth Sprigge, a faithful visitor in these years, and later author of the first memoir). All Ivy's manuscripts were endlessly rewritten, crossed out and gone over before being copied in a neat school-girl's hand quite different from the loopy black scrawl in which she wrote letters and composed her first drafts. But the twelve notebooks which contain the fair copy of this last novel[116] are still miserably expressive of labour and effort. They are written in a mixture of both hands, in parts indecipherable and so disturbed that her final revisions are strung out like a chain of islands across a swamp of alterations—five or ten lines left standing on a page criss-crossed with interpolations, corrections, deletions, as many as three or four alternative versions scored through or scrubbed out; and the twelfth booklet, labelled 'Next!', has been dismembered altogether, containing little more than often incoherent notes on scraps or sheaves of loose paper.

Ivy herself was often despairing as her days grew shorter and more cluttered: she would rise at eight, dress slowly, write a little

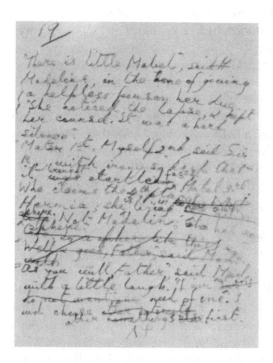

A tentative rough draft written in the mature, loopy hand she used for letters, and showing an early stage in the process of cutting, altering, re-writing and generally working-over to which all her manuscripts were submitted. This is part of a scene omitted from the published text; Mabel was the original name of the child Amy.

with lunch on a trolley, take tea with friends, perhaps write a little more and retire early to bed. She liked to have her hair done for her ('When I was a little girl, I was very particular about my hair'[117]), and, as she became slower and weaker, would permit Mary to help her dress, telling her little practical things about her mother or the nurse who had looked after her as a child. Ivy's sisters came more often to visit her and, now that the relationship no longer grated on any of them, they slipped back easily to the days when Ivy sat over the others as governess in the schoolroom at Hove ('I am coming to the end of trouble with my naughty sisters,' she wrote to Madge on 1 April 1968, when Vera and Juliet, now running a Rudolf Steiner school at King's Langley, had released capital to finance it by buying an annuity 'against the will of the family lawyer'). She talked more freely of Noel and what he had meant to her. Once she gave Kay without explanation a photograph of Dorothy Kidd as a young woman in a large hat ('We lived together before I lived with Margaret,' she said. 'She married'[118]); and another time, when Dorothy telephoned one Thursday afternoon, Madge heard Ivy change as she answered the telephone, laughing and talking very fast in a voice ('It was a young voice, gay, like a girl's') Madge had never heard her use before.

Many of her friends noticed this general sharpening of memory; and the 'little book', too, returned to the situation in Ivy's own family on which she had based *Dolores* more than sixty years earlier. Ivy had been distressed, round about the time she first began complaining of trouble with her new novel, by Barbara saying that people often took her books to show that human beings were incapable of altruism. 'That was not what I meant at all,' Ivy protested to Barbara, 'with a bleak look'; and in *The Last and the First* (the name eventually chosen for the posthumously published version of Ivy's nameless and unfinished manuscript), she reverts to the theme of unselfishness originally broached in *Dolores*. Her dissatisfaction with that novel had if anything increased with time: she told Barbara how much she envied painters for being able to destroy their early work, and she was scathing whenever admirers—'people who think they are clever'[119]—managed to unearth a copy. Her own published copy is disfigured with a mass of pencilled alterations, crossings-out and rearrangements, showing how endlessly Ivy must have tinkered with it in the fallow period when, for fourteen years after the publication of *Dolores*, she wrote nothing at all. Her first and last books both deal among other things with friction between a strong-minded, undervalued, unwanted eldest stepdaughter and a jealous stepmother ('Whose house is it? Hers or mine?'[120]) closely based in the first instance on Ivy's mother. Dr Compton Burnett had eased the tension in his own household by removing his eldest daughter bodily (Olive Compton-Burnett had died in 1963, the year Ivy started thinking about *The Last and the First*), setting her up as partner in a girls' school, which is Hermia Heriot's solution to the same problem in *The Last and the First*.

But Dolores Hutton—a characteristically extreme variation on the emotionally agonized, intellectually stultified, morally obdurate Victorian heroine idealized by Mrs Humphry Ward and Charlotte M. Yonge—had insisted on renouncing her own teaching career, her financial independence and hopes of love and marriage, for her family's sake (Ivy, even at this stage, was too honest to represent the recipients of Dolores' repeated sacrifices as anything but ungrateful). Hermia's opportunity for spectacular selflessness comes when, inheriting a small fortune from a rejected elderly suitor, she makes the money over to her father, thereby simultaneously retrieving the family's financial position and exposing the duplicity of her disgruntled and resentful stepmother. The contrast could hardly be more emphatic. Dolores, conceived by a profoundly logical mind in terms of a no less profoundly disingenuous morality, remained obstinately blind to the pernicious consequences of her saintly self-immolation, while Hermia, embarking on an act of unequivocal altruism, 'behaved as she did as a matter of practical common sense, openly relishing moreover the hold she thus acquired over her stepmother' (the analysis comes from Walter Robinson,[121] always one of Ivy's most perceptive critics). Virtue—the generous virtue of intelligence—prospers for Hermia who puts her trust, as poor Dolores never could, in candour and a shrewd appraisal of the realities of power politics.

But, if *The Last and the First* has an autumnal clarity, there is also an autumnal dryness about this last book which looks back, over more than sixty years and eighteen intervening novels, to the archetypal shapes and outlines laid down in Ivy's childhood. Angus and Roberta Heriot, Hermia's half-brother and -sister by her father's second marriage, are a subdued and chastened pair, hardly more than horrified spectators at a drama in which their own role is negligible ('We have seen some real life, Roberta, a thing I have always wanted to see. But now I don't want to see any more as long as I live'[122]). Madeline, Hermia's cheerful, compliant younger sister, is the last in a long line of optimists, always anxious to smooth over trouble and think only of the happy part ('What is the happy part?' asks one of Ivy's dreadful children, told to run along and not worry about a death in the family in *Darkness and Day*[123]), whose provenance goes back ultimately to Olive's missionary sister, Daisy, the only one of Dr Compton Burnett's first family on reasonable terms with their stepmother. If there are traces of Ivy herself, they are most evident in young Amy Grimstone, child of a neighbouring household, whose successive mortifications at Hermia's school reflect her creator's experience (Amy's homework essay, quoted verbatim in a cancelled passage of the manuscript, comes in both style and content closer to *Dolores* than anything else in Ivy's subsequent writings[124]); and also perhaps in Amy's grandmother, Jocasta Grimstone, whose laconic speech was recognized by several of Ivy's friends. Hermia's father is an ineffectual figure, kindly but (like Dr Compton Burnett) too hopeful—or too well-schooled in self-preservation—to register fully the misery and injustice arbitrarily imposed on the whole household by his wife ('You might be a figure in history corrupted by power,' says Hermia to her stepmother. 'It is what you are, only you are not in history'[125]).

Eliza Heriot is unmistakably descended from silly, comic, peevish Mrs Hutton, but the distance Ivy had travelled since *Dolores* may be gauged by the compassion and tragic penetration of this last un-finished, condensed and abstracted portrait of her mother. The last chapter of the printed text of *The Last and the First* was extracted by Cicely, after Ivy's death, from a maze of cancellations (including incestuous complications among the Grimstones, and a whole clutch of alternative marriages for Hermia and others); and among these jumbled and abandoned workings is an episode dealing far more fully than the published Chapter XI with Eliza's public exposure and humiliation: a kind of hunting scene, evidently composed (unlike anything else on this manuscript) straight on to the page, in rich and sombre colours with Eliza hounded and brought down to the horror of her pursuers before staggering, damaged and in pain, to her feet again. The writing—huge, wild, fierce, lurching diagonally across the page as though the hand that wrote it could scarcely hold a pen—gives a miserable impression of difficulty and weakness. But the scene itself is as crisp in its opening stages, as tautly organized and searching in its exploration of fear, rage, shame, betrayal and their squalid aftermath as anything Ivy ever wrote; and the whole suggests that, if things had not got the better of her in the end, *The Last and the First* might have been a formidable work.

'About a week before she died, she told me it would be "a terrible ms". Her exhaustion was terrible to see,' wrote Cicely[126] who had begged in vain to be allowed to type the manuscript in the summer of 1969. Ivy complained constantly of being short of time, paying less and less attention to the outside world and seeming scarcely to notice what proved to be a particularly lovely summer. She told Cicely, the last time they stepped out together into a stiff breeze on the balcony, that England was growing windier,[127] as well as emptier. 'It is a dreadful year. Everyone is sick or having operations or gone before. Life is framed in blanks,' she wrote to Katie on 17 February 1969. Ivy, who had been in bed with bronchitis for most of the previous month, was grieving bitterly for Theodora who had died suddenly at Christmas: all that spring she watched over a pot plant that had been Theodora's last present to her, and on 27 February—two months after Theodora's death—she changed her will for the last time.

This was a very long, carefully composed and original document, beginning with twenty-three small bequests: a dozen mirrors were left to friends, mostly other novelists—Olivia Manning, Francis King, Kay Dick, Kathleen Farrell, Lettice Cooper and Julian Mitchell—her diamonds to Carol, her Chinese glass painting (originally a present to Margaret from Soame, it hung over Ivy's desk and was the only picture in the whole flat) to Madge because she loved colour, two urns apiece to Herman and Jim Brandreth (Jim Lees-Milne had a vase, and so did Robin McDouall), small tables to Ivo Pakenham and Cecil Gould, three mirrors to Janet and everything else in the flat to Hester. £15,000 was set aside for Gollancz to produce the collected edition against which Victor had so firmly set his face (he had died at the end of 1967 and been succeeded by his daughter, Livia, who had named half that sum when Ivy asked out of the blue one day at tea how much would be sufficient[128]). The copyrights went to Anthony Compton-Burnett, who was to divide the residue of the estate with Ivy's five friends: Madge, Herman, Robert, Soame and Dorothy's son, Roger Kidd.

Ivy kept her secrets to the end: no one in her lifetime could do more than form often highly inaccurate guesses as to the extent of her resources (eventually sworn at £86,000), her family origins or even her date of birth. She grew desperately frail towards the end, often ill or in pain, and increasingly protected by Mary who did her best in these last months to keep callers at bay. For some time Mary's behaviour had disturbed Ivy's friends. She had long since put a stop to minor pleasures like sitting by a coal fire, or inviting people to lunch, and the thermos flask teas she left out on her afternoons off were generally considered undrinkable so that tea was available as often as not only to visitors prepared to get it themselves. Access to the flat was in any case not always easy: Mary would invent unlikely excuses, sometimes even try to shut the door in the face of anyone not already deterred by her rudeness, and she frequently refused to fetch Ivy to the telephone on grounds that 'the Dame' was unavailable, resting or 'out'. People disliked her bullying manner, and visitors who knew that Ivy was sometimes pitifully lonely were naturally infuriated by being turned away at the door.

But Mary was probably the only person who realized the full extent of her employer's dependence and weakness; and Ivy, who refused point blank many times to contemplate any change, always said that she and Mary understood each other pretty well. Ivy needed someone who could be relied on to help her dress, move, get about, who would nurse her if necessary without protest or question, someone who would accept both Ivy's helplessness and her reluctance to be coddled or taken in charge. The clause in her will leaving Mary £70 for each year in Ivy's service, provided she was still in it when Ivy died, was a bribe to which Mary responded, enjoying the sense of importance 'the Dame's' celebrity gave her, taking pride in her illustrious visitors (though she remained hazy as to the difference between, say, Lettice and Gladys Cooper), grateful to the Dame as the only employer who had ever given her a radio of her own, let alone promised her money.

In June, just after her eighty-sixth birthday, Ivy, who was in bed with bronchitis again, began hearing hostile foreign voices ('You know I am a writer and have imagination,' she explained afterwards to Hester. 'Perhaps some of the voices were in my imagination, but this did not make them hurt any the less'[129]). Shortage of time worried her dreadfully. Vera and Cicely, meeting over tea at Braemar Mansions in early June, agreed that she could not live very much longer. She re-read *Stepsons* which was at last published that summer:

June 3, 1969

Dear Robert,

I settled back into the old atmosphere with so much ease and pleasure, that I am reluctant to leave it, and other books suffer inattention.

More, I *can't* leave it yet, and other books must suffer.

I hear you have another book on the way, and that must shape the lot of all. But for the moment I am satisfied, and ask no more of Heaven, oblivious of the fact that others may ask much. I hear of you from Olivia and others, and *Stepsons* brings us very near.

Yours affectionately,
Ivy.

Another great pleasure was the diamond brooch which she bought, using up an unexpected windfall from Margaret's American royalties, with a great sense of daring and in defiance of Mr Mowll ('He doesn't understand about a brooch,' said Ivy,[130] clearly thrilled at behaving for once as irresponsibly as her sisters). Hester and Elizabeth Sprigge came to inspect a selection of brooches supplied by a charming young man from a Bond Street shop who produced more and more diamonds as if by magic from his pockets until 'Ivy's eyes shone like the jewels as they were spread on the dining room table'.[131] She chose the prettiest (also, to Hester's consternation, the scratchiest), 'sending us out of the room like schoolchildren while she discussed the price', and afterwards wearing it pinned high up on her dress or her bedjacket, or keeping it by her in a bag with other treasures like her little pearl-studded watch.

On 22 June she wrote a last cryptic letter to Francis King (who was immersed in libel difficulties over his novel, *A Domestic Animal*):

Dear Francis,

You must be fearing I had left the earth; and its binding forces hardly increase. May I ask one question? Has this double world the same significance as it would have here, or anything approaching it? Just *Yes* or *No*, and we will pass on.

The book is the strongest you have done, and quality seems to break in everywhere, or perhaps rather to break out. You have great gifts, and the present misfortunes will not alter its inevitable end. You may come to say you are glad it all happened. It is better to be drunk with loss and to beat the ground, than to let the deeper things gradually escape.

Do come and see me when you can.

Yours always with love,
Ivy.

Vera came for the last time, and they talked about the day that Noel was born. Ivy was becoming too frail to walk easily, her skin irritated her, she had difficulty in eating and sleeping. Julian came on 27 June bringing a friend who had made her a pot of the sort of strawberry jam she liked best with whole berries in it: 'She talked lovingly of Robert Liddell and his novel *Stepsons*. But what really pleased her was the jam. Sometimes she could suddenly shed eighty years and look quite girlish. She did so that afternoon. My last memory is of her licking the jam spoon.'[132] All through July she entertained a procession of old and new friends, seeing someone most days for tea. She had a disconcerting trick of cat-napping, dropping off sometimes in the middle of a sentence. 'I'm not tired, I'm sleepy,' she said sharply to Robin McDouall the last time he saw her on 8 August: 'They are very different things. And I'm surprised that *you* should say tired when you mean sleepy.'[133] On the thirteenth, one of Herman's young friends, Simon Blow, brought a contemporary from Cambridge and Ivy talked without being prompted about Thackeray, saying she was reading *Vanity Fair* and urging them both to another slice of Rex Britcher's plum cake (' "It was made by a member of your own sex," she said encouragingly'[134]).

Soon afterwards she was confined to bed again with bronchitis, and the doctor (Pasmore was away) arranged for a night nurse so as to spare Mary. At their last meeting she had electrified Julian by saying under her breath, as her head went down after a particularly sweet goodbye, 'Why doesn't he go away and leave me alone?' Herman sat with her for the last time on 26 August, and her last words that evening to Mary, who had gone in later to ask if she needed anything, were 'Leave me alone'.[135] That night she took the nurse for her brother. She died the next day, Wednesday, 27 August, at about half past nine in the morning. The night nurse had gone off duty, Ivy had said she would like breakfast and, when Mary returned with tea, toast and marmalade, had asked for a cup of hot milk: by the time Mary got back with it, Ivy was dead.

Her mind was clear, her death peaceful, she had kept her maid to the end. Whatever the question in her last letter to Francis may have meant, there can, as he said, be no doubt that Ivy herself had been drunk with loss and beat the ground, and that she had never let the deeper things escape. She was missed long and sadly by an unusually large circle of friends. Mourners at her funeral, instructed to return from Putney Vale crematorium to collect their bequests at a last tea party in Braemar Mansions—many of them meeting for the first time as they jostled in the hall with their loot—felt they were taking part in a final strange scene of Ivy's making. She herself had perhaps foreseen something of the sort when she drew up her will;

and perhaps her own deathbed had not been entirely out of mind when she made Selina Middleton take to hers in *The Mighty and Their Fall*:

'You don't sound as if you were going to die,' said Hugo.

'No,' said Selina, almost smiling. 'And I can see the nurse agrees. She feels I am not fit for a higher life; and I would choose the lower one. And she thinks I should be afraid to die.'

'And you are afraid of nothing,' said her son.

'I don't feel I am going to meet my Maker. And if I were, I should not fear him. He has not earned the feeling. I almost think he ought to fear me.'[136]

APPENDICES

GENEALOGICAL TREE

NOTES

SELECT BIBLIOGRAPHY

INDEX

APPENDIX ONE

Burnetts and Comptons

SO MANY MISLEADING claims have been made for I. Compton-Burnett's family tree that it is perhaps worth summarizing what little factual evidence survives. The earliest Burnett transactions which I have succeeded in tracing are the marriages of Ivy's great-grandfather, Richard Burnett, at St Maurice's in 1803, and his presumed brother William at St Bartholomew Hyde, Winchester, in 1811. Richard came from Wherwell, William from Barton Stacey. The explanation of this discrepancy seems to be that Gavelacre Farm, which was rented by Burnetts between 1790 and 1835, lies at the meeting place of three parishes, the farmhouse itself being just within Longparish boundary on one bank of the Test and much of its land in Barton Stacey on the other side of the river, a few hundred yards upstream from Wherwell parish boundary. A family living at Gavelacre would have been free to take its choice between these three parishes.

Barton Stacey Churchwarden's Accounts record Burnetts paying rent on Gavelacre land, while a 'Sarah Burnett of Gavelacre' was married at Longparish in 1812 (perhaps the same Sarah Burnett who had witnessed the marriage of William Burnett of Barton Stacey to Anne Compton at Winchester the year before). A witness to this wedding was the John Burnett who rented Gavelacre land from 1811 until his death in 1835, and who must have been kinsman to Richard and William, possibly their eldest brother. There are no entries in Barton Stacey rate books between 1794 and 1811, but before that a William Burnett was tenant of Gavelacre. None of these Burnetts left wills. A search of the registers at Longparish, Barton Stacey, Wherwell and the neighbouring parishes (Whitchurch, Stockbridge, Upper Clatford and Chilbolton, as well as the voluminous records at Andover which contain a fair number of Burnetts) reveals nothing of interest* save that,

---

* The only Burnetts recorded at Wherwell are Ann, wife of James, buried in 1754 and —more promising—Harry, son of Richard and Mary, baptized in 1793 (Ivy's great-grandfather, Richard Burnett of Wherwell, was born in 1790); Barton Stacey has only two baptisms—John, bastard son of Ann Burnett, and the daughter of Isaac and Mary Burnett, travellers, both in 1795.

between 1737 and 1759, Henry and Hannah Burnett brought nine children
to be baptized at Longparish: a Richard, a William and a John were among
this couple's six sons, any one of whom might have been father to Richard of
Wherwell and William of Barton Stacey.

Their marked absence from Church of England records of birth, marriage
and death almost certainly means that the Gavelacre Burnetts were nonconformist. There was a chapel at Wherwell from 1712 (Willis' *Dissenters'
Meeting House Certificates*) but no records survive. The flourishing Independent Chapel four miles away at Andover, where 'Mr Burnet gave the charge'
at the ordination of a new minister in 1739, records no other Burnetts among
its congregation between 1730 and 1790 (when records cease for the next
sixteen years)—but its members were Congregationalists, which may perhaps cast some light on why Ivy's two uncles (grandsons to Richard Burnett
of Wherwell) later became Congregationalist ministers.

Richard and William become easier to trace after their marriages: William
settled as a tenant farmer at Baybridge in the parish of Owslebury, Richard
returned to Wherwell where his seven children were baptized between 1804
and 1815. He is not listed in the Wherwell Poor Book as a ratepayer, but
from 1804 to 1816 he appears on Land Tax Assessments as a tenant of John
Iremonger who was lord of the manor of Wherwell. Two notes on a
disputed right-of-way in the parish register, dated 1805 and 1812, are signed
by Richard Burnett as parish overseer and churchwarden to the vicar,
Richard Iremonger (the squire's family, being patrons of the living, were
often incumbents as well). Probably Richard Burnett had obtained this
tenancy a year after his marriage on the strength of the loan from his father-
in-law, John Compton,* who died in 1814 and whose will records that he
had already lent £300 each to Richard and William Burnett; he left the
interest in her lifetime to his widow and required her to bequeath the original
capital sums to his sons-in-law—which she did, providing only that there
should be enough money left after paying other legacies, and signing the
will with her mark on 1 May 1814. She died the year after and it must have
been a considerable relief to the Burnetts when the estate was sworn at
£1500, a sum amply sufficient to provide for both daughters' inheritances.
Richard seems to have left Wherwell round about this time and is next heard
of in 1834, living thirty miles away at Alverstoke where four of his children
married Wilsons in the parish church of St Mary.

These Wilsons do not seem to have been persons of consequence in Alverstoke. Their family left no wills (or not at any rate wills proved in the Arch-

---

* The registers of St Bartholomew Hyde, Winchester, record the marriage of John
Compton to Elizabeth Ellis in 1771, and the baptism of his son and three daughters—
Catherine Maria, Ivy's great-grandmother, in March 1774, and Anne Hutchins, Ivy's
great-great-aunt by blood and by marriage, in 1785.

deacons and Bishops and peculiar courts of the diocese of Winchester), no certain entries in the copious parish registers at Alverstoke and Gosport (apart from their marriages—which suggests that they too were nonconformist, since nonconformists at that time were commonly married, though not baptized or buried, by the Church of England), and no records in Land Tax Assessments (unless perhaps the 'J. Wilson' who had a small holding assessed at one shilling and eightpence in 1810 and 1820 might be identified with the 'James Wilson, farmer' who was Jesse's father).

I can find no trace of Richard Burnett's son Charles and his wife Sarah (née Wilson) in the first six years of their marriage; the 1841 census records that Charles Compton Burnett was then living at Hamptonworth, a hamlet in the eastern part of Redlynch, that his household included no servants, and that (since his three elder children, born in 1835, 1837 and 1839, were not born in Wiltshire) he had been there for at most two years. The birth of James Compton Burnett in 1840 is recorded in the Redlynch register and at the Principal Probate Registry. Such information as I have on Charles' subsequent career comes chiefly from entries in local directories,* from which it is possible to piece together a complicated pattern of business relationships. Ivy's great uncle Richard Compton Burnett (who gave his occupation as 'labourer' on the birth certificate of his daughter Sarah in 1847) and his wife, Agnes the bonnet-maker, are found from 1847 at 3 West Street, Southampton, moving in 1853 to 5 Pembroke Square, and being joined in 1851 by Charles Compton Burnett, who describes himself as a shopkeeper at 74 French Street. Four years later Charles begins dealing in coal and corn and by 1859 there is a joint operation, Richard advertising as a coal carrier from Church Lane, French Street, and Charles as a coal dealer from Richard's old address in Pembroke Square, while a '— Burnett' has appeared selling coal at Millbrook. (One may suspect that this is Charles Compton, using the Pembroke Square address for business purposes.) In 1861 'Charles C. Burnett' is back as a coal dealer at 74 French Street and there is another Charles (possibly a nephew—it can hardly have been his eldest son, who obtained his first Congregational ministry at Sheerness the following year) dealing in coal at Pembroke Square. The situation is the same in 1862 but by 1865 Charles Compton has become a dairyman at Mousehole, Millbrook, and in 1869 has moved to Pinks Farm at Dibden, while a Charles Burnett is shown at Mousehole and a William Wilson Burnett deals in coal and corn at Millbrook.

By 1880 Charles Compton Burnett has disappeared for ever from the

---

* *Southampton Directories* for 1803, 1811 (ed. Cunningham), 1836 (Fletcher), 1845, 1849 (Rayner), 1851, 1853, 1855, 1857 (Forbes), 1859 (Forbes), 1861 (Forbes), 1863, 1865, 1876 (Cox), 1878 (Cox), 1880 (Cox). Also *Post Office Directory of Hampshire* 1867 and 1875; *Mercer and Crocker's General, Topographical and Historical Directory for Hampshire* 1871, and *William White's Directory of Hampshire* 1878.

Hampshire directories. He seems to have moved to the Midlands to be near his son John, who lived at Bedford; his death certificate records that he was an annuitant when he died aged seventy-two of a diseased liver, 'A Feble Heart' and 'A Fainting Fit' on 21 August 1883, at Leighton Buzzard, being attended by his son John and leaving no will.

APPENDIX TWO

Helen Cam's key to Dolores

DR HELEN CAM (1885–1968) was not only a student at Holloway in Ivy's last two years but also a lecturer at the college from 1912 to 1921. She later became Vice-Principal of Girton and, in 1948, the first woman to hold a chair at Harvard; her reputation as an historian for scrupulous factual accuracy, and her knowledge of both senior and junior common rooms at Holloway, suggest that one could hardly ask for more reliable evidence. Her key, written at the back of a copy of *Dolores* which is signed at the front 'H. M. Cam 1912', runs as follows:

Miss Cliff	=	K. S. Block
„ Butler	=	M. E. J. Taylor
„ Dorrington	=	M. Cunningham
„ Greenlow	=	C. Frost
„ Lemaître	=	M. Péchinet
„ Adam	=	M. Hayes Robinson
Claverhouse? (looks only)		T. Seccombe
		Visiting lecturer in history
		1905—

A brief survey of the evidence suggests that 'actual life' supplied Ivy, at the start of her career, with characters who were not so much developed or made over as simply transferred direct from fact to fiction. Photographs in the archive at Holloway (mostly taken by Miss Frost, who was a keen amateur photographer) confirm that the six staff portraits in *Dolores* were faithfully copied from the models listed above; and the reader may like to compare the photograph following page 430 with the relevant passages from pages 97–100 of the novel, printed below together with biographical and other details:

The dispenser of the beverage is crossing the room with movements of easy briskness. She is a woman of forty, older at a glance; with a well-cut, dark-skinned face, iron-grey hair whose waving is conquered by its drawing to the knot in the neck, and dark eyes keen under thick, black brows. That is Miss Cliff, the lecturer in English literature.

[Miss Cliff's chief characteristics are her keen feminism and a 'half-philosophizing interest in her kind', both undoubtedly shared by Katharine Block who was Senior Staff Lecturer in English at Holloway, and who had her fortieth birthday in Ivy's third year. Miss Block, known to her colleagues as 'our intellectual conscience', had joined the college in 1899 and left it only on her retirement twenty-seven years later: 'There was iron in her; she went through the bogus, the pretentious, the sentimental like a knife through cheese. . . . She worked hard herself and would tolerate no slackers, but she invested the routine of the business of teaching and learning with an aura of greatness.' (*R.H.C. College Letter*, December 1954). She also wrote the college song:

> Our College is well-founded,
> Foursquare a stately pile . . .
> Great women watched it growing,
> Just women, steadfast, wise;
> They set the roses blowing,
> They planted memories.
>
> The sacred torch of learning
> They in our halls did light;
> The right to keep it burning,
> They won for us in fight. . . .]

The companion to whom she is handing a cup—the lecturer in classics, Miss Butler,—and who takes it with a word in a vein of pleasantry, is a small, straight woman, a few years younger; whose parted hair leaves the forehead fully shown, and whose hazel eyes have humour in their rapid glancing.

[For a comparison between Miss Butler and Margaret Taylor, see p. 140. Miss Taylor, who had come to Holloway from a lecturing post at Girton, retired in 1954 and died in 1964: 'She watched firmly over our morals and could be highly outspoken—a grand fighter for causes she approved of: Women in the Church, and Woman's Suffrage, and an equally fierce denouncer of things she disliked, such as bad grammar and slovenly speech.']*

'I remember the last time you made it,' said a genial, guttural voice at the side of Miss Butler—the voice of Miss Dorrington, the lecturer in German,

* All the quotations marked with an asterisk come from Miss Delp's pamphlet, *Royal Holloway College 1908-1914*.

and a strong illustration of the power of moral attractiveness over the physical opposite; which, in her case, depended on uncouth features, an eruptive skin, and general ungainliness.

[Miss Dorrington is given no particular characteristic beyond her geniality, which is several times employed in the novel to soothe other people's ruffled feelings. Marjorie Cunningham, head of the German department at Holloway from 1900 to 1906 (when she left to become Warden of Trinity Hall, Dublin), had also suffered from an unsightly skin disease. 'She was Irish . . . and she brought a breath of untrammelled gaiety into the SCR', wrote Miss Block in the *College Letter* for November 1941. 'She had a heart overflowing with loving kindness, and no one who sought her in trouble for advice or for comfort went unhelped away.']

A short, quaint-looking, middle-aged lady, with a pathetic manner which somehow was comical in its union with her calling of mathematical teacher, looked up with a slow smile.

[This is Miss Greenlow, whose 'comical pathos' is mentioned whenever she puts in an appearance. Catherine Frost was senior lecturer in mathematics at Holloway from 1887 to 1907, and the jubilee booklet, *Royal Holloway College 1887–1937*, refers on page 28 to 'Miss Frost, demurely concealing a bagful of mirth and mimicry. . . .']

A lady who was standing apart came forward to join in the talk. She was a Frenchwoman, over fifty, with a sallow, clever face, and sad brown eyes which lighted with her smile; who had led a difficult life in the land of her forced adoption, and lived with its daughters, feeling that she owed it no gratitude.

[This is Miss Lemaître, who is something of a wit—the most nearly frivolous member of *Dolores'* staff common room—and whose ironic levity is keenly resented by its sterner inmates. Marie Péchinet, head of the French department at Holloway from 1887 to 1909 (Pernel Strachey was her assistant in Ivy's day), was 'commonly called "Peck" and not without reason—her Gallic wit was *very* sure of aim. She once returned the essay of a rather cocksure first year scholar with: "Here is your essay, Miss So-and-so, I don't mark below delta minus."'* People who were not afraid of her found her enchanting ('just meeting her in the corridor or at her door allowed me to catch something of her sparkle')*; and both Miss Delp and the anonymous obituarist in the *College Letter* for July 1912 pay tribute to her stoicism in a life dogged by 'bad health' and 'disappointments'.]

The speaker was Miss Adam, the lecturer in history—younger than the others, and young for her youth; with her zeal for the world where she had her life, not untempered by a wistfulness on the world outside, and her faith in the creed of her nurture as untouched by any of the usual shattering forces, as by her special knowledge of its growth.

[Miss Adam is alternately petted and teased by her colleagues, who find something irresistibly fetching in her combination of youth and innocence with learning (and, when someone suggests that she may once have had a proposal, 'Miss Adam yielded without great unwillingness to the impulse to look conscious', p. 329). Margaret Hayes Robinson, head of the History department, had come to Holloway straight from taking a first at Oxford in 1898; she was a good ten years younger than any of the others except Miss Taylor, and the only one who married (an Oxford don in 1916). 'To work with her was not so much to become her pupil as to share an adventure: friendliness and democracy were the natural traditions of the history school she founded. . . . In that smaller Holloway of twenty to thirty years ago, many outside her own school knew her well, and to know her was to love her,' wrote Dr Cam in the *College Letter* when she died in 1930.]

[Thomas Seccombe's influence on Claverhouse is examined in the text on pp. 157-9; and it is perhaps not uninteresting to note that three of these comparatively crude copies in *Dolores* provided starting points for some rather more complex characters among the staff of Josephine Napier's school in *More Women Than Men*, where Miss Lemaître's neutral attitude to Miss Adam has grown into the highly charged relationship between Maria Rosetti and the young and charming newcomer from Oxford, Helen Keats; while traces of Miss Greenlow may still be seen in Miss Munday's subtle and secretive sense of humour.]

GENEALOGICAL TREE

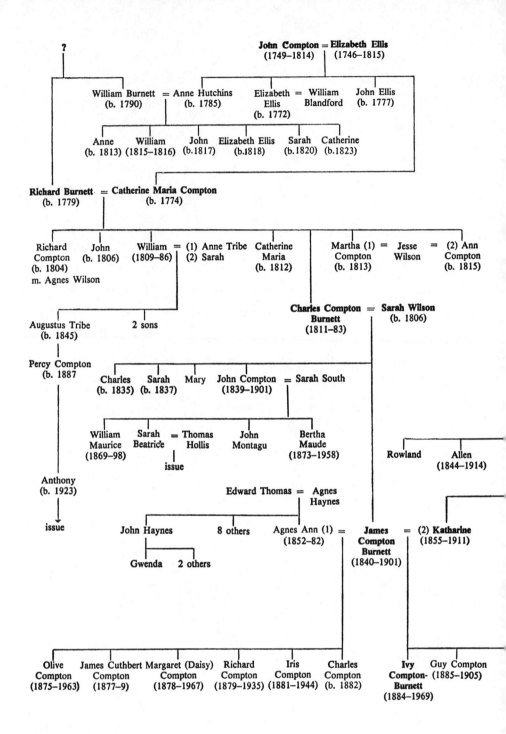

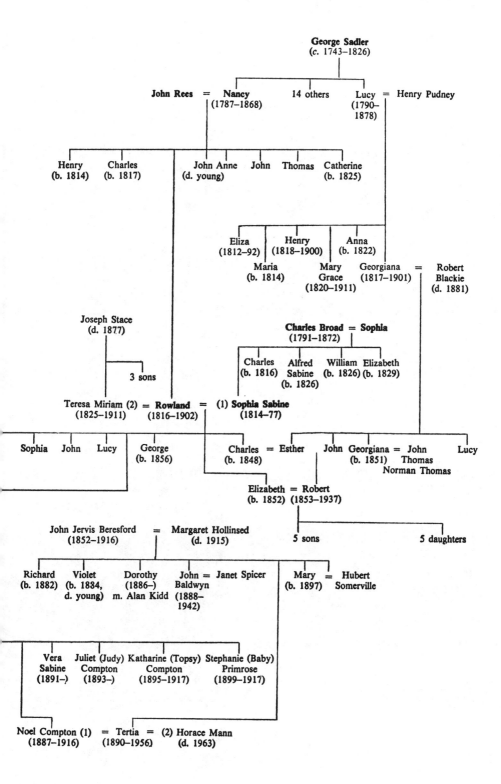

NOTES

By far the greater part of my information came from talking to people who knew Ivy, so the reader may safely assume that the formula 'x or y said something' means (unless another source is given) that x or y said it to me. Any unattributed quotation about the Compton-Burnett family comes from my many conversations with Ivy's sisters, Vera and Juliet Compton-Burnett.

Noel Compton-Burnett's letters to Oscar Browning are in Hastings Public Library; his letters to Sir Charles Webster are among Webster's papers at the London School of Economics; those to Ivy and to Elliott Felkin are among the Marsden-Smedley papers; and those to Jack Beresford belong to the Beresford family. Apart from these, all letters belong, unless otherwise indicated, to the people to whom they were written.

Abbreviations used in the notes

The works of I. Compton-Burnett distinguished by initials, as P&M = *Pastors and Masters*, B&S = *Brothers and Sisters*, F&Fate = *A Father and His Fate*, F&Fortune = *A Family and a Fortune*, H&Head = *A House and Its Head*, H&History = *A Heritage and Its History*, etc. With the exception of *Dolores* (published by Blackwood, Edinburgh and London, 1971), page numbers refer to Gollancz's uniform edition published in 1972, and are the same for all subsequent reissues.

Burkhart 1	*The Art of I. Compton-Burnett* ed. Charles Burkhart
Burkhart 2	*Herman and Nancy and Ivy* by Charles Burkhart
Burkhart 3	*Twentieth Century Literature*, 'Ivy Compton-Burnett Issue', 1979, guest ed. Charles Burkhart
Butler	*The Note-Books of Samuel Butler*
Clarke	*Life and Work of James Compton Burnett, M.D.*, by J. H. Clarke
Dick	*Ivy and Stevie* by Kay Dick
DC	*Dover Chronicle*
DE	*Dover Express*
DT	*Dover Telegraph*
Fedden	'Recollections of Ivy Compton-Burnett' by Robin Fedden, *Cornhill Magazine*, Winter 1969/70

50 Reasons	*Fifty Reasons for Being a Homoeopath* by James Compton Burnett
Forster	*Goldsworthy Lowes Dickinson* by E. M. Forster
Greig	*Ivy Compton-Burnett: A Memoir* by Cicely Greig
HW	*Homoeopathic World*
Marsden-Smedley papers	Miscellaneous documents belonging to I.C.B. and M.J., inherited by Hester Marsden-Smedley and now in the possession of her daughter, Henrietta Williamson
Mitchell NS	Julian Mitchell in the *New Statesman*, 5 September 1969
Mowll	Compton Burnett papers in the possession of Mowll and Mowll of Dover
Sprigge	*The Life of Ivy Compton-Burnett* by Elizabeth Sprigge
V&A papers	Miscellaneous waste papers on the backs of which M.J. compiled her furniture notes, deposited with the Furniture and Woodwork Dept. of the Victoria and Albert Museum
Wortham	*Victorian Eton and Cambridge* by H. E. Wortham.

PREFACE

1 *The Writing on the Wall and Other Literary Essays* by Mary McCarthy, p.143; the luncheon at the Ritz was arranged by Sonia Orwell who described it to me, and so did Miss McCarthy, in a letter, 25 July 1983.

2 Blurb to early Penguin editions of her novels.

3 BBC Radio interview with H.S., May 1984.

4 E&B p.289.

5 D&S p.149.

6 BBC Radio interview with John Bowen, see Chapter XIV, pp.418–19 and note 57.

7 B&S p.144.

8 D&S p.183.

CHAPTER I   Parents and Grandparents

1 This and the previous quotation from Clarke, p.4.

2 The Earl of Dartmouth, quoted in *Bishop Burnet's History of His Own Times,* edited by His Son, Oxford, 1833, vol. I, p.5 note.

3 See 'The Family Burnett of Leys' from the mss. of the late George Burnett, LL.D, Lyon King of Arms, *Aberdeen University Studies No. 4,* Aberdeen, 1906, p.140.

4 Clarke, p.5; the next two quotations in this paragraph from *50 Reasons,* p.46, and Clarke, p.5.

5 *Ecce Medicus,* p.41. (Dr Burnett afterwards claimed to have been at Edinburgh

University, where records show only a 'James Burnett' who matriculated in arts subjects 1865–6; Ivy's father is said to have hesitated at first between philology and medicine so, if this was our man, he must promptly have abandoned the arts in favour of medicine at Vienna, where he was duly awarded an honorary M.B.)

6   Miss Vera and Miss Juliet Compton-Burnett; further quotations about their family come from Ivy's sisters, unless otherwise attributed.

7   *50 Reasons*, p.38.

8   Clarke, p.8; the next quotation from *50 Reasons*, p.38.

9   *50 Reasons*, pp.32–5. There is an excellent account of conditions in the Glasgow Medical School at this time in *Reminiscences of an Old Physician* by Robert Bell (John Murray, 1924.)

10 *50 Reasons*, p.158; the comparison with St Paul comes in *Tumours of the Breast*, p.15; the next two quotations in this paragraph from Clarke, p.44, and from Dr Bodman's 'Richard Hughes Memorial Lecture'.

11 Annual Report of the Chester Free Homoeopathic Dispensary, HW November 1882, *Diseases of the Veins*, p.61, and *Curability of Cataract*, p.177.

12 Dr Burnett sold 17 Hamilton Square in 1879 (Mowll). His earlier addresses from his marriage certificate, the birth certificates of his children and medical directories; information on the Thomas family from Miss Gwenda Haynes-Thomas; the advertisement from the *Homoeopathic Directory* for 1853 (Edward Thomas later moved both businesses from Bridge Street to Pepper Street).

13 Clarke, p.iii; the previous quotation from *Gout and Its Cure*, p.158.

14 *Diseases of the Liver*, p.33; the other case histories cited in this paragraph from *50 Reasons*, pp.220–6; *Curability of Cataract* pp.2–14; *Diseases of the Skin*, p.17.

15 HW July 1880; the next two quotations from HW August 1880 and September 1879.

16 James Cuthbert Compton Burnett was born at 51 Hamilton Square on 17 July 1877, and died on 29 May 1879 at Moselle Villa, Lee Road, Lee, of 'concussion of the brain 25 days'; the death was certified by his father. I can find no report of an inquest (or of any accident on 4 May) in the local papers, and Ivy's sisters have no recollection of this half-brother's existence.

17 HW January 1882 (Edward Thomas was a fully qualified member of the Pharmaceutical Association of Great Britain).

18 B&S pp.7–8; Ivy's sisters confirm that this is an exact likeness of their mother.

19 See family tree. One of Rowland Rees' first cousins had married a Robert Blackie of Liverpool whose daughter Georgiana was married in 1871 to a Liverpool businessman named John Thomas Norman Thomas. I have found no connection between this John Thomas and Agnes Thomas' family in Chester; but in 1875 Georgiana's brother and sister, Robert and Esther Blackie, married their second cousins, Elizabeth and Charles Rees (sister and brother to Ivy's mother), and it was Robert Blackie who—acting presumably on advice from the Thomases in Liverpool—took Katharine up to London to see Dr Burnett.

20   *50 Reasons*, pp.153–6; Ivy's sisters confirm that their mother was 'the patient in question'.

21   *Dolores*, p.39.

22   M&F p.43.

23   Information from Miss Gwenda Haynes-Thomas (who had met her much older cousins, Olive and Daisy Compton-Burnett, on visits to her parents' home, and remembered hearing as a child the sad story of her Aunt Agnes: 'My mother used to say that all her brothers and sisters had been deeply fond of her and greatly mourned her').

24   *Vaccinosis*, preface dated March 1884 (this, like several of Dr Burnett's early books, was printed by Edward Thomas in Chester).

25   Mitchell NS.

26   See Kenneth Walker's *Martello Towers and the Defence of N.E. Essex in the Napoleonic War* for a detailed account of John Rees' activities at Clacton. Mr Walker assures me that 'Charles Rees' in this article is a misprint for 'John Rees', and I am greatly indebted to him for information about the marriage of Ivy's great-grandparents on 23 December 1813, at the Great Clacton parish church where their eight children were baptized between 1814 and 1825; the ancient inhabitant who told Mr Walker about the coal business was born round about 1860.

27   Mitchell NS.

28   Believed by her Compton-Burnett grandchildren to have been named for a Huguenot ancestor, Sir Avery Sabine, which is perfectly possible since the name is common among Kentish families and seems to have come originally from Avery Sabine, *c.* 1580–1648, a wealthy woollen-merchant and three times Mayor of Canterbury; a kinsman of his was Sir Avery Sabine, Bart., whose younger brother Phillip took as his second wife in the late seventeenth century Elizabeth Woodward of St Mary's, Dover (*Sabin(e): The History of an English Surname* by W.H.W. Sabine [London and New York, 1953]). Sophia's father died in 1872, leaving £4000 among his surviving children and grandchildren.

29   B&S p.5.

30   Rule's *Recollections*, p.77; the next quotation in this paragraph is from *Wesleyan Local Preachers* by the author of 'Tyneside Celebrities' (W. D. Lawson) (New-castle-upon-Tyne, 1874), p.297, which contains an enthusiastic account of con-temporary mission work. Rowland Rees' conversion, his subsequent religious activity, his keen support of foreign missions and his address to the China Breakfast Meeting were reported throughout his life in the local press and summed up in the *Methodist Recorder*, 30 July 1878 and 14 August 1902, and the *Methodist Times*, 31 July 1902.

31   This and the next two quotations from an article, 'Mr Rowland Rees, J.P.', in a series on 'The Mayors of Dover' published *c.* 1890 in a local paper (almost certainly the *Dover Express*) and kindly supplied by the Librarian of Dover Public Library.

32 DC 22 June 1850; for the development of this rearguard action see also DC 22 December 1849, 13 July 1850, 3 August 1850 and DT 14 June 1849, 4 August 1849.

33 DC 26 October 1851; the following quotations in this paragraph from DT 13 November 1858, DC 23 June 1860, DT 15 December 1860.

34 DC 10 August 1861; the next three quotations from DC 11 May and 16 March 1861, and the whole affair is reported blow by blow in both papers from March to mid-November (when Rowland Rees triumphantly settled his libel action out of court).

35 *The Life of Hugh Price Hughes*, p.78.

36 DC 18 February 1871.

37 She was the only daughter of Joseph Stace who died on 23 January 1877, leaving £20,000 to be divided equally between 'my dear daughter' and his three sons; her marriage settlement assigning the capital to her trustees in her lifetime was drawn up on 29 January 1879 (Mowll).

38 Mitchell NS.

39 DE 27 February 1885.

40 DE 18 January 1884; the previous quotation from DE 23 November 1883.

41 This and the next quotation from *The Life of Hugh Price Hughes*, pp.78–9; the *Spectator*'s comment is cited in Maldwyn Edwards' *Methodism and England*, p.150.

42 This and the next quotation from DE 5 June 1885 (Rowland Rees was asked to retire, and did so on 25 February 1885; a contemporary minute at the Harbour Board records that he felt himself entitled to £70 more than the £250 pension accorded him by his employers).

43 DE 11 January 1884 (further reports on 1 and 8 February); the next two quotations from HW January 1883 and *50 Reasons*, p.151.

44 HW January 1882.

CHAPTER II 1884–1896

1 To Barbara Robinson.

2 Burkhart 1, pp.28–9.

3 Information from Maureen Beresford.

4 P&C pp.122–3.

5 MWTM p.9.

6 P&C p.253.

7 This and the previous quotation from G&G pp.168 and 171–2.

8 *Further Extracts from the Notebooks of Samuel Butler*, edited by T. A. Bartholomew (Cape, 1934), p.112.

9 Dick, p.4.

10 *Delicate, Backward, Puny and Stunted Children*, pp.12–13; Ivy's sisters confirm that the family described here is Dr Burnett's own.

11   Mitchell NS.

12   B&S p.10; there is a portrait of Minnie following page 174.

13   Joseph Smith, Master Draper, died on 7 October 1912 (leaving his house called 'Boscombe' and chattels—including 'my oil painting "Highland Cattle"' but excluding 'my presentation clock in oak case with bracket'—and the income from £17,737 to his second wife in her lifetime, with instructions that she provide a home for her stepdaughters, Ellen, Alice and Emily Smith, each of whom would come into an annuity of £150 on her death).

14   Mitchell NS.

15   Letter from Ivy to Barbara Robinson, 21 November 1964.

16   P&P p.10.

17   This and the next quotation from Mitchell NS.

18   *Delicate, Backward, Puny and Stunted Children*, p.65; for Dr Burnett's advanced views on the health and punishment of children, *ibid*, pp.71, 43 and 151; for his views on vegetables, *Gout and Its Cure*, pp.135–6.

19   'Harrow, including Pinner' by Diane K. Bolton, *Victoria County History, Middlesex*, vol.iv; information on Dr Burnett's acquisition of property from Mowll.

20   *Pike's Directory of Brighton and Hove*, 1895.

21   Dick, p.5.

22   Simon Blow.

23   Letter from Elizabeth Taylor to Robert Liddell, undated, *c.* 1964; the next two memories of Ivy's childhood come from Francis King and Julian Mitchell.

24   D&D p.92.

25   P&C p.42.

26   P&C pp.51–2.

27   This and the next quotation from P&C p.307 and P&P p.46.

28   E&B p.47.

29   Burkhart 1, p.31.

30   E&B p.49; the next three quotations from E&B pp.81, 246 and 254.

31   D&S p.144.

32   D&D p.125.

33   Dick, pp.2–3.

34   P&P p.12.

35   *The Daisy Chain*, pp.163–4; the next two quotations from *The One Too Many*, vol.1, pp.151 and 104.

36   *Delicate, Backward, Puny and Stunted Children*, pp.89–92. (The phrase 'and twelve of them make a dozen'—meaning that the things in question were adequate but no more—was such a favourite with Dr Burnett that it became a family joke.)

37   Dick, p.8.

38   P&P p.15.

CHAPTER III 1897–1901

1 H&Head p.20.

2 Julian Mitchell (his notes), who also remembered Ivy's description of her Uncle George.

3 M&W p.8.

4 Contemporary cutting, supplied by Kenneth Walker, to whom I am indebted for this account of Robert Blackie's career; details of property transactions from Mowll; and the wills of Robert Blackie, Robert Blackie senior and James Compton Burnett.

5 M&W p.271.

6 This and the previous quotations about missionary work among Ivy's relations come from the section entitled 'Two Elect Ladies and a Nephew' in a pamphlet, 'Lest We Forget. The Record of Fifty Years' Work in the Clacton-on-Sea Circuit of the Wesleyan Methodist Church. 1875–1925' by the Rev. George C. Gould (Clacton, 1925).

7 *Dolores* p.72.

8 The Rev. John Brown's funeral oration for John Compton Burnett, reported in the *Bedfordshire Times*, 21 March 1901. ('. . . It is no mere figure of speech to say that he [Mr Burnett] gave his very heart and life to the village churches and the village pastors of this country. It is simply true to say that for them he laboured up to and beyond his strength.') For an account of religious life in Bedford at this time, see *Gathering Up the Threads* by Florence Ada Keynes (who was John Brown's daughter and Maynard Keynes' mother); (W. Heffer, Cambridge, 1950); *Bunyan Meeting Bedford 1650–1950* by H. G. Tibbut (Bedford, 1950); and *The Life of Mark Rutherford* by Himself (William Hale White) (O.U.P. 1913).

9 'Touchstone' in 'Bedfordian's Diary', *Bedfordshire Times*, 29 March 1963.

10 F&Fortune p.20; see also pp.25, 292 *et passim*.

11 Dick p.3.

12 M&F p.18.

13 Butler, p.35 (Ivy's copy of the *Note-Books,* with her annotations, is among the Marsden-Smedley papers.

14 D&S p.125.

15 B&S p.7; the following quotation about Ivy's mother from Dick, p.4.

16 B&S p.28; the previous quotation from P&C p.52.

17 M&M p.151; the following quotation from M&W p.272.

18 TWTW p.212; the next quotation from p.109.

19 TWTW p.85.

20 L&F p.62.

21 TWTW p.137; the previous quotation from p.21.

22 E&B p.53.

23 *Delicate, Backward, Puny and Stunted Children,* p.13 (see Chapter II, note 10).

24 Mrs J. A. Elliott; the previous quotation from Dick, p.2.

25 P&P p.17.

26 *The Daisy Chain,* p.163; the previous quotation from *The One Too Many,* vol. I, p.3.

27 Mrs Elliott.

28 TWTW p.93 (Miss Marathon teaches mathematics at Clemence's school, like Miss Marsland at Ivy's; Miss Laurence, like Miss Laura Cadwallader, is the classics mistress).

29 P&M p.51.

30 This and the two previous quotations from Mr L. R. Conisbee's recollections of Bedford at the turn of the century, in correspondence with the author.

31 This and the two following quotations about Howard College from Miss Grace J. Fothergill, who was a pupil at the school 1898–1902; Ivy's anecdote about her cousin from Soame Jenyns.

32 TWTW pp.108–9.

33 TWTW p.79; the next quotation from p.21.

34 *Period Piece,* p.72.

35 TWTW p.214.

36 L&F p.62.

37 TWTW p.126; the two previous quotations from pp.118 and 125.

CHAPTER IV   James Compton Burnett

1 Clarke, p.55.

2 *50 Reasons,* p.281.

3 B&S p.7; the next quotation from p.104.

4 Dr Kraft, quoted by Clarke (p.68), who also reprints obituaries from *The Times* (5 April), the *Westminster Gazette* (14 April), the *Monthly Homoeopathic Review* (May), and his own from HW (May). The quotation from TWTW is on p.241.

5 *Diseases of the Spleen,* pp.59–60.

6 HW December 1880; the three previous quotations from *New Cure of Consumption,* first preface, *Ecce Medicus,* p.3, *Tumours of the Breast,* p.15, and *50 Reasons,* p.293.

7 HW Sept. 1879; the previous quotation from *50 Reasons,* p.75.

8 B&S p.29.

9 *Tumours of the Breast,* pp.84–6 (needless to say, the clergyman retired in disarray and the lady's tumour was with time duly cured).

10 M&F p.166.

11 *Tumours of the Breast,* p.147; the previous quotation from HW November 1883.

12 'Richard Hughes Memorial Lecture' by Frank Bodman (to whom I am greatly indebted for this account of homoeopathic internal politics).

13 Clarke's *Life of Dr. Skinner*, p.86; the next two quotations from HW May 1901 (unsigned editorial, but Clarke was then editor and the style is recognizably his) and Clarke, p.44.

14 *Cure of Consumption*, p.184; the next three quotations from *50 Reasons*, p.219, *On Neuralgia*, p. 139, and *Gout and Its Cure*, p.27.

15 *Ecce Medicus*, p.52; the next quotation from Clarke, p.41.

16 *50 Reasons*, pp.3–4.

17 Prescribed in *Diseases of the Spleen*, pp.97 and 11; *50 Reasons*, pp.73 and 252–5; *Gout and Its Cure*, pp.41–8; and *Diseases of the Liver*, p.30.

18 Unsigned, but identified by Dr Bodman; the following quotation from Bodman's 'Memorial Lecture'.

19 *Dolores*, pp.9 and 10.

20 *Curability of Tumours*, p.163.

21 *50 Reasons*, p.24.

22 HW September 1879.

23 Information from Alison Waley; the previous quotations from B&S pp.7 and 25.

24 F&Fortune p.16; for Dr Burnett's similar sentiments, see Chapter I, p.12.

25 D&S p.183.

26 *Diseases of the Spleen*, pp.19–20.

27 *50 Reasons*, p.93; the next two quotations from Clarke, p.106, and HW December 1880.

28 *Cure of Consumption*, pp.141 and 92.

29 Clarke, p.6.

30 G&G pp.17 and 62; the next four quotations from G&G pp.24 and 63, D&S p.23.

31 D&S p.215; for Dr Burnett's identical sentiments, see Chapter II, p.54.

32 *Cure of Consumption*, second preface.

33 F&Fortune p.186; the previous quotation from pp.57–8.

34 Information from Madge Ashland.

35 B&S pp.25–6; the previous quotation on p.25.

36 Arthur Waley said so to Barbara and Walter Robinson; Elliott Felkin told Raisley Moorsom.

37 B&S p.32.

38 Butler, p.26; the two previous quotations from Clarke, p.55.

39 *On Neuralgia*, p.167.

40 *On the Prevention of Hare-Lip*, p.7.

CHAPTER V   Katharine Compton Burnett

1 B&S p.125.

2 MWTM p.104.

3 M&S p.110.

4   B&S p.119; quotations from B&S in this and the next two paragraphs all come from pp.118–28.

5   E&B p.251.

6   D&S p.43.

7   D&S p.39.

8   P&C p.34.

9   B&S pp.131–2.

10   D&D p.85.

11   D&S pp.114–15; the next quotation from p.10.

12   P&C p.242.

13   E&B p.242.

14   Burkhart 1, pp.27–8; the next quotation on p.31.

15   B&S p.87.

16   B&S p.152.

17   L&F p.9; the previous quotation from F&Fate p.33 (for Sophia Stace's looks, see Chapter I, p.17).

18   F&Fate p.23.

19   F&Fate p.35; the next quotation from p.36.

20   *Dolores*, p.45.

21   L&F p.18.

22   P&C p.142.

23   Olive, according to her half-sisters, had 'a tyrannical nature' bravely borne by Miss Pope; but Mr Percy Compton-Burnett and his family, who first met their cousin ('Olive was a great dear') after the second war and visited her thereafter regularly until her death in 1963, take the opposite view.

24   M&W p.53.

25   Dr Frank Bodman (who, as Daisy Compton-Burnett's G. P. in the 1930s and as an authority on homoeopathic history well acquainted with her father's career, was admirably placed to draw comparisons between the two).

26   The Rev. Edward Hayward, of the C.M.S. Mission at Panyam, 1911–20, and examining chaplain to the Bishop of W. Equatorial Africa. (Mr Hayward remained a friend of Daisy Compton-Burnett to the end of her life, and I am much indebted to him for information about her career.)

27   H&Head p.23; Ivy's similar jokes about her half-sister recalled by Janet Beresford.

28   P&P p.41.

29   B&S p.6.

30   F&Fate p.156.

31   DC 1 November 1862; the next two quotations from DE 23 November 1883 and 27 March 1885.

32   F&Fate p.191.

33   Arthur Waley told Francis King (and others seem to have heard the same thing from Ivy herself).

34   M&W p.200.
35   This affair reported in DC 11, 18 and 25 March 1871.
36   DT 7 February 1906.
37   This and the following quotation from M&W, p.176.
38   Information from Francis King and Janet Beresford.
39   Burkhart 1, p.30.
40   *A History of Brighton College* compiled by G. P. Burstow and M. B. Whittaker (London, 1957), pp.70 and 75. (See also *Brighton College Register,* 1922, ed. by E. K. Milliken.)
41   B&S p.125.

CHAPTER VI   1902–1911

1   Thomas Davison, later Archbishop of Canterbury, quoted by John H. Ellison in 'Early Days' from the anniversary pamphlet, 'Royal Holloway College 1887–1937'.
2   'Social Life at R.H.C. 1887–1937', an unpublished ms., in the archive at Holloway by Marion Pick, who was a year behind Ivy at college and who returned as a lecturer from 1911 to 1946 (when her departure was lamented in a masque with the refrain: 'Who now shall keep the ancestral altars green?/Miss Pick forsakes the Hollowegian scene'; 'R.H.C. has produced no more devoted a Hollowegian,' wrote the *College Letter* when she died in 1968). Quotations about Holloway not otherwise attributed in this chapter come from her 'Social Life', and from a talk given at the college on 21 June 1969, by Miss W. E. Delp, later issued as a pamphlet, 'Royal Holloway College 1908–1914'.
3   Joan Evans' *Prelude and Fugue,* p.114.
4   *Dolores,* p.109.
5   *Dolores,* p.110 (the same comparison had occurred to Miss Pick, and to Lilian M. Faithful in her autobiography, *In the House of My Pilgrimage* [Chatto, 1924], p.93).
6   Information from Barbara and Walter Robinson.
7   *RHC College Letter,* 1904 (Pernel Strachey was assistant lecturer in French, and her sister Marjorie a student at the college from 1901 to 1904).
8   Information from Barbara and Walter Robinson.
9   Miss Mabel Eastaugh (E III was the third floor corridor in the eastern block of the building); see also Chapter III, p.69, for the view of another contemporary who thought Ivy 'not at all popular', and who wishes to remain anonymous.
10   Daisy Elizabeth Harvey (b. 3 September 1883, daughter of George Harvey, metal merchant, of Eltham Road, Lewisham, educated at Lewisham Grammar School before being sent to spend a year at a pension in Brunswick and two more at Howard College) took her B.Sc. in 1906, after which the college

records contain no further reference to her (nor is there any record at Somerset House of her marriage or death in the next four years).

11   *Dolores*, p.115.

12   Identified by Helen Cam, see Appendix Two.

13   Mrs A. E. Rampal, a friend who often partnered Ivy at dinner (the article, not in any *College Letter* or other periodical preserved in the archive at Holloway, must have appeared in one of the students' own more ephemeral productions which I am unable to trace).

14   Walter Robinson.

15   'A Visit to Royal Holloway College' by Greta Hahn, *Our Magazine*, N. London Collegiate School for Girls, November 1892.

16   *Dictionary of National Biography 1941–50*.

17   *Dolores*, p.98; for Miss Cam's key see Appendix Two.

18   *The Tragic Drama of the Greeks* by A. E. Haigh (O.U.P., 1896), p.280 (Ivy's copy given to the author by Hester Marsden-Smedley).

19   Burkhart 1, pp.24–5.

20   Letter from Ivy to Oscar Browning, 30 December 1911 (Hastings Public Library).

21   P&P p.63.

22   A Founder's scholarship was not the highest award at Holloway: a resolution of the staff-meeting on 5 May 1904 proposed that 'the standard be such that the student might be expected to obtain at least a second class in Finals'. (The college produced one first in 1905, two in 1906 and eight—out of twenty-one honours degrees—in 1907.)

23   Mitchell NS.

24   *Beginning Again*, p.34.

25   *Lytton Strachey* by Michael Holroyd, vol. 1, p.34.

26   Letter to O.B., 29 January 1909.

27   *Rupert Brooke* by Christopher Hassall, p.121. (Noel lived from 1908 to 1911 in Room 13, Staircase A, Wilkins Buildings—Hassall has 'Fellows Building' but this must be a misprint since Brooke, by his own account, lived 'on a landing opposite Oscar Browning'.)

28   Forster, p.29.

29   Wortham, p.284.

30   *Dolores*, p.97.

31   *Dolores*, p.151.

32   Information from Simon Blow.

33   M&W p.153.

34   *Dolores*, p.150; the next five quotations from pp.211, 168, 210, 207 and 157.

35   HW November 1883.

36   *Scenes of Clerical Life* (O.U.P. World's Classics, 1909), p.48; the previous quotation from *Dolores*, p.32.

37   *Dolores*, p.3; the next quotation from p.4.

38 *Scenes of Clerical Life,* p.53; the next two quotations from *Dolores,* pp.82 and 24.

39 *Dolores,* pp.40–43; the two previous quotations from pp.62 and 63.

40 H&Head, p.274.

41 *Dolores,* p.152; the next two quotations from pp.90 and 20.

42 *Dolores,* p.166; the next quotation from p.140.

43 *Dolores,* p.138.

44 Burkhart 1, p.46; the next quotation from *Dolores,* p.112.

45 *Dolores,* p.199.

46 George Furlong and Rex Britcher.

47 *Dolores,* p.164; the next three quotations from pp.207, 197 and 257.

48 *Robert Elsmere,* p.153.

49 E&B p.138.

50 Address to the Dover Youths Institute, DE 29 February 1884; the next two quotations from D&S, p.16 and G&G, p.18.

51 Dick, p.7; the previous quotation from F&F, p.195.

52 Mrs Marsden-Smedley papers (though Ivy inscribed her book to 'Noël', her brother himself dropped the dots after he reached King's).

53 A second letter, dated 11 August 1909, from Noel to O.B. acknowledges the return of Blackwood's letter (which has since disappeared) and thanks him for writing to John Lane, but there is no relevant reply filed under L in O.B.'s correspondence at Hastings.

54 D&S p.154.

55 Letter to O.B., 12 August 1911.

56 This is one of three letters to Ivy preserved in Blackwood's business files (the fact that her original application and subsequent replies have disappeared suggests that she dealt only with the firm's London office in Paternoster Row, which was destroyed in 1940 when all documents were lost); further information on sales from Blackwood's ledger.

57 'M.M.' in the *Daily Mail,* 3 March 1911; the next two quotations from the *T.L.S.,* 2 March, and the *Bystander,* 12 April.

58 *Krapp's Last Tape* (Faber, 1959), p.17.

CHAPTER VII   1911–1915

1 Mr Noel-Baker is not sure whether this was May Week 1911 or 1912, but Juliet Compton-Burnett is convinced it was 1911 (Ivy had also spent May Week 1910 with her mother in Cambridge, according to a letter from Noel to O.B., 13 June 1910).

2 *Cambridge Review,* 1 November 1916; Noel's speeches at the Union criticized in *ibid.,* 27 February and 4 June 1908.

3 Letter undated, probably late November 1915; quotations from Noel's corre-

spondence in this and the next chapter are from letters to Jack Beresford unless otherwise attributed.

4 *Basileon*, no.11, June 1909; anon. review identified in the King's Library copy as the work of O. L. Richmond. (Professor Richmond, who was an undergraduate and Fellow of King's at roughly the same time as Noel, has 'absolutely *no* recollection of him ... it is extraordinary that I do not remember that name among the many undergraduates I knew. It even supplies a bit of negative evidence about him. He cannot have been at all interested in music, since no musician escaped my net.') The following quotation from Arthur Schloss comes from the same source; Mr Noel-Baker (who was present at the 1909 dinner and remembers that Noel was too) and Mr Haslam recall respectively the debagging of Dalton and ducking of Birrell.

5 Wortham, p.179.

6 Forster, p.101; the two previous quotations from Dalton's *Call Back Yesterday*, p.57, and Christopher Morris in *Portrait of Lowes Dickinson*, BBC Radio programme produced by Maurice Brown, 19 January 1960.

7 Forster, p.119; the previous quotation on p.228.

8 P&M p.23.

9 P&M p.19; identified by Leigh Farnell.

10 Information from Raisley Moorsom.

11 Forster, p.120.

12 P&M p.24; the previous quotation from p.23.

13 *Lytton Strachey* by Michael Holroyd, vol.1, p.200; the next two quotations from *ibid.* p.256 and *Sowing* by Leonard Woolf, p.160.

14 Forster, p.66.

15 Forster, p.31; the next four quotations from P&M p.19, Wortham pp.230–1, and P&M p.83.

16 Lady Darling, quoted in *Portrait of Lowes Dickinson*, BBC Radio, 19 January 1960.

17 P&M p.36.

18 Forster, p.155.

19 'Charles Kingsley Webster' by S. T. Bindoff, PBA.

20 A typescript of the thesis is in the London Library, bequeathed by Horace Mann who had married Noel's widow.

21 This and the previous quotation from Clapham's obituary of Noel, *Cambridge Review*, 1 November 1916.

22 P&M p.78.

23 *A Bundle of Time* by Harriet Cohen (Faber, 1969), p.36.

24 B&S p.203.

25 Butler, p.29.

26 Greig, p.105.

27 M&S p.11.

28 Butler, p.31.

29 D&S p.41.
30 Greig, p.39.
31 B&S pp.215–16.
32 MWTM p.55.
33 *Spectator,* 6 September 1969.
34 See *Beresford of Beresford: Eight Centuries of a Gentle Family* by the Rev. E. A. Beresford, S. B. Beresford and the Rev. William Beresford (privately printed, 1893), according to which Beresfords fought at Crécy and Poitiers, at Agincourt and under the red rose for the Lancastrians.
35 *Cambridge Review,* 23 January 1908; the following quotation from Clapham, *Cambridge Review,* 1 November 1916.
36 *Goodbye To All That* by Robert Graves, p.288.
37 *Goldsworthy Lowes Dickinson* by Roger Fry and John T. Sheppard.
38 M&S p.158.
39 P&C p.82; the previous quotation from D&S p.126.
40 B&S p.231.
41 Butler, p.31.

CHAPTER VIII 1915–1919

1   F&Fortune, p.260.
2   *Testament of Youth* by Vera Brittain, p.200.
3   P&M, p.17.
4   Information from Kenneth Walker (Winifred's mother had been an Amelia Elliott, granddaughter of a farmer named Daniels whose family belonged to the same little farming community as the Sadlers and Pudneys).
5   B&S p.215.
6   *Testament of Youth* by Vera Brittain, p.143.
7   *The Big Push* by Brian Gardner, p.81; the previous quotation from *The World Crisis* by Winston Churchill (Odhams, 1938), p.1070. See also the *Official History of the War. France and Belgium 1916* (Macmillan, 1932), vol.1, p.485. ('The VII Corps, before Gommecourt, having played its part in the preparatory period by attracting an extra enemy division, the assault *"à fond"* at that spot should have been countermanded by G.H.Q. order.')
8   The prize was £10 in books, but what book or books Noel bought with it I am unable to discover.
9   MWTM, p.214.
10 *Letters of the Earl of Oxford and Asquith to a Friend. 1915–1922,* p.7.
11 Captain T. C. Howitt had been a second lieutenant with Noel at the start of the war.
12 *Testament of Youth* by Vera Brittain, p.450; the next quotation from Dick, p.8.
13 *Tell England* by Ernest Raymond (Cassell, 7th ed. 1929), p.167.
14 E&B pp.55, 96 and 268; the next quotation from p.169.

15 To Robert Liddell.

16 D&D p.216.

17 Information from Barbara and Walter Robinson; the following quotation from *Delicate, Backwood, Puny and Stunted Children*, p.152. (Trine's works on thought power include *What all the World's a-seeking: or, the Vital Law of True Life*, *The Greatest Thing Ever Known*, *The Higher Powers of Mind and Spirit*, *This Mystical Life of Ours: a book of suggestive thoughts for each week through the year*, etc., all of which went through many editions in America and were reissued in London between 1897 and 1918.)

18 Death certificates of Katharine and Primrose Compton-Burnett; further information from Vera and Juliet Compton-Burnett, Janet Beresford, *The Times* and *Morning Post*, 29 and 31 December 1917, *Kilburn Times*, 4 January 1918. (The official record of the inquest, held at Marylebone on 29 December, was destroyed after fifteen years.)

19 TWTW p.68.

20 Butler, p.30.

21 Dick, p.22.

22 Mitchell NS.

23 Dick, p.7; there is an excellent account of this influenza epidemic in Ursula Bloom's *Youth at the Gate* (Hutchinson, London), 1959.

24 F&Fortune, p.270; the previous quotation from MWTM, p.158.

25 Information from Alison Waley; the next two quotations from Barbara and Walter Robinson, and from Sonia Orwell.

26 Information on Jourdain ancestors from *Ranging Memories* by Lt.-Col. H.F.N. Jourdain (Oxford, privately printed, 1934), pp.7ff. (the crusaders' exploits were commemorated in the family arms by an heraldic pun—two bars wavy—on the River Jordan).

27 *Ottoline. The Early Memoirs of Lady Ottoline Morrell* edited by Robert Gathorne-Hardy (Faber, London, 1963), p.113.

28 *The Odes of Horace* collected and arranged by M. Jourdain (Temple Classics, London, 1904). Further information on Margaret's career from Hester Marsden-Smedley and Raisley Moorsom, and from Margaret's diaries, Account Book and papers (Marsden-Smedley papers).

29 *Practically True* by Ernest Thesiger, p.1.

30 Butler, pp.22–3.

31 *Testament of Youth* by Vera Brittain, pp.470–1; the previous quotation from Clarke, p.109.

32 D&S p.148; the next quotation from p.197.

33 E&B p.100.

34 *Samuel Butler* by H. Festing Jones, vol.2, p.412 (for Ivy's tribute to Butler, see page 362ff).

35 *Samuel Butler* by P. N. Furbank, p.13.

36 MWTM p.19; the following quotation from Furbank's *Samuel Butler*, p.32.

37 B&S p.132 (in a cancelled passage from the MS. of L&F, chap. 2, Hermia Heriot says about leaving home: 'If relief is the strongest form of joy, this is an illustration of it').

38 Dick, p.7.

39 L&F MS. (the last five words are omitted in the published text, p.136).

40 B&S, p.27.

41 *The European Anarchy* by Goldsworthy Lowes Dickinson (Allen and Unwin, 1916), p.138.

42 Mrs. C. R. Ashbee in *Portrait of Lowes Dickinson,* BBC Radio, 19 January 1960.

43 Quoted in *Essays in Biography* by J. M. Keynes (Macmillan, 1933), pp.302–3.

CHAPTER IX 1920–1929

1 Information from Francis Wyndham (who had it from M.J.).

2 Hester Marsden-Smedley in Burkhart 3.

3 Information from Viva King.

4 Burkhart 2, p.77.

5 Information from Robert Liddell.

6 David Garnett, letter to H.S., 19 June 1979. The lunch was given by Francis Birrell.

7 Information from R. Mortimer.

8 M.J. was born on 15 August 1876, though Ivy (born in 1884) apparently told Herman and others that there was a gap of ten years between them.

9 P&P, p.12.

10 P&C, p.70.

11 *The Weeping and the Laughter,* pp.126–7.

12 *The Familiar Faces* by David Garnett, p.221; Lord Hampton (then Humphrey Pakington), another regular on Ivy and Margaret's dining circuit in the early 1920s, said much the same in a letter to H.S., 22 March 1971.

13 D&S, p.94.

14 D&S, p.90.

15 Interview with Michael Millgate in 1962, Burkhart 1, p.35.

16 E. H. Cranton ran this firm, apparently singlehanded, at 6, Fleet Lane, E. C.4, until the Second World War; M. J.'s V&A papers contained fragments of letters to I.C.-B. and statements from Cranton dated 30 September 1933, 31 March 1934, 4 November 1935 and September 1937.

17 Information from Joan Evans.

18 G&G, p.17.

19 N.S., 20 June 1925.

20 Information from Ralph Edwards who reviewed B&S, M&W and MWTM anonymously in *Country Life* on 8 June 1929, 6 June 1931 and 26 August 1933 respectively.

21 Hester Marsden-Smedley, Burkhart 3.

22   G&G, p.21.

23   Burkhart 2, p.83.

24   MWTM, p.27.

25   B&S, p.144.

26   TWTW, p.149.

27   *Harold Nicolson. A Biography,* vol. 1, by James Lees-Milne (Chatto & Windus, 1980); this account confirmed in conversation with H.S. by Raymond Mortimer, who reviewed P&M in *Vogue,* early April 1925, and H&Head in N.S., 13 July 1935.

28   *A Boy at the Hogarth Press* by Richard Kennedy, p.69.

29   Correspondence with I.C.-B. (V&A papers); information from Eric Hiscock of *The Bookseller* who worked for the *Evening Standard* when Arnold Bennett's review of B&S was published on 30 May 1929, and discussed it at the time with Cranton.

30   *The Graphic,* 25 May 1929.

31   *Nation and Athenaeum,* 30 March 1929.

32   Letter, V.S.-W. to H.N., 10 April 1929; the diaries of V.S.-W. and I.C.-B. confirm this and subsequent meetings; V.S.-W.'s broadcast review published in *The Listener,* 28 May 1929.

33   Letters to I.C.-B. from David Higham, 12 August 1929, Sylvia Lynd (who had been one of the Book Society's judging panel along with Clemence Dane, J. B. Priestley and George Gordon in May), 7 August, and Donald Brace (V&A papers).

34   P&M, p.25.

35   Burkhart 1, p.33.

36   See p.244.

37   MWTM, p.23.

38   See p.193.

39   Mitchell NS.

40   B&S, p.102.

41   P&M, p.26.

42   P. C. Kennedy, N.S. 20 June 1925. I am assured by Richard Kennedy that P. C. Kennedy was no relation of his uncle, the architect George Kennedy, who subsequently read B&S in manuscript for Leonard Woolf at the Hogarth Press and was the first to pronounce it a work of genius (see *A Boy at the Hogarth Press*).

43   P&M, p.47.

44   B&S, p.39.

45   M&W, p.203.

46   P&M, p.32.

47   *New Republic,* 15 January 1930; see also Leo Kennedy, *Commonweal,* 2 April 1930.

48   *Saturday Review,* N.Y., 30 November 1929.

49 Information from Francis Wyndham.

50 Burkhart 1, p.87.

51 Review of E&B, *Cornhill Magazine,* 1944, reprinted in Burkhart 1, p.61.

52 D&D, pp.112–17.

53 MWTM, p.122.

54 M&W, p.261.

55 B&S, p.95.

56 B&S, p.226.

57 B&S, p.64.

58 Information from Willie Ranken's niece, Anne Doe; this and subsequent accounts of Ernest Thesiger are largely based on information, papers, press cuttings and the unpublished second half of E.T.'s memoirs provided by his nephew Richard Thesiger.

59 *Eve,* 24 February 1926. (*Eve* was then edited by Ivy's subsequent friend, Madge Garland.)

60 *Pall Mall Gazette,* 28 October 1915.

61 *London Mail,* 20 October 1915.

62 *The Queen,* 19 May 1919.

63 *The Outlook,* 10 May 1919.

64 Information from Francis King.

65 *Daily Sketch,* 22 April 1927.

66 E.T., unpublished memoir.

67 Information from Violet Henriques (daughter of the Hon. Nelly Levy).

68 *Practically True,* p.159.

69 *Practically True,* p.31.

70 Information from Yvonne ffrench.

71 *Practically True,* p.188.

72 *The Sketch,* 26 May 1926.

73 P&P, p.69.

74 Burkhart 2, p.33. This and later accounts of Herman's career based on conversations with him, on Burkhart's admirable memoir, on information supplied by Herman's sister, Elka Schrijver, and on her unpublished ms., 'The Diamonds That Never Were'.

75 £3 a week is the sum given in Burkhart 2 (p.15), but in fact this was Herman's wage in his first, thoroughly uncongenial job as clerk in a Swiss bank.

76 Information from Jim Brandreth.

77 Burkhart 2, pp.77 and 79.

78 Sonia Orwell.

79 P&C, p.126.

80 P&C, p.79.

81 Burkhart 2, p.89.

82 Burkhart 2, p.44.

83 E&B, pp.14–15.

84 MWTM, p.33.

85 MWTM, p.222.

86 Quoted by Arthur Calder-Marshall in *Lewd, Blasphemous and Obscene* (Hutch-inson, 1972).

87 C.L., 26 August 1933.

88 *S. Times*, 6 August 1933.

89 N.S., 5 August 1933.

90 Burkhart 3.

91 MWTM, p.85.

92 Alice Herbert, *Yorkshire Post*, 9 August 1933.

93 See p.180.

94 *A Reflection of the Other Person. The Letters of Virginia Woolf, vol. IV 1929–31*, ed. Nigel Nicolson (Hogarth Press, 1978), p.92.

95 Nathalie Sarraute to H.S., 30 March 1973; see Chapter XVII for a fuller account of this meeting.

96 Information from B. Robinson.

97 Information about Strachey and Cox from Gerald Brenan, letter to H.S., April 1974. (The comment on Cox comes from H. G. Wells.)

98 *Messengers of Day* (Heinemann, 1978), p.5.

99 *A Writer's Diary* (Hogarth Press, 1954), p.280.

100 E.W., conversation with H.S.

Chapter X 1930–1936

1 F&Fortune, p.25.

2 P&C, p.86.

3 MWTM, p.84.

4 M&W, p.103.

5 Unpublished memoir.

6 *Eve*, 11 January 1922.

7 *A Moveable Feast* by Ernest Hemingway (Cape, 1964), p.19.

8 P&P, p.12.

9 V&A papers.

10 Letter, I.C.-B. to her cousin Katharine (Katie) Blackie, 3 November 1919.

11 Sprigge, p.94.

12 M&S, p.79.

13 Robert Liddell in Burkhart 3.

14 Barbara Robinson.

15 Marsden-Smedley papers.

16 D&S, p.77.

17 M. J., note in diary for 1926; her diary for 1928 records her decreasing weight

'on Dr Heyman's scales' at 27, New Cavendish Street; both her diaries and I.C.-B.'s record regular weighings and trips to fetch pills, etc., from 1929–33. M.J. described this cure and its cost to Ralph Edwards at the time.

18 Hester Marsden-Smedley's account, confirmed by other close friends; but Ivy told James Lees-Milne in 1947 that she always wrote at her little walnut bureau by the window, *Caves of Ice*, p.248.

19 P&M, p.35.

20 This and subsequent accounts of Dorothy Beresford based on an interview with H.S. (1970), also on conversations with her son, Roger Kidd, her sister-in-law, Janet Beresford, and their respective families.

21 Dorothy Kidd, unpublished writings supplied by Roger Kidd.

22 G&G, p.17.

23 Quoted in Sprigge, p.95.

24 Letter, D.K. to R.K., 27 July 1943.

25 B&S, p.204.

26 Rosemary Beresford.

27 Burkhart 1, pp.27–8.

28 Sprigge, p.95.

29 J. A. Laurence of Laurence, Keen and Gardener.

30 Mowll.

31 Letter, N.C.-B. to I.C.-B., 24 June 1916, see p.224.

32 Letter, Roy Fuller to H.S., 30 July 1974.

33 J. A. Laurence.

34 P&C, pp.87–8.

35 Their careers reconstructed from conversations with Vera and Juliet Compton-Burnett, and papers, letters, etc., belonging to Mowll & Mowll.

36 D&S, p.115.

37 Sprigge, pp.94–5.

38 Information from Sonia Orwell.

39 P&C, p.70.

40 P&C, p.185.

41 Burkhart 3, p.173.

42 H.M.-S., unpublished memoir.

43 Burkhart 3, p.177.

44 Information from Margaret Hawkins, who worked for the Misses Noyes before and after the Second World War at Sutton Veney, and remembered 'Miss Burnett's' visits, and often heard them talk about her books.

45 G&G, p.153.

46 Burkhart 2, p.93.

47 This and subsequent quotations from Hester Marsden-Smedley come, unless otherwise attributed, from conversations with H.S. between 1970 and her death in 1982.

48 *Regency Furniture 1795–1820*, p.41.

49 *Ibid.*

50 *Prophesying Peace*, p.223.

51 Quoted in *Decoration in England from 1660–1760* by Francis Lenygon, p.12.

52 P&P, p.68.

53 Sprigge, p.86.

54 Burkhart 2, p.81.

55 *Prophesying Peace*, p.223.

56 *The Work of William Kent*, p.12.

57 H.M.-S., unpublished memoir.

58 Quoted by M.J. in *Eve*, 7 December 1921.

59 M&S, p.80.

60 Burkhart 2, p.75.

61 *The Flowers of the Forest* by David Garnett (Chatto and Windus, 1955), p.209; so little impression did Ivy make on Birrell at the time that Garnett subsequently confused her and M. J. with the then far more celebrated couple, Miss Moberly and Eleanor Jourdain; and Garnett was obliged to make amends ('Ivy Compton-Burnett was naturally furious with me, and my most abject apologies failed to satisfy her,' D.G. to H.S., 19 June 1979) in his next autobiographical volume, *The Familiar Faces*, p.221.

62 *Ezra Pound* by Charles Norman (Macmillan, N. Y., 1960), p.246.

63 M&W, p.264.

64 Fedden (Renée Fedden confirms that the anonymous admirer in her husband's anecdote was Toynbee). Unless both these well-known stories are true, it is the second that must be a myth since Ivy tacitly confirmed the Birrell version in a scathing postcard about Garnett's book to Cicely Greig, dated 5 December 1955.

65 Fedden, p.429.

66 Burkhart 2, p.80.

67 This and subsequent attempts to establish M. J.'s financial circumstances are based on her Account Book, which gives detailed figures and sources of income for the years 1902–1924 (Marsden-Smedley papers), and various notes, bills, receipts, bank statements etc. among her V&A papers; figures for Ivy's income from Mowll & Mowll.

68 MWTM, p.22.

CHAPTER XI Margaret Jourdain

1 D&S, p.68.

2 G&G, p.62.

3 Letter, R.M. to H.S., 21 September 1980.

4   I.C.-B. to R.L. (Mrs Philipps), 20 March 1938, King's College Library, Cambridge; and conversation with R.L.

5   A typescript of *Buchanan's Hotel*, dated 1933, was loaned to me in 1973 by Ralph Edwards (who had it from the V&A Furniture Department, where it had been found among M.J.'s papers deposited there after her death in 1951), but has apparently since disappeared; Rosamond Lehmann had certainly heard of it, and Hester Marsden-Smedley remembered much talk about it in the mid-1930s when M.J. was applying in vain to London managements.

6   Letters from F. Surgey of Acton Surgey, and several from Hugh Phillips, among the Marsden-Smedley papers; the following account is based also on M.J.'s diaries, trade address book, fragments among her V&A papers; and conversations with Herman Schrijver.

7   *Private History* by Derek Patmore (Cape, 1960).

8   Herman Schrijver; information also from Raisley Moorsom, Mrs Henriques, Viva King; and see 'An Architect's Debt to Country Life' by Oliver Hill, C.L., 12 June 1967.

9   G&G, p.66.

10 Burkhart 2, p.96.

11 MWTM, p.43.

12 P&M, p.35.

13 Joan Evans, preface to *An Adventure*, p.15; the following account owes much to conversations with Dame Joan.

14 Conversation with I.C.-B. in February 1957, written down at the time by Rosamond Lehmann.

15 *The Ghosts of Versailles* by Lucille Iremonger, p.65.

16 To Dr John Rollett, 3 January 1970.

17 Information from Viva King.

18 To Ivo Pakenham.

19 *The Reluctant Pioneer. The Life of Elizabeth Wordsworth* by Georgina Battiscombe (Constable, 1978), pp.101–2.

20 *Prelude and Fugue. An Autobiography* by Joan Evans, p.76.

21 *A Childhood*, p.48.

22 'Reminiscences' by C. M. Jourdain, 1911 (the first part of this typescript is a more intimate, early draft for *A Childhood*, the second is an account of the onset of Milly's illness, her terror, shame, despair and gradual acceptance of her condition). Add. ms., British Library, Darwin and Cornford Papers (these include a correspondence between Milly and her friend, the poet Frances Cornford, giving a detailed picture of the Jourdains at home between 1902 and 1926).

23 Letter, Elizabeth Taylor to Robert Liddell, n.d.

24 D&S, p.148.

25 Ralph Edwards.

26 Burkhart 2, p.96.

27 *An Outdoor Breviary*, p.105, previous reference, p.84 (the places described are nameless in the published text but identified in M.J.'s handwriting in the margins of the copy she gave Joan Evans).

28 Memoir of Philip by Milly Jourdain, quoted by A. E. Heath in *The Monist*, vol. XXX, April 1920 (a typescript of this essay, 'Philip', corrected in Milly's own hand, is in the library of Trinity College, Cambridge, together with other P.E.B.J. papers deposited by Livia Breglia, Laura Jourdain's daughter by a second marriage). There is another detailed obituary by George Sarton, including a memoir by Philip's wife Laura, in *Isis* (Brussells), vol. V, 1923; and a fascinating account of the relationship with Russell in 'Russell and Philip Jourdain', by I. Grattan-Guinness, greatly expanded in Grattan-Guinness's *Dear Russell—Dear Jourdain*. My account is further indebted to Dr John Rollett for a generous supply of insights, information and Jourdain papers.

29 Russell's journal, November 1902, quoted by Grattan-Guinness, *op. cit.*

30 Frances Cornford to C.M.J., July 1906, B. Lib.

31 C.M.J., *Monist, op. cit.*

32 To Esther Millar, housekeeper to Janette Thesiger.

33 'Philip', *op. cit.*

34 D&S, p.203.

35 'Some Aspects of Samuel Butler' by M. Jourdain, *Open Court*, vol. XXVII, no. 10, October 1913. (*The Open Court* belonged, with *The Monist* and *The International Journal of Ethics*, to a stable of international, U.S.-based, intellectual journals run by Paul Carus, in all of which P.E.B.J. had an editorial hand.)

36 *Monist, op. cit.;* the original proposal and development of this scheme traced in Cornford papers, B. Lib.

37 P.E.B.J. to Russell, 24 May 1919, *Dear Russell—Dear Jourdain*, p.150.

38 This was an expanded, updated edition (pub. Marston, 1902) of a work first published in 1865 by Fanny Bury Palliser (Captain Marryat's sister) who had catalogued the lace collection at the S. Kensington (V&A) museum.

39 'Northamptonshire Memories' by W. W. Hadley, *Northamptonshire Past and Present*, vol. II, no. 4; see also 'Alice Dryden' by Joan Wake, *Ibid.*, vol. II, no. 3, 1956; further information from Joan Evans and M.J.'s V&A papers.

40 'Canons Ashby', C.L., 9 April 1981; I am greatly indebted to Mr Cornforth for further advice and information about M.J. and the Drydens.

41 *Dictionary of National Biography.*

42 H.M.-S., unpublished memoir; further quotations and information about the Jourdains at Broadwindsor come from the same source, unless otherwise attributed, or from conversations with H.S.

43 MWTM, p.213.

44 'The Literary Associations of Dorset' by M. Jourdain, *Memorials of Old Dorset* (Benrose & Sons, 1907).

45 *Outdoor Breviary*, p.98.

46 *Unfulfilment*, title poem.

47 *Outdoor Breviary*, p.49.

48 P.E.B.J.'s note scribbled on a letter, 6 March 1911, from Arthur L. Humphreys setting out Hatchard's terms (the *Poems* were eventually published by Truslove and Hanson), V&A papers.

49 M.J.'s salary from Lenygon given in her Account Book; information about Lenygon and his firm from the historian Sarah Coffin, Ralph Edwards, Peter Thornton of the V&A and James Kiddell of Sothebys; M.J.'s authorship of the Lenygon books confirmed by a fragment of a letter to her from the leading American authority on the decorative arts, Fiske Kimball, among her V&A papers (probably written round about the time he published Kent's Houses of Parliament designs in the *RIBA Journal*, August and September 1932): 'I have known and admired your work for a long time—longer than the public, for Francis Lenygon betrayed to me that his two books were written for him, I presume by you. They were the earliest of all recognitions of Burlington and Kent.' See also *English Decoration in the Eighteenth Century* by John Fowler and John Cornforth (Barrie and Jenkins, 1978), pp.16–17.

50 Fragments of M.J.'s correspondence with Mulliner and Hudson among her V&A papers; their financial transactions listed in her Account Book.

51 'Percy Macquoid and Others' by Ralph Edwards, *Apollo* 4, 1974; see also 'Edward Hudson' by Christopher Hussey, *Country Life*, 26 September 1936, 'Portrait of a Perfectionist. Edward Hudson' by Pamela Maude, *ibid.*, 12 January 1967.

52 Editorial, *Country Life* (opening number), 8 June 1897.

53 Information from Dr Rollett, who had it from a friend of P.E.B.J., Prof. C. D. Broad ('At that time he shared very much the same views of the then war as did Bertrand Russell, and I used to hear from Jourdain a good deal about these matters . . .').

54 Letter, P.E.B.J. to Laura J., 4 July 1915, Trinity College, Cambridge.

55 Frances Cornford to C.M.J., B. Lib. (quotations from F.C.'s and C.M.J.'s letters all come from this correspondence, quotations from P.E.B.J. are from the Jourdain papers, Trinity College, Cambridge).

56 Burkhart 3, p.175.

57 To Dr Rollett, 26 January 1970; further quotations from V.C.-S. come from the same source.

58 G&G, p.5.

59 V&A papers; Joan Evans said the *Poems* were financed by Janette.

60 Information from Richard Thesiger, who had it from Janette.

61 *Outdoor Breviary*, p.103.

62 To Dr Rollett, 26 January 1970.

63 D&S, p.94.

64 Joan Evans, to whom I am indebted for an account of this affair.

65 A fuller account is in *Dear Russell—Dear Jourdain*, pp.146–53.

66 *The Work of William Kent*, p.30.

67 Conditions laid down in correspondence with Waltons of Leadenhall Street (Mrs Levy's solicitors), 26 September 1924–29 September 1931, Marsden-Smedley papers; further correspondence up to and including 1945, V&A papers; Mrs Levy's daughter, Violet Henriques, confirms that the anonymous benefactor was almost certainly her mother, see footnote p. 342.

68 Violet Henriques.

69 Information from Kathleen Farrell, who had it from Elizabeth Sprigge.

70 See p.18.

71 Sprigge, p.95.

72 See p.244; M.J. endorsed Butler in *The Open Court,* October 1913.

73 *Traveller's Prelude* by Freya Stark (John Murray, 1950), p.129.

74 P&M, p.35.

75 D&S, p.65.

76 *Spectator,* 19 March 1937.

77 Burkhart 2, p.79.

78 Information from R. Liddell (letter to H.S., 7 December 1970), who had it from R. Mortimer.

79 *An Adventure,* p.85.

80 Information from Carol Rygate who was a pupil at St Hugh's at the time; this version of the St Hugh's affair based on Joan Evans' recollections, C.M.J.'s letters, *The Ghosts of Versailles* by Lucille Iremonger and an unpublished, pro-Jourdain memoir by another St Hugh's pupil, 'The Row' by Eveleen Stopford (lent to me by Robert Liddell).

81 Letter, R.L. to H.S., 7 December 1970.

82 Story from Kay Dick, confirmed by Sheila Bush, letter to H.S., 8 April 1983.

83 P&M, p.26.

CHAPTER XII Ivy

1 TWTW, p.6.

2 Information from Sonia Orwell.

3 Information from B. Robinson.

4 Detonated by Carol Rygate, whose stories of this affair subsequently gave Ivy much pleasure.

5 Information from Madge Garland.

6 Information from Herman Schrijver; see also Burkhart 2, p.88.

7 Ivy said this explicitly to Sonia Orwell, and discussed the book's influence on her in more general terms with Francis King and Marion Rawson.

8 *The Real Charlotte,* p.250.

9 *Week End Review,* 2 September 1933.

10 MWTM, pp.34 and 37; *The Ghosts of Versailles, op. cit.;* information from Joan Evans.

11 See p.167.

12 MWTM, p.85.

13 MWTM, p.87.

14 MWTM, p.140.

15 MWTM, p.142.

16 See pp.227–8.

17 MWTM, p.157.

18 MWTM, p.158.

19 *The Real Charlotte*, p.291.

20 MWTM, p.199.

21 MWTM, p.173.

22 F&Fortune, p.235.

23 *Ibid.*, pp.236–7.

24 In 'Conversation et Sous-Conversation', *Nouvelle Revue Française*, January–
    February 1956 (reprinted in *Tropisms and the Age of Suspicion*, pp.117–20).

25 MWTM, p. 265; the comparison with Ivy's illness based on information from
    Vera Compton-Burnett, who nursed her through it; and see pp.238–9.

26 F&Fortune, p.271; cf. M&M, p.290.

27 To James Lees-Milne, *Ancestral Voices*, p.71.

28 *Lord Byron's Family. Annabella, Ada and Augusta. 1816–24* by Malcolm Elwin
    (John Murray, 1975), p.102.

29 MWTM, p.304.

30 Fedden.

31 MWTM, p.104.

32 P&P, p.71.

33 D&S, p.256.

34 Burkhart 2, p.30 (the N.S. reviewer was Philip Toynbee on 29 January 1944).

35 Information from Janet Beresford.

36 MWTM, p.176.

37 MWTM, p.143.

38 MWTM, pp.142–3.

39 See Chapter VIII for a fuller account of this debt; Ivy had certainly read H.
    Festing Jones' *Samuel Butler. A Memoir* (Macmillan, 1919) when it came out
    (perhaps also Clara Stillman's excellent account of the 'long and painful' corre-
    spondence between father and son in *Samuel Butler. A Mid-Victorian Modern*,
    1932), and seems to have borrowed among other things Butler's habit of
    annotating minutes and letters from his father in the same way as Felix inter-
    sperses his own comments in reports of his father's letters and telephone calls.

40 MWTM, p.20.

41 MWTM, p.97.

42 MWTM, p.86.

43 MWTM, pp.61–2.

44 Interview with Brodie, *Books of Today*, April 1950.

45 MWTM, p.143.

46 Dick, p.18.
47 MWTM, p.174.
48 Burkhart 2, p.14.
49 *Ibid.,* p.36.
50 *At Lady Molly's* (Heinemann, 1957), p.211.
51 This fraud is recorded in 'The Diamonds That Never Were', unpublished ms. by Elka Schrijver, and my account of Herman's professional and private life is largely based on conversations with her in Amsterdam in 1981.
52 *Boswell's Life of Johnson,* ed. G. B. Hill (O.U.P., 1971), vol. IV, p.86.
53 Letter, Elka Schrijver to H.S., 24 October 1981.
54 D&S, p.182.
55 Burkhart 2, p.49.
56 *Ibid.,* p.96.
57 *Ibid.,* p.86.
58 E&B, p.63.
59 Burkhart 2, p.93.
60 *Ibid.,* p.95.
61 Dick, p.17.
62 *Ibid.,* p.9.
63 See p.253.

CHAPTER XIII   1937–1939

1 D&S, p.123.
2 Information from Barbara Robinson.
3 Letter, D.H. to I.C.-B., July 1935, V&A papers; see also *Literary Gent,* p.154.
4 Letter, V.G. to I.C.-B., 26 June 1940.
5 *New York Times,* 23 July 1937.
6 Information from Sybille Bedford.
7 R. Ellis-Roberts, *News Chronicle,* 26 May 1937.
8 I.C.-B. to R.L., 27 November 1961.
9 Letter, V.G. to Blanche Knopf, 3 December 1952; information from Livia Gollancz.
10 *Literary Gent,* p.171.
11 Information from Rupert Hart-Davis.
12 Information from Christopher Sykes.
13 Information from B. Robinson.
14 Burkhart 1, p.26.
15 C.S. to I.C.-B., 29 March 1937, Marsden-Smedley papers.
16 *Caves of Ice,* p.115.
17 Information from Cecil Gould.
18 G&G, p.20.
19 Burkhart 2, p.100.

20 Quoted in *Rose Macaulay* by Constance Babington-Smith, p.225.

21 Information from James Brandreth.

22 Greig, p.26.

23 *Reminiscences of Affection* by Victor Gollancz (Gollancz, 1968), p.80.

24 Burkhart 2, p.87.

25 G&G, p.51.

26 *Ancestral Voices*, p.61.

27 Greig, pp.44–5.

28 G&G, p.63.

29 Liza Banks, to whom I am greatly indebted for information about the Noyeses at Sutton Veney; the following account also owes much to her sister, Anne Northcroft; to Mrs Hawkins and Mrs Gertrude McCracken (both of whom had known and worked intermittently for the Noyeses all their lives); to Mrs John Walker; and to the younger Nicholsons' friends, Humphrey Spender and Clissold Tuely.

30 *Salisbury Plain*, pp.292–3.

31 Letter, A.N. to H.S., 1 July 1981.

32 Information from the Noyeses' great-niece, Jennifer Adamson; see also *Two Worlds for Memory* by Alfred Noyes (Sheed and Ward, 1953), pp.9, 42–3, 188.

33 P&C, p.134.

34 P&C, p.129.

35 P&C, p.226.

36 P&C, p.130.

37 P&C, p.139.

38 P&C, p.143.

39 P&C, p.147.

40 P&C, p.143.

41 P&C, p.147.

42 P&C, p.144.

43 P&C, p.168.

44 TWTW, p.310.

45 P&C, p.129.

46 'Some Notes About Ivy Compton-Burnett, 21 April 1942', unpublished ms. by Lady Anne Hill.

47 Burkhart 1, p.27.

48 *Ibid.*, p.192.

49 Typist's bill dated 8 December 1938, V&A papers.

50 Burkhart 2, p.90, and conversation with Herman Schrijver; but see H.M.-S. in Burkhart 3, pp.178–9; M. J.'s movements at this time, given in her diary for 1938, were confirmed by Peter Wilson.

51 H.M.-S., unpublished memoir.

52 Letter, Robert Liddell to H.S., 7 December 1970.

53 H.M.-S., unpublished memoir.

54 *Boswell's Life of Johnson, op. cit.,* vol. iii, p.48.

55 Information from Soame Jenyns, to whom this account is largely indebted.

56 *The Weeping and the Laughter,* p.167.

57 Story from Angus Wilson.

58 TWTW, p.5.

59 M&M, pp.12 and 35.

60 D&S, p.37.

61 Information from Angus Wilson.

62 P&P, p.155.

63 D&D, p.19.

64 'Distinguished Evacuee—Miss Ivy Compton-Burnett' unpublished ms. by Dulcie Pendred; further accounts of Ivy at Bottisham supplied by Anna Browne and Ann Graham Bell, both of whom were there at the time.

65 P&M, p.17; the book in question was identified for me as P&M by Soame Jenyns.

66 'Distinguished Evacuee', *op. cit.*

CHAPTER XIV   1940–1945

1   Burkhart 2, p.90.

2   N.S., 13 July 1935.

3   'Notes on Ivy Compton-Burnett' by Robert Liddell, Burkhart 3, p.135; subsequent quotations come from the same source unless otherwise attributed.

4   Letter, R.L. to H.S., 29 November 1970.

5   Burkhart 2, p.101 (Herman puts this visit after the war but M.J.'s diary and R.L.'s recollection date it 4–10 May 1940).

6   Letter, R.L. to H.S., 7 December 1970.

7   Letter, R.L. to H.S., 13 December 1982.

8   *Ancestral Voices* by James Lees-Milne, p.71.

9   *Ibid.,* p.43.

10 Dorothy Kerr, letter to H.S., 30 January 1975; further information from Lady Medawar, and the villagers of Sutton Veney.

11 H&Head, p.274.

12 I.C.-B. to R.L., 5 January 1942.

13 P&C, p.127.

14 V&A papers.

15 Burkhart 3, p.179; further information about this period from H.M.-S., her daughter Henrietta Williamson, Michael Pinney and Marion Rawson.

16 I.C.-B. to R.L., 5 January 1942.

17 N.S., 24 May 1941, reprinted in Burkhart 1, p.55.

18 Burkhart 2, p.91.

19 See pp.78–9.

20 Information from Francis Wyndham.

21 Letter, I.C.-B. to B. Robinson, 21 November 1964; she had said the same to R.L. in a letter dated 26 July 1950.

22 18 December 1941, V&A papers.

23 V&A papers.

24 E.T., unpublished memoirs.

25 *Ancestral Voices*, pp.42–3.

26 *Ibid.*, p.61.

27 Letter from Routledge and Sons, Ltd, 9 July 1941, V&A papers.

28 Susan Miles, Sutton Rectory, Sandy, Berks., to I.C.-B., 5 September 1941.

29 *Ancestral Voices*, p.61.

30 Anne Hill, 'Some Notes About Ivy Compton-Burnett'.

31 *Ancestral Voices*, p.220.

32 *Julia Strachey* by Herself and Frances Partridge (Gollancz, 1983), p.190.

33 Letter, John Pope-Hennessy to H.S., 1 June 1981.

34 *Ancestral Voices*, p.223.

35 Information from James Lees-Milne.

36 *Prophesying Peace* by James Lees-Milne, p.63.

37 Letter, J.P.-H. to H.S., 1 June 1981.

38 *Ancestral Voices*, p.65.

39 *Autobiography of Bertrand Russell*, vol. ii, p.158.

40 F&Fortune, p.17.

41 Edith Shackleton in *The Lady*, 20 January 1944.

42 M&M, p.55.

43 M&M, p.35.

44 Letter, D.G. Muir to I.C.-B., 23 July 1944, Marsden-Smedley papers.

45 D.K. to R.K., 26 January and 9 February 1944.

46 *David Blaize* (Hodder and Stoughton, 1916), p.149.

47 Letter, n.d., M.J. to Heywood Hill.

48 Information from Livia Gollancz.

49 D.G. Muir to I.C.-B., 23 July 1944, Marsden-Smedley papers.

50 *Collected Poems* by Keith Douglas, ed. John Walker, G. S. Fraser and J. C. Hall (Faber, 1966), p.150.

51 D.K. to R.K., Royal Lion, Lyme Regis, 18 January 1944.

52 Letter, M.J. to Anne Hill, Cliff Bank, Lyme Regis, 10 February 1944.

53 H.M.-S., unpublished ms.

54 R. Lehmann, 'Tribute to Ivy Compton-Burnett', delivered at the memorial meeting at Crosby Hall on 24 October 1969.

55 'A Conversation between I. Compton-Burnett and M. Jourdain', *Orion*, No. 1, 1945; reprinted in Burkhart 1, pp.21–2.

56 *Ibid.*, p.27.

57 Reported in a letter from Elizabeth Taylor to Robert Liddell, quoted in his unpublished ms., 'Elizabeth and Ivy'; a slightly different version of this passage appears in the transcript of this interview published in Burkhart 3, pp.168–9.

58 'An Appraisal. Ivy Compton-Burnett and Elizabeth Bowen', *Horizon,* June 1946; reprinted in Burkhart 1, p.108.

59 H&Head, p.172.

60 M&M, p.22.

61 p.112.

62 Letter, M.J. to Anne Hill, 10 February 1944.

63 Burkhart 1, p. 22; subsequent quotations come from pp. 23, 25 and 29 respectively.

64 *Regency Furniture, op. cit.,* pp.41, 47–8, etc.

65 Burkhart 3, p.139.

66 M.J. to H.H., 22 June 1944.

67 *Ibid.*

68 M.J. to J. Lees-Milne, 5 November 1944.

69 M.J. to H.H., January 1945.

70 M.J. to H.H., 22 June 1944.

71 *Prophesying Peace* by James Lees-Milne, p.72.

72 M.J. to J.L.-M., 5 November 1944 and 3 March 1945.

73 M.J. to J.L.-M., 3 March 1945.

74 M.J. to H.H., December 1944.

75 Letter, R.L. to H.S., 7 December 1970. Another version appears in Burkhart 3, p.141.

76 *Ibid.*

77 See p.232.

78 Burkhart 3, p.142.

79 R.L. to H.S., 7 December 1970.

80 Burkhart 3, p.142.

81 *Ibid.*

82 I.C.-B. to R.L., 17 September 1957 and 2 June 1960.

83 I.C.-B. to R.L., 1 June 1953.

84 On p.62.

85 I.C.-B. to R.L., 3 June 1969.

86 R.L. to H.S., 7 December 1970.

CHAPTER XV   1946–1951

1 Letter, I.C.-B. to Cicely Greig, 27 March 1946.

2 I.C.-B. to E.T., 16 July 1947.

3 I.C.-B. to E.T., 28 June 1947.

4 On p.133.

5 I.C.-B. to R.L., 26 July 1950.

6 P&P, pp.62 and 66.

7 Greig, p.33.

8   Review of *Darkness and Day, Sunday Times,* 5 April 1951.

9   M&M, p.183.

10 Information from Sonia Orwell.

11 Described in a letter, Rutley Mowll to I.C.-B., 8 January 1946, V&A papers.

12 This and the following quotation from Fedden.

13 Burkhart 1, p.187 (A. Powell assures me that the boat race party in question took place in 1952).

14 Letter, Elizabeth Taylor to Robert Liddell, n.d.

15 This and the following quotation from Fedden.

16 Greig, p.49; the next four quotations are from pp.17, 36, 20 and 24 respectively.

17 Letter, Graham Greene to H.S., 7 April 1983; the following account is largely based on a three-cornered correspondence between I.C.-B., Victor Gollancz and Spencer Curtis Brown in Gollancz's files.

18 G.G. to I.C.-B., 8 October 1948, Gollancz papers.

19 *Daily Telegraph,* 21 February 1947.

20 I.C.-B. to E.T., 16 July 1947.

21 Information from Elizabeth Taylor.

22 Charles Poore, *New York Times,* 20 June 1948.

23 Greig, p.43.

24 Cecil Gould, unpublished ms., 1 January 1971.

25 *Important to Me,* p.193.

26 M&M, p.67.

27 D&S, p.69.

28 John Farrelly, *New Republic,* 14 June 1948.

29 Greig, p.80; the next three quotations from pp.75, 39 and 44 respectively.

30 Greig, p.43; possibly there was some confusion about the magazine in question, since *Time*'s verdict ('*Bullivant and the Lambs* . . . is perhaps Author Compton-Burnett's finest novel. Its principal character, Family-Head Horace Lamb, is a typical Compton-Burnett tyrant . . .' 19 July 1948) was by no means among the most perceptive or enthusiastic American review.

31 Information from Vere Watson-Gandy and James Brandreth.

32 Dick, p.16.

33 Letter, E.T. to H.S., July 1971.

34 Greig, p.32.

35 Dick, pp.21–2.

36 Information from Joan Evans.

37 *Caves of Ice* by James Lees-Milne, p.214.

38 I.C.-B. to V.W.-G, 4 July 1950.

39 Information from Carol Rygate.

40 *Caves of Ice,* p.254.

41 *Ibid.,* p.215.

42 Greig, pp.54–5.

43 *Ibid.*

44 Hester Marsden-Smedley, unpublished ms.

45 D&D, p.117.

46 D&D, p.81.

47 *Important to Me,* pp.188–9.

48 Letter, R.L. to H.S., 7 December 1970.

49 Information from E.T.

50 Summary of medical treatment in M.J.'s diary for 1951.

51 Burkhart 2, p.76; this scene and its consequences were confirmed privately to me by both Herman Schrijver and Peter Wilson.

52 Information from Margaret Branch.

53 See p.243.

54 *Important to Me,* p.190.

55 See p.159.

56 D&D, p.27.

57 D&D, p.40.

58 D&D, p.209.

59 D&D, p.214.

60 Information from Dr Pasmore.

61 R.E. to H.S., 23 April 1974.

62 Herman Schrijver's version; another, probably apocryphal but much appreciated in design and architectural circles, was 'Ivy, be sure to lock up the whisky and the biscuits.'

63 F&Fortune, p.229.

64 I.C.-B. to R.M., 14 April 1951.

65 Information from Joyce Felkin.

66 Information from Olivia Manning, who had it from Basil M.-S.

67 Burkhart 2, p.76.

68 I.C.-B. to Robin McDouall, 14 April 1951.

69 Information from V. Sackville-West's biographer, Victoria Glendinning.

70 Sprigge, p.129.

71 Information from James Lees-Milne and Olivia Manning respectively.

72 D&D, p.215.

73 I.C.-B. to K. Blackie, 14 June 1951.

74 Greig, p.61.

75 Letter, I.C.-B. to C.G., 4 June 1951.

76 Fedden.

77 Information from Margaret Branch.

78 Letters and information from Dame Janet Vaughan; Lady Mander thought Ivy had also applied to Lady Margaret Hall, Oxford, but the College Secretary was unable to find any evidence among Dame Lucy Sutherland's papers.

79 Information from Ivo Pakenham.

CHAPTER XVI 1952–1959

1 *Caves of Ice* by James Lees-Milne, p.192.
2 P&P, p.8.
3 P&P, p.44.
4 P&P, p.164.
5 P&P, p.188.
6 Information from Sybille Bedford.
7 Fedden.
8 C. Sykes, tribute to Dame Ivy, read at the memorial meeting, Crosby Hall, 24 October 1969.
9 Sprigge, p.135.
10 Information from B. Robinson.
11 Information from Sybille Bedford.
12 Greig, p.69.
13 Burkhart 2, p.100.
14 'A Friendship Without a Thorn', unpublished ms. by Madge Garland.
15 Information from Angus Wilson.
16 Madge Garland.
17 Fedden.
18 I.C.-B. to R.L., 20 October 1954.
19 Burkhart 2, p.104.
20 I.C.-B. to R.L., 1 August 1951.
21 Letter, I.C.-B. to B. and W. Robinson, 31 January 1965.
22 Burkhart 1, p.187.
23 Fedden.
24 Anne Hill, diary, 11 February 1956.
25 Fedden.
26 To Robert Liddell.
27 Information from R. Lehmann.
28 Letter, John Pope-Hennessy to H.S., 1 June 1981.
29 *Ancestral Voices*, p.65; see also Fedden.
30 Betty Miller-Jones.
31 Information from Herman Schrijver.
32 Burkhart 2, pp.105–7.
33 *Ibid.*, p.82.
34 J.L.-M. to Madge Garland, 31 August 1969.
35 Fedden.
36 P&C, p.191.
37 Sprigge, p.133; the following account based largely on information from O. Manning.
38 E.T. to R.L., n.d.

39   Information from N. Wright.
40   Burkhart 2, p.96.
41   'A Friendship Without a Thorn', unpublished ms.
42   B&S, p.88.
43   This and subsequent quotations from Elizabeth Taylor come, unless otherwise acknowledged, from her letters to Robert Liddell, hardly any of which are dated (or dateable, except by internal evidence), and many of which survive only in fragments, the rest having been destroyed at the author's request by R. L. who incorporated much of this extraordinary correspondence in his book, 'Elizabeth and Ivy' (as yet unpublished).
44   *The Bookman,* April 1949.
45   *The Echoing Grove* (it was after this meeting that Ivy came to know Rosamond Lehmann better).
46   Elizabeth Taylor was painfully conscious of some small, barely noticeable burn marks left by a firework on her throat; the heroine of her novel, *The Sleeping Beauty,* had been unrecognizably changed by plastic surgery after a road accident.
47   Information from Angus Wilson.
48   Blanche Knopf to Victor Gollancz, 3 December 1952.
49   M&S, p.73.
50   M&S, p.67.
51   Information from Lord Goodman.
52   Information from Sybille Bedford.
53   Information from A. J. Ayer.
54   Dick, p.25.
55   'A Friendship Without a Thorn', unpublished ms.
56   *Ibid.,* see photograph opposite p.169.
57   Letter, I.C.-B. to C.G., 22 June 1954.
58   I.C.-B. to B. Robinson, 26 April 1960.
59   Sprigge, p.151.
60   Letter, Mrs C. C. Baines of Canterbury to C. Greig, 3 June 1972.
61   Sprigge, p.151.
62   *The Life of Charlotte Brontë,* by E. C. Gaskell (Smith, Elder, 1857), vol. ii, pp.8–9.
63   G&G, pp.19 and 51.
64   Dick, p.14.
65   Letter, I.C.-B. to C. Greig, 5 December 1962; see Greig, p.88.
66   Dick, p.18.
67   I.C.-B. to R.L., 29 January 1959.
68   Fedden.
69   This and subsequent quotations from Barbara and Walter Robinson come, unless otherwise attributed, from many conversations with H.S., also from their unpublished ms. notes, 'Conversations Between Ourselves and Ivy'.

70 Greig, p.21.
71 G&G, pp.66–7.
72 Information from B. Robinson.
73 Burkhart 2, p.92.
74 Letter, Valerie Eliot to H.S., 14 June 1983.
75 E.T. to R.L., n.d. (1957).
76 Information from George Furlong and Rex Britcher.
77 This and the subsequent account from 'Some Notes About Ivy Compton-Burnett', unpub. ms. by Anne Hill, 11 March 1958.
78 *Tropisms and the Age of Suspicion*, p.118.
79 Nathalie Sarraute to H.S., 30 March 1973; this account confirmed by Sonia Orwell.
80 MWTM, p.92.
81 Burkhart 2, p.99.
82 I.C.-B. to K. Blackie, 19 December 1959.
83 N.S. to H.S., 30 March 1973.
84 Information from Robin McDouall.
85 *Ibid.*
86 Mowll.
87 Letter, I.C.-B. to B. and W. Robinson, 9 April 1958.
88 Presumably Henrietta Day, whose illness (followed by a change of housekeeper for Ivy) is described in an undated letter which also refers to the murder of a friend and neighbour of E.T.'s by Ruth Ellis in April 1955.
89 I.C.-B. to P.M., 25 July 1954.
90 Greig, pp.73–5.
91 *The Ghosts of Versailles*, p.104.
92 Burkhart 3, p.174.
93 Information from Lucille Iremonger.
94 I.C.-B. to K. Blackie, 14 June 1951.
95 Cancelled passage from 'Herman's Memoir of Ivy', not published in Burkhart 2 but kindly shown me by Professor Burkhart.
96 I.C.-B. to Lady MacAlister, 19 April 1968; see also Sprigge, p.150.
97 See pp.112–13.
98 F&Fate, p.194.
99 F&Fate, p.75.
100 *Recollections of Virginia Woolf*, ed. Joan Russell Noble (Peter Owen, 1972), p.172.
101 R.L. to H.S., 25 February 1983.
102 E.T. to R.L., n.d.
103 I.C.-B. to Robin McDouall, 7 October 1955.
104 I.C.-B. to V. Watson-Gandy, 4 July 1950.
105 Ernest Thesiger, unpublished memoir.
106 Information from Cecil Gould.

107 Burkhart 3, p.182.
108 E.T. to H.S., n.d. (1971).
109 *Rose Macaulay* by Constance Babington Smith, p.227.
110 I.C.-B. to R.L., 21 January 1959.
111 H&History, p.25.
112 I.C.-B. to C.G., 4 November 1958.
113 I.C.-B. to R.L., 17 September 1957.
114 This and the following quotation from H&History, pp.98 and 134.
115 Letter from I.C.-B., quoted in E.T.'s report to R.L.

CHAPTER XVII 1960–1969

1 Dick, p.24.
2 This and subsequent quotations from Kay Dick come, unless otherwise attributed, from conversation with H.S.
3 This and the next two quotations from Ivy come from Dick, pp.12, 13 and 9.
4 Mitchell NS; this account also based on conversation with J.M.
5 *Important to Me*, p.193.
6 Information from Madge Garland.
7 Dick, p.11.
8 Dick, p.10.
9 Information from Sonia Orwell.
10 I.C.-B. to B. Robinson, 1 October 1959.
11 *Ibid.*, 7 October 1961.
12 *Ibid.*, 21 November 1964.
13 E.T. to R.L., n.d. (1964).
14 Information from Herman Schrijver; my account of this luncheon and what followed is based on conversations with both Herman and Sonia Orwell.
15 TWTW, p.66.
16 'A Friendship Without a Thorn', unpublished ms.
17 Information from Madge Garland.
18 M&F, p.101.
19 M&F, p.60.
20 M&F, p.102.
21 *The Mighty and Their Fall* 'just coming' on 20 November 1959 (Burkhart, p.46) and ready for typing by 10 February 1961 (letter, I.C.-B. to C. Greig).
22 M&F, p.6.
23 M&F, p.48.
24 M&F, p.64.
25 Dick, p.19.
26 Information from Madge Garland.
27 See Burkhart 2, p.84; Madge Garland confirms that the woman mentioned in this passage was the one with the roses on Brighton Pier.

28 P&C, p.126.

29 Dick, p.7.

30 Information from Hester Marsden-Smedley.

31 Kathleen Farrell.

32 'A Friendship Without a Thorn', unpublished ms.

33 I.C.-B. to B. Robinson, 26 April 1960.

34 Christopher Sykes, Sprigge p.135; Jonathan Cecil and Dorothy Reynolds said the same.

35 Burkhart 2, p.117. (Balthus' real name was Stanislas Klossowski.)

36 Fedden.

37 'I am well aware . . .' E.T., unpublished memoirs.

38 Information from George Furlong, Rex Britcher and Madge Garland (who were there).

39 'Thé chez Miss Compton-Burnett', Les Nouvelles Littéraires 10 March 1960 (my translation in this and the following quotations); information from Robin McDouall.

40 E.T. to R.L., n.d.; Madge Garland confirms this account.

41 The following account of Gollancz's dealings with Ivy is largely based on correspondence in Gollancz's files; see also Gollancz: The Story of a Publishing House by Sheila Hodges.

42 Greig, p.41.

43 J. A. Laurence.

44 I.C.-B. to B. Robinson, 1 October 1959.

45 Sprigge, p.96.

46 Information from Lettice Cooper.

47 Information from Soame Jenyns.

48 I.C.-B. to B. Robinson, 6 January 1960.

49 Burkhart 2, p.100.

50 I am grateful to Livia Gollancz for a comprehensive survey of Ivy's sales figures, 1937 to date, from which it seems that she sold decidedly more than the 'steady 6,000 copies' quoted on p.99 of Sheila Hodges' Gollancz: The Story of a Publishing House.

51 Sunday Times, 8 April 1951.

52 P&C, p.127.

53 Mowll.

54 Information from Lettice Cooper, to whom V.G. described this meeting.

55 I.C.-B. to K. Blackie, 30 July 1963.

56 I.C.-B. to R. L., 14 December 1964.

57 I.C.-B. to E. Taylor, 1 September 1965.

58 Burkhart 2, p.96.

59 Anne Hill, 'Notes', 11 February 1956.

60 I.C.-B. to R.L., 5 July 1963; the ms. was ready for typing by 5 April 1963 (p.c., I.C.-B. to C. Greig).

61 Greig, p.90.
62 Burkhart 2, p.99.
63 Information from Alison Waley.
64 G&G, p.53.
65 G&G, p.10.
66 G&G, p.38.
67 G&G, p.39.
68 G&G, p.49.
69 I.C.-B. to R.L., 20 November 1960.
70 *Ibid.*, 12 March 1963.
71 *Ibid.*, 18 October 1961.
72 *Ibid.*, 10 December 1963.
73 The cast was headed by Dorothy Reynolds as Julia Challoner with James Cairncross as Sir Edward, Christopher Guinee and Alan Howard as Walter and Simon, and a memorable performance from Jonathan Cecil as Simon's youngest child, Ralph; Julian Mitchell's *A Family and a Fortune* was put on the following July at the Yvonne Arnaud Theatre, Guildford, directed by Donald Haworth, designed by Cecil Beaton, with Raymond Huntley as Edgar Gaveston, Catherine Lacey as Blanche, George Benson as Dudley, Avril Elgar as Justine and Joyce Carey as Aunt Mattie.
74 Information from Francis King.
75 E.T. to R.L., n.d.
76 D&S, p.76.
77 E.T. to R.L., n.d.
78 Information from Sonia Orwell (the other guests included Herman and Dorothy Stroud; and Mrs King did indeed enjoy the situation, see *The Weeping and the Laughter*, p.236 *et passim*).
79 I.C.-B. to C. Greig, 25 May 1965.
80 Information from Ivo Pakenham.
81 E.T. to R.L., n.d.
82 Greig, p.102.
83 'Herman's Memoir of Ivy', cancelled passage not published in Burkhart 2.
84 Information from Lettice Cooper.
85 I.C.-B. to S.O., 28 December 1967.
86 E.T. to H.S., 11 May 1971.
87 I.C.-B. to Madge Garland, 29 June 1968.
88 Burkhart 1, p.196.
89 Greig, pp.101–2 and 104.
90 I.C.-B. to R. McDouall, 19 April 1966.
91 E.T. to R.L., n.d., but they discussed Truman Capote's *In Cold Blood*, published in February 1966.
92 Burkhart 2, p.88.
93 Information from Kathleen Farrell.

94 *The Weeping and the Laughter,* p.237.

95 Reprinted in Burkhart 1; Sr Praz's visit to Braemar Mansions described in his diary for 9 June 1967.

96 Burkhart 2, p.78; Mario Praz contradicted Herman's report in a letter to Elka Schrijver, 22 December 1981.

97 Burkhart 1, p.196.

98 I.C.-B. to R.L., 21 May 1968.

99 Interview with I.C.-B., *The Times,* 21 November 1963.

100 E.T. to R.L., n.d.

101 Fedden.

102 Greig, p.27.

103 Information from Barbara Robinson.

104 Information from Vera Compton-Burnett; and from Madge Garland.

105 I.C.-B. to M.G., 7 June 1968.

106 Letter, I.C.-B. to M.G., 20 June 1968.

107 'Conversation with Miss Compton-Burnett 18 July 1968', unpublished notes by Dr Pasmore.

108 M&W, p.113.

109 Burkhart 1, p.196.

110 M&F, p.60.

111 I.C.-B. to Anne Hill, 17 July 1967.

112 Greig, p.117.

113 I.C.-B. to M.G., 10 July 1968.

114 Information from J. Mitchell.

115 I.C.-B. to R.L., 14 December 1964; she said much the same to C. Greig and B. Robinson.

116 The ms. of L&F, comprising twelve notebooks (see Sprigge, p. 175), is now in the British Library; the remaining eighteen notebooks, mostly first drafts, all cancelled in Ivy's hand, are in the possession of Henrietta Williamson.

117 Information from Mary Maguire.

118 Dick, p.29.

119 Information from Lady Mander.

120 L&F, p.12.

121 Letter, W.R. to H.S., 4 January 1971.

122 L&F, p.144 (the last five words excised from the published text).

123 D&D, p.233.

124 See p.168.

125 L&F, p.79.

126 C.G. to H.S., 1 January 1971.

127 Greig, p.116.

128 Information from Livia Gollancz.

129 Sprigge, p.171.

130 Information from H. Marsden-Smedley.

131   Sprigge, pp.172–3.
132   Mitchell NS, and conversation with H.S.
133   Information from R. McDouall.
134   Glen Cavaliero, letter to H.S., 11 March 1974.
135   Information from Mary Maguire.
136   M&F, pp.63–4.

SELECT BIBLIOGRAPHY

ARDEN, JOAN (C.E.M. Jourdain), *A Childhood*, Bowes & Bowes, Cambridge, 1913.

———— *Unfulfilment*, Basil Blackwell, Oxford, 1924.

BALDANZA, FRANK, *Ivy Compton-Burnett*, Twayne, New York, 1964.

BINDOFF, S. T., 'Charles Kingsley Webster, 1886–1961', *Proceedings of the British Academy*, vol. xlviii, O.U.P., London.

BODMAN, FRANK, 'Richard Hughes Memorial Lecture', *British Homoeopathic Journal*, vol. lix no. 4, October 1970.

BOWEN, ELIZABETH, *Collected Impressions*, Alfred A. Knopf, New York, 1950.

BRITTAIN, VERA, *Testament of Youth*, Macmillan, New York, 1937.

BROWNING, OSCAR, *Memories of Sixty Years*, John Lane, London, 1910.

BURKHART, CHARLES (ed.), *The Art of I. Compton-Burnett. A Collection of Critical Essays*, Gollancz, London, 1972.

———— *Herman and Nancy and Ivy. Three Lives in Art*, Gollancz, London, 1977.

———— *I. Compton-Burnett*, Gollancz, London, 1965.

———— (guest ed.), 'Ivy Compton-Burnett Issue', *Twentieth Century Literature*, vol. 25 no. 2, Summer 1979.

CLARKE, J. H., *Life and Work of James Compton Burnett, M.D.*, Homoeopathic Publishing Company (HPC), London, 1904.

———— *The Life of Dr. Skinner*, HPC, London, 1907.

COMPTON BURNETT, JAMES, *Cataract, Its Nature, Causes, Prevention and Cure*, HPC, London, 1889.

———— *The Change of Life in Women*, HPC, London, 1898.

———— *Curability of Cataract with Medicines*, HPC, London, 1880.

———— *Curability of Tumours by Medicines*, HPC, London, 1893.

———— *Delicate, Backward, Puny and Stunted Children*, HPC, London, 1895.

———— *Diseases of the Skin*, HPC, London, 1898 ed.

———— *Diseases of the Spleen*, James Epps, London, 1887.

———— *Ecce Medicus, or Hahnemann as a Physician*, HPC, London, 1881.

———— *Eight Years Experience in the New Cure of Consumption*, HPC, London, 1894.

———— *Enlarged Tonsils Cured by Medicines*, HPC, London, 1901.

———— *Fevers and Blood-Poisoning, and their Treatment*, James Epps, London, 1888.

———— *Fifty Reasons for Being a Homoeopath*, HPC, London, 1896 ed.

———— *Gold as a Remedy in Disease*, HPC, London, 1879.

———— *Gout and Its Cure*, James Epps, London, 1895.

——— *Greater Diseases of the Liver,* HPC, London, 1891.

——— *The Medicinal Treatment of Diseases of the Veins,* HPC, London, 1881.

——— *Natrum Muriaticum as Test of the Doctrine of Drug Dynamisation,* Gould, London, 1878.

——— *On Fistula and Its Radical Cure by Medicines,* James Epps, London, 1889.

——— *On Neuralgia: its causes and remedies,* HPC, London, 1894 ed.

——— *On the Prevention of Hare-Lip, Cleft Palate and Other Congenital Defects,* HPC, London, 1880.

——— *Organ Diseases of Women,* HPC, London, 1896.

——— *Ringworm: its constitutional nature and cure,* HPC, London, 1892.

——— *Supersalinity of the Blood,* HPC, London, 1882.

——— *Tumours of the Breast,* James Epps, London, 1888.

——— *Vaccinosis and Its Cure by Thuja,* HPC, London, 1884.

——— *Valvular Disease of the Heart from a New Standpoint,* Leath and Ross, London, 1885.

DALTON, HUGH, *Call Back Yesterday. Memoirs 1887–1931,* Muller, London, 1953.

DELP, W. E., *Royal Holloway College 1908–1914,* text of a talk given at the college on 21 January 1969, privately printed.

DICK, KAY, *Ivy and Stevie. Conversations and Reflections,* Duckworth, London, 1971.

EVANS, JOAN (ed.), *An Adventure by C.A.E. Moberly and E. F. Jourdain,* Faber, London, 1955 (5th ed.).

——— *Prelude and Fugue. An Autobiography,* Museum Press, London, 1964.

FEDDEN, ROBIN, 'Recollections of Ivy Compton-Burnett', *Cornhill,* no. 1062, Winter 1969/70.

FORSTER, E. M., *Goldsworthy Lowes Dickinson,* Harcourt, Brace & Co., New York, 1934.

FRY, ROGER, and SHEPPARD, JOHN T., *Goldsworthy Lowes Dickinson, 6 August 1862–3 August 1932,* privately printed, Cambridge, 1933.

FURBANK, P. N., *Samuel Butler,* C.U.P., London, 1948.

GARDNER, BRIAN, *The Big Push,* Cassell, London, 1961.

GARNETT, DAVID, *The Familiar Faces,* Chatto & Windus, London, 1962.

——— *The Flowers of the Forest,* Chatto & Windus, London, 1955.

GRATTAN-GUINNESS, I., *Dear Russell–Dear Jourdain,* Duckworth, London, 1977.

——— 'Russell and Philip Jourdain', *Russell: The Journal of the Bertrand Russell Archives* vol. 8, Winter 1972/73.

GRAVES, ROBERT, *Goodbye To All That,* Blue Ribbon Books, New York, 1930.

GREIG, CICELY, *Ivy Compton-Burnett. A Memoir,* Garnstone Press, London, 1972.

GRILLS, ROSALIE GLYNN, *I. Compton-Burnett, Writers and Their Work,* Longmans, London, 1971.

HASSALL, CHRISTOPHER, *Rupert Brooke,* Faber, London, 1964.

HIGHAM, DAVID, *Literary Gent,* Cape, London, 1978.

HODGES, SHEILA, *Gollancz: The Story of a Publishing House 1928–1978,* Gollancz, London, 1978.

HOLROYD, MICHAEL, *Lytton Strachey,* vol. I. *The Unknown Years,* Heinemann, London, 1967.

HUGHES, MISS, *The Life of Hugh Price Hughes, by his daughter,* Hodder and Stoughton, London, 1904.

IREMONGER, LUCILLE, *The Ghosts of Versailles,* Faber, London, 1957.

JOHNSON, PAMELA HANSFORD, *I. Compton-Burnett,* British Council, Longmans, London, 1951.

—— *Important to Me. Personalia,* Macmillan, London, 1974.

JONES, HENRY FESTING, *Samuel Butler: A Memoir,* 2 vols., Macmillan, London, 1919; Octagon Books, New York, 1968.

—— (ed.), *The Note-Books of Samuel Butler,* A. C. Fifield, London, 1918.

JOURDAIN, C.E.M. (Melicent), see Arden, Joan.

JOURDAIN, E. F. (Eleanor), see Evans, Joan.

JOURDAIN, LT. COL. H.F.N., *Ranging Memories,* John Johnson at the O.U.P., Oxford, 1934.

JOURDAIN, MARGARET (see also Lenygon, Francis), *An Outdoor Breviary,* Academy Press, London, 1909.

—— *Poems,* Truslove and Hanson, London, 1911.

—— *Regency Furniture 1795–1820,* Country Life, London, 1934.

—— *The Work of William Kent,* Country Life, London, 1948.

JOURDAIN, P.E.B. (ed.), *The Philosophy of Mr. B*rtr*nd R*ss*ll,* Allen & Unwin, London, 1918.

KENNEDY, RICHARD, *A Boy at the Hogarth Press,* Heinemann, London, 1972.

KING, VIVA, *The Weeping and the Laughter,* Macdonald & Jane, London, 1976.

LEES-MILNE, JAMES, *Ancestral Voices,* Chatto & Windus, London, 1975.

—— *Caves of Ice,* Chatto & Windus, London, 1983.

—— *Prophesying Peace,* Charles Scribners & Sons, New York, 1978.

LENYGON, FRANCIS (M. Jourdain), *Decoration and Furniture of English Mansions During the Seventeenth and Eighteenth Centuries,* T. Werner Laurie, London, 1909.

—— *Decoration in England from 1660–1760,* Charles Scribners & Sons, New York, 1927.

—— *Furniture in England from 1660–1760,* Charles Scribners & Sons, New York, 1914.

LIDDELL, ROBERT, *A Treatise on the Novel,* Cape, London, 1947.

—— *Kind Relations,* Cape, London, 1939.

—— *The Last Enchantments,* Cape, London, 1948.

—— *The Novels of Ivy Compton-Burnett,* Gollancz, London, 1955.

—— *Stepsons,* Longmans, London, 1969.

—— *Unreal City,* Cape, London, 1952.

LINTON, MRS. LYNN, *The One Too Many,* 3 vols. Chatto, London, 1894.

MACCARTHY, DESMOND (ed.), *Letters of the Earl of Oxford and Asquith to a Friend, 1915–1922* (Hilda Harrisson), Geoffrey Bles, London, 1933.

McCarthy, Mary, *The Writing on the Wall and Other Literary Essays,* Weidenfeld & Nicolson, London, 1970.

Mitchell, Julian, 'Ivy Compton-Burnett', *New Statesman,* 5 September 1969, London.

Moberly, C.A.E., see Evans, Joan.

Noyes, Ella, illustrated by Dora Noyes, *Salisbury Plain. Its Stones, Cathedral, City, Valleys and Folk,* Dent, London, 1913.

Powell, Margaret, *My Mother and I,* Michael Joseph, London, 1972.

Powell, Lady Violet, *A Compton-Burnett Compendium,* Heinemann, London, 1973.

Raverat, Gwen, *Period Piece,* Faber, London, 1952.

Russell, Bertrand, *Autobiography,* vols. i–iii, Allen & Unwin, London, 1967–9.

Rule, William Harris, *Recollections of My Life and Work at Home and Abroad in Connection with the Wesleyan Methodist Conference,* London, 1886.

———— *Wesleyan Methodism in the British Army,* London, 1883.

Sackville-West, Edward, *Inclinations,* Secker & Warburg, London, 1949.

Sarraute, Nathalie, *L'Ere du Soupçon,* Gallimard, Paris, 1959, trans. by Maria Jolas in *Tropisms and The Age of Suspicion,* Calder & Boyers, London, 1963.

Sassoon, Siegfried, *Memoirs of an Infantry Officer,* Coward, McCann, New York, 1930.

Smith, Constance Babington, *Rose Macaulay,* Collins, London, 1972.

Somerville, E., & Ross, Martin, *The Real Charlotte,* Longmans, London, 1918.

Sprigge, Elizabeth, *The Life of Ivy Compton-Burnett,* Gollancz, London, 1973.

Thesiger, Ernest, *Practically True,* Heinemann, London, 1927.

Trevelyan, G. M., and others, *John Harold Clapham, 1873–1946,* privately printed, Cambridge, 1949.

Trine, Ralph Waldo, *In Tune with the Infinite, or, fullness of peace, power, and plenty,* G. Bell & Sons, London, 1900; Bobbs-Merrill, New York, 1947.

Walker, Kenneth, 'Martello Towers and the Defence of N.E. Essex in the Napoleonic War', *Essex Review,* vol. xlvii, October 1938.

———— *The Story of Little Clacton—an Essex Village,* Little Clacton, 1959.

Ward, Mrs. Humphrey, *Robert Elsmere,* Smith, Elder, London, 1900.

Woolf, Leonard, *Beginning Again: An Autobiography of the Years 1911 to 1918,* Hogarth Press, London, 1964.

———— *Sowing: An Autobiography of the Years 1880 to 1904,* Harcourt, Brace, New York, 1960.

Wortham, H. E., *Victorian Eton and Cambridge: Being the Life and Times of Oscar Browning,* Arthur Barker, London, 1956 (2nd ed.).

Yonge, Charlotte M., *The Daisy Chain,* Macmillan, New York, 1856; London, 1911 ed.

———— *The Trial: More Links of the Daisy Chain,* Appleton & Co., New York, 1866; Macmillan, London, 1911.

WORKS OF I. COMPTON-BURNETT

(Dates are those of first editions)

Dolores, 1911.

Pastors and Masters, 1925.

Brothers and Sisters, 1929.

Men and Wives, 1931.

More Women Than Men, 1933.

A House and Its Head, 1935.

Daughters and Sons, 1937.

A Family and a Fortune, 1939.

Parents and Children, 1941.

Elders and Betters, 1944.

Manservant and Maidservant, 1947.

Two Worlds and Their Ways, 1949.

Darkness and Day, 1951.

The Present and the Past, 1953.

Mother and Son, 1955.

A Father and His Fate, 1957.

A Heritage and Its History, 1959.

The Mighty and Their Fall, 1961.

A God and His Gifts, 1963.

The Last and the First, 1971.

INDEX

PHOTOGRAPHIC CREDITS

FOLLOWING PAGE *174*

plate

1 *top:* Grossman; lower right: Lambert and Weston
2 Gunn and Stewart
3 *upper left:* Edmund Wheeler; upper right: Edmund Wheeler
4 *top:* Mayall and Co.
5 *top and bottom:* Courtesy of Royal Holloway College
8 *upper left:* Courtesy of the Librarian, King's College, Cambridge
9 *lower right:* Appeared in *Dear Russell-Dear Jourdain* by I. Grattan-Guinness and is reproduced by kind permission of the publisher, Gerald Duckworth & Co.
10 Claude Harris
11 Star Photographic Co.
12 *bottom:* Lee Miller, reproduced by kind permission of Vogue

FOLLOWING PAGE *430*

plate

1 Cecil Beaton, courtesy of Sotheby's London
2 *left:* Courtesy of Elka Schrijver; right: Photopress
3 *upper left:* Courtesy of Constance Babington Smith; upper right: Cecil Beaton; *bottom;* Appeared in *Gollancz: The Story of a Publishing House* by Shelia Hodges and is reproduced by kind permission of Victor Gollancz Ltd.
4 *top:* Drawing by Rodrigo Moynihan, courtesy of Mrs. J. Routledge
5 Edith Lamont, courtesy of Nigel Nicolson
7 John Vere Brown
8 Hans Beacham